Practical .NET for Financial Markets

■ ■ ■

Yogesh Shetty
Samir Jayaswal

Apress®

Practical .NET for Financial Markets

Copyright © 2006 by Yogesh Shetty and Samir Jayaswal

ISBN-13: 978-1-59059-564-0

ISBN-10: 1-59059-564-5

Printed and bound in the United States of America 9 8 7 6 5 4 3 2 1

Trademarked names may appear in this book. Rather than use a trademark symbol with every occurrence of a trademarked name, we use the names only in an editorial fashion and to the benefit of the trademark owner, with no intention of infringement of the trademark.

Lead Editor: Ewan Buckingham
Technical Reviewer: Ravi Anand
Editorial Board: Steve Anglin, Dan Appleman, Ewan Buckingham, Gary Cornell, Jonathan Gennick, Jason Gilmore, Jonathan Hassell, James Huddleston, Chris Mills, Matthew Moodie, Dominic Shakeshaft, Jim Sumser, Keir Thomas, Matt Wade
Project Manager and Production Director: Grace Wong
Copy Edit Manager: Nicole LeClerc
Copy Editor: Kim Wimpsett
Assistant Production Director: Kari Brooks-Copony
Production Editor: Lori Bring
Compositor and Production Artist: Kinetic Publishing Services, LLC
Proofreader: April Eddy
Indexer: Valerie Perry
Cover Designer: Kurt Krames
Manufacturing Director: Tom Debolski

Distributed to the book trade worldwide by Springer-Verlag New York, Inc., 233 Spring Street, 6th Floor, New York, NY 10013. Phone 1-800-SPRINGER, fax 201-348-4505, e-mail orders-ny@springer-sbm.com, or visit http://www.springeronline.com.

For information on translations, please contact Apress directly at 2560 Ninth Street, Suite 219, Berkeley, CA 94710. Phone 510-549-5930, fax 510-549-5939, e-mail info@apress.com, or visit http://www.apress.com.

The information in this book is distributed on an "as is" basis, without warranty. Although every precaution has been taken in the preparation of this work, neither the author(s) nor Apress shall have any liability to any person or entity with respect to any loss or damage caused or alleged to be caused directly or indirectly by the information contained in this work.

The source code for this book is available to readers at http://www.apress.com in the Source Code section. You will need to answer questions pertaining to this book in order to successfully download the code.

I dedicate this book to my father, Narshima, and to my mother,
Saroja—without her sacrifices I wouldn't have reached so far.
—Yogesh Shetty

I dedicate this book to my father, who, despite being from a small city,
had a vision of providing the best education and life to his children
three decades ago, and to my mother, who relentlessly furthered his vision for
20 long years after he passed away.
—Samir Jayaswal

We also collectively dedicate this book to our dear friend, Rajesh Mestry,
who was with us for a very short time before he left for the other world.
—Yogesh Shetty and Samir Jayaswal

Contents at a Glance

About the Authors... xiii

About the Technical Reviewer xv

Acknowledgments.. xvii

Introduction.. xix

■**CHAPTER 1** Introducing the Equities Market..................................... 1

■**CHAPTER 2** The Order-Matching Engine... 41

■**CHAPTER 3** The Data Conversion Engine 105

■**CHAPTER 4** The Broadcast Engine 171

■**CHAPTER 5** The Application Operation Engine 235

■**CHAPTER 6** STP Security... 299

■**CHAPTER 7** STP Interoperability 347

■**CHAPTER 8** Equity Arbitrage.. 403

■**CHAPTER 9** .NET 2.0... 447

■**APPENDIX A** .NET Tools 477

■**APPENDIX B** References 481

■**INDEX** 483

Contents

About the Authors. xiii

About the Technical Reviewer xv

Acknowledgments. xvii

Introduction xix

CHAPTER 1   Introducing the Equities Market 1

What Is a Capital Market?. 1
What Is Equity, and What Are Equity Shares? 2
Why Do People Trade?. 3
Understanding Entities in the Equities Market 5
    Stock Exchanges 6
    Members of the Exchange 8
    Indexes 12
    Clearing Corporations 14
    Banks 15
    Depositories 15
Exploring the Life Cycle of a Trade 18
    Order Initiation and Delivery 19
    Risk Management and Order Routing 20
    Order Matching and Conversion into Trade. 22
    Affirmation and Confirmation 23
    Clearing and Settlement 24
Exploring the Precursor to Straight Through Processing (STP) 28
Understanding .NET in an Equities Market 30
What Is a Techno-Domain Architect?. 34
Understanding the Three I's (Intelligence) of Performance
    in Capital Markets 35
    Machine Intelligence 36
    Domain Intelligence. 37
    Human Intelligence 37
Introducing the Upcoming Business Cases 38

CHAPTER 2   The Order-Matching Engine 41

Understanding the Business Context of Order Matching 41
    The Need for Efficient Order Matching 41
    Actors: Exchanges and Brokers 42

Types of Orders 43

Order Precedence Rules 44

Introducing .NET Collections 48

Introducing Specialized Collections 58

ListDictionary 58

HybridDictionary 58

Introducing Multithreading 59

Thread Pools 59

Asynchronous Delegate Infrastructure 60

Manual Thread Management 63

UI Widgets and Multithreading 81

Server Timer 83

Examining the Business-Technology Mapping 84

Class Details 88

Code Snippets 88

Summary 103

■CHAPTER 3   **The Data Conversion Engine** 105

Introducing Data Management 105

Understanding the Business Infoset 106

Reference Data 107

Variable Data 107

Derived Data 107

Computed Data 108

Static Data 108

Introducing Reference Data 108

Framework for Data Conversion 111

Entering the XML World 115

Reading and Writing Data 117

Introducing Specialized Streams 119

TextReader and TextWriter 120

BinaryReader and BinaryWriter 120

XmlReader and XmlWriter 121

Looking at the Types of Parsers 122

Tree-Based Parser 122

Fast-Forward Parser 122

Reading XML 123

Writing XML 128

Introducing XML Serialization 131

Introducing XML Schema Document (XSD) 136

Examining the Business-Technology Mapping 143

CSV Conversion Rule 148

Class Details 151

Conversion Example 166
XML Output. 167
Refined Conversion Rule 167
XML Output. 168
Summary 169

CHAPTER 4   The Broadcast Engine 171

What Is Market Data? 171
Participants in the Market Data Industry 172
Example of Market Data 173
Role of Market Data. 173
Market Data Service 175
Why Is the Timeliness of Market Data Important? 175
Level Playing Field 177
Introducing Networking 177
Internet Protocol. 179
Transport Layer (User Datagram Protocol) 185
Transport Layer (Transmission Control Protocol) 191
Asynchronous Market Data Producer and Consumer 195
Network Byte Order 201
Message Framing 202
Broadcast 209
Unsolicited Broadcast 210
Solicited Broadcast 213
Protocol Tweaking 216
Exploring the Business-Technology Mapping 220
Class Details. 222
Summary 234

CHAPTER 5   The Application Operation Engine 235

Understanding the Trading Operational Requirement 235
Exploring the Multiple Facets of an Object 238
Understanding .NET Remoting Infrastructure 240
Exploring the Multiple Facets of a Remoting Object. 242
Introducing Local Process Communication (LPC) 244
Configuring Infrastructure Services 250
Shadow Copying Infrastructure Services. 252
Finding the AppDomain Treasure 253
Introducing Remote Process Communication (RPC). 254
Understanding Proxies. 261
Understanding Distributed Garbage Collection 267
Configuring Remoting 271

Lifetime Management 273
Versioning. 274
Error Handling 274
Security. 275
Debugging 275
Understanding Aspect-Oriented Programming (AOP) in .NET 275
Examining the Business-Technology Mapping 283
Class Details. 284
PrimaryController. 290
AgentInfo. 292
LogManagement 293
Primary Controller Remoting Configuration 293
Primary Controller Host. 294
AgentController 294
AppManagement 295
Agent Remoting Configuration 296
Agent Host 297
Order-Matching Application 297
Summary 298

■CHAPTER 6   STP Security 299

Exploring the Business Context 299
Custodian Service Provider. 299
STP Service Provider. 300
Driving Factors Behind STP 300
A Perspective of STP 301
How Is STP Achieved?. 303
Implementing Security in the STP Space 307
Confidentiality. 308
Integrity. 322
Digital Signatures. 324
Digital Certificates 327
Exploring the Business-Technology Mapping 331
Class Details. 333
Code Example 343
Summary 344

■CHAPTER 7   STP Interoperability 347

What Is Interoperability? 347
Why Is Interoperability Required? 349
Challenges in Achieving Interoperability 350

Introducing Service-Oriented Architecture 351
    Web Services 352
    WSDL 354
    SOAP 358
    Platform Infrastructure for Web Services 359
    STP and Web Services.. 360
    STP Provider Consortium: Using UDDI........................... 370
    WS-Specification (WS-*).. 379
    Web Services Enhancement (WSE) 2.0 380
    WS-Security 384
    WS-Policy 395
    WS-Addressing 397
    WS-MetadataExchange.. 398
    WS-Referral 399
    Web Service Performance in the Financial Market................. 400
Exploring the Business-Technology Mapping 400
Summary 402

CHAPTER 8   Equity Arbitrage 403

Introducing Arbitrage.. 403
    Costs Involved in Arbitrage Transactions......................... 404
    Other Forms of Arbitrage... 405
    Pure and Speculative Arbitrage 406
    Risks Associated in Arbitrage 407
    Building an Equity Arbitrage Engine: Arbitrage in Equity Shares........ 407
Introducing Code Generation 415
    Types of Code Generators.. 416
    Code Generation and Reflection................................. 417
    User Interface.. 418
    Code Wizards 420
    Code Documentation.. 420
    Code Inflator... 422
    Model-Driven Generator 422
    Specialized Class... 423
    Just-in-Time Code Cutting 423
Introducing the CodeDOM... 424
Introducing Reflection 434
    Code Generation Using Reflection.Emit........................... 439
Examining the Business-Technology Mapping 442
Summary 445

■CHAPTER 9   .NET 2.0 447

Language Improvements. 447
    Generics 447
    Inheritance on Generic Types 451
    Constraints on Generic Types 452
    Anonymous Methods. 457
    Iterators. 459
    Partial Types 460
    Nullable Types 461
Counting Semaphore 462
Memory Gate 464
Garbage Collector 464
SGen 465
Data Compression 467
Network Information 468
Remoting. 471
    Shared Assembly 472
    Implementation of Market Info Cache Server 472
    Remoting Configuration of Market Info Cache Server 472
    Market Info Cache Server Host. 473
    Market Info Cache Client (Back-Office Applications) 473
    Remoting and Generics. 474
Summary 476

■APPENDIX A   .NET Tools 477

■APPENDIX B   References 481

■INDEX 483

About the Authors

YOGESH SHETTY is an expert in development for financial markets, with more than eight years of experience in Microsoft technologies. He has extensive knowledge and experience in the design and development of trading engines, using the Microsoft .NET Framework, ADO.NET, C#, VB .NET, SQL Server, and other technologies. Yogesh has built and deployed front-office and back-office solutions for major financial institutions. He was responsible for developing a Straight Through Processing (STP) back-office product with real-time connectivity to exchanges and has participated in the Microsoft .NET Center of Excellence for Financial Markets. Yogesh is currently consulting for a major investment bank on WallStreet where he is responsible for delivering .NET based solutions for algorithmic trading and electronic market-making business. You can contact Yogesh at Yogesh.Shetty@gmail.com.

SAMIR JAYASWAL heads the Product Management & Product Development Group for treasury and risk management products at 3i Infotech Limited (http://www.3i-infotech.com). He has about a decade of experience in conceptualizing, leading, and managing product development for financial markets in domains such as fixed income, equities, foreign exchange, commodities, and derivatives. These products have been successfully deployed in banks, exchanges, financial institutions, and brokerages worldwide and have fulfilled functions such as trading, surveillance, risk management, and settlements. He is a computer science graduate and a postgraduate in international finance. He is an avid investor and a voracious reader. You can contact Samir at leosamir@yahoo.com.

About the Technical Reviewer

 **RAVI ANAND** is a technical manager and vice president at a large investment bank in midtown Manhattan. Ravi has an executive MBA degree from Rutgers University in New Jersey and has more than 13 years of experience in software architecture and development, primarily using Microsoft technologies. In his current role, Ravi has been intensely involved with C# and WinForms to develop solutions for algorithmic trading.

Acknowledgments

Writing this book was an extremely long journey for me. The toughest part was balancing full-time work and writing. I wish there were banks that could loan time instead of money!

I started programming at a very young age and entered the financial world at the age of 18. The credit for this goes to Sajit Dayanand, who hired me as a programmer. Thanks, Sajit, for trusting my knowledge and giving me the opportunity to unleash my potential. I also want to thank Dewang Neralla and Jignesh Shah, who played equally important roles in shaping my professional life.

My interest in computers started when I was in the fifth grade, and at that time, I made up my mind to follow a career in some computer-related field. During those days, learning computers was expensive, and only a few people could afford to do it. Seeing my enthusiasm, one of my good friends, Agnel Tangaraj, stepped forward and helped me financially in obtaining basic education from a highly reputed institute. Thanks, Agnel—needless to say, I couldn't have come this far without your support. I also want to thank some other people—S.P Sir, Fabian Dias, and Prabhakar—who helped me during difficult days to shape my career.

I would also like to take this opportunity to thank my friends Jaideep, Ashish, Prasad, Kiran, Ramkrishna, Bala, Prateek, Mala, and Shonali for their love and support. My special thanks to Ravi and Gulzar for always being there for me. Thanks to my naughty brother, Mukesh, for his support and encouragement; you are the best, and I am fortunate to have you as my younger brother. Thanks to Nishtha for showering me with lots of love and her million-dollar smiles. Many thanks to Parag Ajmera for providing me with support, especially when I needed it the most. I also want to thank Leon Pesenson for giving me the opportunity to further explore my potential. I may have missed many other friends who have walked with me in various phases of life and made impressions on me that have one way or another contributed to this success that I wish to share with them today.

Writing a book is not an individual effort. It is a team effort, and many people worked in the background to make this book. First I would like to thank Dominic Shakeshaft, who went through our proposal and believed in our vision. Thanks to Jayashree Raghunathan, who worked very hard and helped me in making the book proposal presentable. My sincerest thanks to Kim Wimpsett, who was our copy editor and who went through every single detail to ensure quality and readability. Many thanks to Grace Wong for keeping us all on track. I finally would like to thank Ewan Buckingham, Lori Bring, and the entire production staff who worked on this book.

My final gratitude to the Almighty, who has been there with me at every step as he guided me, kept me in good health, gave me opportunities, encouraged me to purse my dream, and helped me stay motivated and focused while bringing a new challenge every day.

Yogesh Shetty

While this book was written because of our interest in the techno-financial issues faced in financial markets, there are several individuals without whom this book would have never seen light.

I would like to thank my family members—my wife, Shalika; my sister, Surbhi; my mother; my uncle; and Mr. Awtar Singh for helping me at every point of my life and career and motivating me to pursue writing as an activity despite severe time constraints.

I would also like to acknowledge my first employers—Jignesh Shah, Sajit Dayanandan, and Dewang Neralla—who were responsible for grooming me professionally and providing me with rare insight and experience in this market. They also taught me an important lesson—age is never a factor for attempting to achieve anything. I have never met someone who can see the future as clearly as Jignesh. Thanks, Jignesh, for recruiting me when I needed it most.

A few teachers helped me in school and later years—Mrs. Bhat, Mr. Narang, Mrs. D'Souza, Mrs. Abedin, Mr. and Mrs. Arun, Mr. Prakash, Mr. Natarajan, Mrs Joglekar, Mrs. Kankane, Mrs. Gupte, and Dr. Chopa. Thanks also to teachers who weren't designated as teachers but who taught me nonetheless—Mr. Utpal, Mr. Deval, and Mr. Anjal.

Thanks to my friends Hem and Yash who were there with me since my childhood, watching and helping me in every step I took. Thanks to Jayashree and Anjali who took on the onus of editing the chapters in this book but could not continue because of lack of time.

Special thanks to my coauthor, Yogesh, for his relentless follow-ups, which kept the momentum for this entire project intact.

Big thanks to Dominic Shakeshaft and his entire team for believing in our vision and working hard to publish this book. Thanks to Kim Wimpsett, our copy editor, who tightened every line we wrote to make it more interesting. Thanks to Grace Wong for keeping us all on schedule. I would also like to thank Lori Bring, Ewan Buckingham, Tom Debolski, Kurt Krames, and the entire production staff.

Samir Jayaswal

Introduction

Practical .NET for Financial Markets was born because we were convinced no focused literature existed for people involved in application/product development in financial markets using .NET. Although a lot of .NET-related material is available, most often it is not relevant for developers in the finance domain. The finance domain poses some interesting issues and challenges. Reliability, accuracy, and performance are tested to the hilt.

Given the number of professionals worldwide who are engaged in implementing solutions using Microsoft technologies as well as the impending changes that .NET will bring about in all future applications, this book will be of considerable interest to a lot of readers. While the same concepts can be extrapolated to various types of markets, we have kept our discussion restricted to equities markets because most readers are familiar with them and because the level of technology absorption in equities markets is quite high when compared to other markets.

Strictly speaking, this book is for those who want to understand the nuances of financial applications and the implementation of technologies in financial markets using .NET. Solution providers for financial markets in general and equities markets in particular will find this book exceptionally useful. Developers who want to understand .NET and also get exposed to the fundamentals of financial markets will also find this book invaluable. The book covers techno-domain issues in an unprecedented way. The issues discussed are practical in nature, and readers will almost immediately start relating issues discussed in this book with their day-to-day work.

This book is clearly divided into business sections and technical sections. The business sections first discuss the functional aspects of the issues that the market is facing. Once you read the business section in each chapter, you will have a reasonable grasp of the business flow for that particular topic. The technical section picks up where the business section leaves off and discusses the issues faced and their possible solutions using .NET. We do not stop at merely discussing the .NET Framework. In most places, we have written a small prototype to make each topic easy to understand and easy to implement.

The implicit goal of the book is to provide insight into the practical, day-to-day challenges posed by domain-specific issues. The book provides in-depth engineering solutions for the exchange markets while covering all aspects of the .NET Framework. We believe that multiple solutions to a problem may coexist. The solutions provided in this book may or may not be an optimized solution for a particular problem but will surely be one of the solutions to address the issue.

Because both problems and solutions are interwoven in every chapter, you will get a sense of completeness with each chapter, which covers both the business aspects and the relevant .NET features and framework. This also means we will deal with every aspect of .NET in its proper context by explaining how the features are relevant and applicable to a real-life business case.

Our aim in writing this book is twofold. We want to educate readers on Microsoft .NET technology, and we want to discuss key challenges that developers and solutions architects in the financial technology space face in their day-to-day development.

CHAPTER 1

Introducing the Equities Market

Luck in life always exists in the form of an abstract class that cannot be instantiated directly and needs to be inherited by hard work and dedication.

This chapter provides a broad overview of the equities market by explaining its fundamental concepts. It does not assume any understanding of financial markets. Our goal is to give you a brief tour of the trading world. After reading this chapter, you will appreciate the basics of capital markets (more specifically, the equities market), and you will understand the various entities that come together to create a marketplace and how trading and settlement take place. As you read this book, the coverage of markets becomes more detailed. Although all the other chapters cover technical aspects of markets, this chapter covers only the business aspects of the equities market. The business topics covered in this chapter are by themselves a vast subject, and it is nearly impossible to address every facet of them. Therefore, we will focus on the entities and basic workflow involved in the trading and settlement business.

What Is a Capital Market?

A *capital market* is the part of a financial market where companies in need of capital come forward and look for people to invest in them in search of returns. Companies raise money either through bonds or through stocks. *Bonds* are issued against an interest-bearing loan that the company takes. The loan assures that bondholders will get periodic interest payments, which are more or less guaranteed by the company that issues the bonds. Investors who are risk averse or who want to diversify their portfolios in safer areas invest in bonds. *Stocks* do not assure periodic payments like bonds do. Hence, stocks are considered riskier than bonds. Companies raise money to fund a new venture, an existing operation, or a new takeover; to purchase new equipment; to open new facilities; to expand into new markets; to launch new products; and so on. Companies list their stocks on stock exchanges to create a market for them and to allow their shares to be traded subsequently. (We discuss listings in more detail in a moment.) Sometimes companies can issue stocks even when the company is not listed but has the intention of getting listed.

■Note Stocks of companies are also popularly called *scrips*, *instruments*, and *securities*.

Sometimes a company directly approaches a market in search of investors and issues securities. The company hooks up with agencies called *lead managers,* or *merchant bankers,* that help the company raise money. In cases where investors are directly providing money to companies, the process is called a *public offering.* If it's the first time the company is raising money from the public, the process is called an *initial public offering* (IPO). A market where a public offering is made and companies raise money directly from investors is called a *primary market.*

Once the public offering takes place, investors have the securities, and the company has the money. The company then *lists* the securities on one or multiple stock exchanges. Companies apply to the exchange to get their stocks listed. They pay a *listing fee* to the exchange for listing and comply with the exchange's specified listing requirements. Listing makes the securities available for subsequent buying and selling through current and potential investors. This enables investors to make profits, cut risks, invest in potential growth areas, and so on. A market where shares are subsequently traded after issuance is called a *secondary market.*

What Is Equity, and What Are Equity Shares?

Equity is the capital that is deployed to start a company. It has all the risk and gives a share in the profit that the corporation makes. *Equity shares* are instruments that grant ownership on equity and thus the underlying company. *Shareholders* are owners of a company. Their ownership is proportional to the percentage of shares held in the company. Usually shareholders and managers of the company are different, but they can also be the same. Shareholders appoint the company's board and chief executive officers (CEOs). The company makes profits and losses in the usual course of its business. The profit that the company makes is distributed amongst the shareholders in proportion to the number of shares they hold. The profit shared with shareholders is a *dividend.* When the company incurs a loss, no dividend is paid, and shareholders have to wait for a better year that brings in profits.

Owning stocks has some other benefits. If you buy stocks at an attractive price in a profit-making company, chances are you will witness capital appreciation as stock prices rise. Prices rise because people are willing to pay higher prices in anticipation of an increase in a company's profit. Simply put, these shares are not merely pieces of paper—they have real companies behind them. When the fortunes of these companies improve because of improved business conditions or an increase in the demands of a company's products, the value of shares representing the company also rises, resulting in profits for shareholders. However, during times of losses, the share prices can decline; and at times these declines can be substantial. These declines can hurt shareholders by eroding their holding values. Buying and holding shares thus requires patience, insight, and risk-taking ability on the part of the shareholder.

When a company whose securities are traded on a stock exchange tries to issue stock, its already prevailing prices determine how much money the company can raise per share for its fresh issue. Investors and researchers do an inherent valuation of the company's stock to arrive at the price the shares will trade at after the stock issue and then, depending on the offer price, invest accordingly. A company whose offer price is lower than the intrinsic value will receive a good response in terms of investor participation, and a company whose offer price is at a premium will receive a lukewarm response.

This form of financing is not available to sole proprietorships and partnerships.

Why Do People Trade?

Several entities—such as banks, mutual funds, pension funds, brokering firms, insurance companies, corporations, and individuals who possess resources for investments—classify as *investors*, or *traders*. Throughout the book, we will use the words *investors*, *traders*, and *dealers* interchangeably because they are more or less the same. They access the markets with a motive of making profits; the differences are in their approaches, frequency of trading, and aggression of trading. Although dealers and traders are the same, the term *investor* implies people who are a tad risk averse and whose trading frequency is less. Investors usually remain with a specific position for a longer term than dealers/traders. We will ignore these differences, however, because these are general distinctions. Investors trade to invest in an asset class, to speculate, or to hedge their risks. Investors trade with an objective of profiting from the transaction by buying and holding securities in the case of rising prices and by selling and protecting themselves from price declines in the case of a falling market.

Trading is a two-person, zero-sum game. In each transaction, one party makes money, and the other loses money. Since the prices of shares or any asset traded is bidirectional, you generally have a 50 percent chance of making a profit and a 50 percent chance of losing money. Traders know this, yet they trade. This is because they have a price and value forecast/view of the security that they believe is correct, and they want to profit from the view.

Transactions are normally driven by two factors:

Information: The purchaser/seller genuinely thinks the prices will go up/down. This understanding is usually backed by some commercial development, news, research, or belief. An asset is *undervalued* when the ongoing market price is less than the intrinsic worth of the asset and *overvalued* when the ongoing market price is higher than the intrinsic worth.

Buyers buy and hold securities because they think prices will go up. This simple strategy is called *going long*, and this position is called a *long position*. Buyers of securities may or may not have the money to finance their purchases. Buyers who don't have the money to pay can look out for financing their positions. Similarly, investors sell securities if they anticipate a price decline. They usually sell and deliver securities to the buyer. However, certain categories of sellers sell but don't have the securities to deliver. These types of sellers are called *short sellers*, and this position is called a *short position*. Short sellers either close out their position by accepting profit/loss or look for a *securities lender* to lend them securities so they can meet their delivery obligations.

Liquidity: Holders of securities know they need to hold securities longer in order to make a reasonable profit but are unable to hold them because they need money urgently for some other reason. Traders keep shuffling between assets in search of superior returns. If they know one particular security gives them a better opportunity to earn, they might liquidate investments made in another security even if their investment objective in that particular security has not matured. Such transactions are *liquidity-driven transactions*. Even when traders are not shuffling between asset classes, they may be forced to liquidate positions simply because they have monetary obligations that they can no longer postpone.

It is not difficult to visualize that most trades happen because of differences in opinion about a stock's price (see Figure 1-1). Therefore, the value of securities fluctuates from time to time. Buyers are thinking a particular security has a potential upside, and sellers are thinking the opposite. In certain extreme conditions, no difference in opinion exists. In such cases, markets really become illiquid, and it becomes difficult to push through transactions. One such example was the condition of stock markets worldwide after the September 11 disaster.

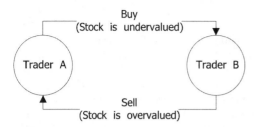

Figure 1-1. *Trades happen because of differences in opinion.*

Although traders knew for certain there would be value erosion in most securities because of the loss and resultant slowdown in the economy, they did not agree on the quantum, and no one was even willing to hazard a guess. More specifically, no one knew what the economic impact would be on the share prices of companies and at what levels prices would stagnant. Security prices went into a free fall. While prices fell, the entire market was of the view that prices should fall; hence, no difference of opinion existed, and therefore no buyers existed. Buyers surfaced only after a large fall. At these levels, potential buyers were convinced they were once again getting value for their money; hence, they became counterparties to sale transactions, and that is when transactions started happening. Such conditions of market stress directly impact liquidity.

Liquidity is the ease at which you can trade a particular asset. When traders demand liquidity, they expect their transactions to be executed immediately. Liquidity is also determined by *market width*, which is the cost of executing the transaction of a specified size, and by *market depth*, which is how much quantity can be executed at a given cost. In markets where securities are relatively illiquid, possibilities exist that the market is willing to bet on only one side; that is, either the players are willing only to buy or only to sell. Even when two-way quotes exist, the depth could be small. This means not enough orders could be in the system to match a large order. This will make traders go through an agonizing wait if not enough takers exist for their orders. This is a condition most traders/investors abhor. In fact, large investors are known to avoid stocks that are illiquid.

Traders go long on a stock they think will go up in price. Such traders are called *bullish* on the stock. Similarly, traders go short on stocks they think will decline in price. Such traders are called *bearish* on the stock. At any given time, a trader could be bullish on one stock while being bearish on another. Or, even for a particular stock, the trader could be bullish at a particular price and bearish at another price. To see the price at which a security is trading, traders need to refer to a *quote*. A quote could be a purchase price or a sale price. It could also be a *two-way quote*. A two-way quote comprises a *bid price* (the purchase price) and an *offer price* (the sale price). The bid price is the price a counterparty is willing to pay you in case you want to sell your securities to that party. The *offer price* is the price the party is asking for in case you want to buy securities from that party.

The offer price will logically be higher than the bid price. When you ask for a quote, for example, you will get a figure such as $54.10/$54.15 (see Figure 1-2).

Figure 1-2. *Two-way quote comprising bid price and offer price*

In a two-way quote, the first price is the bid price. In other words, $54.10 is the price you will get if you want to sell your securities; the condition is called *hitting the bid*. If you want to buy, the trader will sell that security to you for $54.15. This is called *taking the offer*. The difference between the bid price and offer price is called the *spread*. The spread is the profit the trader makes by providing a two-way quote and doing a *round-turn* transaction (both buy and sell) at that quote. In this example, the spread is $0.05. Spread is thus a profit for the quote-providing trader and a cost for the investor.

Some traders also do *arbitrage*. Arbitrage is buying a stock (or any asset) from a market where its quote is cheaper and selling it in a different market simultaneously where its quote is at a higher rate. Though it sounds simple, arbitrage has its own nuances and risks. We will discuss the arbitrage business in more detail in Chapter 8.

Understanding Entities in the Equities Market

Generally, you can divide an entire market into a buy side and a sell side (see Figure 1-3). The *buy side* includes fund managers, institutions, individual investors, corporations, and governments that are looking for investment avenues and solutions to issues they face. For example, corporations could be looking to issue fresh equity and thus be looking for investors. Corporations could also be hedging their existing exposure. This means they would be buying or selling some assets to cut risk they are already facing. Fund managers could be looking for avenues to *park* their funds to provide returns to their unit holders. Portfolio managers play a similar role and could be looking for opportunities to sell and make profits.

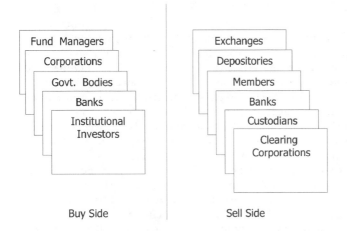

Figure 1-3. *Markets can be divided into a buy side and a sell side. Banks are both investors and settlement facilitators and hence appear on both sides.*

The *sell side* includes entities that provide liquidity services and solutions to the buy side. Examples of sell-side entities include stock exchanges, clearing corporations, and depositories. Fund managers and portfolio managers could trade on an exchange and settle their transactions through clearing corporations. Corporations could access the market's issuance mechanism to raise money. In short, the sell side comes forward to provide services to the buy side.

The equity market comprises a lot of entities, including stock exchanges, clearing corporations, clearing members, members of the exchange, depositories, banks, and so on. In the subsequent sections, we will describe the roles played by individual entities in the equities market.

Stock Exchanges

Stock exchanges are organized markets for buying and selling securities. These securities include bonds, stocks, and derivative instruments such as options and futures. Because stock exchanges are one of the most important entities in a capital market, this section discusses them in more detail. A stock exchange provides players with a platform where transactions can take place. The function of a stock exchange is to bring all the buyers and sellers together in order to minimize transaction costs, which are a reality of life and have to be incurred by traders and investors. Apart from obvious costs such as commissions, taxes, and statutory levies, other costs such as spreads, impact costs, and search costs are built into the transaction costs.

We have explained *spread* as a round-turn cost. It is the cost you will incur if you buy some shares and sell them immediately. Exchanges minimize spreads by taking steps to improve the overall liquidity in stocks. Since exchanges bring all the participants interested in a security together, liquidity improves dramatically. Traders now compete with each other to buy and sell securities, and rates become realistic. The better the rates become, the narrower the spread becomes.

Impact cost is the cost incurred when someone is trying to push a large trade or when an informed trader wants to deal with someone in particular. Counterparties become suspicious when a large order is pushed through, especially when someone known to be an informed trader pushes it. For such orders, they don't want to transact at the prevailing price and want to include a risk premium. The counterparty is thus subjected to a different price immediately, which is inferior to the ongoing price. This difference becomes an impact cost.

Bringing buyers and sellers together reduces the *search cost* dramatically. Assume, for example, that you want to buy a secondhand car. Usually, people who want to sell their cars put an advertisement in the classifieds column of a newspaper. Potential buyers read this listing and contact the sellers. When the basic price details and requirements match, they travel to meet face to face, inspect the car, and sometimes get a mechanic to do an appraisal. They negotiate the rates and other terms, and then the sale takes place. This entire process takes a couple of days to a week's time. Such secondhand car markets are relatively illiquid. To improve liquidity in such a market, some second-hand car dealers organize sales where they request all sellers to display their cars in a fair. They also organize such meetings online. Potential buyers then visit the area (or log on to the Internet) and negotiate terms there and then. They also feel comfortable because they can compare all offers simultaneously. Suddenly, liquidity increases. Such markets have a potential of doing a lot more transactions in the same time frame, which benefits the buyers and the sellers. Both incur fewer costs in doing the deal, and both get the best possible price. Thus, getting buyers and sellers together improves liquidity, reduces search costs, and increases the confidence of the participants. A stock exchange performs precisely this function.

Stock exchanges worldwide are going through a lot of transformation. You probably remember seeing television footage of a typical stock exchange where thousands of traders shout in order to place orders. Since an exchange's trading floor is a big area and the number of traders is large, how could it then be possible or at least easy for people to find interested counterparties in a particular security? What if one trader wanted to transact on a security that is not so popular? It wouldn't be easy to find a counterparty.

In reality, an exchange floor has areas earmarked for each security. Traders desirous to trade a certain security have to go to the area demarcated for that security and find counterparties. What you usually see on television is traders shouting their bids or offer prices for a particular security. Others listen to their prices and commit to transactions when they hear favorable prices. Once a transaction is committed, it is immediately recorded manually so that it is honored later even when prices turn against one of the parties.

Note To cut down on shouting, traders devised methods of negotiating by using actions through their fingers and palms. This method of trading is, however, fraught with a lot of lacunae.

Stock exchanges usually never accept orders directly from investors; instead, order requests are directed to exchanges via *brokers*. A broker is a member of an exchange who acts as an intermediate agent between an investor and the exchange. (We will discuss brokers in the "Members of the Exchange" section.) We will use the words *broker* and *member* interchangeably because they both refer to members of a stock exchange. To place an order, investors have to call/meet their brokers or brokers' agents and dictate their orders. (A broker's agent would forward the order to the broker.) The broker would then go or send a representative to the floor of the exchange to execute the order. Once the execution is done, the investor is informed about the execution. In the past, it was not unusual for the broker to *club* (aggregate) the order from various investors in a common security while going to get it executed. This execution could have then happened in multiple *fills* at different prices. Brokers then decided which price to pass on to which investor. Investors had no mechanism to know whether the purchase/sale price being passed to them by their brokers was correct and meant for them. This area was ambiguous and fraught with manipulation. In less-advanced financial markets, brokers would normally pass on purchase requests from customers at the highest price of the day and pass on sale transactions at the lowest price of the share on that day. Brokers would pocket the difference between the highest/lowest price and actual purchase/sale prices. This became a good form of earning for the brokers, and in many cases, income from this was even higher than the commissions they earned.

With the advancement of technology and expectation of markets came the desire to reduce dependency on such traders and bring about transparency in the entire trading process. When you have a huge nation with vibrant retail participation, the potential number of orders that hit the exchange is large. It becomes virtually impossible for brokers to do justice to individual investors, which in turn affects the quality and price of execution and raises a lot of ethics-related issues. This problem gave birth to *screen-based trading*.

Most advanced nations have adopted screen-based trading. All the crowded and noisy exchanges are a thing of past now in most countries. All brokers are connected electronically to their exchanges through their trading terminals. Brokers can see every order that hits the exchange on their trading terminals and can bid or offer shares for an order by entering their corresponding buy/sell orders. These trading terminals are installed at the brokers' offices, thereby dramatically increasing the reach of exchanges to the common trading public. This virtually brings the exchange to an investor's doorstep. In some countries, investors connect to the exchange directly by trading software provided by their brokers. Their orders are first routed to the broker's surveillance system, which conducts the necessary risk management checks and then routes the order to the exchange for execution.

The screen-based trading system has many advantages over the traditional system. First, the process of trading has a lot of transparency. Traders know the exact prices at which their transactions go through. They also can access the exchange's order books (with, of course, certain restrictions) and know the *touchline prices*, which are the last transacted prices. Access to the order books also helps traders know the best bid and offer rates prevailing in the markets. This means they know at what prices their next orders are likely to be transacted.

Second, trading systems have broken geographical barriers and reduced communication costs drastically. In the earlier model, a lot of trading was centered in large cities that had a physical presence of a stock exchange. Investors from other cities were required to hook up with representatives of members of these exchanges, and the order flow used to happen on the phone. A large number of orders used to miss out or sometimes used to get transacted on a security different from what the investor had demanded. Many exchanges still prefer floor-based trading because dealers see their counterparties in person and decide immediately whether they are more informed or less informed than them and whether trading with them will prove profitable. In adverse cases, dealers get an opportunity to revise their quotes to suit themselves.

Exchanges provide fair access to all members, and members expect that their orders will be executed in a fair manner without bias. Automated trading provides them with comfort because computers behave the way they have been programmed without any bias. Exchanges are usually open between fixed times during the day, and they allow all members to log in and trade during this time. This time slot is called the *trading session*. Most exchanges allow order entry even before the trading session in a session called the *pre-opening session*. This session is a slot of about 15 to 20 minutes before the trading session commences. Members are allowed to enter orders in this session, but the orders don't get transacted. Exchanges arrive at the fair opening prices of all scrips by getting a feel of prices contained in the orders for all securities. This is also useful because it prevents the exchange system from being burdened by a huge number of orders being entered when the trading starts. Trading stops at a designated time. Exchanges are particular about timing because even a few seconds' deviation could benefit some members at the cost of others.

Historically, most exchanges worldwide were nonprofit organizations owned by their members. This ownership structure has continued for more than a century now. This, however, raised a lot of governance issues in many countries because members made policies suiting them at the cost of their clients. Clients started shying away from such exchanges, and liquidity shifted to other exchanges that had better and more transparent ownership and management structures.

Many exchanges are now trying to de-link ownership and membership on the lines of professionally managed companies. They are now offering shares to institutions and listing those shares on the same/multiple exchanges. Once a share is listed on an exchange, the exchange and its functioning, fundamentals, and financials become the subject of public scrutiny. This form of change is called the *demutualization* of the exchange. Exchanges make money from charging listing fees, membership fees, and transaction charges and by selling market data. Market data is trading- and settlement-related data and is used by most market participants who base their trading decisions on this information. (We will cover market data and its importance in the trading business in Chapter 4.) Apart from exchanges, brokers get data from a variety of sources, including depositories, clearing corporations, and third-party agencies such as Reuters, Bloomberg, and internal data repositories. (We discuss the various kinds of data required for trading activities and related issues in Chapter 3.)

The New York Stock Exchange (NYSE) and the American Stock Exchange (AMEX) are the major stock exchanges in the United States; both are located in New York City. Some regional stock exchanges operate in Boston, Cincinnati, Chicago, Los Angeles, Miami, Philadelphia, Salt Lake City, San Francisco, and Spokane. In addition, most of the world's developed nations have stock exchanges. The larger and more successful international exchanges are in London, Paris, Hong Kong, Singapore, Australia, Toronto, and Tokyo. Another major market in the United States is the NASDAQ stock market (formerly known as the National Association of Securities Dealers Automated Quotation system). The European Association of Securities Dealers Automated Quotation system (EASDAQ) is the major market for the European Union (EU). NASDAQ is a major shareholder in EASDAQ.

Members of the Exchange

Members of the exchange are also called *brokers*. On the NYSE today, two kinds of brokers exist: floor brokers and specialists.

Floor Brokers

Floor brokers act as agents of their customers and buy and sell on their customers' behalf and for the organizations for which they work (see Figure 1-4). It is mandatory for clients to access the exchange only through designated brokers. Clients cannot do trades otherwise. Brokers solicit business from clients, get their orders to the exchange, and match them on the exchange's matching system. They also settle their clients' trades. Some even get the orders matched outside the system, but most countries have a regulation that trades resulting from such orders be reported immediately to the exchange system for the entire market to know.

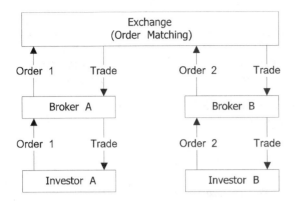

Figure 1-4. *Brokers help investors access the pool of liquidity that is otherwise not available to investors.*

Clients specify which security they want to trade and under what conditions. Some clients want to trade immediately regardless of the prevailing price. Some are willing to wait the entire day for a good price, and some are willing to wait for several days for a favorable price. These restrictions are explained to the brokers, and the brokers try to arrange trades accordingly. These conditions can be captured gracefully in *order attributes*, or *order terms*. (We cover various attributes associated with orders in Chapter 2.)

Though clients pay commissions to floor traders to get their transactions executed, they get a lot of benefits indirectly. Brokers have access to an exchange's order-matching system where they execute orders at competitive prices. They undertake the responsibility of clearing and settling those trades in a hassle-free, standardized, transparent method. In addition, brokers are generally better informed than their customers. Sometimes their advice can be valuable. Professional brokers, however, concentrate only on brokering and refrain from giving advice. They normally execute what their clients instruct. Some brokers give advice as a value-added service but don't accept any liability for that advice not materializing. Brokers also extend a credit facility to customers in need who have a good reputation with the broker. They execute the orders on behalf of the customer first and collect money from the customer later. In many markets, brokers extend a similar facility through banks. This is called *margin trading*.

Brokers also execute transactions on their own accounts through *house accounts*. Profits and losses from these trades accrue to the broker and not to any client. Such transactions are called *principal transactions*. Floor brokers thus perform the role of agents as well as principals. Acting as an agent as well as a principal becomes an ethical issue and is a cause of key concern in many markets, especially in those markets that are not very advanced. When brokers buy the same security for themselves that they also buy for their customers, how can the customers be sure brokers are passing on transacted prices to them?

For example, assume a stock has moved from $40 to $42 during a trading session. A client has placed an order to buy this stock at $41. Assume that the broker also has interest in this stock and wants to purchase at roughly the same rate. When the broker goes to the floor to trade, the broker executes two buy orders. One gets filled at $41, and the other gets filled at $40.75. Now it's a tough decision for the broker. If the broker has not segregated the order initially before executing, he will not know which one to pass on to his customer and which one to keep for himself. If he passes on the lot executed at $40.75, he keeps the customer happy but loses money (it's still debatable whether this money was his to begin with), and if he passes the execution of $41, then it's an ethics issue. Automated trading systems have a neat method of solving this problem. At an order level, the broker has to specify whether the order is meant for the customer or for his own account. If it's for the customer, the broker also has to specify the client code of the customer. The code is required so the broker does not pass on an execution meant for one customer to another.

Dishonest brokers also do *front running*. When they receive a large order from an informed investor, they first trade on their own accounts in the same security and build up a similar interest as the client wants to build up, and then they trade for the client. In this case, the client builds the position she desires, but she may be saddled with relatively inferior prices as compared to the broker who traded *before* the client and thereby put his own interest ahead of the client's. Front running is a punishable offense.

Many brokers also solicit business through Internet trading sites where customers who want to trade log on and place their orders. These brokers are also floor traders.

Specialists

Specialists are a second category of brokers; they provide two-way quotes and execute orders for floor brokers (see Figure 1-5). They are also called *market makers* for their designated securities and maintain their own inventories of shares (for which they are specialists). They will buy from anyone who wants to sell and sell to anyone who wants to buy. They are key liquidity providers. Designated market makers exist in many securities in many markets. They provide liquidity to anyone who wants to buy/sell in the absence of other counterparties. Specialists wait for others to trade with them. Thus, they are brokers who will be always willing to act as counterparties to anyone who wants to buy or sell. Anyone who wants to transact with such specialists will ask for a quote. Since they don't initiate transactions, they have to be extra careful about the rates at which they choose to transact.

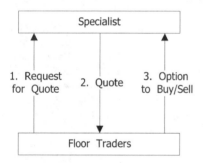

Figure 1-5. *Specialists provide quotes on request and give others the option to trade with them.*

Specialists normally provide a two-way quote. Depending upon the quote, traders decide whether to trade immediately or wait for a more favorable price to be quoted. Depending upon a quote, a trader may also decide whether to buy or sell at that particular price. While providing a two-way quote, specialists don't really know whether the trader wants to buy from him or sell to him. Actually, it does not make much of a difference to them because they earn through spreads and through price changes on the inventories of shares they maintain (provided the quantity is small and the counterparty is less informed). When specialists want to trade aggressively, they narrow the spread by bringing the bid price and offer price closer to each other. When they want to be cautious and want to discourage others from trading, they widen the spread. This increases the cost of doing a round-turn transaction for other traders, and it discourages others from trading with specialists. Note that liquidity in most securities is high, and adjusting the bid/offer rates even by a couple of cents creates a large difference in the demand and supply. Millions of shares can be bought or sold in a matter of seconds.

The quotes provided by specialists are often referred to as firm or soft. A *firm quote* is a quote that, once provided, cannot be changed. When a specialist provides a quote to any trader, the specialist becomes liable to trade with the trader at that particular price should the trader so desire. On the other hand, the specialist can modify a *soft quote* once the trader wants to transact. After giving a soft quote, a specialist can also refuse to transact with the trader. Specialists are generally wary of transacting with traders who potentially know more than them. This apprehension is obvious—if an owner of a company is trying to sell a large block of her own company's shares and it is known that the transaction is not liquidity driven, it is obvious that she thinks her company's stock is fully valued and that chances of further appreciation are rare. People who are more informed than the specialists are normally those who have an insider view of the company. If specialists are wary that they will lose out financially to the trader if they enter into the trade, they are likely to back out before transacting or at least modify the quote to suit them. People who know about corporate developments and trade to profit from them before the news comes out in the public domain are called *insiders*. Insider trading is an offense and is punishable in all markets.

A specialist's business is interesting as well as important for the overall market. They help in the price discovery process and help the market reach an equilibrium position. During times of market stress, they provide necessary liquidity, thereby giving opportunity to others to invest/exit. They are generally better informed about the security than other traders. Depending upon the urgency of other traders, the outlook of the company behind the security, and the overall market conditions, specialists determine the bid and offer prices. Needless to say, just like other traders, they like to keep a larger inventory of shares when the prices are looking up and want to cut their inventories when the prices seem to be going down. The size of the inventory that they maintain largely depends upon the bid and offer rates they are quoting.

Since all other traders looking for liquidity want to transact with specialists, a high offer price from a specialist will tempt traders to sell their holdings to the specialist. This in turn will increase the inventory size the specialist is holding. A price rise will then benefit the specialist. Conversely, when the outlook is grim and the specialist wants to offload inventory, the specialist will revise the prices and quote a lower offer price. This will tempt other traders to buy shares from the specialist at the lower price. The specialist will then manage to offload his position in favor of other traders. Thus, you have seen how specialists trade on both the buy side and the sell side and how they attract and regulate liquidity by adjusting the bid and offer prices. At a particular level of inventory, however, they would want to maintain a constant stock. In such cases, they quote bid and offer prices in such a way that the rate at which other traders sell to them matches the rate at which other traders buy from them, and at this point demand for that stock equals the supply available. This position is called an *equilibrium position*, and this price is called the *equilibrium price*.

Becoming a Member

Through this entire discussion, it would seem that brokers are individuals. Some of them are. However, brokering as a business requires tremendous power and operational and marketing strength. Most members (brokers) are thus institutions. Even individuals who hold membership rights maintain a corporate structure and employ people who run the entire business for them. So, are the members the same people who you see trading on the exchange floor? Maybe, but in most cases they are not. They are member representatives who are authorized by the members to trade for them.

Large institutions and traders prefer to become members themselves to protect their interests and have better control over the entire trading and settlement process. In case volumes of their proprietary transactions are very high, they save good money that would have otherwise been spent on commissions.

To become an exchange member, a trader or an institution must acquire a membership in the exchange. Each exchange has a different set of norms and requirements. Indeed, having a membership in any renowned exchange is a matter of prestige. In most exchanges, memberships can be bought and sold like any stock. The cost at which membership can be acquired fluctuates and is a function of the demand and supply of memberships. However, money alone cannot buy membership. Most exchanges have strict screening criteria, and the candidates have to demonstrate a good understanding of the securities business, a commitment to their customers, and financial integrity. Membership on the NYSE is called a *seat* because in the earlier years of its existence, members had to sit in assigned seats during roll calls. In December 2005, two seats sold on the NYSE for $3,500,000 each.

The highest price paid for a membership in the history of the NYSE was $4,000,000 in December 2005. As of December 15, 2005, the NYSE had 1,366 members.

Although some exchanges do not issue fresh memberships easily (thereby forcing potential members to buy from existing members), some exchanges offer memberships on a *tap basis*. This means that anyone wanting a membership can approach the exchange anytime and complete the necessary formalities to become a member.

Indexes

Though an index is not a real entity, any discussion of the equities market cannot be complete without a discussion of indexes. The movement of indexes has now become synonymous with the movement of markets and stocks. An index's price is undoubtedly the most sought after number or piece of information by traders, investors, researchers, and so on. Investors and researchers do a lot of analysis to predict where an index is headed and what its direction means to each market participant.

Basically, an *index* is a measure of relative values. When discussed in equities market parlance, changes in an index measure changes in market values and hence the market capitalization of underlying securities. If someone says, "stock prices rose" or "the market was up," they're generally referring to an index. A stock index is built on a specific group of stocks. Whether its value is up or down reflects the combined price movements of all the stocks in the index.

Indexes are created and maintained by exchanges normally through an index committee. However, several popular indexes are created and maintained by external companies, agencies, and newspaper houses.

Widely cited indexes include the following:

- The Dow Jones Industrial Average (DJIA) tracks stock prices of 30 major companies.
- Standard & Poor's 500, commonly referred to as the S&P 500, combines the stock prices of 500 large companies.
- The NYSE Composite Index includes all common stocks traded on the NYSE.

Apart from miming trends in the market, indexes provide investors with a cheaper method of creating interest in a market. Most popular indexes are heavily traded, and they enjoy extremely good liquidity. The impact cost of trading in these indexes is low, and they enjoy good spreads. Indexes are also not bound by the limitation of availability as compared to corporate stocks. (Corporate stocks are finite in number; indexes are not finite because they are just numbers.) All these factors make indexes a desirable product on which to trade. You can track indexes through an index fund or through index options and futures. Some investors prefer taking a position in an index itself rather than investing in individual securities. Mutual fund managers build a position in indexes to hedge their positions in stocks.

Suppose a fund manager holds $10 billion worth of securities in a portfolio. Also assume that the fund manager expects the market to fall in the medium term by 10 percent. Assuming that the securities in the portfolio are perfectly correlated with the market and the market actually falls by 10 percent, the portfolio should also see an erosion of about 10 percent. Now the fund manager faces a strange situation. Although she knows the market will fall, she cannot go ahead and sell individual securities because if she sells them individually, their prices would fall anyway because of impact. Since impact cost is much less in an index than in individual securities, the fund manager can go short (sell) on the index. Now if the market actually declines, the fund manager will lose money on the portfolio but will buy back the index she short sold and make money on her short position on the index. If the quantum of index that is sold short is calculated scientifically, the losses on the portfolio of stocks will be more or less covered by the profit on the index position. Indexes thus provide an inexpensive but potent way of eliminating portfolio risk.

We will now show how a basic index is computed and what it means when someone says that "the index has gone up by 100 points." As discussed earlier, an index is a relative measure. But what does it measure, and what does it mean?

Market capitalization measures the total current replacement value of a company. In other words, it is the price you would have to pay if you wanted to buy out the company fully (with the assumption that the prices would not rise with the buying, an unlikely case). In other words, it also indicates the amount of money it would take if someone decided to create an exact replica of the company with the same products, manufacturing, and distribution capabilities and the same brand value (in an environment where the first company is absent so the two don't compete with each other).

Market capitalization is measured by multiplying the total number of outstanding shares that the company has issued by its current market price:

Market capitalization = Total number of outstanding shares * Current market price

While constructing any index, some stocks from industries that best represent the economy are selected for inclusion in the index. These stocks are the best representatives of companies in the industry they represent. Selecting stocks that will participate in an index requires considering a number of criteria. Some of these are as follows:

- The quality of representation of the company in the industry segment to which the company belongs

- How much less the impact cost is when a transaction on this stock is executed

- The liquidity of the stock on the exchanges on which it is listed and traded

- The stock holding pattern—how widely the stock is held

Normally, the 80-20 rule applies here, meaning 20 percent of the stocks usually represent 80 percent of the market capitalization. So, a handful of about 30–50 stocks are selected. Which stocks are selected and what criteria was used is public domain information; you can get it for any index from the exchange/index owner. With about 30 stocks, their market capitalizations are added up to arrive at the market capitalization of the entire market. Thus, the market capitalization of an entire market (assuming 30 stocks have been selected) for the creation of an index is as follows (where market capitalization equals i):

Σ i = 1 to 30

Since an index is a relative measure of market capitalization, the current market capitalization is compared to the market capitalization of a selected base year. And usually 100 is taken as the starting point of the index. Using this concept, you can arrive at a number. Thus, the index is as follows:

(Current market capitalization / Average market capitalization in the base year) * 100

So, when you read that some index is at 4,000, it means the market capitalization of that particular market has gone up 40 times compared to the market capitalization of the base year. Note that you divide 4,000 by 100 in this interpretation because you multiplied the index by 100 to start. It is not compulsory that all indexes are multiplied by 100, though; it depends upon the calculation used from index to index.

If the index adds 100 points in one day and moves from 4,000 to 4,100, it means that the relative market capitalization has gone up from 40 times to 41 times. In other words, it means the market has added the kind of worth in one day that is equal to its total worth during the base year. The base year that is chosen for computing the index whose market capitalization is used as a benchmark is one where the markets were relatively stable and were not characterized by a bull or bear run. The average market capitalization is public domain information and can be calculated/obtained from the exchange/index owner.

Since market capitalization uses the current market prices of stocks and these prices change every second, the index changes every second. With the previous formula of the index and all other factors being constant, you can now compute the effect of change in an index with a change of prices in any security dollar by dollar.

Clearing Corporations

A stock exchange is an interesting market. Traders enter into hundreds of thousands of transactions with other traders without settling them immediately. They simply trust that other traders/members will honor their purchases and sale commitments. In reality, with such a complex web of transactions, any default could start a chain of defaults and could prove catastrophic. Therefore, a *clearing corporation* settles all trades executed in a stock exchange. In this section, we will first cover the importance of the role played by clearing corporations, and then we will cover how a clearing corporation functions.

Even with differences in opinion about the value of a security, trades will happen only when the parties involved in the trade are comfortable with each other, especially on the front of financial soundness. When members transact with each other, they need to believe their trade commitments will be honored. Large institutions would otherwise shy away from trading with smaller traders if they perceive the risk that small traders will not honor their commitments. Advanced exchanges have thousands of members. Even assuming 1,000 members, there could be 999,000 potential trading relationships. It is not possible for each member to verify the financial stability of the others before they enter into a trade, especially on an ongoing basis. The costs associated with this verification would be immense, and this would make markets very illiquid. In a market that does not foster confidence, few will come forward to trade.

Clearing corporations take on the onus of doing credit checks on each member. They lay down capital adequacy guidelines and make the members adhere to them. They provide exposure limits on the amount of collateral collected from members. This collateral is in the form of cash, fixed deposits, and bank guarantees. In addition to this collateral, clearing corporations ask for day-to-day margins, which are commensurate to the positions that members take on a daily basis. The position limits of members are monitored closely. Margin calls are made to members who the clearing corporation thinks can endanger the financial integrity of the overall market. In the event of a member breaching his limits, the clearing corporation immediately recommends disconnecting the trading facility for that particular member until the member brings additional collateral.

Most clearing corporations identify only members. They don't identify a member's customers and don't maintain personal- and trading-related data for a member's customers. However, in reality it is a member's customers who place the majority of orders on any exchange. Just as the clearing corporation takes responsibility of verifying the credit worthiness of its members, it leaves the verification of credit worthiness of end customers to its members. Members by and large use the same concept of asking for margins and collateral from their customers to cover their risks, and they in turn validate a customer's exposure vis-à-vis collateral and margins submitted.

Running credit checks only does not suffice, though. What if a member or customer defaults after all the precautions have been taken? A member might not put in fresh trades, but adverse price changes could result in severe losses and could make him a defaulter. In addition to having stringent credit checks, clearing corporations also guarantee transaction settlement through the concept of *novation*, discussed in detail in Chapter 2.

The level of guarantee that clearing corporations provide goes a long way in providing peace of mind to institutions and large investors, so much so that now most trading is anonymous. This means that while trading on a screen-based system, traders don't even know who they are trading with. With novation, they know that legally, their counterparty is the clearing corporation itself, and in case the counterparty defaults, the clearing corporation will make their losses good.

Every exchange usually hooks up with one or more clearing corporations to settle its trades. The clearing corporation normally levies a small fee and builds a corpus of funds over a period of time to provide this kind of guarantee. This fund is normally called a *trade guarantee fund*. Some even buy insurance policies to cover this kind of default risk.

Every member of the exchange either has a clearing agreement with one of the members of a clearing corporation or directly holds membership in the clearing corporation. Members of a clearing corporation settle either their own trades or the trades of other trading members. One trading member who is a member of a clearing corporation may sometimes choose to route trades through other clearing members because they have reached their clearing limits.

For trades executed on the NYSE, the National Securities Clearing Corporation (NSCC) acts as the clearing corporation and guarantees and settles transactions between market professionals and ensures sellers are paid and buyers receive their securities in a manner that reduces risk, cost, and post-trade uncertainties.

Since losses arising from becoming a central counterparty could be huge, clearinghouses pay a lot of attention to the credit quality of members. They also pay a lot of attention to the settlement risks faced by the clearing corporation from time to time. Risk is also controlled by the imposition of margins from members in correlation to the position they hold in the market at any given point of time.

We will now discuss how settlement takes place in brief and cover it in detail in subsequent sections. At the end of every trading period (also known as the *settlement period*), the clearing corporation arrives at figures relating to every member's obligation toward the clearing corporation and the clearing corporation's obligation toward the members. The members deliver securities and cash to discharge their obligations at the time of pay-in and receive money from the clearing corporation at the time of pay-out. Cash is interchanged through the banking channel, and securities are moved through *demat* accounts. This entire process is called *settlement*.

In terms of technology and capacity, clearing corporations must be able to handle average volumes but also peak volumes, such as the market could have witnessed after the September 11 disaster. Any shortfall in handling capacity could potentially doom the entire financial market, which in turn would become a catalyst to its demise.

Banks

Banks play two roles. Some banks are designated as *clearing banks* with whom members of a clearing corporation open *clearing accounts*. All settlement between the clearing member and clearing corporation relating to funds happens through debit and credit in this account only.

Investors and traders also maintain bank accounts, and fund-related settlements happen from these bank accounts. It is never mandatory for the investor and broker to have accounts in the same bank. Having a swift and robust banking infrastructure is highly desirable to enable initiatives such as STP and T+1 settlements. (STP and T+1 are marketwide initiatives to reduce the settlement period. We will discuss these in detail in subsequent sections of this chapter.) If transferring money from one account to another is enabled only through conventional methods such as checks and takes three days to clear, how can market participants honor their monetary obligations within one day or two days as stipulated by the T+1 and T+2 regimes? A lot of study and changes are being made/suggested in the banking sector so that it can meet this kind of challenge.

Banks play a crucial role in enabling online trading. Members enable online trading by providing a browser-based interface. Such members hook up with banks where investors are asked to open accounts. For any buy order that the investor places through the Internet, the trading system routes the order to the bank, which in turn debits the investor's account to the extent of the value of shares purchased. Investors are required to maintain either a separate account or a normal account where the bank holds a power of attorney to debit the client's account.

Depositories

A *depository* can be compared to a bank for shares. Just as a bank holds cash in your account and provides all services related to transactions of cash, a depository holds securities in electronic form and provides all services related to transactions of equity shares, debt instruments, or other securities.

A depository plays an important role in settling transactions. To increase their reach, just like banks, depositories have accredited agencies that represent them. In many countries, members of the clearing corporation themselves become agencies of the depository and provide brokering as well as depository services to their customers. In other countries, the agency is called a *depository participant*. Apart from brokers, banks and financial institutions also become depository participants. The Depository Trust Corporation (DTC) is the largest depository in the world.

An investor requiring depository services has to approach the member or the depository participant to open an account. The investor has to fill out an account opening form and fulfill some documentation requirements. Once the documentation is complete, the agency interacts with the depository and opens the account. The investor is given an account number, which he has to provide for reference for all future transactions. Shares are then kept in electronic form in this account just like money is kept in the form of electronic credits in any bank account.

The type of accounts depositories have vary from country to country. Two types of accounts are found in most depositories:

- A *beneficiary account* is an account held by an investor. As the name suggests, this type of investor enjoys all the benefits that accrue to him as a virtue of being a shareholder. These benefits include price appreciation and benefits arising from corporate actions such as dividends, bonuses, rights issues, and so on, declared on the stocks held in the beneficiary account.

- A *clearing member account* is held by a clearing member and used for facilitating settlements. This account works as a conduit, and shares flow from investors into this account and from this account to clearing corporations for pay-in, and vice versa for pay-out.

Worldwide depositories operate on a variety of architectures. Some hold the details of an investor's accounts, including details of the shares held. Others maintain details at the agency level and require that agencies maintain the details of investors and investor accounts. Some depositories use a hybrid model, meaning they hold details about the holdings of an investor and also make it mandatory for agencies to hold the same information. Though this setup means redundancy in data, at times it may be a good approach if the connectivity between the depository and the agency is not reliable or the depository is untested and is working in a relatively new environment.

The kind of transactions that depositories support varies from country to country and from market to market. Some common types of transactions in every market are as follows:

Off-market transfer: As the name suggests, these are transfers that are not backed by any market transactions on the exchange. These are transfers from one beneficiary account to another. A friend giving shares to another friend or a husband moving shares from his account to his wife's account is an example of off-market transfers where no market buying/selling is involved. This type of transfer usually takes place in large corporate deals such as acquisitions and stake sales where shares are transferred from one corporate entity to another.

Market transfers: These are transfers that result from the purchase/sale of transactions in the market (read: exchange). An investor doing a sale transaction, for example, will have to go to the depository agency and give an instruction to debit his account and credit the account of the broker through which the transaction was conducted. Similarly, if he has done a buy transaction and the broker has received securities in his account on behalf of the investor, the broker will have to give a debit instruction to debit his account and credit the account of the investor.

Interdepository transfers: This is the transfer of securities from one account in one depository to another account maintained in another depository. Depositories normally maintain connectivity with each other for these kinds of transactions, and such transactions take place as a batch process at one time or at multiple times during the day.

Pledge: An investor holding securities can pledge his securities in favor of someone to raise money or for any other reason. The securities that have been pledged cannot be transferred. When the term of the pledge expires or when both parties agree, the pledge can be closed, and the securities are again moved to the free balance. Once securities move to the free balance, they can be transferred freely.

Most of these instructions are tagged with an execution date. When the investor/broker gives a debit or credit instruction, they also specify when the transfer has to take place. The depository conducts the transfers on that particular date. All transactions within the depository can be executed instantaneously. All transfers that happen are irrevocable in nature, which means that once the transfer is complete, it cannot be transferred back without the consent and signature of the recipient.

Note that a risk is associated with a debit instruction from any investor's account. Hence, it is mandatory that investors include their signatures and expressly give all debit instructions. Credit instruction has no such risk. The investors are required to give a *standing instruction* once, and then all credits will flow automatically into their account. This method reduces the number of instructions flowing to the depository and provides convenience to investors. An analogy of this is a bank where you need to write a check to get your account debited, but for any credits coming in, you don't give any instructions. The credit just flows in. Institutions, however, don't use this facility much. They also keep a check on what securities are flowing into their accounts. Hence, they expressly give instructions for crediting their accounts.

Most brokers make investors sign a power of attorney. They use this power of attorney to generate debit instructions automatically on behalf of the investors for sale transactions they do on behalf of the investors. This saves an investor's time and effort, considering the strict timelines imposed for meeting T+2 settlements.

Depositories perform millions of such transfers daily. Apart from the transfers, depositories also safely keep shares. Instead of keeping their shares with themselves, investors hold them in a depository and don't risk losing them. Depositories also keep track of corporate actions and facilitate in providing benefits of these corporate actions to investors. For all these services, depositories levy a small fee. The agencies of depositories with which the investors interact increase these charges to levy their own charges.

Having shares in a dematerialized form is a prerequisite for T+1 and T+2 settlements. This eliminates the risk of bad deliveries to a large extent and provides a lot of operational convenience. It was not unusual during the physical certificate days to see truckloads of certificates being brought to a clearing corporation for the delivery of large orders. Imagine the effort it took for the clearinghouse to count, sort, and redistribute those shares to the buyers. In all, it used to take a lot of time and effort. In the depository system, the ownership and transfer of securities takes place by means of electronic book entries. At the outset, this system rids the capital market of the dangers related to handling paper. This system provides a lot of other benefits too:

Elimination of risks associated with physical certificates: Dealing in physical securities has the associated security risks of theft of stocks, mutilation of certificates, loss of certificates during movements through and from the registrars (thus exposing the investor to the cost of obtaining duplicate certificates and advertisements), and so on. This risk does not arise in the depository environment.

Some governments exempt stamp-duty requirements for transferring any kind of securities in the depository. This waiver extends to equity shares, debt instruments, and units of mutual funds.

Immediate transfer and registration of securities: In the depository environment, once the securities are credited to the investor's account on pay-out, the investor becomes the legal owner of the securities. The investor has no further need to send the security to the company for registration. Having purchased securities in the physical environment, the investor has to send it to the company's registrar so that the change of ownership can be registered. This process is cumbersome and takes a lot of time.

Faster settlement cycle: Markets could offer T+3, T+2, and so on—down from T+5—because dematerialized mode enables faster turnover of stock and more liquidity with the investor.

Having discussed various important entities, we will now provide a brief overview of how a typical trade life cycle moves from the order initiation phase to the final settlement phase.

Exploring the Life Cycle of a Trade

In this section, we will show how an order flows from an investor to an exchange, how it gets converted into a trade, and how it gets settled. Each order that is initiated by an investor follows a defined life cycle from initiation to settlement (see Figure 1-6). This life cycle is defined worldwide by the existing operational practices of most institutions, and the processes are more or less similar. The emphasis is on getting the orders transacted at the best possible price and on getting trades settled with the least possible risk and at manageable costs. Designated employees in the member's office ensure that each trade that takes place through them or in their house account gets settled properly. Unsettled trades lead to liability, risk, and unnecessary costs.

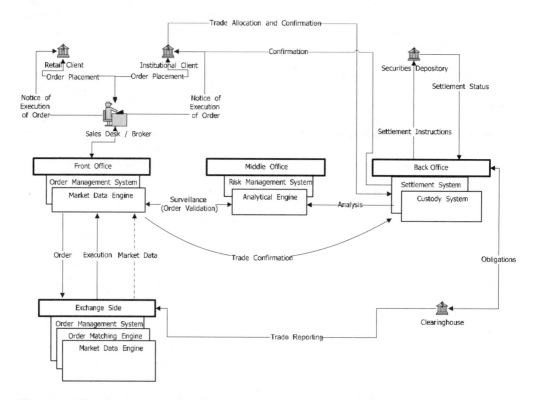

Figure 1-6. *Life cycle of a trade: schematic view*

The following steps are involved in a trade's life cycle:

1. Order initiation and delivery

2. Risk management and order routing

3. Order matching and conversion into trade

4. Affirmation and confirmation (this step is relevant for institutional trades only)

5. Clearing and settlement

Steps 1 and 3 are generally called *front-office* functions, and steps 4–5 are called *back-office* functions. The risk management part in step 2 is a *middle-office* function, and the routing part is again a front-office function. In the trading and settlement value chain, steps that take place before the order gets executed are called *pre-trade*. These include order initiation, order delivery, order management and routing, order-level risk management, and so on. Similarly, steps that take place after the order is matched and converted into a trade are called *post-trade*. The entire gamut of clearing and settlement is known as *post-trade activity*.

We will cover each of these steps in detail in the following sections. Though the underlying philosophies of executing orders at the lowest costs and performing risk-free settlements remain the same, the operational steps differ from member to member and also from country to country. Also, given an institution, the steps followed differ from client to client. This is actually more linked to the client type rather than to the client. An individual person trading is classified as a *retail customer* and is hence considered risky. Corporate customers, funds, banks, and financial institutions are called *institutional investors*. For example, risk management before order routing may be a step that takes place compulsorily for a retail client but could be waived for an institutional client, especially if the institution has a sound financial standing in the market. Additional steps are involved in settling an institutional trade in comparison to a retail trade. This difference is because institutions normally outsource their settlement function, and members have to talk to this additional agency. Institutions also have a number of checks and balances that each member has to follow.

Order Initiation and Delivery

This is the first step, and it involves accepting orders from a client and forwarding them to the exchange after doing risk management checks.

Clients keep a close eye on the markets and keep scouting for investment opportunities. They form a view about the market. View alone, however, is not enough to produce profits. Profits come from maintaining a position in the market. Positions are the results of trades that investors execute in the markets. Clients place orders with their brokers through multiple delivery channels. Some popular channels for placing orders include phones, faxes, the Internet, and interactive voice response systems (IVRSs). The majority of brokers have built-in capabilities to allow clients to submit their orders through personal digital assistants (PDAs) and other handheld devices. Institutions usually place a large number of orders. Most institutions submit their orders in soft-copy format through a floppy disk or any other bulk-upload medium.

Those who trade a lot in a particular market may even demand that the broker gives them a dedicated trading terminal. They may also set up their own trading terminal that connects to the broker's trading terminal/server through a proprietary protocol or industry-standard protocol such as Financial Information Exchange (FIX), which is a technical specification prepared in collaboration with brokers, exchanges, banks, and institutional investors to enable the seamless exchange of trading information between their systems. Systems with broker and trading institutions generate orders automatically depending upon the market conditions. Trading on such automatically generated orders is called *program trading* and is not allowed in some markets because it is perceived to cause volatility. Regardless of the methodology used for order delivery, the broker carefully records the orders so that there is no ambiguity or mistakes in processing. Almost all brokers record the conversation between clients and brokers, which can be used later for dispute resolution in case any ambiguity exists over what was communicated and what was interpreted and executed.

Institutions normally speak to a *sales desk* of the broker and get a feel for the market. An institution or the fund manager who places the order may be managing multiple funds. At the time of placing the order, however, the fund manager may not know to which fund he will allocate the securities bought/sold. At the point of placing the order, the fund manager just instructs the sales desk of the broker to execute the order.

An individual order received from a client is tagged with some special conditions such as good till cancelled (GTC), good till date (GTD), limit order, market order, and so on. These conditions dictate the rate and condition at which the customer expects the orders to be executed. (We will discuss these conditions in more detail in Chapter 2.) The member on a best-effort basis accepts the order. Unless an institution specifically demands it, there is no standard practice of giving back-order confirmation details. This essentially means that the clients work with brokers on good faith that the broker has understood their order terms clearly and will get it executed at the best possible price. It is important that brokers preserve the sanctity of the conditions specified and get the orders executed within the boundaries of specification. Failure to do so will result in the client moving to a different brokerage house.

Note Reputation is far more important than any other attribute in this business. Institutions like brokers who get their orders executed at the best possible prices and save them money. Standard methodologies are available for institutions to measure the performance of brokers.

Risk Management and Order Routing

Regardless of how an order gets generated or delivered, it passes through a risk management matrix. This matrix is a series of risk management checks that an order undergoes before it is forwarded to the exchange. We discussed earlier that the onus of getting the trades settled resides with the broker. Any client default will have to be made good to the clearing corporation by the broker. Credit defaults are thus undesirable from the point of view of the broker who puts money and credibility on the line on behalf of the customer. Hence, these credit and risk management checks are deemed necessary.

Institutions are normally considered less risky than retail customers. That is because they have a large balance sheet compared to the size of orders they want to place. They also maintain a lot of collateral with the members they push their trades through. Their trades are hence subjected to fewer risk management checks than retail clients.

The mechanisms followed when orders are accepted and sent to exchanges for matching are the same for both institutions and retail clients. However, for retail customers the orders are subjected to tighter risk management checks and scrutiny. The underlying assumption in all such risk management checks is that retail clients are less credit worthy and hence more susceptible to defaulting than institutions. A recent extension of retail trading has been trading through the Internet. This exposes brokers to even more risk because the clients become faceless. In the good old days of "call and trade" (receiving orders by phone), most brokers executed transactions of clients they knew. With the advancement in trading channels, the process of account opening became more institutionalized, and the numbers came at the expense of client scrutiny. Most brokers who operate on behalf of retail clients these days operate on the *full-covered* concept. This means that while accepting orders from retail clients, they cover their risks as much as possible by demanding an equal value of cash or near cash securities.

We'll briefly cover how a retail transaction is conducted so you can understand the benefit provided by risk management. The method utilized is more or less the same in call and trade as in Internet trading. The order delivery mechanism changes, but the basic risk management principle implemented remains the same. Here are the steps:

1. The client calls the broker to give the orders for a transaction (in Internet trading the client logs on to the Internet trading site, provides credentials, and enters orders).

2. The broker validates that the order is coming from a correct and reliable source.

3. In case the client gives a buy order, the broker's system makes a query to ascertain whether the client has enough balance in a bank account or in the account the client maintains with the broker. In case the client does not have enough balance, the order is rejected even before forwarding to the exchange. If the client has the balance, the order is accepted, but the value of the order is deducted from the client's balance to ensure that he does not send a series of orders for which he cannot make an upfront payment. Many brokers still do not have direct interfaces to a banking system. In such cases, they ask the client to maintain a deposit and collateral in the form of cash and other securities; they keep the ledger balances of a client's cash and collateral account in their back-office system and query this system while placing the order to ensure that the client has enough money in his account (see Figure 1-7).

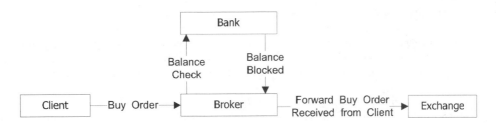

Figure 1-7. *Buy orders of retail clients are usually validated against the amount held in the bank/account with the broker.*

4. In case a client gives a sell order, the broker checks the client's custody/demat account to ensure that he has a sufficient balance of securities to honor the sale transaction. Short selling is prohibited in most countries, and brokers need to ensure that the client is not short of securities at the time of settlement, especially in markets that do not have an adequate stock-lending mechanism in place. Most markets have an auction mechanism in place for bailing out people with short positions, but such bailouts could be very expensive. Once the sale transaction is executed, the broker keeps a record and updates the custody balance's system if it is in-house or keeps reducing the figures from the figures returned by the depository to reflect the client's true stock account position. In many countries, brokers have a direct interface with the depository system that lets them query the amount of shares of a particular company in which the client has balances. Wherever a direct interface is absent, the broker maintains the figures in parallel; the broker then does a periodic refresh of this data by uploading the figures provided by the depository and maintains a proper intraday position by debiting figures in his system when the clients give sale orders that are executed on the exchange (see Figure 1-8).

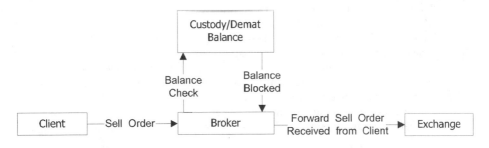

Figure 1-8. *Sell orders are validated against the stock balance held by the client in the custody/demat account.*

5. Once the risk management check passes, the client's order is forwarded to the exchange.

6. On receipt of the order, the exchange immediately sends an order confirmation to the broker's trading system.

7. Depending upon the order terms and the actual prices prevailing in the market, the order could get executed immediately or remain pending in the order book of the exchange.

You can appreciate the role technology plays when you consider that the entire process of receiving the order, doing risk management checks, forwarding the order to the exchange, and getting back the confirmation is expected to take a few hundredths of a second. Any performance not conforming to this standard is considered unacceptable and could be a serious reason for clients to look for other brokers who can transact faster and get them more aggressive prices.

One of the ways of implementing risk management is through *margining*. A margin is an amount that clearing corporations levy on the brokers for maintaining positions on the exchange. The amount of margin levied is proportional to the exposure and risk the broker is carrying. Since positions may belong to a broker's clients, it is the broker's responsibility to recover margins from clients. Margins make the client stand by trades in case the market goes against the client by the time the trades get settled.

Let's examine this concept using an example: Suppose a client purchased 1,000 Microsoft shares at $45 per share. The total amount needed to be paid to the clearing corporation at the time of settling the transaction is $45,000. But this is payable only after two days of executing the transaction. This is because in most markets there is a lag of two days between executing the transaction and finally settling it. Assume on the next day of transacting—that is, T+1—there is adverse news about Microsoft that causes the stock price to drop 10 percent. The client would see an erosion of $4,500 straight from his account if he has to honor the position. The client would have a strong incentive to default in this transaction merely by not showing up to the broker to make the payment. To protect the market from such defaulters, clearing corporations levy margins on the date of the trade. Margins are computed and applied to a client's position in many ways, but the underlying philosophy of levying margins is to tie the customer to a position and preserve the integrity of the market even if a large drop in stock prices occurs.

Order Matching and Conversion into Trade

All orders are aggregated and sent to an exchange for execution. Chapter 2 explains the entire process of order matching in detail. Stock exchanges follow defined rules for matching all the orders they receive. While protecting the interests of each client, the exchange tries to execute orders at the best possible rates. The broker's trading system communicates with the exchange's trading system on a real-time basis to know the fate of orders it has submitted.

A broker keeps a record of which orders were entered during the day, by whom, and on behalf of which client. A broker also maintains details of how many orders were transacted and how many are still pending to be executed. Using this system, a broker can modify the order and order terms, cancel the order, and also split the order if required depending upon the behavior of the market and instructions from the clients. Once the order is executed, it gets converted to a trade. The exchange passes the trade numbers to the broker's system. The broker in turn communicates these trade details to the client either during the day or by the end of the day through a *contract note* or through an *account activity statement*. The contract note is a legal document that binds the broker and the client. Contract note delivery is a legal requirement in many countries. Apart from the execution details, the contract note contains brokerage fees and other fees that brokers levy for themselves or collect on behalf of other agencies such as the clearing corporation, exchange, or state.

Affirmation and Confirmation

This step is present only when the trading client is an institution. Every institution engages the services of an agency called a *custodian* to assist them in clearing and settlement activities (see Figure 1-9). As the name suggests, a custodian works in the interest of the institution that has engaged its services. Institutions specialize in taking positions and holding. To outsource the activity of getting their trades settled and to protect themselves and their shareholder's interests, they hire a local custodian in the country where they trade. When they trade in multiple countries, they also have a global custodian who ensures that settlements are taking place seamlessly in local markets using local custodians.

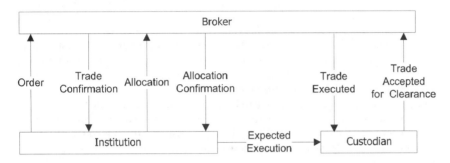

Figure 1-9. *Affirmation and confirmation process*

As discussed earlier, while giving the orders for the purchase/sale of a particular security, the fund manager may just be in a hurry to build a position. He may be managing multiple funds or portfolios. At the time of giving the orders, the fund managers may not really have a fund in mind in which to allocate the shares. To avoid a market turning unfavorable, the fund manager will usually give a large order with the intention of splitting the position into multiple funds. This is to ensure that when he makes profits in a large position, it gets divided into multiple funds, and many funds benefit.

The broker accepts this order for execution. On successful execution, the broker sends the trade confirmations to the institution. The fund manager at the institution during the day makes up his mind about how many shares have to be allocated to which fund and by evening sends the broker these details. These details are also called *allocation details* in market parlance. Brokers then prepare the contract notes in the names of the funds in which the fund manager has requested allocation.

Along with the broker, the institution also has to liaise with the custodian for the orders it has given to the broker. The institution provides allocation details to the custodian as well. It also provides the name of the securities, the price range, and the quantity of shares ordered. This prepares the custodian, who is updated about the information expected to be received from the broker. The custodian also knows the commission structure the broker is expected to charge the institution and the other fees and statutory levies.

Using the allocation details, the broker prepares the contract note and sends it to the custodian and institution. In many countries, communications between broker, custodian, and institutions are now part of an STP process. This enables the contract to be generated electronically and be sent through the STP network. In countries where STP is still not in place, all this communication is manual through hand delivery, phone, or fax.

On receipt of the trade details, the custodian sends an affirmation to the broker indicating that the trades have been received and are being reviewed. From here onward, the custodian initiates a *trade reconciliation process* where the custodian examines individual trades that arrive from the broker and the resultant position that gets built for the client. Trades are validated to check the following:

- The trade happened on the desired security.

- The trade is on the correct side (that is, it is actually buy and not sell when buy was specified).

- The price at which the trade happened is within the price range specified by the institution.

- Brokerage and other fees levied are as per the agreement with the institution and are correct.

The custodian usually runs a software back-office system to do this checking. Once the trade details match, the custodian sends a confirmation to the broker and to the clearing corporation that the trade executed is fine and acceptable. A copy of the confirmation also goes to the institutional client. On generation of this confirmation, obligation of getting the trade settled shifts to the custodian (a custodian is also a clearing member of the clearing corporation).

In case the trade details do not match, the custodian rejects the trade, and the trades shift to the broker's books. It is then the broker's decision whether to keep the trade (and face the associated price risk) or square it at the prevailing market prices. The overall risk that the custodian is bearing by accepting the trade is constantly measured against the collateral that the institution submits to the custodian for providing this service.

Clearing and Settlement

With hundreds of thousands of trades being executed every day and thousands of members getting involved in the entire trading process, clearing and settling these trades seamlessly becomes a humungous task. The beauty of this entire trading and settlement process is that it has been taking place on a daily basis without a glitch happening at any major clearing corporation for decades. We discussed earlier that apart from providing a counterguarantee, one of the key roles of a clearing corporation is getting trades settled after being executed. We will now cover in brief how this entire process works.

After the trades are executed on the exchange, the exchange passes the trade details to the clearing corporation for initiating settlement. Clearing is the activity of determining the answers to who owes the following:

- What?

- To whom?

- When?

- Where?

The entire process of clearing is directed toward answering these questions unambiguously. Getting these questions answered and moving assets in response to these findings to settle obligations toward each other is *settlement* (see Figure 1-10). Thus, *clearing* is the process of determining obligations, after which the obligations are discharged by settlement. It provides a clean slate for members to start a new day and transact with each other.

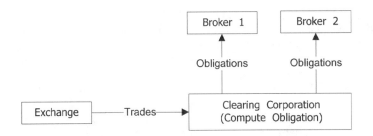

Figure 1-10. *The clearing corporation computes the obligations for every member arising from trades and communicates it to members as a first step toward settlement.*

When members trade with each other, they generate obligations toward each other. These obligations are in the form of the following:

- Funds (for all buy transactions done and that are not squared by existing sale positions)

- Securities (for all sale transactions done)

Normally, in a T+2 environment, members are expected to settle their transactions after two days of executing them. The terms *T+2*, *T+3*, and so on, are the standard market nomenclature used to indicate the number of days after which the transactions will get settled after being executed. A trade done on Monday, for example, has to be settled on Wednesday in a T+2 environment.

As a first step toward settlement, the clearing corporation tries to answer the "what?" portion of the clearing problem. It calculates and informs the members of what their obligations are on the funds side (cash) and on the securities side. These obligations are net obligations with respect to the clearing corporation. Since the clearing corporation identifies only the members, the obligations of all the customers of the members are netted across each other, and the final obligation is at the member level. This means if a member sold 5,000 shares of Microsoft for client A and purchased 1,000 shares for client B, the member's net obligation will be 4,000 shares to be delivered to the clearing corporation. Because most clearing corporations provide novation (splitting of trades, discussed in more detail in Chapter 2), these obligations are broken into obligations from members toward the clearing corporation and from the clearing corporation toward the members. The clearing corporation communicates obligations though its clearing system that members can access. The member will normally reconcile these figures using data available from its own back-office system. This reconciliation is necessary so that both the broker and the clearing corporation are in agreement with what is to be exchanged and when.

In an exchange-traded scenario, answers to "whom?" and "where?" are normally known to all and are a given. "Whom?" in all such settlement obligations is the clearing corporation itself. Of course, the clearing corporation also has to work out its own obligations toward the members. Clearing members are expected to open clearing accounts with certain banks specified by the clearing corporation as clearing banks. They are also expected to open clearing accounts with the depository. They are expected to keep a ready balance for their fund obligations in the bank account and similarly maintain stock balances in their clearing demat account. In the questions on clearing, the answer to "where?" is the funds settlement account and the securities settlement account.

The answers to "what?" and "when?" can change dramatically. The answer to "when?" is provided by the pay-in and pay-out dates. Since the clearing corporation takes responsibility for settling all transactions, it first takes all that is due to it from the market (members) and then distributes what it owes to the members. Note that the clearing corporation just acts as a conduit and agent for settling transactions and does not have a position of its own. This means all it gets must normally match all it has to distribute.

Two dates play an important role of determining when the obligation needs to be settled. These are called the *pay-in date* and the *pay-out date*. Once the clearing corporation informs all members of their obligations, it is the responsibility of the clearing members to ensure that they make available their obligations (shares and money) in the clearing corporation's account on the date of pay-in, before the pay-in time. At a designated time, the clearing corporation debits the funds and securities account of the member in order to discharge an obligation toward the clearing corporation. The clearing corporation takes some time in processing the pay-in it has received and then delivers the obligation it has toward clearing members at a designated time on the date of pay-out. It is generally desired that there should be minimal gap between pay-in and pay-out to avoid risk to the market. Earlier this difference used to be as large as three days in some markets. With advancement in technology, the processing time has come down, and now it normally takes a few hours from pay-in to pay-out. Less time means less risk and more effective fund allocation by members and investors. The answer to "when?" is satisfied by the pay-in and pay-out calendar of the clearing corporation, which in turn is calculated depending upon the settlement cycle (T+1, T+2, or T+3).

Answers to "what?" depend on the transactions of each member and their final positions with respect to the exchange. Suppose a member has done a net of buy transactions; he will owe money to the clearing corporation in contrast to members who have done net sell transactions, who will owe securities to the clearing corporation. To effect settlements, the clearing corporation hooks up with banks (which it normally calls *clearing banks*) and depositories. It has a clearing account with the clearing bank and a clearing account with the depository as well. A clearing bank account is used to settle cash obligations, and a clearing account with a depository is used to settle securities obligations.

Funds Settlement

Funds settlement is relevant for all buy transactions that are not *netted off* by offsetting the sale transaction. This is required because brokers have to pay for all the securities they have purchased. For funds settlement, every broker is required to open a clearing account with a clearing bank designated by the clearing corporation. The broker then needs to ensure that he parks the required amount, as specified in funds obligation by the clearing corporation, in the clearing account before the pay-in.

For obligations arising because of transactions done by the client, the broker has to collect money from the client. Hence, the following takes place:

1. For a buy transaction, the client issues a check-in favor of his broker or pays money through other acceptable payment channels.

2. The broker calculates (and also receives as a notice from a clearing corporation) his total monetary obligation and deposits money accordingly in the clearing account. (Since this deposit is a routine activity, he normally keeps a deposit in the clearing account much like a current account, and the clearing corporation keeps debiting and crediting his account depending upon whose obligation is toward whom. The clearing corporation also pays money to the clearing member in case a member is a net seller of securities; in this case, the money is the sale proceeds of the member.)

3. The clearing corporation debits this clearing account by the amount of money required to meet the settlement obligation at the time of pay-in. As discussed in the previous step, if the obligation is in favor of the broker, the clearing corporation credits the broker's clearing account during pay-out.

In case a client has sold securities and needs to be paid, the broker will issue a check after receiving the money from the clearing corporation during pay-out.

All funds obligation is therefore managed by debiting and crediting this clearing account. Moving money from and to this account rarely takes place through checks these days. Standard banking interfaces and electronic funds movement channels move money from one account to another.

Also note that the clients can be based in a city that is different from where the broker has a clearing account. Clients are not required to deposit checks directly in the clearing account. They submit their checks locally to the broker's office, and the broker's staff can deposit the check in a local branch or forward it to the head office. As discussed earlier, all money required to meet the obligation has to reach the clearing account by T+2 in a T+2 settlement regime. This makes keeping large working capital necessary. In some countries, brokers have special arrangements with their banks to treat money in the local branch accounts as money in the clearing account and will honor the clearing request made by the clearing corporation as long as the sum of all money in such accounts is more than the demand made by the clearing corporation. They also have the facility to move this money swiftly, often on an intraday or next-day basis, so that such obligations can be met.

With funds settlement, settlement is only partially complete. Even the securities side has to be settled for settlement to be complete.

Securities Obligation

All efforts are directed toward ensuring that the clearing corporation receives the shares before the pay-in time. Just like a broker maintains a clearing account for funds with a designated clearing bank, brokers are required to maintain a clearing account for securities with the depository. At the time of pay-in, the clearing corporation just puts its hands in this clearing account and takes whatever has been placed there for meeting the securities obligation.

The clearing account for the securities of a broker can be logically divided into three parts, as shown in Figure 1-11.

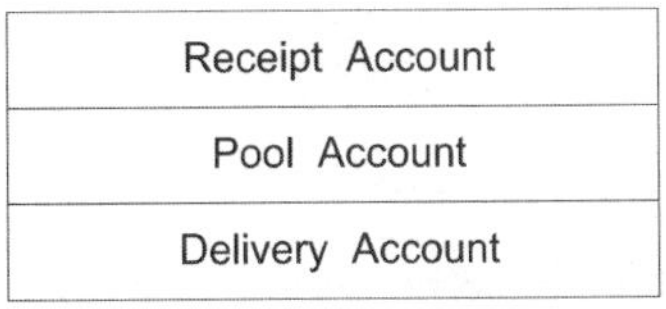

| Receipt Account |
| Pool Account |
| Delivery Account |

Figure 1-11. *Logical breakdown of a securities clearing account*

Whatever securities the broker is required to deliver to meet his pay-in requirements move to the delivery account. Note that the existence of a delivery account is logical only in theory. Hence, there is no movement of shares per se. What actually happens is that brokers give special instructions earmarking securities for pay-in. It is an express statement that authorizes the clearing corporation to pick up these shares and use them toward the discharge of a broker's obligation. This express statement is necessary because at the time of pay-in, the broker may have a large reserve of securities in his pool account that may not be meant for delivery, and all such securities need to be ignored while picking up the securities.

Just like funds obligation arises from purchase transactions, securities obligation arises from sale transactions of a client. To discharge this obligation, clients need to move securities from their accounts to the clearing corporation accounts. They do this using a three-step process:

1. The client gives a debit instruction in his account and credits the broker's securities account with the required number of shares. With completion of this step, the shares move from the client's securities account to the broker's pool account.

2. The broker marks these securities for pay-in and moves them logically from his pool account to the delivery account.

3. At the time of pay-in, the clearing corporation takes all the securities in the delivery account to discharge the broker's securities obligation.

This, however, does not complete settlement. Note that the broker could also be a buyer of some securities. He will receive these securities in his receipt account during pay-out. This receipt account is also a logical account. The shares will actually reside in the pool account itself, but they will be properly classified as "received in pay-out for a particular settlement."

For the settlement of securities that clients have purchased through a broker, the broker gives a debit instruction in his securities account favoring the client. As a result, shares move from the broker's account to the client's account. A broker will move shares to the client's account after the client has paid for the purchase. Figure 1-12 illustrates this process.

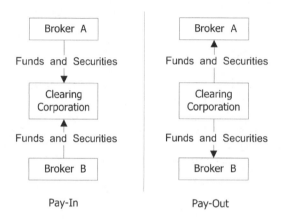

Figure 1-12. *Settlement comprises pay-in and pay-out.*

Transactions are thus called *settled* when both the funds part and the securities part are settled. This provides traders with a clean slate to trade afresh without worrying about the consequences of trades they did in the past. Settlements ensure that their transactions have reached finality and that the benefits of executing the transactions will accrue to them.

After understanding the basics of how transactions are executed and settled, you will now explore another important aspect, STP. STP plays an important role in getting all the participants together in a way that good synergy is achieved and that the operational time, risk, and cost of getting this entire cycle from order initiation to settlement is automated.

Exploring the Precursor to Straight Through Processing (STP)

To understand STP, you need to understand the concepts of the *front office, middle office,* and *back office* (see Figure 1-13). These are, role-wise, the segregation in a member's office or trading institution's office. The front office is responsible for trading. In a broker's office, the front office speaks to various customers and solicits business. The front-office staff is also responsible for managing orders and executing them. The back-office staff is responsible for settling transactions. The back office ensures that all obligations toward the clearing corporation are met seamlessly and that the member receives its share during pay-out. While this entire process is happening, the middle office monitors all limits and exposures, and thus risks, that the firm is assuming. The middle office is also responsible for reporting, especially where corporate-level reporting is required. Since a broker's office is organized into front, middle, and back offices, solution providers structure their products in the same fashion in the form of *modules*. Although many vendors provide solutions for all three sections, it is not mandatory for a broker to buy all three modules from the same vendor. If a broker goes for different vendors, though, then they have an issue of intermodule communication. Most brokers want all the three modules to be integrated. If they are not, then data will have to be entered multiple times in these modules. To obviate from this problem, brokers rely on a concept called STP (see Figure 1-14).

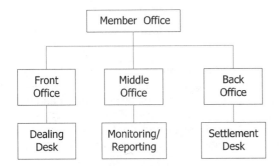

Figure 1-13. *Front, middle, and back offices*

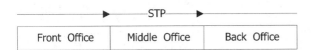

Figure 1-14. *Conceptual view of STP*

STP, as defined by the Securities Industry Association (SIA), is "...the process of seamlessly passing financial information to all parties involved in the transaction process, spanning the investment manager decision through to reconciliation and statement production, without manual handling or redundant processing in real time."

Two types of STP exist: internal and external. In the case just discussed, *internal STP* is required because you need to connect modules installed in a broker's office. But some other entities such as custodians, fund managers, and so on, play an equally important role in settlement. To achieve true STP, even these need to be connected to each other. Any attempt to connect such entities beyond the organization in pursuit of STP is called *external STP*. We will lay the foundation for STP in this section and discuss some related but advanced concepts in Chapters 6 and 7.

The industry wants to put processes in place that will allow an order to flow right from deal entry to conversion to trade to affirmation and confirmation and finally through settlement and accounting without manual intervention. This is because the industry wants to move toward T+1 settlement. This means trades done on one day will get settled the next day. This is an ambitious plan because it will call for a lot of process change, technology change, and industry change. Applications will have to come together and orchestrate the entire business process.

STP provides a lot of benefits to industry participants:

- STP reduces settlement time. This essentially reduces risk because transactions will be settled faster and will be irrevocable. Settlements are said to be *irrevocable* when they are considered to be final and cannot be reversed. Reduced settlement time also means better utilization of capital.

- Less manual intervention will mean fewer operational risks and errors. It will also mean fewer costs.

- STP will force the entire industry to move toward standard communication protocols. This will mean standardized systems and fewer system development and maintenance costs. Interoperability will be a prerequisite for this to happen; we will go into depth about this in Chapter 7.

- Increased automation will lead to increased throughput in transaction processing, thereby enabling institutions to achieve greater transaction volumes.

Equity trading and STP by itself are vast subjects, and understanding every minute business detail in a single go is not possible; furthermore, the functioning of every stock exchange is different from one another (though the concepts are fairly standard). We hope you by now understand the importance of financial markets, why equities are issued, and how they are traded and settled. We will discuss STP concepts in more detail in Chapters 6 and 7. You should also be in a position to understand the various entities in a financial system relating to equities trading and settlement.

Understanding .NET in an Equities Market

Figure 1-6 clearly demonstrates the amount of business complexity involved in achieving end-to-end automation. To technically realize this entire business case, you need a rock-solid technology platform that is capable of providing an intelligent solution to various aspects of the business. In the equities market, we broadly categorize business functionality in the form of the front office, middle office, and back office. The target audiences of this business are different, and obviously their expectations from the system are different. For instance, front-office systems are highly performance-oriented, and the audience using them demands an instant response. Front-office systems are (near) real-time systems, and their core responsibility is to open new business opportunities by providing the correct information at the correct time. On the other hand, back-office systems are database oriented and somewhat relaxed in terms of real-time performance. Back-office systems are the information backbone of the organization and provide a strong reporting and regulatory compliance feature. Similarly, middle-office systems are designed for managing risk and are used by both front-office and back-office systems. Performance is important in all phases of a trade's life cycle, but a tolerance factor determines to what extent systems can bend and lends itself to quirks and rapid changes in market conditions. In the front-office system, the tolerance factor needs to be absolutely low, but the same may not be true for back-office systems.

Figure 1-15 depicts the technology stack used in the pre-.NET days to implement front-office, middle-office, and back-office functionality. C/C++ stands out as the most favorable candidate in designing front-office systems, and the primary reason behind such a decision is the multitude of resources offered by the language. C/C++ offers a broad range of programming features to equip developers so they can deal with all spectrums of programming such as the operating system, graphical user interface, network, multithreaded programming, and so on. Back-office systems are designed using rapid application development (RAD) tools such as Visual Basic and are backed with extremely powerful relational database management systems (RDBMSs) such as SQL Server or Sybase. Finally, a middle-office system's implementation varies and is mainly driven by the business requirement. If a lot of analytics are involved that require complex mathematical calculation, then Microsoft Excel is the primary programming tool.

Figure 1-15. *Pre-.NET days*

There is no doubt that when performance forms the key factor to success of the trading business, then C/C++ is used. C/C++ has both a bright side and a dark side. The dark side is the time-consuming coding tasks and hard-to-detect memory leaks faced in a production environment. Some good integrated development environments (IDEs) are available to bring down the development time to some extent, but they never meet a developer's satisfaction. Despite all these problems, you must appreciate that Microsoft is always full of new ideas.

For example, Microsoft introduced the Component Object Model (COM) technology with an aim of revolutionizing the Microsoft programming world. COM architecture heavily promoted reusability among Microsoft programming languages, which in turn opened the door for implementing a new hybrid programming approach, as depicted in Figure 1-16. The performance-critical code was developed in C++ and happily exposed to the outside world as COM components. The consumers of these components could be any COM-aware programming language. The organization started devising a new strategy in which the majority of tasks were implemented using RAD tools, and only the small portion that is performance sensitive is implemented in C/C++ and exposed as COM components. This in turn increased developer productivity and promoted faster development time.

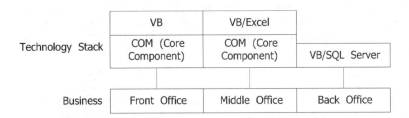

Figure 1-16. *COM days*

But such language monogamy among Microsoft products was not striking enough to face the competition from its rivals, and with business complexities growing day by day Microsoft clearly needed a deeply integrated programming model. This is where .NET came to the rescue (see Figure 1-17).

Figure 1-17. *.NET days*

Innovation is the culmination of an individual's imagination, and .NET innovation is the culmination of the "Redmondian" imagination. It filled many of the gaps and also answered many of the key decisions in determining the platform selection. The whole programming model was revisited and reengineered from the ground up, giving birth to the common language runtime (CLR). The CLR is a modern run-time system and welcomes developers into a new "managed world" where *managed code* is written in a *managed language* and executed in a *managed environment*. The CLR provides the execution environment and other core services to managed code that form one of the strong foundations in designing a robust and secure application.

.NET as a language offers rich programming features and also overcomes most of the deficiencies that were evident in the earlier Windows programming languages. Because of this, .NET gave impetus to major financial organizations to look at their business realms and reconsider their decisions and investments. .NET clearly provides all the features of a good programming language:

Automatic garbage collection: Trading-related applications usually fall prey to memory-related problems, and diagnosing such leaks is every programmer's nightmare. Even though one of the basic tenets of programming is to allocate resources when required and reclaim the memory when it is not required, this is an explicit step that a programmer needs to strictly follow. Although most programmers follow this discipline religiously, as with all human endeavors, mistakes tend to creep in. .NET relieved developers from battling these memory leaks by introducing nondeterministic garbage collection. Programs written in .NET completely depend upon garbage collection, which uses a heuristics-based algorithm to reclaim memory from unused or unreachable resources. It is also nondeterministic because the timing of performing garbage collection is not determined and comes into action when memory pressure is felt, finally freeing up memory space.

Deployment: The ease of deploying applications is considered to be one of the key attributes in determining the adaptability of applications. Deployment was extremely painful during the COM days; with advent of .NET, this task is made extremely simple by embracing the XCOPY-style deployment approach. The only prerequisite required to execute .NET-based applications is the .NET Framework; after installing the framework, developers or users can install .NET applications simply by copying the binaries.

Openness: With .NET, Microsoft has entered into community development for the first time, breaking the long-standing wall between consumers and producers. This is made possible by outlining a specification known as the Common Language Infrastructure (CLI). The specification defines everything from execution environment to metadata information that would enable anyone to build a concrete implementation. The .NET Framework itself adheres to this specification. To encourage community participation, Microsoft released Shared Source CLI, popularly known as Rotor, which basically is a spin-off from the original .NET Framework. Shared Source CLI contains source code that provides a deep understanding of the language infrastructure.

Platform neutrality: Applications written in .NET are no longer limited to the Windows platform; they can be targeted on any platform as long as the underlying execution runtime is available and adheres to the CLI standard. Mono (http://www.go-mono.com) is one of the successful implementations of CLR available for the Linux platform.

Security: In the olden days, application security was always an afterthought. But with the advent of .NET, the equation has changed; security is given important consideration and is baked into every aspect of the framework. Security is branched into two forms: code access security and data security. *Code access security* is all about protecting resources based on the identity and origin of the code. This is in contrast to *data security*, which is used to enable secure message exchange using various cryptographic algorithms.

Interoperability: The base framework in .NET provides most of the features required for day-to-day operation. However, it still falls short of some of the functionality available in the Win32 world. The same applies to the COM technology. .NET provides backward compatibility and allows seamless integration with legacy COM components or Win32 DLLs by using the Platform-Invoke (P/Invoke) API. This will motivate organizations to migrate to this new platform without losing the investment done on legacy code.

Business-to-business integration: The next big wave in software development is connecting various heterogeneous systems deployed in an organization. The biggest problems faced are integration and interoperability between systems; to resolve these issues, you need a platform that connects this system and takes advantage of investments made in existing systems. .NET heavily promotes this goal by providing unconditional and unstinted support to Web services–based development. Web services are the implementation backbone and vehicle for connecting systems using industry-established open standards and protocols.

Language rich: .NET is language rich. Currently, more than 20 programming languages are available, and such an influx of languages completely eliminates the steep learning curve required for an individual. Organizations can smoothly mobilize their development forces based on the favored in-house programming language. For example, if COBOL is the most suitable language for the organization's software automation, then the developers can use COBOL.NET.

Handheld computing: The .NET Compact Framework is a slim version of the .NET Framework that facilitates the development of applications targeted for handheld and mobile devices. The overall resource bandwidth in handheld devices is limited and hence needs to be judiciously utilized. Considering this resource limitation, Microsoft shipped Compact Framework, which is optimized for both the time and space dimensions of an application. Even though not all features of the .NET Framework are available in the Compact Framework, the available class hierarchy is inline with .NET Framework classes. This provides a smooth learning curve and transition for any developer who wants to develop programs for handheld devices.

Productivity: Visual Studio .NET 2003/2005 is a full-blown IDE that offers RAD, deployment and packaging, versioning, debugging, IntelliSense help, dynamic help, and many more features that help to increase software development productivity. Furthermore, the VS .NET IDE is fully extensible to allow developers to automate most common routine daily tasks by packaging them inside *macros*. Macros are .NET-based executables written in VB .NET or C# but are designated to execute inside the IDE shell.

Community support: You can gauge the growing popularity of .NET by the amount of contribution from the open source development community. . NET introduced a new posture toward the open source initiative by encouraging thousands of developers around the globe to develop open source applications based on the .NET Framework. This support is further backed by the strong community support available in the form of blogs and newsgroups.

Academic research: .NET has not only gained success in the commercial world but has also stretched its wings into academic research. Popular universities now consider .NET a part of their course curriculums. Several new research projects are also underway. Such solid commitments will further help reshape the future of .NET-related technologies.

Development methodology: .NET has emerged as a leading platform that makes software quality endeavors much simpler to implement. With .NET, most of the manual development processes are automated, thereby infusing discipline into every stage of the software life cycle. This automation has resulted in higher productivity and fewer software defects.

Potentiality: With the industry already moving toward a 64-bit computing initiative, there is heavy demand for the 64-bit CLR. As of this writing, Microsoft has already floated a 64-bit CLR designed to work with Windows 2003 64-bit editions. There is virtually no rework involved in moving the existing 32-bit versions of .NET applications, and the existing managed code base can be migrated to the 64-bit CLR with little or no change.

So far we have discussed only the most important features of .NET. We will discuss several other important aspects of .NET in subsequent chapters.

What Is a Techno-Domain Architect?

An *architect* is a creator who crafts the destiny of a vision or a goal, and a *software architect* is no different from a civil architect in this aspect. When it comes to the final objective, a software architect's ultimate mission is to provide a strong foundation. It is important for a civil architect to build a strong base for constructing a building. If the foundation is weak, it will create a devastating effect and even risk lives. The same analogy applies to a software architect; a loose foundation will shake the business of an organization. As the first person to enter the application development arena, the software architect's primary role is to understand the requirements of the organization and apply the appropriate technology mix that is best suited for the organization.

In today's world where every area of computer science has seen many forms of growth and given the depth and breadth of current technologies, it is extremely challenging to keep abreast of all these aspects. It is virtually impossible to achieve mastery over all areas. To keep pace with growing technologies, software architects have started to specialize in various forms, including as enterprise architects, security architects, infrastructure architects, interoperability architects, information architects, and so on. As their names suggest, each architect's roles and responsibilities are clearly defined, which in turn helps to clearly articulate their technical strengths.

Techno-domain architects can be considered as one of the branches of the software architect tree. Unlike architects from other branches whose core focus is sharpening only technical skills, a techno-domain architect has excellent command over both the domain and the technology. Such specialized architects are limited in number because people's skill sets are usually one-sided: a person is specialized either in the hard-core technology or in the business aspects of the domain. Thus, a techno-domain architect is a vertical specialist who has gathered tremendous knowledge in a particular niche area by designing and executing real-life systems and in the process assimilated both the nutrients of the system (that is, the domain knowledge and the underlying technology to realize the business case).

Techno-domain architects are not meant to replace business analysts. Business analysts will continue to play a key role in the requirements-gathering phase. Vertical specialists, with their knowledge of the particular niche area, will help to strengthen the team as a whole.

Both technology and businesses change over a period of time. But changes in business are frequent and are driven by changes in the external environment. Moreover, there is no longevity associated with business; once a business feature is outdated, it carries no further value. However, technology has an associated aging factor and is a slowly decaying process. Thus, keeping abreast of both these aspects of a system is a challenging task for a vertical specialist.

Understanding the Three I's (Intelligence) of Performance in Capital Markets

Performance is the mantra for all high-performance or mission-critical applications. This is generally overlooked in small-scale applications where the number of users is limited and the number of transactions conducted is relatively small. Performance goals in such small-scale applications are often sidelined or considered only during the design phase, and no additional thought process is usually invested subsequently. This is in direct contrast to mission-critical applications where performance is given serious thought in every phase, is continuously refined, and is constantly evidenced in the form of significant growth and improvement in the overall functioning of the system.

Efficiency of applications revolves around the following main objectives of performance:

Responsiveness: Responsiveness is measured by how fast the system reacts to a user request.

Latency: Latency is the quantum of time taken to get a response. Latency is usually high in a networked application.

Throughput: Throughput is often measured during a peak time and depicts the application's full potential to handle the maximum load in a given amount of time.

Scalability: Scalability is often overstressed, but in reality it relates to the scaling of hardware resources.

Several guidelines provide a wealth of information about how to achieve these objectives, and even some best programming practices will elevate the performance of an application to a certain level. However, remember that performance is an art and cannot be achieved by applying some straightforward cookbook rules. You can achieve these goals only by closely evaluating the environment under which the application is sheltered and then applying the appropriate intelligence that best suits the environment. In fact, sometimes techniques applied to boost performance in one environment prove to be ill-suited for another environment.

In the financial world, performance holds center stage, and a lack of good performance is a primary reason for discarding an existing application and then rebuilding it from scratch. It also means that the performance of an application is tightly coupled with its underlying design. It is the application's design that is not capable of meeting the required quality of service that a typical business demands. Also, such problems do not spring up immediately but become evident as time passes. It also implies a direct relationship between design and time, as shown in Figure 1-18.

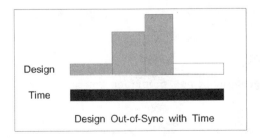
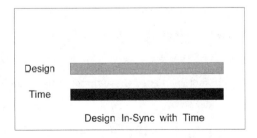

Figure 1-18. *Relationship between an application's design and time*

In Figure 1-18, the lower rectangular bar represents time, and the upper bar represents design. On the left, notice that until a certain point, design is completely in sync with time; however, design loses track as the height of the design bar increases. This phase reflects a change in design either because of a drastic change in the business requirement that was unwarranted at this stage of time or because of some poor assumption based on which the design was realized and finally failed to meet the required expectations. In the final stage, the design bar returns to its original shape and size, but notice that the inner filling in the bar is shaded, which is different from the original bar. This indicates that the old design has been completely scrapped, resulting in a completely new design. On the right, the design is completely in sync with time and therefore considered to be a good design.

So, what makes a good design? Some audiences consider even a badly designed application that has the potential to cater to a business expectation as a good design. Therefore, it is difficult to provide a definition of good design; however, a good design is one that considers the three constellations of time: past, present, and future. A rock-solid design must be designed from the past, designed with the present, and designed for the future. It means a design must fill all the missing gaps in the past, must handle all the current requirements, and must handle any future needs. In a nutshell, a good design is a time traveler.

Although performance is an important aspect of design, you must consider another important aspect: user requirements. At the end of the day, if the application fails to win customer hearts by not meeting their business needs, it would still be considered a bad design even if it is free from any architectural flaws. In the financial world, both performance and user requirements are key sensitive areas. User requirements are expected to change, which is inevitable, but performance-related issues are avoidable. In a broader sense, you can achieve good performance by applying the three levels of intelligence in an application shown in Figure 1-19.

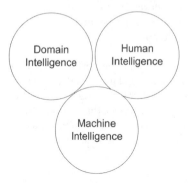

Figure 1-19. *The three levels of intelligence*

In fact, by mixing these three levels of intelligence in the right proportion, you can develop a rock-solid application.

Machine Intelligence

Machine intelligence is inclined toward the programmatic perspective of an application. The best way to implement this intelligence is by religiously following the best programming practices and applying well-proven architectural standards. The most common practices followed in high-performance applications are applying parallelism, which is achieved using multithreading; devising a highly optimized algorithm; and exploiting platform- or hardware-specific capabilities.

Domain Intelligence

Domain intelligence goes hand in hand with machine intelligence. To apply such intelligence, the team must be cognizant of both domain- and technology-specific details. When domain intelligence is applied at the right place, it gives a multifold increase in the performance of the application. This intelligence is often ignored during the performance-engineering phase of a system where a team's energy is primarily mobilized toward implementing all sorts of machine-level intelligence.

Let's take a market data example where introducing domain intelligence along with machine intelligence provides a tremendous performance boost: Market data applications broadcast the latest price of a stock. Several consumers then process this information. These real-time prices are often displayed on most financial Web sites. The price of stocks tends to lose tempo whenever there is a swing in the market behavior. This swing period lasts for a short span of time, and during this period almost every stock price is affected. This period is called a *data-quake* because the system will notice a huge surge of data, and this sometimes may even lead to a system crash. Even if you assume that the first line of defense is strong and the market data service is able to survive this data-quake, remember that this information needs to further trickle down to the consumers; thus, the consumers of this information could also face the same disaster.

So, how do you escape from such a deluge of data? Although no easy solution exists, you can deal with this by applying domain-level intelligence. Before applying this intelligence, you need to understand the business implication behind this data that will help control the flow of data. Let's say your investigation disclosed that most stock prices tend to change at least 100 times a second. So, instead of pushing this change immediately to downstream systems, you can throttle it for a second. During this throttling period, data will not be pushed; rather, it will undergo a price-replacement process that will blindly override the old price of a stock with the new price. As data gets published only after the expiry of 1 second, it effectively controls the flow of data from flooding the market data ecosystems. Even though the first line of market data service will receive roughly about 100 messages per second for any given stock, this will not affect downstream systems because they will receive throttled messages at the rate of one message per second.

Human Intelligence

Human intelligence is user-centric. This may come as a surprise; the question that is immediately raised is, what type of contribution will users make toward improving the performance of the application? To be more precise, it is not the performance specification from users but their postures toward the system that will drive the performance of the application. You must follow the important principle What-You-Ask-Is-What-You-Get (WYAIWYG) to provide users with what they demand rather than what is merely provided by the system. For example, it does not make sense to paint the user screen with thousands of orders that are far beyond the range of the human eyeball, even if the system has the capacity to provide this. It is also important to keep a close eye on a user's behavior toward applications and also spend a fair amount of effort gathering this intelligence by spending time with users and watching their screen interactions and mouse movements.

You can further optimize the market data service discussed in the earlier "Domain Intelligence" section by infusing elements of human intelligence into it. You already know that any given stock price is updated at least 100 times a second, and if the user has subscribed to 100 stocks, this would result in the system processing 10,000 message per second. But in reality, the user may not view all 100 stocks but keep a watch over only a few volatile stocks. So, if the system temporarily suspends subscribing to a stock that is not viewed by the user, then it would give a fair amount of breathing space to system resources, which would in turn be less taxed and also effectively utilized. This clearly explains the merit of applying human intelligence, which is often overlooked.

Thus, it is important to apply both domain and human intelligence to extract every bit of performance. Furthermore, it is also important to understand that a threshold factor is associated with machine-level intelligence. After a certain level, you will have no room left for any kind of improvement, and once you have exhausted this resource, the only alternative is to leverage the domain and human intelligence in a balanced manner.

Introducing the Upcoming Business Cases

The rest of the chapters in this book elaborate on business cases that play important roles in the trading life cycle. Individual chapters cover both domain and technology know-how in specific areas. The implicit theme of each chapter is to provide insight into the practical day-to-day challenges posed by domain-specific issues and how you can address these issues using the .NET technology. The motive of this book is to deeply explore the .NET Framework base class library (BCL).

The .NET Framework BCL is an exhaustive collection of reusable types that facilitates the faster development of applications (see Figure 1-20). The BCL arms you with the ability to develop nearly all kinds of applications spanning from GUI-based to (near) real-time applications. It is impossible to explore this library in one gulp. Hence, the next step will be to cover some of the important libraries and their immediate counterparts in the business world. The primary goal of this exercise is to provide theoretical insight into .NET and its practical applications and discuss solutions to challenges faced in the real world.

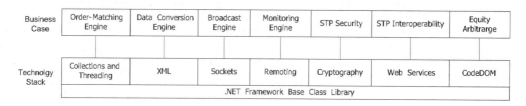

Figure 1-20. *The .NET Framework and solutions for the financial world*

The following are the areas that will be covered in depth in subsequent chapters:

Order-matching engine (collections and threading): The order-matching engine satisfies the quest for moving toward a centralized order book. Order matching represents the exchange-side process that receives orders from different sources, and based on various parameters associated with an individual order, it performs a matching process. Chapter 2 discusses the important data structures and threading features available as part of the BCL and demonstrates their usability by showing how to build a simple-to-use order-matching engine.

Data conversion engine (XML): It is well-known that in spite of advances in technology, the communication of information using flat files is still prevalent and considered to be one of the most reliable vehicles for packaging and delivering information to the final end system. Chapter 3 recognizes this and addresses the issue usually encountered in systems where information originates from different sources, particularly flat files, instead of data entered by a data-entry operator. File import and export activity are commonly encountered in a settlement system where various kinds of data are required for reporting purposes. Such systems are flooded with data import and export code, so Chapter 3 discusses the need for a generic conversion framework and also designs one using XML.

Broadcast engine (sockets): A broadcast engine is the heart of a trading system. The main goal of a broadcast engine is to publish the best asking and offer prices prevailing in the exchange. However, this doesn't restrict using a broadcast engine to only market data; it can also be used in implementing other types of trading broadcasts. The most important aspect that needs serious thought in realizing this engine is the timely delivery of data. Furthermore, a large number of users would be using this data, and users are also geographically distributed. Chapter 4 covers the .NET socket programming domain and shows how you can leverage it to build a simple-to-use broadcast engine.

Application-monitoring engine (remoting): A trading system is built upon several individual subcomponents. Each subcomponent is physically distributed on a separate machine and shares a particular piece of task. In such an environment, it is important to manage and monitor the task of all subcomponents from one central location. An application-monitoring engine is tasked with this responsibility of hosting the individual subcomponents and periodically monitoring the activity. Chapter 5 discusses how to create an application-monitoring engine using .NET Remoting as an underlying infrastructure for managing the subcomponents of an application.

STP security (data security): Security is a key concern for all market participants, and its implementation remains the greatest challenge in the current vulnerable markets. In an STP space where interaction among business participants cross organizations and geographic boundaries, it is important to have the proper mechanisms in place to ensure the legitimacy of a business participant and also shield the confidentiality of business transactions. Chapter 6 covers cryptography and discusses various security measures that you can implement to achieve both internal and external STP.

STP interoperability (Web services): Chapter 7 is geared toward the implementation of external STP where the goal is to bring entities such as the broker, fund manager, and clearing corporation under one common roof in pursuit of achieving T+1. Chapter 7 will explore the Web services platform and the WS-* standards in achieving integration and interoperability among different entities.

Equity arbitrage engine (CodeDOM): With millions of data packets hitting a system every second and price ticks being revised tens of times every second, evaluating scenarios and generating orders automatically are challenges for all solution providers. Chapter 8 talks about leveraging automated code generation and how you can use it in designing a simple rule-based arbitrage system.

Each chapter provides insight into how you can address issues confronting the financial markets using the .NET Framework BCL. This means we will deal with every aspect of .NET in its proper context by explaining how it is applicable to real-life business cases. Interweaving both domain and technology aspects in every chapter will further solidify your understanding of the class library by specializing it to the specific needs of a business. Finally, at the end of this book, we will give overview of .NET 2.0 and explain some of the important features that further solidify .NET as a complete end-to-end technology platform.

CHAPTER 2

The Order-Matching Engine

The beauty of time is that it controls the construction and destruction of each instance of the human type.

This chapter discusses an important wing of the trading system—the order-matching decision process. All trading systems must be able to process orders placed by multiple customers from multiple locations, with several orders arriving at the same time and desperately trying to grab the best price in the market at that particular moment. Therefore, it is not surprising to note that trading systems face an influx of data during peak periods. Thus, the systems must easily withstand the heavy traffic of orders and still be able to judiciously find the best price in the market for a given order at the given time.

In this chapter, we explain how an order is matched as soon as it is received and explain the variants that an order exhibits, which in turn affects the matching process. The first part of this chapter discusses the business know-how; then the chapter covers the .NET Framework and exposes the tools that will enable the fulfillment of the discussed business case. Specifically, we explain the different types of collection classes available in the .NET Framework, and we then continue the technical exploration with in-depth coverage of the threading features and the types of synchronization methods that are essential for building a thread-safe system. This is followed by the merging stage where every aspect of business is directly mapped to its low-level technical implementation. Finally, we provide illustrative code samples for the prototype of an order-matching engine written in C#.

Understanding the Business Context of Order Matching

The following sections cover the business context of the order-matching engine.

The Need for Efficient Order Matching

The two primary objectives in the financial marketplace are to keep transaction costs at a minimum and to avoid credit defaults. Although several market practices have been devised to fulfill these objectives, efficient order matching is an important factor for achieving these goals.

A market's liquidity is measured by how easily a trader can acquire (or dispose of) a financial asset and by the cost associated with each transaction. For example, if you wanted to sell a house, you could place an advertisement or go through a real estate agent. Both of these options have costs associated with them. It may also take a month to locate a buyer who is willing to match the price you desire. In this case, the house is considered to be relatively illiquid. But imagine a marketplace where all sellers and buyers of houses in the city came together in one area and tried to find a match—the search would be easier, the chances for finding a buyer would be greater, and the convergence of all buyers and sellers would result in price discovery and hence better prices. In this case, the house is considered highly liquid. If you extend this example to a marketplace where company instruments (shares and debt instruments) are traded, you get a *stock exchange*, as introduced in Chapter 1. To avoid search costs (and of course to enforce other legal statutes), buyers and sellers come together in a stock exchange on a common platform to transact. Since many buyers and sellers are present at any point in time, searching for a counterpart for an order is relatively easy.

An *order* is an intention to enter into a transaction. Each order has certain characteristics such as type of security, quantity, price, and so on. Initiators of orders notionally announce their willingness to transact with the specified parameters.

Each player in the market wants to get the best possible price. There is a huge scramble to get one's order executed at the right time and at the best available market price. Efficient order matching is thus a highly desirable tenet of an advanced market.

Also, anonymity is considered good for a financial market. This means traders do not know any information about the people with whom they are trading. This is desirable when the participants in the market do not have the same financial strength and when it becomes important for the market to protect the interests of the small players. Anonymity also prevents large players from exerting undue influence on the trade conditions. In such a situation, to protect the integrity of the market, precautions must be taken to ensure that no credit defaults take place. As mentioned in Chapter 1, this is the job of a clearing corporation, which takes away the credit risk concerns of large players through novation. This process also takes care of matching large orders with several potential small players.

Actors: Exchanges and Brokers

Let's examine who the actors are in this matching process. Two counterparties, at a minimum, are required with opposing views to trade with each other—after all, one must be willing to buy when another is willing to sell. And their orders must converge on a common platform, which is the exchange. Generally, exchanges support two forms of trading:

- Oral auctions

- Electronic trading

In an oral auction, traders meet each other face to face on the exchange's trading floor. They shout their bids and offer prices for other traders to hear; the other traders constantly write down these quotes. When two traders agree on a price and an associated quantity, a transaction takes place. Some traders may provide a two-way quotation (a bid price and an asking price) and enter into a transaction only with another trader willing to take the offer or accept the bid.

Oral auctions are the conventional form of trading used in absence of automation, but with the advent of electronic trading, they are on verge of decline. Electronic trading offers the same function through a computer and a trading screen. Traders log their orders through the trading system, and their orders are recorded in the exchange's order book. These orders are then considered for potential matches as designated per the order-matching rules and algorithm defined by exchange.

The most common matching logic uses the concept of priority based on price and time:

- All buy orders received by the exchange are first sorted in descending order of bid price and in ascending order of time for the same prices. This means orders where traders are willing to pay the highest price are kept on the top, reflecting the highest priority. If two orders have the same bid price, the one entered earlier gains a higher priority over the one entered later.

- All sell orders are sorted in ascending order by offer price and in ascending order of time for the same offer prices. This means orders where traders are willing to accept the lowest rate are kept on the top, giving them the highest priority. Two orders asking the same price would be prioritized such that the one entered earlier gets a higher priority.

For example, consider traders A, B, and C who want to buy shares of Microsoft and traders D, E, and F who want to sell shares of Microsoft. Assuming the last traded price of Microsoft (MSFT) shares was $40, consider the scenario shown in Table 2-1.

Table 2-1. *Traders Who Want to Buy/Sell MSFT Orders*

Traders Who Want to Buy	Traders Who Want to Sell
A wants to buy 1,000 @ $40.	D wants to sell 250 @ $40.10.
B wants to buy 500 @ $40.10.	E wants to sell 500 @ $41.20.
C wants to buy 10,000 @ $39.50.	F wants to sell 250 @ $41.50.

A separate *bucket* is assigned for each company's stock, and all orders for the company are grouped into the specific bucket. In business lingua, this bucket is called the *order book*. Thus, the order book for the example in Table 2-1 will look like Table 2-2.

Table 2-2. *MSFT Order Book*

Buy		Sell	
Quantity	Rate	Rate	Quantity
500	$40.10	$40.10	250
1,000	$40	$41.20	500
10,000	$39.50	$41.50	250

All transactions happen on the rate reflected in the topmost row of the order book. This price is popularly called the *touchline price*. The touchline price represents the best ask (lowest sell) price and best bid (highest buy) price of a stock.

In the previous example, because there is a consensus on the rates from both the buyer and the seller, at the touchline price the order will get matched to the extent of 250 shares at $40.10. Thus, the order book will look like Table 2-3.

Table 2-3. *Updated MSFT Order Book After Buy and Sell Order Matched at Touchline Price*

Buy		Sell	
Quantity	Rate	Rate	Quantity
250	$40.10	$41.20	500
1,000	$40	$41.50	250
10,000	$39.50		

Types of Orders

The following are the most common types of orders:

Good till cancelled (GTC) order: A GTC order is an order that remains in the system until the trading member cancels it. It will therefore be able to span several trading days until the time it gets matched. The exchange specifies the maximum number of days a GTC order can remain in the system from time to time.

Good till date (GTD) order: A GTD order allows the trading member to specify the days or a date up to which the order should stay in the system. At the end of this period, the order will automatically get flushed from the system. All calendar days, including the starting day in which the order is placed and holidays, are counted. Once again, the exchange specifies the maximum number of days a GTD order can remain in the system from time to time.

Immediate or cancel (IOC) order: An IOC order allows a trading member to buy or sell a security as soon as the order is released into the market; failing that, the order will be removed from the market. If a partial match is found for the order, the unmatched portion of the order is cancelled immediately.

Price conditions/limit price order: This type of order allows the price to be specified when the order is entered into the system.

Market price order: This type of order allows buying or selling securities at the best price, obtainable at the time of entering the order. The price for such orders is left blank and is filled at the time of the trade with the latest running price in the exchange.

Stop loss (SL) price/order: SL orders allow the trading member to place an order that gets activated when the market price of the relevant security reaches or crosses a threshold price. Until then, the order does not enter the market. A sell order in the SL book gets triggered when the last traded price in the normal market reaches or falls below the trigger price of the order.

Note that for all of these order types, the behavior of an order is determined by a set of special attributes. Every order entered by a buyer or seller follows the same basic principle of trading, but this special attribute further augments the nature of an order by having a direct (or indirect) effect on the profitability of a business. For example, if an order's last traded price was $15 and a limit buy order was placed with a limit price of $15.45 with a stop loss at $15.50, this order would be sent to the market only after the last traded price is $15.50, and it would be placed as a limit price order with the limit price of $15.45.

Order Precedence Rules

The order precedence rules of an oral auction determine who can bid (or offer) and whose bids and offers traders can accept. To arrange trades, markets with order-matching systems use their order precedence rules to separately rank all buy and sell orders in the order of increasing precedence. In other words, they match orders with the highest precedence first.

The order precedence rules are hierarchical. Markets first rank orders using their primary order precedence rules. If two or more orders have the same primary precedence, markets then apply their secondary precedence rules to rank them. They apply these rules one at a time until they rank all orders by precedence.

All order-matching markets use *price priority* as their primary order precedence rule. Under price priority, buy orders that bid the highest prices and sell orders that offer the lowest prices rank the highest on their respective sides. Markets use various secondary precedence rules to rank orders that have the same price. The most commonly used secondary precedence rules rank orders based on their times of submission.

Most exchanges give an option to traders to hide the total quantity of shares they want to transact. This is to discourage other traders from changing their bids/offers in case a large order hits the market. In this case, displayed orders are given higher precedence over undisclosed orders at the same price. Markets give precedence to the displayed orders in order to encourage traders to expose their orders. Though disclosure is encouraged, traders also have the option of not displaying the price in order to protect their interests.

Size (quantity) precedence varies by market. In some markets, small orders have precedence over large ones, and in some markets the opposite is true. Most exchanges allow traders to issue orders with size restrictions. Traders can specify that their entire order must be filled at once, or they can specify a minimum size for partial execution. Orders with quantity restriction usually have lower precedence than unrestricted orders because they are harder to fill.

Order Precedence Ranking Example

Assume that some traders enter the orders shown in Table 2-4 for a particular security.

Table 2-4. *Buy and Sell Orders Sorted Based on Order Arrival Time*

Time (a.m.)	Trader	Buy/Sell	Quantity	Price
10:01	Anthony	Buy	300	$20
10:05	Anu	Sell	300	$20.10
10:08	Nicola	Buy	200	$20
10:09	Jason	Sell	500	$19.80
10:10	Jeff	Sell	400	$20.20
10:15	Nicholas	Buy	500	Market price order
10:18	Kumar	Buy	300	$20.10
10:20	Doe	Sell	600	$20
10:29	Sally	Buy	700	$19.80

The exchange will send an order acknowledgment to the traders' trading terminals and fill the order book as shown in Table 2-5.

Table 2-5. *Order Book (Pre-Match)*

Buy Order Time Stamp	Buy Order Quantity	Buy Price	Buyer	Sell Price	Sell Order Quantity	Seller	Sell Order Time Stamp
10:15	500	Market	Nicholas	$19.80	500	Jason	10:09
10:18	300	$20.10	Kumar	$20	600	Doe	10:20
10:01	300	$20	Anthony	$20.10	300	Anu	10:05
10:08	200	$20	Nicola	$20.20	400	Jeff	10:10
10:29	700	$19.80	Sally				

Note the following in the order book:

- Jason's sell order has the highest precedence on the sell side because it offers the lowest price.

- Nicholas' buy order has the highest precedence on the buy side because it is a market price order.

- Anthony's order and Nicola's order have the same price priority, but Anthony's order has time precedence over Nicola's order because it arrived first.

- In the actual order book, names are not stored and not displayed to traders because the trading system preserves anonymity.

The Matching Procedure

The first step is to rank the orders. Ranking happens on a continuous basis when new orders arrive.

Then the market matches the highest-ranking buy and sell orders to each other. If the buyer is willing to pay as much as the seller demands, the order will be matched, resulting in a trade.

A trade essentially binds the two counterparties to a particular price and quantity of a specific security for which the trade is conducted.

If one order is smaller than the other, the smaller order will fill completely. The market will then match the remainder of the larger order with the next highest-ranking order on the opposite side of the market. If the first two orders are of the same size, both will fill completely. The market will then match the next highest-ranking buy and sell orders. This continues until the market arranges all possible trades.

Order-Matching Example

If the traders in the previous example (see Table 2-5) submit their orders, the market will match the orders as follows:

1. Nicholas's buy order at market price will match Jason's sell order. This will result in the first trade, and both the orders will be removed from the order book.

2. Kumar's order of 300 buy will get matched to Doe's order of 600 sell. Interestingly, this order will get matched at $20.10 even though Doe wanted to sell at $20. Exchange systems are designed to protect the interests of both buyers and sellers. Since there was a passive order from Kumar willing to buy at $20.10 and Doe's order comes in later asking only for $20, she will still get $20.10. Since Kumar's order is completely filled, it will be removed completely from the order book. However, Doe's order of 600 is only half-filled. So, 300 shares of Doe will remain in the order book.

3. In the next step, Anthony's buy order of 300 shares will get fully filled by Doe's balance of 300 at $20, and both orders will be removed from the order book.

4. Now Nicola wants to buy 200 at $20, but Jeff will sell only at $20.20. There is no agreement in price; hence, there will be no further matching, and the matching system will wait either for one of the parties to adjust the price or for a new order at a price where either a buy or a sell can be matched.

Table 2-6 shows the trade book for trades resulting from these orders.

Table 2-6. *Trade Book*

Trade	Buyer	Seller	Quantity	Price
1	Nicholas	Jason	500	$19.80
2	Kumar	Doe	300	$20.10
3	Anthony	Doe	300	$20

Table 2-7 shows the order book after matching.

Table 2-7. *Order Book (Post-Match)*

Buy Order Time Stamp	Buy Order Quantity	Buy Price	Buyer	Sell Price	Sell Order Quantity	Seller	Sell Order Time Stamp
10:08	200	$20	Nicola	$20.20	400	Jeff	10:10
10:29	700	$19.80	Sally				

When the buy side matches with the sell side at an agreed price, the order finds a match, thereby converting it to a trade. Each order can get converted into a single trade or multiple trades, in case the order size is large. Traders whose orders get executed have to make payments when they buy or have to deliver the securities when they sell.

Containment of Credit Risk and the Concept of Novation

Millions of orders get executed everyday, with each trader transacting hundreds and sometimes thousands of trades. In such a process, traders potentially commit to pay others (from whom they bought) and anticipate the receipt of money from others (to whom they sold). Imagine if one of the traders exhausted his payment capacity and defaulted. His default would actually give rise to a chain of defaults, and the integrity of the market as a whole would be in danger. In such a scenario, it would be difficult for large traders to transact with small traders. This, in turn, would raise transaction costs, because traders would start selectively trading with each other. To circumvent this credit risk and bring about confidence in the minds of traders, clearing corporations implement novation.

■**Note** *Novation* is a Latin word that means *splitting.*

Novation essentially splits every transaction into two parts and replaces one party in the trade with the clearing corporation. So, each party in the transaction feels they have transacted with the clearing corporation.

For example, assume that the orders of buyer A and seller B match for 10,000 shares of Microsoft. In the absence of novation, the trade will look like Figure 2-1.

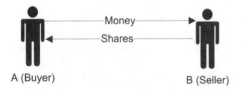

Figure 2-1. *Example of trade without novation*

With novation in place, the trade gets split in two and looks like Figure 2-2.

Figure 2-2. *Example of trade with novation*

Buyer A pays money and receives the shares from the clearing corporation. The clearing corporation, in turn, collects the shares and pays the money to seller B.

This brings us to the end of the discussion about the business know-how of order matching. The next section explains the relevant features of .NET that you can use to automate this business case.

Introducing .NET Collections

Data structures provide a container for storing "arbitrary" data and provide a uniform mechanism to operate on this data. Data structures and algorithms share a bloodline relationship—each algorithm is specifically designed and tuned to work with a specific data structure. Therefore, when a specific algorithm is applied on the appropriate data structure, it yields the best possible result. For instance, numerous algorithms can iterate over data stored in a data structure, but often one will work faster than the other when applied in the appropriate environment.

The real litmus test for the performance of an algorithm is to apply it on a huge collection of data elements and then compare the results with that of other similar algorithms. The reason for such an evaluation is that algorithms tend to predict satisfactory results—or at worst only marginal differences when applied on a small amount of data with poor data density. It is only when the number of elements in the data structure increases that the algorithm loses its strength and eventually deteriorates in performance.

The venture of a right algorithm and data structure is the Holy Grail of any good data operation exercise. The scope of a data operation is not only limited to inserting or deleting a data element but, more important, is also limited to seeking data elements. The key to the success of any "data-seeking" activity is directly attributed to the efficiency of the algorithm, denoted by the *number of iterations* it takes to locate an item. This number is derived from the worst-case scenario list; for example, in a linear list of 50 elements where items are inserted in sequential order, it can take at most 50 iterations to locate an item. So, the efficiency of the algorithm is determined by the number of elements stored inside the data structure and is measured based on the following two factors:

- Time (the amount of computation required by the algorithm)

- Space (the amount of memory required by the algorithm)

The efficiency of an algorithm is represented in *Big-O notation*, which acts as a barometer for measuring the efficiency of algorithms. Big-O notation allows a direct comparison of one algorithm over another. The value denoted by Big-O form is sufficient enough to draw a rational comparison between two algorithms without looking at the real code and understanding the real mechanics.

This concludes the brief introductory journey into algorithms; it is time to step back into the .NET world and understand the various types of data structures defined under the System.Collections namespace.

Arrays

Arrays have been in existence since the genesis of the computing world. They are a basic necessity of every developer; hence, you will find their implementations molded into all programming languages. Arrays are tightly coupled types, and therefore they are known as *homogenous data structures* (see Figure 2-3). This means once an array of a particular data type is declared, it ensures that the data elements stored must be of the same type.

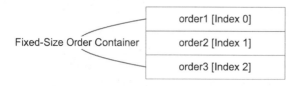

Figure 2-3. *Linear arrangement of a homogeneous order using an array*

The following code example demonstrates how to use an array data structure in .NET:

```
using System;

class ArrayContainer
{
  class Order
  {}
  static void Main(string[] args)
  {
    //Create orders
    Order order1 = new Order();
    Order order2 = new Order();
    Order order3 = new Order();

    //Declare array of order type
    //and add the above three order instance
    Order[] orderList = { order1,order2,order3};

    //Access the order
    Order curOrder = orderList[1] as Order;
  }
}
```

In the previous code, an array of the Order type is declared by allocating space for three elements. Then the code assigns a value to an individual element of an array. The primary benefit of using an array is the simplicity it provides in manipulating data elements. An individual data element is accessed by its ordinal position, using an index. An array is extremely efficient when it comes to searching for a data element, even if the number of elements stored in the array is large. Another benefit of using an array is it provides good locality of reference because data elements are arranged in a contiguous block of memory. An array is one of the basic foundations for building sophisticated data structures. These data structures are queues, stacks, and hash tables, and their underlying implementations in .NET are based on arrays.

Array Lists

Array lists inherit the same characteristics of arrays but are specifically designed to address the shortcomings of arrays (see Figure 2-4).

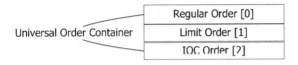

Figure 2-4. *Linear arrangement of a heterogeneous order using an array list*

The foremost problem faced by an array is it is a fixed size—once allocated, an array cannot be resized in a straightforward manner. The array size is defined either during runtime or during compile time. After that, the size remains fixed for the entire duration of the program. The only way to redimension an array is to apply a crude approach—by allocating a separate temporary array (which acts as a temporary storage container for the old data elements), moving the elements from the source array to the temporary array, and then reallocating a different size to the source array, as illustrated in the following code:

```
using System;

class ArrayCopy
{
  class Order{}
  [STAThread]
  static void Main(string[] args)
  {
    //Create an order array
    Order[] orderList = { new Order(),new Order(),
                          new Order(),new Order()};

    //Create a temp array of exactly the same size
    //as original order container
    Order[] tempList = new Order[4];

    //copy the actual items stored in the order array
    //to temp order array
    Array.Copy(orderList,0,tempList,0,4);

    //resize the order array
    orderList = new Order[5];

    //copy the order items from the temp order array
    //to the original order array
    Array.Copy(tempList,0,orderList,0,4);
  }
}
```

Array lists alleviate the fixed-size problem faced by arrays. Behind the scenes, array lists follow the same crude mechanism demonstrated in the previous code, but the mechanism is transparent to developers. Developers, without worrying about dimension issues, can add data element at runtime.

The other major problem faced by an array is the "type coupleness" behavior. An array list solves this problem by acting as a universal container and allows you to insert a data element of any data type. This means an instance of both the value types and the reference type is allowed. However, be careful when dealing with value types because of the implicit boxing and unboxing penalty cost incurred at runtime. The internal storage implementation of an array list is of the reference type, and an instance of the value type that is allocated on the stack cannot be straightforwardly assigned to a reference type. To achieve this task, the instance of the value type needs to be converted to a reference type through a process known as *boxing*. Similarly, in the reverse process known as *unboxing*, the boxed value type that is a reference type is converted to its original value type.

The following code example demonstrates various operations performed on array lists and how different types of orders are added, retrieved, and finally removed:

```
using System;
using System.Collections;

class ArrayListContainer
{
  class Order
  {}
  class LimitOrder
  {}
  class IOCOrder
  {}
  [STAThread]
  static void Main(string[] args)
```

```
{
   ArrayList orderContainer;
   orderContainer  = new ArrayList();
   //Add regular order
   Order order = new Order();
   orderContainer.Add(order);

   //Add limit order
   LimitOrder limOrder = new LimitOrder();
   orderContainer.Add(limOrder);

   //Add IOC order
   IOCOrder iocOrder =new IOCOrder();
   orderContainer.Add(iocOrder );

   //Access limit order
   limOrder = orderContainer[0] as LimitOrder;

   //Remove limit order
   orderContainer.RemoveAt(0);

   //Display total elements
   Console.WriteLine("Total Elements : " +orderContainer.Count);
  }
}
```

Quick Sort and Binary Search

Both arrays and array lists provide a simple way to insert and delete an item. However, you must also take into account the cost involved in locating a specific data element. The simple technique is to conduct a sequential search where the entire array is enumerated element by element. This approach sounds sensible if you have only a few elements but proves to be inefficient for large numbers of items. Additionally, often you have requirements to sort arrays in either ascending order or descending order. This requirement for both searching and sorting elements illustrates the need for efficient searching and sorting algorithms. Although several well-known, robust sorting and searching algorithms exist, .NET provides out-of-the-box quick sort and binary search algorithms to cater to the sort and search requirements. The quick sort is considered to be one of the most highly efficient sorting algorithms.

The following code demonstrates how elements of arrays are sorted using the quick sort algorithm:

```
using System;

class QuickSort
{
   static void Main(string[] args)
   {
      //elements arranged in unsorted order
      int[] elements = {12,98,95,1,6,4,101};

      //sort element using QuickSort
      Array.Sort(elements,0,elements.Length);

      //display output of sorted elements
      for(int ctr=0;ctr<elements.Length;ctr++)
      {
```

```
        Console.WriteLine(elements[ctr]);
      }
    }
  }
```

Similarly, to locate items in an array, the .NET Framework provides a binary search algorithm. The only prerequisite required for this search algorithm is that the array must be sorted. So, the first step is to apply a quick sort to ensure that the arrays are sorted either in ascending order or in descending order. With the incredible increase in the processing power of computers, a search conducted on 1,000 elements using either sequential search or binary search would make no difference to the overall performance of an application. However, the binary search technique would easily outperform the sequential search when the underlying array contains an extremely large number of items.

The following code demonstrates how to use the built-in binary search algorithm to locate a specific item in an array:

```
using System;

class BinarySearch
{
  static void Main(string[] args)
  {
    //elements arranged in unsorted order
    int[] elements = {12,98,95,1,6,4,101};

    //sort element using quick sort
    Array.Sort(elements,0,elements.Length);

    //find element using binary search
    //i.e find 95
    int elementPos = Array.BinarySearch(elements,0,elements.Length,95);

    //if exact match found
    if ( elementPos >= 0 )
    {
      Console.WriteLine("Exact Match Found : " +elementPos);
    }
    else
    //nearest match found
    {
      //bitwise complement operator
      elementPos = ~elementPos;
      Console.WriteLine("Nearest Match : " +elementPos);
    }
  }
}
```

The search is initiated by calling the Array.BinarySearch static method. If this method returns a positive value, then it is a success indicator and represents the index of the searched item. However, if the method fails to find the specified value, then it returns a negative integer, and to interpret it correctly, you need to apply a bitwise complement operator. By applying this operator, you get a positive index, which is the index of the first element that is larger than the search value. If the search value is greater than any of the elements in the array, then the index of the last element plus 1 is returned.

The code for the binary search and quick sort demonstrated is based on a single-dimensional fixed array. But in the real world, you will be using an array list to store custom objects such as instruments and order information. Moreover, the binary search and sorting will be based on some specific attributes of custom objects. So, the interesting question is, how do you apply sorting on specific user-defined attributes of the data element? This is possible with the help of the IComparer interface. The role of this interface is to provide a custom hookup that influences the decision made by the quick sort and binary search algorithms.

The following code example shows how orders stored in an order container of the ArrayList type are sorted by order price in ascending order and by quantity in descending order:

```
using System;
using System.Collections;

class OrderComparer
{
  public class Order
  {
    public string Instrument;
    public int Qty;
    public int Price;
    public Order(string inst, int price,int qty)
    {
      Instrument= inst;
      Qty= qty;
      Price= price;
    }
  }
  [STAThread]
  static void Main(string[] args)
  {
    //order collection
    ArrayList orderCol = new ArrayList();

    //add five orders
    orderCol.Add(new Order("MSFT",25,100));
    orderCol.Add(new Order("MSFT",25,110));
    orderCol.Add(new Order("MSFT",23,95));
    orderCol.Add(new Order("MSFT",25,105));

    //Invoke the sort function of the ArrayList, and pass the custom
    //order comparer
    orderCol.Sort(new OrderSort());

    //Print the result of the sort
    for ( int ctr = 0;ctr<orderCol.Count;ctr++)
    {
      Order curOrder = (Order)orderCol[ctr];
      Console.WriteLine(curOrder.Instrument+ ":"
                    +curOrder.Price +"-" +curOrder.Qty);
    }
  }

  public class OrderSort : IComparer
  {
    public int Compare(object x, object y)
    {
      Order ox = (Order)x;
      Order oy = (Order)y;
      //Compare the price
      int priceCompare = ox.Price.CompareTo(oy.Price);
```

```
      //Compare the quantity
      int qtyCompare = ox.Qty.CompareTo(oy.Qty);
      if ( priceCompare == 0 )
      {
        //return value multiplied with -1
        //will sort quantity in descending order
        return qtyCompare * -1;
      }

      //returns indication of price comparison value
      return priceCompare;
    }
  }
}
```

In this code, a new instance of OrderSort is created that implements IComparer and is passed as an argument to the Sort method of ArrayList. OrderSort implements the Compare method of IComparer. This method compares two values and returns 0 if the first argument is equal to the second argument. Similarly, if the first argument is less than the second argument, then it returns -1; and in case the first argument is greater than the second argument, then it returns 1. The value 0, -1, or 1 determines the sort order position of an element in an array. To sort an array in descending order, you simply multiply this value with -1, which basically reverses the original logical operator.

Queues

In real life, thousands of orders are submitted to the trading system for final processing. These orders originate from different sources, and it is important to process each order based on its arrival time. It is also important to acknowledge these individual orders first and then process them asynchronously. Processing each order synchronously would lead to a higher turn-around time to traders/system users, which is totally unacceptable during peak trading hours. This scenario demands a data structure that can do both of these tasks—storing and retrieving data based on its arrival time. A *queue* is a data structure that meets this condition. It places data at one end called the *entry point* and removes it from the other end called the *exit point*. Because of this characteristic, a queue is called a *first-in, first-out* (FIFO) data structure (see Figure 2-5).

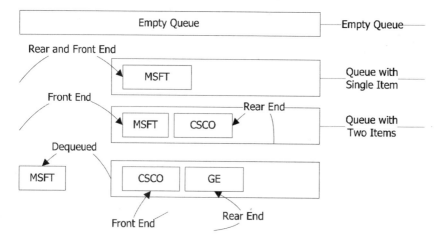

Figure 2-5. *Order processed in a FIFO manner*

The following code demonstrates how orders are processed in a FIFO manner using a queue data structure:

```
using System;
using System.Collections;

class OrderQueue
{
  class Order
  {
    public string Instrument;
    public Order(string inst)
    {
      Instrument = inst;
    }
  }
  static void Main(string[] args)
  {
    //Create Queue collection
    Queue orderQueue = new Queue();

    //Add MSFT order
    orderQueue.Enqueue(new Order("MSFT"));
    //Add CSCO order
    orderQueue.Enqueue(new Order("CSCO"));
    //Add GE order
    orderQueue.Enqueue(new Order("GE"));

    //retrieves MSFT order
    Order dequedOrder = orderQueue.Dequeue() as Order;

    //peek at CSCO order but do not remove from the queue
    Order peekedOrder = orderQueue.Peek() as Order;
  }
}
```

In this code, a queue data structure is constructed by creating an instance of Queue. This class provides Enqueue and Dequeue methods. Enqueue adds an order at the rear end of the queue, and Dequeue removes the order from the front end of the queue. Oftentimes you may want to peek at the front end of the queue and not remove it; in such cases you can use the Peek method, which does not modify the queue and returns the item without removing it. Also, you can use a Count property to return the total number of items in Queue.

Stacks

Stacks are popularly known as *last-in, first-out* (LIFO) data structures (see Figure 2-6); from a functionality point of view, they do the reverse of queues. In a queue, items are served based on a FIFO basis, whereas in a stack, items are served on a LIFO basis. Stacks push the new item on top of all the other items, and when requesting data, they pop up the topmost item. Modern compilers use a stack data structure extensively during the parsing and compilation process.

Figure 2-6. *Order processed in a LIFO manner*

The following code demonstrates how orders are processed in a LIFO manner using a stack data structure:

```
using System;
using System.Collections;

class OrderStack
{
  class Order
  {
    public string Instrument;
    public Order(string inst)
    {
      Instrument = inst;
    }
  }

  static void Main(string[] args)
  {
    //create empty stack
    Stack orderStack = new Stack();

    //push MSFT order
    orderStack.Push(new Order("MSFT"));
    //push CSCO order
    orderStack.Push(new Order("CSCO"));
    //pop CSCO order
    Order poppedOrder = orderStack.Pop() as Order;
  }
}
```

In this code, a stack data structure is constructed by creating an instance of Stack. This class provides Push and Pop methods. Push places the new order on top of all orders, and Pop removes and returns the topmost order. Also, a Count property returns the total number of orders stored in Stack.

Hash Tables

Consider a scenario where a humongous list of orders is stored in an array list. Rarely would you access an order by its array index; instead, you will be interested in accessing an individual order by its unique order ID. To accomplish this, you will build your own custom search implementation using IComparer, apply a quick sort on the array list, and finally search the order using the binary search technique. But when the size of the list starts growing at a rapid rate, then this approach sounds inefficient because on every order insert or delete activity the entire array list needs to be re-sorted. This is clearly unacceptable from a performance point of view, and therefore you need a different data structure that conducts efficient searching even during stress conditions. This is where you can use a hash table. A hash table is one of the most commonly used data structures, and its primary goal is to increase search efficiency. The search cost incurred by a hash table to locate an item easily out-performs an array list. Furthermore, this data structure allows you to associate a unique key identifier to an individual data element to form the base for all kinds of activity. So, any subsequent operation (such as the search, update, or delete) of a data element on a hash table is conducted using this unique key identifier.

The following code shows how orders stored in a hash table are tagged by order ID. This key value then forms the basis for all other operations such as searching or deleting a specific order.

```
using System;
using System.Collections;

class HashTbl
{
  //Order Domain class
  public class Order
  {}
  static void Main(string[] args)
  {
    //create empty hash table
    Hashtable orderHash = new Hashtable();

    //add multiple order, order ID is the key
    //and the actual instance of Order is the value
    orderHash.Add("1",new Order());
    orderHash.Add("2",new Order());
    orderHash.Add("3",new Order());

    //locate a specific order using order ID
    Order order = orderHash["1"] as Order;

    //Remove a particular order
    orderHash.Remove("1");

    //check whether order exists with a particular ID
    if ( orderHash.ContainsKey("2") == true )
    {
      Console.WriteLine("This order already exist");
    }
  }
}
```

In this code, the Hashtable class represents a hash table data structure, and orders are added using the Add method. This method has two arguments; the first argument is a unique key identifier, which in this case is the order ID, and the second argument is the actual data element, which is an instance of Order. After inserting a new order, you can retrieve it using its unique order ID. You can also delete orders from Hashtable using the Remove method. The previous code also demonstrates the ContainsKey method, which is used to validate duplicate orders.

Introducing Specialized Collections

The .NET Framework provides other types of collections specifically tuned for performance and storage. These collections are grouped under the System.Collections.Specialized namespace.

ListDictionary

ListDictionary is primarily used when the total number of elements to be stored is relatively small. The internal storage implementation of any data structures is realized in two ways: a linked list or a vector (array). But in .NET the majority of important data structures such as Hashtable, Queue, and Stack are based on vectors. ListDictionary is the only collection in which the underlying storage implementation is based on a linked list. The benefit of using a linked list is that you conserve storage cost by allocating space only when needed. ListDictionary is recommended only when the total number of data elements is ten or fewer.

The following code example demonstrates how to use the ListDictionary data structure:

```
using System;
using System.Collections.Specialized;

class ListDict
{
  class Order
  {
    public string Instrument;
    public Order(string inst)
    {
      Instrument = inst;
    }
  }
  static void Main(string[] args)
  {
    //create empty list dictionary
    ListDictionary listDict = new ListDictionary();

    //add MSFT order
    listDict.Add("MSFT",new Order("MSFT"));
    //add CSCO order
    listDict.Add("CSCO",new Order("CSCO"));

    //retrieve MSFT order
    Order order = listDict["MSFT"] as Order;
    Console.WriteLine(order.Instrument);
  }
}
```

HybridDictionary

HybridDictionary, as the name suggests, provides the characteristics of both ListDictionary and Hashtable. The internal storage implementation of this collection initially uses ListDictionary; however, as soon as the collection starts growing, it switches to Hashtable, and subsequent operations are performed on the Hashtable. This decision-making process is completely transparent to developers. So, in a nutshell, this collection offers the best of both worlds.

Introducing Multithreading

Financial applications, particularly server-side applications, demand high performance and increased throughput. The tasks executed by this application are both computational and input/output (I/O) intensive. Therefore, applications of this kind are usually deployed on multiprocessor machines where tasks can execute concurrently. Multithreaded programming is the optimal way of leveraging these hardware resources to their maximum potential. The bright side of multithreading is it is easy to implement but requires a good amount of understanding of the application design and the underlying hardware infrastructure. Threads are one of the expensive resources, and creating too many threads will impose a serious penalty on the overall performance of applications; on other hand, fewer threads will result in the underutilization of the processor. Hence, you need to plan a balanced approach; this is what you will do in the following sections. The .NET Framework offers several ways of implementing concurrency in managed applications:

- Using .NET thread-pool capabilities
- Using asynchronous delegate infrastructure
- Manually managing threads

Thread Pools

The rationale behind the design of a thread pool in .NET is to utilize the available limited resources effectively. Although threads are an easy way to achieve parallelism, more threads by any means don't represent a scalable application. A hidden cost is associated with an individual thread in terms of high memory consumption and context switches. Therefore, to reduce this cost, .NET introduces the concept of a *thread pool*. Using a thread pool relieves the developer of having to know the details of how threads are created and managed. This responsibility shifts to the CLR, which creates a pool of reusable threads to process any type of request. By default, the pool is empty and contains no threads, but as soon as a new task is allocated, it creates a new thread and starts processing the task. After completing the task, the thread is not immediately destroyed. Instead, it is recycled back to the pool, waiting for the arrival of a new task request. When a new task arrives, then the reused thread immediately picks it up.

The algorithm of a thread pool in .NET is implemented in such a way that when receiving multiple task requests, the number of threads in the pool increases. However, an upper limit exists on the number of threads, and no new threads are spawned once this maximum value is reached. A thread pool by default is allowed to create a maximum of 25 worker threads and 25 I/O threads per available processor. The I/O threads are specifically used to execute I/O-related operations such as reading data from a disk or network socket. Now, what happens when the pool hits its limit? In this case, the task request gets queued and is processed as soon as busy threads in the pool complete executing the allocated task. The pool also has sophisticated logic that monitors the processor utilization before creating a new thread. If the processor utilization is at its fullest extent, then no new threads are created. On other hand, when there are no more tasks to execute, then (after a preconfigured time interval that is internally maintained) the threads in the pool are automatically released.

In .NET the `System.Threading.ThreadPool` class represents a thread pool. The following code demonstrates how orders are processed concurrently using a thread pool:

```
using System;
using System.Threading;

class OrderProcessor
{
  public class Order
  {
```

```
    public string Instrument;
    public Order(string inst)
    {
      Instrument=inst;
    }
  }

  static void Main(string[] args)
  {
    //Process order using a thread pool
    ThreadPool.QueueUserWorkItem(new WaitCallback(ProcessOrder),
                          new Order("MSFT"));
    ThreadPool.QueueUserWorkItem(new WaitCallback(ProcessOrder),
                          new Order("CSCO"));
    Console.ReadLine();
  }
  public static void ProcessOrder(object order)
  {
    Order curOrder = order as Order;
    Console.WriteLine("Processing Order :" + curOrder.Instrument);
  }
}
```

Tasks in the thread pool are queued by calling the QueueUserWorkItem static method. This method accepts two arguments; the first argument represents the method to be executed on thread-pool threads and is defined by an instance of the WaitCallBack delegate. The second argument specifies user-defined data passed to the method referenced by the WaitCallBack delegate instance. Based on this declaration, you define the ProcessOrder static method, which drives the actual processing logic of an individual order.

Asynchronous Delegate Infrastructure

The .NET Framework, with the help a delegate, provides a new asynchronous execution pattern that allows you to execute any method asynchronously. As you know, a *delegate* is basically an object-oriented representation of a function pointer, and it can represent any method as long as the method signature matches the delegate declaration. This is one of the benefits of using a delegate, but the most important feature is the standard asynchronous infrastructure to execute asynchronous operations. Typically, when an instance of a delegate is invoked, the underlying method referenced is executed synchronously. What is interesting is that you can use the same delegate instance to initiate an asynchronous execution of the method, and you can do this with the help of the BeginInvoke and EndInvoke methods that are automatically defined by the CLR. Additionally, the runtime uses a thread pool to process the request received from a delegate's asynchronous method, thus ensuring the effective utilization of resources.

BeginInvoke defines the asynchronous execution of a method, and upon invocation the control is immediately returned to the caller. EndInvoke then collects the actual result of the method initiated by BeginInvoke. Of course, the initiation of the asynchronous method always takes place on a worker thread and not on the caller thread; however, when it comes to collecting an execution result, an asynchronous infrastructure offers several approaches to obtain it. In the rest of this section, we discuss this approach with the help of the following order-processing code example that uses the delegate's asynchronous infrastructure to process the order, which in turn generates trades:

```
using System;

class AsyncDelegate
{
  //Order Domain class
```

```
public class Order{}
//Trade Domain class
public class Trade{}

//Delegate used to process order, which in turn returns trades
//generated as a result of this new order
public delegate Trade[] OrderHandler(Order order);
static void Main(string[] args)
{
  //instantiate a new order
  Order newOrder = new Order();

  //create a delegate instance that refers to the processing order
  //method
  OrderHandler processOrder = new OrderHandler(ProcessOrder);

  //begin the processing order in an asynchronous fashion
  IAsyncResult orderResult = processOrder.BeginInvoke(newOrder,null,null);

  //blocks the current thread until the processing of the order
  //that is executed on a thread-pool thread is completed
  orderResult.AsyncWaitHandle.WaitOne();

  //collect the trades generated as a result of
  //asynchronous order processing
  Trade[] trades = processOrder.EndInvoke(orderResult);

  //display the trades
  Console.WriteLine("Total Trade Generated : " +trades.Length);
}

//order processing
public static Trade[] ProcessOrder(Order order)
{
  //Process the order
  //ideally submit it to matching engine
  //and get the trades

  //Let's assume we hit some trades for this order
  return new Trade[]{new Trade()};
}
}
```

The previous code example uses a blocking approach to collect the asynchronous method output. Let's start with the declaration of BeginInvoke. The signature of this method contains the same parameters as the underlying method referenced by the delegate instance in addition to two extra parameters that are explained shortly. Using BeginInvoke, the asynchronous processing of the order is initiated, which is implemented inside ProcessOrder. Upon queuing this task successfully, an asynchronous token is returned to the caller of the asynchronous method, which is represented by an instance of IAsyncResult.

The beautiful thing about IAsyncResult is it provides multiple ways of querying the status of an asynchronous operation; one of them is the blocking approach. Using this approach, the caller thread is blocked until the asynchronous operation completes. The caller, instead of blocking for an indefinite period of time, can also specify a timeout value that after expiration resumes executing the caller thread regardless of the status of the asynchronous operation. Both of these flavors of blocking are achieved with the help of the AsyncWaitHandle property of IAsyncResult. This property returns a WaitHandle object, and the actual blocking happens on the invocation of WaitOne, which is an overloaded method that supports both indefinite and timeout-based blocking.

When the asynchronous call is completed, the next step is to call EndInvoke to collect the result. EndInvoke takes an asynchronous token to identify the correct asynchronous operation and return the method result. Similarly, in the previous code example, to retrieve trades, you call EndInvoke on an instance of an OrderHandler delegate by correctly passing the IAsyncResult object.

In most situations, you will want to use the callback notification approach to obtain the result of the asynchronous operation. The callback approach relieves the caller from actively monitoring the status of the asynchronous operation; instead, a notification method is registered during the initiation of the asynchronous operation, and the asynchronous infrastructure invokes this method on the completion of the operation. Another great benefit of this approach is that the processing of both the asynchronous operation and the notifications are executed on thread-pool threads.

To further demonstrate this concept, the following code notifies trades using a callback mechanism:

```
using System;

class OrderProcessorCallback
{
  //Order Domain class
  public class Order{}
  //Trade Domain class
  public class Trade{}

  //Delegate used to process order, which in turn returns trades
  //generated as a result of this new order
  public delegate Trade[] OrderHandler(Order order);

  static void Main(string[] args)
  {
    //instantiate a new order
    Order newOrder = new Order();

    //create a delegate instance that refers to the processing order
    //function
    OrderHandler processOrder = new OrderHandler(ProcessOrder);

    //callback function to be invoked when order processing is completed
    AsyncCallback processComplete = new AsyncCallback(TradeGenerated);

    //begin the processing order in an asynchronous fashion
    //passing the callback delegate instance
    IAsyncResult orderResult =
            processOrder.BeginInvoke(newOrder,processComplete,processOrder);
    Console.ReadLine();
  }

  //order processing
  public static Trade[] ProcessOrder(Order order)
  {
    //Process the order
    //ideally submit it to the matching engine
    //and get the trades
```

```
    //Let's assume we hit some trades for this order
    return new Trade[]{new Trade()};
}

//callback notification after successfully processing order
public static void TradeGenerated(IAsyncResult result)
{
    //retrieve the correct method delegate reference
    OrderHandler processOrder = ((AsyncResult)result).AsyncDelegate as OrderHandler;

    //collect the trades generated as a result of
    //asynchronous order processing
    Trade[] trades = processOrder.EndInvoke(result);

    //display the trades
    Console.WriteLine("Total Trade Generated : " +trades.Length);
}

}
```

To enable asynchronous callback notification, the caller must register the callback method during the initiation of BeginInvoke. This method accepts two extra parameters that are specifically related to the callback notification. The first parameter is an instance of the AsyncCallback delegate that represents the callback method to be invoked when the asynchronous operation completes. The second parameter represents user-defined information passed to the callback method.

When the operation completes, the asynchronous infrastructure invokes the method referenced by the AsyncCallback instance. The signature of AsyncCallback contains the IAsyncResult parameter that represents the asynchronous token. On receiving the method completion notification, the code inside the callback method must invoke EndInvoke on the correct delegate instance to obtain the result. To do this, you must cast the IAsyncResult parameter to the AsyncResult object in order to access the AsyncDelegate property that returns the correct delegate instance.

Manual Thread Management

Creating threads manually is the most conventional approach of handling asynchronous-based operations or introducing parallelism in applications. When threads are constructed manually, developers are solely responsible for the proper synchronization and handling of interthread communications either using callbacks or using some other mechanism. Developers use this approach when they require absolute control over the execution of threads. You have to keep a few things in mind when adopting this approach:

- Code synchronization
- Deadlock prevention
- Interthread notification

Code Synchronization

A program's execution is said to be consistent when its data or variables' values are not unintentionally modified, staying intact and consistent. These are key indicators that drive the overall consistency of a program. A wrong variable value can change the program execution adversely, giving unexpected results. Such diversion in the execution of programs to an unexpected state or inconsistent state is highly visible in multithreaded applications. This is because usually one copy of data is shared across multiple threads. So, when multiple threads read shared data at the same time and issue an update operation, then the last thread update is preserved, overwriting the previous thread's update.

This is called a *race condition* and, if not handled properly, could result in corrupted data and could seriously hamper the overall flow of the application. To avoid race conditions, you must protect the code in such a way that it is accessible to only one thread at a time; in other words, the code must be *synchronized*. This will ensure that at any moment, no more than one thread will execute the code.

In .NET, you can use Monitor to ensure thread-safe access to shared resources. Monitor is a lightweight and efficient locking mechanism available in a managed environment. It weaves a thread synchronization block, and code defined inside this block is known as a *critical section* and is always thread-safe. The idea is that when a thread tries to execute a critical section of code, it must first request exclusive ownership on that code, which is initiated by Monitor.Enter. This method accepts an Object instance on which the exclusive ownership is requested. The key point is that the ownership can be provided to only one thread at a time. So, if multiple threads are requesting at the same time, then Monitor.Enter guarantees that only a single thread can safely enter and execute the critical section of code. This way, the execution of code is serialized, and the access to shared resources is synchronized. A thread, after successfully acquiring ownership on the Object instance, must also release it to give an opportunity to other blocked threads that require exclusive access to the critical section of code. To release the exclusive ownership, use Monitor.Exit. Notice that both Monitor.Enter and Monitor.Exit are paired methods and weave thread-safe code.

The following code example demonstrates how to use Monitor in implementing a central order book in which multiple threads access this shared resource:

```
using System;
using System.Collections;
using System.Threading;

class SyncOrder
{
  //Order Domain Model
  public class Order
  {
    public string Instrument;
    public Order(string inst)
    {
      Instrument = inst;
    }
  }

  //Order book that stores an individual order
  public class OrderBook
  {
    //arrays to hold orders
    ArrayList orderList = new ArrayList();

    //synchronization object
    private object syncObj = new object();

    public void Add(object order)
    {
      Order newOrder = order as Order;
      //acquire exclusive synchronization lock
      //start of critical section
      lock(syncObj)
      {
        Console.WriteLine("Order Received : " +newOrder.Instrument);
        //Add order into array list
        orderList.Add(order);
        //update the downstream system
```

```
      }
      //end of critical section
    }
  }

  static void Main(string[] args)
  {
    //create order book
    OrderBook orderBook = new OrderBook();

    //start pumping orders
    Order order = new Order("MSFT");
    Order order1 = new Order("GE");

    //start updating the order book with multiple orders on multiple threads
    ThreadPool.QueueUserWorkItem(new WaitCallback(orderBook.Add),order);
    ThreadPool.QueueUserWorkItem(new WaitCallback(orderBook.Add),order1);
    Console.ReadLine();
  }
}
```

This code example depicts a real-life scenario of a central order book that is a shared resource and is subject to concurrent access by multiple threads. The operation typically performed on this shared resource is usually an insert or update of orders. Therefore, it is extremely important to serialize access to an order book to maintain the integrity of information. You do this with the help of the lock statement, which is a compiler-synthesized statement for Monitor.Enter and Monitor.Exit.

Deadlock Prevention

Multithreading brings better performance to an application. But it also introduces complexity into the overall execution of the application. To be precise, it is extremely difficult to debug a multithreaded program, particularly in a situation where bugs are unusual and hard to reproduce. Deadlock between threads is one of the toughest problems to detect.

The following code explains the cause of deadlock:

```
using System;
using System.Collections;
using System.Threading;

class DeadLock
{
  //Order Domain Model
  public class Order
  {}

  //Position book that maintains instrument net position
  public class PositionBook
  {
    //position book synchronization object
    public object posSync = new object();
    public OrderBook OBook;

    //update and reevaluate instrument position
    public void UpdateOrder(object order)
    {
      //acquire exclusive ownership on position book
      lock(posSync)
      {
```

```
          //acquire exclusive ownership on order book
          lock(OBook.orderSync)
          {}
        }
      }
    }
  }

  //Order book that stores individual order
  public class OrderBook
  {
    public PositionBook PBook;
    //order book synchronization object
    public object orderSync = new object();

    public void Add(object order)
    {
      //acquire exclusive ownership on order book
      lock(orderSync)
      {
        //acquire exclusive ownership on position book
        lock(PBook.posSync)
        {}
      }
    }
  }

  static void Main(string[] args)
  {
    //create order book
    OrderBook orderBook = new OrderBook();

    //create position book
    PositionBook posBook = new PositionBook();

    //assign reference to respective books
    orderBook.PBook = posBook;
    posBook.OBook = orderBook;

    //create order
    Order order = new Order();

    //update order book
    ThreadPool.QueueUserWorkItem(new WaitCallback(orderBook.Add),order);

    //update position service
    ThreadPool.QueueUserWorkItem(new WaitCallback(posBook.UpdateOrder),order);
    Console.ReadLine();
  }
}
```

This code demonstrates how the order book and position book are interrelated; the order book maintains the orders, and similarly, the position book maintains the net position of the individual instrument. By looking at the code, it may seem foolproof and free from any kind of error. However, upon execution, you will notice that the application occasionally goes into a hung state. The code is clearly the victim of deadlock because both the order book and position book updates are executed on a separate thread, and each of these threads is waiting for each other to release exclusive owner-ship on the shared resources. Assume that the order book successfully acquires a lock on orderSync

and then attempts to obtain exclusive access on the position book by requesting a lock on
PBook.posSync. This request will never get satisfied because the position book, which has received
an update request from another thread, has already acquired a lock on posSync and is trying to
obtain exclusive access on the order book by requesting a lock on OBook.orderSync. In a nutshell,
neither the order book nor the position book will release its acquired lock, and both will go into an
indefinite waiting period.

The solution to solving deadlock problems resides in the Monitor class. It provides a TryEnter
that is similar to Enter, but it will never go into an indefinite waiting period; instead, it accepts a timeout value, specifying how long the thread should wait for the lock. When the timeout value expires,
TryEnter returns a value of false, which is an indicator of a deadlock problem in the program.

The following code explains it well:

```
using System;
using System.Threading;

class DeadLockFree
{
  public class PositionBook
  {
    public object posSync = new object();
    public OrderBook OBook;

    public void UpdateOrder(object order)
    {
      //try to obtain position book lock
      if ( !Monitor.TryEnter(posSync,TimeSpan.FromSeconds(5)))
        throw new ApplicationException("Failed to obtain Position Book Lock");

      try
      {
        //try to obtain order book lock
        if ( !Monitor.TryEnter(OBook.orderSync,TimeSpan.FromSeconds(5)))
          throw new ApplicationException("Failed to obtain Order Book Lock");

        try
        {
          //update order book
        }
        finally
        {
          //release order book lock
          Monitor.Exit(OBook.orderSync);
        }
      }
      finally
      {
        //release position book lock
        Monitor.Exit(posSync);
      }
    }
  }

  public class OrderBook
  {
    public PositionBook PBook;
    public object orderSync = new object();
```

```
      public void Add(object order)
      {
        //try to obtain order book lock
        if ( !Monitor.TryEnter(orderSync,TimeSpan.FromSeconds(5)))
          throw new ApplicationException("Failed to obtain Order Book Lock");

        try
        {
          //try to obtain position book lock
          if ( !Monitor.TryEnter(PBook.posSync,TimeSpan.FromSeconds(5)))
            throw new ApplicationException("Failed to obtain Position Book Lock");

          try
          {
            //update position book
          }
          finally
          {
            //release position book lock
            Monitor.Exit(PBook.posSync);
          }
        }
        finally
        {
          //release order book lock
          Monitor.Exit(orderSync);
        }
      }
    }
  }
}
```

Interthread Notification

Interthread notification is the most common requirement in a multithreaded application where the action of one thread depends upon the action of other threads. More simply, the thread is waiting on a specific condition that is supposed to be satisfied by another thread. For example, say you have a central order book where orders are queued by one thread, and a dedicated thread is assigned to dequeuing and processing these orders. This is the most commonly used threading pattern, and we will demonstrate it by creating a managed thread that provides full control over the execution of the underlying operating system thread. This is in contrast to the thread pool and asynchronous delegate where developers are shielded from the underlying complexities of manual thread management.

Here's the code:

```
using System;
using System.Collections;
using System.Threading;

class InterThreadSignal
{
  public class Order
  {}
  public class OrderBook
  {
    Thread orderSweeper;
    //event object initially set to nonsignal state
    ManualResetEvent manualEvent = new ManualResetEvent(false);
```

```
    //create a thread-safe version of queue
    Queue orderQueue = Queue.Synchronized(new Queue());

    public OrderBook()
    {
      //create order sweeper thread
      orderSweeper = new Thread(new ThreadStart(Process));

      //start thread execution
      orderSweeper.Start();
    }

    public void Add(Order order)
    {
      //enqueue the order
      orderQueue.Enqueue(order);

      //signal the sweeper thread about arrival of new order
      manualEvent.Set();
    }

    public void Process()
    {
      while(true)
      {
        //wait for order to be enqueued
        manualEvent.WaitOne();

        //set the event to nonsignal state
        manualEvent.Reset();

        //process the order
        while(orderQueue.Count > 0 )
        {
          Console.WriteLine("Processing Order");
          //dequeue the order
          orderQueue.Dequeue();
        }
      }
    }
  }

  static void Main(string[] args)
  {
    //create order book
    OrderBook orderBook = new OrderBook();

    //start pumping orders
    //that will be concurrently processed by sweeper thread
    for(int ctr=0;ctr<=10;ctr++)
    {
      orderBook.Add(new Order());
    }
    Console.ReadLine();
  }
}
```

This code is structured in such a way that the queuing of orders is happening on the application's default thread, and the processing of orders takes place on a separate worker thread (an order sweeper thread) that is manually created by instantiating an instance of `Thread`. This class contains an overloaded constructor method that takes an instance of the `ThreadStart` delegate, which represents the method to be executed on this new thread. Calling `Start` on an instance of `Thread` starts the actual execution of the managed thread.

It is possible for the order sweeper thread to monitor the arrival of the new order by continuously iterating over the order queue. But this is not an efficient approach; imagine the amount of processor utilization consumed when iterating over the queue in a tight-loop fashion, especially when the queue is empty. What you need is some of kind of notification mechanism that will inform the order sweeper thread about the arrival of a new order. This is where `ManualResetEvent` and `AutoResetEvent` come to the rescue.

`ManualResetEvent` and `AutoResetEvent` are the synchronization event classes used for cross-thread notification. This notification takes the form of signal state and nonsignal state. *Signal state* indicates that the event has occurred, and *nonsignal state* indicates that the event has yet to occur. So, generally, threads wait on this event by calling `ManualResetEvent.WaitOne` or `AutoResetEvent.WaitOne`, and if the event is in a nonsignal state, then the thread will get blocked until some action puts it in a signal state by calling `ManualResetEvent.Set` or `AutoResetEvent.Set`. But when it comes to resetting signal state to nonsignal state, then both `ManualResetEvent` and `AutoResetEvent` adopt a different approach. If `ManualResetEvent` is used, then you need to explicitly call `ManualResetEvent.Reset` to set it back to nonsignal state. In the case of `AutoResetEvent`, it will automatically reset to nonsignal state as soon as the waiting thread is notified. To achieve event synchronization in the previous code, we used an instance of `ManualResetEvent` that is by default initialized to nonsignal state. This way, the order sweeper thread will get blocked until it receives a signal, which happens as soon as a new order is inserted in the queue. After processing all orders from the queue, the order sweeper thread again blocks, waiting for a signal.

Another important difference between `AutoResetEvent` and `ManualResetEvent` is their way of notifying waiting threads about the signal event. `ManualResetEvent` is suitable for notifying one or multiple waiting threads, which is different from `AutoResetEvent` where only one waiting thread is notified at a time.

Mutex

`Mutex` is another form of synchronization mechanism similar to the `Monitor` class. The mission of both of these classes is to emit thread-safe code and grant the exclusive access of shared resources to only one thread at a time. Locks acquired using `Mutex` are known as *heavyweight locks*; locks acquired using `Monitor` are known as *lightweight locks*. `Mutex` gets its heavyweight title because acquiring and releasing a `Mutex`-based lock incurs an extra amount of processing overhead. Furthermore, lightweight locks are highly optimized but are specifically tuned to work within the boundaries of a currently running process. On the other hand, a `Mutex` is capable of synchronizing code across multiple processes. Such types of mutexes are known as *system-named* mutexes.

To illustrate the benefit of a mutex, we'll show an example of thread synchronization among multiple processes. In a capital market, most trading systems installed on the trading member end use a proprietary class library provided by the exchange itself to communicate with their systems. These libraries are usually single-threaded, and even exchange systems are designed in such a way that only one request at a time is allowed from an individual broker or institution. Various reasons exist for such limitations, primarily that exchange systems are legacy systems and are not equipped to handle the current market infrastructure's expectations. Therefore, various services running on the broker or institution end must ensure that only one request at a time is issued to the exchange system.

This scenario is clearly depicted in the following code where the order management service and the exchange market data service are running as two separate operating system processes. The order management service is responsible for sending orders to the exchange, and the market data service is tasked with the responsibility of periodically retrieving market data from the exchange system. It is extremely important for both these services to synchronize their interaction with the exchange, and this is achieved with the help of a Mutex.

```
using System;
using System.Threading;

class OrderMgmtSvc
{
  class Order{}
  class OrderBook
  {
    //create system named mutex
    Mutex syncExchange = new Mutex(false,"SyncExchange");

    //send order to exchange
    public void SendToExchange(Order order)
    {
      //only one request is allowed to submit to exchange
      //therefore it is important to synchronize this access
      //among all services
      //acquire exclusive ownership
      syncExchange.WaitOne();

      //send order to exchange
      Console.WriteLine("Order sent to Exchange");
      Console.ReadLine();

      //release the lock allowing other service
      //such as exchange mkt data to interact
      //with exchange
      syncExchange.ReleaseMutex();
    }
  }
  static void Main(string[] args)
  {
    //create order book
    OrderBook orderBook = new OrderBook();

    //create order
    Order order = new Order();

    //send order to exchange
    orderBook.SendToExchange(order);
  }
}
```

This code mimics the functionality of an order management service, and its primary task is sending orders to the exchange that are defined in the SendToExchange method of OrderBook. To ensure that at any given point of time only one thread is allowed to send a request, you use a system-named Mutex to achieve this goal. You create a system-named mutex by passing two parameters to the overloaded constructor method of Mutex. The first parameter indicates whether the ownership of this mutex is to be given to the calling thread, and the second argument represents a user-friendly name of the Mutex. In the previous code example, we specified a default value of false, which doesn't provide exclusive ownership of the mutex, followed by a unique mutex name—SyncExchange. When it comes to sending data to the exchange, at that time the Mutex.WaitOne method is invoked to request the exclusive ownership of a mutex. If ownership is granted, then the requesting thread resumes its execution, or else it is blocked until the mutex is released by its current owner. Assuming the thread acquires a mutex, then it can safely perform its exchange-related operations, and after completing this activity, the ownership of the mutex is released by calling Mutex.ReleaseMutex.

The next part of the code describes the market data service that is responsible for market data management:

```
using System;
using System.Threading;

class ExchangeMktDataSvc
{
  class MktDataManager
  {
    //create system named mutex
    Mutex syncExchange = new Mutex(false,"SyncExchange");

    public void RetrieveData()
    {
      //since we know only one request at a time
      //is allowed to submit to exchange
      //therefore it is important to
      //synchronize this access among all services
      syncExchange.WaitOne();

      //retrieve market data from exchange
      Console.WriteLine("Market Data Service");

      //release the lock allowing other service
      //such as order mgmt service to interact
      //with exchange
      syncExchange.ReleaseMutex();
    }
  }

  static void Main(string[] args)
  {
    //create market data mgr; its primary
    //responsibility is retrieving market data published by exchange
    MktDataManager mktData = new MktDataManager();

    //retrieve market data
    mktData.RetrieveData();
    Console.ReadLine();
  }
}
```

The importance of the Mutex is clearly highlighted in the RetrieveData method defined in MktDataManager. To ensure thread synchronization with the order management service, which is a separate process, an instance of a system mutex is created by passing the same name used by the order management service. It is important to know the user-friendly name beforehand because that is the only way to get hold of a shared system mutex.

Atomic Operation

In a multithreaded environment, an operation is said to be *atomic* when its multiple steps are combined and executed as a single operation and the current executing thread will not be preempted by another thread during the execution of this atomic operation. .NET's Interlocked class provides atomic operation for variables that are accessed or updated from multiple threads:

```
using System;
using System.Threading;

class InterLock
{
  //Order Domain Model
  public class Order
  {
    public int OrderID;
  }
  //Order Book
  class OrderBook
  {
    //Static variable that keeps track of last order ID generated
    public static int orderId;

    //factory method to create new order
    public Order CreateOrder()
    {
      //create order
      Order newOrder = new Order();

      //create unique order ID
      //increment the shared variable value in an atomic manner
      int newOrderId = Interlocked.Increment(ref orderId);

      //assign the new order ID
      newOrder.OrderID = newOrderId;
      return newOrder;
    }
  }
  static void Main(string[] args)
  {
    //create order book
    OrderBook orderBook = new OrderBook();
    //create new order
    Order newOrder = orderBook.CreateOrder();
  }
}
```

The previous code depicts a scenario of generating a unique order ID and assigning it to a newly created order. To keep a track of this order ID, a static variable of the integer data type is declared in OrderBook. This variable is accessed and updated by multiple threads, and therefore you need to implement some kind of synchronization mechanism to maintain the integrity of this value. The Interlocked class provides methods that enable the synchronization of shared variables in an atomic manner. Furthermore, the intelligence behind Interlocked is directly implemented inside processor hardware; therefore, it is faster than other synchronization primitives such as mutexes and critical sections. Interlocked also provides a Decrement method that is used to decrement values as an atomic operation.

Thread Scheduling

When building highly multithreaded applications, the question that is often debated is, what is the upper limit on the number of threads an individual application can create? Well, the basic rule is to use as few threads as possible—possibly that the total number of threads must not exceed the total number of processors installed in a machine—but this is not how it works in the real world. The purpose of this section is to highlight some important facts about multithreading that will help you devise a better strategy in outlining the design of a server-side trading application.

Threads are the basic unit of execution, and multiple threads are executed on a single-processor system. This is possible because of the preemptive scheduling system implemented by Windows where multiple threads are allowed to create and execute, giving the illusion of parallel execution even though in reality at any point of time only one thread is being addressed by an individual processor. A thread is scheduled to execute by the operating system scheduler for a particular amount of time called a *quantum*. This quantum value differs from system to system and is managed by the operating system, but by default on Windows XP the thread length time is 20 milliseconds, and on Windows 2003 it is 120 milliseconds. When a thread is scheduled to run by the scheduler, the thread runs for its allocated quantum; after this quantum expires, the scheduler initiates a process known as *context switching* in which the currently active thread state information is saved, a new thread is selected to run, and its state is loaded and finally executed. Context switching also happens for the following reasons:

- A high-priority thread preempts a low-priority thread.
- A running thread enters a wait state when trying to get exclusive ownership on a resource.
- An active running thread suspends its operation.
- An active running thread enters sleep mode.

Context switching is an expensive operation, and a system with a high number of threads will encounter a high number of context switches. Therefore, a common solution to reduce context switches is to create a pool of reusable threads and use this pool to process all application requests. The System.Threading.ThreadPool class already offers this functionality, and we already covered it in the "Thread Pools" section.

As already noted, threads are scheduled in a round-robin fashion, but the most important factor that drives the internal thread-scheduling algorithm is the priority levels associated with an individual thread. Without going into the low-level details, Figure 2-7 shows how the priority of threads affects the scheduler's scheduling policy.

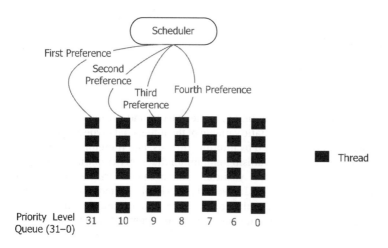

Figure 2-7. *Thread scheduling*

By default, when a managed thread is created in .NET, it is assigned a normal thread priority. You can assign the priority of a thread with the help of the Thread.Priority property. This property accepts an enumerated value of the ThreadPriority type. Even though ThreadPriority defines five levels of thread priorities, in reality Windows internally uses 32 priority levels from 0–31; Table 2-8 represents this mapping.

Table 2-8. *Thread Priority Levels*

Managed Thread Priority Level	Windows Internal Thread Priority Level
ThreadPriority.Lowest	6
ThreadPriority.BelowNormal	7
ThreadPriority.Normal	8
ThreadPriority.AboveNormal	9
ThreadPriority.Highest	10

The Windows scheduler internally maintains a queue for the individual priority level. This individual queue contains a list of ready threads waiting to be executed. The scheduler schedules threads stored in this queue, which starts at priority level 31. Note that a higher number indicates a higher priority level. Threads with higher priority values will always run and preempt lower-priority threads. This also means a high-priority thread will always get a much larger share of the processor compared to a low-priority thread.

When building front-office systems, sometimes it is necessary to tweak a thread's priority level to get better performance. For example, multiple order books are created for individual instruments, and during peak times not all instruments are active. It is only a few specific instruments that are highly volatile in nature. So, assuming that the processing of an individual order book is assigned to an individual thread, then you can lift the thread priority of a highly volatile instrument order book to a higher level so that it gets a good amount of processor time to process orders quickly.

The following code example illustrates this scenario where a thread assigned to process the MSFT order book gets a higher priority:

```
using System;
using System.Threading;

class OrderBookPriority
{
  class OrderBook
  {
    //dedicated thread to process orders
    private Thread orderSweeper;

    public OrderBook(string instrument,bool highPriority)
    {
      orderSweeper = new Thread(new ThreadStart(Process));

      //if it is a high-priority order book
      //then we need to ensure that this order book
      //gets maximum processing time
      if ( highPriority == true )
        orderSweeper.Priority = ThreadPriority.Highest;

      //start thread execution
      orderSweeper.Start();
    }
```

```
  public void Process()
  {
    //order-processing code goes here
  }
}

static void Main(string[] args)
{
  //create MSFT order book
  //we want to make sure the orders of Microsoft are quickly processed
  //and therefore we raised the thread priority to highest
  OrderBook orderBook = new OrderBook("MSFT",true);
  Console.ReadLine();
}
}
```

On a multiprocessor system, the scheduler schedules an individual thread's execution on an available processor. The scheduler will always attempt to schedule an individual thread on its previously assigned processor, but during a heavy system load it may not always succeed and will be forced to assign a different processor. The scheduler also supports *thread affinity*, which enables a thread to be affinitized on a specific processor. In the trading world, this feature proves extremely useful in establishing a processor balance between multiple threads. For example, imagine an order book–processing application installed on a multiprocessor machine. This machine contains four processors and handles the load of twenty instruments, with individual instrument processing offloaded to a dedicated thread. So, the Windows scheduler will schedule these twenty newly created threads on four processors. But from a business point of view, out of twenty instruments, only ten of them will be highly volatile, and the rest of them will not be that active. Taking this into account, we affinitized the first three processors with threads of the highly volatile instruments, and the remaining threads were assigned to the last processor. This will ensure that the scheduler will schedule all three threads on an individual processor that is different from the last processor in which a total of ten threads are configured to run. This is equivalent to assigning a dedicated processor to process only three instruments.

The following code demonstrates this example:

```
using System;
using System.Threading;
using System.Diagnostics;

class InstrumentBalancing
{
  //Enumerated flag used to specify
  //the list of processor on which threads are
  //affinitized
  [Flags]
  public enum Processor
  {
    CPU1=1, //1st bit
    CPU2=2, //2nd bit
    CPU3=4, //3rd bit
    CPU4=8  //4th bit
  }

  class OrderBook
  {
    //dedicated thread to process orders
    private Thread orderSweeper;
    Processor procMask;
```

```
    public OrderBook(string instrument,Processor mask)
    {
      procMask = mask;

      //create order sweeper thread
      orderSweeper = new Thread(new ThreadStart(OrderProcess));
      orderSweeper.Start();
    }


    public void OrderProcess()
    {
      //Get current running process instance
      Process curProcess = Process.GetCurrentProcess();

      //Get the list of threads running in this process
      foreach(ProcessThread osThread in curProcess.Threads)
      {
        //ProcessThread represents an operating system thread
        //whereas Thread represents managed thread
        //we need to find the corresponding OS thread for the
        //current managing thread
        //Get managed thread ID
        int threadId = AppDomain.GetCurrentThreadId();

        //check thread ID with current as thread ID
        if ( osThread.Id == threadId )
        {
          int mask = (int)procMask;
          //Set processor affinity
          osThread.ProcessorAffinity = (IntPtr)mask ;
        }
      }

      //start processing the order
    }
  }

  static void Main(string[] args)
  {
    //Allocate first CPU for processing MSFT orders
    OrderBook msftBook = new OrderBook("MSFT",Processor.CPU2);

    //Allocate second CPU for processing IBM orders
    OrderBook ibmBook  = new OrderBook("IBM",Processor.CPU2);

    //Allocate third and fourth CPUs for processing GE orders
    OrderBook geBook= new OrderBook("GE",Processor.CPU3 | Processor.CPU4 );
    Console.ReadLine();
  }
}
```

Collections and Multithreading

Data structures such as arrays, queues, and so on, are the primary storage mechanisms used for storing in-memory data. It also means that data will be simultaneously accessed or updated by multiple threads. .NET offers two variants of data structures primarily for a queue, hash table, stack, and array list. The first variant is meant to be used in single-threaded applications, and the second variant is specifically meant to be used in multithreaded applications.

The following code represents a list data structure that is not thread-safe and, when accessed by multiple threads, results in inconsistent program output:

```
using System;
using System.Collections;

class SingleThreadArray
{
  static void Main(string[] args)
  {
    //not a thread-safe list
    ArrayList orderList = new ArrayList();
  }
}
```

To guarantee thread safety, you need to use a thread-safe list, as illustrated in the following code example:

```
using System;
using System.Collections;

class MultiThreadArray
{
  static void Main(string[] args)
  {
    //thread-safe list
    ArrayList orderList = ArrayList.Synchronized(new ArrayList());
  }
}
```

You obtain a thread-safe version of the list data structure by invoking the Synchronized static method defined in the ArrayList class. Such a similar method is available on the Hashtable, Stack, and Queue classes. Upon the successful invocation of the Synchronized method, a new instance of SyncArrayList is created, which is basically a thread-safe wrapper over ArrayList. For example:

```
public static ArrayList Synchronized(ArrayList list)
{
  if (list == null)
  {
    throw new ArgumentNullException("list");
  }
  return new ArrayList.SyncArrayList(list);
}
```

SyncArrayList is derived from ArrayList, and its visibility mode is private, which means it is not publicly accessible to the external world. The internal implementation of this class overrides only those methods that modify or access shared data. For instance, as shown in the following code, the Add and Remove methods are overridden because both of these methods can be invoked by multiple threads and the operation performed by them directly affects the state of the shared data.

```
[Serializable()]
private class SyncArrayList : ArrayList
{
  private ArrayList _list;
  //sync root
  private object _root;
```

```
internal SyncArrayList(ArrayList list) : base(false)
{
  this._list = list;
  this._root = list.SyncRoot;
}

public override int Add(object value)
{
  int num1;
  //acquire lock
  lock (this._root)
  {
    num1 = this._list.Add(value);
  }
  return num1;
}
public override void Remove(object value)
{
  //acquire lock
  lock (this._root)
  {
    this._list.Remove(value);
  }
}
}
}
```

The previous code snippet is a partial implementation of SyncArrayList. By looking at the code of the Add and Remove methods, you should be able to understand the technique used in achieving code synchronization. A monitor object, _root, is used to guarantee thread safety.

The other interesting property of ArrayList is SyncRoot, which returns the internal root object used by SyncArrayList to gain an exclusive lock before performing any update operations. The purpose of this property is to provide a way for other parts of the application code that are beyond the control of SyncArrayList to synchronize with collections. For example, the order book container that uses ArrayList to store orders also provides support to enumerate an individual order such as *top-five* functionality. Top-five functionality refers to the best five orders at that moment in time. The biggest problem with enumeration is that it is not a thread-safe operation, and other threads can still add or remove orders from the order book while enumeration is in progress. To guarantee thread safety, you should lock the list.

The following code shows how to achieve this:

```
using System;
using System.Threading;
using System.Collections;

class SyncRoot
{
  //Order Domain model
  class Order{}
  //Order Book
  class OrderBook
  {
    //create thread-safe list
    ArrayList orderList = ArrayList.Synchronized(new ArrayList());

    public void Add(object order)
    {
```

```
      //Add order
      orderList.Add(order);
    }
    public void Remove(object order)
    {
      //Remove order
    }

    public ArrayList TopFive()
    {
      //create temporary list to hold top-five orders
      ArrayList topFive = new ArrayList();

      //Lock the collection so that the orders
      //returned are accurate
      lock(orderList.SyncRoot)
      {
        //Iterate and retrieve top-five orders
        int ctr=0;
        foreach(Order order in orderList)
        {
          topFive.Add(order);
          if ( ctr > 5 )
            break;
          else
            ctr++;
        }
      }
      return topFive;
    }
  }
  static void Main(string[] args)
  {
    //create order book
    OrderBook orderBook = new OrderBook();

    //start inserting orders on different thread
    Order newOrder = new Order();
    ThreadPool.QueueUserWorkItem(new WaitCallback(orderBook.Add),newOrder);

    //create another new order
    newOrder = new Order();
    ThreadPool.QueueUserWorkItem(new WaitCallback(orderBook.Add),newOrder);

    //Retrieve top-five orders on different thread
    ThreadPool.QueueUserWorkItem(new WaitCallback(TopFiveOrder),orderBook);
  }

  public static void TopFiveOrder(object oBook)
  {
    //Retrieve top-five orders
    OrderBook orderBook = oBook as OrderBook;
    ArrayList topFive = orderBook.TopFive();
  }
}
```

UI Widgets and Multithreading

Even though we have not covered anything about user interface (UI) widgets, it is essential for you to know the quirks and foibles of implementing multithreading in Windows form–based applications. It is true that the user interface for an application is the first step of attracting user attention. It also stamps an indelible impression that has a long-lasting effect. Most of the time, developers do a pretty decent job of embellishing the user interfaces of applications by using sophisticated UI controls. After completing the look-and-feel task, the next biggest challenge is to increase user responsiveness by allowing users to perform multiple tasks at the same time and also provide a way to abort a long-running task.

An example commonly found in the financial world is implementing parallelism in a bulk order upload form. This form uploads bulk order information that is stored in a tab- or comma-delimited text file. Such upload activity is a time-consuming process, and sometimes the total number of orders to be uploaded is significantly large. To stop users from falling sleep, developers make the upload activity more interactive by displaying a progress bar that continuously displays the status of the upload along with a cancel button that allows users to abandon the entire upload process.

Developing this type of upload program is pretty simple. You need to create a new form, lay out the appropriate widgets such as a progress bar and a cancel button on the form, and eventually write a code that spawns an additional worker thread along with the default thread created by the application. This worker thread is assigned the task of reading individual order information from a source file and notifying the progress bar control of its status. With the worker thread doing the heavy lifting, the default application thread becomes highly responsive to user actions.

Now imagine if you offload this heavy-lifting task from the worker thread to the default application thread; the user interface activities freeze, and the application remains unresponsive until the upload activity completes. The reason for this kind of behavior is that even though the application's default thread shares the same characteristics of the worker thread, the default thread is assigned the additional task of processing user interface–related messages. The application thread spawned by a Windows form application, because of its special purpose, is called a *UI thread*, as shown in Figure 2-8.

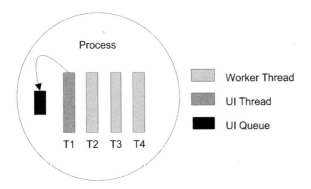

Figure 2-8. *UI thread processing messages stored in a UI queue*

From a technical implementation perspective, every UI action (such as a form click, a button click, a window move, a window resize, and so on) that is triggered by users is materialized in the form of a UI message. You have two ways of generating UI messages. One is an implicit way, which is generated as a result of a user action, and the other one is the explicit way, which is triggered when widget aesthetic characteristics are programmatically modified, which in turn forces a repaint of the controls. The UI messages are stored in a special queue known as the *UI message queue*, and an individual message is then processed by a UI thread in a sequential manner. A strong bond exists between the UI queue and the UI thread, because the UI thread is aware of this queue and knows how to honor messages residing in this queue.

So, what are the repercussions of modifying UI widget properties from a worker thread? Well, this certainly shakes the fundamentals of GUI programming in Windows. The general principle is that the widget member must be invoked only from the UI thread and not from any other thread. So, when the worker thread wants to update the widget, it must employ a bit of a trick. Widgets available in a Windows control collection expose thread-safe members, Invoke and BeginInvoke, that allow freehand invocation from any thread. BeginInvoke is an asynchronous version of Invoke, and both methods are defined in System.Windows.Forms.Control, which is a base class for UI controls. These members are termed as *thread-safe* because the execution of these members always happens on the UI thread, regardless of the thread from which they are being invoked.

To further simplify this concept, we have designed a WinForm application, as depicted in Figure 2-9, with a progress bar and two command buttons rendered on a bulk order upload form.

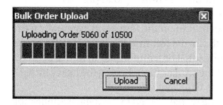

Figure 2-9. *Bulk order upload form*

By clicking the Upload button, the bulk order import activity starts and is executed on the worker thread. The code for achieving this task is as follows:

```
private void btnUpload_Click(object sender, System.EventArgs e)
{
    //Starts the bulk order upload on worker thread
    ThreadPool.QueueUserWorkItem(new WaitCallback(BulkOrderUpload));
}
```

The core logic of uploading the bulk order is defined in BulkOrderUpload, which is executed on one of the threads from the thread pool. With the help of a progress bar control, users are informed about the progress of this bulk import activity. So, somehow the worker thread must send a message to the UI thread to update the progress bar control; this happens by calling the Invoke method on the progress bar control, as shown in the following code. The Invoke method accepts a delegate and an optional parameter list and always arranges the execution of the delegate on the UI thread.

```
public delegate void SetProgressBar(int value);

private void UpdateProgressBar(int current)
{
    //update the progress bar control
    uploadProgressBar.Value = current;
}

private void BulkOrderUpload(object state)
{
    int ctr=0;
    int totalRecords=1;
```

```
//Read bulk order import file, and initialize the values
//such as total number of orders to import

//start iterating individual order
while(ctr < totalRecords)
{
  //update progress bar control value
  //this needs to be done on UI thread
  uploadProgressBar.Invoke(new SetProgressBar(UpdateProgressBar),
                           new object[]{ctr});
}
}
```

Server Timer

An *event* is a notification that is triggered in response to an action. This action could be initiated by users or could be because of a change in state. Based on this action, events are broadly classified as user events, state-change events, and timer events:

- *User events* are generated as a result of user actions. Examples of such events are the user clicking the mouse or navigating around controls using the keyboard.
- *State-change events* are generated as a result of programmatic action. For example, programmatically updating the text of a textbox widget forces a redraw of the UI control and also raises an event.
- *Timer events* are recurring events and are triggered at particular intervals.

Timer events play an important role in implementing actions that are configured to occur at a predefined interval. In the financial world, the most notable example of a timer event is the periodic exchange of heartbeat messages between a trader's system and the exchange's system. Failure to dispatch a message by the trader's system in a timely manner would sometimes result in the abrupt termination of a session with the exchange system, which in turn would bring the trading operation to a complete halt. So, from a technical implementation perspective, you need an effective timer architecture that provides both accuracy and scalability, and this is where the Timer class defined in the System.Threading namespace comes into action. This class uses threads in a .NET thread pool to raise and execute events when the user-defined timer interval expires.

The following code illustrates how a server timer is configured to send a heartbeat message to the exchange system at an interval of 2 seconds:

```
using System;
using System.Threading;

class ServerTimer
{
  class ExchangeGateway
  {
    //Server Timer
    public Timer hbTimer;

    //Callback method invoked at an interval of 2 seconds
    public void SendHeartBeat(object state)
    {
      //Disable the timer
      //to avoid code-reentrancy problem
      hbTimer.Change(Timeout.Infinite,Timeout.Infinite);

      //Send message to exchange
```

```
      //Enable the timer
      //schedule start and subsequent invocation of callback
      //after every two seconds
      hbTimer.Change(TimeSpan.FromSeconds(2),TimeSpan.FromSeconds(2));
    }

    public ExchangeGateway()
    {
      //Create server timer, and pass the callback method that
      //is periodically notified at an interval of two seconds
      //start the timer immediately
      hbTimer = new Timer(new TimerCallback(SendHeartBeat),null,0,2000);
    }
  }

  static void Main(string[] args)
  {
    //create exchange gateway responsible
    //for all communication with exchange
    ExchangeGateway gateWay = new ExchangeGateway();
    Console.ReadLine();
  }
}
```

You can enable a server timer by constructing an instance of Timer. This class has four overloaded constructors, and each one differs mainly by how timer interval values are assigned. The first parameter requires an instance of the TimerCallback delegate, which actually represents the timer callback method. The second parameter defines application-specific information that is supplied to the callback method. The third and fourth arguments are essential and determine the timer interval. To immediately schedule the timer, pass a value of 0 to the third argument, or you can also specify an amount of time (in milliseconds) to wait before scheduling the first timer execution. The last argument determines the frequency of the timer (in milliseconds). In the previous code, we immediately start the timer and configure it to send a heartbeat message to the exchange, which is defined in SendHeartBeat of ExchangeGateway at a 2-second interval.

Since the execution of a callback method always takes place on thread-pool threads, it may lead to a code-reentrancy problem. This may happen if the total execution time of the callback method exceeds a timer's firing interval. To guard timer code from multithreaded problems, the timer must be disabled and reenabled on the entry and exit of the callback method. You can do this by invoking the Change method, which reconfigures the start time and frequency of the timer.

Examining the Business-Technology Mapping

This section covers how to translate the order-matching business requirement into a technical implementation. The key element in designing an order-matching engine is *efficiency*, which is how quickly an order gets matched with its counterpart. Furthermore, when the market is at its peak, thousands of orders are queued, with each order trying to locate its best fit and eventually resulting in a successful trade. If you analyze this scenario from a technical standpoint, it would involve some kind of data container that holds all these orders. Data containers are usually built based on the nature of an order, that is, one container for buy orders and another for sell orders. Each order searches through the other container to find a successful match. Matching can be further categorized as follows:

- In-memory matching

- Out-memory matching

In-memory matching, as the name indicates, is a match that is performed in the memory. Such matching demands a larger memory capacity, because the entire data needs to be hosted in memory. Data constructed in the memory results in a fast pass-through, and orders are quickly located. Absolutely no disk I/O activity is involved.

On the other hand, out-memory matching is conducted with the help of a commercial, off-the-shelf database product such as Sybase, Oracle, or SQL Server. Here data is stored in database tables in the form of rows and columns. This is less efficient than in-memory because it brings relational database overheads. Also, every data read/write operation needs to be transaction aware and logging aware, which leads to a heavy amount of disk I/O operations. This also brings some attention to the three aspects that are crucial from a data container design perspective:

- How fast an item gets attached to its underlying container (insertion)

- How fast an item gets detached from its underlying container (deletion)

- How efficiently an item gets sought (search)

It is clear that the underlying storage mechanism of data containers must be efficient and provide support for an implementation of a time-proven search algorithm. The search algorithm must not only allow for the faster seeking of an individual item but also must live up to its promise of not deteriorating performance when the items in the container keep increasing exponentially.

If you extend the concept of algorithm implementation to the relational database world, data is stored in the form of rows and columns and encapsulated inside a table. This is an abstraction wrapped over the actual data container by the vendor. However, the underlying implementation is kept close to the vendor's chest and hence provides fewer controls for fine-tuning. This does not mean it is not optimal to use a relational database; rather, it requires a developer to take advantage of RDBMS indexes and the power of Transact-SQL to perform a one-to-one match. In addition to this, each database vendor provides specific database settings that are exclusively designed to work in their own database products, which ultimately give a double-edged performance boost.

But in the case of in-memory matching, many options are available. In-memory matching brings together the virtues of both a robust data container and an efficient algorithm. It also allows working at low levels of precision wherever possible. However, the business requirement is the key driver that influences the decision of out-memory over in-memory matching. Also, keep in mind that extra features come with extra cost. The cost associated with in-memory matching is that the data is held in volatile storage, making it transient in nature. In the event of an abrupt failure, data will be wiped out. To overcome this problem, you may require a fair amount of "plumbing" code to make the data immortal. In the case of out-memory matching, data is persistent and hence automatically reconstructible.

Now that you understand the domain problems, it's time to implement the data structures and threading covered in the earlier technical sections of this chapter. Order-matching applications are mainly founded upon data structures, and so far we have covered the basic data structures (such as arrays, array lists, hash tables, queues, and so on) that come as part and parcel of the base framework. You can easily extend these basic collections to form new specialized data containers. Moreover, another rationale behind in-memory matching is the need for high-end performance, which is possible only when data is manipulated in memory. The candidates that best fit this list are the classes under the System.Collection namespace that provide the virtues of both a robust data container and an efficient algorithm.

In Figure 2-10, various sources provide orders. Some of these orders originate from a broker's trading desk, and some of them come directly from customers through the Internet. These orders are then funneled into what we will call a *business domain*. A business domain maps a business entity or a business unit. The equities market is treated as a separate domain from the foreign currency market domain.

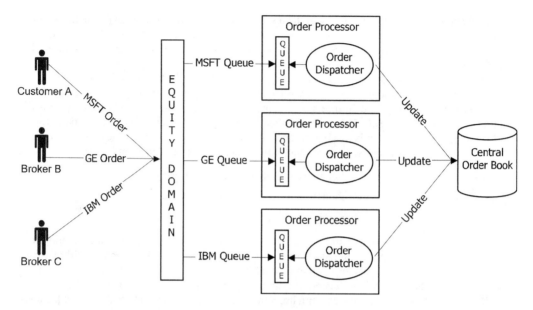

Figure 2-10. *High-level implementation of an order-matching engine*

Once the business domain receives orders, the orders are then handed over to an order processor that handles the scalability aspects of the framework by providing an order-processing platform for a single instrument or a group of instruments. The order processor is built upon a queue in which orders are queued based on arrival time, and a dedicated order dispatcher continuously monitors and processes this queue. When new orders arrive, the order dispatcher processes them, and the central order book is updated. From an implementation point of view, the queue of the order processor is realized by the `System.Collections.Queue` class, and the order dispatcher responsible for processing orders from the queue is realized by the `System.Threading.Thread` class. To further optimize the monitoring of operations performed by the order dispatcher, a signal-based notification approach is adopted. This approach uses `System.Threading.ManualResetEvent`, which will signal the order dispatcher thread on the arrival of a new order.

Figure 2-10 shows a one-to-one mapping between the order processor and instrument. So, if there are 250 instruments, then 250 order processors will be created. But you should avoid this strategy; because every new order processor results in the creation of one dedicated thread, too many threads will result in a higher number of context switches, eventually deteriorating performance. The most sensible approach is to create a dedicated order processor for highly volatile instruments and then create the necessary order processor for a group of instruments.

The next step that the order processor undertakes is to perform bookkeeping by placing the new order in the central order book, as shown in Figure 2-11.

From a conceptual standpoint, the order book represents the massive storage of orders arranged in a table. If you transform this conceptual view into a technical implementation, then you can nest orders in the `System.Collections.ArrayList` class. Using `System.Collections.ArrayList` undoubtedly meets this requirement; from a flexibility standpoint, it is a hardwired approach. Hence, you can adopt a mixed approach by using both `System.Collections.Hashtable` and `System.Collections.ArrayList`.

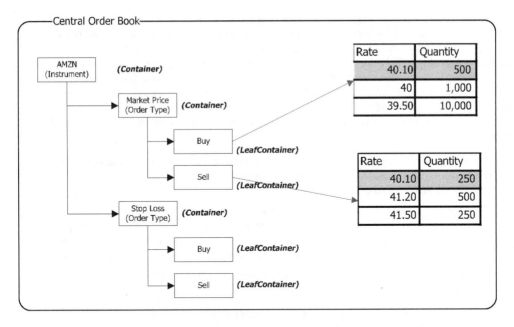

Figure 2-11. *Central order book*

The monolithic order book is segregated into a tree structure, where every node occupies one of the key attributes of the order. Such hierarchical arrangement of data compared to raw tabulated data gives further flexibility in grouping orders. Orders can now be easily classified based on certain business characteristics. These business characteristics are laid down in the form of individual tree nodes, and three levels have been identified in the tree:

- Level 1 (Instrument)
- Level 2 (Order Type)
- Level 3 (Buy/Sell)

Level 1 of the tree is mapped to an instrument; for example, MSFT and IBM will form two nodes at Level 1. Level 2 is defined according to the order types that are categorized based on a special set of attributes associated with every order. This attribute identifies the type of order, such as a market price order, limit price order, IOC order, and so on. The final leaf level in the tree is mapped to the buy and sell legs of an order. Hence, it is logical to have two nodes representing Buy and Sell, because the business logic performed on these leaf levels will be different. Below the leaf level resides the internal storage implementation of the order book where orders are finally seated.

A tree is implemented using the System.Collections.Hashtable class; similarly, System.Collections.ArrayList is used to store orders. The reason for using System.Collections.ArrayList is that, besides its programming simplicity combined with its sequential nature of arranging elements, it also offers ready-to-use sort (quick sort) and search (binary search) algorithms. Figure 2-11 illustrated the need for quick sort and also explained that in the business specification the buy-side orders are arranged in descending order of bid prices and the sell-side orders are arranged in ascending order of offer prices. Although the quick sort algorithm solved one of the most important requirements of the business, elements stored inside System.Collections.ArrayList are custom order objects. So, to sort these data elements based on a particular field, the System.Collections.IComparer class is used. This drives both sort and search behavior in an ArrayList.

So far, we have discussed the storage aspect of an order, not the matching component. The matching component hides the core matching logic and varies from market to market. Therefore, the matching component needs to be separated from the order-matching framework. In this way, the order-matching framework is solely responsible for looking after the infrastructure details such as optimizing data structure, parallelism, and so on, and the business logic is defined outside the context of the framework and plugged at runtime. The operations performed inside this matching component have a direct effect on the state of an order. Orders are classified into three states, as follows, and the transition from one state to another is determined by a condition that usually differs from business to business:

Active (pre-insert): The order before insertion is in the "active" state. It gives an opportunity to the business component to execute any business-related logic that may even cancel this insert operation based on certain conditions.

Passive (insert): The order when permanently stored in the order container is considered to be in the "passive" state. It is not necessary for every order to go into the passive state. It is possible that an active order, when passed to a business-matching component, may immediately find a counterpart order and not satisfy the condition required to go into the passive state.

Inactive (removed): The order when finally removed from the underlying container is switched to an "inactive" state.

This concludes the business-technology mapping section. The next section covers the code-level details required to implement a prototype of an order-matching engine.

Class Details

Figure 2-12 shows the order-matching engine class diagram, and Figure 2-13 shows the order-matching engine VS .NET project structure.

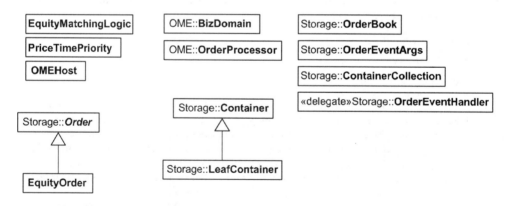

Figure 2-12. *Order-matching engine class diagram*

Code Snippets

The following sections show the code for each class of the order-matching engine.

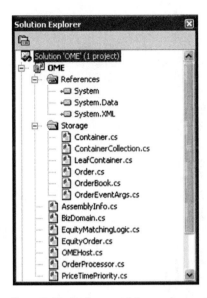

Figure 2-13. *Order-matching engine project structure*

Order

Order is the triggering point of a successful transaction, and its values directly contribute to the overall functioning of the order-matching engine. But in the real world, you can further classify information that constitutes an order by its commonality and variability attributes. Every order, regardless of the context in which it is created (*context* in this sense implies the underlying market such as the equities market, the derivatives market, the forex market, or the auction market), comprises the following common attributes:

Instrument: This is the name of the product for which an order is initiated. *Product* is a more generic term and often gets translated to more domain-specific terms that fit well in the domain's vocabulary. In the equities world, an instrument maps to a symbol; similarly, in a book's auction market, an instrument maps to the name of the book that is to be traded.

Order type: This represents the nature of an order that allows the imbibing of some domain-specific peculiarities.

Buy or sell: This attribute represents the actual motive or intention of an order.

Price: This is the price at which the buyer or seller is willing to offer this order.

Quantity: The number of shares.

Order ID: The unique ID that allows easy traceability of an order.

Time stamp: The creation time of an order.

The previous common information is captured in an abstract Order class from which every concrete order class must derive.

Here's the code for Order:

```
using System;
using System.Threading;

namespace OME.Storage
{
  public abstract class Order
```

```csharp
{
  string instrument;
  string buySell;
  string orderType;
  double price;
  int quantity;
  static long globalOrderId;
  long orderId;
  DateTime orderTimeStamp;
  public Order()
  {
    //Generate Default Values
    //Global unique order ID
    orderId = Interlocked.Increment(ref globalOrderId);
    //Order Time Stamp
    orderTimeStamp = DateTime.Now;
  }

  public DateTime TimeStamp
  {
    get{return orderTimeStamp;}
  }

  public string Instrument
  {
    get{return instrument;}
    set{instrument=value;}
  }

  public string OrderType
  {
    get{return orderType;}
    set{orderType=value;}
  }

  public string BuySell
  {
    get{return buySell;}
    set{buySell=value;}
  }

  public double Price
  {
    get{return price;}
    set{price=value;}
  }

  public int Quantity
  {
    get{return quantity;}
    set{
        if ( value < 0 )
          quantity = 0;
        else
          quantity=value;
      }
  }
}
```

```
    public long OrderID
    {
      get{return orderId;}
      set{orderId=value;}
    }
  }
}
```

EquityOrder

EquityOrder is a specialized order inherited from the Order abstract class. This class allows the further augmentation of an order by allowing annotation of additional information that is applicable only in an equities market.

Here's the code for EquityOrder:

```
using System;
using OME.Storage;

namespace EquityMatchingEngine
{
  public class EquityOrder : Order
  {
    public EquityOrder(string instrument,string orderType,
                       string buySell,double price,int quantity)
    {
      this.Instrument = instrument;
      this.OrderType = orderType;
      this.BuySell = buySell;
      this.Price = price;
      this.Quantity = quantity;
    }
  }
}
```

PriceTimePriority

The PriceTimePriority class defines the logic of how orders are ranked; this determines the positional placement of an order in an order book. You are already aware that in an equities market orders are arranged by price and time priority and matching is performed at a touchline price. In an order book, the highest buy price and the lowest sell price occupy the top positions. This class is decoupled from the framework's internal implementation, which allows developers to easily replace the order-ranking logic.

Here's the code for PriceTimePriority:

```
using System;
using System.Collections;
using OME.Storage;

namespace EquityMatchingEngine
{
  public class PriceTimePriority:IComparer
  {
    public int CompareOrder(Order orderX,Order orderY,int sortingOrder)
    {
      //Compares the current order price with another order price
      int priceComp = orderX.Price.CompareTo(orderY.Price);
```

```
            //If both prices are equal, then we also need to sort according to
            //order time stamp
            if ( priceComp == 0 )
            {
              //Compare the current order time stamp with another order time stamp
              int timeComp = orderX.TimeStamp.CompareTo(orderY.TimeStamp);
              return timeComp;
            }

            //since the sorting order for the buy and sell order book is different
            //we need to ensure that orders are arranged accordingly
            //buy order book - highest buy price occupies top position
            //sell order book - lowest sell price occupies top position
            //therefore, sortingOrder helps to achieve this ranking
            //a value of -1 sorts orders in descending order of price and ascending
            //order of time
            //similarly, a value of 1 sorts orders in ascending order of price
            //and ascending order of time
            return priceComp * sortingOrder;
        }

        public int Compare(object x, object y)
        {
          Order orderX = x as Order;
          Order orderY = y as Order;

          //For a buy order, the highest buy price occupies the top position
          if ( orderX.BuySell == "B" )
            return CompareOrder(orderX,orderY,-1);
          else
            //For a sell order, the lowest sell price occupies the top position
            return CompareOrder(orderX,orderY,1);
        }
    }
}
```

Container

Container to the outside world is a repository of orders. It is important to raise the abstraction level to the outside world of how orders are inserted and deleted in a repository by wrapping them inside a Container class; remember, the deletion, insertion, and search (DIS) ingredients play a key role in determining the storage efficiency of an order-matching engine. If a particular data structure proves to be inefficient in meeting a business need, then it can be transparently replaced with no intervention from the outside world.

Here's the code for Container:

```
using System;
using System.Collections;
using System.Data;

namespace OME.Storage
{
  public class Container : IEnumerable
  {
    //Container Name
    protected string contName;
    //Reference to Leaf items where the actual order are stored
```

```
      protected ContainerCollection leafItems = new ContainerCollection();
      protected OrderBook orderBook;
      //Reference to Parent Container
      protected Container parentContainer;

      public ContainerCollection ChildContainers
      {
        get{return leafItems;}
      }

      public Container(OrderBook oBook,string name,Container parent)
      {
        orderBook=oBook;
        contName=name;
        parentContainer=parent;
      }

      //This method determines the order-processing logic
      public virtual void ProcessOrder(Order newOrder)
      {}

      //Order Iteration Support
      public virtual IEnumerator GetEnumerator()
      {
        return null;
      }
    }
}
```

ContainerCollection

ContainerCollection is a container for the collection of Container. It allows a reference to a specific Container with the help of an indexer method.

Here's the code for ContainerCollection:

```
using System;
using System.Collections;

namespace OME.Storage
{
  public class ContainerCollection
  {
    //Container collection represents individual container
    //For example, all regular orders for MSFT will be arranged
    //in a separate container; similarly, all buy orders falling under
    //regular order category will form a separate container but with
    //reference to its parent container, which is "regular order container"
    Hashtable contCollection = new Hashtable();

    //Check for existence of specific container
    public bool Exists(string containerName)
    {
      return contCollection.ContainsKey(containerName);
    }

    //Get reference to specific container
    public Container this[string name]
```

```
      {
        get{return contCollection[name] as Container;}
        set{contCollection[name]=value;}
      }
    }
}
```

LeafContainer

LeafContainer represents the final leaf level in the tree depicted in Figure 2-11. This class extends
the Container class, thus inheriting all the behavior supported by a container. The actual order is
stored and arranged at this level and hence considered to be the core class mainly when it comes to
boosting the performance of the order-matching engine. The data structure used by this class to store
orders is an ArrayList.

Here's the code for LeafContainer:

```
using System;
using System.Collections;

namespace OME.Storage
{
  public class LeafContainer : Container , IEnumerable , IEnumerator
  {
    private int rowPos = -1;
    //The internal implementation of the order is based on an ArrayList,
    //but, remember, based on performance criteria this implementation
    //can be easily changed without affecting the business component code
    ArrayList orderDataStore = ArrayList.Synchronized(new ArrayList());

    public LeafContainer(OrderBook oBook,string name,Container parent)
    :base(oBook,name,parent)
    {}

    public override IEnumerator GetEnumerator()
    {
      Reset();
      return this;
    }

    public override void ProcessOrder(Order newOrder)
    {
      //Access the buy order book of this instrument
      Container buyBook = parentContainer.ChildContainers["B"] ;

      //Access the sell order book of this instrument
      Container sellBook = parentContainer.ChildContainers["S"] ;

      //create a event arg object containing reference to newly created
      //order along with reference to buy and sell order book
      OrderEventArgs orderArg = new OrderEventArgs(newOrder,buyBook,sellBook);

      //Invoke the OrderBeforeInsert event, which will also notify
      //the matching business component, which will then perform
      //its internal matching
      //the order becomes active in this stage
      orderBook.OnOrderBeforeInsert(orderArg);
```

```
  //Check the quantity of the newly created order
  //because if the order has been successfully matched by matching
  //business component, then quantity will be 0
  if ( newOrder.Quantity > 0 )
  {
    //If order is partially or not at all matched,
    //then it is inserted in the order collection
    orderDataStore.Add(newOrder);

    //Re-sort the order collection because of addition
    //of new order
    orderDataStore.Sort(orderBook.OrderPriority);

    //Invoke the OrderInsert event,
    //which will again notify the matching business component
    //the order becomes passive in this stage
    orderBook.OnOrderInsert(orderArg);
  }
}

//This group of code is scoped toward controlling the
//iteration behavior. C# introduced a convenient way of
//iterating over elements of an array using a foreach statement.
//We have provided similar support to the Container class that allows
//developer to iterate through orders stored inside the Container class.
//In the case of the LeafContainer class, this behavior is overridden by
//implementing the IEnumerable and IEnumerator interfaces. We provided
//a custom implementation to the Reset, Current, and MoveNext methods.
//The Boolean value returned by the MoveNext method acts as a terminator
//condition of a foreach loop.
public void Reset()
{
  rowPos=-1;
}

public object Current
{
  get{return orderDataStore[rowPos];}
}

public bool MoveNext()
{
  //The code in the MoveNext method validates an order by checking
  //its quantity. If the quantity is equal to zero,
  //then it is deleted from ArrayList
  //and the row pointer is positioned to the next element in the ArrayList.
  //This check is continuously repeated inside a loop until it encounters an
  //Order whose quantity is greater than zero.
  rowPos++;
  while(rowPos < orderDataStore.Count)
  {
    Order curOrder = orderDataStore[rowPos] as Order;
    if ( curOrder.Quantity == 0 )
      orderDataStore.RemoveAt(rowPos);
    else
      return true;
  }
```

```
        Reset();
        return false;
      }
    }
}
```

OrderBook

OrderBook is the facade exposed to the outside world to access the order book. OrderBook is a focal point when it comes to tweaking the behavior of the order book; the important feature it offers is the assignment of order-matching priority logic. It provides various kinds of order notification events that allow you to hook up custom business logic implementations.

Here's the code for OrderBook:

```
using System;
using System.Collections;

namespace OME.Storage
{
  public delegate void OrderEventHandler(object sender,OrderEventArgs e);

  public class OrderBook
  {
    //Event invoked before inserting order - active order
    public event OrderEventHandler OrderBeforeInsert;
    //Event invoked after inserting order - passive order
    public event OrderEventHandler OrderInsert;

    //Order-ranking logic
    private IComparer orderPriority;
    //This variable holds the root node of the order tree
    //that in turn allows navigating the entire tree.
    private ContainerCollection bookRoot;

    public ContainerCollection Containers
    {
      get{return bookRoot;}
    }

    //Internal method to trigger active order notification
    //to external business component
    internal void OnOrderBeforeInsert(OrderEventArgs e)
    {
      if ( OrderBeforeInsert != null )
        OrderBeforeInsert(this,e);
    }

    //Internal method to trigger passive order notification
    //to external business component
    internal void OnOrderInsert(OrderEventArgs e)
    {
      if ( OrderInsert != null )
        OrderInsert(this,e);
    }

    public IComparer OrderPriority
    {
```

```csharp
  get{return orderPriority;}
  set{orderPriority=value;}
}

public OrderBook()
{
  //instantiate the root container of the order tree
  bookRoot = new ContainerCollection();
}

private Container ProcessContainers(ContainerCollection contCollection,
                                    string name,Order order,Container parent)
{
  //Check for presence of this specific container
  //in the case it is not found, then create a new container
  if ( contCollection.Exists(name) == false )
    contCollection[name] = new OME.Storage.Container(this,name,parent);

  OME.Storage.Container currentContainer = contCollection[name];

  //invoke the order processing on that container
  currentContainer.ProcessOrder(order);
  return currentContainer;
}

//This method looks after the arrangement of order in the order tree,
//based on key attributes of the order, it seeks appropriate node
//in tree; in the case a node doesn't exist, it creates a new node
//by instantiating the appropriate Container class. The logic deviates
//a bit when it comes to the creation of leaf node of the tree
//(i.e. Buy or Sell Node); we fall back to LeafContainer class that is
//where the actual order is rested.
public void Process(Order order)
{
  Container container = ProcessContainers(bookRoot,order.Instrument,
                                          order,null);
  container = ProcessContainers(container.ChildContainers,
                                order.OrderType,order,container);

  //Logic deviates a bit; if it is a buy or sell node,
  //then leafcontainer is created that actually holds the order
  if ( container.ChildContainers.Exists(order.BuySell.ToString()) == false )
  {
    //create buy and sell leaf container
    LeafContainer buyContainer = new LeafContainer(this,"B",container);
    LeafContainer sellContainer = new LeafContainer(this,"S",container);
    container.ChildContainers["B"] = buyContainer;
    container.ChildContainers["S"] = sellContainer;
  }

  //Based on the buy/sell attribute of the order
  //access the underlying leaf container
  LeafContainer leafContainer =
        container.ChildContainers[order.BuySell.ToString()] as LeafContainer;

  //process the order
  leafContainer.ProcessOrder(order);
```

```
        }
    }
}
```

OrderEventArgs

The OrderEventArgs class works closely with the OrderBook class. We discussed the various event
notification mechanisms that OrderBook supports. When events are notified to interested subscribers, an instance of OrderEventArgs is created that is passed along with the event. The class
encapsulates the handy information along with an instance of Order that triggered this event.

Here's the code for OrderEventArgs:

```
using System;

namespace OME.Storage
{
  public class OrderEventArgs
  {
    private Order order;
    private Container buyBook;
    private Container sellBook;

    public OrderEventArgs(Order newOrder,Container bBook,Container sBook)
    {
      order = newOrder;
      buyBook = bBook;
      sellBook = sBook;
    }

    public Order Order
    {
      get{return order;}
    }

    public Container BuyBook
    {
      get{return buyBook;}
    }

    public Container SellBook
    {
      get{return sellBook;}
    }

  }
}
```

OrderProcessor

OrderProcessor spawns a separate processing thread and allocates a dedicated queue in which
orders targeted for a particular order processor are queued. The processing thread dequeues the
orders and passes them to the next chain in the processing; in this case, it is submitted to OrderBook.
To enable the efficient utilization of processor, ManualResetEvent is used to signal the start of the
dequeuing processing, and during idle time the thread is put in a waiting state.

Here's the code for OrderProcessor:

```
using System;
using System.Threading;
using System.Collections;
using OME.Storage;

namespace OME
{
  public class OrderProcessor
  {
    Queue msgQueue ;
    Thread msgDispatcher;
    ManualResetEvent processSignaller;
    BizDomain bizDomain;

    public OrderProcessor(BizDomain domain,string wspName)
    {
      //Domain under which this order processor is assigned
      bizDomain = domain;
      //create a order queue
      msgQueue = Queue.Synchronized(new Queue());

      //create a event notification object
      //which notifies the enqueuing of a new order
      processSignaller = new ManualResetEvent(false);

      //create a dedicated thread to process the order stored
      //in queue collection
      msgDispatcher = new Thread(new ThreadStart(ProcessQueue));

      //start the processing
      msgDispatcher.Start();
    }

    public void EnQueue(object newOrder)
    {
      //Enqueue the order, and signal the event object
      msgQueue.Enqueue(newOrder);
      processSignaller.Set();
    }

    private void ProcessQueue()
    {
      //start of order-draining process
      while(true)
      {
        //wait for signal notification
        processSignaller.WaitOne(1000,false);

        //iterate through queue
        while(msgQueue.Count > 0)
        {
          //dequeue the order
          Order order = msgQueue.Dequeue() as Order;
```

```
          //submit it to order book for further processing
          bizDomain.OrderBook.Process(order);
        }
      }
    }
  }
}
```

BizDomain

BizDomain is a business-level abstraction imposed by the order-matching engine. It is by using this class that a single instance of the order-matching engine can satisfy the interest of multiple stakeholders of different business origins. BizDomain is also responsible for managing and creating the order processor.

Here's the code for BizDomain:

```
using System;
using System.Collections;
using OME.Storage;

namespace OME
{
  public class BizDomain
  {
    //Hashtable to store order processor instances
    private Hashtable oprocItems = Hashtable.Synchronized(new Hashtable());
    //array of order processor name to be created under this biz domain
    private string[] oprocNames;
    //creation of order book
    private OrderBook orderBook = new OrderBook();

    public BizDomain(string domainName,string[] workNames)
    {
      oprocNames= workNames;
    }

    public OrderBook OrderBook
    {
      get{return orderBook;}
    }

    public void Start()
    {
      //Iterate through all order processor names, and
      //create a new order processor object
      for (int ctr=0;ctr<oprocNames.Length;ctr++)
      {
        //Instantiates new order processor that in turn creates a
        //dedicated thread and queue
        OrderProcessor wrkObj= new OrderProcessor(this,oprocNames[ctr]);
        oprocItems[oprocNames[ctr]] = wrkObj;
      }
    }

    //A facade method to the outside world,
    //through which orders are submitted and queued in
    //appropriate order processor.
```

```
    public void SubmitOrder(string procName,Order order)
    {
      OrderProcessor orderProcessor = oprocItems[procName] as OrderProcessor;
      orderProcessor.EnQueue(order);
    }
  }
}
```

EquityMatchingLogic

The real business logic of order matching is fanned out inside the EquityMatchingLogic class. The business logic is folded with the order-matching engine infrastructure by subscribing to the OrderBeforeInsert event of OrderBook. The matching logic is partitioned based on the buy or sell type of an order.

Here's the code for EquityMatchingLogic:

```
using System;
using OME;
using OME.Storage;
using System.Collections;

namespace EquityMatchingEngine
{
  public class EquityMatchingLogic
  {
    public EquityMatchingLogic(BizDomain bizDomain)
    {
      //Hook up to active order event of the order book
      bizDomain.OrderBook.OrderBeforeInsert +=
              new OrderEventHandler(OrderBook_OrderBeforeInsert);
    }

    private void OrderBook_OrderBeforeInsert(object sender, OrderEventArgs e)
    {
      //Check buy/sell leg of the order
      //as the matching logic is different
      if ( e.Order.BuySell == "B" )
        MatchBuyLogic(e);
      else
        MatchSellLogic(e);
    }

    private void MatchBuyLogic(OrderEventArgs e)
    {
      //since the order to be matched is a buy order,
      //start iterating orders in sell order book
      foreach(Order curOrder in e.SellBook)
      {
        //If the current price of sell order price is less
        //than the price of buy order, then it is a best match
        if ( curOrder.Price <= e.Order.Price && e.Order.Quantity > 0 )
        {
          //Generate Trade
          Console.WriteLine("Match found..Generate Trade..");

          //get the buy order quantity
          int quantity = e.Order.Quantity;
```

```
            //subtract the buy order quantity from current sell order quantity
            curOrder.Quantity = curOrder.Quantity - e.Order.Quantity;

            //assign the remaining quantity to buy order
            e.Order.Quantity = e.Order.Quantity - quantity;
          }
          else
          {
            break;
          }
        }
      }
    }

    private void MatchSellLogic(OrderEventArgs e)
    {
      //since the order to be matched is a sell order,
      //start iterating orders in buy order book
      foreach(Order curOrder in e.BuyBook)
      {
        //If the current price of buy order is greater
        //than the price of sell order, then it is a best match
        if ( curOrder.Price >= e.Order.Price && e.Order.Quantity > 0 )
        {
          //Generate Trade
          Console.WriteLine("Match found..Generate Trade..");

          //get sell order quantity
          int quantity = curOrder.Quantity;

          //subtract sell order quantity from current buy order quantity
          curOrder.Quantity = curOrder.Quantity - e.Order.Quantity;

          //assign the remaining quantity to sell order
          e.Order.Quantity = e.Order.Quantity - quantity;
        }
        else
        {
          break;
        }
      }
    }
  }
}
```

OMEHost

OMEHost is the host class that loads the matching infrastructure, creates a new BizDomain along with three new order processors, instantiates the appropriate business logic class, and assigns the matching priority logic. Several orders are generated and submitted to the matching infrastructure that are ranked and matched based on the price and time priority rule.

Here's the code for OMEHost:

```
using System;
using OME.Storage;
using OME;
```

```
namespace EquityMatchingEngine
{
  class OMEHost
  {
    [STAThread]
    static void Main(string[] args)
    {
      BizDomain equityDomain;
      //Create equity domain with three order processors dedicated to process
      //MSFT, IBM, and GE orders
      equityDomain = new BizDomain("Equity Domain",
                               new string[]{"MSFT","IBM","GE"});

      //Assign the order-ranking logic
      equityDomain.OrderBook.OrderPriority = new PriceTimePriority();

      //Assign the business component
      EquityMatchingLogic equityMatchingLogic =
                  new EquityMatchingLogic(equityDomain);

      //Start the matching engine
      equityDomain.Start();

      //Submit buy order
      equityDomain.SubmitOrder("MSFT",new EquityOrder("MSFT","Regular","B",20,3));

      //Submit sell order
      //this will also generate a trade because
      //there is a matching counter buy order
      equityDomain.SubmitOrder("MSFT",new EquityOrder("MSFT","Regular","S",20,2));
      Console.WriteLine("Press any key to Stop");
      Console.ReadLine();
    }
  }
}
```

Summary

This chapter covered the following points:

- We explained how the order decision process takes place based on various matching criteria such as price and time priority.

- We provided a basic overview of the important data structures available in the .NET Framework.

- We discussed various approaches provided by the .NET Framework to achieve parallelism in processing orders.

- We covered different types of thread synchronization techniques that are essential for protecting the integrity of shared data from multiple thread access.

- We introduced thread scheduling and how thread priority and CPU affinitization further allows you to balance the processor utilization.

- We discussed the advantages of using server timers.

- Finally, we implemented a prototype of an order-matching engine that basically sums up the important features discussed in this chapter.

CHAPTER 3

■■■

The Data Conversion Engine

Parents are the real programmers who programmed us. It is because of their continuous refactoring and unit testing effort that we turn out to live a bug-free life in this unmanaged world.

This chapter provides insight into the problems encountered during data conversion. Simply defined, *data conversion* is the process of decomposing data structured in an incompatible data format and recomposing it again using different semantics and a different data format. During this conversion, data is structurally rearranged. Data conversion occupies a central place in organizations with business goals that depend on the integration of multiple applications. These applications may be legacy systems, homegrown applications, or vendor-based applications. In this chapter, we discuss the various hurdles faced in the financial world during the data conversion process and how XML provides a solution to these problems.

Introducing Data Management

Data originates from a variety of sources. Many times, the same data is presented in different formats. Figure 3-1 illustrates how information is consumed from different newspapers. Although the information produced in each of these newspapers is the same, the information differs in style, representation, and structure. For example, the *New York Times* may publish sports news on page 16 in a columnar format, the *Star Ledger* may produce the same information as a summary on page 1 with details on the last page of the paper, and *Fox Magazine* may publish the same information with less verbiage and more emphasis on pictures and a small description at the bottom of each picture. The primary objective of all these newspapers is to publish accurate information/data, but each one adopts a totally different approach and style. This is called *information enlargement* where the integrity of data is maintained but presented differently.

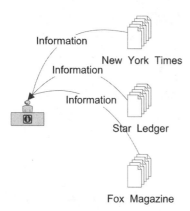

Figure 3-1. *The same information originates from multiple sources and in a different format.*

A human brain weighs just 3.5 pounds, but it is one of the most complex organs and continuously interprets data for us. In the computing world, however, things are different—machines lack consciousness, intellect, and capacity for thought. Although computers are better than the human brain in calculating speed and power, they have to be specifically instructed/coded to conduct/perform/execute an activity. However, it will always be true no matter how much progress we make in technology advancements that there is no substitute for human creativity, diligence, and judgment.

Thus, if Figure 3-1 is to be replicated in a computing environment, a new program has to be developed to interpret the needs of the *New York Times*, the *Star Ledger*, and *Fox Magazine*. This trend does not stop here; in the future, if a new newspaper comes into the market, then a new program specifically to interpret the information published by this newspaper needs to be developed. The truth is that every organization reinvests/mobilizes funds for "interpreting" already "interpreted" data.

In the financial world, various applications use a lot of data related to securities, prices, market conditions, clients, and other entities for the fulfillment of trade. Applications do trade enrichment on the basis of this data and also make a lot of decisions. Data comes from a variety of sources. Market data, news, and analysis are bought from third-party content service providers such as Reuters, and the institutions generate the rest themselves in the normal course of their day-to-day activities. The latter relates to transaction- and settlement-related data. Institutions obtain some data from agencies such as stock exchanges, clearing corporations, regulators, and so on, by virtue of being members of those agencies. Maintaining this data is expensive. Some data has to be purchased, and some has to be filtered (unnecessary data has to be removed), validated, and stored.

Understanding the Business Infoset

Business infoset is synonymous to information; it comprises a lot of data items in various forms. What and how an organization decides on various issues largely depends upon the kind of data that is presented to its business managers, including its presentation format and perspective. Business infoset can be decomposed into granular data elements. Each data element has its own characteristics and can be classified as one of the following:

- Reference data
- Variable data
- Derived data
- Computed data
- Static data

To understand this classification, let's discuss various attributes of an order, as shown in Table 3-1.

Table 3-1. *Attributes of an Order*

Order Attribute	Description	Type of Data
Market of operation	Geography from where order is placed	Static data
Client code	Client placing the order	Reference data
Exchange	Stock exchange on which the order is being placed	Reference data
Traded asset/ISIN/SEDOL/ scrip code	Security that needs to be transacted	Reference data
Company name	Name of the company issuing shares	Derived data
Order type	Buy/sell	Static data
Quantity	Number of shares to be purchased	Variable data
Order price	Price at which the client expects his order to get through	Variable data
Currency	Currency of transaction	Reference data
Segment	Exchange segment	Reference data
Broker code/Counterparty	Counterparty	Reference data
Order validity	Date and time conditions	Variable data

Reference Data

Reference data is any data that is created and maintained outside the purview of the system but is required by the system to meet business or computational needs. To meet these needs, systems may decide to maintain a copy of reference data or have links to other systems and use the link to access this data on an online or real-time basis. Reference data is used to categorize transactional data and can be used to link to data from other organizations.

Variable Data

Data whose value changes over a period of time is called *variable data*. Variable data may or may not lie in a fixed range, but its values can be random and unpredictable. A typical example is a stock price. Stock prices depend upon the market perception of the earnings and on the cash flows a company can generate, but the day-to-day price is impossible to predict. Prices also keep changing on a daily basis. Hence, stock prices fall under variable data. Similarly, a company's earnings keep changing from quarter to quarter so can also be classified as variable data.

Derived Data

Derived data is any data that derives its value from any other data. For example, if you have a list of countries and capitals and you try to access the capital using a country—say by retrieving the capital by using "United States of America" and getting the value "Washington DC"—then "Washington DC" (capital) becomes derived data since its value is based on the value "United States of America" (country). In this chapter's example of order attributes (see Table 3-1), the company name becomes derived data, because its value depends upon the International Securities Identification Number (ISIN) code.

Computed Data

Any data that results from manipulating other data or another set of data is called *computed data*. For example, if you attempt to calculate the average stock price quoted across the month, the resulting average figure will be computed data because its value is derived using some computation over some other set of base data.

Static Data

Static data is data whose value does not change over a period of time. In the order attribute example in Table 3-1, the order type (that is, "buy" or "sell") is an example of static data. Even if you revisit the order type after a long time, each order will still be either "buy" or "sell."

Introducing Reference Data

Data is the lifeblood of any organization. The success of an organization also depends on the quality of data it possesses, because strategic decisions may be based on the data. Every act of an organization requires input of data and generates (or enhances) data at the end of the activity. Financial institutions and organizations are making a lot of investments in the area of reference data management. Though institutions maintain reference data for their quick reference, they rely on other agencies to create this data and supply it to them. They then upload a copy of this data in their system and use it for quick reference to add value to their transactional data. Departments and operations have traditionally been compartmentalized in the form of front, middle, and back offices, and each department forms its own systems to cater to its needs. This results in the duplication of activity because each operational area tends to replicate a lot of referential data within its own system to reduce its interdependence on other systems. This also gives rise to another problem of having and managing redundant reference data.

   Note that even when institutions import required reference data in their systems, they also need to convert it into a format defined in their systems and acceptable to it. This acceptable format and content changes as data moves down from one link in the value chain to another. This calls for a lot of conversion even during the life cycle of a single trade. Let's examine the business need of converting this data using the trading value chain and examine this concept in more detail (see Figure 3-2).

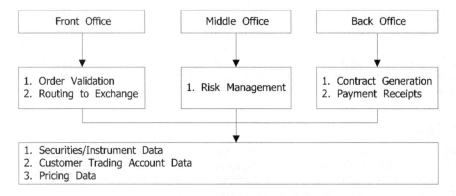

Figure 3-2. *Reference data plays a central role in all functions.*

The trading value chain is divided into front office, middle office, and back office (described in Chapter 1). We will look at these concepts in more detail here. An order is originated and is delivered to the exchange by the front office. Dealers interact with investing institutions to get their orders, and when the order is executed, they charge brokerage from those deals. The order flows through a defined process (discussed in Chapter 1).

The middle office holds the reference data that is shared between the front office and the back office. At most places, the middle office is also responsible for risk management on the orders that hit the trading system and for orders getting converted into trades during the process. The middle office conducts a lot of validations, checks limits, and validates the resulting trade values against the ledger balances that clients hold with the broker, who is executing the order.

Once a trade gets generated and hits the trading system, it is routed to the back office for settlement. On the basis of trades, the settlement obligation of every client is determined, and the payment/receipts are generated and affect the settlements. Let's revisit each of these steps to analyze the data requirements and also examine why data conversion is necessary when organizations are forced to maintain multiple copies of data. To illustrate these steps, we will use the example of an instrument *master* that is extensively used in the trading chain.

When a client calls up the broker to place the order, he will either give the company name or use a popular code to refer to the security. For example, if the customer wants to purchase Microsoft shares, he will either say "Buy equity of Microsoft Corporation" or say "Buy MSFT.N." If the order originates from a different country, chances are that the institution placing the order will use a code that is completely different from the code used by the exchange. Even though a standard unique code called an *ISIN code* is associated with every security, each exchange (instead of adhering to this ISIN code) devises its own local security code.

The ISIN code is a standard code for a security that is supposed to be unique across the world. The ISIN for each security is generated by the regulatory body of a country or by any other agency mandated by the regulatory agency. Though ISIN codes are standard codes that are supposed to be used worldwide, trading systems rarely (almost never) use ISIN codes. Most settlements, however, happen on ISIN codes. No specific reason exists for this anomaly. ISIN codes are longer to use and confusing to type; hence, they are kept out of trading systems. Additionally, other codes such as the Stock Exchange Daily Official List (SEDOL) have been popular for a long time among the dealing circles. Dealers tend to understand each other without ambiguity when they use SEDOL codes while referring to any security. A fixed format is defined for constructing an ISIN code. An ISIN code has a 12-character structure in the following format: USAAAABBBCCD. The characters break down as follows:

- The first two characters ("US" in this example) stand for the country code.

- The next four characters (represented by "AAAA") are alphanumeric and represent the issuer.

- The next three characters (represented here as "BBB") stand for the type of asset. The second and third position can also be used as a running serial number.

- The next two characters (represented as "CC") are alphanumeric and represent the type of stock issued. These two are also used as the sequence number for every security issuance.

- The last character (represented as "D") is a control digit.

It is not mandatory that the exchange where the transaction is routed uses the SEDOL or ISIN code for its reference. Each exchange uses its own proprietary code for trading, and their systems are designed to support their proprietary codes. In the front office itself, we come across the potential to use three different codes while referring to one security. A data mapping mechanism will hence be required to interpret these codes while the information passes on so that each entity understands the information completely and without ambiguity, as shown in Figure 3-3.

Figure 3-3. *Instrument mapping in the front office*

Now let's examine where reference data comes into use in this entire order flow chain. The institution placing the order will use a system to maintain a portfolio. Assuming a global investor, the client holding the position will be maintained locally in different countries, and each will have a local name and sometimes even different code for the same security. While placing the order, the institution will reference its database to arrive at the exact name of the security to be transacted. The institution will give the order as the name appears in its database. Assume that the database lists "Microsoft Corporation equity shares" as "MICROSOFT EQ." Thus, the order from the institution to the brokerage house will look like this: Buy 10000 MICROSOFT EQ.

The dealer or sales desk person in the brokerage house will now enter the order in the broker's system. Let's assume the broker's system is configured using SEDOL. Hence, in this case, the system will not understand "MICROSOFT EQ," and therefore the broker will manually convert the order to "2588173" (the SEDOL of Microsoft) and place the order. If the institution provided the order as a soft copy, the order will get validated in the broker's system, resulting in an exception stating that it does not understand "MICROSOFT EQ." The user will then override these cases and manually replace all "MICROSOFT EQ" instances with "2588173." If the broker does a lot of business with this institution (and receives a lot of orders from it on a daily basis), it will not be long before someone realizes that it will be worthwhile to maintain a mapping in the system to convert the institution's codes to the SEDOL codes, as shown in Table 3-2.

Table 3-2. *Mapping Between Institution and SEDOL Code*

Institution Code	SEDOL Code
Microsoft EQ	2588173
INTEL EQ	2463247

The order for Microsoft EQ is now interpreted by the broker system. The issue, however, does not get resolved here. As discussed, each exchange may use its own local code. To forward the order to the exchange in a way that the exchange recognizes the order properly, it needs to provide the exchange with its local code. This in turn means the broker system will have to maintain an additional mapping between the SEDOL codes and the local codes understood by the exchange, as shown in Table 3-3.

Table 3-3. *Mapping Between SEDOL and Local Exchange Code*

SEDOL Code	Local Exchange Code (NASDAQ)
2588173	MSFT.O
2463247	INTC.O

The need for security code mapping does not end here. After the exchange confirms that orders have been executed, the broker needs to send a trade confirmation to the institution and institution's custodian. The broker needs to remap the exchange codes to the language understood by the institution. Additionally, to get the trades settled, the broker will have to interact with the clearing corporation and depository. Chances are that the clearing corporation and depository will communicate using ISIN codes. The broker will thus have to maintain an additional mapping of exchange codes vis-à-vis ISIN codes in the back office system, as shown in Table 3-4.

Table 3-4. *Exchange Code Mapped to ISIN Code for Settlement*

Local Exchange Code (NASDAQ)	ISIN Code
MSFT.O	US5949181045
INTC.O	US4581401001

Figure 3-4 shows the flow of the order confirmation back to the broker and from the broker back to the client, clearing corporation, and depository.

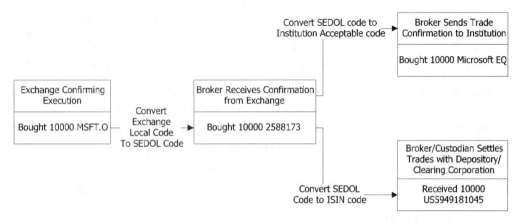

Figure 3-4. *The trade confirmation must happen in a language understood by the client, and the settlement must happen in a language understood by the clearing corporation and depository.*

All communication that the clearing corporation and depository has with the member will be in ISIN codes. It is hence important for the broker's system to understand and convert these codes and then communicate this information to their clients.

Framework for Data Conversion

Data conversion means different things to different people and institutions. To a stock exchange, it could mean converting very old prices into electronic format. To a museum, it could mean creating a soft-copy repository of images of the priceless paintings it possesses. Whatever the notion, data conversion involves taking data from one system (which could be any legacy system, hard copy, digital media, analog device, and so on) and migrating to another. Usually the target system is a new system.

Getting a new system to accept any data is a big process, especially if the data is coming from a legacy system and the target system is a new system built on more recent technologies and not built with the thought that reference data would be coming from a legacy system. There is an established methodology for migrating/importing this data in the new system. Of course, the first-time migration/import takes a lot of time because of field-level mapping and the finalization of the structure. However, once the structure is finalized, subsequent imports do not require this kind of effort. Let's examine the conversion methodology in some detail.

The entire step of populating data from a legacy system to a new system comprises the following two broad processes:

- Cleansing the data received from the source system

- Changing the data format to suit the new system and translating/integrating it into a structure where it can be stored in the database of the new system

Data cleansing is a method or series of steps to address the cleaning of dirty data that is inconsistent, incomplete, and/or not uniform. Data could be dirty because of typing mistakes or missing essential entries, or it could be inconsistently coded. Before data is converted and migrated in a new system, it needs to be cleaned. It is not uncommon to see institutions maintaining several copies of such data; unfortunately, this compounds creation, storage, and referring costs. Apart from actual costs, this also creates the problem of duplication where the institution is really not sure which data has to be used.

For example, assume that a client has specified two different addresses and phone numbers in two different systems. Until the systems are integrated, both systems' users are unaware of the existence of a different address and phone number in the other system. If the institution undertakes the exercise of integrating the two systems, it will be meaningless to maintain two different sets of addresses and phone numbers; if they decide to merge the data, they will be in a state of confusion as to which address and phone number is correct, and a decision may be made to retain the more recent information. This is a simple example. If this same thing is extrapolated over a number of instruments, markets, trades, and settlement-related data, this problem tends to be overwhelming.

The presence of data in silos raises a number of issues:

- Institutions have to manage a lot of external vendors who manage/maintain external systems.

- Since data is parked in multiple systems, the institution may be forced to maintain a number of licensed copies of software used for maintenance.

- A lot of storage space and hardware is utilized.

- Data definition standards are poor; hence, the same data cannot be referenced by multiple systems.

- Trades have to be frequently corrected, leading to high operational costs.

- Making data corrections is time-consuming and expensive.

Recently, financial institutions and banks are under greater regulatory and market scrutiny because of compliance requirements for the Sarbanes-Oxley and Patriot Acts. Market forces have compelled institutions to take a consolidated view of risk management and other financial numbers. Institutions are now trying to integrate all data that is present in silos. Reference data management is a huge challenge for institutions that operate from multiple geographies and that trade in multiple products.

Cleaning dirty reference data has its own methodology, and the approach depends purely on the complexity of data and the extent of its inconsistency. Most cleansing processes and methodologies use application programs to convert data from proprietary formats to standardized formats. Extensible Markup Language (XML) is widely used in the cleansing process.

The deployment of XML for the data cleansing process provides speedy and effective resolution. In its basic form, the data cleansing process has three stages, as shown in Figure 3-5:

- Import and conversion

- Cleansing

- Enrichment

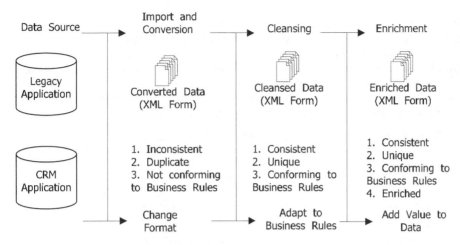

Figure 3-5. *Steps in cleaning reference data*

Import and Conversion

In the first step, data is extracted from multiple sources such as legacy applications, customer relationship management (CRM) applications, and current settlement systems. It is converted to basic XML format. During the conversion process, care is exercised to see that no data is lost or dropped. Converting data is a tedious process. A lot of data could be in an unorganized form. For example, libraries could have data in the form of printed books. Stock exchanges could have stock rates in magnetic tapes with defined reference structures. The reference structure itself could differ from time to time. Analysts doing data-cleansing activities must refer to these structures and convert data appropriately and carefully. After the conversion process is over, a warehouse of XML data is created.

Cleansing

In this step, imported data is verified for missing items, duplicates, and referential integrity. For example, if you refer to the earlier ISIN master example where the following business rules must be followed:

- All securities must have ISIN codes assigned.

- ISIN codes must be unique.

- ISIN codes must be 12 characters in length.

- The first two characters of the ISIN code must be a country-specific prefix.

In the cleansing process, if the system comes across cases where the ISIN code is not populated against a security or is not 12 characters in length, or cases where the same ISIN code is allotted to two securities, then the system needs to analyze such cases and correct them. All such cases are collected, and correct codes are found by checking other systems, by contacting a third-party data service provider, or by contacting the agency that generates ISIN codes in the specific country. Multiple scans of the same data through the same business validations may be required to arrive at a correct and clean repository.

Enrichment

In this step, the existing data set is analyzed critically to see whether any further information needs to be tagged along with the data that is being cleaned. For example, while compiling the ISIN-related data, it could be beneficial to tag the face value of the securities along with the existing data (assuming that the face value is not in the existing data). The face value will have to be extracted from a different data source and updated along with current ISIN codes using a join or some other update method.

The presence of clean reference data can deliver the following benefits to the organization:

- It can help in the availability of accurate and timely data on which business decisions can be based. Data forms the heart of all CRM activities. Good-quality data has a direct correlation to customer satisfaction.

- It frees up software and hardware resources, thereby lowering operational costs.

- Software licenses can be used more effectively. Manual development and maintenance costs are reduced.

- It requires less manual intervention, which results in fewer trade failures, which in turn reduces the operational costs.

- Redundant operations can be combined, resulting in operational efficiency.

- Clean and accurate data benefits several downstream applications, ensuring their proper functioning.

If these benefits were summarized, they would fall under the following headings:

Operational benefits: Helps in cost reduction, improves efficiency in operations, and removes redundancy.

Technology benefits: Reduces total cost of ownership and reduces pain involved in maintaining several applications and silos of data.

Organizational benefits: Improves risk management and compliance. Better performance leads to greater client satisfaction.

Several vendors provide reference data solutions. Each vendor, however, has a different approach. Whatever the method or approach, the following common threads run through a successful reference data implementation:

- The underlying data needs to be clean. No amount of technical approach will help if the underlying data is not clean. While implementing a reference data solution, care has to be taken to clean the data and remove any format/version issues.

- Pareto's 80-20 rule works here as well. This means that some steps will give magnified benefits with small and incremental effort. Such steps have to be identified and implemented first.

- The build or buy dilemma is common in the case of reference data solutions. It is not a good approach to implement both in isolation. Most of the time a mix of both is required. Many financial institutions are looking at outsourcing the data management and exception-handling process to further reduce costs.

Note Vilfredo Pareto was an economist who during 1906 created a theory that 20 percent of the population in his country owns 80 percent of the wealth. This principle was then followed in various other areas such as quality management, marketing management, and business.

This brings an end to the business section, and we will continue the ISIN master example to see how to do data conversion from a technical perspective. We will discuss the technical issues encountered in each step so you can understand how the concepts are implemented in real life.

Entering the XML World

In the computing world, XML is a basic necessity. It is the equivalent of food, clothes, and shelter to a human being; life would be crippled without it. Today millions of systems are using XML as their basic foundation in one form or another. XML has established itself as the building block of a good system design, and therefore every new system design built today is centered on XML.

XML is a markup language, and the success of XML is based primarily on its most important quality—its ability to describe both the data and the intelligence behind the data. This ability to model a data branch under the category of data-oriented language is the unique strength of XML.

An XML document is a new form of content extension that is similar to an executable file or dynamic link library. But the comparison ends there; XML documents contain ordinary text that is expressed using XML syntax instead of low-level machine instruction. The plain-text data is easy to read and is primarily comprised of elements and attributes. Elements are represented in the form of start and end angle brackets, and the data is enclosed between these angle brackets. Attributes are the equivalent of a name-value pair, where the value represents the actual data. Both elements and attributes are tagged with a meaningful name that is easy to understand. Although no cookbook rules exist for naming conventions used in XML documents, it's a basic tenet of good XML document design that an element or attribute name must express the real hidden meaning of the data encapsulated within the markup. The formation of an XML document is simple; the Notepad application is sufficient for creating an XML-based document. No additional or special tools are required.

This innate ability of XML to engineer the information in a plain-text format has formed the important glue in achieving integration among heterogeneous systems. The plain text is encoded and decoded using ASCII standards. Data based on ASCII standards are understood by most of the commercially available operating systems and applications. Such standardization of data emphasizes an important fact: XML is platform neutral and a perfect candidate in achieving enterprise application integration (EAI). Over the last decade, EAI has been in the limelight and has also become one of the key factors in determining the growth of an organization. In a typical large-scale organization, thousands of systems are hosted in a multiplatform environment. Most of these systems run independently, catering to the needs of the individual departments/divisions within an organization. The industry needed a universal language that would enable these systems to communicate with each other. XML, with its innate characteristic of platform neutrality, bridges this gap. It has further enlarged the scope of integration by crossing the periphery of organizational boundaries to establish the free flow of information exchange with business partners as well.

To further illustrate the power of XML, let's take the following real-life example of an ISIN master file that also forms the basis of the discussion in the rest of this chapter. Listing 3-1 and Listing 3-2 represent different formats of the ISIN master. Listing 3-1 is an ordinary comma-delimited text file, and Listing 3-2 is an XML file.

Listing 3-1. *ISIN Master (CSV Format)*

```
ISINMASTER12122004
US5949181045,MSFT,10,5,Active
EXCHANGE,NASDAQ,MSFT.O
EXCHANGE,NYSE,MSFT.N
ISINEOF
```

Listing 3-2. *ISIN Master (XML Format)*

```
<ISINMaster>
  <ISIN  ISINCode="US5949181045"
         Symbol="MSFT"
         FaceValue="10"
         MarketLot="5"
         Status="Active" >
  <Exchanges>
   <Exchange Code="NASDAQ"
             ScripCode="MSFT.O" />
   <Exchange Code="NYSE"
             ScripCode="MSFT.N" />
  </Exchanges>
  </ISIN>
</ISINMaster>
```

If you quickly compare these two versions, the XML version is an eye-catcher and is more intuitive compared to the text-based version. In addition, the XML version also offers other important characteristics, as described next.

Domain Knowledge

In the XML version of the ISIN master, the real content is enclosed between start and end tags. This clearly helps you recognize both the content and the underlying domain knowledge supporting this content. This is remarkable compared to the text version, which is not easy to understand unless it is supplemented by some user documentation that describes the offset of every field and its business-level interpretation. XML is called a *self-describing* document because of its unique ability to convey both data and metadata (domain knowledge). This self-describing nature of the document breaks all kinds of barriers arising in information sharing and makes it possible to share XML documents with all types of audiences such as business analysts, developers, and users.

Data Arrangement Uniformity

The most noticeable difference between the CSV and XML versions is the arrangement of data. The CSV version has a tabular arrangement with every field delimited by a comma. However, keep in mind that text files have different structural representations as well, including tab-delimited, fixed-delimited, and custom-delimited representations. Such structural-level inconsistency completely shuts down the door to standardization. This is in direct contrast to the XML version where data is arranged hierarchically and follows certain well-established vocabulary such as an element name being represented inside angled brackets with every start tag having a corresponding end tag, and so on. The XML version of the ISIN master can be categorized as a *well-formed* document because it meets the structural criteria of an XML document. Such well-formed documents are boons because several parser tools are currently available that can help you iterate, read, and easily understand any XML document as long as it is well-formed.

Context-Oriented Data (COD)

Context-oriented data (COD) cannot be accessed on its own; it must be referenced from its context. For example, referring to the CSV version of the ISIN master (in Listing 3-1), it would be difficult to extract the data "MSFT" because multiple occurrences of "MSFT" exist. You can extract the data only after providing the context in the form of row and column numbers. Hence, in this example, you must provide row 2 and column 2 to obtain the data "MSFT" falling under this context. Once again, keep in mind that this context may differ for different types of text files. For example, in a fixed-based file format, you can extract the context by passing the offset position and length of the data to be extracted. In an XML-based document, the context is provided in the form of an element or attribute name. Such uniformity in the context allows a standard mechanism to programmatically access the data.

Extensibility

The CSV version of the ISIN master is fragile—if you insert a new column at the beginning of a row, then it will completely distort your interpretation. Starting from the user specification document and continuing to the data converter program, everything will need to be fixed. Fixed-based file formats are highly vulnerable to such changes because they completely break down the whole offset number-crunching process. Such types of breaking changes are harmful to applications and leave no room for extensibility. XML is free from such curse and provides complete freedom to mix new elements or attributes with no side effects.

The previously mentioned benefits by themselves are sufficient to show the advantages of using XML-based data; the rest of this chapter highlights the various XML-related features available in the .NET Framework that will further encourage you to drive in the XML highway.

Reading and Writing Data

Data is valuable and precious. Hence, every effort must be undertaken to preserve and store data in a *data store*. A data store is an abstract container that allows you to store and query data. A data store can take the form of a file on disk or in memory. (In other words, data can be either saved as a disk file or stored in memory or on a central Web site.) The underlying common storage denominator of any data is a collection of bits, but the retrieval implementation of the stored bits differs based on the kind of data store used.

A *stream* is a generic wrapper around a data store. The rationale behind a stream is to abstract the intricacies involved in handling data and also provide a uniform interface for all types of data input- or output-related operations. The .NET Framework respects this uniformity by encapsulating all read/write operations in a common Stream class. It is an abstract class and is packaged inside the System.IO namespace. All concrete stream providers are inherited from this abstract class. Developers are not required to learn the know-how of the underlying storage devices. As long as they are under the shelter of the Stream class, they can perform basic operations such as reading and writing data. Table 3-5 describes the Stream subclasses.

Table 3-5. Stream *Subclasses*

Subclass	Description
FileStream	FileStream is the commonly used class for reading or writing data to a file. This stream also supports the random seeking of data in the file. Furthermore, this stream can operate on *process standard* input and output. By default, the keyboard is the process standard input stream, and the monitor is the standard output and error stream. You can use FileStream to redirect the standard input stream (from a keyboard) and output stream (to a monitor) to a file.
MemoryStream	MemoryStream is the equivalent of FileStream from the perspective of its functionality. However, data is fetched/persisted solely in memory rather than in a physical file on disk. MemoryStream is a perfect candidate for short-lived temporary data that is generated on the fly and is accessed multiple times and eventually discarded upon the termination of an application.

Continued

Table 3-5. *Continued*

Subclass	Description
BufferedStream	Disk I/O–related operations, with their heavy-duty data spinning (reading or writing operations), are the most expensive operations in an application. They can easily bring down the performance of the application. In such a scenario it is always advisable to perform read/write operations in a chunk of bytes instead of an individual byte. BufferedStream is intended for this purpose and used in conjunction with FileStream and MemoryStream to provide caching service. This improves the read/write performance. FileStream is buffered internally, so there is no need to wrap the BufferedStream shield around this class.
NetworkStream	NetworkStream is specifically designed to handle the intercommunication aspects between applications. It is used in network-related data I/O operations. This class allows reading or writing data to or from a network pipe, which is usually a Socket.
CryptoStream	CryptoStream is the focal class of the .NET cryptography kingdom. This stream is used in conjunction with any data stream to perform cryptographic transformation (encryption or decryption).

The subclasses mentioned in Table 3-5 share the same goal—to provide uniform access to data. But each stream's underlying characteristics are different and tuned to meet specific data needs. Table 3-6 describes some of the common properties and methods that Stream and its descendant classes provide.

Table 3-6. *Common Properties/Methods Provided by the* Stream *Class*

Property/Method	Description
Length	This property returns the length of data.
Position	The Position property allows you to get or set the seek pointer in the stream. Even though the stream supports the random seeking of data; the seeking behavior is not welcomed by all Stream subclasses, particularly the NetworkStream class.
CanRead	This property determines whether the stream supports read operations.
CanWrite	This property determines whether the stream supports write operations.
CanSeek	This property determines whether the stream supports seek operations.
Read	This method reads raw bytes from a stream.
Write	This method writes raw bytes to a stream. Both the Read and Write methods allow the reading or writing of data in chunks. You can do this by specifying the number of bytes to read/write from/to a stream.
Close	This method closes the stream and also reclaims the memory by releasing the operating system resource used by the Stream class.

The Stream class also provides an asynchronous version of read and write operations. Asynchronous-based operations are the building blocks for designing highly scalable applications. These asynchronous flavors are available through the BeginRead and BeginWrite methods.

The Stream class is fairly simple to use from a coding perspective. To prove it, we will demonstrate a code example that reads a comma-delimited text version of the ISIN master file from Listing 3-1. Stream is an abstract class; therefore, you need to use the FileStream class to read the contents of this file.

Listing 3-3 shows the example code.

Listing 3-3. *Reading the Comma-Delimited Version of the ISIN Master*

```
using System;
using System.IO;
using System.Text;

class StreamExample
{
  [STAThread]
  static void Main(string[] args)
  {
    //File to read
    string csvFile = @"C:\CodeExample\Chpt3\StreamExample\CSVISINMaster.csv";
    //Open a file stream in read/access mode
    FileStream isinStream = new FileStream(csvFile,FileMode.Open,FileAccess.Read);
    //allocate a byte array of size 10
    byte[] byteBuffer = new byte[10];
    //read until the stream pointer reaches the end of the file
    while (isinStream.Position < isinStream.Length )
    {
      //read data
      int byteRead= isinStream.Read(byteBuffer,0,byteBuffer.Length);
      //display data
      Console.Write(Encoding.ASCII.GetString(byteBuffer,0,byteRead));
    }
    //close stream
    isinStream.Close();
  }
}
```

The code shown in Listing 3-3 is pretty straightforward; you first allocate a byte array of size 10 and then enter a loop that reads raw bytes into this byte array with the help of the Read method. The loop will terminate as soon as you have read all the bytes, which is determined with the help of the Position and Length properties of a Stream class. To display this raw byte on the console, you need to convert it into a string, which you do using the Encoding class available as part of the System.Text namespace.

Introducing Specialized Streams

The .NET Framework provides special-purpose reader and writer classes whose inner workings are specialized based on specific characteristics of data. These classes are not inherited from the Stream class but are directly related to it when it comes to reading or writing data. The need for specialization arises from the byte-oriented nature—only bytes are used to push in or pull out from a stream. Such flexibility of working at the byte level provides absolute power because it allows you to regulate the flow of data. But this may not be feasible in certain scenarios. In Listing 3-3, while reading the content of the ISIN master, you are forced to convert an array of bytes read from a FileStream to the string data type before displaying it on the console.

Specialized stream classes are paired classes with the read and write operations decoupled and placed in their own separate classes. This is in direct contrast to the Stream class, which provides both the reads and writes under one roof. The following sections cover some common reader and writer classes available within the .NET Framework.

TextReader and TextWriter

Both TextReader and TextWriter classes are designed to read or write series of characters. The TextReader class allows reading groups of characters from an underlying stream. This underlying stream could fall under any one of the concrete stream classes such as MemoryStream or FileStream. TextReader is intelligent enough to understand the semantics of a text file and is highly recommended when it comes to reading data from an ordinary text file. It provides a ReadToEnd method that allows reading the content of the entire text file in a single iteration.

It also provides a ReadLine method, which can be used to read a group of characters until a carriage return is reached. TextReader is an abstract class and cannot be instantiated directly by the code. It needs to be used in conjunction with StreamReader and StringReader, which are concrete classes and are inherited from TextReader. The underlying data source of StreamReader is backed by Stream, and similarly, the underlying data source of StringReader is backed by string.

The following code demonstrates how to use TextReader when reading the content of the CSV version of the ISIN master:

```
using System;
using System.IO;

class TextStreamExample
{
  [STAThread]
  static void Main(string[] args)
  {
    string csvFile = @"C:\CodeExample\Chpt3\TextStreamExample\CSVISINMaster.csv";
    //Open the CSV file
    TextReader isinReader = new StreamReader(csvFile);
    //read the entire content of the file
    string content = isinReader.ReadToEnd();
    //display content
    Console.WriteLine(content);
    //close the stream
    isinReader.Close();
  }
}
```

BinaryReader and BinaryWriter

Unlike TextReader and TextWriter, which were meant to handle ordinary text data, BinaryReader and BinaryWriter are designed to read and write primitive data types. Both classes preserve the encoding scheme, which is by default UTF-8, during read and write operations. BinaryReader and BinaryWriter are recommended for reading and writing data where the underlying precision of the data type in the data needs to be preserved.

This feature is implemented by providing a collection of ReadXXX and overloaded Write methods that are specialized for reading or writing data of a particular data type. The following code demonstrates how to read and write ISIN data in the form of binary values:

```
using System;
using System.IO;

namespace BinaryExample
{
  struct ISINRecord
```

```
{
  public string isinCode;
  public char securityType;
  public double faceValue;
  public long lotSize;
}
class BinaryExample
{
  [STAThread]
  static void Main(string[] args)
  {
    string filePath = @"C:\CodeExample\Chpt3\isin.dat";
    //Initialize the ISIN data
    ISINRecord newRecord = new ISINRecord();
    newRecord.isinCode = "US5949181045";
    newRecord.faceValue = 10;
    newRecord.lotSize = 100;

    //Open binary file for writing
    FileStream fStream = new
                FileStream(filePath,FileMode.CreateNew,FileAccess.Write);
    //Create a binary writer
    BinaryWriter bwrt = new BinaryWriter(fStream);

    //write ISIN data
    bwrt.Write(newRecord.isinCode);
    bwrt.Write(newRecord.securityType);
    bwrt.Write(newRecord.faceValue);
    bwrt.Write(newRecord.lotSize);

    //Close the stream
    fStream.Close();

    ISINRecord isinRecord;
    //Open the binary file
    fStream = new FileStream(filePath,FileMode.Open,FileAccess.Read);
    //Create a binary reader
    BinaryReader br = new BinaryReader(fStream);
    //read ISIN code
    isinRecord.isinCode= br.ReadString();
    //read security type
    isinRecord.securityType= br.ReadChar();
    //read face value
    isinRecord.faceValue= br.ReadDouble();
    //read lot size
    isinRecord.lotSize = br.ReadInt32();
  }
}
}
```

XmlReader and XmlWriter

Considering the popularity of XML, the .NET Framework introduced two additional special-purpose XML classes that understand the well-formed discipline of XML data. These classes have been designed from the ground up to gain performance. The next sections discuss these classes and their important members in detail.

Looking at the Types of Parsers

The .NET Framework provides several ways to read an XML document by offering different types of XML parsers. In the pre-.NET days, the only way to read an XML document was to install a separate set of Microsoft XML libraries. With the advent of .NET, XML parsers are built in and bundled as part of the framework, and hence no additional deployment is required. The core responsibility of these parsers is to ensure that each document adheres to the XML discipline and vocabulary, mainly verifying whether the document is well-formed. If the document fails to meet the well-formed criteria, then it provides a detailed error message in the form of a .NET exception. These exceptions provide the appropriate element name or attribute name in which the structural inconsistency was found. The parsers are realized in a separate class altogether, and they provide rich functionality in the form of members and properties that allow you to tweak every nook and cranny of an XML document.

XML parsers are broadly categorized into two forms, discussed in the following sections.

Tree-Based Parser

A *tree-based parser* is drawn upon a tree-based model. It loads an XML document as an in-memory collection of objects that are arranged hierarchically. This parser is similar to the TreeView widget, which we have all worked with in some form or the other. The TreeView widget provides a programmatic way of traversing and manipulating every node in a tree. An XML document is intrinsically structured in a tree form. Therefore, every element and attribute is accessible in the form of a concrete node object. An element may become a parent node or leaf node based on the number of child elements. From an object-oriented perspective, an XML document represents a tree of objects. This parser has both an upside and a downside. It is extremely unhealthy for the application if the XML document is massive in size. The entire document needs to be flattened in memory, which means that loading several large documents will tax both the memory and the efficiency of the application. On a brighter side, this parser is highly suited for hosting a low-end mini–data store, thus avoiding the need for a mid-scale database engine. Most commonly used application data is persisted in an XML file and fetched into memory with the help of this parser. A tree-based parser is realized in the form of an XML Document Object Model (XML DOM) parser. This parser is part of the .NET Framework and available in the form of the `System.Xml.XmlDocument` class.

Fast-Forward Parser

This parser is the equivalent of a server-side fast-forward database cursor. The fast-forward nature of the cursor makes it highly efficient when it comes to iterating a large number of records. The only caveat is that it provides access to only one record at a time. A forward-only XML parser inherits the same behavior of a database cursor. It too provides access to only one node at a time. This is in sharp contrast to a tree-based parser, which allows free-flow navigation from the top to the bottom of a tree, or vice versa. This stateless nature of parsers offloads the responsibility of retaining the state of a document to the caller. The most unique benefit this parser offers is that it demands a slim memory footprint, which makes it highly attractive when it comes to reading huge documents. A forward-only parser is available in the following two flavors. These flavors are differentiated based on how the data is made available to the application.

> *Push*: A parser of this type publishes data to the application using a callback mechanism. Applications interested in reading XML documents must register a callback handler with a parser, and this handler is invoked whenever a node in the document is visited. The parser controls the modus operandi of reading the document. Hence, it is more parser driven than application driven. Simple API for XML (SAX) parsers fall under this category and are designed specifically to overcome problems faced in the DOM, primarily the memory issue. Even though the .NET Framework has no direct support for SAX parsers, they are still available as part of the Microsoft XML 4.0 COM Library.

Pull: Pull-based parsers are application driven and not parser driven. They provide unstinted and unconditional control to applications. Only applications have the sole authority over interested elements or attributes and are free to discard the remaining unwanted information. The .NET Framework bundles this type of parser in the form of the `System.Xml.XmlReader` class, which is explained in detail later in this section.

Thus, .NET provides the best of both worlds; it has support for tree-based parsers (`XmlDocument`) and fast-forward parsers (`XmlReader`). There are no hard-and-fast rules about which parser is good; rather, the decision of which parser to apply is driven by the scenario because each parser has its own unique selling points. Although there is no out-of-the-box support for the SAX parser in .NET, given the extensibility mechanism the `XmlReader` class offers, it is easy to emulate SAX-based behavior.

Table 3-7 summarizes the important features each parser provides.

Table 3-7. *Important Parser Features*

Feature	Tree-Based Parser (DOM)	Push (SAX)	Pull (XmlReader)
Memory footprint	Fat	Slim	Slim
Cached?	Yes	No	No
Navigation	Free flow	One-way (forward only)	One-way (forward only)
Ownership	Application driven	Parser driven	Application driven
W3C industry standard?	Yes	Yes	No
Functionality	Rich	Limited	Limited
Read/write	Read and write	Read	Read

Reading XML

The necessary ingredients required to read an XML document are enclosed in the `XmlReader` class. `XmlReader` and all the other important classes related to XML are packaged inside the `System.Xml` namespace. This is an abstract class that provides general-purpose functionality and delegates other specific functionality to its descendants. This abstract class is interweaved with a common set of methods and properties that allow the navigation and inspection of every node in an XML document. `XmlReader` has three concrete inherited classes: `XmlTextReader`, `XmlValidatingReader`, and `XmlNodeReader`. Each of these concrete classes is refined to meet the different goals of an XML document.

`XmlValidatingReader` is used when a document needs to be validated with an XML Schema Document (XSD); this is discussed later in the "Introducing XML Schema Document (XSD)" section. `XmlNodeReader` reads XML content from `XmlNode`. `XmlNode` is a fragment that is extracted from a DOM-based XML document. Similarly, `XmlTextReader` allows the reading of XML content from a stream or file on a file system. It supports forward-only navigation and provides read-only access to a document. This one-way, fast-forward nature makes `XmlTextReader` extremely lightweight in terms of memory consumption and allows a large document to easily fit in. However, an inherent constraint at the framework level restricts the size of the file to be smaller than 2GB. Besides this limitation, `XmlTextReader` is ideal when the XML content needs to be processed quickly to extract data that in turn must be provided to an intermediate in-memory data store.

We will now demonstrate how to write your first version of XML-aware code using `XmlTextReader`. Listing 3-4 reads the XML version of the ISIN master file to populate an intermediate in-memory data store.

Listing 3-4. *Reading the XML Version of the ISIN Master*

```
using System;
using System.Collections;
using System.Xml;

class ReadXml
{
  //ISIN Domain Model
  public class ISINInfo
  {
    public string Symbol;
    public double FaceValue;
    public int MarketLot;
    public ArrayList exchangeList =  new ArrayList();
  }

  //Exchange Domain Model
  //that holds exchange-specific instrument
  //code for a particular ISIN
  public class ExchangeInfo
  {
    public string ExchangeCode;
    public string ScripCode;
  }

  [STAThread]
  static void Main(string[] args)
  {
    //declare ArrayList for the in-memory data store
    ArrayList isinDataStore = new ArrayList();

    //ISINMaster XML path
    string xmlPath = @"C:\CodeExample\Chpt3\ReadXml\ISINMaster.xml";
    //Create Xml text reader
    XmlTextReader txtReader = new XmlTextReader(xmlPath);

    //loop until we have read the entire file
    //returns true as long as there is content to be read
    while ( txtReader.Read() )
    {
      //check the type of node that we just read to be an Element type
      switch(txtReader.NodeType)
      {
        case XmlNodeType.Element:
          //check the name of the current node being read
          //If ISIN node is read
          if ( txtReader.LocalName == "ISIN" )
          {
            //create an instance of the ISINInfo class, and
            //assign various properties by querying attribute
            //nodes of the ISIN element
            ISINInfo isinInfo = new ISINInfo();
            isinInfo.Symbol = txtReader.GetAttribute("Symbol");
            isinInfo.FaceValue =
                XmlConvert.ToDouble(txtReader.GetAttribute("FaceValue"));
            isinInfo.MarketLot =
                XmlConvert.ToInt32(txtReader.GetAttribute("MarketLot"));
```

```
            isinDataStore.Add(isinInfo);
          }
          //If Exchange node is read
          if ( txtReader.LocalName == "Exchange" )
          {
            //Get reference to latest isin instance added in arraylist
            ISINInfo isinInfo =
                        isinDataStore[isinDataStore.Count - 1] as ISINInfo;
            //create instance of exchange, and assign various
            //properties by querying attribute node of exchange element
            ExchangeInfo exchInfo = new ExchangeInfo();
            exchInfo.ExchangeCode = txtReader.GetAttribute("Code");
            exchInfo.ScripCode = txtReader.GetAttribute("ScripCode");
            //add exchange instance into isin exchange list
            //reflects isin-exchange mapping
            isinInfo.exchangeList.Add(exchInfo);
          }
          break;
        default:
          break;
      }
    }

    //close the text reader
    txtReader.Close();

    //Display the ISIN
    foreach(ISINInfo isin in isinDataStore)
    {
      Console.WriteLine("ISIN :" +isin.Symbol);
      //Display Exchange
      foreach(ExchangeInfo exchange in isin.exchangeList)
      {
        Console.WriteLine("Exchange {0} Scrip Code {1} ",
                    exchange.ExchangeCode,exchange.ScripCode);
      }
    }
  }
}
```

In Listing 3-4, the first line of code declares an ArrayList that represents an in-memory data store. The array collection holds object instances of ISINInfo, which is basically an object-oriented representation of the ISIN element, fetched from the XML file. ISINInfo also references the ExchangeInfo class, which is an object-oriented representation of the Exchange element defined under the ISIN element.

The XML reading process starts with the instantiation of the XmlTextReader class, which accepts a full path of the XML file. The next line of code is a while loop that gets triggered by invoking the Read method of the XmlTextReader class. This method is the analog to a database cursor row pointer that knows the current row position in a cursor; similarly, the internal implementation of the Read method is such that it also knows the current node position. Thus, the repeated invocation of this method increments its internal position pointer and moves it to the next node in the XML document. The Read method returns a Boolean value to indicate whether a read request was successful in locating the next node in the XML document. A return value of false indicates the end of the file and also the criteria for exiting the loop. Also, an important point to note is that the Read method navigates node by node, and the XML attributes are not considered to be nodes; instead, attributes are treated as the auxiliary information of a node. Figure 3-6 depicts a graphical representation of a node visited in the while loop code.

Figure 3-6. *Graphical representation of* while *loop code*

In Figure 3-6, both start and end tags are considered to be nodes and therefore must be excluded from the evaluation logic. You can do this with the help of the NodeType property. This property returns the type of the visited node, and a list of all possible node types is supplied by the XmlNodeType enumeration. Because you are interested only in the ISIN and Exchange elements that contain the required domain information, you narrow the evaluation logic by favoring only the XmlNodeType.Element node and specifically checking for the existence of both these elements by querying the LocalName property. This property returns the name of the current node; in this example, it returns the name of the element.

So, when the code encounters ISIN and Exchange elements, it enters a conditional block of code that instantiates an appropriate object based on the element name. Elements are just tags to the core information that resides inside an XML attribute. The essential information in this case is stored inside Symbol, FaceValue, and MarketLot attributes that are extracted with the help of the GetAttribute method by passing the correct attribute name. The return value of the GetAttribute method is of string type and needs to be converted to the object field's underlying type. The type conversion takes place with the help of the XmlConvert class. This class is introduced to achieve a locale-independent conversion and to respect the XSD data type specification. With the help of the XmlConvert class, the attribute value is converted to the appropriate underlying CLR type, is assigned to the newly instantiated object field, and finally is inserted into an in-memory data store.

It is also essential to handle the whitespace encountered while reading an XML document. Although in Figure 3-6 whitespace is not discussed explicitly, it is considered a distinct node and therefore forms part of the read iteration process. If efficiency is the key goal of an application where every bit of performance is counted, then it is recommended that you turn off the processing for whitespace nodes using the WhiteSpaceHandling property.

The XmlTextReader class houses several other important members and properties that are useful for handling XML documents from all dimensions. Most of the members and properties are bound contextually, which means their values are dynamic and populated based on the current node. Table 3-8 lists some of the important properties of the XmlTextReader class. Table 3-9 lists the important methods supported by XmlTextReader, and Table 3-10 lists the navigation methods.

Table 3-8. *Important Properties of the* XmlTextReader *Class*

Properties	Description
AttributeCount	This property returns the total number of attributes in the current node.
BaseURI	This property is useful for determining the location of an XML document.
Depth	The XML document is structured in a tree-based fashion, and every element or attribute in the tree belongs to a particular level in the tree. This property returns the tree level of the current node.
EOF	This is useful to determine whether the stream has finished reading the entire document and its position pointer has reached the end of the file.
HasAttribute	This property indicates whether the current node has any attributes.
IsEmptyElement	This property comes in handy when you need to know whether the current node is an empty element. For example, in the ISIN master, an occurrence of text such as <ISIN/> represents an empty element.

Table 3-9. *Important Methods of the* XmlTextReader *Class*

Members	Description
Skip	When invoked, this method skips all the children in the current node, and the node pointer is positioned on the next element in the tree level. For example, if the node pointer was positioned on the Exchanges element and the Skip method was invoked, the node pointer skips the entire children node branching under this element, thereby skipping all Exchange elements. Therefore, the node pointer directly jumps to the end node of the ISINMaster element.

Table 3-10. *Navigation Methods of the* XmlTextReader *Class*

Navigation Members	Description
MoveToAttribute	This is an overloaded method that allows navigation to a specific attribute by passing its attribute name or attribute index position within the element node.
MoveToFirstAttribute	This moves to the first attribute in the element node.
MoveToNextAttribute	This moves to the next attribute in the element node. Both MoveToFirstAttribute and MoveToNextAttribute return a Boolean value that indicates whether traversal to the next attribute was successful.
MoveToElement	This method is useful to reset the navigation pointer to the element in the current attribute node.

To further illustrate the application of navigation methods, we'll show how to add some intelligence to the parsing code. The current parsing code is well-crafted to read mandatory information; ISIN-related information is built upon Symbol, FaceValue, and MarketLot attributes, and Exchange-related information is built upon Code and ScripCode attributes. The following code introduces an additional visual cue in the Exchange element-processing block that will display unwanted information that surfaces in the form of unknown XML attributes:

```
using System;
using System.Xml;

class NodeNavigation
{
  [STAThread]
  static void Main(string[] args)
  {
    //ISINMaster Xml path
    string xmlPath = @"C:\CodeExample\Chpt3\ReadXml\ISINMaster.xml";
    //Create Xml text reader
    XmlTextReader txtReader = new XmlTextReader(xmlPath);
    //loop until we have read the entire file
    //returns true as long as there is content to be read
    while ( txtReader.Read() )
    {
      switch(txtReader.NodeType)
      {
        case XmlNodeType.Element:
          //If Exchange node is read
          if ( txtReader.LocalName == "Exchange" )
          {
            //Iterate through all attributes of the exchange element
```

```
        for(int ctr=0;ctr<=txtReader.AttributeCount-1;ctr++)
        {
          //Move to attribute with specified index
          txtReader.MoveToAttribute(ctr);
          //display additional unwanted attribute
          if ( !(txtReader.Name == "Code" || txtReader.Name == "ScripCode"))
          {
            Console.WriteLine("Unknown Attribute Node "
                                  +txtReader.Name +" Found ");
            Console.WriteLine("Attribute Value : " +txtReader.Value);
          }
        }
      }
      break;
    default:
      break;
    }
   }
  }
}
```

You have seen that XmlTextReader is XML-oriented and can extract XML-based data from any given underlying file or stream. The only feature it does not support is writing XML data that is separated in an XmlTextWriter class, as discussed in the next section.

Writing XML

We see two classifications of developers in our day-to-day work. The first category is adventurous and is always in search of some new programming tools and techniques that will be eagerly implemented in their day-to-day development routines. The second category is more narrow minded and reluctant to adopt new approaches. This classification also applies to writing XML documents. XML documents, because of their text-centric characteristics, can be easily crafted by concatenating a bunch of strings. Such an approach will be happily implemented by the second category of developers using the StringBuilder class. With this approach, although it meets the goal of churning out a well-formed XML document, in reality a lot of time and effort is invested in ensuring that the final output adheres to the XML standards. There are high possibilities for errors, such as missing end tags, missing quotes, and so on.

When adventurous developers look into the .NET Framework, they will discover a new class—XmlWriter—as part of the System.Xml namespace. It is an abstract base class that provides a forward-only and noncached way of generating XML documents. Using this class, developers no longer have to worry about missing angled brackets or missing quotes. The XmlWriter class provides the logic that will help build a well-formed XML document. It offers several versions of WriteXXX methods for each possible XML node type.

XmlTextWriter is the immediate specialization of the XmlWriter class. This class writes XML output to a stream or file in a file system. Listing 3-5 illustrates how to use this class by reading the object-oriented format of ISIN data and persisting it in an XML document.

Listing 3-5. *Writing the ISIN Master XML Document*

```
using System;
using System.Collections;
using System.Xml;
using System.Text;
```

```
class WritingXml
{
  public class ExchangeInfo
  {
    public string ExchangeCode;
    public string ScripCode;
  }

  public class ISINInfo
  {
    public string Symbol;
    public double FaceValue;
    public int MarketLot;
    public ArrayList exchangeList = new ArrayList();
  }

  [STAThread]
  static void Main(string[] args)
    {
        //initialize in-memory isin data store
        ArrayList isinList = new ArrayList();

        //create isin
        ISINInfo isinInfo = new ISINInfo();
        isinInfo.Symbol ="MSFT";
        isinInfo.FaceValue = 10;
        isinInfo.MarketLot = 5;

        //create exchange
        ExchangeInfo nasdaqInfo = new ExchangeInfo();
        nasdaqInfo.ExchangeCode = "NASDAQ";
        nasdaqInfo.ScripCode = "MSFT.O";

        //add exchange to isin exchange list
        isinInfo.exchangeList.Add(nasdaqInfo);
        //add isin to array list
        isinList.Add(isinInfo);

        //create XML text writer
        XmlTextWriter xmlWriter = new
                XmlTextWriter(@"C:\ISINMaster.xml",Encoding.UTF8);
        xmlWriter.Formatting = Formatting.Indented;
        //write the root element
        xmlWriter.WriteStartElement("ISINMaster");

        //iterate through individual isin
        foreach(ISINInfo curIsin  in isinList)
        {
          //write isin element
          xmlWriter.WriteStartElement("ISIN");
          //write attributes of isin
          xmlWriter.WriteAttributeString("Symbol",curIsin.Symbol);
          xmlWriter.WriteAttributeString("FaceValue",
                    XmlConvert.ToString(curIsin.FaceValue));
          xmlWriter.WriteAttributeString("MarketLot",
                    XmlConvert.ToString(curIsin.MarketLot));
          //write parent element of exchange
```

```
        xmlWriter.WriteStartElement("Exchanges");
        //iterate through individual exchange
        foreach(ExchangeInfo curExchange in curIsin.exchangeList)
        {
          //write exchange element
          xmlWriter.WriteStartElement("Exchange");
          //write attributes of exchange
          xmlWriter.WriteAttributeString("Code",curExchange.ExchangeCode);
          xmlWriter.WriteAttributeString("ScripCode",curExchange.ScripCode);
          xmlWriter.WriteEndElement();
        }
        //exchange end tag
        xmlWriter.WriteEndElement();
        //exchanges end tag
        xmlWriter.WriteEndElement();
      }
    //root end tag
    xmlWriter.WriteEndElement();
    //close xml text writer
    xmlWriter.Close();
  }
}
```

In Listing 3-5, first an XmlTextWriter object is instantiated by passing the path of the file to which the XML output is redirected. The next line of code is where the XML writing journey begins; first the root element of the document is written with the help of the WriteStartElement method. The method name that starts with WriteStartXXX is called a *paired method*. The first leg of the paired method represents the start of the node with WriteStartElement and WriteStartAttribute, and the final leg indicates the end of the node with WriteEndElement and WriteEndAttribute. So, every WriteStartXX method has a corresponding WriteEndXX method.

After generating an opening angled bracket for the ISINMaster element, the program enters into a loop that reads the ISIN master from an in-memory ArrayList data store. The ISIN element is emitted with the help of WriteStartElement. Information about ISIN—such as Symbol, FaceValue, and MarketLot—forms part of the XML attribute, and this information is written out with the help of the WriteAttributeString method.

You also use the same approach to generate the Exchange information that is inside a nested loop associated with the current ISIN. When the code exits from the nested loop, the WriteEndElement method is invoked two times. The first invocation is meant to close the Exchanges element, and the last invocation is meant to close the ISIN element. The code also includes a final call to WriteEndElement to close the root element.

Observe that the code described in Listing 3-5 does not concatenate the strings to generate the XML document; instead, it leverages the XmlTextWriter class. This guarantees that the generated final document adheres to the well-formed XML standard. Table 3-11 lists the important members available in the XmlTextWriter class, and Table 3-12 lists the important formatting properties.

Table 3-11. *Important Members of the* XmlTextWriter *Class*

Members	Description
WriteComment	This member provides XML-style comments, such as <!--...-->. The comments are passed as a string argument to this method.
WriteBase64	A Base64 encoding scheme is used to convert binary data into ASCII characters. XML documents do not support raw binary data; only ASCII characters are allowed as part of an element value or attribute value. The only mechanism to embed binary data inside an XML document is to convert it into a Base64 encoding scheme. The WriteBase64 method accepts a byte array as the method argument and encodes this byte array to Base64 format.

Table 3-12. *Important Formatting Properties of the* XmlTextWriter *Class*

Formatting Properties	Description
Formatting	This property indicates how the XML output must be formatted, and an appropriate value is assigned using the Formatting enumeration. The possible Formatting enumeration values are None and Indented. By default no formatting is performed, so when the document is opened in Notepad, or any other text editor, the content is arranged in a series of lines instead of in a hierarchical arrangement.
IndentChar	This property defines the character used for indenting.
Indentation	This property defines the number of IndentChar to be written at each level in the hierarchy.
QuoteChar	This defines the quotation mark character to be used to enclose the attribute value.

XmlReader and XmlWriter form the core classes in the .NET Framework. Although they are independent classes, encapsulating read and write operations in a distinct, separate class allows for the cleaner separation of responsibilities. You can extend both of these classes to read and write non-XML data. XmlReader and XmlWriter also provide a strong foundation for designing other XML-based services such as XML integration in ADO.NET, XML serialization, and so on.

Introducing XML Serialization

Modern systems are modeled around the basic tenets of object-oriented programming where business requirements are distilled into fine, granular objects. Undoubtedly, object-oriented programming models are safe bets when the scope of communication is confined to the local periphery of an application. But in today's era, the automation of organizations is built upon disparate systems, and exchanging data between such systems is a major bottleneck. The data required for the exchange purpose is in place and also encapsulated inside an object, but the object itself is a runtime representation and affiliated to a specific runtime system and operating system. For example, an object instantiated by a .NET system cannot be passed, as is, to a Java-based system. This demands a mechanism to hydrate an in-memory representation of an object that can be easily understood by another system. *Serialization* is the process of flattening the in-memory object state into a common representation format that can be easily transferred over the wire or persisted to a stream. Similarly, *deserialization* is the reverse ability to resurrect an in-memory object state from disk storage or any other in-memory data source. The serialization and deserialization process is managed by the serialization engine, which defines the scope of the object to be serialized and the format of the serialized object. The serialization engine not only provides the ability to serialize a given object but also conducts a deep traversal of objects to flush out the entire object graph contents. The serialization engine primarily operates in two modes:

Full-type fidelity mode: In this mode, the object's state and its contextual information or object identity information is serialized. For example, when a .NET type is serialized in full-type fidelity mode, the object's public and private fields—along with its assembly information such as the assembly name, its version number, public key, and assembly culture—also get recorded. The serialization engine enforces stringent norms during the deserialization phase in this mode. An object serialized in one context can be resurrected only when the context at the deserializing end matches the serialized context. Hence, the serialization engine in this mode (in such types) is context-centric; therefore, even if there are no changes in the structure of an object, minor assembly version number increments are sufficient to invalidate the deserialization process. This mode is useful in a distributed environment where both the client and the server are physically separated and the types shared between them demand a strict versioning policy.

Partial-type fidelity mode: In partial-type fidelity mode, only the object state is serialized; contextual information is completely sidelined during the deserialization phase.

Three types of serialization engines are built in and readily available within the .NET Framework:

Binary serializer: The binary serializer is one of the fastest serializers that hydrates object state into raw bytes, and vice versa. The raw bytes generated are compact in size and highly efficient for transfer over the wire. Binary serialization is achieved with the help of the `BinaryFormatter` class and is used heavily by the .NET Remoting Communication Infrastructure.

SOAP serializer: The SOAP serializer converts object state into SOAP messages that are designed upon XML standards. The primary goal of this serializer is to achieve platform neutrality. SOAP serialization is achieved with the help of the `SoapFormatter` class.

XML serializer: The XML serializer serializes object state into XML format. The behavior of this serializer is controlled with the help of .NET attributes and has pioneered a new declarative style of programming.

The declarative style of programming is a novel approach introduced in the C# programming language. It allows annotating additional information called *attributes*. Attributes are simply information markers or additional metadata associated with programming elements such as types, fields, methods, and properties. This metadata augments the functionality of the entity to which it is applied. With the help of the .NET reflection technique, these attributes can be easily queried or inspected, and the appropriate interpretation of the attributes can be performed during either runtime or compile time. Attributes complement the existing coding syntax by allowing a cleaner approach. You do this by decoupling the core logic from the consumer class and allowing the consumer class to consume this logic by explicitly expressing it in the form of attributes. Attributes are easy to debug and locate because of their placement rule; they are allowed only before the declaration of any programming element. Attributes are deeply rooted in the .NET Framework and can handle a variety of tasks such as assembly versioning information, code access security, and so on.

Listing 3-6 demonstrates how to use attributes.

Listing 3-6. *Using Attributes*

```
[Serializable]
public class ISINInfo
{
  public string Symbol;
  public double FaceValue;
```

```
  public int MarketLot;
  public ArrayList exchangeList = new ArrayList();
}
```

In Listing 3-6, you will notice an attribute named Serializable annotated on the ISINInfo type. By annotating this attribute, you augment the functionality of the ISINInfo type by allowing its object instances to be serializable. Attributes themselves are object instances of the Attribute class. Attributes are further classified into custom attributes and pseudo-attributes. Custom attributes are defined by developers, and pseudo-attributes are system-level attributes defined by the CLR. Now that you know about the fundamentals of attributes, you can look at the XmlSerializer class where attributes play an important role in achieving serialization.

XmlSerializer is housed inside the System.Xml.Serialization namespace. It mediates between a CLR type and an XML document and weaves some plumbing code that allows for the seamless translation between a CLR type and an XML document, and vice versa. This plumbing code is generated based on a set of known mapping rules that are defined with the help of an XML serialization attribute that is explained shortly. Attributes are placed on the class property or on fields. Once they are defined, they form input to the XML serialization engine, which dictates how to persist the value of the field or property in XML format—whether to represent the field or property as an XML element or an attribute. Also, certain attributes are driven by the underlying data type of the field or property. They provide additional hints to the XML serialization engine about how to handle a complex data type associated with a field or property. To illustrate this mechanism, let's return to the topic of XML content being read using the XmlReader class. You can achieve the same task with the help of XmlSerializer.

But before that, the following classes need to be persist aware, which is achieved with the help of attributes:

```
public class ISINInfo
{
  [XmlAttribute("Symbol")]
  public string Symbol;
  [XmlAttribute("FaceValue")]
  public double FaceValue;
  [XmlAttribute("MarketLot")]
  public int MarketLot;
  [XmlArray("Exchanges")]
  [XmlArrayItem("Exchange",
               typeof(ExchangeInfo))]
  public ArrayList exchangeList =
               new ArrayList();
}

public class ExchangeInfo
{
  [XmlAttribute("Code")]
  public string ExchangeCode;
  [XmlAttribute("ScripCode")]
  public string ScripCode;
}

[XmlRoot("ISINMaster")]
public class ISINDataStore
{
  private ISINInfo[] isinStore;
```

```
[XmlArray("ISINS")]
[XmlArrayItem("ISIN",typeof(ISINInfo))]
public ISINInfo[] Items
{
  get{return isinStore;}
  set{isinStore=value;}
}
}
```

The only noticeable change is the recruitment of appropriate attributes. You should note that at this point no structural changes have been made to the class in any form either by injecting a new method or by deriving from any existing base classes. Attributes were the only ingredients that were needed to mix with your class to achieve XML serialization. Table 3-13 describes individual attributes in detail.

Table 3-13. *Attributes and Their Descriptions*

Attribute Name	Description
XmlRoot	The valid programming element for this attribute is a CLR type. This attribute represents the root element of an XML document. In the example, ISINMaster is the root element, and therefore you declared this attribute on the ISINDataStore type.
XmlAttribute	This attribute is used on a class public field or property. It accepts the attribute name as part of the argument and persists the value of the field or property to an XML attribute node type. Referring to the previous ISINInfo class, the public field is decorated with XmlAttribute, which in turn gets mapped to the attribute node type when represented in the XML document form.
XmlElement	This attribute maps the field or property value to an XML element node.
XmlIgnore	This is a useful attribute, and it comes in handy when sensitive or unwanted information needs to be excluded from getting serialized. When this attribute is annotated on a public field or property, the serialization engine completely ignores it, and the value of the field or property will not be serialized in any form.
XmlArray XmlArrayItem	These two attributes go hand in hand and are promising when the field or property to be serialized returns an array of objects. The definition of an *array* in this context is any class that implements the IEnumerable interface. This expands the list of classes that are serializable from a simple primitive array to a complex collection of objects. If you look closely at the ISINDataStore and ISINInfo classes, you will find the presence of these attributes declared on a field of the ArrayList data type. We all know that there will be multiple occurrences of ISIN, with each ISIN holding multiple Exchange records. Such one-to-many mappings between ISIN and Exchange can be achieved in conjunction with the XmlArray and XmlArrayItem attributes. XmlArray also allows you to define the name of the parent element node, and XmlArrayItem allows you to define the name of the inner child element node of this parent node. The XmlArrayItem attribute also allows the mapping of the inner child element node to the appropriate CLR type.
XmlEnum	This attribute allows you to tweak the serialization of enumeration values.
XmlAnyAttribute	This attribute is annotated on a field or property that returns an array of XmlAttribute. This array acts as a generic container for storing all attributes that do not have a corresponding mapped field or property.
XmlAnyElement	This attribute is annotated on a field or property that returns an array of XmlNode or XmlElement. The array acts as a generic container for storing all elements that do not have a corresponding mapped field or property.

Now that you have a clear understanding of serialization attributes, let's look at its application. So far, you used `XmlTextReader` and `XmlTextWriter` for reading and writing XML-based data. Using `XmlTextReader`, you read an XML document from a stream and traversed each node, and in the process you extracted the appropriate node value and assigned it to an object public field. You did exactly the reverse using `XmlTextWriter`, where object fields were assigned to an appropriate XML node, and generated a well-formed XML document. The only downside with this approach is that you need to manually hand-roll the code to "XMLify" object fields. With `XmlSerializer` in action, you are relieved from having to write low-level parsing code; you can achieve the same task with a minimum amount of code. The following snippet demonstrates both serialization and deserialization:

```
using System;
using System.Collections;
using System.Xml.Serialization;
using System.IO;

public class XmlPersist
{
  [XmlRoot("ISINMaster")]
  public class ISINDataStore
  {
    [XmlArray("ISINS")]
    [XmlArrayItem("ISIN",typeof(ISINInfo))]
    public ArrayList isinStore = new ArrayList();
  }

  public class ISINInfo
  {
    [XmlAttribute("Symbol")]
    public string Symbol;
    [XmlAttribute("FaceValue")]
    public double FaceValue;
    [XmlAttribute("MarketLot")]
    public int MarketLot;
    [XmlArray("Exchanges")]
    [XmlArrayItem("Exchange",typeof(ExchangeInfo))]
    public ArrayList exchangeList = new ArrayList();
  }

  public class ExchangeInfo
  {
    [XmlAttribute("Code")]
    public string ExchangeCode;
    [XmlAttribute("ScripCode")]
    public string ScripCode;
  }

  [STAThread]
  static void Main(string[] args)
  {
    string isinPath = @"C:\CodeExample\Chpt3\XmlSerialization\ISINMaster.xml";
    //read isin content
    StreamReader xmlDoc = new StreamReader(isinPath);
    //create a new instance of XML serializer
    XmlSerializer isinXml = new XmlSerializer(typeof(ISINDataStore));
    //deserialize isin master
```

```
    ISINDataStore dataStore = isinXml.Deserialize(xmlDoc) as ISINDataStore;
    //write isin content
    StreamWriter newXmlDoc = new StreamWriter(@"C:\NewISINMaster.xml");
    //serialize isin master
    isinXml.Serialize(newXmlDoc,dataStore);
    //close the stream
    xmlDoc.Close();
    newXmlDoc.Close();
  }
}
```

The Serialize and DeSerialize methods of the XmlSerializer class dictate the serialization and deserialization of any arbitrary type. The arbitrary type is supplied as a constructor argument to the XmlSerializer class. Based on this arbitrary type, XmlSerializer implements a just-in-time code-cutting technique that generates code by reflecting a class public field and property that need to be serialized, and then XmlSerializer compiles this code into a .NET assembly that is loaded in the program's memory. Furthermore, the underlying source from which data is fetched during the deserialization phase or persisted during the serialization phase could be any valid Stream object. Chapter 8 describes the inner workings of the XmlSerializer class in detail.

The XmlSerializer class is a powerful weapon in a developer's arsenal. Developers are often faced with a requirement to sprinkle an XML layer over a runtime object, or vice versa. You can use the XML serializer to achieve this layering by abstracting away the core complexities and not forcing parsing code down the developer's throat.

Introducing XML Schema Document (XSD)

Before getting into an explanation of XSD, we'll cover the assumptions made in the ISIN master XML document (refer to Listing 3-2). The XML version of the ISIN document poses some serious short-comings that were overlooked during the parsing stage. Although you can overlook such negligence in a perfect world where everything behaves in an expected manner, this is not true in the real computing world. In the computing world, any action executed based on assumptions tends to be brittle in nature. The following questions, when raised, are sufficient to cripple the strong assumptions used to develop the parsing logic:

- What happens when an XML document deviates from the expected standard? For example, what if there is no occurrence of an ISINMaster element or one of its child elements?

- What happens when the necessary information in the document is arranged in an unordered fashion? For example, what if Exchange elements are nested under ISIN elements instead of the Exchanges element?

- What happens when partial information is received from the XML document? For example, what if a Symbol attribute is missing from an ISIN element?

- What happens when there is a data type mismatch? For example, what if the FaceValue attribute of the ISIN element contains a string value instead of a numeric value?

- What happens when the ISIN master document contains extraneous information that bloats up the size of the document and the visible side effect of such large document is negatively impacted performance?

The previous questions often lead to a common syndrome that is directly related to document structure validation and integrity. To overcome such problems, developers start building a whole suite of validation frameworks to function across different XML node touch points. The addition of a validation framework further increases the development time, and above all it shifts the main focus of a developer. Instead of concentrating on building core domain components, the developer is actively engaged in building a validating parser component. XML Schema comes to the rescue to alleviate this parsing problem. It is one step ahead of parsing.

XML Schema is analogous to a database table in a relational database system. A database table encapsulates the structural information of a row in the form of column definitions and also allows the enforcement of data-level validations, such as defining primary keys, constraints, rules, and so on. In the XML world, XML Schema mimics the functionality of a database table and defines the structural and content aspects of an element and attribute in an XML document.

XML Schema enriches the value of an XML document by mainly capturing three types of information:

Structural information: XML Schema defines the hierarchical arrangement of elements in the XML document. It captures the names of elements and attributes that are considered to be valid nodes in the document.

Content information: In XML documents, node values are represented in text that defaults the underlying data type to string. With the help of XML Schema, it is possible to define the underlying data type of a node. XML Schema supports several data types and includes all primitive types such as string, int, long, datetime, and so on.

Content restriction: XML Schema, along with its ability to define data types, provides the facility to define constraints on the data type. For example, an integer data type could be further customized to create a user-defined data type that accepts a restricted range of numbers.

XML Schema is defined using XML vocabulary and therefore in itself is an XML document. This means it is a well-formed document, and like other XML documents, it can be loaded and inspected by any XML parser. The only striking difference is that XSD is built on a fixed set of XML vocabulary that is leveraged to define the structural model of an XML document. This vocabulary comprises a fixed number of XML elements and attributes, and each of these markup nodes has its own distinct meaning when it comes to validating an XML document. Listing 3-7 is a full-blown XML Schema of the ISIN master.

Listing 3-7. *XML Schema of the ISIN Master*

```
<xs:schema id="ISINSchema" xmlns=""
                         xmlns:mstns="http://tempuri.org/ISINSchema.xsd"
                         xmlns:xs="http://www.w3.org/2001/XmlSchema">
  <xs:complexType name="ISINModel">
    <xs:sequence>
      <xs:element name="Exchanges" type="ExchangesModel" />
    </xs:sequence>
    <xs:attribute name="Symbol" type="xs:string" use="required" />
    <xs:attribute name="FaceValue" type="IntDataType" use="required" />
    <xs:attribute name="MarketLot" type="IntDataType" use="required" />
    <xs:attribute name="Status" type="StatusDataType" use="required" />
    <xs:attribute name="ISINCode" type="ISINCodeDataType" use="required" />
  </xs:complexType>
  <xs:simpleType name="StatusDataType">
    <xs:restriction base="xs:string">
      <xs:enumeration value="Active" />
      <xs:enumeration value="InActive" />
    </xs:restriction>
  </xs:simpleType>
  <xs:complexType name="ExchangeModel">
    <xs:sequence />
    <xs:attribute name="Code" type="xs:string" use="required" />
```

```
      <xs:attribute name="ScripCode" type="xs:string" use="required" />
  </xs:complexType>
  <xs:element name="ISINMaster">
    <xs:complexType>
      <xs:sequence>
        <xs:element name="ISIN" type="ISINModel"
                    minOccurs="1"  maxOccurs="unbounded"/>
      </xs:sequence>
    </xs:complexType>
    <xs:key name="PrimaryKeyISINCode">
      <xs:selector xpath=".//ISIN" />
      <xs:field xpath="@ISINCode" />
    </xs:key>
  </xs:element>
  <xs:complexType name="ExchangesModel">
    <xs:sequence>
      <xs:element name="Exchange" type="ExchangeModel"
                  minOccurs="1" maxOccurs="unbounded" />
    </xs:sequence>
  </xs:complexType>
  <xs:simpleType name="IntDataType">
    <xs:restriction base="xs:int">
      <xs:minExclusive value="0" />
    </xs:restriction>
  </xs:simpleType>
  <xs:simpleType name="ISINCodeDataType">
    <xs:restriction base="xs:string">
      <xs:pattern value="US[A-Z0-9]*" />
      <xs:length value="12" />
    </xs:restriction>
  </xs:simpleType>
</xs:schema>
```

In Listing 3-7, the declaration of xs:schema defines the root element of the XML Schema document. Primarily, three types of elements nest under this xs:schema element:

Complex type elements: A complex type element describes the structural characteristics of the XML elements. It is represented by the xs:complextype element and is composed of the following information:

- A list of all attributes housed inside an element that is defined by the xs:attribute element. This xs:attribute element also exposes a type attribute that allows you to associate the underlying data type of the attribute value. The content of the attribute node can be string, integer, or any custom data type.

- A list of all child elements defined with the help of compositor elements. Child elements are represented by xs:element but are defined within the scope of the compositor element. Compositors are also the driving force in ensuring elements are arranged in the appropriate order. Compositor elements are nested under the xs:complextype element. The xs:sequence element is a commonly used compositor element, and it directs the order of the nested child elements. Furthermore, xs:element also allows you to define the occurrence constraint that controls the minimum and maximum number of child elements. This element range restriction is fed to the minOccurs and maxOccurs attributes of xs:element.

Simple type elements: Simple type elements provide the notion of user-defined data types. This is inclined more toward content, unlike complex type elements that are centered on the structural aspects of the content. Simple type elements are derivations of built-in data types, but they offer additional flexibility to developers to customize this base data type to accept only a subset of data. Such restriction on data is usually determined by business requirements. A simple type element is analogous to a user-defined data type in a relational database and is represented by the xs:simpletype element.

Document root elements: A root element is represented by xs:element, but it directly branches as a child of the xs:schema element. This element determines the starting root element of the underlying XML document.

Although manually designing XML Schema documents is time-consuming, this should not be used as an excuse for not adopting this approach. The development community has addressed this problem well, and hence you will find a plethora of XML Schema designing tools that make the job easier by overcoming many challenges and drastically increasing productivity. The VS .NET IDE comes with a sophisticated XML Schema designer tool. With a few clicks and a drag-and-drop interface, you can quickly generate an XSD. In fact, the XML Schema described in Listing 3-7 was generated using VS .NET Schema Designer.

We'll now walk through the XML schema file described in Listing 3-8 and explain the one-to-one mapping of individual schema elements with the ISIN XML document, which will further solidify your understanding. The following is an XML fragment of the ISIN element described in Listing 3-2:

```
<ISIN ISINCode="US5949181045"
      Symbol="MSFT"
      FaceValue="10"
      MarketLot="5"
      Status="Active">
```

Listing 3-8. *XML Schema of the* ISIN *Element*

```
<xs:complexType name="ISINModel">
  <xs:sequence>
    <xs:element name="Exchanges" type="ExchangesModel" />
  </xs:sequence>
  <xs:attribute name="Symbol" type="xs:string" use="required"/>
  <xs:attribute name="FaceValue" type="IntDataType" use="required"/>
  <xs:attribute name="MarketLot" type="IntDataType" use="required"/>
  <xs:attribute name="Status" type="StatusDataType" use="required"/>
  <xs:attribute name="ISINCode" type="ISINCodeDataType"
                             use="required" />
  <xs:simpleType name="StatusDataType">
    <xs:restriction base="xs:string">
      <xs:enumeration value="Active" />
      <xs:enumeration value="InActive" />
    </xs:restriction>
  </xs:simpleType>
  <xs:simpleType name="IntDataType">
    <xs:restriction base="xs:int">
      <xs:minExclusive value="0" />
    </xs:restriction>
  </xs:simpleType>
  <xs:simpleType name="ISINCodeDataType">
    <xs:restriction base="xs:string">
```

```
      <xs:pattern value="US[A-Z0-9]*" />
      <xs:length value="12" />
    </xs:restriction>
  </xs:simpleType>
```

Listing 3-8 represents the structural model of the ISIN element. The ISIN element is defined as a complex type and is named ISINModel. ISINModel also encloses mandatory attributes such as FaceValue, Symbol, MarketLot, and Status. Also, notice the data type of the FaceValue, MarketLot, and Status attributes. They are based on IntDataType and StatusDataType, which are simple types and are customized to accept only restricted data.

Another good thing about the simple type is that it allows you to apply regular expressions on data. The previous example, as part of the business validation check, defines a rule using the regular expression syntax that states the ISIN code will always start with US as the first two characters and will accept only uppercase characters along with numeric digits. The declaration of the attribute node is further strengthened with the use attribute that instructs the schema parser to treat this attribute as one of the mandatory attributes and also raise an exception when it fails to locate this attribute in the XML document. You will also discover an element named Exchanges. The underlying complex type of this element is ExchangesModel, which is as shown in Listing 3-9. Listing 3-10 represents the structural model of the Exchange element that is enclosed inside the ExchangeModel complex type.

Listing 3-9. *The* Exchange *Element*

```
<Exchanges>

<Exchange
  Code="NASDAQ"
  ScripCode="NMSFT" />
```

Listing 3-10. *XML Schema of the* Exchange *Element*

```
<xs:complexType name="ExchangesModel">
  <xs:sequence>
    <xs:element name="Exchange" type="ExchangeModel"
                minOccurs="1" maxOccurs="unbounded" />
  </xs:sequence>
</xs:complexType>
<xs:complexType name="ExchangeModel">
  <xs:sequence />
  <xs:attribute name="Code" type="xs:string" use="required" />
  <xs:attribute name="ScripCode" type="xs:string" use="required" />
</xs:complexType>
```

The Exchange element does not contain any child elements, so the only node it supports is Code and the ScripCode attributes. Exchange elements are repeatable elements and hence appear multiple times for a particular ISIN. Therefore, it is nested inside the Exchanges element that is schematically mapped to the ExchangesModel complex style. The important attributes to observe are minOccurs and maxOccurs associated with xs:element. These attributes control the minimum and maximum occurrences of the child elements. In Listing 3-10, we expressed a mandatory validation that there should be at least one Exchange but no limit on the maximum number of Exchange. The next and final element to be addressed is the root element, which is as follows:

```
<ISINMaster>
```

Listing 3-11 shows the XML Schema of the root element.

Listing 3-11. *XML Schema of the Root Element*

```
<xs:element name="ISINMaster">
  <xs:complexType>
    <xs:sequence>
      <xs:element name="ISIN" type="ISINModel"
                  minOccurs="1" maxOccurs="unbounded" />
    </xs:sequence>
  </xs:complexType>
  <xs:key name="PrimaryKeyISINCode">
    <xs:selector xpath=".//ISIN" />
    <xs:field xpath="@ISINCode" />
  </xs:key>
</xs:element>
```

The root element of the XML document is ISINMaster, and in Listing 3-7 it is defined as a direct descendant of the xs:schema element. The ISINMaster root element contains multiple ISIN elements, and this arrangement is achieved with the help of xs:element named as ISIN, and the underlying type of this element is mapped to ISINModel, which is a complex type. Another interesting thing to note is that the validation of the XML document is further tightened by defining a primary key constraint on the ISIN code. The benefit of this constraint is reaped during the XML Schema validation stage when the parser checks for the duplicate existence of the ISIN code.

This completes the discussion of the XML Schema. This discussion, so far, has focused on the individual characteristics of both the XML and its underlying schema. In the following section, you will see how to bring these two documents together. In addition, an XML document must satisfy two important conditions. Along with its well-formed nature, it must also gain the status of a valid document. You can accomplish this task by validating the document against the correct schema. Thus, the desperate missing piece is the schema parser that carries an inherent knowledge of the vocabulary in the XML Schema. The schema parser loads both the XML document and the schema document in the memory. After loading, it reads each node from the document and validates both the content and structure of this node against the schema document and ensures that the node is not violating any rule and that it satisfies all the conditions expressed in the schema document. The .NET Framework provides this kind of schema parser in the form of the XmlValidatingReader class.

XmlValidatingReader is also bundled in the System.Xml namespace along with the XmlReader and XmlWriter classes. XmlValidatingReader is a direct descendant of the XmlReader class, and this leaves no room for doubt that its data-reading tactics are based on the pull model. It reads data node by node and then validates it against the specified schema specification. Such step-by-step validation of each individual node, from a performance perspective, is highly rewarding. The following code snippet represents the applicability of XmlValidatingReader that validates the ISIN master XML document (see Listing 3-2) against the ISIN master schema file (see Listing 3-7):

```
using System;
using System.Xml;
using System.Xml.Schema;

class SchemaValidation
{
  public static bool isDocumentValid=true;
  [STAThread]
  static void Main(string[] args)
  {
    string path = @"C:\CodeExample\Chpt3\SchemaValidation\";
    //read ISIN XML
    XmlTextReader reader = new XmlTextReader(path +"ISINMaster.xml");
    //create schema validator
    XmlValidatingReader validateReader = new XmlValidatingReader(reader);
```

```
        //associate validation event handler
        validateReader.ValidationEventHandler +=new
                    System.Xml.Schema.ValidationEventHandler(ValidationEventHandler);
        //add schema file path
        validateReader.Schemas.Add("",path +"ISINSchema.xsd");
        //validate the XML file with XSD
        while(validateReader.Read())
        {
          if ( isDocumentValid == false )
            break;
        }
        //check boolean value; the value of this variable
        //is assigned in validation handler code
        if ( isDocumentValid == true )
        {
          Console.WriteLine("Document is Valid...");
        }
      }

      private static void ValidationEventHandler(object sender,
                              System.Xml.Schema.ValidationEventArgs e)
      {
        //error in XML document
        isDocumentValid=false;
        //display the error message
        Console.WriteLine(e.Message);
      }
    }
```

XmlValidatingReader can read a schema document from a Stream or XmlTextReader. Since you are already familiar with the XmlTextReader class, the previous code uses XmlTextReader, which maps to the ISINMaster.xml file. This newly constructed XmlTextReader object is passed as a constructor argument to the XmlValidatingReader class. The next line of code contains the error-handling code. XmlValidatingReader exposes a ValidationEventHandler event that allows the chaining of a user-defined method with the help of a delegate. This event gets bubbled up as soon as the XmlValidationReader notices a structural ambiguity in the current processing node that does not adhere to a defined structure or rules in the schema document. Because we have associated our own custom ValidationEventHandler method with this event, we must have the necessary error handler code in place along with the correct path of the XML document that needs to be validated. The only missing information is the path to the schema file, and that is provided in the next line of code.

XmlValidatingReader provides a Schemas property. This property returns an XmlSchemaCollection object, which is part of the System.Xml.Schema namespace. XmlSchemaCollection allows multiple schema files to be inserted, and each of these schema files can be identified by a unique namespace. In the previous code, the XML document does not contain a namespace; we have passed an empty string as the namespace name along with an absolute path to the schema file. Once the necessary information is provided to the XmlValidatingReader class, the document validation process starts by declaring an empty body loop that traverses one node at a time. From each traversed node, the XmlValidatingReader locates the structural information in the schema document and, if found, validates it for data sanctity. This happens even though you have not placed any code inside the read loop. The exit criteria for this validating loop is reached either when the end of the file is encountered or when a validation exception occurs because of a structural mismatch between the XML document and schema document, which in turn raises the ValidationEventHandler and also internally triggers the registered error handler method. After exiting the loop, to indicate whether the document validation is successful, the value of the static Boolean variable is inspected. If the resulting value is `true`, it indicates that no errors have been flagged by the parser, and hence the document can be considered to be well-formed and valid. A `false` value assigned by the error-handling code indicates an invalid XML document.

The `XmlValidatingReader` class and XML Schema addressed concerns relating to the data sanctity of the ISIN master XML document. Looking closely at the previous code, notice that not even a single line of code checks for node structural ambiguity or node content data type mismatch. You have completely decoupled the data validation logic, expressed it in a schema document, and used `XmlValidatingReader` to do the rest of the validation magic.

In summary, XML Schema is beneficial because it alleviates the need for programmatically validating the content and structure of an XML document. The business community has adopted XML Schema extensively; we all know that to trade, one party needs to sign a business contract with the counterparty. In today's information exchange world where most business is conducted electronically, it is important to have a data contract mutually agreed on by both parties. An XML Schema is basically a kind of a data contract that is shared with all interested parties; based upon this contract, information is prepared and exchanged.

Examining the Business-Technology Mapping

In this section, we will architect a data conversion framework to address the conversion needs. The whole essence of this framework is to offer a service that is easy and friendly to use and brings higher productivity to a developer. Developers no longer have to undergo the painful task of writing parsing code to extract data from an unstructured file, which basically pollutes the code, losing code legibility, and also becomes a daunting task to reverse engineer the logic from code. The most important goal of the conversion framework is to weed out the parsing logic from the code and strongly motivate developers to develop real code by applying the core domain knowledge on the parsed information.

In the financial world, information built on external data sources passes through the following main stages:

Conversion: This is always the first stage and an entry point to this chain. This stage governs the conversion rule that instructs how raw data needs to be managed. The input to this stage is the raw data that is in an unstructured format, and the output from this stage is data in a structured format that is mainly defined by the developer.

Cleansing: The primary responsibility of this layer is to perform data-level validation and fix grammatical errors with the help of reference data. For example, consider the CSV version of the ISIN master file (refer to Listing 3-1), which is converted to a user-defined format. During this conversion process, the ISIN code is validated against the ISIN master repository. Assuming that this repository is a table stored in a relational database and a query of ISIN code in this central database results in an unsuccessful match, instead of completely grinding the process to a halt at this stage by throwing an exception, developers can undertake an alternate route of applying the cleansing technique. By adopting the cleansing path, the ISIN code can be closely matched to the data in the central repository with the help of a pattern-matching algorithm to find a similar ISIN code to replace the wrong ISIN code with the correct code. Additionally, the cleansing process can also propose alternate values for a bad input value and demand user intervention to ensure correct replacement.

Enrichment: The enrichment layer goes hand in hand with the cleansing layer. But the separation is important because the cleansing layer is meant to operate only on data originating from the original source, but in the enrichment stage the information is further augmented by associating additional missing information that did not originate from the actual data source. Using the ISIN master example, if one of the secondary attributes of ISIN, such as the company name, is missing from the comma-delimited version of the file and is required by the business component in the next stage, it can be fetched from the ISIN central repository, packaged with other primary attributes of the ISIN, and dispatched to the final stage.

Business logic: This is the last stage and is the stage in which core business logic is executed. The business logic component always acts on the finished data.

You saw how data passes through these four stages and how each stage morphs the intent of the data in terms of its usage. Each stage, from a technical architecture view, could be realized as independent subcomponents and later integrated to build a complete end-to-end data management solution. Building such a solution is way beyond the scope of this chapter, and hence the scope of this discussion is limited to how to handle the conversion stage, which provides the business logic with the finished data and also introduces data uniformity.

The merit of using uniform data at the business logic layer is even if a new file format is introduced whose data is structurally rearranged, the conversion layer takes care of this format, leaving the business logic undisturbed. By providing uniform data, the business logic is completely oblivious to the underlying data format and representation and can focus on application-centric concerns instead of data-centric concerns.

It is important to clearly lay out the objectives that every framework must address. The following is a list of the important goals of the conversion framework:

- Use XML as a strong foundation to define conversion rules.

- Act as integration middleware to enable EAI.

- Allow bidirectional data movement to facilitate data import and export activities.

- Provide for faster development time.

- Provide support for any arbitrary text file format, such as CSV, fixed length, SWIFT, EDI, and so on.

- Provide a unified API.

- Bring down software maintenance costs.

It is wiser to solve a problem by first looking at it from a higher level and then slowly factoring in each of the granular problems. Such an approach leads to a vivid and watertight design. As a first step in this exercise, let's analyze the various types of file formats described in Table 3-14 that are normally encountered in the financial world. In Table 3-14, a record represents a unit of information and is composed of rows and columns.

Table 3-14. *Various Types of File Formats Encountered in the Financial World*

File Format	Record-Row-Column Cardinality	Example	Description
Delimited	1-1-*	US5949181045,10,10	A record is represented by a single row and multiple columns, but the length of the column is dynamic and determined by a delimiter, which is usually a comma.

File Format	Record-Row-Column Cardinality	Example	Description
Positional	1-1-*	US594918104500100010	A single row with multiple columns representing a record, but each column is of fixed length, and the column values are retrieved by passing the offset position and length of the character that must be extracted.
SWIFT	1-*-1	US5949181045 10 10	Multiple rows with a single column representing a record.
Master-detail	1-*-*	US5949181045,00100010 EXCHANGEASX,12 EXCHANGENASDAQ,13	A master-detail file format is considered to be a complex file format when it comes to parsing. A record in this context is composed of multiple rows and columns with each row representing a different aspect of the information. For example, ISIN information is defined in the first row followed by the local exchange mapping information.

Having looked at the different file formats, you will see one common element; regardless of its representation, every record finally comes down to a row and column matrix, as represented in Figure 3-7.

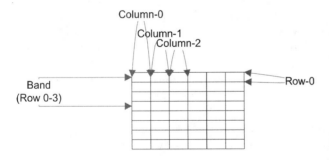

Figure 3-7. *Representation of a record as a matrix*

Data is plotted inside this matrix, and you need to know the proper coordinates—mainly, the row and column position—to access this data. Figure 3-7 depicts a matrix, and each rectangular block inside this matrix stores a series of characters. A *row* represents a collection of *columns* in a horizontal order; similarly, a *band* represents a collection of rows in vertical order. It is necessary to get well-versed with the terms *row*, *column*, and *band* because the following discussion on the framework is based on this concept:

Band: A band is the actual container, and it holds a collection of rows. The decision whether to interpret a particular line in the data source file is determined by the criteria defined at the band level. A band acts as an entry point to the underlying rows and columns; if the current line read from the source file satisfies the band criteria, then the inner row and column is evaluated; else the band is bypassed and skipped to the next band in the chain. The need for this extra shell over rows and columns is to aggregate a collection of rows as a single row. This grouping at the band level comes in handy when the file format is arcane in nature, such as the SWIFT standard, where multiple sections are nested inside a row and each section is an *elastic type*, that is, it can be expanded/collapsed based upon the presence of certain values. The following are important attributes of a band:

- *Identifier*: This attribute is used to search text, which is in turn evaluated by the band to decide whether the inner rows require processing.

- *Loop*: This attribute determines whether the current band supports iterations in the presence of a repetitive value. Iteration is achieved by checking the presence of the `identifier` attribute value in the current processing line. This attribute is useful when the detail rows need to be enumerated line by line. In the case of header and footer lines where the occurrence is only once, the value will be single. To further simplify the loop and identifier concept, let's look at a CSV version of the ISIN master:

```
ISINMASTER12122004
US5949181045,MSFT,10,5,Active
EXCHANGE,NASDAQ,MSFT.O
EXCHANGE,NYSE,MSFT.N
ISINEOF
```

By looking at content, you can visualize four bands altogether. The first band represents the header information, and it is identified by the presence of the `ISINMASTER` text, which also forms the band identifier. Next, you need to find out the number of times the header information is repeated; in this case it is repeated only once at the beginning of file, and therefore the loop attribute value of this band needs to be `single`.

The second band represents ISIN information and contains attributes such as the ISIN code, instrument name, market lot, face value, and instrument status. The ISIN information is identified by the presence of the `US` text that forms the band identifier. Since there will be multiple ISIN information, it is obvious that the loop attribute value of this band will be `repeatable`.

Local exchange information comes under the jurisdiction of the third band, and it is identified by the presence of the `EXCHANGE` text, which is also the band identifier. The loop attribute value of this band will be `repeatable`.

The final band represents the footer information, which is identified by the presence of the `ISINEOF` text. The loop attribute value of this band will be `single`.

- *Start*: This attribute provides the offset position to extract the value of the identifier.

- *Length*: This attribute provides the length of the value of the identifier.

- *Suppress*: A Boolean value of this attribute determines whether to include or exclude data.

Row: A row is similar to a band. Although it inherits all the properties of a band, it is a container for a collection of columns or a *child band*. A child band provides enormous flexibility in the form of recursiveness. It is a perfect candidate to cater to the complex requirements of a master-detail file format. SWIFT-based formats contain various subsections that are a part of a distinct record but are repetitive and dynamic in nature. The effectiveness of a child band is maximized in this kind of scenario. The absence of this feature would have given rise to a lot of common inherent problems associated with SWIFT formats.

Column: A column is the final element in the matrix. Rows and bands are the data pathways to get to a column. Columns encapsulate the real field-level mapping that in turns yields the actual data. The following are the important attributes of a column:

- *Start*: Provides offset position to extract the data.
- *Length*: Provides the length of the data.
- *Suppress*: A Boolean value of this attribute determines whether to include or exclude data.

Moving one step further, it is time to compartmentalize your thought process and start mixing the applicability of XML in the data conversion arena. Figure 3-8 depicts a conceptual end-to-end flow of the conversion framework.

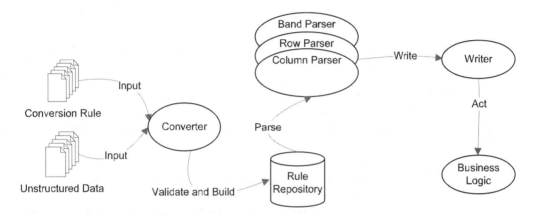

Figure 3-8. *End-to-end flow of a conversion framework*

The central piece of this conceptual model is the converter that knows both sides of the environment. Mainly it has access to all the supporting artifacts that are within the internal conversion framework and also accessible to the external user. External users interact with the converter by feeding two input files. The first file is the primary data file that needs to be converted, and the second file is the rule file that defines the structural representation of the primary file and is embedded with the logic for demystifying the data scattered in the primary file. The rule file is based on the matrix principle described previously. In other words, it contains band-, row-, and column-level information. The rule file is an XML document, and it comprises a series of band, row, and column elements. Each of these elements is further supported by attributes that capture mandatory information associated with them. It is necessary for the rule file to be free from any ambiguous information because this may negatively impact the parsing behavior, resulting in the wrong finished information.

To ensure that rule file is free from errors, an XSD document is created that forms a part of the *rule repository*. This schema document exactly represents the structural content of the rule file and sanitizes the data by enforcing all possible data-level validation. Both the rule file and the schema document are brought together using the XmlTextReader and XmlValidatingReader classes to verify whether the files are well-formed and valid. Using the schema document at this stage proves to be nifty because it saves you from writing a whole bunch of validation code.

The next step is to blend the contents of the rule file in an object representation form so that it can be accessed by the downstream components. The straightforward approach is to read the content using the XmlTextReader class and traverse each node to determine the appropriate node type and assign its value to an object field or property. However, because this method involves writing a large amount of code, you can use the XML serialization technique to achieve the same task. XML serialization eases the coding burden when it comes to deserializing the XML content to an object and provides for a declarative style of programming.

So far you have put all the necessary apparatus in place; you have passed through a battery of checks such as ensuring that the rule file is well-formed and valid and also eventually serializing it into an object. Next you step into the parsing stage, which plays an important role in breaking up the unstructured data and providing it in the finished form. Parsing heavily relies upon the rule information because it is just a driver that blindly drives based on the direction plotted inside the rule file. Three types of parsers are specialized to meet the distinct needs of band, row, and column. The parser reads raw data from the primary data file using the TextReader class and with the help of the rule definition extracts the appropriate chunk of data. This extracted data is then handed over to the writer, which is entrusted with the responsibility of creating the parsed information in a format that can be easily understood by developers creating the business logic component. This extra layer helps developers take advantage of the fact that the final parsed information can be easily molded as per the needs of the technology. The writer can be technically materialized in the following flavors:

> *XML data writer:* This writer enriches the data by surrounding it with angle brackets like XML attributes and elements. The business logic component then fully leverages the capabilities of the built-in XML classes of the .NET Framework to operate on this data. We will bundle this as the default writer of the conversion framework.

> *DataSet writer:* This writer arranges the data in the form of relational table rows and columns, packaging it in the form of a DataSet. The business logic component can then use most of the ADO.NET features to access the data.

Because there are no limits to the different types of writers, the data conversion framework has appropriately outsourced writers as pluggable components instead of providing them as built-in functionality. This opens the door for developers to write their own custom writers that suit their need. Once the writer finishes its job, the business logic can start to process the finished information, completely unaware of the various cycles that the information has gone through to reach this stage.

It is time to use some real code to illustrate this. In the next section, we will use a comma-delimited version of the ISIN master as a real-life example to write a conversion rule that will transform an unstructured format to XML format. This XML format will be considered as the uniform format on which the business logic will depend.

CSV Conversion Rule

The conversion rule described in Listing 3-12 embodies the structural description of the ISIN master CSV file. This rule file is also the technical realization of the conceptual matrix depicted in Figure 3-7—it flawlessly interprets the band, row, and column concept. A row is sandwiched between a band, and a column is placed between rows. Both the header information and the footer information in the CSV file are repeated once, so the loop attribute of their band is assigned a single value. The detail band is interesting; its loop attribute is marked repeatable, and it nests both a row and a child band named Exchanges. This child band iterates over all exchange-related rows. The identifier attribute available at the band or row level acts as a marker, and with its help, the parser interprets information correctly and knows where to draw an end-of-information (EOI) mark.

Listing 3-12. *ISIN Master CSV Conversion Rule File*

```
<?xml version="1.0" encoding="utf-8" ?>
<matrix>
<bands>
  <band name="Header" identifier="ISINMASTER" start="0" loop="single">
  <rows>
    <row name="HeaderInfo" identifier="" length="0" coldelimeter="">
```

```
        <cols>
          <col name="InfoDateTime" length="7" start="11"/>
        </cols>
        </row>
      </rows>
    </band>
    <band name="Detail" identifier="US" start="0" loop="repeatable">
    <rows>
      <row name="ISIN" identifier="" length="0" coldelimeter=",">
      <cols>
        <col name="ISINCode"  length="12" start="0"/>
        <col name="Symbol"    length="12" start="0"/>
        <col name="FaceValue" length="12" start="0"/>
        <col name="MarketLot" length="12" start="0"/>
        <col name="Status"    length="12" start="0"/>
      </cols>
      </row>
      <row>
        <band name="Exchanges" identifier="EXCHANGE" start="0" loop="repeatable">
        <rows>
          <row name="Exchange" identifier="" length="0" coldelimeter=",">
          <cols>
            <col name="ExchangeTag" length="12" start="0"/>
            <col name="Code" length="12" start="0"/>
            <col name="ScripCode" length="12" start="0"/>
          </cols>
          </row>
        </rows>
        </band>
      </row>
    </rows>
    </band>
    <band name="Footer" identifier="ISINEOF" start="0" loop="single">
    <rows>
      <row name="FooterInfo" identifier="" length="0" coldelimeter="">
      <cols>
        <col name="FooterTag" length="7" start="0"/>
      </cols>
      </row>
    </rows>
    </band>
  </bands>
</matrix>
```

Rule Schema

The following XSD dictates both the content and structural layout of the conversion rule file. Rule
files are first validated against this schema before forwarding it to the parsing stage.

```
<?xml version="1.0" encoding="UTF-8" ?>
<xs:schema xmlns:xs="http://www.w3.org/2001/XmlSchema"
           elementFormDefault="qualified">
  <xs:simpleType name="IntAttribute">
    <xs:restriction base="xs:int" />
  </xs:simpleType>
  <xs:complexType name="bandType">
    <xs:sequence>
```

```xml
      <xs:element name="rows" type="rowsType" />
   </xs:sequence>
   <xs:attribute name="name" type="xs:string" use="required" />
   <xs:attribute name="identifier" type="xs:string" use="required" />
   <xs:attribute name="start" type="IntAttribute" use="required" />
   <xs:attribute name="loop" type="LoopDataType" use="required" />
   <xs:attribute name="suppress" type="xs:boolean" use="optional" />
 </xs:complexType>
 <xs:simpleType name="LoopDataType">
   <xs:restriction base="xs:string">
     <xs:enumeration value="single" />
     <xs:enumeration value="repeatable" />
   </xs:restriction>
 </xs:simpleType>
 <xs:complexType name="bandsType">
   <xs:sequence>
     <xs:element name="band" type="bandType" maxOccurs="unbounded" />
   </xs:sequence>
 </xs:complexType>
 <xs:complexType name="colType">
   <xs:attribute name="name" type="xs:string" use="required" />
   <xs:attribute name="length" type="IntAttribute" use="required" />
   <xs:attribute name="start" type="IntAttribute" use="required" />
   <xs:attribute name="suppress" type="xs:boolean" use="optional" />
 </xs:complexType>
 <xs:complexType name="colsType">
   <xs:sequence>
     <xs:element name="col" type="colType" maxOccurs="unbounded" />
   </xs:sequence>
 </xs:complexType>
 <xs:element name="matrix">
   <xs:complexType>
     <xs:sequence>
       <xs:element name="bands" type="bandsType" />
     </xs:sequence>
   </xs:complexType>
 </xs:element>
 <xs:complexType name="rowType">
   <xs:choice>
     <xs:element name="cols" type="colsType" />
     <xs:element name="band" type="bandType" />
   </xs:choice>
   <xs:attribute name="name" type="xs:string" use="optional" />
   <xs:attribute name="identifier" type="xs:string" use="optional" />
   <xs:attribute name="length" type="IntAttribute" use="optional" />
   <xs:attribute name="coldelimeter" type="xs:string" use="optional" />
   <xs:attribute name="suppress" type="xs:boolean" use="optional" />
 </xs:complexType>
 <xs:complexType name="rowsType">
   <xs:sequence>
     <xs:element name="row" type="rowType" maxOccurs="unbounded" />
   </xs:sequence>
 </xs:complexType>
</xs:schema>
```

Class Details

Figure 3-9 shows the data conversion framework class diagram, and Figure 3-10 shows the data conversion framework project structure.

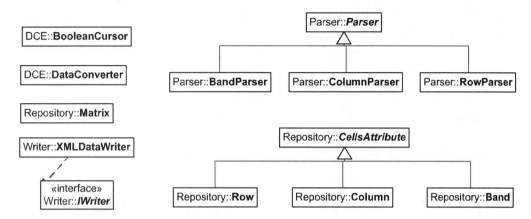

Figure 3-9. *Data conversion framework class diagram*

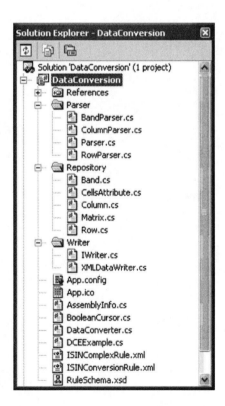

Figure 3-10. *Data conversion framework project structure*

CellsAttribute

CellsAttribute is an abstract class inherited by the Band, Row, and Column classes. The intent of this abstract class is to group all common properties.

This is the CellsAttribute class:

```
using System;
using System.Xml.Serialization;
namespace DCE.Repository
{
  public abstract class CellsAttribute
  {
    private string  dataIdentifer;
    private int  offSet;
    private string name;
    private int  index;
    private int  dataLength;
    private CellsAttribute  parentCell;
    private bool isSuppressed;

    [XmlIgnore]
    public CellsAttribute ParentCell
    {
      get{return  parentCell;}
      set{ parentCell= value;}
    }

    [XmlIgnore]
    public int Index
    {
      get{return  index;}
      set{ index=value;}
    }

    [XmlAttribute("name")]
    public string Name
    {
      get{return  name;}
      set{ name= value;}
    }

    [XmlAttribute("identifier")]
    public string Identifier
    {
      get{return  dataIdentifer;}
      set{ dataIdentifer=value;}
    }

    [XmlAttribute("start")]
    public int Start
    {
      get{return  offSet;}
      set{ offSet= value;}
    }
```

```
    [XmlAttribute("length")]
    public int Length
    {
      get{return  dataLength;}
      set{ dataLength = value;}
    }

    [XmlAttribute("suppress")]
    public bool IsSuppressed
    {
      get{return  isSuppressed;}
      set{ isSuppressed= value;}
    }

  }
}
```

Band

The Band class is an object-oriented representation of the band element defined in the conversion rule file. It is inherited from the CellsAttribute abstract class and introduces some additional attributes specific to the band.

This is the Band class:

```
using System;
using System.Xml.Serialization;

namespace DCE.Repository
{
  public enum LoopType
  {
    [XmlEnum("repeatable")]
    Repeatable,
    [XmlEnum("single")]
    Single
  }

  public class Band : CellsAttribute
  {
    private Row[] rows = {};
    private LoopType loopMode;

    public Band()
    {
    }

    [XmlAttribute("loop")]
    public LoopType LoopMode
    {
      get{return loopMode;}
      set{loopMode=value;}
    }
```

```
    [XmlArray("rows")]
    [XmlArrayItem("row",typeof(Row))]
    public Row[] Rows
    {
      get{return rows;}
      set{rows = value;}
    }
  }
}
```

Row

The Row class is an object-oriented representation of the row element defined in the conversion rule file.

This is the Row class:

```
using System;
using System.Xml.Serialization;

namespace DCE.Repository
{
  public class Row  : CellsAttribute
  {
    private Column[] columns = {};
    private Band childBand;
    private string colDelimeter;

    public Row()
    {
    }

    [XmlAttribute("coldelimeter")]
    public string ColDelimeter
    {
      get{return colDelimeter;}
      set{colDelimeter=value;}
    }

    [XmlElement("band")]
    public Band ChildBand
    {
      get{return childBand;}
      set{childBand= value;}
    }

    [XmlArray("cols")]
    [XmlArrayItem("col",typeof(Column))]
    public Column[] Columns
    {
      get{return columns;}
      set{columns= value;}
    }
  }
}
```

Column

The Column class is an object-oriented representation of the column element defined in the conversion rule file.

This is the Column class:

```
using System;
using System.Xml.Serialization;
using System.Runtime.InteropServices;

namespace DCE.Repository
{
  public class Column : CellsAttribute
  {
    private string dataPrefix;

    public Column()
    {
    }

    [XmlAttribute("prefix")]
    public string Prefix
    {
      get{return dataPrefix;}
      set{dataPrefix = value;}
    }
  }
}
```

Matrix

The Matrix class represents an object-oriented form of the dce element, which is a root container. This class acts as a surrogate container for the collection of all bands, and therefore there is no need to inherit it from the CellsAttribute class.

This is the Matrix class:

```
using System;
using System.Xml.Serialization;

namespace DCE.Repository
{
  [XmlRoot("matrix")]
  public class Matrix
  {
    private Band[] bands = {};
    public Matrix()
    {
    }

    [XmlArray("bands")]
    [XmlArrayItem("band",typeof(Band))]
    public Band[] Bands
    {
      get{return bands;}
      set{bands = value;}
    }
  }
}
```

All the classes discussed so far belong to the illustrated conceptual matrix depicted in Figure 3-7. Each class maps to a particular section of the conversion rule file and is appropriately annotated with a serialization attribute. Certain properties, specifically ParentCell and Index of the CellAttribute class, are ignored during the serialization phase. The purpose of both these properties is explained in the DataConverter class.

BooleanCursor

BooleanCursor is the internal data source reader class of the data conversion framework. This class supplies unstructured data to the framework; basically, it reads data from the source file. BooleanCursor is the equivalent of a Boolean variable that can hold two specific states. Thus, BooleanCursor also stores two copies of data. The first copy represents the previously read data, and the final copy represents the latest read data. Using such a caching technique is extremely beneficial and provides the in-memory file-seeking capability.

This is the BooleanCursor class:

```
using System;
using System.Collections;
using System.IO;

namespace DCE
{
  public class BooleanCursor
  {
    private TextReader _dataReader;
    private string[] _data;
    private int _readCounter = 0;

    public BooleanCursor(TextReader dataSource)
    {
      _dataReader = dataSource;
      _data = new string[2];
      _readCounter = 1;
    }

    public TextReader BaseReader
    {
      get{return _dataReader;}
    }

    public string Previous()
    {
      _readCounter = 0 ;
      return _data[_readCounter];
    }

    public string Next()
    {
      if ( _readCounter == 0 )
      {
        _readCounter = 1;
      }
      else
      {
        _readCounter = 1;
        _data[0] = _data[1];
```

```
        _data[1] = _dataReader.ReadLine();
      }
      return _data[_readCounter];
    }
  }
}
```

Parser

The Parser class groups all the common behavior that a parser should provide, specifically the abstract Parse method. RowParser, ColumnParser, and BandParser are inherited from this abstract class and override the Parse method by supplying a concrete implementation. The concrete Parser class is driven by the information provided to them. This information is none other than the conversion rule that is wrapped inside the Matrix class.

This is the Parser class:

```
using System;
using DCE.Repository;
using DCE;

namespace DCE.Parser
{
  public abstract class Parser
  {
    private string  data;
    private BooleanCursor  dataReader;
    private CellsAttribute cellInfo;

    public Parser(BooleanCursor reader)
    {
      dataReader = reader;
    }

    //The value of this property governs the entire parsing process.
    //It represents the conversion rule and must be a Band or Row or Column class.
    public CellsAttribute CellsAttribute
    {
      get{return cellInfo;}
      set{cellInfo = value;}
    }

    //This property gives the parser class access to the
    //underlying information data source.
    public BooleanCursor Reader
    {
      get{return  dataReader;}
    }

    //Parser needs to have access to the raw data before it
    //could apply its parsing logic. It is with the help of this property that
    //data is retrieved or assigned.
    public string Data
    {
      get{return  data;}
      set{ data = value;}
    }
```

```
  public abstract bool Parse();
  }
}
```

BandParser

BandParser provides the concrete implementation of parsing the band section of the conversion rule file.

This is the BandParser class:

```
using System;
using System.IO;
using DCE.Repository;
using DCE;

namespace DCE.Parser
{
  public class BandParser : Parser
  {
    private int _iterationCount = 0;

    public BandParser(BooleanCursor dataReader, string data,
                      CellsAttribute cellInfo) :base(dataReader)
    {
      this.Data = data;
      this.CellsAttribute = cellInfo;
    }

    public override bool Parse()
    {
      //Retrieve the band information
      Band curBand = (Band)CellsAttribute;

      //If data to be processed is null, then terminate the parsing
      if ( Data == null )
        return false;

      //Referring to the band section, specifically the loop attribute,
      //if the current loop mode is single, then it needs to process
      //only once for the current section.
      if ( curBand.LoopMode == LoopType.Single)
      {
        if ( _iterationCount >= 1 )
        {
          _iterationCount  = 0 ;
          Reader.Previous();
          return false;
        }
        else
        {
          _iterationCount++;
          return true;
        }
      }
```

```
        //If the loop attribute is of repeatable type, then it
        //evaluates data for the presence of an identifier-defined band
        //section of the conversion rule file. If parser is not able to
        //locate the identifier in the data, then it resets the
        //read pointer of the data source to its previous location by
        //invoking the Previous member of the BooleanCursor class.
        if ( curBand.LoopMode == LoopType.Repeatable)
        {
          if ( ( curBand.Identifier.Length <= Data.Length - curBand.Start ) &&
                  Data.Substring(curBand.Start,curBand.Identifier.Length) ==
                                              curBand.Identifier )
          {
            return true;
          }
          Reader.Previous();
        }
        _iterationCount = 0 ;
        return false;
      }
    }
}
```

RowParser

RowParser provides a concrete implementation of parsing the row section of the conversion rule file.

This is the RowParser class:

```
using System;
using DCE;
using DCE.Repository;

namespace DCE.Parser
{
  public class RowParser : Parser
  {
    public RowParser(BooleanCursor dataReader,
                     string data, CellsAttribute cellInfo)
    :base(dataReader)
    {
      this.Data = data;
      this.CellsAttribute = cellInfo;
    }

    public override bool Parse()
    {
      //The parser checks for the presence of a identifier
      //defined in the row section of rule file. If the parser is
      //not able to locate the identifier in the data, then it
      //resets the read pointer of the data source to its previous
      //location by invoking the Previous member of the BooleanCursor class.
      if ( CellsAttribute.Identifier.Length > 0 &&
          Data.Substring(CellsAttribute.Start,CellsAttribute.Length) !=
                      CellsAttribute.Identifier )
      {
        Reader.Previous();
        return false;
      }
```

```
        return true;
      }
    }
  }
```

ColumnParser

ColumnParser provides a concrete implementation of parsing the col section of the conversion rule file.

This is the ColumnParser class:

```
using System;
using DCE.Repository;
using DCE;

namespace DCE.Parser
{
  public class ColumnParser : Parser
  {
    private string[] splittedData;

    public ColumnParser(BooleanCursor dataReader)
    :base(dataReader)
    {
    }

    public override bool Parse()
    {
      Row curRow = (Row)CellsAttribute.ParentCell;
      //This is the final processing logic in the parsing chain.
      //A check is performed to see whether a column delimiter has
      //been specified. If a column delimiter is found, then a Split
      //operation is performed that splits out an array of strings based
      //on the character delimiter passed to it. The array of string returned
      //from the Split operation is assigned to the array. This splitting process
      //is conducted only once - during the parsing of first column - and
      //subsequent access to data is retrieved from a cached array.
      if (curRow.ColDelimeter.Length > 0 )
      {
        if ( this.CellsAttribute.Index == 1 )
          splittedData = Data.Split(curRow.ColDelimeter.ToCharArray());
        this.Data = splittedData[this.CellsAttribute.Index - 1];
      }
      else
      {
        //If there is no delimiter specified, then it is assumed that it is a
        //fixed-length file format, and data is retrieved using the offset position
        //and length of data.
        this.Data =
            this.Data.Substring(CellsAttribute.Start,CellsAttribute.Length);
      }
      return true;
    }
  }
}
```

IWriter

IWriter is the interface implemented by the concrete data writer class. The responsibility of this class is to furnish finished information that is in turn submitted to the business logic component. Using this interface ensures full cooperation by concrete classes that provide real code implementation. This interface is referenced by the Parser class to invoke the appropriate operation during important stages of parsing.

This is the IWriter class:

```
using System;
using System.IO;
using DCE.Repository;
using DCE.Parser;

namespace DCE.Writer
{
  public interface IWriter
  {
    //This paired method is invoked by ColumnParser during the parsing phase
    void WriteStartColumn(CellsAttribute metaDataInfo, string data);
    void WriteEndColumn(CellsAttribute metaDataInfo);
    //This paired method is invoked by RowParser during the parsing phase
    void WriteStartRow(CellsAttribute metaDataInfo,string data);
    void WriteEndRow(CellsAttribute metaDataInfo);
    //This paired method is invoked by BandParser during the parsing phase
    void WriteStartBand(CellsAttribute metaDataInfo,string data);
    void WriteEndBand(CellsAttribute metaDataInfo);
    TextWriter BaseWriter{get;}
  }
}
```

XmlDataWriter

XmlDataWriter realizes a concrete XML writer and annotates semifinished data with elements and attributes to produce the finished information.

This is the XmlDataWriter class:

```
using System;
using System.Xml;
using System.IO;
using DCE.Repository;
using DCE.Parser;

namespace DCE.Writer
{
  public class XmlDataWriter: IWriter
  {
    private XmlTextWriter xmlWriter;
    private TextWriter baseWriter;

    public XmlDataWriter(TextWriter dataWriter)
    {
      xmlWriter = new XmlTextWriter(dataWriter);
      xmlWriter.Formatting=  Formatting.Indented;
      xmlWriter.Indentation = 4;
      baseWriter = dataWriter;
    }
```

```csharp
    public void WriteStartColumn(CellsAttribute metaDataInfo, string data)
    {
      if ( metaDataInfo.IsSuppressed == true ) return;
      xmlWriter.WriteStartAttribute(metaDataInfo.Name,"");
      xmlWriter.WriteString(data);
    }

    public void WriteEndColumn(CellsAttribute metaDataInfo)
    {
      if ( metaDataInfo.IsSuppressed == true ) return;
      Row rowCell = metaDataInfo.ParentCell as Row;
      xmlWriter.WriteEndAttribute();
    }

    public void WriteStartRow(CellsAttribute metaDataInfo, string data)
    {
      if ( metaDataInfo.IsSuppressed == true ) return;
        xmlWriter.WriteStartElement(metaDataInfo.Name);
    }

    public void WriteEndRow(CellsAttribute metaDataInfo)
    {
      if ( metaDataInfo.IsSuppressed == true ) return;
      xmlWriter.WriteEndElement();
    }

    public void WriteStartBand(CellsAttribute metaDataInfo, string data)
    {
      if ( metaDataInfo.IsSuppressed == true ) return;
      xmlWriter.WriteStartElement(metaDataInfo.Name);
    }

    public void WriteEndBand(CellsAttribute metaDataInfo)
    {
      if ( metaDataInfo.IsSuppressed == true ) return;
      xmlWriter.WriteEndElement();
    }

    public TextWriter BaseWriter
    {
      get{return baseWriter;}
    }
  }
}
```

DataConverter

DataConverter is the facade class that is visible to the outside world. The responsibility of this class is to dovetail the classes discussed so far by instantiating them and initializing them with an appropriate state. The important member in this class is Convert, which kicks off the conversion stage. On its successful completion, this method gathers the finished data with the help of an underlying stream wrapped inside the XmlDataWriter class.

This is the DataConverter class:

```csharp
using System;
using System.IO;
using System.Xml.Serialization;
```

```
using DCE.Repository;
using DCE.Parser;
using DCE;
using DCE.Writer;
using System.Xml;
using System.Xml.Schema;
using System.Configuration;

namespace DCE
{
  public class DataConverter
  {
    private Matrix  dceSchema;
    private IWriter  dataWriter;
    private BooleanCursor  dataReader;
    private string ruleFile;
    private string ruleSchema;

    public DataConverter(string rulePath,string ruleSchemaPath)
    {
      //Rule file is validated with a framework schema file
      //that checks for well-formed characteristics and conformity,
      //ensuring that all mandatory attributes/elements are present
      //and arranged in a defined order.
      ruleFile = rulePath;
      ruleSchema = ruleSchemaPath;

      XmlTextReader xmlRule = new XmlTextReader(ruleFile);
      XmlValidatingReader xsdSchema = new XmlValidatingReader(xmlRule);
      xsdSchema.ValidationEventHandler +=new
                ValidationEventHandler(xsdSchema_ValidationEventHandler);
      xsdSchema.Schemas.Add("", ruleSchema);
      while(xsdSchema .Read()){}

      xsdSchema.Close();
      xmlRule.Close();

      //Rules stored in Xml file are dehydrated
      //in an object representation format.
      FileStream schemaStream = new FileStream(rulePath, FileMode.Open);
      XmlSerializer schemaSz = new XmlSerializer(typeof(Matrix));
      dceSchema = (Matrix)schemaSz.Deserialize(schemaStream );
      schemaStream.Close();

      //This loop invokes the AssignIndex function that
      //assigns a running sequence number to every instance of the Band, Row, and
      //Column objects. This sequence number is assigned recursively to the Index
      //property of CellsAttribute. There is no way to capture this information
      //during the deserialization stage; therefore, it needs to be manually assigned.
      foreach ( Band curBand in dceSchema.Bands)
      {
        AssignIndex(curBand);
      }

    }
```

```
public void Convert(BooleanCursor reader,IWriter writer)
{
  dataWriter = writer;
  dataReader = reader;

  //Parsing kicks off with the invocation of this method.
  //The parsing code has been packaged inside the ConvertBand, ConvertRow, and
  //ConvertCol methods. These methods instantiate an appropriate parser, and
  //based on the return value of Parse method, it invokes
  //the Writer WriteXXX method.
  foreach ( Band curBand in  dceSchema.Bands )
  {
    ConvertBand(curBand, dataReader.Next());
  }

  //Close the underlying reader and writer
  dataReader.BaseReader.Close();
  dataWriter.BaseWriter.Close();
}

private void ConvertBand(Band band,string data)
{
  //This method is responsible for the initiating parsing of the
  //band section. A new instance of band parser is created
  //by passing the current data and band information
  BandParser bandParser;
  bandParser = new BandParser( dataReader,data,band);
  //loop until data contains the appropriate band identifer
  while ( bandParser.Parse()== true )
  {
    //invoke the writer band start method
    dataWriter.WriteStartBand(band,bandParser.Data);
    //iterate through individual row of band
    foreach ( Row row in band.Rows)
    {
      //a row can be a child band
      //if it is, then a recursive call to CovertBand
      //is triggered
      if ( row.ChildBand != null )
        ConvertBand(row.ChildBand,data);
      else
        ConvertRow(row,data);
      //get the next data
      data =  dataReader.Next();
    }
    //invoke the writer band end method
    dataWriter.WriteEndBand(band);
    bandParser.Data = data;
  }
}

private void ConvertRow(Row row,string data)
{
  //This method is responsible for initiating the parsing of
  //row section. A new instance of row parser is created
  //by passing the current data and row information
```

```
    RowParser rowParser = new RowParser( dataReader,data,row);
    //invoke the writer band start method
    dataWriter.WriteStartRow(row, rowParser.Data);
    //invoke row parser
    if (  rowParser.Parse() == false )
    {
      //if there is no matching data found based on the row identifier,
      //then bypass the column processing and invoke
      //the writer row end method
      dataWriter.WriteEndRow(row);
      return ;
    }
    //initiate the column parsing
    ColumnParser colParser  = new ColumnParser(dataReader);
    //iterate through individual columns
    //and process the column level information
    foreach ( Column col in row.Columns)
    {
      colParser.Data = data;
      colParser.CellsAttribute = col;
      ConvertCol(row,col,data,colParser);
    }
    //invoke the writer row end method
    dataWriter.WriteEndRow(row);

}

private void AssignIndex(Band curBand)
{
  if ( curBand == null ) return ;

  int rowIndex;
  int colIndex;
  rowIndex=1;
  foreach(Row curRow in curBand.Rows)
  {
    curRow.Index = rowIndex;
    curRow.ParentCell= curBand;
    AssignIndex(curRow.ChildBand);
    colIndex=1;
    foreach(Column curCol in curRow.Columns)
    {
      curCol.Index = colIndex;
      curCol.ParentCell= curRow;
      colIndex++;
    }
    rowIndex++;
  }
}

private void ConvertCol(Row row,Column col,string data,ColumnParser colParser)
{
  //This method is responsible for initiating the parsing of
  //column section
  colParser.Parse();
  //invoke writer column start and end method
```

```
        dataWriter.WriteStartColumn(col, colParser.Data);
        dataWriter.WriteEndColumn(col);
      }

      private void xsdSchema_ValidationEventHandler(object sender,
                                                    ValidationEventArgs e)
      {
        throw new ApplicationException(e.Message);
      }
    }
}
```

Conversion Example

The following sample code illustrates a data conversion example. Before invoking the Convert method of the DataConverter class, it instantiates an appropriate reader and writer object and passes the newly created instance to the Convert method.

```
using System;
using System.IO;
using System.Configuration;
using System.Xml.Serialization;
using DCE.Repository;
using DCE.Parser;
using DCE.Writer;
using DCE;

namespace DCE
{
  class DCEExample
  {
    [STAThread]
    static void Main(string[] args)
    {
      string filePath = @"C:\CodeExample\Chpt3\Framework\";
      //Assign the framework rule schema
      string ruleSchema = filePath +"RuleSchema.xsd";
      //ISIN Master - comma-separated
      BooleanCursor dataRdr = new BooleanCursor(new
                  StreamReader(filePath +"CSVISINMaster.csv"));
      //Create XML data writer
      XmlDataWriter dataWrt= new XmlDataWriter(new StringWriter());
      //Instantiate Data Converter passing the ISIN conversion rule file
      DataConverter _dataConverter= new DataConverter(
                  filePath +"ISINConversionRule.xml",ruleSchema );
      //Start of conversion phase
      _dataConverter.Convert(dataRdr,dataWrt);
      //Display XML output
      Console.WriteLine(dataWrt.BaseWriter.ToString());
    }
  }
}
```

XML Output

The following is the finished data produced by the parser based on the rule defined in the conversion rule file (see Listing 3-12):

```
<Header>
  <HeaderInfo InfoDateTime="2122004" />
</Header>
<Detail>
  <ISIN ISINCode="US5949181045" Symbol="MSFT" FaceValue="10"
                                MarketLot="5" Status="Active" />
    <Exchanges>
      <Exchange ExchangeTag="EXCHANGE" Code="NASDAQ" ScripCode="MSFT.O" />
    </Exchanges>
    <Exchanges>
      <Exchange ExchangeTag="EXCHANGE" Code="NYSE" ScripCode="MSFT.N" />
    </Exchanges>
</Detail>
<Footer>
  <FooterInfo FooterTag="ISINEOF" />
</Footer>
```

The previous XML output doesn't reproduce the ISIN master XML format described in Listing 3-2. We did this for demonstration purposes. We purposely shaped our conversion rule file in such a fashion where every section (that is, band, row, and col) can get its share of pie in the final generated XML document.

Refined Conversion Rule

The whole concept of a matrix upon which the conversion framework is cemented is so rigorous that almost all kinds of file formats can be conceptualized and easily materialized. To prove this, we paid a second visit to the conversion rule and refined it to produce XML output that matches the format described in Listing 3-2.

Here's the code:

```
<?xml version="1.0" encoding="utf-8" ?>
<matrix>
  <bands>
    <band name="ISINMaster" identifier="ISINMASTER" start="0" loop="single"
                                                     suppress="false">
      <rows>
        <row name="HeaderInfo" identifier="" length="0"
             coldelimeter="" suppress="true">
          <cols>
            <col name="InfoDateTime" length-"7" start="11" suppress="true"/>
          </cols>
        </row>
        <row>
          <band name="ISIN" identifier="US" start="0"
                loop="repeatable" suppress="false">
            <rows>
              <row name="ISIN" identifier="" length="0"
                   coldelimeter="," suppress="true">
                <cols>
                  <col name="ISINCode" length="12" start="0"/>
                  <col name="Symbol"   length="12" start="0"/>
                  <col name="FaceValue" length="12" start="0"/>
                  <col name="MarketLot" length="12" start="0"/>
```

```
                        <col name="Status"     length="12" start="0"/>
                    </cols>
                </row>
                <row>
                  <band name="Exchanges" identifier="EXCHANGE" start="0"
                        loop="repeatable" suppress="false">
                    <rows>
                      <row>
                        <band name="Exchanges" identifier="EXCHANGE" start="0"
                              loop="repeatable" suppress="true">
                          <rows>
                            <row name="Exchange" identifier=""
                                 length="0" coldelimeter="," >
                              <cols>
                                <col name="ExchangeTag" length="12" start="0"/>
                                <col name="Code" length="12" start="0"/>
                                <col name="ScripCode" length="12" start="0"/>
                              </cols>
                            </row>
                          </rows>
                        </band>
                      </row>
                    </rows>
                  </band>
                </row>
              </rows>
            </band>
          </row>
        </rows>
      </band>
      <band name="Footer" identifier="ISINEOF" start="0" loop="single"
                                                         suppress="true">
        <rows>
          <row name="FooterInfo" identifier="" length="0" coldelimeter=""
                                                           suppress="true">
            <cols>
              <col name="FooterTag" length="7" start="0" suppress="true"/>
            </cols>
          </row>
        </rows>
      </band>
    </bands>
</matrix>
```

XML Output

Here's the XML output:

```
<ISINMaster>
  <ISIN ISINCode="US5949181045" Symbol="MSFT" FaceValue="10"
        MarketLot="5" Status="Active">
    <Exchanges>
      <Exchange ExchangeTag="EXCHANGE" Code="NASDAQ" ScripCode="MSFT.O" />
      <Exchange ExchangeTag="EXCHANGE" Code="NYSE" ScripCode="MSFT.N" />
    </Exchanges>
  </ISIN>
</ISINMaster>
```

Summary

In this chapter, we covered the following key points:

- Data is the lifeblood of an organization, and the success of an organization depends on the quality of the data it possesses. Data related to securities, prices, market conditions, clients, and trades is used by various trading applications for the fulfillment of trades. Data comes from a variety of sources, and this leads to a data conversion problem where data taken from one system needs to be migrated to another.

- We illustrated the power of XML and how it can act as the glue in enabling data integration among heterogeneous systems.

- We covered the XML classes in the .NET Framework that allow the parsing, reading, and writing of XML documents.

- We explained the benefit of XSD and how it can be used to define and validate the structure of an XML document.

- We provided a basic overview of the declarative style of programming and how it is being leveraged by the XML serializer to convert in-memory objects to XML representation formats.

- We designed a data conversion framework that is built upon XML and supports the conversion of an unstructured text file format to XML format.

■ ■ ■

CHAPTER 4

The Broadcast Engine

99 *percent perspiration + 1 percent luck = 100 percent success*

In this chapter, we explain what *market data* is and its importance in the trading world. Market data reflects information about the performance of an organization as a whole; several actors in the trading world depend upon this information. The important fact about this information is that it is time critical. Furthermore, market data information requires no further intelligence or any kind of sophisticated processing; it just needs to be forwarded from one end to another. Such data forwarding demands a good amount of groundwork from systems that utilize a network communication library, which forms the basis of this chapter's technical sections; we will discuss various aspects of the network programming model in detail.

What Is Market Data?

Financial engineers, dealers, and traders require timely and accurate information about the securities they trade in so they can arrive at a proper price for them. Changing market scenarios and world events keep altering perceptions about the value of financial assets, and hence these factors also change their prices. For most financial assets, these changes are so fast that they translate into price changes every second. Every change in price represents an opportunity for dealers to either buy these assets and build more positions or sell these assets and square these positions to book profit or loss. Dealers and traders whose positions run into the millions of dollars pay special attention to these changing scenarios, which could change the prices of assets they hold or intend to trade in. The moment they see a rate favorable to them, they buy the asset and dispose of it when they have reasons to believe that they are overpriced. These perceptions and beliefs that dealers have about financial assets are made possible by the market data available to them (of course, their judgment is also a key contributor) through an exchange trading system or through other third-party market data service providers such as Reuters, Bloomberg, Moneyline Telerate, and so on.

Market data can be defined as information that traders need for analysis to make informed trading decisions while trading in a market. Since the scope of this book is equities only, we will cover the market data requirements and associated issues for equities. Going by the definition, you can classify the following information as market data:

- Quotes such as bid/offer rates for a particular financial instrument (including stocks, bonds, derivatives, and so on) that is either traded in a market such as an exchange or available for transaction in an interbank or other financial market

- News such as earnings reports, raw news, senior management speeches, and any other information that could impact the profitability and in turn stock prices

- Macro- and micro-economic data and related analysis relating to gross domestic product (GDP), gross national product (GNP), employment ratios, import and export figures, fiscal deficit, and other economic data

- Analyst reports/opinions on stocks, bonds, and other investment instruments

- News about competitors and related information

Market data is normally provided in the form of a broadcast to its subscribed recipients. This broadcast is provided either by exchanges or by third-party market data service providers. The timely receipt of market data is one of the highest priorities for any institution's information technology (IT) and dealing rooms. Stale information could mean delayed action and missed opportunities for the institution; hence, a lot of emphasis is put on obtaining this data on a real-time basis.

Participants in the Market Data Industry

The following are the participants in the market data industry:

Stock exchanges: Stock exchanges are one of the prime generators of market data. They constantly broadcast the prevailing rates of all securities traded on that exchange, as well as volume and depth information. Most exchanges also provide data about the total number of trades, the number of securities advanced in a day, the number of declines, the total volume of transactions, the total percentage of transactions that resulted in delivery, and so on. All this information is useful for traders, analysts, and brokers who have an interest in the securities listed and traded on that stock exchange. Most exchanges sell this data either directly or through other market data service providers such as Reuters and Bloomberg. This is a major source of revenue for many exchanges. Some exchanges are known to earn about 35 percent of their annual revenues through the sale of market data. Since the generation of this data is continuous and a lot of trading interest is built on these exchanges, many firms subscribe to these data services.

Issuers: Since most trading interest is centered on corporate- and government-issued securities, any news related to the performance of corporate changes in prices of their finished goods or raw materials, the fiscal position of the country, and micro- and macro-economic issues forms part of market data. Issuers do not sell market data proactively. Their actions—such as issuing bonuses, issuing rights, consolidating/splitting shares, conducting mergers, and so on—become news. Data related to these actions (also called *corporate action*) becomes relevant market data.

Market data providers: These are agencies/companies that collect data from various sources, do some value addition on it, and send it as a broadcast to all subscribed recipients. Some examples of market data service providers are Reuters, Thomson Financials, Moneyline Telerate, and Bloomberg. These service providers provide data in multiple formats: news broadcasts, streaming quotes, messages, XML dumps, messages on mobile phones, messages on PDAs, and streaming video. Data service providers normally have two kinds of services: delayed and real time. Delayed data has multiple types; data with 5-minute, 10-minute, 15-minute, and 20-minute delays is the most common. Real-time data is far more expensive than delayed data. This distinction exists to provide services at a lower cost to institutions that don't need real-time data.

Recipients: These are institutions/people who are the consumers of market data. They are normally institutions that trade and maintain positions across various markets such as fixed-income securities, foreign exchanges, equities, commodities, and related derivatives. These institutions normally trade across markets in several countries and hence look for service providers that can give them data across various markets, exchanges, and countries. They either analyze raw data mentally or put it through a system that analyzes raw market data and converts it to a meaningful and usable form.

Example of Market Data

Figure 4-1 could qualify as an example of market data.

Stock	Volume	Value	Change	
CPN	160,211,200	$0.28	30.00%	⇩
GE	25,442,60	$35.50	0.70%	⇩
LU	22,354,700	$2.83	0.35%	⇧

Figure 4-1. *Market data (Source:* http://www.nyse.com; *December 2, 2005)*

Role of Market Data

Market data has a lot of meaning and importance to professionals across the financial trading value chain. An institution buys market data to support professionals employed in that institution and to provide them with high-quality information that enables them to make informed decisions. Judgments based on information that is derived from quality data could be superior when compared to those based on low-quality data or data that is not timely in nature.

Market data is important for professionals engaged in the following areas:

- Analysis
- Trading and dealing
- Risk management
- Back office and settlement

Analysts need a lot of information for the valuation of a particular stock. They analyze past dividend statistics, latest earning figures, and news and couple all that with their own judgment about the industry and company to arrive at the future cash flows of a company. Using this kind of market data, they are in a reasonably informed position to arrive at the overall valuation of the company. They also analyze information about the macro- and micro-economic position of the environment under which a particular company is operating. They then refer to the current capital structure of the company to arrive at the per-share net worth of the company and the projected net worth. Since the market price of the company on a stock exchange depends upon the future earning potential and the future net worth of the company, they are in a position to determine whether the company is currently undervalued, overvalued, or reasonably valued on the stock exchange. Market data is crucial in helping analysts decide on these valuations.

All the types of data discussed previously qualify as market data and are exceptionally important for these kinds of analysis. Analysis and investment research are continuous activities. Once a particular valuation is arrived at, analysts keep track of all happenings in that sector through the constant availability of market data.

Once the analysts arrive at these future valuations, they circulate it amongst internal portfolio managers, dealing rooms, private clients, and so on, and these analysis reports result in buy/sell or hold calls for the institutions holding these shares or wanting to get into that security. Interestingly, these analysis reports and buy/sell calls are also circulated as market data. Market data service providers buy these research reports and distribution copyrights and then broadcast the analysts' opinions to their clients. Such types of market data form value-added information for other customers who would have to otherwise process a lot of the raw data discussed earlier to arrive at these buy/sell calls.

On the basis of these reports (of course, the demand to purchase/sell originates from a variety of sources; these reports are only one of them) and depending upon how much an institution needs to invest/divest, the buy or sell order is given to the trading desk. Assume for the purpose of brevity that the call is a purchase call. We will use this example to ascertain the need of market data for traders.

When a purchase order is given to the trading desk or brokerage desk, it is usually given along with a limit within which all purchases have to be made. During trading hours, the trading desk receives a continuous broadcast of bid and offer rates and a minimum volume available against each rate. In this example, the trader has to purchase shares below a certain limit.

Market data received in the broadcast becomes crucial for this trader, too. This data is constantly flashed on the trading terminal. Traders' performance is monitored by their abilities to get the specified number of shares below the limit price (provided the share itself trades below this limit price on that day after the trader has received the order). The share in question may trade below and above the limit specified a number of times during the day. If the stock is relatively illiquid, a small buy order from someone else may push the stock up, and vice versa. This may prove a bit tricky for a trader. The market data about this stock related to the order book position will help the trader ascertain how many of these shares they can get at a particular price (say at the limit price or lower).

Traders will also refer to the volume of shares already transacted during the day. This figure is normally available as part of market data in terms of both the number of shares transacted during the day and the value of shares transacted. Some market data providers also provide the weighted average price for the day. This helps the trader know how far an order's price is from the weighted average price of the day. After knowing all this information, the trader will push through the purchase order either in one go or in multiple lots during the day. The continuous broadcast of market data relating to bid/offer prices, the volumes available, and the volume transacted become the lifeline for such traders.

Subscribers normally call for market data for the same instruments from multiple exchanges and markets. This data is routed in analysis systems to provide various kinds of analysis to help the dealers. Suppose the sales desk receives a relatively large order, say, for the sale of 100,000 shares of Microsoft Corporation. The client demands the best possible rate for this deal. Now, shares of Microsoft Corporation are traded on a number of stock exchanges. Each exchange has its own bid/offer rates, which will be different from each other (but not substantially different). This difference may be large enough to tempt the trader to place the order on multiple exchanges, get it transacted, and get the best available price for the placed order. Such kind of analysis is possible only when the trader has access to a market data system that has the capability of providing real-time bid/offer rates for multiple exchanges. Arbitrageurs also use this kind of data to spot price differences for the same security across markets and exploit these differences by buying on markets where prices are lower and selling simultaneously where prices are higher.

Risk managers who measure and manage risks on a continuous basis feed on market data. Every order that can potentially be converted into a trade is taken, and the order quantity is multiplied by the rates available in a real-time broadcast to arrive at the potential exposure this order would add to the existing portfolio if it were to get transacted. Apart from the orders flowing in, even the existing portfolio is valued constantly to arrive at an overall market-to-market profit/loss. For such computation, every security in the portfolio is chosen, and its valuation is calculated by multiplying the current prevailing price by the number of shares held in the portfolio. Such analysis is required on a continuous basis to take proactive steps for managing and minimizing risk, especially when the market is volatile. Sophisticated risk management techniques such as Value at Risk use the data about prices prevailing in the past five years. Some use data such as current volatility, past volatility, and details about the correlation of movement of the stock with the index, and so on. It is clear that market data service providers cannot provide all these services. Institutions do a careful analysis to check what data they can get ready from market data service providers and what they need to store in their existing application repositories. Data from both sources (from repositories and from market data service providers) is used with a good amount of computation to achieve business results.

A purchase order, once it is a transacted order, needs to be paid for and settled. (Chapter 1 discussed the entire cycle of payment and settlement.) Settlement and back office people require a lot of market data such as ISIN codes, SEDOL codes, the pay-in/pay-out dates of the clearing corporation, and so on, to complete the settlement of these trades. This is required to bring about uniformity in communication.

Thus, you see that the market data service is crucial to everyone in the securities trading value chain. However, most of the time data that is received from such service providers is in a raw form and needs a good amount of cleaning, processing, and value adding before various consumers of the data can use it.

Market Data Service

Market data service providers usually provide the same set of information. This explains why you get the same news when you move from one financial portal to another (chances are they have subscribed to the same service provider). Key differentiators in market service providers revolve around the following:

Timeliness of data: This is whether data is coming real time or is delayed. If historical data is also available, then how long is the history? We devote the next section of this chapter to understanding why timeliness is important as far as market data is concerned.

Coverage of data: This means data is covered across markets such as forex, stocks, bonds, derivatives, and so on. Some market data service providers provide more intensive coverage about some classes of instruments than other service providers and provide preanalyzed (value-added) data.

Geographical reach: Some service providers specialize in certain geographies such as North America, Southeast Asia, Japan, and so on. Institutions that want more intensive coverage of a particular geography subscribe to these services.

Institutional investors whose stakes are high in the market and who can bear the costs normally subscribe to two or three service providers and use each of their strengths.

Why Is the Timeliness of Market Data Important?

Institutions ensure that the market data they receive is absolutely on time. At times, even delays of a few milliseconds are undesirable and could lead to a lot of trading losses and missed opportunities. Several institutions (the number runs into the thousands) have trading interests in financial assets such as government-issued bonds, corporate fixed-income securities, foreign currencies, equities, commodities, real estate, and their related derivatives. As discussed earlier, these institutions continuously price these assets and generate buy/sell orders accordingly. Since so many interested parties exist for any asset/security at any given time, people who have access to the latest or high-quality information will be in a better position to arrive at a future valuation compared to those who receive this information late. Assume that a fund manager sitting in the United States tracks a particular sector such as chemicals closely, has a good grip on the sector, and has been able to make reasonable assessment of the sector and of the major companies in this sector.

The fund manager knows that a company registered in the United States and producing Polypthalic Anhydride (PTA) is facing difficult times because one of its major raw materials, Dimethyl Terephthalate (DMT), has gone up in price drastically. The jump in price is so much that it begins threatening the profitability of the company. The fund manager also knows that the sales of the company are strong but that the rise in raw material prices of DMT is hurting badly; therefore, the fund manager speaks to experts in the chemical industry and finds out that prices of DMT are going to remain high for years to come. In addition, a chance exists that DMT prices will remain high forever, and its consumers must accept this fact. The company in question wants to take drastic steps.

Another company produces Naphtha and sells it in the market. The fund manager understands the chemical business better than the rest of the market and understands well that PTA can also be produced from Naphtha. He speaks to management and learns that management is determined to cut raw material prices. He also comes to know that a series of meetings has been scheduled by the company's senior management with the senior management of the company producing Naphtha. He quickly concludes that the company may be considering abandoning the DMT route to produce PTA and take up the Naphtha route. He calculates the increase in the bottom line from switching raw materials and also calculates the capital expenditure the company will have to undergo to make this change. Finally, he arrives at a per-share rate of the post-change scenario. He can work out the quick numbers on how much more the company could add to its bottom lines because of this change in raw materials. He can then arrive at the change in the company's valuations because of this change. He will then be able to forecast how much change this news will bring to the company's share prices. If the change is large enough to trade on, he will call his broker and place a buy order on this company's shares.

Assume that his news was correct, and the next week the management announces this policy change. Market data service providers will pick up this news and broadcast it worldwide. It will also be reported in all the leading newspapers and broadcast as news on TV. Analysts will then place a buy recommendation on the stock, and a lot of traders will buy. This surge in demand will cause the prices to rise. In this entire euphoria, the biggest beneficiary will be the fund manager who deciphered this vital piece of information and who acted on this news one week prior to the entire market. He ends up making much more profit in percentage terms than any of his peers in the market. One day of lead in getting this crucial information could mean a fortune to a lot of people like the fund manager. Of course, in an attempt to get this kind of news directly from the issuing company (and at most times *before anyone else gets it*), many operators jump the gun and commit insider trading, which is punishable by law in most countries. Insider trading is trading on price-sensitive information that is not available simultaneously to all.

We will introduce another example where a delay of even seconds could mean losses to institutions. As normal practice, institutional investors and fund managers talk to the sales desk in a brokerage house continuously to get feedback on the prices, global and local trends, market outlook, and investment opportunities. These discussions result in orders on securities that are then passed to the brokerage firm, and the brokerage firm executes them. Assume that a sales desk in an institution does not have access to tick-by-tick real-time market data because of system or implementation issues and is working on data that is delayed by a few milliseconds.

The sales desk, however, believes that the data available to them is real time (because they have subscribed to real-time service) and doesn't realize the potential damage the delayed feed can beget. In the course of this discussion, assume that the sales desk convinces the institution that Microsoft Corporation is a good stock to buy at the current trading prices. The institution asks about the prevailing price of Microsoft stocks. The salesperson looks at her terminal and says $45.10. The institution says, "Fine—buy 10,000 for me at $45.10." Now this order can be executed in two ways. It can be sent as a limit order with $45.10 as the limit, or if the salesperson is fast enough, she can risk sending a market order to buy. In case the market price when the market order hits the exchange is still $45.10, she will get the shares at $45.10.

Now assume the salesperson was working on data she thinks is real time but is actually delayed. This means that on volatile days, the prices prevailing on the exchange at any given time are different from the prices the salesperson is seeing on her terminal. In this example, if the salesperson sends a market order to buy Microsoft Corporation stocks and the prices have actually moved to $46 by then, her order will get filled at $46. This could irk the institution on behalf of which the purchase was made, and the salesperson will have to give a lot of explanation to explain this difference between the asked price and the executed price. If the salesperson gives a limit order to curtail this risk of overpriced execution, this order will not be executed since the market price has moved to $46. Nonexecution could mean missed opportunity, which most institutions do not like. A couple of such cases of this would be enough for the institution to start looking for another broker or another salesperson. Delayed market data can thus mean loss of trust, reputation, and eventually loss of business.

Sophisticated clients measure the performance of the executing brokers very closely. Their consistent ability of getting shares/instruments below the specified price is rewarded by giving more execution orders (which in turn means more brokerage). Similarly, those who consistently underperform in terms of getting favorable rates or miss getting orders executed are relied less upon and are not trusted with critical or voluminous orders.

Some market data is sold as delayed data. This comes in about 5 to 15 minutes delayed. Institutions accept these delays because either their trading interest or position in these markets/instruments is not very high or they don't intend to trade in these markets/instruments in the near future. Or, maybe they have subscribed direct services from the exchange that is also providing real-time data through a separate channel and is being monitored by other dealers.

Level Playing Field

After this discussion on the timeliness of market data, you are now in a position to appreciate why the availability of market data to all is important. This is to ensure that one recipient does not have any edge over another in terms of the timeliness of data or its content. The timing of market data is extremely crucial. Traders rely on its timing and accuracy to push through trades worth millions of dollars. Every tick of data coming to them conveys something and means potential opportunity. If market data service providers miss providing some ticks of information or if the tics get delayed, it means loss of trade opportunity for the recipient institution. It is thus highly desirable that the service provider offering the data services provide its direct recipients with a level playing field. This essentially means that no preference must be given to any recipient over another for a particular level of service.

Normally market data service providers inform every recipient institution about their various services and levels of service and provide them an equal opportunity to purchase them. Institutions then purchase services depending upon the cost incurred and the benefits they yield. A particular service could have multiple recipient institutions. Market data service providers ensure that no one gets precedence over the other in terms of the quality of service, level of support and communication, timing of data dissemination, data quality, and provision of data backup and recovery.

This brings an end to the business topics; in next section, we begin the journey into the network programming world and explain the relevant area that plays an important role in realizing this business case study.

Introducing Networking

Networking between computers brought revolutionary changes both in the digital world and in the human world. In the digital world, a new branch named *distributed system* was born. Distributed systems are built around networks, and one of the real-life examples of such a system is the Internet. The Internet is one of the largest distributed systems in the world; it interconnects computers all around the globe using different types of networks, and it provides various other useful services such as e-mail and file transfer. The availability of such services had a direct impact on the human world by forming one of the basic necessities of today's modern life. Moreover, network computing yielded a major shift in software architecture and design space; it revolutionized the way we think about computing by providing the following benefits:

Resource sharing: *Resource* is a general term used to represent both software and hardware resources inside a computer. A hard disk represents hardware resources. Software resources are represented in the form of files, databases, and so on. Resources are scarce and also costly, but with a communication backbone in place, both expensive software and hardware resources are now easily shared with other computers in the network.

Connecting heterogeneous systems: Networks not only opened the communication door to personal desktops but also allowed communications with heterogeneous systems of different breeds such as mainframes, handheld devices, wireless devices, and so on.

Scalability: Software systems have fully embraced a distributed style of architecture, factoring out the code in the form of network components, deploying it on a faster machine, and finally sharing it among all clients.

When it comes to the implementation of a network, it is mainly three major components that cohabit, and their sole interaction and coordination determines the success of the network:

Transmission media: Transmission media plays a pivotal role in a network; it connects media devices such as computers, routers, and hubs to form a network. In a local network environment, cable wire transmits messages from one device to another device. However, in a wide area network, the transmission media could be a telephone device or a dedicated leased line.

Hardware components: Hardware components handle the complexities involved in interfacing with transmission media; additionally, they contain sufficient knowledge to oil the raw messages directly received from the transmission media, translate them to the correct encoding format, and pass them to the software components. The most commonly found hardware components in a network are routers, network interface cards (NICs), and so on.

Software components: Messages received from hardware components are forwarded to network device drivers that reside in the kernel part of the operating system. This message, once processed by the device driver, is then passed over a chain of software abstraction layers where multiple software components employ further application-specific processing logic. Software components such as the Windows socket library or remote procedure library are extensively utilized in building a networked software system. This library abstracts away the low-level network details and provides developer-friendly network programming interfaces.

These three components play a major role by conducting a series of micro-operations under the hood that are totally transparent; discussing each of these micro-operations is outside the scope of this book. However, the software component is the primary target, and the rest of this chapter delves into this topic in detail.

A *protocol* in general terms is an agreed method of exchanging views or opinions. In a network world, identifying and defining a suitable protocol is important, and based on this agreed protocol, the message will then be exchanged among nodes. A *node* is a device such as a computer, hub, router, and so on, that is attached to a network. To meet this need, TCP/IP (Transmission Control Protocol/Internet Protocol) was invented. TCP/IP is a ubiquitous protocol and is universally accepted as a communication backbone of the Internet. TCP/IP is not a one-organization effort; it was the brainchild of many researchers, universities, and organizations. It has been in existence for the last couple of decades, and over this period, it has evolved to form one of the most robust communication protocols.

Communication between two nodes in a network is established using TCP/IP, but TCP/IP is not a single protocol; it is a suite of protocols where each protocol is layered one on top of another. Figure 4-2 shows a condensed version of the most popular Open System Interconnection (OSI) model.

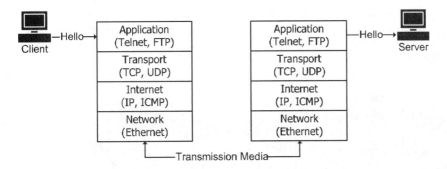

Figure 4-2. *TCP/IP layers*

A message triggered from a client is received and processed by all four layers depicted in Figure 4-2. An individual layer appends its own layer-specific information to the message before dispatching it to the destination. A similar action is carried out on the receiving end (the server); the layer-specific information padded by the client is stripped out as it is promoted to each layer, and finally the message is submitted to the application layer. When an application message is passed from the application layer to the transport layer, this message is padded with additional transport layer information, and the newly formed message is known as a *segment*. A segment is then passed to the Internet layer that is again appended with the Internet layer–specific information to form a *datagram*. The datagram is passed to the final layer that transforms it to a *frame* and finally into *bits* (that is, 0 or 1) that are then delivered over the transmission media. Such a layered architecture model is one of the distinct strengths that singles out TCP/IP from the rest of the other communication protocols. Here are the roles played by individual layers:

Network interface layer: This layer is primarily linked with the transmission media and hardware component; it is responsible for decomposing the network packets into a common transmission medium and recomposing them again on the receiving end.

Internet layer: The Internet layer is responsible for addressing a node on a network and routing a network packet to the destination host in a network. Additionally, this layer also looks after the diagnostic aspect in a network, such as conducting a node health check to find out whether a specific node in a network is reachable.

Transport layer: The transport layer provides advanced functionality to the application layer, such as handling sessions, delivering data reliably, regulating the flow of data on a network, ensuring the ordering of the message during the sending and receiving phases, and so on.

Application layer: The application layer comprises applications that satisfy the network need of the applications. This is the highest layer in the TCP/IP suite, and the most commonly used applications in this layer are Simple Mail Transfer Protocol (SMTP) to exchange mails or File Transfer Protocol (FTP) to upload a file to a remote machine.

Internet Protocol

The first common requirement in any type of communication is to have at least two entities; one is the sender, and the other is the receiver. Both of these entities need to know each other's address. A real-life analogy is a postal mailing address; to deliver an important parcel, it is mandatory to know the destination address as well as the source address, so in the case of a delivery failure, the parcel will be returned to the sender. So, in a TCP/IP-based network world, you need a similar addressing mechanism that allows the individual node to communicate with other nodes in a network. IP is responsible for addressing nodes in a network by assigning a unique 32-bit address known as an *IP address*. The IP address, along with the addressing, is also responsible for the movement of the network packet between nodes. Figure 4-3 depicts a common scenario of finding out the IP address of the local host in a network.

```
C:\WINDOWS\system32\cmd.exe                               _ □ X

C:\>ipconfig

Windows IP Configuration

Ethernet adapter Local Area Connection:

        Media State . . . . . . . . . . : Media disconnected

Ethernet adapter Wireless Network Connection 2:

        Connection-specific DNS Suffix  . : cust.hotspot.t-mobile.com
        IP Address. . . . . . . . . . . : 10.255.243.51
        Subnet Mask . . . . . . . . . . : 255.255.255.224
        Default Gateway . . . . . . . . : 10.255.243.33
```

Figure 4-3. *IPConfig output*

In Figure 4-3, the IP address is denoted in four decimal-based integers, and each delimited digit occupies 8 bits, so a binary representation of 10.255.243.51 is 11000000 10101000 00000000 01100100. A 32-bit IP address would theoretically allow 2^{32} nodes in a network to be addressed, but in reality this is not how it works. The IP address is broken down into two parts; the first part stores the physical network ID, and the second part stores the unique ID of a node in that physical network. Hosts on the same physical network can directly communicate with each other; however, when an individual host wants to exchange data with another host on a different network, then the data need to be handed over to a network router (see Figure 4-4).

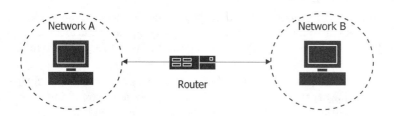

Figure 4-4. *Bridging networks with routers*

A network router is a device that is connected to more than one network, and its primary job is to route packets from one network to another network. So, a router bridges a path between two separate networks, but the actual allotment of IP addresses in a network is implemented by following standard rules established by the Internet community. Five predefined network address classes determine the number of networks and number of hosts in a network (see Table 4-1).

Table 4-1. *Network Address Classes*

Class	Bytes Allocated (Network)	Bytes Allocated (Host)	Binary Format (Network)	Total Network	Number of Hosts per Network	IP Address Range
Class A	1	3	0xxxxxxx	126	16,777,214	1.x.x.x–126.x.x.x
Class B	2	2	10xxxxxx xxxxxxxx	16,384	65,534	128.x.x.x–191.255.x.x
Class C	3	1	110xxxxx xxxxxxxx	2,097,152	254	192.x.x.x–223.255.255.x

As you can see in Table 4-1, only the first three network classes are described because Class D is explained in the "Broadcast" section of this chapter and Class E is used purely for experimentation purposes. Class A has the maximum potential to address the large number of hosts per network compared to Class C, which has a lower capacity to address hosts per network. Additionally, the total number of bytes allocated to the network is not utilized to their full storage capacities; all three network classes mandate a particular portion of high-order bits to follow a specific pattern. For example, in a Class B network, the first two high-order bits are always set to binary 10.

Class A also contains a loopback address, 127.x.x.x, that is used mainly to test network applications that are detached from the physical network. This loopback address is a special-purpose IP address similar to any other IP address; the only difference is that the processing of data terminates at the IP layer instead of at the network layer. Besides the loopback address, there is also a specific range of IP addresses assigned for multicast IP addresses; we cover them in more detail later in the "Broadcast" section.

The IP address, besides containing the network ID and host ID, also contains the subnet ID. With the help of the subnet ID, a large physical network is further partitioned into a logical subnetwork and then accordingly groups relevant nodes in this newly created subnetwork. For example, a small-scale firm assigned with a Class C IP address will allow 254 hosts per network, but in an effort to create a smaller network, this firm can further adopt a strategy to subdivide its existing network based on organizational divisions such as Marketing, HR, and so on. That is the reason you see a subnet mask entry in Figure 4-3; a subnet mask determines the number of subnetworks and hosts inside a network.

The host ID portion is used to create a subnet division, so in a Class C network where 1 byte is assigned to an address host, a network administrator can assign 4 bits of this byte to a subnet ID and the remaining 4 bytes to a host ID. Therefore, according to this new formula, given a single IP address in a physical network, you can form 16 logical subnetworks and 16 hosts per logical subnetwork. The representation format of a subnet mask is similar to the IP address format. For example, the default subnet mask for a Class C address is 255.255.255.0, so to create 16 logical subnetworks and 16 hosts per logical subnetwork, the new subnet mask would be 255.255.255.240. The mask contains 1s for the subnet ID and 0s for the host ID, so the binary representation of this mask would be 11111111 11111111 11111111 11110000.

IP is an unreliable protocol even though it attempts a best-effort delivery service. It poses some serious shortcomings such as it offers no guarantee that the packet will get delivered to the target host. Furthermore, the packet may get delivered in a nonsequential manner; as a result, the target host will notice messages are being received in an out-of-sequence order. Despite such problems, IP is still a cornerstone of the TCP/IP communication backbone, and its limitations are nicely handled by its upper layer.

The IP datagram, along with the actual message to be delivered, also contains its own header fields that are required to properly route a message to the destination host. The following sections describe the key fields of the IP header and are categorized according to their usage.

Addressing

The two most important fields of the IP header are the *source address* and *destination address*. Both addresses represent the IP address of the sender and the destination host in a network, and each field occupies 4 bytes of memory storage.

Data Length

This 2-byte field stores the total length of the IP datagram, which also includes the length of the data. Based on this value, it would allow you to send 65,535 bytes of the IP datagram, but the actual maximum size is determined based on the underlying network maximum transmission unit (MTU). The MTU determines the maximum size of packet that could float on a network. The MTU of a network is computed based on the end-to-end communication link of two hosts. For example, if a sending host in a local area network communicates with a target host that is geographically distributed and connected using telephone lines, then the smallest MTU between the two hosts is computed.

Fragmentation

When the IP datagram size exceeds the MTU capacity, it undertakes a fragmentation and reassembling process. Fragmentation happens on the sender's end, and during this stage, the IP datagram is broken into a smaller datagram to fit within the range of the MTU. The IP datagram is then tagged with the additional information, described as follows, that is important to successfully reassemble the message on the receiving end:

Flags: Based on this field value, it is determined whether the IP datagram is fragmented.

Identification: A 2-byte autoincrement field used to uniquely identify the IP datagram. The IP datagram constructed because of the fragmentation process shares the same identification number; this allows the target host to know how to reassemble this fragmented packet into original data.

Fragment offset: The fragment offset denotes the original position of the fragmented datagram relative to the original unfragmented datagram.

Diagnostic

The following are the important fields that are used to maintain the integrity of a message:

Header checksum: This is a mathematical hashed value of an IP header computed to verify the integrity of the IP datagram.

Time to live: The lifetime of the datagram wandering on a network is based on this value; every time a datagram passes through the router, this value is decremented by a factor of one. When it reaches zero, it is deemed to be a dead packet and finally discarded.

The IP layer is also responsible for monitoring the health status of the network and reporting appropriate error messages or additional information in the case of a network outage. This functionality is not part of IP; it is offloaded to Internet Control Message Protocol (ICMP), which is part of the IP layer. ICMP acts as a messenger that reports errors and feedbacks about activity happening inside a network. Activities such as a failure to transmit packets to a destination host are recorded and encapsulated inside an ICMP message; the sender is then notified of this message using the IP unreliable delivery service. ICMP messages are embedded inside the IP datagram and form part of the data section. The following are some of the most commonly noticed ICMP messages:

Echo request: An echo request message is generated to check the network availability of the remote host

Echo reply: A message generated in response to the echo request message

Destination unreachable: A message generated by intermediate routers to notify the senders about a failure to deliver the datagram to the designated host

The most popular program used by developers to diagnose network-related problems is the Packet Internet Groper Utility (PING). The PING program is bundled with the operating system and used to generate both the echo request and echo reply messages. When a sender initiates a ping to the destination host, the PING program on the sender end generates an echo request message and sends it to the destination host. On receiving this message successfully, the destination host generates an echo reply message and transmits it to the sender. The output of the PING program also contains the round-trip time (RTT) that forms a strong basis to find out the strength of the underlying network (see Figure 4-5). The RTT value computed is the difference of time between the echo request message and the echo reply message.

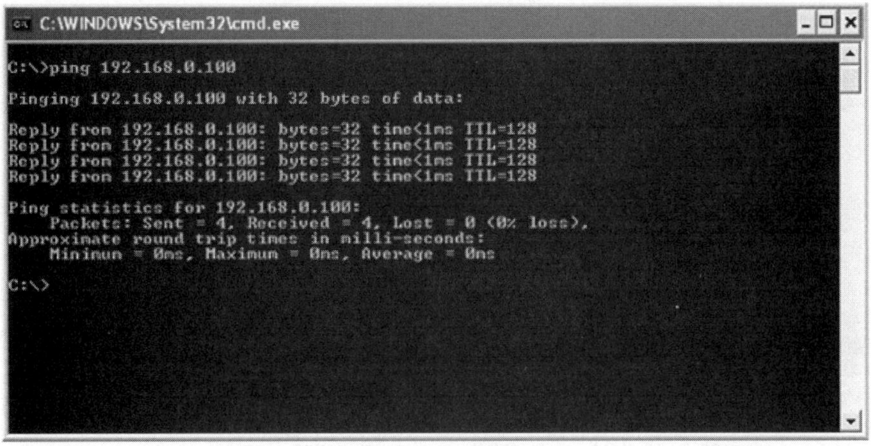

Figure 4-5. *Ping output*

In Figure 4-5, the destination host is addressed using the IP address. There is no doubt that the IP address directs the pathway of a network packet, but given the nature of the IP address, which is encoded in numeric format, it is highly nonintuitive for a human to reckon it. To overcome this problem, a new service, the Domain Name System (DNS), was implemented.

DNS is a set of protocols used in a TCP/IP network environment to assign a human-understandable name to an individual host in a network. Each host name is then mapped to an IP address, and this mapping information is centrally stored and maintained by the DNS server. DNS, because of its mapping capabilities, is also popularly known as a *name server*. It is a central database where the host name and its corresponding IP addresses are stored and retrieved on demand. DNS also provides a bidirectional resolution capability to resolve a host name to an IP address, and vice versa.

The database of DNS is distributed; multiple DNS servers exist and are hierarchically arranged, and individual DNS servers know their parent DNS servers. When a DNS server receives a request to resolve a host name, a search is first conducted against its own local database. If the local database fails to satisfy the request, then DNS undertakes a "recursive resolution" mode where the request starts bubbling up to the parent DNS server. The immediate parent DNS then conducts a similar search operation in its local database, and on failure it delegates to its parent. This escalation is iterative in nature and terminates when it reaches the root DNS server where the final result is determined. To speed up the resolving request, DNS also maintains a cache database; this caching technique is employed to decrease the search cost that is incurred when the recursive-resolution process triggers. DNS along with the local database querying also enumerates the cache database before escalating to its parent DNS.

To demonstrate the benefit provided by the DNS service, we will show the first code of this chapter. The .NET Framework BCL provides a rich set of network class libraries; these libraries allow you to design a highly robust and scalable network application and are available as part of the System.Net and System.Net.Sockets namespaces.

Listing 4-1 shows how to resolve a host name to its IP address.

Listing 4-1. *Host Translator*

```
using System;
using System.Net;

namespace HostTranslator
{
  class Translator
  {
    [STAThread]
    static void Main(string[] args)
    {
      //Get Local Host Name
      string hostName = Dns.GetHostName();
      Console.WriteLine("Local HostName : " +hostName);
      //Ask user to enter IP address or host name
      Console.Write("Enter IP Address or Host Name : ");
      string hostOrip =Console.ReadLine();
      //Resolve the host/IP address
      IPHostEntry entry = Dns.Resolve(hostOrip );
      Console.WriteLine("HostName : " +entry.HostName);
      //Get the IP address list that resolves to the host names
      foreach(IPAddress address in entry.AddressList)
      {
        Console.WriteLine("IP Address : " +address.ToString());
        byte[] addressBytes = address.GetAddressBytes();
        for(int ctr=0;ctr<addressBytes.Length;ctr++)
        {
          Console.WriteLine("Byte : " +ctr +" : " +addressBytes[ctr]);
        }
      }
    }
  }
}
```

In Listing 4-1, the program accepts either an IP address or a host name and then passes this information to the DNS service to resolve it. The DNS resolution service from a programmatic perspective is provided by the Dns class, and it supports both forward-lookup and reverse-lookup capabilities. When resolving is performed using a host name, it is known as *forward lookup*; similarly, when resolving is done using an IP address, it is known as *reverse lookup*. Both resolving techniques take place by a Resolve of the Dns class. Resolve is a time-intensive operation, and keeping this aspect in mind, Dns provides an asynchronous flavor of the Resolve method in the form of BeginResolve and EndResolve.

The result returned by Resolve is encapsulated in an instance of the IPHostEntry class. The IPHostEntry class provides both the host name and IP address information; the host name is displayed by invoking the HostName property, and the IP address is displayed by accessing the AddressList property, which returns an array of IPAddress.

IPAddress is a programmatic representation of the host IP address, and it wraps the dotted quad notation IP address in a byte array and is accessed by invoking the GetAddressBytes method.

When the previous translator program is compiled and executed, it displays the output to the console (see Figure 4-6); the input provided to the program is the host name of the local machine, which returns the IP address.

Figure 4-6. HostTranslator *console output*

Transport Layer (User Datagram Protocol)

The IP layer handles the communication between two hosts; similarly, the transport layer is responsible for the communication between two networked applications. The transport layer provides a data delivery service to the application layer. It is the network face to the applications, and the developer invokes the appropriate API exposed by this layer in order to deliver a message to the destination host. The host in a network is identified by a 4-byte IP address, and the message exchange between two hosts is performed using this IP address. This addressing mechanism is useful only when the communication is between two hosts. When the communication is between applications and with multiple applications running inside a host, you need a different addressing mechanism. To address this requirement, the transport layer contains *network port* information; the network port (the transport layer) and IP address (the IP layer) are combined to form a *network endpoint* that is associated with an individual application.

A perfect example of an endpoint in the real world is the customer service care of a bank. It is almost like a virtual bank that provides all kinds of support such as opening an account, transacting an inquiry, and so on. Customers avail of this support by dialing a toll-free number provided by a bank; after dialing this number, the customer is connected to the Interactive Voice Response System (IVRS) that lists all the bank's services and their corresponding extension numbers. The customer dials the appropriate extension, and the call is transferred to a customer representative who is specifically trained in the selected customer service area. The gist of this example is to further widen your understanding that in the computer network world, the toll-free number is the IP address, and the extension number is the port number. Moreover, multiple applications are specialized to provide different kinds of services. To avail of this service, it is mandatory to know both the IP address and the port number.

The transport layer provides TCP and User Datagram Protocol (UDP), which encapsulates and forwards messages from one network endpoint to another endpoint, and the existence of both of these protocols is meant to cover different goals of the application.

UDP, unlike TCP (discussed in the next section), is a connectionless protocol; communication between applications using UDP is simple and straightforward. There is no set-up cost involved in setting up a UDP communication channel; instead, UDP-driven applications can directly exchange messages with each other solely based on their endpoint information. The only major drawback with UDP is that it provides no guarantee that a message will successfully reach its destination. To address this limitation faced by UDP, applications at the application layer have to devise and implement their own logic that ensures the successful delivery of messages. UDP is just an additional layer above the IP layer, and it blindly forwards the message received from applications to the IP layer with no further intelligence applied to it. This doesn't mean UDP is singled out; UDP is still needed and plays an important role in implementing the network broadcast, which is explained shortly.

UDP and TCP form the message delivery backbone of today's modern distributed application, and network programming using this protocol is fairly easy because of the abstraction provided by the underlying network library; this abstraction is exposed in the form of a *socket*. A socket is a network data conduit that allows the sending and receiving of raw bytes. A socket is similar to a stream that hides the underlying storage details. A socket hides the implementation-level detail of the underlying network protocol such as IP, TCP, UDP, ICMP, and so on, and provides a uniform interface to interact with them. Using a socket, we will show how to implement the first market data example that uses UDP to deliver the message. This example represents a typical data producer and consumer scenario, where there is a single producer and multiple consumers of the market data message (see Figure 4-7).

Figure 4-7. *Market data producer (MDP) and market data consumer (MDC)*

Listing 4-2 shows the code for the market data producer service.

Listing 4-2. *Market Data Producer (Using UDP)*

```csharp
using System;
using System.Collections.Specialized;
using System.Collections;
using System.Net.Sockets;
using System.Net;
using System.Text;

namespace MDP
{
  class MDP
  {
```

```
[STAThread]
static void Main(string[] args)
{
  Console.WriteLine("Market-Data Producer Service Started");
  //Market Data
  string mktPrice = "MSFT;25,IBM;24";
  //Market Data Recipient List
  EndPoint[] mdcEndPointList = new EndPoint[]{new
                              IPEndPoint(IPAddress.Loopback,30000)};
  //Build a network data conduit
  Socket mdpSocket = new
        Socket(AddressFamily.InterNetwork,SocketType.Dgram,ProtocolType.Udp);
  //Convert the data into array of bytes
  byte[] sendBuffer = new byte[512];
  sendBuffer = Encoding.ASCII.GetBytes(mktPrice);
  //Iterate through recipient list, and transmit the data
  foreach(EndPoint mdcEndPoint in mdcEndPointList )
  {
    mdpSocket.SendTo(sendBuffer,mdcEndPoint);
  }
  Console.WriteLine("Market Data Sent to all Market-Data consumer clients");
  Console.ReadLine();
  //Free the resources
  mdpSocket.Close();
  }
 }
}
```

The program described in Listing 4-2 plays the role of a market data producer (the server); it internally maintains a list of clients with whom the market price information is shared. With this code, you also mark the beginning of your journey into the socket programming world. The two important namespaces to add in your mental toolkit are System.Net and System.Net.Sockets. Both these namespaces provide a gamut of network classes.

The actual market data contains the name of the underlying and current price; a semicolon concatenates this information. Also, it's repeatable information, so we have used a comma character as a record delimiter.

```
string mktPrice = "MSFT;25,IBM;24";
```

The information about the market data consumer (the clients) waiting to receive data is stored in an array. The underlying type of array element is EndPoint. EndPoint is an abstract class that encapsulates the address of a network resource and is subclassed by IPEndPoint.

```
EndPoint[] mdcEndPointList = new EndPoint[]{new
                            IPEndPoint(IPAddress.Loopback,30000)};
```

IPEndPoint represents the address of a UDP- or TCP-based application and is created for individual market data consumer clients by combining the IP address and the port number. The first argument of the IPEndPoint constructor method expects an instance of IPAddress, and accordingly IPAddress.Loopback value is passed. IPAddress.Loopback represents a loopback address. The second argument represents the port number.

Next, you create a new instance of Socket. Socket builds a network data conduit that allows the application to send or receive data across the network. Three pieces of information are required to successfully start the data flow. These are the network address type, socket type, and protocol type, as shown here:

```
Socket mdpSocket = new
        Socket(AddressFamily.InterNetwork,SocketType.Dgram,ProtocolType.Udp);
```

The network address type defines the addressing scheme to resolve an EndPoint, and the most commonly used network address type is AddressFamily.InterNetwork that recognizes IPv4 addresses. You then assign the socket type and protocol type; this information goes hand in hand and dictates a strict combination. For instance, when the protocol type is ProtocolType.Udp, the only socket type supported is SocketType.Dgram.

After instantiating a new instance of a Socket, the next step is to deliver data. The data is always encapsulated in a strongly typed object, and it needs to be converted into raw bytes. This conversion is achieved by the Encoding defined in the System.Text namespace. Encoding provides various types of encoding implementations that support converting strings to and from array of bytes.

```
byte[] sendBuffer = new byte[512];
sendBuffer = Encoding.ASCII.GetBytes(mktPrice);
```

The most important code is where individual client endpoint information is retrieved from the MDC recipient list; this information and actual data is then supplied to the SendTo method that finally transmits data to the specified endpoint:

```
foreach(EndPoint mdcEndPoint in mdcEndPointList )
{
  mdpSocket.SendTo(sendBuffer,mdcEndPoint);
}
```

In the final leg of the code, as follows, you close the socket connection, which also releases the underlying memory allocated by Socket. A word of caution: Socket, once closed, can no longer be used to either send or receive messages over a network.

```
Console.WriteLine("Market Data Sent to all Market-Data consumer clients");
Console.ReadLine();
mdpSocket.Close();
```

This brings an end to the market data producer aspect of this example. The next step is to look at the market data consumer code; the main function of the code in Listing 4-3 is to receive data published by the market data producer, so the technique employed is more or less similar to the market data producer service.

Listing 4-3. *Market Data Consumer (Using UDP)*

```
using System;
using System.Collections.Specialized;
using System.Collections;
using System.Net.Sockets;
using System.Net;
using System.Text;

namespace MDC
{
  class MDC
  {
    [STAThread]
    static void Main(string[] args)
    {
      Console.WriteLine("Market-Data Consumer Service Started");
      byte[] receiveBuffer = new byte[512];
      EndPoint bindInfo = new IPEndPoint(IPAddress.Loopback,30000);
      Socket mdcSocket = new
          Socket(AddressFamily.InterNetwork,SocketType.Dgram,ProtocolType.Udp);
```

```
    try
    {
      //Associates socket with a particular local endpoint
      mdcSocket.Bind(bindInfo);
      EndPoint endPoint = new IPEndPoint(IPAddress.Any,0);
      //receives a datagram, and the call blocks until data is received
      int bytesReceived = mdcSocket.ReceiveFrom(receiveBuffer,ref endPoint);
      //market data sender information is recorded
      IPEndPoint mdpEndPoint = (IPEndPoint)endPoint;
      string mktPrice = Encoding.ASCII.GetString(receiveBuffer,0,bytesReceived);
      Console.WriteLine("Market-Data Received : " +mktPrice);
      Console.WriteLine("Market Data Producer IP Address {0} Port {1} "
                  ,mdpEndPoint.Address.ToString(), mdpEndPoint.Port);
    }
    catch(SocketException e)
    {
      Console.WriteLine(e.ToString());
    }
    Console.ReadLine();
    mdcSocket.Close();
  }
 }
}
```

In Listing 4-3, we have explicitly added the socket exception handler that is excluded in the market data producer code. By enclosing network-related operations inside a try-catch block, you get the opportunity to catch SocketException. SocketException provides additional information that is extremely valuable in troubleshooting network-related failures. The ErrorCode property of SocketException returns a socket-specific code, and to correctly interpret it, you will have to refer to Windows Socket Version 2 API error code documentation in MSDN.

Listing 4-3 contains a new instance of IPEndPoint and Socket. The arguments supplied to the IPEndPoint constructor method must match the market data recipient list maintained by the market data producer service.

```
EndPoint bindInfo = new IPEndPoint(IPAddress.Loopback,30000);
Socket mdcSocket = new
      Socket(AddressFamily.InterNetwork,SocketType.Dgram,ProtocolType.Udp);
```

After creating a socket, Bind is invoked, which associates a Socket instance with a particular local endpoint:

```
mdcSocket.Bind(bindInfo);
```

A local endpoint contains both the IP address and the port number, but the IP address is sufficient to identify the underlying NICs associated with it. Bind proves to be very nifty in a multihomed scenario. A multihomed host is equipped with two or more NIC, and each NIC is assigned a different IP address. A multihomed host provides multiple channels to communicate data, and by calling Bind, you explicitly specify the channel from which data is communicated. It is absolutely necessary to call Bind if the application is configured to receive data.

Bind is never called in the market data producer code because during the data delivery phase you were not concerned with any specific local endpoint and instead delegated this task to the underlying network service provider that uses an appropriate local endpoint. But if a need arises to know the local endpoint of a Socket, you can always get this information by accessing the LocalEndPoint property of Socket.

The next step is to receive data, which is done by invoking ReceiveFrom. This method blocks until data is received, so when new data arrives, the method unblocks and populates the byte array and remote host information. The remote endpoint contains the IP address and port number used by the market data producer service to deliver this data. Additionally, this method also returns an exact number of bytes read. Accordingly, you extract that number of bytes using the GetString method of the Encoding.ASCII class.

```
EndPoint endPoint = new IPEndPoint(IPAddress.Any,0);
int bytesReceived = mdcSocket.ReceiveFrom(receiveBuffer,ref endPoint);
IPEndPoint mdpEndPoint = (IPEndPoint)endPoint;
string mktPrice = Encoding.ASCII.GetString(receiveBuffer,0,bytesReceived);
Console.WriteLine("Market-Data Received : " +mktPrice);
Console.WriteLine("Market Data Producer IP Address {0} Port {1} "
                    ,mdpEndPoint.Address.ToString(), mdpEndPoint.Port);
```

Finally, the connection is closed, and the underlying memory used by Socket is released:

```
mdcSocket.Close();
```

With this code, you have completed the first example. Figure 4-8 and Figure 4-9 show the console output generated by the MDC and MDP.

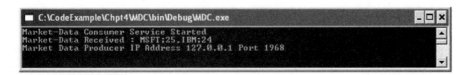

Figure 4-8. *MDC (UDP) console output*

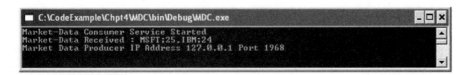

Figure 4-9. *MDP (UDP) console output*

This example provided a first-hand taste of socket programming in the .NET world, and you implemented it using UDP. Although in reality UDP comes into action only in a specific scenario, most of the time applications are designed using TCP. UDP undoubtedly is the fastest delivery transport protocol, but it has some serious drawbacks:

Unreliable: UDP provides no guarantee that data will ever reach its destination; this means in the previous example the market data information published may or may not reach the market data consumer. If you are looking for this kind of reliability feature, then you have no other choice but to hand-roll custom logic at the application level.

Unordered sequence: Consider an example where market data is continuously pumped by the market data producer service, and in such cases the consumer will face a huge surge of data. If you look at the pattern of information published, you will find a case where a price of a stock is sent, and immediately an updated price for the same stock is delivered. In such cases UDP does not guarantee that the updated price information will be delivered only after the old price information is delivered. On the receiving end, you can imagine the impact on the application and its downstream components when it first receives the updated price and when afterward it receives the stale price.

Network congestion: A strong flow control is required that can sense the network, find out its maximum capacity, and based on its current utilization throttle the amount of data pumped on network. This will ensure the optimum utilization of the network, but UDP doesn't support such features, so it is pretty easy to choke the network by continuously generating and sending messages.

UDP is a simple protocol, but it lacks many of the characteristics that are essential for conducting reliable communication. To address the caveats faced by UDP, TCP was invented and is considered to be the most robust transport protocol available for any type of internetwork communication.

Transport Layer (Transmission Control Protocol)

The most appealing features of TCP are its various out-of-band features that are offered to ensure the reliable delivery of application data. The reliability service provided by TCP has strongly established its presence in the Internet world where millions of systems exchange data using TCP. TCP is a connection-oriented protocol; this means both the sender and the receiver must perform a handshaking before exchanging data. After successful handshaking, a TCP connection is established between the sender and the receiver; using this connection, the sending application sends data to the destination application, or vice versa. Many popular protocols such as SMTP, FTP, and HTTP are built on top of TCP. Some of the important features supported by TCP are as follows:

Reliable: TCP implements the reliability service by acknowledging each message sent to the destination host, and the failure to receive an acknowledgment receipt from the destination host within a predefined time will initiate a retransmission of the message. This mechanism is implemented by tagging every TCP segment with a unique sequence number, and both the source and destination applications know each other's last sequence number received or sent by them. Another benefit of the sequence number is it helps to detect and resolve the message duplication or out-of-order issues. In a case where the TCP message arrives out of order, TCP waits for its predecessor message to arrive and reassembles them in the correct order before passing them to the application.

Handshaking: UDP is very informal when it comes to sending or receiving messages; besides knowing each other's endpoint information, no additional steps are needed either from the sending host or from the receiving host. This is in contrast to TCP where before the data exchange takes place, both the sender and the receiver first negotiate the protocol initialization information. This includes information such as the sender and receiver starting sequence number, the TCP window size, and the TCP maximum segment size (MSS). The MSS is equivalent to the MTU, but the MTU represents a network; similarly, the MSS represents TCP. The MSS determines the largest size of the TCP segment, and during the TCP connection set-up phase, both the sender and the receiver announce their MSS values. Most of the time, the MSS mirrors the host MTU. The MSS lessens message fragmentation happening at the IP layer. Fragmentation is an expensive operation and seriously hampers the performance of the application.

TCP follows a similar negotiation technique when the connection is closed. During the connection closing stage, TCP ensures that both the sending and receiving hosts don't have pending data to be delivered or received.

Flow control: TCP handles a fast producer and slow consumer scenario well. In this scenario, the producer generates the message and transmits to the consumer at a rate higher than the consumer ability to consume it. To stop the sender from bursting messages to the receiver, TCP implements an adaptive sliding window technique.

A data receive buffer, also known as *window size*, is allocated for the individual TCP connection established between the client and server. This buffer acts as intermediate storage for the receiver and represents the maximum capacity of data it can handle at one time from the sender. When TCP data is received, it is first copied into this buffer and is emptied only when the application makes an explicit request. Until that time, data is temporarily stored in this TCP buffer. So, if the application is executing computational-intensive tasks in parallel, then it is quite possible that it may not be able to read data in a timely manner, which will introduce a slow consumer scenario. In such cases, the receive buffer will get quickly filled up, and the sender will immediately stop sending more data. Therefore, it is extremely important that the application quickly read data from the TCP buffer and queue it in the application-maintained in-memory storage. An application can request data from this buffer either in a large chunk or in a smaller chunk.

This TCP buffer from the sender point of view becomes the *sender window size* and from the receiver point of view becomes the *receiver window size*. The window size is dynamic in nature and mainly depends on how quickly the application is able to read data from this buffer. The receiver window size value is always stored inside an acknowledgment message sent by the receiver to the sender and forms the basis of implementing a strong flow control. The sender checks the window size published by the receiver as part of the TCP acknowledgment message, and if its value falls below zero, then the sender will stop sending any further data until it notices an increase in window size.

Now we will show how to reimplement the earlier market data example (see Listing 4-2 and Listing 4-3) using TCP. From a coding perspective, Listing 4-4 is more or less similar to its UDP counterpart; however, certain prerequisite are required to be set up before the market data consumer (the client) requests data from the market data producer (the server). The following code is the TCP version of the market data producer (the server) and listens for a request from the market data consumer (the client). As soon as the client connects, the data is prepared and delivered using TCP.

Listing 4-4. *Market Data Producer (Using TCP)*

```
using System;
using System.Net;
using System.Net.Sockets;
using System.Text;

namespace TCPMDP
{
  class MDP
  {
    [STAThread]
    static void Main(string[] args)
    {
      IPEndPoint localEP = new IPEndPoint(IPAddress.Loopback,20000);
      Console.WriteLine("Market-Data Producer Service Started - Using TCP");
      //Market Data
      string mktPrice = "MSFT;25,IBM;24";
      //Create network data conduit
      Socket mdpSocket = new
          Socket(AddressFamily.InterNetwork,SocketType.Stream,ProtocolType.Tcp);
      //Associate socket with particular endpoint
```

```
        mdpSocket.Bind(localEP);
        //server starts listening for client connection
        mdpSocket.Listen(10);
        while(true)
        {
            //synchronously extracts the first pending connection request
            Socket mdcSocket = mdpSocket.Accept();
            IPEndPoint mdcRemoteEP = mdcSocket.RemoteEndPoint as IPEndPoint;
            Console.WriteLine("MDC EndPoint Info {0} {1} :
                        ",mdcRemoteEP.Address.ToString(),mdcRemoteEP.Port);
            //data is flatted into array of bytes and
            //dispatched to client

            byte[] sendBuffer = new byte[512];
            sendBuffer = Encoding.ASCII.GetBytes(mktPrice);
            mdcSocket.Send(sendBuffer);
            //client connection is closed
            mdcSocket.Shutdown(SocketShutdown.Both);
            mdcSocket.Close();
        }
    }
  }
}
```

In the UDP version of the market data producer (described in Listing 4-2), you should have observed the sender directly sending data to a particular endpoint, assuming the receiver on the other end is waiting to receive it. There is no implicit way to determine whether the receiver has successfully received the data. But in a connection-oriented world, it's a different story; the receiver beforehand must know the sender endpoint information and explicitly connect to this endpoint. A connection is deemed to be successful only after the sender accepts it.

In Listing 4-4, the first step is to define a local endpoint to which the market data consumer client will connect to receive market data. In this example, you identify the loopback address and port number 20000. In the next step, a socket is created, the socket type passed is SocketType.Stream, and the protocol type is ProtocolType.Tcp. This newly created Socket is then associated with the local endpoint by invoking the Bind method.

```
IPEndPoint localEP = new IPEndPoint(IPAddress.Loopback,20000);
Console.WriteLine("Market-Data Producer Service Started - Using TCP");
string mktPrice = "MSFT;25,IBM;24";
Socket mdpSocket = new
        Socket(AddressFamily.InterNetwork,SocketType.Stream,ProtocolType.Tcp);
mdpSocket.Bind(localEP);
```

The Listen method, shown next, puts the Socket in listening mode. A Socket in listening mode actively listens for an incoming client connection request. The argument passed to this method determines the maximum number of entries in the TCP incoming connection request queue. When a client connection request arrives, it is first placed in this connection request queue and is dequeued by the application with a call to Accept. In a stress scenario where multiple connection requests arrive in a concurrent fashion, it is important for the application to dequeue this connection request fast enough so that the number of entries in the queue doesn't exceed the maximum limit.

```
mdpSocket.Listen(10);
Socket mdcSocket = mdpSocket.Accept();
IPEndPoint mdcRemoteEP = mdcSocket.RemoteEndPoint as IPEndPoint;
Console.WriteLine("MDC EndPoint Info {0} {1} :
                ",mdcRemoteEP.Address.ToString(),mdcRemoteEP.Port);
```

Accept drains the connection request queue in a FIFO fashion, and on finding no pending connection request, it blocks until a new request gets enqueued. A successful return from Accept establishes a connection between the client and the server. The Socket instance returned by the method represents a client connection. The endpoint information of the client is available through the RemoteEndPoint property.

Two types of Socket exist on the server side; the first one is the listening socket, and the other is the client socket. The purpose of the listening socket is to honor the client connection request; it doesn't support any type of data exchange activity. The Socket returned by the Accept method represents the client socket, and data exchange is performed on this socket.

After the connection is established successfully, market data is serialized into raw bytes, and using Send it is dispatched to the MDC client:

```
byte[] sendBuffer = new byte[512];
sendBuffer = Encoding.ASCII.GetBytes(mktPrice);
mdcSocket.Send(sendBuffer);
```

The TCP connection established between the client and server is *full-duplex* in nature. This means data is allowed to flow from both directions of the connection. TCP provides a feature that allows one end of the connection to disable its sending or receiving activity. For example, if a market data consumer client is never going to send data and its only intention is to receive data, then it may very well block the sending end of the connection. You can apply the same technique to the market data producer server; if it is never going to receive data, then it can block the receiving end of the connection. This feature is called *TCP half-close*, and you use Shutdown to implement it:

```
mdcSocket.Shutdown(SocketShutdown.Both);
```

Shutdown also takes care of any pending data that needs to be delivered or received and ensures data on the connected Socket is flushed out before closing it down. The argument supplied to Shutdown is one of these enumerated values of SocketShutdown:

SocketShutdown.Receive: Disables the receiving end of the Socket

SocketShutdown.Send: Disables the sending end of the Socket

SocketShutdown.Both: Disables both the sending and receiving ends of the Socket

Finally, the TCP connection is closed, and the underlying memory used by Socket is released:

```
mdcSocket.Close();
```

With the code example illustrated in Listing 4-4, you have completed the TCP version of the market data producer service. The next step is to implement the TCP version of the market data consumer service (see Listing 4-5).

Listing 4-5. *Market Data Consumer (Using TCP)*

```
using System;
using System.Net;
using System.Net.Sockets;
using System.Text;

namespace TCPMDC
{
  class MDC
  {
    [STAThread]
    static void Main(string[] args)
    {
```

```
            Console.WriteLine("Market-Data Consumer Service Started - Using TCP");
            IPEndPoint mdpEP = new IPEndPoint(IPAddress.Loopback,20000);
            Socket mdcSocket = new
                 Socket(AddressFamily.InterNetwork,SocketType.Stream,ProtocolType.Tcp);
            //Establishes connection with market data server
            mdcSocket.Connect(mdpEP);
            byte[] receiveBuffer = new byte[512];
            //Receive market data
            int bytesReceived = mdcSocket.Receive(receiveBuffer);
            string mktPrice = Encoding.ASCII.GetString(receiveBuffer,0,bytesReceived);
            Console.WriteLine(mktPrice);
            //Close connection
            mdcSocket.Shutdown(SocketShutdown.Both);
            mdcSocket.Close();
            Console.ReadLine();
        }
    }
}
```

In Listing 4-5, the code works by first identifying the server endpoint information, which is then fed to the Connect method that synchronously establishes a connection with the remote server. After you are connected, the server immediately sends the data. The data is received and converted into a readable format before being displayed on the console. After displaying the data, the connection is closed, and the underlying memory allocated is released. Figure 4-10 and Figure 4-11 show the console output of both the market data producer and the consumer service.

Figure 4-10. *MDP (TCP) console output*

Figure 4-11. *MDC (TCP) console output*

Asynchronous Market Data Producer and Consumer

Socket supports both blocking and nonblocking operations. In blocking mode, the operation being conducted on the socket (such as reading data, writing data, or connecting to the host) gets blocked indefinitely until the requested operation completes successfully. For example, a read issued on a connected socket that contains pending data will return immediately; however, if there is no data, then the read operation is blocked until the arrival of new data. You noticed similar blocking behavior while accepting the client connection; the Accept method blocks until a new connection is established.

To build a scalable application, it is essential to adopt a concurrent programming path. By adopting this path, you break a coarse-grained task into individual subtasks and offload processing of these subtasks to a separate thread. If you implemented this during the design of networked applications, then most of the operations, such as sending data to the client or accepting a client connection, are forked on a separate thread.

To provide such multithreaded behavior, Socket provides both a synchronous and an asynchronous version of the common operation performed on it. This common operation includes connecting to the remote host, accepting the connection from the client, and sending or receiving the data. We have already demonstrated the synchronous version of the market data producer and consumer. In Listing 4-6, we show how to implement an asynchronous version of these services and perform most of the time-consuming operations on a separate thread.

Listing 4-6. *Asynchronous Market Data Producer (Using TCP)*

```
using System;
using System.Threading;
using System.Net;
using System.Net.Sockets;
using System.Text;

namespace AsyncTCPMDP
{
  public class AsyncStateInfo
  {
    public Socket socket;
    public byte[] dataBuffer = new byte[512];

    public AsyncStateInfo(Socket sock)
    {
      socket=sock;
    }
  }

  class MDP
  {
    [STAThread]
    static void Main(string[] args)
    {
      ManualResetEvent shutDownSignal = new ManualResetEvent(false);
      IPEndPoint localEP = new IPEndPoint(IPAddress.Loopback,20000);
      Console.WriteLine("Market-Data Producer Service Started -
                    Using TCP (Async Model)");
      Console.WriteLine("Main Thread : " +Thread.CurrentThread.GetHashCode());
      Socket mdpSocket = new
        Socket(AddressFamily.InterNetwork,SocketType.Stream,ProtocolType.Tcp);
      mdpSocket.Bind(localEP);
      mdpSocket.Listen(10);
      //Starts listening to client connection in an asynchronous mode
      mdpSocket.BeginAccept(new AsyncCallback(AcceptConnection),
                              new AsyncStateInfo(mdpSocket));
      shutDownSignal.WaitOne();
    }

    //Method invoked to accept an incoming connection attempt
    public static void AcceptConnection(IAsyncResult result)
    {
```

```
        Console.WriteLine("Connection Request Thread : "
                    +Thread.CurrentThread.GetHashCode());
        AsyncStateInfo stateInfo = result.AsyncState as AsyncStateInfo;
        //Accepts client connection
        Socket mdcSocket = stateInfo.socket.EndAccept(result);
        //Starts listening to client connection
        stateInfo.socket.BeginAccept(new AsyncCallback(AcceptConnection),
                        new AsyncStateInfo(stateInfo.socket));
        AsyncStateInfo mdcStateInfo = new AsyncStateInfo(mdcSocket);
        string mktPrice = "MSFT;25,IBM;24";
        stateInfo.dataBuffer = Encoding.ASCII.GetBytes(mktPrice);
        //Sends data asynchronously
        mdcSocket.BeginSend(mdcStateInfo.dataBuffer,0,512,SocketFlags.None,
                        new AsyncCallback(SendData),mdcStateInfo);
    }

    public static void SendData(IAsyncResult result)
    {
        Console.WriteLine("Data Sending Thread : "
                    +Thread.CurrentThread.GetHashCode());
        AsyncStateInfo stateInfo = result.AsyncState as AsyncStateInfo;
        //Completes asynchronous send
        stateInfo.socket.EndSend(result);
    }

  }
}
```

The code described in Listing 4-6 is a rehash of the TCP version of the market data producer service but uses asynchronous methods of Socket. Asynchronous methods, as explained in Chapter 2, are paired methods. The execution of the method starts with a call to BeginXXX and ends with a call to the EndXXX method. The logic implemented here is similar to the synchronous version of the market data producer with the only difference being that tasks such as accepting the client connection and sending data to the client are separated in AcceptConnection and the SendData method.

In Listing 4-6, BeginAccept asynchronously notifies the client connection request, the notification happens on a separate thread, and the registered callback method is invoked. The registered callback method is represented by an instance of the AsyncCallback delegate. This delegate expects a method argument to be passed that is later referenced inside the callback method. The argument passed in this case is an instance of AsyncStateInfo that encapsulates the listening socket instance:

```
mdpSocket.BeginAccept(new AsyncCallback(AcceptConnection),
                        new AsyncStateInfo(mdpSocket));
}
```

AcceptConnection completes the connection request received from the client by invoking the EndAccept method. EndAccept returns a new Socket that is then used to send data to the client. Notice that you again trigger a call to the BeginAccept method to process the remaining connection request. After accepting the connection, the data is asynchronously sent using the BeginSend method:

```
public static void AcceptConnection(IAsyncResult result)
{
    Console.WriteLine("Connection Request Thread : "
                +Thread.CurrentThread.GetHashCode());
    AsyncStateInfo stateInfo = result.AsyncState as AsyncStateInfo;
    Socket mdcSocket = stateInfo.socket.EndAccept(result);
    stateInfo.socket.BeginAccept(new AsyncCallback(AcceptConnection),
                    new AsyncStateInfo(stateInfo.socket));
```

```
AsyncStateInfo mdcStateInfo = new AsyncStateInfo(mdcSocket);
string mktPrice = "MSFT;25,IBM;24";
stateInfo.dataBuffer = Encoding.ASCII.GetBytes(mktPrice);
mdcSocket.BeginSend(mdcStateInfo.dataBuffer,0,512,SocketFlags.None,
                           new AsyncCallback(SendData),mdcStateInfo);
```

Finally, SendData completes the asynchronous send operation by invoking EndSend:

```
public static void SendData(IAsyncResult result)
{
  Console.WriteLine("Data Sending Thread : "
                    +Thread.CurrentThread.GetHashCode());
  AsyncStateInfo stateInfo = result.AsyncState as AsyncStateInfo;
  stateInfo.socket.EndSend(result);
}
```

The next step is to demonstrate the market data consumer end, which connects to the market data producer and receives data in an asynchronous manner. Listing 4-7 represents the asynchronous version of the market data consumer service.

Listing 4-7. *Asynchronous Market Data Consumer (Using TCP)*

```
using System;
using System.Threading;
using System.Net;
using System.Net.Sockets;
using System.Text;

namespace AsyncTCPMDC
{
  public class AsyncStateInfo
  {
    public Socket socket;
    public byte[] dataBuffer = new byte[512];

    public AsyncStateInfo(Socket sock)
    {
      socket=sock;
    }
  }

  class MDC
  {
    [STAThread]
    static void Main(string[] args)
    {
      Console.WriteLine("Market-Data Consumer Service Started -
                        Using TCP(Async Model)");
      Console.WriteLine("Main Thread : " +Thread.CurrentThread.GetHashCode());
      IPEndPoint mdpEP = new IPEndPoint(IPAddress.Loopback,20000);
      Socket mdcSocket = new
          Socket(AddressFamily.InterNetwork,SocketType.Stream,ProtocolType.Tcp);
      AsyncStateInfo stateInfo = new AsyncStateInfo(mdcSocket);
      //Begins an asynchronous connection request
      mdcSocket.BeginConnect(mdpEP,new AsyncCallback(MDCConnected),stateInfo);
      Console.ReadLine();
```

```
      if ( mdcSocket.Connected == true )
      {
        mdcSocket.Shutdown(SocketShutdown.Both);
        mdcSocket.Close();
      }
    }

    //Callback method invoked as a result of asynchronous data receive request
    public static void ReceiveData(IAsyncResult result)
    {
      Console.WriteLine("Receiving Thread : "
              +Thread.CurrentThread.GetHashCode());
      AsyncStateInfo stateInfo = result.AsyncState as AsyncStateInfo;
      Socket mdcSocket = stateInfo.socket;
      //Successfully accepts data
      int bytesReceived = mdcSocket.EndReceive(result);
      if ( bytesReceived > 0 )
      {
        string mktPrice =
            Encoding.ASCII.GetString(stateInfo.dataBuffer,0,bytesReceived);
        Console.WriteLine(mktPrice);
        //Begins async. operation to receive more data sent by server
        mdcSocket.BeginReceive(stateInfo.dataBuffer,0,512,SocketFlags.None,
              new AsyncCallback(ReceiveData),stateInfo);
      }
    }

    //Callback method invoked as a result of asynchronous connection request
    public static void MDCConnected(IAsyncResult result)
    {
      Console.WriteLine("Connecting Thread : "
              +Thread.CurrentThread.GetHashCode());
      AsyncStateInfo stateInfo = result.AsyncState as AsyncStateInfo;
      Socket mdcSocket = stateInfo.socket;
      //Successfully connects to market data server
      mdcSocket.EndConnect(result);
      //Begins asynchronous data receive operation
      mdcSocket.BeginReceive(stateInfo.dataBuffer,0,512,SocketFlags.None,
      new AsyncCallback(ReceiveData),stateInfo);
    }
  }
}
```

In Listing 4-7, the connection request to the market data producer service is spawned on a separate thread that is achieved by BeginConnect. The connection to the remote host is successfully established with EndConnect. After connecting, the next step is to receive the data published by the server, and this task is again processed asynchronously with BeginReceive:

```
public static void MDCConnected(IAsyncResult result)
{
  Console.WriteLine("Connecting Thread : "
          +Thread.CurrentThread.GetHashCode());
  AsyncStateInfo stateInfo = result.AsyncState as AsyncStateInfo;
  Socket mdcSocket = stateInfo.socket;
  mdcSocket.EndConnect(result);
  mdcSocket.BeginReceive(stateInfo.dataBuffer,0,512,SocketFlags.None,
      new AsyncCallback(ReceiveData),stateInfo);
}
```

In the following code, ReceiveData is triggered by BeginReceive, which gives the ability to receive data on a separate thread. The actual data is received only after a call to EndReceive. EndReceive returns the total number bytes read, and this value determines any pending data that needs to be read.

```
public static void ReceiveData(IAsyncResult result)
{
  Console.WriteLine("Receiving Thread : "
          +Thread.CurrentThread.GetHashCode());
  AsyncStateInfo stateInfo = result.AsyncState as AsyncStateInfo;
  Socket mdcSocket = stateInfo.socket;
  int bytesReceived = mdcSocket.EndReceive(result);
  if ( bytesReceived > 0 )
  {
    string mktPrice =
      Encoding.ASCII.GetString(stateInfo.dataBuffer,0,bytesReceived);
    Console.WriteLine(mktPrice);
    mdcSocket.BeginReceive(stateInfo.dataBuffer,0,512,SocketFlags.None,
        new AsyncCallback(ReceiveData),stateInfo);
  }
}
```

Figure 4-12 and Figure 4-13 show the console output of the market data producer and the consumer service.

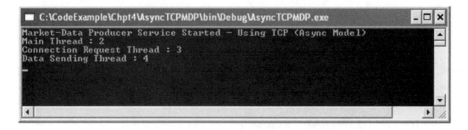

Figure 4-12. *MDP (*Async-TCP*) console output*

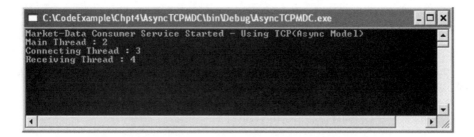

Figure 4-13. *MDC (*Async-TCP*) console output*

Network Byte Order

The standardization of data has always been a focal issue in achieving interoperability between machines where the underlying hardware architecture or operating system is different from each other. A common problem encountered in a network application is the arrangement of the bits of multibyte numbers such as the short, integer, or long data types. The interpretation and packaging of multibyte numbers are different for different types of CPU architecture. Intel-based machines are known as *little-endian* machines where the least significant byte (LSB) is stored at a lower memory address. This is in contrast to Motorola-based machines where the most significant byte (MSB) is stored at a lower memory address. For instance, data triggered from Intel-based machines will be interpreted differently when received by a Motorola machine. Figure 4-14 illustrates this problem where the short value 99 defined by little-endian machines is interpreted wrongly by big-endian machines.

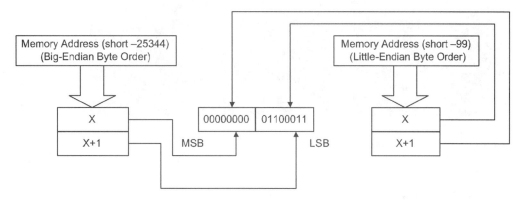

Figure 4-14. *Byte ordering*

To address this inconsistency, a common network representation format is defined that makes no assumptions and ensures the portability of data across different CPU architectures. This format is the same as big-endian. Therefore, both little-endian and big-endian machines, before sending data, convert it to a network representation format. This kind of data portability is required only when the applications communicating with each other use a different CPU architecture. But if they are built on a similar architecture, then there is no need for any intermediate conversion step, and the data is directly exchanged.

To convert a multibyte value from host byte order to network byte order, we will use the NetworkToHostOrder defined in the IPAddress class in the following code. Similarly, HostToNetworkOrder converts from network byte order to host byte order. Both HostToNetworkOrder and NetworkToHostOrder are overloaded methods, and both take a multibyte value and convert it to an appropriate format.

```
using System;
using System.Net;

namespace NetworkByteOrder
{
  class NBO
  {
    [STAThread]
    static void Main(string[] args)
```

```
  {
    short quantity = 99;
    short networkOrder = IPAddress.NetworkToHostOrder(quantity);
    Console.WriteLine("Quantity Converted to Network Byte Order :"
                      +networkOrder);
    short hostOrder = IPAddress.HostToNetworkOrder(networkOrder);
    Console.WriteLine("Quantity Converted to Host Byte Order :" +hostOrder );
  }
 }
}
```

The output in Figure 4-15 shows a multibyte value converted from a host format to a network format, and vice versa.

Figure 4-15. *Network byte order console output*

Message Framing

The earlier code example highlighted the modus operandi of UDP- and TCP-based applications. The data transmitted on the network is first serialized into a byte array of a fixed size. The receiving application knows this fixed size and accordingly allocates a buffer before receiving the data. However, in a real-world application, there are different types of application data, and you cannot expect their data lengths to be the same. Also, both UDP and TCP exhibit a different behavior when it comes to the data transmission stage.

When data is handed over to TCP using Socket.Send, it is first copied into TCP internal data structures, and the control is immediately returned to the caller. In reality, TCP never immediately sends data over the wire; it first buffers the data, so it is likely that a multiple call to Socket.Send will batch the data, and TCP will then transmit this accumulated data in a single TCP segment. The side effect of such optimization is that the receiving application now needs to apply enough intelligence to dissect the correct message. On the other hand, UDP is pretty straightforward, and data dispatched using Socket.Send is considered to be a unique UDP segment and is immediately transmitted over the wire.

As you saw earlier, Socket uses a sequence of bytes when it comes to sending or receiving data. But in reality applications work at a higher abstraction layer and are represented in the form of strongly typed objects. So you need to serialize the actual data that is encapsulated inside a strongly typed object into raw bytes before sending it over a network. The reverse process is applied on the receiving end where a strongly typed object is re-created from the bytes of an array. This process is known as the *serialization* and *deserialization* of objects, as discussed in Chapter 3.

The .NET Framework already provides a binary formatter that serializes the entire object graph into raw byte form. The truth of the matter is sometimes the performance of network applications occupies center stage, and during that period you need to wet your hands with various other alternative message encoding and decoding techniques and select the best that fits your requirement. To demonstrate this alternative solution, we will show how to implement a real-world scenario where market data is encapsulated inside a strongly typed class, as shown in the following code. The data will then be translated into raw bytes and transmitted over a network. Here comes the real complexity; on the receiving end, in order to translate a sequence of bytes into strongly object types, you need to preserve the message boundary (see Listing 4-8).

Listing 4-8. *Application Message Header*

```
using System;
using System.Runtime.InteropServices;

namespace Parsing
{
  public enum MessageHeaderType
  {
    MarketData,
    OrderData,
    TradeData
  }

  [StructLayout(LayoutKind.Sequential,Pack=1,CharSet=CharSet.Ansi)]
  public class MessageHeader
  {
    public int MessageLength;

    [MarshalAs(UnmanagedType.I4)]
    public MessageHeaderType MessageType;

    public MessageHeader()
    {
    }
  }
}
```

In Listing 4-8, MessageHeader wraps the application-related message, and it contains padding information (mainly the length of the message and the type of message). The intent of padding will be revealed shortly. In the next section of code, you declare the market data class, which inherits from MessageHeader and assigns a proper value to MessageType, as shown in Listing 4-9.

Listing 4-9. *Market Data (Stock Price) Class*

```
using System;
using System.Runtime.InteropServices;

namespace Parsing
{
  [StructLayout(LayoutKind.Sequential,Pack=1,CharSet=CharSet.Ansi)]
  public class MarketDataInfo : MessageHeader
  {
    [MarshalAs(UnmanagedType.ByValTStr,SizeConst=20)]
    public string InstrumentName;
    public double BidPrice;
    public double AskPrice;
```

```
    public MarketDataInfo()
    {}

    public MarketDataInfo(string instrumentName,double bidPrice,double askPrice)
    {
      this.MessageType = MessageHeaderType.MarketData;
      InstrumentName = instrumentName;
      BidPrice = bidPrice;
      AskPrice = askPrice;
    }
  }
}
```

By looking at the code described in Listing 4-9, you must have figured out the parsing approach we will implement. We will be using the P/Invoke service provided by the CLR. P/Invoke itself is a vast subject, and covering every aspect of it is beyond the scope of this book. In a nutshell, P/Invoke is a mediator between managed and unmanaged code. It takes into account the difference between managed and unmanaged code and allows managed code to directly invoke functionality provided by unmanaged code. It is obvious that interoperating two different environments is not an easy task, and it is primarily the managed environment where you play by the rules defined by the CLR.

If you glance at MarketDataInfo, you will notice that the class and some of the fields are annotated with interop attributes. These interop attributes are defined in System.Runtime.InteropServices, and basically they provide hints to the P/Invoke service about how to marshal the managed object in an unmanaged environment.

In a managed world, the field layout of a managed object is not fixed; instead, it is dynamically rearranged by the runtime. By annotating StructLayout attributes, you instruct the runtime to not rearrange the field order. Moreover, you can also change the individual field marshaling behavior by annotating them with the MarshalAs attribute. For example, if you look at MessageHeader, described in Listing 4-8, the MessageType field is annotated with interop attributes that instruct the runtime to marshal them as an integer type because in an unmanaged world there is no concept of enumerated types.

The program shown in Listing 4-10 is a generic parser that translates a strongly typed object into an array of bytes, and vice versa. It also implements a common logic for handling the message boundary for all types of objects.

Listing 4-10. *Message Framing*

```
using System;
using System.Runtime.InteropServices;
using System.IO;

namespace Parsing
{
  public delegate void MessageParsedHandler(MessageHeader header);

  public class MessageParser
  {
    public event MessageParsedHandler MessageParsed;
    bool newMsg=true;
    int remainingByte;
    MemoryStream memStream = new MemoryStream();
    int msgLength;
    //Message parsing notification
    private void OnMessageParsed(MessageHeader msgHeader)
    {
```

```
  if ( MessageParsed != null )
    MessageParsed(msgHeader);
}

//Serializes message into array of bytes
public byte[] Serialize(MessageHeader obj)
{
  //Calculate size of object
  int objectSize = Marshal.SizeOf(obj);
  obj.MessageLength = objectSize;
  //Serialize message into array of bytes
  IntPtr memBuffer = Marshal.AllocHGlobal(objectSize);
  Marshal.StructureToPtr(obj,memBuffer,false);
  byte[] byteArray = new byte[objectSize];
  Marshal.Copy(memBuffer,byteArray,0,objectSize);
  Marshal.FreeHGlobal(memBuffer);
  return byteArray;
}

//Convert array of bytes into a managed type
private void ConvertToObject(byte[] msgBytes)
{
  //Extract the message type by reading from 4th position of byte array
  //i.e MessageType field of MessageHeader.
  int msgType = BitConverter.ToInt32(msgBytes,4);
  Type objType = null;
  //Based on the message type determine the underlying type
  if ( msgType == (int) MessageHeaderType.MarketData)
  {
    objType = typeof(MarketDataInfo);
  }
  //Calculate the object size
  int objectSize = Marshal.SizeOf(objType);
  //Convert byte array into object
  IntPtr memBuffer = Marshal.AllocHGlobal(objectSize);
  Marshal.Copy(msgBytes,0,memBuffer,objectSize);
  object obj = Marshal.PtrToStructure(memBuffer,objType);
  Marshal.FreeHGlobal(memBuffer);
  //Invoke the event to notify parsing of new message
  //pass the concrete object instance
  OnMessageParsed(obj);
}

public void DeSerialize(byte[] msgBytes)
{
  AlignMessageBoundary(msgBytes,0);
}

//Code inside this method determines the correct message boundary
public void AlignMessageBoundary(byte[] recvByte,int offSet)
{
  if ( offSet >= recvByte.Length ) return ;
  //The logic has been branched for two types of scenarios
  //first scenario is when framing of message is performed for a new message
  //second scenario applies to messages received on a installment basis
```

```
   if ( newMsg == true )
   {
     //Get the length of message
     msgLength = BitConverter.ToInt32(recvByte,offSet);
     //Determine the message type
     int msgType = BitConverter.ToInt32(recvByte,offSet + 4);
     //If the length of byte array + offset is less than message length,
     //then it indicates a partial message, and there are still
     //remaining bytes pending to be read.
     if ( msgLength > ( recvByte.Length - offSet ) + 1 )
     {
       newMsg=false;
       remainingByte = msgLength - recvByte.Length;
       memStream = new MemoryStream();
       memStream.Write(recvByte,offSet,recvByte.Length);
     }
     else
     {
       //completes reading all pending bytes and converts
       //it into concrete object
       byte[] bytes = new byte[msgLength];
       Array.Copy(recvByte,offSet,bytes,0,msgLength );
       MessageHeader obj = this.ConvertToObject(bytes) as MessageHeader;
       this.OnMessageParsed(obj);
       //Recursive call
       AlignMessageBoundary(recvByte,offSet + msgLength);
     }
   }
   else
   {
     if ( remainingByte > recvByte.Length )
     {
       memStream.Write(recvByte,0,recvByte.Length);
       remainingByte = remainingByte - recvByte.Length;
     }
     else
     {
       memStream.Write(recvByte,offSet,remainingByte);
       byte[] bytes = new byte[msgLength];
       memStream.Seek(0,SeekOrigin.Begin);
       memStream.Read(bytes,0,msgLength);
       memStream.Close();
       MessageHeader obj = this.ConvertToObject(bytes) as MessageHeader;
       this.OnMessageParsed(obj);
       newMsg=true;
       AlignMessageBoundary(recvByte,offSet + remainingByte + 1);
     }
   }
 }
}
}
```

The parser program, along with the serialization and deserialization functionality, also looks after the message boundary issue. The serialization code returns an array of bytes, but the deserialization code never directly returns the object to the caller; instead, it notifies the caller by raising an event. Let's first get started with the serialization code:

```
public byte[] Serialize(MessageHeader obj)
{
  int objectSize = Marshal.SizeOf(obj);
  obj.MessageLength = objectSize;
  IntPtr memBuffer = Marshal.AllocHGlobal(objectSize);
```

Serialize accepts an instance of MessageHeader that is then passed to Marshal.SizeOf. This method computes the unmanaged size of a managed object. The size returned is then assigned to MessageLength. The size also determines the memory required in unmanaged memory of the process and is allocated by Marshal.AllocHGlobal. On successfully allocating memory, it returns a memory pointer that is represented by IntPtr.

Next, Marshal.StructureToPtr flattens the data of the managed object into a continuous stream of bytes and copies them into an allocated block of unmanaged memory. On successfully copying, you invoke Marshal.Copy, which performs a reverse operation of copying data from unmanaged memory to byte array.

```
Marshal.StructureToPtr(obj,memBuffer,false);
byte[] byteArray = new byte[objectSize];
Marshal.Copy(memBuffer,byteArray,0,objectSize);
```

Since you interacted with the unmanaged world where there is no concept of automatic garbage collection to reclaim the memory, it is important to release all resources that were allocated using AllocHGlobal and this is accomplished by Marshal.FreeHGlobal:

```
Marshal.FreeHGlobal(memBuffer);
```

Now comes the important part of the code where the actual message deserialization happens inside ConvertToObject, and it works by first examining the message type:

```
private object ConvertToObject(byte[] msgBytes)
{
  int msgType = BitConverter.ToInt32(msgBytes,4);
  Type objType = null;
  if ( msgType == (int) MessageHeaderType.MarketData)
  {
    objType = typeof(MarketDataInfo);
  }
```

You already know that when an instance of MarketDataInfo is serialized, its field layout will not be reorganized, and the defined order will be maintained. So, you can safely assume the position of the field in a byte array based on its underlying data type and offset. By applying this pattern, you can retrieve the message type from the byte array because you know it is the first field in MarketDataInfo, and being an integer data type, its storage capacity will be exactly 4 bytes. Similarly, you can also retrieve the message length, which is the next field, and its data type is also an integer. This means the offset of the message length in a byte array will start from the fourth position; using this technique, you can traverse the byte array and retrieve the values of all the fields. BitConverter comes in handy in this scenario; it facilitates the easy conversion from a byte array to the appropriate value type.

Based on the message type, you computed the actual unmanaged size of a managed object. This size is then supplied to AllocHGlobal, which finally allocates memory in unmanaged memory of the process. The byte array received as a method argument is then copied into the unmanaged block of memory.

```
int objectSize = Marshal.SizeOf(objType);
IntPtr memBuffer = Marshal.AllocHGlobal(objectSize);
Marshal.Copy(msgBytes,0,memBuffer,objectSize);
```

The following is the important piece of code in which the byte array from the unmanaged section of memory is marshaled and resurrected to a concrete managed object. After casting the object to MessageHeader, it is appropriately notified to the caller by raising the event.

```
MessageHeader obj = Marshal.PtrToStructure(memBuffer,objType) as MessageHeader;
Marshal.FreeHGlobal(memBuffer);
if ( MessageParsed != null )
   MessageParsed(obj);
```

DeSerialize is the method exposed to outside world; this method call is then routed to AlignMessageBoundary, which properly frames the message before invoking ConvertToObject:

```
public void DeSerialize(byte[] msgBytes)
{
   AlignMessageBoundary(msgBytes,0);
}
```

The following code is the last leg of the example; it conducts different types of tests that start with a simple message and then simulates a multiple-message scenario nested in a large byte array:

```
using System;
using System.Runtime.InteropServices;

namespace Parsing
{
  class ParsingExample
  {
    [STAThread]
    static void Main(string[] args)
    {
      //Instantiate new instance of Message parser
      //and also subscribe to its message parsing event
      MessageParser msgParser = new MessageParser();
      msgParser.MessageParsed +=new MessageParsedHandler(msgParser_MessageParsed);

      MarketDataInfo msftData = new MarketDataInfo("MSFT",21.5,22.5);
      MarketDataInfo ibmData = new MarketDataInfo("IBM",23.5,24.5);
      MarketDataInfo geData = new MarketDataInfo("GE",25.5,26.5);

      //Single Message Scenario
      Console.WriteLine("Single Message Scenario");
      byte[] buffer = msgParser.Serialize(msftData);
      msgParser.DeSerialize(buffer);

      //Large Buffer Scenario
      Console.WriteLine("Large Buffer Scenario");
      int typeSize = Marshal.SizeOf(typeof(MarketDataInfo));
      byte[] largeBuffer = new byte[typeSize*3];
      byte[] ibmBuffer = msgParser.Serialize(ibmData);
      byte[] geBuffer = msgParser.Serialize(geData);
      Array.Copy(buffer,0,largeBuffer,0,typeSize);
      Array.Copy(ibmBuffer,0,largeBuffer,buffer.Length,typeSize);
      Array.Copy(geBuffer,0,largeBuffer,buffer.Length +
                         ibmBuffer.Length,typeSize);
      msgParser.DeSerialize(largeBuffer);
```

```
    //Small Buffer Scenario
    Console.WriteLine("Small Buffer Scenario");
    byte[] smallBuffer1= new byte[22];
    byte[] smallBuffer2= new byte[22];
    Array.Copy(buffer,0,smallBuffer1,0,22);
    Array.Copy(buffer,22,smallBuffer2,0,22);
    msgParser.DeSerialize(smallBuffer1);
    msgParser.DeSerialize(smallBuffer2);
  }

  private static void msgParser_MessageParsed(MessageHeader header)
  {
    MarketDataInfo dataInfo = header as MarketDataInfo;
    Console.WriteLine("{0} {1}
        {2}",dataInfo.InstrumentName,dataInfo.BidPrice,dataInfo.AskPrice);
  }
 }
}
```

The code also demonstrates a small buffer case, and the parser is able to intelligently parse the data. Figure 4-16 shows the parsing console output.

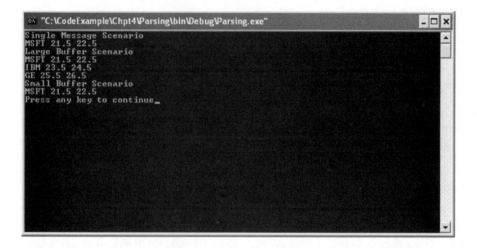

Figure 4-16. *Parsing console output*

Broadcast

The examples demonstrated so far were based on a unicast communication model (see Figure 4-17). In this model, the market data producer (the server) sent data to the individual market data consumer (the client). In UDP, the market data server needs to constantly update its recipient list. However, in the TCP world, the market data consumer explicitly initiates a connection with the server and gets the required data. Regardless of which route you follow, the market data server always needs to know its consumers (clients).

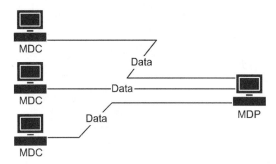

Figure 4-17. *Unicast communication model*

Such one-to-one communication scales poorly, particularly when the number of clients inter-acting with the server is huge. Consider for a moment you were given a design specification of a market data service that should be capable of handling at least 1,000 clients. To implement this system, no doubt you will require the backing of state-of-the-art hardware infrastructure, but one thing you will definitely fall short on is network bandwidth. Network bandwidth in a local area network may not look like a major problem; it is only when communication is spawned on limited-capacity bandwidth that serving 1,000 clients is a different beast.

The server will be sending market data information to individual clients, and if you estimate the size of market data to be around 1KB, then a total of 1MB (1,000 clients * 1KB) of data will be floated on the network at any given point of time. If you extrapolate this equation specifically during peak trading hours when stocks price are highly volatile, then the underlying network bandwidth will not be able to cope with the amount of data produced by the market data service. This problem gets reflected on the consumer end in the form of a market data latency issue. Fortunately, you have a way to resolve this problem, and it is to implement the network broadcast feature.

Using a broadcast, a single copy of data is floated on the network, and this data is sent to all hosts in a network. The immediate benefit reaped here is the optimum utilization of bandwidth; regardless of the number of hosts in a network, data is transferred only once. The underlying network provides two types of broadcasts: unsolicited and solicited. The underlying implementation of both these broadcasts depends upon UDP, and this is where UDP wins over TCP.

Unsolicited Broadcast

Unsolicited broadcast is also known as *local broadcast* because of its limitation to broadcast data only within the subnet of a network (see Figure 4-18). This restriction is inherent to a network where data is never forwarded to another subnet by network routers. A local broadcast is quite useful when both the server and client are located on the same subnet and the nature of information published is the same across all clients.

The broadcast address 255.255.255.255 is a special-purpose address, and the network packet directed toward this IP address is delivered to every host on the specified subnet of the host. From a coding perspective, implementing a broadcast is a trivial task because under the hood it uses UDP to deliver the data. So, the next task is to reimplement the market data solution; unlike in the earlier code example where the server maintained a list of every clients' endpoint information it intended to send data to, in this version the server directly broadcasts data on the broadcast address, and the consumer has to simply listen to this broadcast message.

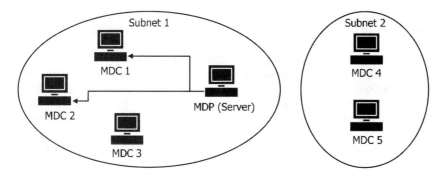

Figure 4-18. *Unsolicited broadcast*

The server and client code shown in Listing 4-11 and Listing 4-12 requires the host to be connected in a network, because the broadcast is a feature supported by the underlying network.

Listing 4-11. *Unsolicited Broadcast of Market Data*

```
using System;
using System.Net.Sockets;
using System.Net;
using System.Text;

namespace UnSolicitedBcastServer
{
  class MDP
  {
    [STAThread]
    static void Main(string[] args)
    {
      Console.WriteLine("Market-Data Producer Service Started -
                        (Unsolicited Broadcast)");
      string mktPrice = "MSFT;25,IBM;24";
      Socket mdpSocket = new
            Socket(AddressFamily.InterNetwork,SocketType.Dgram,ProtocolType.Udp);

      //Broadcast IP address
      IPEndPoint bcastEndPoint = new IPEndPoint(IPAddress.Broadcast,30001);
      //Set socket in broadcast mode
      mdpSocket.SetSocketOption(
                  SocketOptionLevel.Socket,SocketOptionName.Broadcast, 1);

      byte[] sendBuffer = new byte[512];
      sendBuffer = Encoding.ASCII.GetBytes(mktPrice);
      mdpSocket.SendTo(sendBuffer,bcastEndPoint);
      mdpSocket.Close();
      Console.WriteLine("Market Data Broadcasted");
      Console.ReadLine();
    }
  }
}
```

In Listing 4-11, the code introduces two important changes. The first visible change is that a list of recipient endpoint information is missing; it is replaced by a broadcast address. This broadcast address is readily made available by IPAddress.Broadcast, and the port number assigned is 30001.

The next important line of code is SetSocketOption. This method turns on or off some very low-level options of network protocols that are not directly exposed in the form of a property or method. We discuss the possible options supported by this method later in the "Protocol Tweaking" section. Currently, using SetSocketOption, we have enabled the broadcast support that is by default disabled on the socket. After applying this change, the rest of the code looks familiar and requires no further explanation.

The next step is to build the market data consumer that consumes market data published on the broadcast address. The code shown in Listing 4-12 achieves this.

Listing 4-12. *Client Receiving Broadcast Message*

```
using System;
using System.Net.Sockets;
using System.Net;
using System.Text;

namespace UnSolicitedBcastClient
{
  class MDC
  {
    [STAThread]
    static void Main(string[] args)
    {
      Console.WriteLine("Market-Data Consumer Service Started -
              (Unsolicited Broadcast)");
      byte[] receiveBuffer = new byte[512];
      IPHostEntry hostEntry = Dns.GetHostByName(Dns.GetHostName());
      EndPoint bindInfo = new IPEndPoint(hostEntry.AddressList[0],30001);
      Socket mdcSocket = new
            Socket(AddressFamily.InterNetwork,SocketType.Dgram,ProtocolType.Udp);
      mdcSocket.Bind(bindInfo);
      EndPoint endPoint = new IPEndPoint(IPAddress.Any,0);
      int bytesReceived = mdcSocket.ReceiveFrom(receiveBuffer,ref endPoint);
      IPEndPoint mdpEndPoint = (IPEndPoint)endPoint;
      string mktPrice = Encoding.ASCII.GetString(receiveBuffer,0,bytesReceived);
      Console.WriteLine("Market-Data Received : " +mktPrice);
      Console.WriteLine("Market Data Producer IP Address {0} Port {1} "
                  ,mdpEndPoint.Address.ToString(), mdpEndPoint.Port);
      Console.ReadLine();
      mdcSocket.Close();
    }
  }
}
```

There is hardly any difference in the code described in Listing 4-12 compared to the UDP unicast version of this code (see Listing 4-3). The only point to keep in mind is that the local endpoint on which the bind is performed belongs to the same subnet of server. Of course, the port number needs to be the same, or the client will fail to receive the broadcast message. So now that both the client and server are in place, let's compile and run the client before running the server. Figure 4-19 shows the UnsolicitedBCastServer console output, and Figure 4-20 shows the UnsolicitedBCastClient console output.

```
"C:\CodeExample\Chpt4\UnSolicitedBcastServer\bin\Debug\UnSolicitedBcastServer.exe"    [-][□][x]
Market-Data Producer Service Started - (Unsolicited Broadcast)
Market Data Broadcasted
```

Figure 4-19. UnsolicitedBCastServer *console output*

```
"C:\CodeExample\Chpt4\UnSolicitedBcastClient\bin\Debug\UnSolicitedBcastClient.exe"    [-][□][x]
Market-Data Consumer Service Started - (Unsolicited Broadcast)
Market-Data Received : MSFT;25,IBM;24
Market Data Producer IP Address 10.255.243.55 Port 2271
```

Figure 4-20. UnsolicitedBCastClient *console output*

However, the unsolicited broadcast introduces a performance hit on every host within the
subnet. A UDP datagram, when broadcast, is received and processed by all hosts in a subnet. This
additional processing performed by an individual host terminates at the transport layer when it
notices that no application has shown interest in receiving this broadcast message. From a performance viewpoint, you are wasting a few CPU cycles, so you need to find a more elegant solution
where only the interested host receives the broadcast message. This is where solicited broadcast
comes to the rescue.

Solicited Broadcast

Solicited broadcast, popularly known as *multicast*, allows broadcasts within a group of hosts in
a network (see Figure 4-21). Multiple multicast groups may be formed, and each group is uniquely
identified. Based on this group identification, an individual host in a network joins or leaves the
groups. This is analogous to a publisher-subscriber model where the subscriber needs to register
with the publisher if it wants to be notified of a particular action.

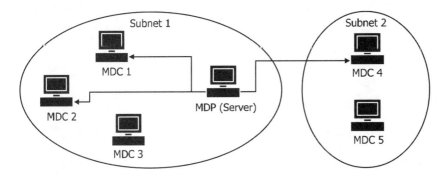

Figure 4-21. *Solicited broadcast*

Another advantage of multicast over unsolicited broadcast is that routers recognize multicast messages, and this allows messages to pass across different networks. On a surface level, this may look like a major issue because it is easy for a malicious user to bombard the entire network by sending a multicast message. But in reality, this is not how it works; a multicast message that originated from a particular network is first received by a router. The router forwards this message to the designated network only if at least one host in that network has explicitly expressed an interest in receiving this multicast message by joining the multicast group. Routers among themselves use Internet Group Management Protocol (IGMP) to notify about a host joining or leaving a multicast group. IGMP forms part of the IP layer and, like ICMP, is encapsulated inside an IP datagram.

Multicast groups are formed by selecting an IP address from a Class D address range. Class D addresses are from 224.0.0.0 to 239.255.255.255 and are allocated especially for multicast-based applications. However, a few multicast addresses, particularly the ones in the range from 224.0.0.0 to 224.0.0.255, are unusable. The multicast address acts as a unique group identifier, and any host in a network can join a multicast group by providing the correct multicast address. This golden rule also applies to a host located in a different network. Similarly, a host can also drop its membership at any given time. Such dynamic group membership makes it highly favorable for building applications where the number of subscribers is not predetermined.

The next task is to implement the same market data example (see Listing 4-13); however, remember in this version, the market data consumer will be able to receive data only if it joins a multicast group to which the server broadcasts data.

Listing 4-13. *Solicited Broadcast of Market Data*

```
using System;
using System.Net.Sockets;
using System.Net;
using System.Text;

namespace MCastServer
{
  class MDP
  {
    [STAThread]
    static void Main(string[] args)
    {
      Console.WriteLine("Market-Data Producer Service Started -
                (Using MultiCast)");
      string mktPrice = "MSFT;25,IBM;24";
      //IP Multicast address
      IPAddress groupAddress =IPAddress.Parse("224.5.6.7");
      IPEndPoint mcastEP = new IPEndPoint(groupAddress,30002);
      Socket mdpSocket = new
          Socket(AddressFamily.InterNetwork,SocketType.Dgram,ProtocolType.Udp);
      byte[] sendBuffer = new byte[512];
      sendBuffer = Encoding.ASCII.GetBytes(mktPrice);
      //Set multicast TTL
      mdpSocket.SetSocketOption(SocketOptionLevel.IP,
                SocketOptionName.MulticastTimeToLive, 3);
      //Send data to multicast address
      mdpSocket.SendTo(sendBuffer,mcastEP);
      mdpSocket.Close();
      Console.WriteLine("Market Data sent to group of consumers");
      Console.ReadLine();
    }
  }
}
```

The first step in a multicast-based application is to define a multicast group, and in Listing 4-13 you perform this step by identifying 224.5.6.7 as the multicast address. However, in the real world, this multicast group information must be made available to all interested hosts, and the mechanism implemented to achieve this may vary. But usually this information is recorded in either a common configuration file or a database. After defining the multicast address, you create a multicast endpoint and port number, defined in this case as 30002.

The next line of code is important, especially when multicast data is suppose to span several routers in a network; the importance of this value has been explained in the "Protocol Tweaking" section of this chapter:

```
mdpSocket.SetSocketOption(SocketOptionLevel.IP,
                    SocketOptionName.MulticastTimeToLive, 3);
```

Market data is finally sent to multicast groups, and the market data consumers that have joined this group will receive the data. The code to send this multicast data is as follows:

```
mdpSocket.SendTo(sendBuffer,mcastEP);
```

The final step is to build market data consumers that consume market data published on a multicast address:

```
using System;
using System.Net.Sockets;
using System.Net;
using System.Text;

namespace MCastClient
{
  class MDC
  {
    [STAThread]
    static void Main(string[] args)
    {
      Console.WriteLine("Market-Data Consumer Service Started -
                    (Using MultiCast)");
      byte[] receiveBuffer = new byte[512];
      IPHostEntry entry = Dns.GetHostByName(Dns.GetHostName());
      EndPoint localEP = new IPEndPoint(entry.AddressList[0],30002);
      Socket mdcSocket = new
        Socket(AddressFamily.InterNetwork,SocketType.Dgram,ProtocolType.Udp);
      mdcSocket.Bind(localEP);
      //Start receiving multicast data by subscribing
      //to below multicast address
      IPAddress groupAddress = IPAddress.Parse("224.5.6.7");
      MulticastOption mcastOption = new MulticastOption(groupAddress);
      mdcSocket.SetSocketOption(SocketOptionLevel.IP,
                  SocketOptionName.AddMembership,mcastOption);
      EndPoint endPoint = new IPEndPoint(IPAddress.Any,0);
      int bytesReceived = mdcSocket.ReceiveFrom(receiveBuffer,ref endPoint);
      IPEndPoint mdpEndPoint = (IPEndPoint)endPoint;
      string mktPrice = Encoding.ASCII.GetString(receiveBuffer,0,bytesReceived);
      Console.WriteLine("Market-Data Received : " +mktPrice);
      Console.WriteLine("Market Data Producer IP Address {0} Port {1} "
                  ,mdpEndPoint.Address.ToString(), mdpEndPoint.Port);
      mdcSocket.SetSocketOption(SocketOptionLevel.IP,
                        SocketOptionName.DropMembership,mcastOption);
      mdcSocket.Close();
      Console.ReadLine();
```

```
      }
    }
}
```

Building a multicast client involves slightly more code than building a multicast server. The first step is to define the multicast group address, and this address needs to be mutually agreed upon and known to both the server and the client. In this case, the agreed multicast address is 224.5.6.7.

The multicast address is then wrapped inside `MulticastOption`. This information is then passed to `SetSocketOption`, which announces the host group joining membership. After successful registration, the host is eligible to receive data published on this multicast group:

```
MulticastOption mcastOption = new MulticastOption(groupAddress);
mdcSocket.SetSocketOption(SocketOptionLevel.IP,
                SocketOptionName.AddMembership,mcastOption);
```

Similarly, the host can leave a multicast group at any moment of time by invoking the `SetSocketOption` method:

```
mdcSocket.SetSocketOption(SocketOptionLevel.IP,
                    SocketOptionName.DropMembership,mcastOption);
```

It is now time to run the multicast server and client. Note that despite the message originating from the multicast group, the consumer is still able to know the originator of this information; this is true for both unsolicited and solicited broadcasts. Figure 4-22 shows the `MCastServer` console output, and Figure 4-23 shows the `MCastClient` console output.

Figure 4-22. `MCastServer` *console output*

Figure 4-23. `MCastClient` *console output*

Protocol Tweaking

You will always encounter edge cases during application development that require a deep dive into the low-level details of a protocol. This means understanding and tweaking some of the important fields of the protocol's data structure. This is especially true for applications that are sensitive in nature. Socket allows such mechanisms through `SetSocketOption` and `GetSocketOption`. Using these methods, you can change the behavior of almost all protocols (including IP, TCP, and UDP). This releases you from knowing the nitty-gritty of the field offset in the protocol structure, the number of bytes, the possible values supported by field, and so on. However, it is essential to know the implication of these changes, and that is what we will cover in the next sections where we discuss some of the important fields and the corresponding impacts on an application's behavior.

IP: DontFragment

When the size of any IP datagram exceeds the underlying network MTU, then it undertakes a fragmentation process where the datagram is broken into small pieces that fit the network MTU capacity. Applications using UDP are the victims of such problems because UDP directly forwards the data received from the application layer to the IP layer. This means if applications pass data of a large buffer size, then it is surely fragmented by the IP layer. However, such problems are not experienced if the application is using TCP; remember, TCP creates a segment of a size equal to the MSS before forwarding it to the IP layer. Using the DontFragment flag, you can instruct the IP layer whether it can fragment a large datagram.

Here's the code that disables IP fragmentation:

```
using System;
using System.Net;
using System.Net.Sockets;

class ProtocolTweaking
{
  public void IPFragment(Socket sockInstance)
  {
    //Disable the Fragmentation
    sockInstance.SetSocketOption(SocketOptionLevel.IP,
                        SocketOptionName.DontFragment,1);
    //Get Assigned Fragmentation Value
    int isFragmented = (int)
            sockInstance.GetSocketOption(SocketOptionLevel.IP,
                            SocketOptionName.DontFragment);
    Console.WriteLine(isFragmented);
  }
}
```

IP: Time to Live (TTL) and Multicast TTL

The IP TTL determines the age of a packet in a network, and the routers on receiving these packets decrement it by one. This prevents a dead packet from wandering in the network. On the other hand, the multicast TTL restricts the scope of a multicast packet in a network. For instance, every multicast-aware router in the network is configured with a TTL limit that determines the reach of a multicast transmission. Table 4-2 shows the recommended threshold values and their scopes.

Table 4-2. *Multicast TTL Scope*

Scope Range	Description
0	Interface
1–31	Subnet
32–63	Site
64–127	Region
127–255	Continent

So, based on Table 4-2, let's say if a router is configured with a threshold value of 32, then when it receives a multicast packet whose MulticastTTL value exceeds the threshold value, then this packet will be discarded by the routers. Hence, it is important to know the scope of the multicast transmission.

Here's the code that demonstrates how to configure both multicast and IP TTL:

```
using System;
using System.Net;
using System.Net.Sockets;

class ProtocolTweaking
{
  public void MultiCastTTL(Socket sockInstance)
  {
    //Subnet Scope
    sockInstance.SetSocketOption(SocketOptionLevel.IP,
                    SocketOptionName.MulticastTimeToLive,3);
  }

  public void IPTTL(Socket sockInstance)
  {
    //Set the TTL to 4
    sockInstance.SetSocketOption(SocketOptionLevel.IP,
                    SocketOptionName.IpTimeToLive,4);
    int ipTTL= (int)sockInstance.GetSocketOption(SocketOptionLevel.IP,
                    SocketOptionName.IpTimeToLive);
    Console.WriteLine(ipTTL);
  }
}
```

IP: MulticastLoopback

This option comes in handy when both the multicast sender and receiver applications are installed on the same host and when the receiver wants to loop back the multicast packet sent by the sender. By default, MulticastLoopback is turned on, and the receiver application can turn it off by executing the following command:

```
using System;
using System.Net;
using System.Net.Sockets;

class ProtocolTweaking
{
  public void DisableMulticastLoopBack(Socket sockInstance)
  {
    //disable multicast loopback
    sockInstance.SetSocketOption(SocketOptionLevel.IP,
                    SocketOptionName.MulticastLoopback,0);
  }
}
```

Socket: ReuseAddress

A Socket, before binding (using Socket.Bind) to a particular endpoint, checks whether it is already being used by an existing instance of Socket. An exception of Socket already in use is thrown if a match is found. The most fertile source of such a problem is an application going into a hung state because of which it fails to gracefully clean up the resources. However, the ReuseAddress option allows you to override this behavior; it permits sockets to bind to an already existing endpoint without throwing an exception:

```
using System;
using System.Net;
```

```
using System.Net.Sockets;

class ProtocolTweaking
{
  public void ReuseSocket(Socket sockInstance)
  {
    sockInstance.SetSocketOption(SocketOptionLevel.Socket,
                            SocketOptionName.ReuseAddress,1);
  }
}
```

Socket: Buffers

Socket maintains two kinds of buffers: a send buffer and a receive buffer. The data before delivering to the destination host is first stored in the send buffer; similarly, the data received from the sender is first stored in the receive buffer before it is submitted to the receiving application. The default size of this buffer is 8KB, but when the application is sending or receiving a large amount of data, then it is important to increase this buffer size to achieve a better throughput.

Here's an example that reconfigures the sending and receiving buffer sizes:

```
using System;
using System.Net;
using System.Net.Sockets;

class ProtocolTweaking
{
  public void SetBufferSize(Socket sockInstance,int recvBuffer,int sendBuffer)
  {
    sockInstance.SetSocketOption(SocketOptionLevel.Socket,
                            SocketOptionName.SendBuffer,sendBuffer);
    sockInstance.SetSocketOption(SocketOptionLevel.Socket,
                            SocketOptionName.ReceiveBuffer,recvBuffer);
  }
}
```

Socket: Timeout

By default, Socket in blocking mode blocks on a read or write operation. You can override this behavior by assigning a timeout value with each operation. The timeout value determines the blocking time, and on timeout expiry, it raises a SocketException.

Here's an example that assigns a timeout value to the send and receive operations:

```
using System;
using System.Net;
using System.Net.Sockets;

class ProtocolTweaking
{
  public void SetTimeOut(Socket sockInstance,int recvBuffer,int sendBuffer)
  {
    sockInstance.SetSocketOption(SocketOptionLevel.Socket,
                            SocketOptionName.SendTimeout,10);
    sockInstance.SetSocketOption(SocketOptionLevel.Socket,
                            SocketOptionName.ReceiveTimeout,10);
  }
}
```

TCP: NoDelay

TCP implements the Nagle algorithm that throttles data before transmission over the wire. Such low-level optimizations are extremely helpful in a low-bandwidth link where applications exchange a TCP segment of a small size. With the help of this algorithm, data is held back for a particular time period before transmitting on the network.

Here's an example that disables the Nagle algorithm:

```
using System;
using System.Net;
using System.Net.Sockets;

class ProtocolTweaking
{
  public void DisableNagle(Socket sockInstance)
  {
    sockInstance.SetSocketOption
        (SocketOptionLevel.Tcp,SocketOptionName.NoDelay,1);
  }
}
```

Exploring the Business-Technology Mapping

As you know, the primary role of the broadcast engine is to publish the latest price information about a stock. It also provides ancillary services such as federal announcements, breaking news, and so on. Such services are provided by market data vendors; they collect data from various exchanges and provide this consolidated data to organizations. Because of this responsibility, they are often considered to be the information backbone of an organization, and this creates huge pressure on them to meet their goal of timely delivery of data. While adhering to this goal, they often face two important problems:

Data-quake: Data-quake erupts at a particular stage in trading hours where almost all stocks undergo a price change. This change occurs as a result of some breaking news that directly/ indirectly impacts the economy of a country or the profitability of an organization or a particular industry segment. But regardless of the source, the amount of data received by the market data vendor is enormous in comparison to the data received during normal trading hours. The equities market is in a much less controllable shape during this stage because of the number of instruments transacted in the market; however, in the derivatives market, particularly the option instrument, the amount of data received is sufficient to bring down the trading systems.

Network efficiency: It is expected that when the amount of data is huge, then the underlying network link used to transfer it must be strong enough to cope with the speed at which data is thrown over the wire. To handle such a massive load, many organizations use state-of-art network infrastructure between the market data vendor system and the organization's internal system.

Figure 4-24 represents a high-level overview of producers and consumers of market data information. Let's begin with systems that directly fall under the market data vendor domain. A market data vendor creates a ticker plant, also known as a *market data farm*. It is actually from here that the information is propagated to its premium subscribers. So, you should not be surprised when you notice two different organizations subscribing to data from the same ticker plant.

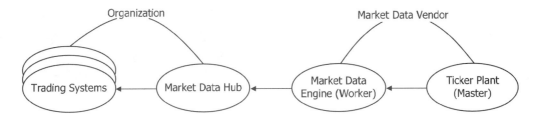

Figure 4-24. *Conceptual overview of market data producers and consumers*

The market data farm connects to various exchanges and gathers data published by them. This gathered data is then packaged in a suitable format and delivered to the market data engine. The market data engine is the actual application that sits at the organization end and receives the data published by its master. Also, the ticker plant falls outside the organization network periphery because the network bandwidth available between the market data engine and its corresponding plant is usually limited in nature.

The market data vendor considers the bandwidth constraint and diverts a major chunk of effort to fine-tuning the interaction between the worker and master both from a message processing and a communication perspective. Once the market data engine receives a message, the message is then made available to internal applications inside the organization. Imagine for a moment what would happen if individual applications inside an organization started requesting market data directly from the market data engine. This would directly result in a tight coupling between the market data vendor and the applications. Furthermore, the message format and communication style adopted by an individual market data vendor is truly proprietary in nature and incompatible with other market data vendors. (Standards such as Market Data Definition Language [MDDL] are defined by groups of financial institutions, but they have yet to be fully embraced by the financial community.)

However, in the real word, the story is different. No organization depends upon a single market data vendor; instead, they spread their risk by subscribing to services of at least two market data vendors so in case of the nonavailability of data from one vendor, they can fall back on the other. So how do you stop applications from directly communicating with the market data engine? The solution to this problem is to introduce another entity market data hub that abstracts away vendor-specific differences.

The market data hub directly speaks to the vendor market data engine and collects this data, transforms it to a uniform format, and finally makes this information available to internal applications. The upside of such an implementation is that applications are completely immune to any new changes implemented by vendors, and this responsibility shifts to the market data hub to accommodate such changes. Another benefit reaped by applications is they can enjoy the data streaming from multiple vendors with just the flip of a switch. With the market data hub acting as an information mediator, it is also possible to build sophisticated intelligence by consolidating data from multiple data vendors, comparing individual stock prices and their arrival times with individual vendor data, and then publishing the latest price information. In this way, applications can ensure that the price information received is on par with the price published in the exchange at that particular time.

Now that we have covered both the business and technology topics, it is time to introduce the solution. Building a broadcast engine generally involves two components; these are the producer and consumer components. The real complexity lurks at the producer end, so we will not cover the consumer end, which is relatively easy to build once you understand the design of the producer component. Figure 4-25 shows the implementation overview.

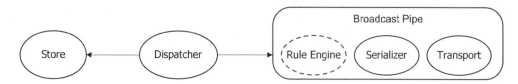

Figure 4-25. *Implementation overview*

The components depicted in Figure 4-25 are as follows:

Store: The store is a repository where the actual market data messages are stored. Stores are created for individual stocks, and the underlying nature of the store is such that it arranges messages in a FIFO fashion. From an implementation point of view, you can materialize this store either by using homegrown in-memory queues or by directly leveraging the Microsoft Messaging Queue (MSMQ) service.

Dispatcher: The dispatcher first ignites the launch of the broadcast event. The dispatcher retrieves an individual store and submits it to downstream components (the broadcast pipe) for further processing. The strength of the dispatcher is its scheduling behavior. It schedules the broadcast event on a defined time interval; this drastically decreases the number of messages published on the network. The other important characteristic of the dispatcher is the strategy implemented to dispatch the processing of the store. Processing stores in a round-robin fashion is a simple strategy, but more complex strategies can be implemented, such as processing stores based on the volatility of the underlying stock. This ensures that messages of highly volatile stocks are first pushed on the network before all other stocks.

Broadcast pipe: The broadcast pipe is formed by chaining individual discrete components. The first component in this chain is the rule engine. The rule engine allows subscribers to express the subscription rule. Based on this rule, the rule engine examines an individual market data message. If it finds a subscriber that satisfies the rules, then it forwards the message to the serializer component in the chain. The serializer converts the message to a byte array that is then passed to the transport. The transport is the final component in the chain, and it transmits data to its recipients.

In the following sections, we'll cover the code that more or less illustrates these concepts. The only component that is not covered is the rule engine.

Class Details

Figure 4-26 shows the broadcast engine class diagram, and Figure 4-27 shows the broadcast engine project structure.

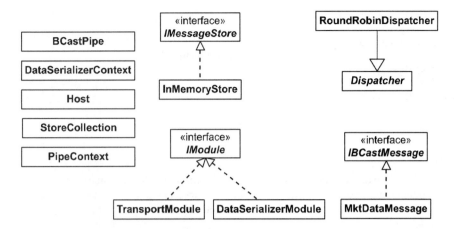

Figure 4-26. *Broadcast engine class diagram*

Figure 4-27. *Broadcast engine project structure*

IBCastMessage

IBCastMessage defines the common behavior implemented by application messages and is required
for broadcast purposes.

Here's the code:

```
using System;
namespace BCastServer
{
```

```
public interface IBCastMessage
{
    //Identifies broadcast message type
    //for example market data broadcast, exchange bulletin broadcast
    int MessageType{get;}
    //Length of Message
    int MessageLength{get;set;}
}
}
```

IMessageStore

The IMessageStore interface defines the common functionality implemented by concrete message stores. This functionality includes inserting and removing messages, assigning store names, and finding the run-time state of the store with the help of enumerated values.

Here's the code:

```
using System;

namespace BCastServer
{
    public enum StoreState
    {
        Idle,
        Busy
    }

    public interface IMessageStore
    {
        //Enqueue broadcast message
        void EnQueue(IBCastMessage bcastMessage);
        //Dequeue broadcast message
        IBCastMessage DeQueue();
        StoreState State{get;set;}
        //Total message in the store
        int Count{get;}
        //User friendly name of the store
        string Name{get;}
    }
}
```

InMemoryStore

InMemoryStore is an in-memory queue that uses System.Collections.Queue to store market data messages. The store is created by accepting a unique user-friendly name that is easy to recall; additionally, it is used by the consumer of market data information during the subscriptions stage.

Here's the code:

```
using System;
using System.Collections;

namespace BCastServer
{
    public class InMemoryStore : IMessageStore
    {
        Queue msgStore = Queue.Synchronized(new Queue());
```

```csharp
    StoreState storeState;
    string storeName;

    public InMemoryStore(string name)
    {
      storeName = name;
    }

    public string Name
    {
      get{return storeName;}
    }

    public int Count
    {
      get{return msgStore.Count;}
    }

    public void EnQueue(IBCastMessage bcastMessage)
    {
      msgStore.Enqueue(bcastMessage);
    }

    public IBCastMessage DeQueue()
    {
      return msgStore.Dequeue() as IBCastMessage;
    }

    public StoreState State
    {
      get{return storeState;}
      set{storeState=value;}
    }
  }
}
```

StoreCollection

StoreCollection represents collections of message stores. Multiple stores exist, and the convention followed here is to create stores based on individual stock names.

Here's the code:

```csharp
using System;
using System.Collections;

namespace BCastServer
{
  public class StoreCollection : IEnumerable
  {
    Hashtable storeTable = Hashtable.Synchronized(new Hashtable());

    public StoreCollection()
    {
    }

    public IMessageStore this[string storeName]
```

```
    {
      get{return storeTable[storeName] as IMessageStore;}
    }

    public void CreateStore(string storeName)
    {
      storeTable[storeName] = new InMemoryStore(storeName);
    }

    public IEnumerator GetEnumerator()
    {
      return storeTable.Values.GetEnumerator();
    }
  }
}
```

Dispatcher

This is an abstract class. The most important method is Schedule, and its implementation is mainly driven by the concrete dispatcher class:

```
using System;
using System.Threading;

namespace BCastServer
{
  public abstract class Dispatcher
  {
    StoreCollection storeCollection;

    public Dispatcher()
    {
    }

    //Returns the store collection that is then iterated
    //by dispatcher, dequeuing individual message from the store
    //and dispatching it to its subscriber
    public StoreCollection Stores
    {
      set{storeCollection=value;}
      get{return storeCollection;}
    }

    //This is an abstract method that basically determines
    //the strategy for dispatching broadcast data
    public abstract void Schedule();
  }
}
```

RoundRobinDispatcher

The code inside the RoundRobinDispatcher class triggers the actual broadcast of messages. The strategy adopted by the dispatcher depends mainly upon the business scenario, but this dispatcher schedules the broadcast of individual stores in a round-robin fashion.

Here's the code:

```csharp
using System;
using System.Threading;

namespace BCastServer
{
  public class RoundRobinDispatcher : Dispatcher
  {
    Thread scheduleThread;
    int sleepPeriod=100;

    public RoundRobinDispatcher()
    {
      //A new schedule thread is created that starts the message-
      //dispatching process.
      scheduleThread = new Thread(new ThreadStart(MessageDispatch));
    }

    private void MessageDispatch()
    {
      //In this section of code, the message store is fetched
      //from the store collection and processing of individual
      //store is then offloaded on a dedicated thread made
      //available from the thread pool. So effectively messages
      //from individual stores are concurrently broadcasted to recipients.
      //The schedule thread sleeps for 100ms before it again reschedules
      //the broadcast. Before rescheduling takes place, we make sure that
      //we don't face the reentrancy problem. This problem is tackled by
      //associating a state to a store.
      while(true)
      {
        foreach(IMessageStore store in Stores)
        {
          if ( store.State == StoreState.Idle )
          {
            store.State = StoreState.Busy;
            ThreadPool.QueueUserWorkItem(new
                WaitCallback(BCastPipe.Instance.ProcessModules),store);
          }
        }
        Thread.Sleep(sleepPeriod);
      }
    }

    public override void Schedule()
    {
      scheduleThread.Start();
    }
  }
}
```

IModule

In the "Examining the Business-Technology Mapping" section, we broadly discussed the broadcast pipe and listed the components chained inside this pipe. Components are allowed to be chained only when they implement the IModule interface.

Here's the code:

```
using System;

namespace BCastServer
{
  public interface IModule
  {
    object Process(PipeContext pipeCtx);
  }
}
```

PipeContext

The PipeContext class provides contextual information to an individual component in the chain. It provides store information and the actual broadcast message. The component uses the Data property to assign component-specific information that is required by the next component in the chain to perform further processing on it.

Here's the code:

```
using System;
using System.Collections.Specialized;

namespace BCastServer
{
  public class PipeContext
  {
    object ctxData;
    IMessageStore msgStore;
    IBCastMessage message;

    public PipeContext(IMessageStore store)
    {
      msgStore=store;
    }

    //Returns the current store
    public IMessageStore Store
    {
      get{return msgStore;}
    }

    //Returns the current message
    public IBCastMessage Message
    {
      get{return message;}
      set{message=value;}
    }

    //Returns the contextual data
    public object Data
    {
      get{return ctxData;}
      set{ctxData=value;}
    }
  }
}
```

BCastPipe

BCastPipe does the work of chaining individual components, dequeuing the message from the store, and handing over the message to the first component in the chain. This entire operation takes place on a dedicated thread (from a thread pool) assigned by the dispatcher component.

Here's the code:

```
using System;
using System.Collections;

namespace BCastServer
{
  public class BCastPipe
  {
    ArrayList moduleChain = new ArrayList();
    private static BCastPipe pipeInstance = new BCastPipe();

    public static BCastPipe Instance
    {
      get{return pipeInstance;}
    }

    public BCastPipe()
    {
      //This is the chain formation code; in an ideal world
      //the chain will be dynamically populated from an XML configuration file.
      //Currently data serialization and data transport module are associated
      //with this chain
      moduleChain.Add(new DataSerializerModule());
      moduleChain.Add(new TransportModule());
    }

    public void ProcessModules(object objState)
    {
      //A loop is carried out where messages are dequeued one by one
      //and are submitted first to serializer component.
      //Serializer component converts the message into raw bytes, and
      //it is made available as part of return argument of Process.
      //The returned information then becomes part of contextual information
      //and is assigned to Data property, which is then passed to Transport
      //component. Also after processing all messages inside the store, the state
      //of store is reset to idle state.
      IMessageStore store = objState as IMessageStore;
      if ( store.Count > 0 )
        Console.WriteLine("Dispatching Store : " +store.Count);
      while(store.Count > 0 )
      {
        PipeContext pipeCtx = new PipeContext(store);
        pipeCtx.Message = store.DeQueue();
        for(int ctr=0;ctr<moduleChain.Count;ctr++)
        {
          IModule module = moduleChain[ctr] as IModule;
          object ctxData = module.Process(pipeCtx);
          pipeCtx.Data = ctxData;
        }
      }
      store.State = StoreState.Idle;
```

```
    }
  }
}
```

DataSerializerModule

The DataSerializerModule module serializes the message received into an array of bytes; the serialization technique used is the same as explained in the "Message Framing" section of this chapter. The array of bytes is encapsulated in an instance of DataSerializerContext that is accessed by the transport module.

Here's the code:

```
using System;
using System.Runtime.InteropServices;

namespace BCastServer
{
  public class DataSerializerContext
  {
    byte[] rawData;

    public DataSerializerContext(byte[] data)
    {
      rawData = data;
    }

    public byte[] Data
    {
      get{return rawData;}
    }
  }

  public class DataSerializerModule : IModule
  {
    public object Process(PipeContext pipeCtx)
    {
      //Receive the strongly typed broadcast message
      IBCastMessage msg = pipeCtx.Message;
      //Calculate the object size
      int objectSize = Marshal.SizeOf(msg);
      //Assign the length of message
      msg.MessageLength= objectSize;
      //convert the managed object into an array of bytes
      IntPtr memBuffer = Marshal.AllocHGlobal(objectSize);
      Marshal.StructureToPtr(msg,memBuffer,false);
      byte[] byteArray = new byte[objectSize];
      Marshal.Copy(memBuffer,byteArray,0,objectSize);
      Marshal.FreeHGlobal(memBuffer);
      //Return the byte array that will then be
      //used by transport module to deliver to its destination
      return new DataSerializerContext(byteArray);
    }
  }
}
```

TransportModule

The `TransportModule` is the final leg in the chain that uses multicast features to deliver data to the consumer of this information.

Here's the code:

```csharp
using System;
using System.Net.Sockets;
using System.Net;

namespace BCastServer
{
  public class TransportModule : IModule
  {
    Socket serverSocket;
    IPEndPoint mcastEP;

    public TransportModule()
    {
      //Create a multicast IP address
      IPAddress bcastAddress =IPAddress.Parse("224.5.6.7");
      mcastEP = new IPEndPoint(bcastAddress ,30002);
      serverSocket = new
          Socket(AddressFamily.InterNetwork,SocketType.Dgram,ProtocolType.Udp);
      serverSocket.SetSocketOption(SocketOptionLevel.IP,
                SocketOptionName.MulticastTimeToLive, 3);
    }

    public object Process(PipeContext pipeCtx)
    {
      //data is broadcast after it is received
      //from serializer module
      DataSerializerContext szCtx =  pipeCtx.Data as DataSerializerContext;
      serverSocket.BeginSendTo(szCtx.Data,0,szCtx.Data.Length,
          SocketFlags.None,mcastEP,new AsyncCallback(SendData),null);
      return null;
    }

    private void SendData(IAsyncResult result)
    {
      serverSocket.EndSend(result);
    }
  }
}
```

MktDataMessage

The `MktDataMessage` is a concrete market data message class; we have annotated the fields with the appropriate marshaling attributes.

Here's the code:

```csharp
using System;
using System.Runtime.InteropServices;

namespace BCastServer
{
  [StructLayout(LayoutKind.Sequential,Pack=1,CharSet=CharSet.Ansi)]
  public class MktDataMessage : IBCastMessage
```

```
{
  int msgLength;

  [MarshalAs(UnmanagedType.ByValTStr,SizeConst=10)]
  string underlyingName;
  double askPrice;
  int askSize;
  double bidPrice;
  int bidSize;

  public string Underlying
  {
    get{return underlyingName;}
    set{underlyingName=value;}
  }

  public double Ask
  {
    get{return askPrice;}
    set{askPrice=value;}
  }

  public double Bid
  {
    get{return bidPrice;}
    set{bidPrice=value;}
  }

  public int AskSize
  {
    get{return askSize;}
    set{askSize=value;}
  }

  public int BidSize
  {
    get{return bidSize;}
    set{bidSize=value;}
  }


  public MktDataMessage(string underlying,double ask,int askSz,
                        double bid,int bidSz)
  {
    underlyingName=underlying;
    askPrice=ask;
    askSize=askSz;
    bidPrice=bid;
    bidSize=bidSz;
  }

  public int MessageType
  {
    get{return 1;}
  }

  public int MessageLength
```

```
        {
          get{return msgLength;}
          set{msgLength=value;}
        }
      }
    }
}
```

Host

The code inside the Host class creates stores, then initializes the dispatcher component, and finally submits messages to stores that are then delivered to the final recipients.

Here's the code:

```
using System;

namespace BCastServer
{
  public class Host
  {

    public static void Main(string[] args)
    {
      StoreCollection storeCollection = new StoreCollection();
      //Create a dedicated store for MSFT,YHOO,GE
      storeCollection.CreateStore(@"store\MSFT");
      storeCollection.CreateStore(@"store\YHOO");
      storeCollection.CreateStore(@"store\GE");

      //Create the Message Dispatching Scheduler
      RoundRobinDispatcher dispatcher = new RoundRobinDispatcher();
      dispatcher.Stores = storeCollection;
      dispatcher.Schedule();

      //Enqueue market data message in MSFT store
      MktDataMessage mktData= new MktDataMessage("MSFT",24.5,100,50,25);
      IMessageStore msgStore = storeCollection[@"store\" +mktData.Underlying];
      msgStore.EnQueue(mktData);

      //Enqueue market data message in GE store
      mktData= new MktDataMessage("GE",24.5,100,50,25);
      msgStore = storeCollection[@"store\" +mktData.Underlying];
      msgStore.EnQueue(mktData);
    }
  }
}
```

Figure 4-28 shows the BCastServer console output.

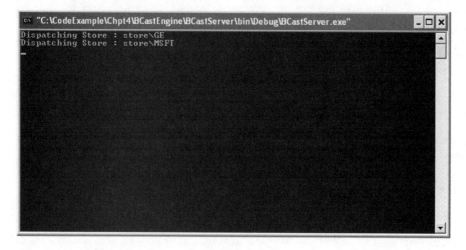

Figure 4-28. BCastServer *console output*

Summary

The following are the key points covered in this chapter:

- We talked about the importance of market data and how it is consumed by market professionals across the financial trading value chain to arrive at informed trading decisions.

- We provided a basic overview of the important network concepts and protocols such as the TCP/IP core stack, IP, and ICMP.

- We covered the advantages of using DNS, which provides better name resolution functionality.

- We demonstrated how to use UDP with the help of a market data producer and consumer example.

- We discussed the advantages of using TCP over UDP.

- We discussed the types of conventions followed by computers when interpreting and packaging multibyte numbers.

- We showed how to implement a generic code to preserve a message boundary.

- We covered the different types of network broadcast techniques: solicited and unsolicited broadcast.

- Finally, we showed how to implement a prototype of a broadcast engine that uses a network multicast feature to publish market data.

CHAPTER 5

■■■

The Application Operation Engine

Struggles in life are like tight while *loops; success comes only when you break this loop.*

This chapter is devoted to the operational requirements of a trading system and is unlike other chapters so far because it does not cover any hard-core business topics. Operational features such as security, logging, configuration, and heartbeat checks are part of any good trading system. But they are usually bundled with the real business component and executed within the same address space of the business component. In this chapter, using the .NET Remoting framework, we will show how to physically separate this operational need and construct a strong foundation to centralize the monitoring and the management of subcomponents within trading systems.

Understanding the Trading Operational Requirement

In bygone days, the design of a trading application was centered on the idea of a stand-alone architecture where the user interface, data store, and business logic were located on one computer. But as business complexities started growing, the demand rose for breaking up these applications and carving out distinct components for them. This led to a new component-oriented architecture. Referring to the trading life cycle in Chapter 1 (Figure 1-6), you'll see it is impossible to meet the end-to-end business requirements if you shy away from a component-oriented architecture.

Returning to a real-life trading scenario, a system is partitioned into subcomponents, also called the *business component*. A business component in this context is a unit of deployment that subsumes a part of the business requirement and is heavily specialized to meet this business need. As a result of this component-decomposing exercise, a system would have a number of business components, and collaboration among these components is the primary key to successfully representing the system as a single entity to the outside world. Hence, to facilitate this integration, a business component needs to contain three types of channels: inbound, outbound, and operational channels. The component listens on the inbound channel, and therefore requests from other components are directed to this channel. Similarly, the business component uses the outbound channel to communicate with other components. The intent of the operational channel is to allow the operational activity of a business component (which is discussed later in this section).

Figure 5-1 provides an abstract view of a business component. From an implementation point of view, you can implement both inbound and outbound channels using a fast enterprise messaging bus. The most popular messaging backbones used in today's Windows world are TIBCO-Rendezvous, Microsoft MSMQ, and IBM MQ-Series.

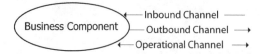

Figure 5-1. *Business component*

Clearly, modularizing trading applications in the form of components has some major benefits:

Scalability: The loose-coupling characteristic of a component makes it a perfect candidate to be deployed on a dedicated high-end machine that would tremendously increase the performance of the application. Moreover, this also opens the door to incorporating advanced capabilities, such as load balancing and fault tolerance, which would further increase the application's robustness.

Pluggability, extensibility, and reusability: A system is usually combined and built from both homegrown and off-the-shelf components, and if an individual component based its communication strictly on the notion of inbound and outbound channels, then it could easily be replaced with a new component without affecting the other dependent business components. Moreover, a business component built in such a fashion will always promote heavy reusability across organizations.

In the trading world, the most commonly found business components that religiously follow these disciplines are the following:

- The order-matching system
- The order management system
- Market data
- Risk management
- The limit-monitoring system
- The position system
- The exchange gateway
- The settlement system

Although business components are essential, operational (infrastructure) components that look after the operational requirements of the business components are equally important (see Figure 5-2).

Figure 5-2. *Operational service common across all business components*

These operational requirements are common among all business components and do not consider any kind of business know-how in their implementation. The frequently needed operational components encountered in day-to-day development are as follows:

Logging component: The role of the logging component is to provide a logging infrastructure that allows an application to log its activity. Application logs play an important role in troubleshooting hard-to-find failures. Additionally, they are also one of the mandatory audit requirements of an organization.

Configuration component: Storing application-related settings in a configuration file is considered a good development practice. Moreover, the configuration file can drive a system's ability to adapt to the external environment. The configuration component is tasked with the responsibility of centralizing and bookkeeping the system's related settings and providing a uniform way of accessing these settings from all business components.

Heartbeat component: With so many critical business components running in a system and with each component hosted on a dedicated machine, it becomes crucial to carefully watch the health of these components. The first step to lessen this problem is to modify the business component to continuously send a heartbeat message to the heartbeat component. This heartbeat message is configured to trigger at predefined intervals, and a failure to receive this message will be raised in the form of a red-flag alert by the heartbeat component.

Data management: The data management service provides a golden copy of static data that is not updated on a regular basis. The data that falls under such a category is the ISIN master, exchange master, client master, and so on. Most of the business components utilize these types of data, and hence it is advisable to centralize this data under a data management service and also provide a uniform data access mechanism.

User authentication and profile component: This component monitors all login requests by performing password and user profile checks. It ensures that individual login requests are valid and are originating from legitimate users. Similarly, it also monitors logout requests and invokes all defined processes (such as saving user profile settings, writing session details to log files, and so on) when a logout request is received.

Instrumentation component: It is absolutely necessary for critical applications to collect performance-related data in the production environment and analyze this data to close any missing gaps that are hard to trace in the development environment. With the instrumentation component in place, the performance-related data collected by various business components is stored and analyzed from a central place.

Application management component: The application management component is considered to be the remote control of a business component mainly because of its ability to manage the startup and shutdown of business components. Moreover, this operational service is further augmented by introducing other value-added features such as the autodeployment of a business component, the scheduling of the business component to start at a particular time, application recoverability, and so on.

You can take many approaches to team operational components with business components, and this depends mainly upon the nature of the system. But as mentioned earlier, a trading-based system is composed of multiple business components. Hence, it becomes important to deviate from the traditional approach. The most optimal way to integrate is to centralize all operational services and host them on a dedicated machine. In a sense, you completely offload the infrastructure-processing requirements of the business component, thus making them further scalable. Furthermore, it is now possible to take a complete snapshot of the system. For example, by implementing a centralized logging component, you can easily build a logging graphical user interface (GUI) that would display the activity in the system in real time. You can also reap the same benefit from the configuration component because now the application configuration information is also centralized in one place, and therefore you can easily implement any changes to the application settings. So, how do the business components communicate with the operational components? To answer this question, let's revisit Figure 5-1 where we talk about an operational channel. It is with the help of this channel that individual business components communicate with the operational components.

Although there are various ways of technically implementing the conceptual model in Figure 5-3, with the advent of .NET Remoting it is a piece of cake. .NET Remoting has modernized the concept of interprocess communication. Considering the breadth and depth of features currently provided by .NET Remoting, it would be extremely disappointing if we failed to leverage it in this scenario. The rest of the chapter is devoted to exploring .NET Remoting and explaining other important topics in detail.

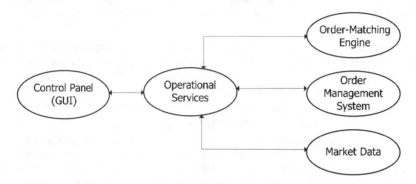

Figure 5-3. *Centralization of operational services*

Exploring the Multiple Facets of an Object

A business requirement is the raw material for software development that is gathered, analyzed, and refined to build a system. Therefore, a well-defined business requirement is undoubtedly the first step in any software development. Requirements fall under the user's domain and are described in plain and simple text. However, from a system implementation point of view, requirements need to be translated into a language that is complex in nature and therefore demands a strict formalism. This process of translation is called *requirement distillation* where requirements from the user domain are condensed and mapped to fine-grained objects in the system domain (see Figure 5-4). Requirements are high-level abstractions of objects; to be more precise, the collection of distinct objects is closely collaborated on to meet the need of a requirement. This raises the question, what is an object? An *object* is a run-time representation of a class. A *class* encapsulates the real intention of a business requirement in the form of state and behavior. State and behavior are evidenced inside a class in the form of *variables* and *members*, respectively. Members are the key drivers, and with the help of variables they orchestrate a specific aspect of the requirement.

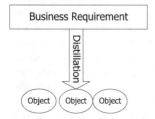

Figure 5-4. *Requirement distillation*

An object is like a multifaceted actor who plays different roles based on the script and story. An object is also bestowed with similar characteristics and sports new behavior based on its underlying context (see Figure 5-5).

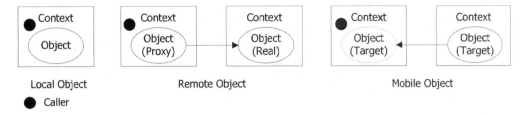

Local Object   Remote Object   Mobile Object

● Caller

Figure 5-5. *Multiple facets of object*

An object is incubated inside a context; a context in a broader sense provides services that are availed by an object.

This includes the creation of the object, which costs few bytes of physical memory and allows seamless access to other objects inside the context. *Context* is an abstract term, and in the computing world it materializes in the form of an application process, thread, or .NET application domain. Based on the dynamics of the context, the object is classified into the following types:

Local object: An object earns the title of local object when both the caller and the real object are citizens of the same context.

Remote object: An object is known as a remote object when its caller resides in a different context. In spite of the context's partition, the caller is able to access the object and leverage its services. In a real world, this depicts interprocess communications where objects from one application process invoke the services of another object hosted in a different application process. The caller accesses the remote object using a proxy object that mimics a real object in the caller context but in reality delegates the request to the actual object. This sort of transparent intercontext communication is achieved by some sort of black-box component that hides the inherent complexities involved in invoking methods on remote objects.

Mobile object: An object is known as a mobile object when it is instantiated in a context that is different from the caller context, but subsequent method invocation on this object is served from the caller context rather than the context in which it was created. This unique ability of the object to package itself and resurrect in a caller context is a mobile object.

By default, objects are created as local objects. To promote them to a remote or mobile object, you need an infrastructure that bridges the path and allows seamless communication between these objects, regardless of the underlying context. The context could also be located in a different machine. This means that the infrastructure should be intelligent enough to understand network quirks. Such infrastructures are developed to link computing and communication in a revolutionary way. The presence of such infrastructures leads to the design of distributed applications, and well-known infrastructures such as DCOM, CORBA, DCE-RPC, and so on, have strong roots in today's modern distributed applications. These kinds of infrastructures have been instrumental in building highly scalable architectures. With .NET Remoting joining this bandwagon, building distributed applications in .NET is even simpler when compared to its predecessor, DCOM. The .NET Remoting Framework removes all the hurdles usually faced in building distributed applications and provides a powerful framework that is easily extensible to meet the needs of an application.

Understanding .NET Remoting Infrastructure

In the preceding section, we discussed a black-box component/infrastructure that acts as the glue to establish communication between objects, irrespective of their underlying context. This black-box component is known as *middleware*. Middleware provides the scaffolding on which distributed systems are designed and developed. In a distributed system, three components—namely, software, hardware, and network components—are involved and closely work with each other. Massive complexities are involved in interacting with hardware and network components. These complexities are unpleasant and therefore result in restricting most software systems from adopting a distributed path. With the advent of middleware, which by itself is a software framework, most of these complexities are hidden, thereby providing an easy-to-use programming model with the necessary building blocks for designing distributed systems.

The latitude of services offered by middleware is praiseworthy and can be categorized into the following types:

Communication services: The communication service is the core and distinguishing feature that all middleware implements. This service shields the application from knowing the underlying raw communication protocol details such as TCP/IP, UDP, Named Pipes, and so on. Instead, it provides applications with a cherry-picking feature—it allows the application to pick which communication protocol to use to exchange messages with the other end of systems.

Infrastructural services: Middleware has further made inroads into the domain realm of systems. The infrastructural service is geared toward providing domain-related features that are available out of the box and directly consumed by applications. For example, services such as transactions, security, and persistence are readily available in most of today's modern middleware systems.

.NET Remoting is communication middleware designed to build .NET-based distributed systems. Although it primarily provides communication services, it came as a bold stroke at the right time when its predecessor, DCOM, was already in the stage of losing market share. The chronic problems rooted in DCOM were carefully considered, and as a result, .NET Remoting was designed from scratch to address all the issues faced in DCOM. The most important theme of .NET Remoting is its ease of use and extensibility. It is so versatile that it allows developers to fine-tune practically every aspect of its framework.

Figure 5-6 depicts a bird's-eye view of the remoting framework. The framework is modeled around the principle of layered architecture. Each layer provides a specific responsibility, which in turn promotes loose coupling between layers. Such layer-wise separation provides complete flexibility when it comes to extending each of these layers.

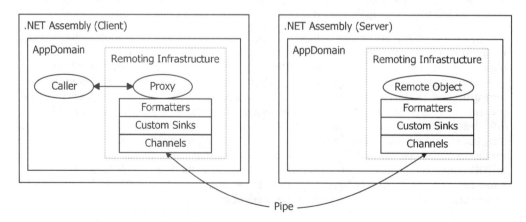

Figure 5-6. *High-level view of the remoting framework*

Note that in Figure 5-6, both the remote object and the caller are hosted inside a separate .NET executable. A .NET executable is a Win32 process partially baked with Intermediate Language (IL) code instead of native instruction and executed under the surveillance of the CLR. The Win32 process is an environment provided by the operating system (OS) and is equipped with all the necessary run-time facilities such as memory and other system-related resources. Another important feature of the Win32 process is that it acts as a fault isolation gate; in other words, failure in one process will not affect other processes running in the system.

The CLR extends the concept of the Win32 process one step further in the form of an *application domain*. An application domain, which is the brainchild of the CLR, offers a fault isolation environment to managed applications. In a nutshell, managed applications are executed inside a default application domain created by the CLR. The most striking feature is that the CLR allows the creation of multiple application domains inside a single Win32 process and also treats each of these application domains as a separate unit of processing. So, if multiple instances of the managed application are executed in multiple application domains and if one application executes error-prone code resulting in an unexpected crash, then only the crashed application domain is affected. The other application domains are completely untouched. Previously, the only way to achieve such fault isolation was to spawn each application as a separate, independent Win32 process. Although the Win32 process is definitely the nicest thing available, it comes with a cost in terms of the additional processing overhead. On the other hand, the application domain is very lightweight and consumes less memory. The application domain is also touted for its dynamic capability to load and unload itself during the execution of the program. Keep in mind that the application domain is an abstraction provided by the CLR, and therefore to the OS it appears as a big chunk of the Win32 process. Hence, when a Win32 process is terminated, all application domains will be effectively terminated.

As depicted in Figure 5-5, an object is always incubated inside a context. In the .NET world, the context is none other than the application domain. So, every object is affiliated with an application domain. Also, no two objects instantiated on a different application's domain running under the same application process will be able to access each other's methods or properties. This is similar to two people living in two different rooms under the same roof but who are still strangers to each other. So, how do these .NET objects communicate with each other? The answer is .NET Remoting, which addresses the need of both local process communication (LPC) and remote process communication (RPC). LPC is the communication between two application domains inside the same application process, and RPC is when the communication spans two application domains hosted on a different application process.

Let's examine Figure 5-6 more closely using a detailed flow-wise explanation. You are aware of how the caller interacts with a remote object with the help of a proxy that masquerades as a real object in the caller application domain. The proxy, after intercepting calls from the caller, forwards them to the next layer in the remoting framework, as described here:

Formatter layer: This layer is tasked with the responsibility of marshaling the intercepted message from the proxy into a specific format. This message, along with the method name and arguments, contains other remoting-specific information that identifies the target remote object on which this method is invoked. The format type of this message could be a raw binary or XML or custom format. By default, the remoting framework provides support for both binary format and SOAP format. The binary formatter undoubtedly is the fastest formatter but when interoperability is at stake, then SOAP is the way to go. The formatter plays a dual role. On the receiving end (the server side), it unmarshals the message back to the appropriate CLR type; on the sending end, it serializes the CLR type to the appropriate wire-encoding format.

Custom sink layer: Compared to its predecessor, the remoting architecture provides a mind-blowing level of extensibility. The custom sink layer allows developers to plug their custom logic. Such custom logic provides the means to introduce additional features, be it business features or infrastructure-related features. One of the most commonly used features is securing the message by applying a strong encryption technique. A mind-numbing way to implement this feature is to change both the proxy and the remote objects and inject additional security code into every method. A much smarter way to achieve this is with the help of a custom sink that is transparently plugged, and then every message is passed through this custom sink layer, thus providing complete liberty to sinks to further change the characteristics of the message.

Channel layer: The channel layer is the backbone for message delivery within the remoting framework. This layer is responsible for transporting a message to its destination, which could be a separate application domain hosted on either the same machine or a different machine. The merits of decoupling transport-level details into a separate layer are that it allows developers to experiment with a wide range of protocols, and both the caller (client) and the remote object (server) are completely unaware of how messages are received and delivered to the destination. By default, TCP and HTTP channels are bundled as part of the remoting framework.

Pipe: The pipe is an abstract wire that builds a data conduit between two applications, and data is pushed in or out of this conduit. A pipe could be further classified as a logical and physical pipe. A *logical* pipe is built when the scope of communication is confined within the same machine and between two separate application domains. A *physical* pipe is implemented with network cables that connect machines to form a network.

Exploring the Multiple Facets of a Remoting Object

The remoting infrastructure allows the creation of both mobile and remote objects. Mobile objects and remote objects are also popularly known as marshal-by-value (MBV) and marshal-by-reference (MBR) objects, respectively. MBR objects in the remoting platform are broadly categorized as server-activated objects (SAOs) and client-activated objects (CAOs). Both SAOs and CAOs vary in how the object state, lifetime, and activation are managed. The lifetime of an SAO-based object is directly controlled by the context in which it is hosted (the server), and the lifetime of a CAO-based object depends on the lifetime of the caller (the client).

We will now describe the two types of remoting objects:

Stateless object: In the remoting context, a stateless remote object is devoid of any state management features. The lifetime of a stateless remote object is very short. It begins with method invocation and ends with the execution of the method. It also means that for every method invocation received from the caller, a new instance of the remote object is created and finally destroyed. Such immediate recycling of remote objects provides no room for preserving any state that could later be accessed on a subsequent method invocation. Remoting supports stateless objects in the form of *SingleCall* objects, which are categorized under SAO. In a SingleCall object, every new request triggered from the caller is handled by a unique instance of the remote object. This instance is constructed upon method request and is subject to garbage collection upon the completion of the method execution.

Stateful object: In the remoting context, a stateful remote object is provided with state management features. It goes one step further by allowing the state of an object to be manipulated both at the global level and at the session level. Remoting allows the construction of stateful objects in the form of a Singleton or CAO object. *Singleton* objects, like SingleCall objects, are categorized under SAO, but the similarities end there. Singleton objects are stateful objects, and this means their state is preserved across method calls. Another important feature of Singleton objects is that only a single instance of the remote object exists at any point of time. Figure 5-7 shows this in action where a single instance of a remote object is served to multiple callers. A Singleton object also allows for easy data sharing because a change in the state of a Singleton object is immediately visible to the callers. On the other hand, CAO-based objects are the equivalent of local objects whose lifetimes are directly controlled by the caller, but the instantiation still happens in the context in which the CAO object is hosted, which is usually the server. CAO, unlike Singleton, allows the creation of multiple instances, and each instance is uniquely distinguishable by the caller.

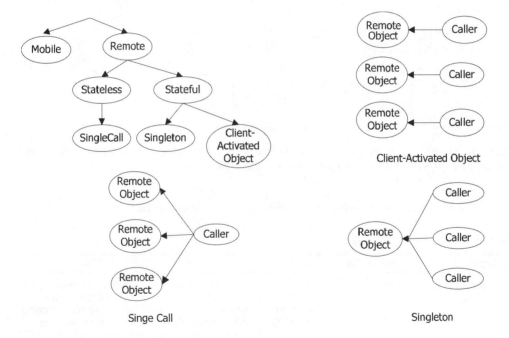

Figure 5-7. *Multiple facets of a remoting object*

The flexibility that remoting provides is evident in the different types of MBR objects described. Merits and demerits are associated with the different types, but the decision to choose the correct one is mainly an architectural decision.

Introducing Local Process Communication (LPC)

In this section, we will demystify the process of how communication is established between two application domains. To illustrate this, we will show how to build a service controller. A *service controller* is the equivalent of a Windows service manager that controls the startup, shutdown, and other maintenance-related activities of a service. The only difference between the Windows service manager and the service controller is that although the former is meant to manage application process, the latter is meant to control trading operation–related services. A real-life example of trading operation–related services is the heartbeat service (see Figure 5-8). The heartbeat service periodically monitors the heartbeat of the important trading components. For example, an order management system depends upon several subcomponents such as a bookkeeping service, an exchange routing gateway, and a market data service that are installed on a separate machine. In this type of environment, it is extremely important to keep a close watch on the health of all these services, and this is where the heartbeat service plays an important role. The heartbeat service forms the basic requirement of the trading operational requirements, and we will use this as the code example throughout the chapter.

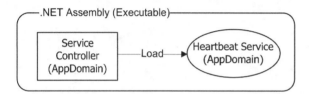

Figure 5-8. *The service controller and heartbeat service are loaded in a different application domain; communication between them takes place through remoting.*

To build this example, you will need the three projects mentioned in Table 5-1.

Table 5-1. *LPC assembly structure*

Project Name	Assembly Type	Description
LPC.Common	Class library	The interdomain communication between two processes or between two machines imposes a particular posture toward the composition of the class (in other words, adopting interface-based polymorphism). The interface defines a contract that needs to be adhered to by the class implementing it. This contract does not provide core implementation; rather, it defines a skeletal implementation of members and properties. The advantage of using the interface is that it decouples the caller from knowing the underlying class implementation, allowing the caller to communicate to any object instance of the class as long as it adheres to the defined contract. This particular posture of programming has already been well established and religiously followed in other distributed programming environments such as CORBA, DCOM, and so on. This class library contains shared interfaces that are referenced by both the service controller (LPC.ServiceHost) and the service provider (LPC.Services).

Project Name	Assembly Type	Description
LPC.ServiceHost	Executable	This is the service controller application that is responsible for managing various infrastructure-related services such as the heartbeat service, instrumentation service, roles entitlement service, and so on. The management task includes starting a service, suspending a service, and stopping a service.
LPC.Services	Class library	This library includes all the core infrastructure services such as the heartbeat service, the instrumentation service, and so on. Packaging core infrastructure services into a separate class library allows the easy maintenance of code.

We begin our remoting journey with the declaration of IService. This interface defines two important members that are implemented by the core infrastructure services:

```
using System;

namespace LPC.Common
{
  public interface IService
  {
    void Start();
    void Stop();
  }
}
```

IService defines the skeletal implementation and is inherited by a concrete infrastructure service, and the heartbeat service is one of them. The heartbeat service is a core infrastructure service that continuously generates a heartbeat message. In reality, a lot of steps are involved before generating a heartbeat, but for demonstration purposes we have ignored those steps. Start and Stop are the two important methods defined in the HeartBeatService class (see Listing 5-1).

Listing 5-1. *Heartbeat Service (LPC Version)*

```
using System;
using System.Configuration;
using System.Threading;
using LPC.Common;

namespace LPC.Services
{
  public class HeartBeatService : MarshalByRefObject,IService
  {
    bool stopFlag=true;
    int hbInterval;


    public HeartBeatService()
    {
      //Configure this service to check for heartbeat messages
      //at an interval of two seconds
      hbInterval=2000;
    }
```

```
    public void Start()
    {
      //This method triggers the heartbeat check activity at a predefined interval
      while(stopFlag)
      {
        Console.WriteLine("Checking HeartBeat");
        Thread.Sleep(hbInterval);
      }
    }

    public void Stop()
    {
      stopFlag = false;
    }
  }
}
```

The Start method contains the while loop code that displays a message on the console every two seconds. The loop termination logic is determined by the code inside the Stop method. Both these methods adhere to the members defined in the IService interface by supplying a concrete code implementation. The interesting piece of code to look at is MarshalByRefObject, which is inherited by the HeartBeatService class. By inheriting from MarshalByRefObject, HeartBeatService is promoted to a remotable class, and with the help of the remoting infrastructure, its public members can be invoked remotely.

After finishing with the implementation of the heartbeat service, the next step is to spin off the execution of this service in a separate application domain. In this way, individual infrastructure services will be running in their own application domains. To achieve this, a new LogicalProcess class is defined that provides an execution environment to the individual infrastructure service:

```
using System;
using System.Reflection;
using System.Runtime.Remoting;
using System.Threading;
using LPC.Common;

namespace LPC.ServiceHost
{
  public class LogicalProcess
  {
    AppDomain appDomain;
    Thread appThread;
    IService serviceProxy;

    public LogicalProcess(string serviceName)
    {
      //Derives type to be instantiated in a new appdomain
      //It is important to specify type name along with its namespace
      string typeName = "LPC.Services." +serviceName;

      //Create a new application domain
      appDomain = AppDomain.CreateDomain(serviceName);

      //The next step is to load LPC.Services assembly in this newly created
      //application domain and also instantiate the appropriate type.
      //Both these  tasks
      //are achieved with the help of CreateInstanceAndUnwrap that returns
```

```
        //a proxy reference that is cast back to the IService interface
        IService serviceProxy =
                appDomain.CreateInstanceAndUnwrap("LPC.Services",typeName) as IService;

        //After instantiating the new service, the processing of service
        //is offloaded to a new thread. This is similar to spawning
        //a new Win32 process, which by default creates a new thread and executes
        //the entry point method
        appThread = new Thread(new ThreadStart(serviceProxy.Start));
    }

    public void Start()
    {
        //The newly created thread begins its execution
        //i.e. invokes the Start method of the service
        appThread.Start();
    }

    public void Stop()
    {
    }

    }
}
```

The core implementation of LogicalProcess resides in the constructor method, where a new application domain is created using the CreateDomain static method of the AppDomain class. The AppDomain class represents the programming aspect of application domains and provides a broad spectrum of features related to application domain management. One of the important features AppDomain provides is the creation of a new application domain using the CreateDomain method. This method returns a reference to the newly created AppDomain, which could then be used to load assemblies. Assemblies, as you know, are either executables or dynamic link libraries, and AppDomain supports loading both these assembly types.

In the constructor method of LogicalProcess, you create a new AppDomain by passing a friendly name as the method argument. Once AppDomain is successfully created, the assembly is loaded, and an appropriate type is instantiated. Both these tasks are achieved with a call to the CreateInstanceAndUnwrap method. This method accepts the assembly name as the first argument and the type's full name as the second argument. In this code, you pass both the infrastructure service assembly name (LPC.Services) and the concrete service name (LPC.Services.HeartBeatService) to the CreateInstanceAndUnwrap method, which in turn loads the assembly, instantiates the type, and finally returns a proxy reference to the newly created service that is then cast back to the IService interface. The proxy reference then paves the way to the real object hosted in a different AppDomain.

Finally, ServiceHost gives the finishing touch to this example. It is a console-based host application that by default runs on an application domain created by the CLR during the initial loading phase of the application. ServiceHost acts as a single point of management, and its primary responsibilities include loading the individual infrastructure service in a separate application domain and unloading it when not required.

```
using System;
using System.Reflection;

namespace LPC.ServiceHost
{
  class ServiceHost
  {
    static void Main(string[] args)
```

```
    {
      //The heartbeat service is launched in a new application domain
      LogicalProcess serviceProcess = new LogicalProcess("HeartBeatService");
      serviceProcess.Start();
      Console.WriteLine("Press any key to Stop Service");
      Console.ReadLine();
      serviceProcess.Stop();
    }
  }
}
```

To compile and execute ServiceHost, you need to ensure the LPC.Services assembly is success-fully copied into the service controller executable directory. With this example, you have scratched the surface of .NET Remoting. To further expand this example, we will slightly modify the code to demonstrate the appropriate fit for the mobile object (in other words, the MBV object). You know that MBV objects are instantiated and serialized from one context to another context. So, to integrate this flavor of communication, we will introduce a new class named ServiceInfo. This class captures important attributes that provide additional information about the infrastructure service to the service controller. Although the information inside this class will be populated in the callee's context, being an MBV object, the complete state of object is serialized and resurrected in the caller's context. This means ServiceInfo will be accessed both by the callee and by the caller, and hence it becomes a perfect candidate to be part of the shared (LPC.Common) assembly.

```
using System;
using System.Collections;

namespace LPC.Common
{
  [Serializable]
  public class ServiceInfo
  {
    //User-Friendly Name of this service specifically used to
    //uniquely identify this service
    public string FriendlyName;
    //A very detailed description of features offered by this service
    public string Description;
    //List of dependent services
    public ArrayList DependentServices;
    //Indicates the start date and time of the service useful for audit purpose
    public DateTime StartDate;
  }
}
```

Annotating the Serializable attribute indicates to the remoting infrastructure that the ServiceInfo class needs to be marshaled by value instead of marshaled by reference. So, to access ServiceInfo, the IService interface needs to be changed and is introduced in the form of an additional method (see Listing 5-2).

Listing 5-2. *Common Operations Supported by Infrastructure Services*

```
using System;

namespace LPC.Common
{
  public interface IService
  {
    void Start();
```

```
    void Stop();
    ServiceInfo QueryServiceInfo();
  }
}
```

In Listing 5-2, a new QueryServiceInfo method was introduced. This method will then be
implemented by the infrastructure service (in other words, HeartBeatService) to furnish additional
information:

```
using System;
using System.Configuration;
using System.Threading;
using LPC.Common;

namespace LPC.Services
{
  public class HeartBeatService : MarshalByRefObject,IService
  {
    public ServiceInfo QueryServiceInfo()
    {
      //This method publishes meta-information about service
      ServiceInfo srvInfo = new ServiceInfo();
      srvInfo.FriendlyName = "Service HeartBeat Service";
      srvInfo.Description =
          "Checks HeartBeat of services at a regular interval of 2 seconds";
      return srvInfo;
    }
  }
}
```

The necessary modifications required to access the service information have been applied to
both the IService interface and the HeartBeatService class. So, the next task is to provide this information to the service controller. However, the service controller never directly interacts with the
infrastructure service; it adopts an indirect route to communicate with the service with the help of
LogicalProcess. The following code modification in the LogicalProcess class is necessary to allow
the service controller to query the service information:

```
using System;
using System.Reflection;
using System.Threading;
using LPC.Common;

namespace LPC.ServiceHost
{
  public class LogicalProcess
  {
    public ServiceInfo ProcessInfo
    {
      get{return serviceProxy.QueryServiceInfo();}
    }
  }
}
```

The updated ServiceHost now uses the ProcessInfo property of the LogicalProcess class to
retrieve and display the service information:

```
using System;
using System.Reflection;
using LPC.Common;
```

```
namespace LPC.ServiceHost
{
  class ServiceHost
  {
    static void Main(string[] args)
    {
      //The heartbeat service is launched in a new application domain
      LogicalProcess serviceProcess = new LogicalProcess("HeartBeatService");
      serviceProcess.Start();

      //The meta-information about service is retrieved
      //and stored in an instance of ServiceInfo. Although this call is processed
      //in a callee application domain, the result is marshaled by value
      //in a caller application domain
      ServiceInfo srvInfo = serviceProcess.ProcessInfo;

      //The meta-information about service is displayed
      Console.WriteLine("Service Info");
      Console.WriteLine("------------");
      Console.WriteLine("Name : " +srvInfo.FriendlyName);
      Console.WriteLine("Description : " +srvInfo.Description);
      Console.WriteLine("Press any key to Stop Service");
      Console.ReadLine();
      serviceProcess.Stop();
    }
  }
}
```

Configuring Infrastructure Services

Application configuration files contain information such as database connection strings, application run-time information, and so on, that is vital for building highly adaptive applications. In bygone days, this information was stored in INI files or the Windows registry database. With the advent of .NET, this practice has changed, and application configurations are stored in XML files. Furthermore, the framework provides a special pack of configuration helper classes to read information from these XML-based configuration files.

By default, .NET executables are mapped to a default configuration file. This default configuration file is in the same directory as the application, and the name of the configuration file is derived from the executable name and appended with the .config extension. For example, if the executable name is LPC.ServiceHost.exe, then the name of its corresponding configuration file would be LPC. ServiceHost.exe.config. In addition to the custom application configuration, the .NET Framework provides a machine.config file installed under the C:\WINDOWS\Microsoft.NET\Framework\v1.1.4322\ CONFIG directory. The machine.config file contains settings that are globally applied to all .NET assemblies. The configuration framework in .NET first probes into the machine configuration file, before looking into the application configuration file. It is considered a best practice to separate global settings from application-specific settings and store them in the machine configuration file. However, settings defined in the custom application configuration can still override machine.config settings.

The configuration file is composed of information that is specific to both applications and the CLR. The application configuration details are defined in the form of key-value pairs inside the <appSettings> element of the configuration file.

To get a feel of the .NET configuration framework, we will modify the heartbeat service code described in Listing 5-1. Currently, the heartbeat interval of the heartbeat service is configured to two seconds and is hard-coded inside the code. Ideally, the configuration file should drive this interval, and this is what the code in Listing 5-3 achieves.

Listing 5-3. *Heartbeat Service Configuration Settings*

```
<configuration>
 <appSettings>
  <add key="HeartBeatInterval" value="2000"/>
 </appSettings>
</configuration>
```

The configuration information described in Listing 5-3 is saved in the LPC.Services.dll.config file. It captures the heartbeat interval information in the form of a key-value pair. To access this configuration information, you need to use the ConfigurationSettings class defined in the System.Configuration namespace, and accordingly HeartBeatService is updated:

```
using System;
using System.Configuration;
using System.Threading;
using LPC.Common;

namespace LPC.Services
{
  public class HeartBeatService : MarshalByRefObject,IService
  {
    public HeartBeatService()
    {
      //Heartbeat interval is read from an application configuration file
      //i.e. the value is read from LPC.Services.dll.config
      int hbInterval =
          Convert.ToInt32(ConfigurationSettings.AppSettings["HeartBeatInterval"]);
    }
  }
}
```

ConfigurationSettings exposes the AppSettings property that is a run-time representation of the <appSettings> element. The AppSettings property returns a NameValueCollection class populated with a list of keys and values defined inside the <appSettings> element. The constructor method of HeartBeatService is modified to read the heartbeat interval from the configuration file. Additionally, you also need to update the LogicalPocess class with an additional overloaded constructor method, as shown in Listing 5-4.

Listing 5-4. *Assigning a Custom Configuration File*

```
using System;
using System.Reflection;
using System.Threading;
using LPC.Common;

namespace LPC.ServiceHost
{
  public class LogicalProcess
  {
    public LogicalProcess(string serviceName,string configurationFile)
    {
      //Binding decision of a new application domain is dictated by
      //creating a new instance of AppDomainSetup
      AppDomainSetup domainSetup = new AppDomainSetup();
```

```
        //Custom Configuration File Path
        domainSetup.ConfigurationFile = configurationFile;
        string typeName = "LPC.Services." +serviceName;
        appDomain = AppDomain.CreateDomain(serviceName,null,domainSetup);
        serviceProxy = appDomain.CreateInstanceAndUnwrap("LPC.Services",typeName)
                    as IService;
        appThread = new Thread(new ThreadStart(serviceProxy.Start));
    }
  }
}
```

In Listing 5-4, the constructor method accepts the full path of the configuration file as an additional argument. This configuration path is then assigned to the `ConfigurationFile` property of the `AppDomainSetup` class. The `AppDomainSetup` class stores information related to binding decisions in an application domain. This binding information is then passed to the `CreateDomain` method.

With this example, we implemented an element of adaptiveness by separating the custom configuration of an individual infrastructure service and driving its execution behavior based on values defined in the configuration file.

Shadow Copying Infrastructure Services

Developers familiar with programming in ASP and IIS must have wrestled with the DLL locking problem. This locking problem completely handcuffed developers from overwriting old files with new versions because of IIS exclusively locking these files. This problem is exacerbated particularly when the IIS service needs to be restarted in order to allow these DLLs to be overwritten. However, today's .NET landscape gives you new ammunition named *shadow copy* to battle this kind of problem.

Shadow copy is a mechanism where the libraries or executables are replicated from a launching directory (the master directory) to a mirrored directory (the cache directory). This cache directory then becomes the active location, and files from this location are served to the main memory. This certainly eases the problem of deployment, and developers are now free to overwrite the files at any point of time without bringing down the entire application. .NET supports shadow copying at the application domain level. Assemblies loaded inside the shadow copy–enabled application domain are copied into a cache directory and accessed from this new location. The following code introduces this feature in the `LogicalProcess` class to support the shadow-copying infrastructure service assembly:

```
using System;
using System.Reflection;
using System.Threading;
using LPC.Common;

namespace LPC.ServiceHost
{
  public class LogicalProcess
  {
    public LogicalProcess(string serviceName,bool shadowCopy)
    {
      AppDomainSetup domainSetup = new AppDomainSetup();
      //Assign the list of directory from which the assemblies
      //are shadow copied.
      domainSetup.ShadowCopyDirectories = AppDomain.CurrentDomain.BaseDirectory;

      //A boolean value that indicates whether all assemblies loaded in
      //application domain are shadow copied
      domainSetup.ShadowCopyFiles = shadowCopy.ToString();
```

```
            //Service name by default represents application name
            domainSetup.ApplicationName = serviceName;

            //Cache Path represents the physical location where assemblies loaded
            //inside application domain are mirrored and then executed from this
            //directory. However, in reality the assemblies are copied into
            //the CachePath\ApplicationName directory
            domainSetup.CachePath = @"C:\CacheLocation";
            string typeName = "LPC.Services." +serviceName;
            appDomain = AppDomain.CreateDomain(serviceName,null,domainSetup);
            serviceProxy = appDomain.CreateInstanceAndUnwrap("LPC.Services",typeName)
                        as IService;
            appThread = new Thread(new ThreadStart(serviceProxy.Start));
        }
    }
}
```

The AppDomainSetup class provides four important properties that need to be correctly assigned in order to turn on the shadow-copy feature. The ShadowCopyFiles property accepts a Boolean value of true or false. Even though there is no support for shadow copying individual assemblies, with the help of the ShadowCopyDirectories property developers can specify a list of directory names separated by a semicolon, and assemblies loaded from this directory will be shadow copied. Both the CachePath and ApplicationName properties indicate the name of a directory from which all assemblies loaded in a shadow copy–enabled application domain will be copied. The assemblies are copied into the CachePath\ApplicationName directory.

Finding the AppDomain Treasure

Along with the important features discussed in the previous section, the AppDomain type also provides a handful of properties and events that prove extremely beneficial in day-to-day development (see Table 5-2).

Table 5-2. *Methods and Events of Application Domain*

Method/Event	Description
FriendlyName	Returns a friendly name for the application domain.
GetAssemblies()	Returns the list of assemblies loaded in the application domain.
ExecuteAssemblies()	Executes the assembly in the application domain. This method is invoked to launch .NET executables.
GetData() and SetData()	The application domain provides a name-value pair data bag that allows storing application-related custom data. This data bag is freely accessible from other application domains. Most of the system-level configuration data such as application directory, configuration file, cache directory, and so on, are stored in this data bag.
AssemblyLoad	This event is raised when the assembly is loaded.
AssemblyResolve	This event occurs when the runtime fails to locate a particular assembly.
DomainUnload	This event is raised when the application domain is about to shut down. This event notification allows handlers of these events to perform the final cleanup activities.
TypeResolve	This event occurs when the runtime fails to resolve any types in an application domain.
UnhandledException	This event is the equivalent of a global exception handler but works only in the default application domain.

Introducing Remote Process Communication (RPC)

In this section, we will build a distributed version of the service controller example that will be grafted on top of the remoting infrastructure. Both the infrastructure service and the service controller are hosted on a separate machine, and this example is similar to a real-life environment where in fact infrastructure services are distributed across several machines. This also leads to a client-server architecture where the service controller is a client and the individual infrastructure service is a server. As a first step, we have identified the required assemblies, as shown in Table 5-3.

Table 5-3. *RPC Assembly Structure*

Project Name	Assembly Type	Description
RPC.Common	Class library	This class library contains shared interfaces that are referenced by both the client (RPC.ServiceController) and the server (RPC.Services).
RPC.ServiceController	Executable	This is the service controller (client) application that controls the management of infrastructure services.
RPC.Services	Executable	This is the application (server) that hosts infrastructure services.

Now you will begin the journey in the distributed world with the declaration of the IService interface that forms part of the shared RPC.Common class library. This exercise is similar to one we presented in the "Introducing Local Process Communication (LPC)" section of this chapter.

```
using System;

namespace RPC.Common
{
  public interface IService
  {
    void Start();
    void Stop();
  }
}
```

IService defines members that are supported by core infrastructure services. The only difference you will notice is that it doesn't support the QueryServiceInfo member. This has been separated into the new interface IServiceInfo, as follows:

```
using System;

namespace RPC.Common
{
  public interface IServiceInfo
  {
    ServiceInfo QueryServiceInfo{get;}
  }
}
```

The final class in the shared library is ServiceInfo, as shown in Listing 5-5.

Listing 5-5. *Meta-information About Infrastructure Service*

```
using System;
using System.Collections;

namespace RPC.Common
{
  [Serializable]
  public class ServiceInfo
  {
    public string FriendlyName;
    public string Description;
    public ArrayList DependentServices;
    public string Location;
  }
}
```

In Listing 5-5, along with basic information, you will find a new `Location` field. We will explain the intent of this field in a moment. With this class, we have completed the task of defining all shared interfaces that will be used in this example. In the next step, we will define the server-side implementation that hosts infrastructure services packaged inside the `RPC.Services` assembly (see Listing 5-6).

Listing 5-6. *Heartbeat Service (RPC Version)*

```
using System;
using System.Threading;
using RPC.Common;

namespace RPC.Services
{
  //By inheriting from MarshalByRefObject, we have made it a remotable class
  //The heartbeart functionality defined here is more or less similar to
  //its LPC version
  public class HeartBeatService : MarshalByRefObject,IService
  {
    Thread serviceThread;
    bool serviceStop;
    public HeartBeatService()
    {
    }

    public void Start()
    {
      Console.WriteLine("HeartBeat Service Started...");
      serviceThread = new Thread(new ThreadStart(Run));
      serviceStop=true;
      serviceThread.Start();
    }

    public void Run()
    {
      while(serviceStop)
      {
        Console.WriteLine("Sending HeartBeat Message...");
        Thread.Sleep(2000);
      }
    }
```

```
   public void Stop()
   {
     serviceStop=false;
   }

   public override object InitializeLifetimeService()
   {
     return null;
   }

 }
}
```

In Listing 5-6, HeartBeatService is inherited from MarshalByRefObject and also implements the IService interface defined in the shared (RPC.Common) library. The code is more or less similar to the HeartBeatService class defined in the cross-application domain example (see Listing 5-1), except that in Listing 5-6 the service is responsible for spawning a thread and running its code in this new thread. Also, a new overridden member, InitializeLifetimeService, relates to the object lifetime, which is explained in detail in the "Understanding Distributed Garbage Collection" section. After defining the heartbeat service, the next step is to define meta-information that provides the remote location of the heartbeat service to the service controller (the client), as shown in Listing 5-7.

Listing 5-7. *Heartbeat Service Meta-Information*

```
using System;
using RPC.Common;

namespace RPC.Services
{
  //This remote class provides meta-information about the heartbeart service
  public class HeartBeatServiceInfo : MarshalByRefObject, IServiceInfo
  {
    ServiceInfo srvInfo = new ServiceInfo();
    public HeartBeatServiceInfo()
    {
      srvInfo.FriendlyName = "Service HeartBeat Service";
      srvInfo.Description =
          "Checks HeartBeat of services at a regular interval of 2 seconds";
      //This is an important attribute because it represents
      //the remote location of the actual heartbeat service
      srvInfo.Location = "tcp://localhost:15000/HeartBeatService.rem";
    }

    public ServiceInfo QueryServiceInfo
    {
      get{return srvInfo;}
    }

  }
}
```

In Listing 5-7, the HeartBeatServiceInfo class provides additional information about the heartbeat service. This class is also inherited from MarshalByRefObject and implements the IServiceInfo interface. The motive behind this class is to emit metadata information about the service. We could have mixed this logic with the core service, but for demonstration purpose we factored it out as a different class.

The last and the important leg of the server-side implementation is to pepper HeartBeatService and HeartBeatServiceInfo with remoting ingredients so that they will be accessible from the service controller. The code shown in Listing 5-8 achieves this objective.

Listing 5-8. *Hosting Infrastructure Services*

```
using System;
using System.Runtime.Remoting;
using System.Runtime.Remoting.Channels;
using System.Runtime.Remoting.Channels.Tcp;

namespace RPC.Services
{
  class Host
  {
    static void Main(string[] args)
    {
      Console.WriteLine("HeartBeat Service Console..");
      //Identify the wire-encoding format; in this case we have selected
      //BinaryFormatter
      BinaryServerFormatterSinkProvider svrFormatter =
                  new BinaryServerFormatterSinkProvider();

      //Identify the communication protocol used to deliver the data.
      //The wire-encoding details are also specified here
      TcpServerChannel svrChannel =
                  new TcpServerChannel("ServiceChannel",15000,svrFormatter);

      //Registration of communication protocol and wire-encoding format to be used
      //by the remoting infrastructure
      ChannelServices.RegisterChannel(svrChannel);

      //Registration of Singleton remote types
      RemotingConfiguration.RegisterWellKnownServiceType(typeof(HeartBeatService),
                      "HeartBeatService.rem",WellKnownObjectMode.Singleton);

      //Registration of singlecall remote types
      RemotingConfiguration.RegisterWellKnownServiceType(
                  typeof(HeartBeatServiceInfo),
                  "HeartBeatServiceInfo.rem",WellKnownObjectMode.SingleCall);
      Console.WriteLine("Infrastructure service host started...");
      Console.ReadLine();
    }
  }
}
```

In Listing 5-8, the Host class defines the executable entry point method, and inside this method we configure the various aspects of the remoting infrastructure and finally listen to the client request. To provide better clarity, we will break each of these aspects down and explain them line by line.

Remoting classes are packaged inside the System.Runtime.Remoting assembly available from the Global Assembly Cache (GAC). You need to reference this assembly in the current project, which will then allow access to the whole suite of remoting classes:

```
using System;
using System.Runtime.Remoting;
using System.Runtime.Remoting.Channels;
using System.Runtime.Remoting.Channels.Tcp;
```

Communication between two application processes located on different machines is a different beast in comparison with communications on the same machine. The most notable problem that arises in remote communication is how to package the data and deliver it to a remote host. A developer will be completely immersed in handling the low-level details. With remoting there is no need to worry because it is a matter of selecting the appropriate formatter (the data packaging protocol) and channel (the data delivery protocol). Remoting provides two types of formatters, namely, binary and SOAP formatters. Both these formatters dictate the wire-encoding format and are designed to meet the different needs of a requirement. Amongst the two, the binary formatter is the fastest formatter but is strictly meant for when both the client and the server are running on the same platform, such as Windows. The SOAP formatter targets the portability requirement of the application and is effective only when both the client and the server are running on different platforms. The formatter solves half of the equation; to solve the other half, remoting provides two types of channels: HTTP and TCP. Both these channels support the reliable delivery of data, but usually the TCP channel is used with the binary formatter, and the HTTP channel is used with the SOAP formatter.

```
BinaryServerFormatterSinkProvider svrFormatter =
            new BinaryServerFormatterSinkProvider();
TcpServerChannel svrChannel =
            new TcpServerChannel("ServiceChannel",15000,svrFormatter);
```

The .NET Framework is bundled with two predefined channels and formatter classes. The classes are separated based on their usage (in other words, whether they are referenced by the server or by the client). In Listing 5-8, the `BinaryServerFormatterSinkProvider` and `TcpServerChannel` classes will serialize the message in binary format and deliver it using TCP. `TcpServerChannel` is assigned a unique channel name and is configured to listen to client requests on port 15000. If you happen to change our minds and favor the portability requirements of the application, then the `SoapServerFormatterSinkProvider` and `HttpServerChannel` classes are your friends. Even though both the binary and SOAP formatters are grouped under the `System.Runtime.Remoting.Channels` namespace, in the case of channels both TCP and HTTP are grouped under the `System.Runtime.Remoting.Channels.Tcp` and `System.Runtime.Remoting.Channels.Http` namespaces, respectively.

After the selection of the appropriate channel and formatter, the next step is to register this information with the remoting infrastructure, and this is done with the help of `RegisterChannel`, which is a static method of the `ChannelServices` class. This method enlists the channels with the remoting infrastructure. Using this method, you can register multiple channels as long as they share a unique channel name:

```
ChannelServices.RegisterChannel(svrChannel);
```

After successfully configuring the communication infrastructure, you then head to the registration of the remote object, and this is done with the help of `RegisterWellKnownServiceType`, which is an important static member of the `RemotingConfiguration` class:

```
RemotingConfiguration.RegisterWellKnownServiceType(typeof(HeartBeatService),
                "HeartBeatService.rem",WellKnownObjectMode.Singleton);
```

`RegisterWellKnownServiceType` exposes the type to the outside world, giving it a final remotable touch. This remotable type, whose instance will be created on the server as a result of a remote object creation request received from the client, is supplied as a first argument to the method. The next argument defines the object uniform resource identifier (URI) that provides unique endpoint information about an object. The last and important argument defines the activation mode, and the only acceptable enumerated value in this case is SingleCall or Singleton. Because the `HeartBeatService` type holds the state and you want to have only a single instance of this service running, the right approach is to make it Singleton. A Singleton type will never have more than one instance created on the server, and this single unique instance along with its state will be shared across all clients.

The next step is to register the `HeartBeatServiceInfo` type, also making it remotely accessible by clients:

```
RemotingConfiguration.RegisterWellKnownServiceType(typeof(HeartBeatServiceInfo),
    "HeartBeatServiceInfo.rem",WellKnownObjectMode.SingleCall);
```

HeartBeatServiceInfo provides additional information about the heartbeat service and is passed as a first argument to RegisterWellKnownServiceType. Remember, because this type does not perform any kind of state management features, the activation mode is defined as SingleCall. The second argument assigns unique object endpoint information. It is with the help of this endpoint information that the remoting infrastructure identifies and forwards the request received from clients to the correct object instance. Another important fact is that there is a relaxed relationship between the remotable type and channel. A single channel can support listening on multiple remotable types, or multiple channels can listen on a single remotable type. In this example, both HeartBeatService and HeartBeatServiceInfo are accepting requests on the same channel (that is, TCP port 15000).

The server application is now up and ready to service client requests:

```
Console.WriteLine("Infrastructure service host started...");
Console.ReadLine();
```

The next part of the code will demonstrate the second leg of this example (that is, the service controller connecting to the heartbeat service), as shown in Listing 5-9.

Listing 5-9. *Hosting Service Controller*

```
using System;
using System.Runtime.Remoting;
using System.Runtime.Remoting.Channels;
using System.Runtime.Remoting.Channels.Tcp;
using System.Runtime.Remoting.Channels.Http;
using RPC.Common;

namespace RPC.ServiceController
{
  class Host
  {
    static void Main(string[] args)
    {
      Console.WriteLine("Service Controller Console..");
      //Identify the wire-encoding format; in this case we have selected
      //BinaryFormatter
      BinaryClientFormatterSinkProvider cltFormatter =
                  new BinaryClientFormatterSinkProvider();

      //Identify the communication protocol used to interact with server.
      //The wire-encoding details are also specified here
      TcpClientChannel cltChannel =
                  new TcpClientChannel("ControllerChannel",cltFormatter);

      //Registration of communication protocol and wire-encoding format to be used
      //by remoting infrastructure
      ChannelServices.RegisterChannel(cltChannel);

      //Instantiation of Remote type  (Service MetaInformation)
      IServiceInfo serviceInfo =  Activator.GetObject(typeof(IServiceInfo),
            "tcp://localhost:15000/HeartBeatServiceInfo.rem") as IServiceInfo;

      //Service meta-information is retrieved to determine the actual
      //location of the heartbeat service
      ServiceInfo heartBeatInfo = serviceInfo.QueryServiceInfo;
      Console.WriteLine("Starting Service : " +heartBeatInfo.FriendlyName);
```

```
        //Instantiation of heartbeat service
        IService hbService = Activator.GetObject(typeof(IService),
                          heartBeatInfo.Location) as IService;
        hbService.Start();
        Console.ReadLine();
      }
   }
}
```

In Listing 5-9, the Host class represents the consumer end in the communication chain that connects to the appropriate infrastructure service with the help of the remoting infrastructure and invokes its members. You will notice that both the formatter and channel configurations are set up with the help of the BinaryClientFormatter and TcpClientChannel classes:

```
BinaryClientFormatterSinkProvider cltFormatter =
            new BinaryClientFormatterSinkProvider();
TcpClientChannel cltChannel =
            new TcpClientChannel("ControllerChannel",cltFormatter);
ChannelServices.RegisterChannel(cltChannel);
```

To create an instance of a remote object, you need to use the Activator class, which is an object factory that supports the creation of both local and remote objects:

```
IServiceInfo serviceInfo = Activator.GetObject(typeof(IServiceInfo),
        "tcp://localhost:15000/HeartBeatServiceInfo.rem") as IServiceInfo;
```

The important method in Activator is GetObject, which is used to create a proxy for the remotable service. This method accepts the type as the first argument for which a proxy will be created, and the second argument indicates the URL of the remote object. The remote object URL follows a fixed naming convention that captures three important attributes required to establish a communication with the remote object. The important attributes are the transport protocol, the host name, and the port number on which the remote object is listening. These values are concatenated with object endpoint information.

As you know, the HeartBeatServiceInfo type acts as the information marker for the heartbeat service, and the important information it encapsulates is the URL location of the heartbeat service. This knowledge about the core service is packaged inside the ServiceInfo serializable class and is accessible by invoking the QueryServiceInfo property. The URL location of the heartbeat service is stored inside the Location property, and the value returned by this property is used to create a proxy instance to the real heartbeat service.

```
ServiceInfo heartBeatInfo = serviceInfo.QueryServiceInfo;
Console.WriteLine("Starting Service : " +heartBeatInfo.FriendlyName);
IService hbService =
    Activator.GetObject(typeof(IService),heartBeatInfo.Location) as IService;
```

By invoking the Start method, the heartbeat service on the remote machine starts:

```
hbService.Start();
```

Also an important fact of remoting is even though you are able to get the proxy instance on the remotable type using the GetObject method of the Activator class, a successful instantiation of a proxy is by no means a success indicator. In reality, the real communication handshaking between the client and the server happens only when a method is called on the proxy. Figure 5-9 shows the console output of the service controller and heartbeat service.

Figure 5-9. *Console output of service controller and heartbeat service*

Understanding Proxies

Proxy objects act as mediators between clients and remote objects (see Figure 5-10). Their primary responsibility is to honor the method invocation received from the client and transparently forward it again to the remote object. In the .NET arena, the remoting infrastructure creates two types of proxy objects when it receives a remote object creation request from a client. Transparent proxies and real proxies are the two proxy objects created by the remoting framework. Both these proxies are instances of the `System.Runtime.Remoting.Proxies.__TransparentProxy` and `System.Runtime.Remoting.Proxies.RealProxy` classes.

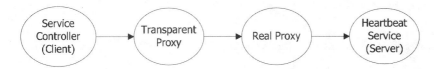

Figure 5-10. *Remote calls triggered by the client forwarded to a remote object via transparent and real proxies*

Although dealing with two types looks like additional overhead imposed by the framework, in reality both of these proxies undertake a different task.

When a client issues a request to create a remote instance object, it is returned with an instance of a transparent proxy.

A transparent proxy is a special class that mimics all methods and properties defined in the remote object and provides an illusion of the remote object residing within the client's context. It is also the first in the call chain to receive all method calls invoked by the client. The client is completely unaware of the existence of a real proxy and always interacts with the transparent proxy. However, the existence of a transparent proxy sometimes causes confusion because the application developer is not able to make a distinction between the real object reference and proxy references. To solve this problem, the framework provides a special helper static method, `IsTransparentProxy`, in the `RemotingServices` class. This method, which is based on the object passed as an argument, returns a Boolean value indicating whether the object is a real object or a transparent proxy object.

```
using System;
using System.Runtime.Remoting;

class TProxy
{
  static void Main(string[] args)
  {
    object newObj= new object();
```

```
    bool isProxy = RemotingServices.IsTransparentProxy(newObj);
    Console.WriteLine(isProxy);
  }
}
```

A transparent proxy examines the method and its arguments, packages them in an IMessage object, and hands them over to the real proxy. From here onward, the real proxy takes charge and completes the rest of the operation, eventually delivering the message to the server. The real proxy also looks after the extensibility aspects of the remoting framework. This is in contrast to the transparent proxy, which allows no room for any sort of customization. Another important fact is that the instance of the real proxy is housed inside the transparent proxy and is easily accessible with the help of another helper method provided by the RemotingServices class, as shown here:

```
using System;
using System.Runtime.Remoting;
using System.Runtime.Remoting.Proxies;

class RProxy
{
  static void Main(string[] args)
  {
    object mbrObj=null;

    //Get a reference to mbrObj
    //mbrObj = <MBR Object>

    //Real Proxy instance
    RealProxy rp=RemotingServices.GetRealProxy(mbrObj);
  }
}
```

A transparent proxy is also serializable in nature. This allows a reference to the proxy to be marshaled by value on different application domains located on different machines. This proxy-forwarding approach proves to be nifty in a scenario where a client itself is playing the role of a server to another client, which is explained later in the service directory code example. The secret behind proxy serialization resides in the System.Runtime.Remoting.ObjRef class. The instance of this class wraps bare-minimum information about the remotable type, which is sufficient for the remoting infrastructure to create a suitable proxy. Under the hood, when a proxy is marshaled, it is the instance of the ObjRef class that gets serialized and transferred over the wire. The CLR is intelligent enough to understand the semantics of remoting, so during the deserialization phase, when it discovers an instance of ObjRef, it immediately creates the transparent and real proxies. The most important information stored inside ObjRef is as follows:

- Channel information that includes machine address and port number.

- Remote object endpoint information.

- Complete chain of type information including the assembly name, culture, version, and public key. The type chain also includes information about base types.

The whole concept of proxy serialization falls squarely in line with the new service directory example that sits between the service controller and the heartbeat service. In the heartbeat service code example described in the "Introducing Remote Process Communication (RPC)" section, the service controller could directly talk to the heartbeat service, but if you exaggerate the example a bit by fanning out more services such as the instrumentation service, the configuration service, and so on, then life gets tougher because now in order to connect to these services, the service controller needs to know their physical locations, port numbers, and object endpoint information. So, by introducing a service directory, you are blending the location transparency feature that will relieve the service controller from knowing the location details. With the help of the service directory, all infrastructure service–related information will be tucked into a central place. This centralization approach also allows for easy maintenance and migration of infrastructure services to another machine without affecting the downstream components.

As illustrated in Figure 5-11, the service controller's first request is targeted toward the service directory, which in turn gets satisfied with the return of a proxy reference to the controller, and after that, the controller directly starts interacting with the heartbeat service, bypassing the service directory route.

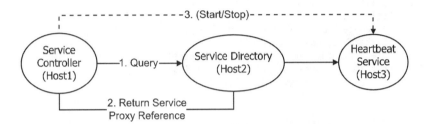

Figure 5-11. *Service directory*

To implement the service directory functionality, we have determined a need for the new interface ILookUp. Obviously, this interface will be included in the shared RPC.Common library and will be made accessible to both the client and the server. The interface declaration code is as follows:

```
using System;

namespace RPC.Common
{
  public interface ILookUp
  {
    IService LookUp(string serviceName);
  }
}
```

The service directory is an independent service and is possibly hosted on the same machine where infrastructure services are hosted or could be on a different machine. So, in this example, we will host the service directory as an executable and, to accommodate this requirement, create the new console project RPC.ServiceDirectory. This project is identical to the RPC.Services project and is mainly composed of two classes: the core lookup service class and the host class that exposes the lookup service to the outside world. The code snippet for the lookup service class is as shown in Listing 5-10.

Listing 5-10. *Infrastructure Service Lookup*

```
using System;
using System.Collections;
using RPC.Common;
using System.Runtime.Remoting;
using System.Runtime.Remoting.Channels;
using System.Runtime.Remoting.Channels.Tcp;
using System.Runtime.Remoting.Channels.Http;
```

```
namespace RPC.ServiceDirectory
{
  public class ServiceLookUp : MarshalByRefObject,ILookUp
  {
    Hashtable connectedServices = new Hashtable();

    public ServiceLookUp()
    {
      BinaryClientFormatterSinkProvider cltFormatter =
              new BinaryClientFormatterSinkProvider();
      TcpClientChannel cltChannel =
              new TcpClientChannel("ControllerChannel",cltFormatter);
      ChannelServices.RegisterChannel(cltChannel);
      //Instantiation of remote heartbeat service and its proxy reference
      //is cached in a hash table, keyed by service name
      IService hbService = Activator.GetObject(typeof(IService),
          "tcp://localhost:15000/HeartBeatService.rem") as IService;
      connectedServices.Add("HeartBeatService",hbService);
    }

    public override object InitializeLifetimeService()
    {
      return null;
    }

    public IService LookUp(string serviceName)
    {
      return connectedServices[serviceName] as IService;
    }

  }
}
```

In Listing 5-10, ServiceLookUp is derived from MarshalByRefObject, which makes it a perfect remoting candidate; additionally, it implements the ILookUp interface by supplying a concrete method body to the LookUp method. To gain a deeper understanding, let's do a step-by-step walk-through of the code described in Listing 5-10.

With the declaration of a Hashtable, you have built a cache container that stores proxy references of infrastructure services:

```
Hashtable connectedServices = new Hashtable();
```

This container is populated only once, as demonstrated in the following constructor code:

```
public ServiceLookUp()
{
  BinaryClientFormatterSinkProvider cltFormatter =
          new BinaryClientFormatterSinkProvider();
  TcpClientChannel cltChannel =
          new TcpClientChannel("ControllerChannel",cltFormatter);
  ChannelServices.RegisterChannel(cltChannel);
  IService hbService = Activator.GetObject(typeof(IService),
          "tcp://localhost:15000/HeartBeatService.rem") as IService;
  connectedServices.Add("HeartBeatService",hbService);
}
```

Inside the constructor method, you connect to all the required infrastructure services and cache their proxy references inside a Hashtable. Proxy references are identified by a suitable name, and based on this service name, they are fetched from the Hashtable.

After populating the proxy cache container, the next step is to make it available to the service controller, which is done using LookUp. This method is the one that will be invoked by external clients. It peeks into the cached hash table to locate an appropriate proxy reference that matches the service name passed as a method argument. On finding a successful match, it returns the proxy reference to the caller. This proxy reference is then marshaled back to the client context. Remember, it is the ObjRef that gets serialized over the wire.

```
public IService LookUp(string serviceName)
{
  Console.WriteLine("Lookup Request Received For : " +serviceName);
  return connectedServices[serviceName] as IService;
}
```

The final part of service directory is to honor the service controller request on port 12000 (see Listing 5-11).

Listing 5-11. *Hosting of Service Directory*

```
using System;
using System.Runtime.Remoting;
using System.Runtime.Remoting.Channels;
using System.Runtime.Remoting.Channels.Tcp;
using System.Runtime.Remoting.Channels.Http;

namespace RPC.ServiceDirectory
{
  class Host
  {
    static void Main(string[] args)
    {
      ServiceLookUp serviceLookUp = new ServiceLookUp();
      BinaryServerFormatterSinkProvider svrFormatter =
                  new BinaryServerFormatterSinkProvider();
      TcpServerChannel svrChannel =
                  new TcpServerChannel("ServiceChannel",12000,svrFormatter);
      RemotingServices.Marshal(serviceLookUp,"ServiceDirectory.rem");
      Console.WriteLine("LookUp Service Started...");
      Console.ReadLine();
    }
  }
}
```

In Listing 5-11, you will notice that Host has not used the RemotingConfiguration. RegisterWellKnownServiceType method to publish the objects. Instead, you use the RemotingServices. Marshal method that registers the precreated instance of the ServiceLookUp instance. Even though using this approach is the equivalent of registering a Singleton object, in this case the object needs to be created beforehand. By hand-rolling the instance of the ServiceLookUp class, you ensure that the service cache is populated completely before making it available to the external world.

The final and last piece of the code is to update the service controller to make it interact with the heartbeat service via the service directory (see Listing 5-12).

Listing 5-12. *Hosting of Infrastructure Service Controller*

```
using System;
using System.Runtime.Remoting;
using System.Runtime.Remoting.Proxies;
using System.Runtime.Remoting.Channels;
using System.Runtime.Remoting.Channels.Tcp;
using System.Runtime.Remoting.Channels.Http;
using RPC.Common;

namespace RPC.ServiceController
{
  class Host
  {
    static void Main(string[] args)
    {
      Console.WriteLine("Service Controller Console..");
      BinaryClientFormatterSinkProvider cltFormatter =
              new BinaryClientFormatterSinkProvider();
      TcpClientChannel cltChannel =
              new TcpClientChannel("ControllerChannel",cltFormatter);
      ChannelServices.RegisterChannel(cltChannel);
      //Instantiation of lookup service that is then used to locate
      //the heartbeat service
      ILookUp serviceLookUp= Activator.GetObject(typeof(ILookUp),
              "tcp://localhost:12000/ServiceDirectory.rem") as ILookUp;

      //Retrieves the proxy reference of the heartbeat service
      //In this case the proxy reference is marshaled by value
      IService hbService = serviceLookUp.LookUp("HeartBeatService");

      //Start the heartbeat service
      hbService.Start();
      Console.ReadLine();

    }
  }
}
```

When the code described in Listing 5-12 is compiled and executed, it will connect to the service directory and invoke its LookUp method. This method will return a proxy reference to the heartbeat service, and using this marshaled proxy reference, you start the heartbeat service as shown in the output windows in Figure 5-12.

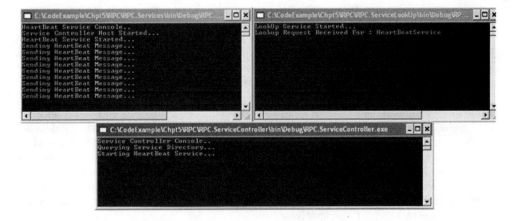

Figure 5-12. *Console output of the service directory*

Understanding Distributed Garbage Collection

The most touted feature of the CLR is the automatic reclamation of memory that frees developers from memory-related wrinkles. However, when you step down to a distributed world, the fundamental change you will notice is that both the client and server objects are no longer within the jurisdiction of the same application process. They are separated into different application processes that are usually running on different machines. It is quite common for complexities to increase when communication spreads its wings, and techniques applied in a local environment may become invalidated in a distributed environment. In the case of garbage collection, the algorithm employed searches for reachable objects, and if it finds some, it marks them as alive and discards the unreachable objects, eventually reclaiming the memory. This logic works flawlessly because the garbage collector (GC) has complete knowledge about its local environment; however, in the case of remoting where server objects are hosted on different application processes or machines, the garbage collector has no way to determine whether the server object is accessed by a client.

To circumvent this problem, .NET adopted a leasing approach that controls the destruction of a remote object. By default, every remote object is assigned a lease. Upon expiration of this lease, the remote object is considered to be garbage and handed over to the garbage collector. Figure 5-13 illustrates the leasing architecture.

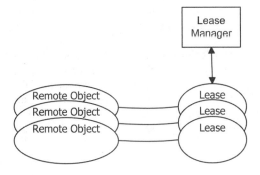

Figure 5-13. *Object lifetime with leasing*

On receiving an object creation request from a client, the remoting framework constructs a new instance of the remote object. As part of this creation process, it also associates a new instance of the Lease object defined in the System.Runtime.Remoting.Lifetime namespace. InitialLeaseTime and RenewOnCallTime are the important properties provided by the Lease object, and the value assigned to this property dictates the overall lifetime of a remote object. InitialLeaseTime assigns the default initial lease time to the remote object, which is by default configured to five minutes, and RenewOnCallTime defines the increment factor. Based on this value, the life of the remote object is further extended. The default renewal time is two minutes. Also, a CurrentLeaseTime property is defined in the Lease object that returns the remaining lease time of a remote object. The default lease values provided by a Lease object can be easily customized on a per-remote-object basis. This is possible by overriding the InitializeLifetimeService method of the MarshalRefObject class. The InitializeLifetimeService method is automatically called by the remoting framework during the remote object creation stage, and upon invoking this method, it returns a Lease object. Based on these returned values, the object lifetime is determined. The code snippet shown in Listing 5-13 demonstrates how to override the default lease behavior.

Listing 5-13. *Overriding Remote Object Lease Time*

```
using System;
using System.Runtime.Remoting.Lifetime;

class MBRLease : MarshalByRefObject
{
  public override object InitializeLifetimeService()
  {
    //Default lease associated with remote object is retrieved
    ILease objLease = (ILease)base.InitializeLifetimeService();
    //Initial Lease time is updated to three minutes
    objLease.InitialLeaseTime=TimeSpan.FromMinutes(3);
    //Renewal time is updated to one minute
    objLease.RenewOnCallTime=TimeSpan.FromMinutes(1);
    return objLease;
  }
}
```

Lease is an internal class and hence not accessible to the outside world. So, the only mechanism to control it is by casting it back to the ILease interface. It is also mandatory to invoke the base class InitializeLifetimeService, which returns the lease object associated with the current instance of the remote object. The instance is then cast back to the ILease interface, and both its initial lease time and renewal time are overridden with new values. In Listing 5-13, the initial lease time is updated from five minutes to three minutes and the renewal time from two minutes to one minute. Note that lease renewal happens only when there is a subsequent method call received from the client and the renewal time is added to the current lease time.

As already mentioned, each remote object is assigned a default lease time by the remoting framework. These default values are easily modifiable with the help of the LifeTimeServices class grouped under the System.Runtime.Remoting.Lifetime.LifetimeServices namespace. For example, the following code decreases the default initial lease time from five minutes to three minutes and increases the renewal time from two minutes to four minutes. After executing the following code, all newly created remote objects will inherit these values unless specifically overridden by their InitializeLifetimeService methods.

```
using System;
using System.Runtime.Remoting.Lifetime;
```

```
class DefaultLease
{
  static void Main(string[] args)
  {
    //Change the default lease time
    LifetimeServices.LeaseTime = TimeSpan.FromMinutes(3);
    //Change the default lease renewal time
    LifetimeServices.RenewOnCallTime = TimeSpan.FromMinutes(4);
  }
}
```

It is also possible to provide an infinite lifetime to a remote object, preventing it from being garbage collected until the application domain in which it is created is unloaded. In the following code, by returning null inside the InitializeLifetimeService method, you grant an infinite lifetime to remote objects:

```
using System;

class ImmortalMBR : MarshalByRefObject
{
  public override object InitializeLifetimeService()
  {
    //By returning null, we have granted infinite lifetime to remote object
    return null;
  }
}
```

If you look at the code of the remoting classes discussed so far—specifically the HeartBeatService (see Listing 5-6) and ServiceLookUp (see Listing 5-10)—both these classes override InitializeLifetimeService and return null values. This step is inevitable in this case where both the remote objects are configured as a Singleton object.

Every lease object is registered with the lease manager. The lease manager is created for each application domain and can be considered as a garbage collector for remote objects; however, it is deterministic in nature. The implementation of the lease manager is straightforward. It internally maintains a collection of Lease objects, and after every configured interval, it iterates through this collection to check for expired leases. On the expiry of a lease, the lease manager simply removes the Lease object from its collection, thus marking it unreachable; in the subsequent garbage collection, memory occupied by an instance of Lease, and its underlying remote object, is reclaimed. The default polling time used by the lease manager to check for expired leases is configured to ten seconds. You can change this default polling value with the help of the LeaseManagerPollTime property defined in the LifeTimeServices class:

```
using System;
using System.Runtime.Remoting.Lifetime;

class LeasePollTime
{
  static void Main(string[] args)
  {
    LifetimeServices.LeaseManagerPollTime=TimeSpan.FromSeconds(20);
  }
}
```

The lease manager also provides one final chance to the remote objects to renew its lease before it gets discarded completely. This opportunity is gifted in the form of sponsorship. A *sponsor* is an entity that is given the final authority to decide whether an object is in need of additional lease time. An affirmative reply from the sponsor at this final stage can extend the lifetime of the remote object. Each sponsor is registered with the lease, and multiple sponsors can be registered at a time.

From an implementation point of view, the sponsor itself is derived from MarshalByRefObject and implements the ISponsor interface defined in System.Runtime.Remoting.Lifetime. The ISponsor interface supports the Renewal method, which decides the fate of the remote object. This method is invoked by the lease manager to get the additional lease time assigned by the sponsor to the remote object.

The concept of sponsorship blends well with the service controller example. Although we have assigned an infinite time-to-live lease to the remote service object (that is, HeartBeatService) by returning a null value inside the InitializeLifetimeService method, you can adopt a different approach, assuming the resource allocated by individual infrastructure services is expensive in nature. Taking into account the limited hardware resources available, you need to ensure an optimum utilization of it. In the world of the front office, most of the core system services are not expected to run 24×7. Rather, the working hours of trading applications never exceed more than seven to eight hours. Considering this, you need to build a sponsor that examines the current system time. If the time computed is not between the start and end of the trading time, then it can be easily concluded that there is no need to renew the lease, and thus the remote object will be freely discarded. For example, the following code checks the current time, and if it doesn't fall between the trading hours, it expresses its clear intention to not renew the lease by returning the TimeSpan.Zero value:

```
using System;
using System.Runtime.Remoting.Lifetime;

namespace RPC.Services
{
  public class BODEODSponsor : MarshalByRefObject, ISponsor
  {
    public BODEODSponsor()
    {
    }

    public TimeSpan Renewal(ILease lease)
    {
      //The logic here clearly determines the object lifetime based on
      //trading hours
      int tradingBod=9;
      int tradingEod=16;
      DateTime bodTime = DateTime.Now;
      if ( bodTime.Hour >= tradingBod && bodTime.Hour <= tradingEod)
      {
        DateTime eodTime =
              new DateTime(bodTime.Year,bodTime.Month,bodTime.Day,tradingEod,5,0);
        TimeSpan diffTime = eodTime-bodTime;
        Console.WriteLine(diffTime.TotalMinutes);
        return diffTime.TotalMinutes > 0 ? diffTime : TimeSpan.Zero;
      }
      return TimeSpan.Zero;
    }
  }
}
```

Note that because the registration of a sponsor takes place on a lease object, you need to get a reference to the lease object. You do this with the help of the GetLifetimeService static method defined in the RemotingServices class. The GetLifetimeService method returns the lease object associated with the instance of MarshalByRefObject. This returned instance of Lease needs to be cast to the ILease interface in order to access its member, specifically the Register and Unregister methods. As the name indicates, the Register method is invoked to register a new sponsor, and the UnRegister method is invoked to unregister an existing sponsor.

Configuring Remoting

So far you have learned the various features offered by the remoting framework and also have learned how easy it is to customize each of the aspects supported by these features. But the truth of the matter is that the example adopted a programmatic path; to change the lease manager's default poll time, you hard-coded the values inside the code. The same problem applies to the registration of the remote object, where you hard-coded the port number and channel information. From a deployment perspective, this is an unhealthy practice because even a simple change such as changing the port number will demand a complete recompilation and deployment of the program. However, don't get disappointed—the remoting framework addresses these deployment issues by allowing developers to tweak the remoting infrastructure through a configuration file. Almost every single aspect of the remoting object can now be regulated using a configuration file. To boot the remoting infrastructure using a configuration file, you need to use the Configure method provided by the RemotingConfiguration class. This method, based on the name of the configuration file passed as the argument, reads the contents and appropriately configures the remoting infrastructure:

```
using System;
using System.Runtime.Remoting;

class RemotingConfig
{
  static void Main(string[] args)
  {
    string configFile = null;
    //Assign valid name of the configuration file
    //configFile = "C:\RemotingConfig.config"

    //Configure the Remoting Infrastructure
    RemotingConfiguration.Configure(configFile);
  }
}
```

There is no restriction on the location of the configuration file. However, the contents arranged inside this configuration file need to adhere to a predefined remoting schema layout. A skeletal view of a typical remoting configuration file is as follows:

```
<configuration>
  <system.runtime.remoting>
    <application name="AppName">
      <lifetime/>
      <channels/>
      <service/>
      <client/>
    </application>
  </system.runtime.remoting>
</configuration>
```

Information about the remoting infrastructure is branched under the <system.runtime.remoting> element, and each of the child elements map to a specific aspect of the infrastructure. The <lifetime> element hosts information about the remote object's lifetime. Similarly, the <service> element provides the remote object's registration information. The <client> element looks after the connectivity information required to connect and instantiate an instance of a remote type. The last and final element is the <channel> element, which defines the low-level transport and wire-encoding details.

Considering the infrastructure hosting code described in Listing 5-8, you will now revisit the code and tailor it to use the configuration file. The first step in customizing the code is to separate the remote object registration and channel information from the code and store this information in the configuration file. Assume that a new configuration file, RPC.Services.exe.config, is created and located in the same folder where the actual executable is stored:

```xml
<?xml version="1.0" encoding="utf-8" ?>
<configuration>
    <system.runtime.remoting>
        <application>
            <service>
                <!-- Registration of Singleton Remote Type (HeartBeatService) -->
                <wellknown mode="Singleton" objectUri="HeartBeatService.rem"
                        type="RPC.Services.HeartBeatService, RPC.Services" />
                <!-- Registration of SingleCall Remote Type
                    (HeartBeat Service Meta-Info) -->
                <wellknown mode="SingleCall" objectUri="HeartBeatServiceInfo.rem"
                    type="RPC.Services.HeartBeatServiceInfo, RPC.Services" />
            </service>
            <channels>
                <!-- Registration of TCP channel and binary encoding format -->
                <channel ref="tcp" port="15000">
                    <formatter ref="binary"/>
                </channel>
                <!-- Registration of HTTP channel and SOAP encoding format -->
                <channel ref="http" port="16000">
                    <formatter ref="soap"/>
                </channel>
            </channels>
        </application>
    </system.runtime.remoting>
</configuration>
```

The information captured in the XML fragment is the same as the actual code, but the infrastructure service host code is much cleaner now and contains a single configuration statement, as shown here:

```csharp
using System;
using System.Runtime.Remoting;
using RPC.Common;

class HostUsingConfig
{
  static void Main(string[] args)
  {
    RemotingConfiguration.Configure(@"RPC.Services.exe.config");
    Console.WriteLine("Infrastructure service host Started...");
    Console.ReadLine();
  }
}
```

On the service controller end (see Listing 5-9), you will implement a similar configuration porting exercise, as shown in Listing 5-14.

Listing 5-14. *Service Controller Remoting Configuration*

```xml
<configuration>
    <system.runtime.remoting>
        <application>
            <channels>
                <channel ref="tcp" port="0">
                    <formatter ref="binary"/>
```

```
            </channel>
          </channels>
      <client>
          <!-- Description of remote object information -->
          <wellknown url="tcp://localhost:15000/HeartBeatService.rem"
                     type="RPC.Common.IService, RPC.Common" />
      </client>
    </application>
  </system.runtime.remoting>
</configuration>
```

Assuming that the XML snippet described in Listing 5-14 is stored in the `RPC.ServiceController.exe.config` file, you modify the client-side host code to use the information contained inside this configuration file:

```
using System;
using System.Runtime.Remoting;
using RPC.Common;

class HostUsingConfig
{
  static void Main(string[] args)
  {
    RemotingConfiguration.Configure(@"RPC.ServiceController.exe.config");
    WellKnownClientTypeEntry[] clientEntry =
            RemotingConfiguration.GetRegisteredWellKnownClientTypes();
    IService hbService = Activator.GetObject(typeof(IService),
                          clientEntry[0].ObjectUrl) as IService;

  }
}
```

By separating out the configuration details for both the client and the server, you have drastically eased the deployment burden. Changes to the remoting behavior can now be heartily welcomed because the only candidate that would be affected is the configuration file. There are other areas in remoting such as lifetime management, versioning, error handling, security, debugging, and so on, where the recruitment of a configuration file technique will further increase the efficiency of application deployment.

Lifetime Management

Even if all the facets of a distributed garbage collection cannot be dictated through configuration files, the object default lifetime and lease manager poll time are allowed to reside within the configuration file:

```
<?xml version="1.0" encoding="utf-8" ?>
<configuration>
    <system.runtime.remoting>
        <application>
                <lifetime
            leaseTime="1S"
            renewOnCallTime="1S"
            leaseManagerPollTime="1S"/>
        </application>
    </system.runtime.remoting>
</configuration>
```

Versioning

Versioning of an assembly plays an important role, especially in a distributed scenario where both the client and the server are physically separated. In the service controller example, you saw the benefit of a shared assembly, but envisage a scenario where a client and a server hold different versions of the shared assembly. How would remoting handle this version mismatch when it receives a call from the client to the server, or vice versa? Two attributes, includeVersions and strictBinding, are associated with formatters to determine the version tolerant levels:

```
<configuration>
  <system.runtime.remoting>
    <application>
      <channels>
        <channel ref="tcp" port="15000">
          <serverProviders>
            <formatter ref="binary" includeVersions="false"
                                     strictBinding="false"/>
          </serverProviders>
        </channel>
      </channels>
    </application>
  </system.runtime.remoting>
</configuration>
```

A TypeLoadException is thrown if the remoting framework fails to load the type based on the four conditions shown in Table 5-4.

Table 5-4. *Versioning Parameters*

includeVersions (Sending Formatter)	strictBinding (Receiving Formatter)	Behavior
true	true	Exact type is loaded by the remoting framework.
false	true	Type is loaded using the type name and assembly name.
true	false	The remoting framework first attempts to load the exact type. If it fails to load, then it makes a second attempt to load a type using the type name and assembly name.
false	false	Type is loaded using the type name and assembly name.

Error Handling

Remoting supports the propagation of exceptions raised on the server side back to the original caller (the client). But the amount of information transferred to the caller is controlled by the mode attribute value defined in the customErrors element:

```
<configuration>
  <system.runtime.remoting>
    <customErrors mode="off"/>
  </system.runtime.remoting>
</configuration>
```

Table 5-5 lists the possible values that control the propagation of remoting exceptions from server to client.

Table 5-5. *Remoting Exceptions*

Value	Behavior
off	Callers receive complete exception information including the server stack trace.
on	Callers receive filtered exception information.
remoteOnly	Local callers (a client running on the same machine as the server) receive complete exception information, but remote callers receive filtered exception information.

Security

To protect a system from unwarranted attacks, the remoting framework supports two levels of automatic deserialization. These levels are defined at the formatter level, and by default they are configured at restricted levels where only limited types required for basic remoting functionality are allowed to serialize. To remove this restriction, the following entry must be present in the configuration file:

```
<configuration>
  <system.runtime.remoting>
    <application>
      <channel ref="tcp" port="15000">
        <serverProviders>
          <formatter ref="binary" typeFilterLevel="Full"/>
        </serverProviders>
      </channel>
    </application>
  </system.runtime.remoting>
</configuration>
```

Debugging

By default, the remoting framework implements a lazy-loading technique, where the underlying remote type on the server is brought into memory only when it receives the first call from the client. But developers often tend to make typing errors while entering the type and assembly name. These mistakes get manifested in the form of run-time exceptions. To avoid this and catch the exception early during application startup time, you need to add a debug element in the configuration file, as shown here:

```
<configuration>
    <system.runtime.remoting>
        <debug loadTypes="true"/>
    </system.runtime.remoting>
</configuration>
```

Understanding Aspect-Oriented Programming (AOP) in .NET

There is a popular quote that says, "Innovation is the creation of the new or the rearranging of the old in a new way." This statement gives you a good sense of the evolution evidenced in the field of programming methodologies. In bygone days, procedural-oriented programming (POP) was considered to be the de facto programming methodology. Then came object-oriented programming (OOP), which was a great boon and also forms the basis for today's modern systems. The important principle followed in both OOP and POP is to raise the level of abstractions and encourage developers to model applications from a particular viewpoint. In the POP world, the viewpoint is the functional requirement itself from which the procedures are directly defined. This is in direct contrast to the OOP world where functional requirements are decomposed into granular classes, and each individual class then folds a specific aspect of the overall requirement by encapsulating both data and behavior. OOP provided best-of-breed features such as encapsulation, inheritance, polymorphism, and so on, that allowed for the efficient reuse of the code. However, currently the OOP world has some short-comings, and this is where AOP comes to the rescue. AOP is not meant to replace OOP; instead, it is considered to be a complementary programming technique to OOP.

Before delving into the explanation of AOP, refer to the following code (see Listing 5-15 and Listing 5-16). This code is no different from the heartbeat service code described in Listing 5-6 except this version shields the start and stop functionality of the service with proper authorization checks. Only users belonging to manager roles are allowed to start and stop the service. As you will notice, this authorization code is spread in all of the infrastructure services executed under the control of the central service controller.

Listing 5-15. *Heartbeat Message Targeted to Monitor NYSE Exchange Gateway*

```
using System;
using System.Threading;

namespace AOP
{
  public class NYSEHeartBeatService
  {
    public NYSEHeartBeatService()
    {
    }

    public void Start()
    {
      if ( !Thread.CurrentPrincipal.IsInRole("Manager"))
        throw new ApplicationException("Access Denied");

      //Exchange-Specific Operation
    }

    public void Stop()
    {
      if ( !Thread.CurrentPrincipal.IsInRole("Manager"))
        throw new ApplicationException("Access Denied");

      //Exchange-Specific Operation
    }

  }
}
```

Listing 5-16. *Heartbeat Message Targeted to Monitor NASDAQ Exchange Gateway*

```
using System;
using System.Threading;

namespace AOP
{
  public class NASDAQHeartBeatService
  {
    public NASDAQHeartBeatService()
    {
    }

    public void Start()
    {
      if ( !Thread.CurrentPrincipal.IsInRole("Manager"))
        throw new ApplicationException("Access Denied");

      //Exchange-Specific Operation
    }

    public void Stop()
    {
      if ( !Thread.CurrentPrincipal.IsInRole("Manager"))
        throw new ApplicationException("Access Denied");

      //Exchange-Specific Operation
    }

  }
}
```

Both the NASDAQHeartBeatService and NYSEHeartBeatService classes are composed of two types of requirements. The first and the most important is the functional requirement itself, which is satisfied by sending a heartbeat message to the exchange. The second type is the operational requirement, which is sprinkled on top of the functional requirement. The most commonly found operational requirement in enterprise-based applications are logging, exception handling, authorization, and thread synchronization. These requirements are scattered inside the functional requirement, and the code needed to perform its services are the same across all functional requirements. For example, if you look at the NYSEHeartBeatService class, there is an explicit authorization check as a first line of code inside the Start and Stop methods. This validation is also applied in the NASDAQHeartBeatService class, and this doesn't stop here. If a new exchange is introduced, then it also inherits this validation. Operational requirements always tend to crosscut the functional requirement, resulting in the tight coupling of functional and system classes. For example, if you need to introduce a new logging feature in Listing 5-15 and Listing 5-16, then you will face a swirl of change, and each of the functional classes needs to be changed. Figure 5-14 shows the integration of operational requirements with functional requirements.

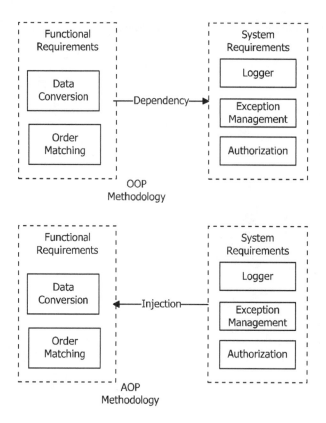

Figure 5-14. *Integration of operational requirements with functional requirements*

AOP promotes the cleaner responsibility of modules in the subsystem by identifying and separating crosscutting concerns (operational requirements) and then transparently injecting them inside functional modules. This transparent injection technique removes the static dependency required from the functional modules to the system modules. Furthermore, it is the power of AOP tools that allows both the functional and system modules to adopt an independent development thread without knowing the existence of each other and in the end transparently combines the features provided by both these modules. To continue the journey with AOP, you need to first download Aspect# from `http://aspectsharp.sourceforge.net/`. Aspect# is an open source AOP framework for .NET-based applications. To demonstrate the power of AOP, we will show how to rewrite the `NASDAQHeartBeatService` and `NYSEHeartBeatService` classes using the Aspect# framework. Figure 5-15 shows the AOP architecture.

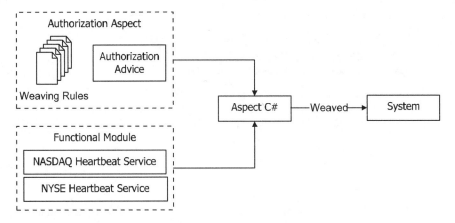

Figure 5-15. *AOP architecture*

AOP has coined its own terminology, and understanding these terms and definitions is important to becoming acquainted with the AOP-based programming environment:

Point-cut: The point-cut is the location in the code where the crosscutting concerns are injected. The point-cut is technically represented in the form of a method, constructor, property, and so on. For example, referring to the NASDAQHeartBeatService class, the point-cuts that can be identified are the Start and Stop methods where the actual authorization check is performed.

Advice: The advice encapsulates logic that is transparently injected inside the code identified by the point-cut. Advice is usually composed as a separate entity. For example, an authorization advice is a different class that hosts the authorization logic.

Aspect: The aspect is the final unit of work in the AOP world. It declares the weaving rules by combining the advice and point-cut.

Before we start, it is mandatory to reference two important assemblies of the Aspect# framework inside the project. These two important assemblies are AspectSharp and AopAlliance. The next step is to construct the AuthorizationAdvice class, which separates out the necessary authorization logic. In the earlier OOP version, this logic was sprinkled all over the functional classes.

Here's the code for AuthorizationAdvice:

```
using System;
using AopAlliance.Intercept;
using System.Threading;
using AOPServices.Services;

namespace AOPServices.Aspects
{
  public class AuthorizationAdvice : IMethodInterceptor
  {
    public AuthorizationAdvice()
    {
    }
```

```
      public object Invoke(IMethodInvocation invocation)
      {
        //Perform Authorization Check
        /*if ( !Thread.CurrentPrincipal.IsInRole("Manager"))
          throw new ApplicationException("Access Denied");*/

        Console.WriteLine("Pre-Authorization Code");
        invocation.Proceed();
        Console.WriteLine("Post-Authorization Code");
        return null;
      }

    }
}
```

The AuthorizationAdvice class implements the IMethodInterceptor interface declared in the AopAlliance assembly. The nice thing about the AuthorizationAdvice class is that it captures only the functionality it is meant to capture. If you take a deep plunge into the class, specifically the Invoke method, you will notice no other logic except the authorization check code. This authorization logic will then be injected in the core functional class.

Next, you can rewrite the functional class, as shown here:

```
using System;

namespace AOPServices.Services
{
  public class NASDAQHeartBeatService
  {
    public NASDAQHeartBeatService()
    {
    }

    public virtual void Start()
    {
      //Exchange-Specific Operation
      Console.WriteLine("Exchange Started");
    }

    public virtual void Stop()
    {
      //Exchange-Specific Operation
      Console.WriteLine("Exchange Stopped");
    }
  }
}
```

The only difference you will notice in NASDAQHeartBeatService is that the authorization logic code is removed from both the Start and Stop methods. Another important fact to note is that both the Start and Stop methods are now declared virtual. This is a mandatory declaration required by the Aspect# framework in order to successfully conduct its injection activity.

The next and final step of this program is to define the Authorization aspect that composes the weaving rules (see Listing 5-17).

Listing 5-17. *AOP-Based Heartbeat Service*

```
using System;
using AspectSharp;
using AspectSharp.Builder;
using AOPServices.Services;

namespace AOPServices
{
  class Class1
  {
    static void Main(string[] args)
    {
      String weavingRules =
        " import AOPServices.Aspects " +
        " " +
        " aspect AuthorizationAspect for [ AOPServices.Services ] " +
        "    " +
        "   pointcut method(* Start())" +
        "     advice(AuthorizationAdvice)" +
        "   end" +
        "    " +
        "   pointcut method(* Stop())" +
        "     advice(AuthorizationAdvice)" +
        "   end" +
        "    " +
        " end ";

      AspectLanguageEngineBuilder builder =
          new AspectLanguageEngineBuilder( weavingRules  );
      AspectEngine engine = builder.Build();

      NASDAQHeartBeatService nasdaqService=
          engine.WrapClass(typeof(NASDAQHeartBeatService)) as NASDAQHeartBeatService;
      nasdaqService.Start();
      Console.ReadLine();
    }

  }
}
```

Let's do a step-by-step walk-through of the code described in Listing 5-17. The most interesting and important piece of code is the weaving rules. The weaving rules are plain, ordinary text where the source could be an XML file or a database. It is defined in accordance with the Aspect# framework, and based on this rule definition, the framework initiates its code injection process.

The import section captures the required namespaces to be imported. This is required by the framework to successfully resolve the advice and point-cut. The next section deals with the aspect by declaring a friendly name and capturing the list of classes on which this aspect needs to be applied. With the help of namespace features, you group the service and aspect classes. Hence, the rule definition states the intention of applying AuthorizationAspect on all classes grouped under the AOPServices. Services namespace. The last section is a repeatable section composed of information related to the point-cut and advice. The two methods identified as point-cut are the Start and Stop methods, and at this point you inject the Authorization advice. This also marks the end of the rule definition step.

```
String weavingRules =
  " import AOPServices.Aspects " +
  " " +
  " aspect AuthorizationAspect for [ AOPServices.Services ] " +
  "    " +
  "    pointcut method(* Start())" +
  "      advice(AuthorizationAdvice)" +
  "    end" +
  "    " +
  "    pointcut method(* Stop())" +
  "      advice(AuthorizationAdvice)" +
  "    end" +
  "    " +
  " end ";
```

The final phase of the code is to use AspectLanguageEngineBuilder and AspectEngine defined in the Aspect# framework that will then dynamically inject these rules:

```
AspectLanguageEngineBuilder builder =
    new AspectLanguageEngineBuilder( weavingRules );
AspectEngine engine = builder.Build();
```

Once the rules are fed to the Aspect#'s core engine, a new instance of NASDAQHeartBeatService is created using the framework WrapClass factory method. If you compile and run this program, you will see the output shown in Figure 5-16 displayed on the screen.

```
NASDAQHeartBeatService nasdaqService=
    engine.WrapClass(typeof(NASDAQHeartBeatService)) as NASDAQHeartBeatService;
nasdaqService.Start();
```

Figure 5-16. *Console output of AOP-enabled heartbeat service*

This demonstrates the power of AOP. An important point to add to your knowledge bank is that the advice has complete knowledge about its calling method execution context. For example, in the AuthorizationAdvice class, you can easily examine and modify the injected method's incoming arguments by inspecting the appropriate properties of the IMethodInvocation interface.

AOP is not a new concept. The ideas adopted by AOP have been prevalent in the Microsoft world for quite a while and can be tracked to the COM days when infrastructure services such as thread safety, object pooling, transaction support, authentication, and authorization were provided by flipping the appropriate switches in the component configuration UI window. AOP has recently started gaining a lot of recognition as one of the techniques to further raise the level of abstraction in designing an easy-to-maintain system. However, AOP is not a panacea to all problems. You must continue to keep your foot in the OOP territory. But, with the passage of time, the adoption rate of AOP in real-life applications will probably increase; we would not be surprised to see it prevailing in the mainstream software development.

Examining the Business-Technology Mapping

Before you step into the actual design, it is important to look at the important role played by the operations team in an organization. Within most companies, a dedicated team known as the *operations team* is appointed. The important task of continuously monitoring the activity of trading applications in the production environment and raising an alarm in the case of abnormal behavior rests on their shoulders. The development team relies on the information gathered by the operations team when it comes to fixing bugs or fine-tuning application behavior. The existence of an operations team relieves the development team from intervening in the day-to-day application hitches and allows them to actively focus on their core task of designing and building applications.

It also means the development team needs to equip the operations team with a rich set of information that will allow them to get thorough insight into the underpinnings of the applications. This is where a need for implementing a centralized application operation engine that will allow the operations team to monitor and administer applications running in an organization is determined. The application operation engine will act as the eyes and ears of the trading applications, which allows the operations team to watch the status of the application's health and activity and also acts as a central information repository for trading applications. From a features perspective, this engine will support all kinds of operational features such as centralized logging, security, configuration, and so on.

The framework of the application operation engine is pretty straightforward. It is similar to the master-slave architecture style where there is one primary application controller and multiple application agents. The primary controller is installed on a dedicated machine and separate from the core trading applications. Agents are installed on the machine where the core trading application resides, as depicted in Figure 5-17.

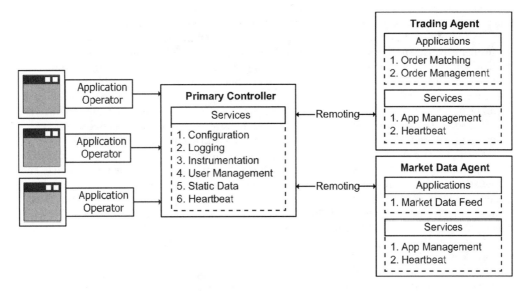

Figure 5-17. *Application operation engine*

In Figure 5-17 both trading and market data agents are assigned the task of managing order-matching and market data applications, respectively. The primary controller, besides being aware of the active agents, also provides various services that are leveraged by applications controlled by these agents. These services take the form of server-side services and agent-side services. Server-side services are those services that are executed under the context of the primary controller. Similarly, agent-side services execute under the context of the agent. A typical example of agent-side services is an application management service that includes logic to load and unload trading applications, so it is quite obvious that such logic needs to be executed on the actual machine where the applications are installed. Services hosted by the primary controller include logging, instrumentation, health monitoring, and so on, that is executed inside the context of the server. The final piece in Figure 5-17 is the application operator GUI, which is responsible for the visual representation of information collected from the primary controller. In other words, it is through this GUI application that the operator or development team will be able to watch and monitor the application's activity.

.NET Remoting is the mainstream approach for building a centralized application controller. First you must identify the important components of remoting, which are the server application and client application, and finally you define a list of classes that needs to be exposed remotely. The first step is to model both the primary controller and the agent as separate distinct Singleton remotable classes that will be extended from `MarshalByRefObject`. Also, both the agent and primary controller will be physically separated so you require a host application that will register the channel and formatting information. Hence, we have adopted `TCPChannel` as the primary communication channel between the agent and the primary controller and `BinaryFormatter` as the data-encoding standard. The next part of the implementation is to understand how you make the trading application aware of the existence of a service controller and allow it to use the features provided by the controller.

The primary controller owns complete knowledge of trading applications to be monitored along with its designated agent. Let's assume that the mapping information between the agent and application is recorded in an XML configuration file. After reading this mapping information, the primary controller will notify agents with the list of trading applications assigned to it and also instructs them to start the application. There is an initial handshake conducted between the agent and primary controller, and during this handshaking phase both the agent and the primary controller create a unique instance of `DomainApp` at their ends. `DomainApp`, also called the *domain application*, is our own internal implementation and encapsulates the infrastructure services discussed previously such as logging, configuration, and so on. To be more precise, an instance of `DomainApp` created by the primary controller encapsulates the server-side services, and an instance of `DomainApp` created by the agent encapsulates the agent-side services. For each trading application managed by a primary controller, a unique instance of `DomainApp` is created on both sides, but the underlying class of this instance itself is derived from `MarshalByRefObject`. So if a reference is passed outside its default application domain, it will be passed as marshaled by reference, and this is what happens during the handshake stage. Both the agent and primary controller receive proxy references to each other's instance of `DomainApp`, which in turn would allow them to invoke both server-side and agent-side services.

The next part is to launch trading applications, and this functionality is considered to be an agent-side service, so you will package this logic in the form of an application management service. The application management service creates a new application domain and executes the application inside this newly created application domain. Before executing, it assigns a reference of `DomainApp` to this newly created application domain using the `SetData` method of the `AppDomain` class. The trading application accesses this `DomainApp` reference using the `GetData` method defined in the `AppDomain` class and starts using the services provided by the application controller engine.

The only missing part that we will not cover is the GUI portion of the application operation engine. But once you get a strong understanding of the components implemented in the operation engine, then it is just a question of invoking the appropriate calls from the GUI. Then, the rest of the job is performed by the primary controller and the agents.

Class Details

In this section, you will develop a scaled-down version of an application operation engine. Although it will not support all the operational features, the motive is to prove that remoting is an ideal fit for building these kinds of monitoring applications. However, keep in mind that because the monitoring applications depend upon the nature of the requirement, in some exceptional cases remoting may not look like a perfect fit. Before you start with the low-level code details, you need to be acquainted with the project hierarchy (see Table 5-6).

Table 5-6. *Application Operation Engine Assembly Structure*

Assembly Type	Project Name	References	Description
Console application	AppController	Common	AppController is the primary controller, so it contains the code to connect to agents, to assign agents a list of trading applications to monitor, and also to provide server-side services.
Console application	AppAgent	Common	AppAgent is the agent that executes the actions issued by the primary controller.
Shared library	Common		The shared library contains both classes and interfaces shared among the primary controller, agents, and domain applications.
Console application	OrderMatching	Common	OrderMatching represents a real-life trading application that will be under the surveillance of an application agent.

In this scenario, ideally, all console applications must be ported to a Windows service so that they can be launched from the Windows startup without any user intervention. But for demonstration purposes, the console applications will always be our friend. Figure 5-18 shows the application operation engine class diagram, and Figure 5-19 shows the application operation engine's project structure.

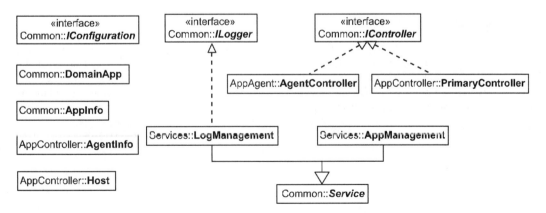

Figure 5-18. *Application operation engine class diagram*

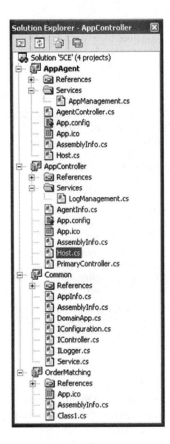

Figure 5-19. *Application operation engine project structure*

IController

The IController interface is shared between both the agent and the primary controller application. A controller from a simple definition point of view is an entity that is assigned the task of controlling or organizing something. So, in both the primary controller and the agent application, you need an entity that will supervise and coordinate the application's activity. IController defines a list of members and properties that is implemented by the concrete controller class of the primary controller and agent.

Here's the code for IController:

```
using System;
using System.Collections;

namespace Common
{
  public interface IController
  {
    //This method is invoked on the agent by the primary controller.
    //It is with the help of this method that the primary controller empowers
    //the agent by assigning a list of applications that directly fall
    //under the agent's control.
    DomainApp CreateApplication(AppInfo appInfo, DomainApp serverApp);
```

```
        //This property determines whether the controller
        //is an agent or a primary controller.
        bool IsAgent{get;}

        //The concept of data bag is not unique. Its existence could be
        //drawn from Windows OS that provides similar features in the form
        //of environment variables. With the help of environment variables,
        //important configuration information are shared among OS processes.
        //We are following a similar path by introducing the data bag, but the
        //information is shared among services. With the help of this method, the
        //primary controller passes the information to the agent that is then
        //shared with agent-side services.
        void InitializeDataBag(Hashtable dataBag);
    }

}
```

AppInfo

AppInfo is a serializable class that acts as an information holder for the primary controller and its agents. We discussed the primary controller assigning a list of trading applications to the agent, so this task is encapsulated inside an instance of the AppInfo class and passed to the agent. It contains information such as the assembly path, assembly name, and so on, that is finally resolved by the agent.

Here's the code for AppInfo:

```
using System;
using System.Collections;

namespace Common
{
    [Serializable]
    public class AppInfo
    {
        string appName, assemblyName;
        string assemblyPath;

        public string AssemblyPath
        {
            get{return assemblyPath;}
            set{assemblyPath=value;}
        }

        public AppInfo(string name)
        {
            appName = name;
        }

        public string Name
        {
            get{return appName;}
            set{appName=value;}
        }

        public string AssemblyName
        {
            get{return assemblyName;}
```

```
    set{assemblyName=value;}
  }

 }
}
```

DomainApp

DomainApp is an important class inside the applications operation framework because the various services such as logging, configuration, application management, and so on, are made accessible through the instance of this class. DomainApp is derived from the MarshalByRefObject type, and hence its instance is also remotely accessible.

Here's the code for DomainApp:

```
using System;

namespace Common
{
  public class DomainApp: MarshalByRefObject
  {
    AppInfo appInfo;
    ILogger logger;
    IConfiguration configuration;
    Service appMgmt;


    //The underlying information about the actual application
    //is available with the help of the AppInfo property.

    public AppInfo Info
    {
      get{return appInfo;}
    }

    public DomainApp(AppInfo info)
    {
      appInfo = info;
    }

    //This property allows accessing the functionality provided
    //by the Application management service.
    public Service AppManagement
    {
      get{return appMgmt;}
      set{appMgmt=value;}
    }

    //The Logger property encapsulates centralized logging features.
    public ILogger Logger
    {
      get{return logger;}
      set{logger =value;}
    }
  }
}
```

IConfiguration

The IConfiguration interface is implemented by the configuration management service. It contains only one method, GetConfig, which is invoked to get configuration information about the application.

Here's the code for IConfiguration:

```
using System;
using System.Xml;

namespace Common
{
  public interface IConfiguration
  {
    XmlElement GetConfig();
  }
}
```

ILogger

The ILogger interface defines the contract that every logging service must implement.

Here's the code for ILogger:

```
using System;

namespace Common
{

  public interface ILogger
  {
    void Log(string logMsg);
  }
}
```

Service

Service is the common base class for all operational services and includes both agent-side and server-side services. This class defines common behaviors that are applied to all services, and it includes behavior to start and stop services or to suspend and resume services. The methods are marked *virtual*, which would allow the concrete service class to override the default behavior to suit its custom requirement.

Here's the code for Service:

```
using System;

namespace Common
{

  public abstract class Service : MarshalByRefObject
  {
    protected IController serviceController;
    protected DomainApp domainApp;

    //The overloaded constructor accepts two arguments;
    //the first argument is an instance of IController, and the
    //second argument is an instance of DomainApp. It is important
    //to educate the service about the underlying controller (primary controller
    //or agent) and domain application inside which it is hosted.
```

```
      //Effectively, by providing this hosting context information,
      //we allow the service to directly interact with the controller or
      //domain application and allow them to leverage other services
      //provided by the domain application; to sum up, we are laying a strong
      //foundation to achieve interservice communication.
      public Service(IController controller,DomainApp app)
      {
        serviceController = controller;
        domainApp=app;
      }

      public virtual void Start()
      {
      }

      public virtual void Stop()
      {
      }

      public virtual void Suspend()
      {
      }

      public virtual void Resume()
      {
      }
   }
}
```

PrimaryController

The first concrete implementation of the controller, PrimaryController is derived from
MarshalByRefObject and also implements the IController interface. This class contains the
most important logic of connecting to agents and loading the server-side services.

Here's the code for PrimaryController:

```
using System;
using System.Runtime.Remoting;
using System.Collections;
using Common;
using AppController.Services;

namespace AppController
{

  public class PrimaryController: MarshalByRefObject,IController
  {
    Hashtable agents = new Hashtable();
    Hashtable dataBag = new Hashtable();

    //The constructor method populates the data bag by
    //invoking the InitializeDataBag method. The body of the method
    //is empty, but ideally the data bag values will be fetched
    //from the XML File or database or some other data source.
    public PrimaryController()
    {
```

```
  InitializeDataBag(dataBag);
}

public AgentInfo this[string agentName]
{
  get{return agents[agentName] as AgentInfo;}
}

public void Start()
{
  ConnectAgents();
}

public void InitializeDataBag(Hashtable data)
{
}


//The real handshaking among agents is performed inside this code.
//The list of agents, primarily their locations, is stored in a application
//configuration file as part of remoting section; after reading this
//location values with help of remoting helper method, we enter
//a foreach loop. It is inside this loop a remote instance
//of agent is created on remote server and its reference is stored for
//subsequent access. After successful creation of agent, the next step
//is to assign it the list of applications that are directly under its
//supervision.
public void ConnectAgents()
{
  foreach(WellKnownClientTypeEntry clientEntry in
      RemotingConfiguration.GetRegisteredWellKnownClientTypes())
  {
    Console.WriteLine("Connecting to Agent : " +clientEntry.ObjectUrl);
    IController agent = Activator.GetObject(typeof(IController),
                              clientEntry.ObjectUrl) as IController;
    agent.InitializeDataBag(dataBag);
    AgentInfo agentInfo = new AgentInfo(agent);
    agents[clientEntry.ObjectUrl] = agentInfo;
    InitializeApplications(agentInfo);
  }
}


//In this section of code both primary controller and agent
//creates an instance of domain applications and attach the
//list of services applicable on their end. Again for sake
//of simplicity, we have hardwired the application name,
//the application path, and the assembly name inside the code,
//but the best approach is to separate this information
//in a configuration file and also assign the agent controlling
//these applications. You will also notice a call to
//CreateApplication method happening on both the primary controller
//and agent; this method invocation will ensure that both agent and
//primary controller have performed the necessary required set-up.
//Another important section of code to look is the exchange of remote
//references, particularly an instance of the AppManagement class reference.
//When we invoke CreateApplication method on an instance of agent, we
//also pass a reference to server-side domain application, and on successful
```

```
//execution of this method it returns a reference to agent-side domain
//application, which itself is a remote reference. We know that both
//server-side and agent-side services are derived from the common base class
//Service, so by accessing the AppManagement property of remote instance of
//domain applications, we will be returned with proxy reference.
public void InitializeApplications(AgentInfo agentInfo)
{
  AppInfo appInfo = new AppInfo("Order Matching");
  appInfo.AssemblyName = "OrderMatching.exe";
  appInfo.AssemblyPath = @"C:\CodeExample\Chpt5\SCE\OrderMatching\bin\Debug";
  DomainApp omeServer= this.CreateApplication(appInfo,null);
  DomainApp omeClient= agentInfo.Agent.CreateApplication(appInfo,omeServer);
  omeServer.AppManagement = omeClient.AppManagement;
  agentInfo.Applications.Add(omeServer.Info.Name,omeServer);
}

//The required initialization of domain application is performed
//inside this code, what we meant by initialization is configuring
//the services and assigning its reference back to the domain application.
public DomainApp CreateApplication(AppInfo appInfo, DomainApp serverApp)
{
  DomainApp newApp = new DomainApp(appInfo);
  LogManagement logMgmt = new LogManagement(this,newApp);
  return newApp;
}

public bool IsAgent
{
  get{return false;}
}

  }
}
```

AgentInfo

The AgentInfo class stores information related to an agent. Besides storing agent remote references, it also stores the instances of applications that are controlled by an agent.

Here's the code for AgentInfo:

```
using System;
using System.Collections;
using Common;

namespace AppController
{
  public class AgentInfo
  {
    IController agent;
    Hashtable applications = new Hashtable();

    public Hashtable Applications
    {
      get{return applications;}
    }
```

```
public IController Agent
{
  get{return agent;}
}

public AgentInfo(IController controller)
{
  agent=controller;
}
}
}
```

LogManagement

The LogManagement service addresses the logging aspect of a trading application and is categorized under server-side services. The code is pretty straightforward and, depending upon the business requirement implementation of the Log method, can be tweaked to suit the need of application:

```
using System;
using Common;

namespace AppController.Services
{
  public class LogManagement : Service,ILogger
  {
    public LogManagement(IController controller,DomainApp app)
    :base(controller,app)
    {
      app.Logger = this;
    }

    //Logging of Messages
    public void Log(string logMsg)
    {
      Console.WriteLine(logMsg);
    }
  }
}
```

Primary Controller Remoting Configuration

This is the primary controller remoting configuration:

```
<?xml version="1.0" encoding="utf-8" ?>
<configuration>
    <system.runtime.remoting>
        <application>
            <channels>
                <channel ref="tcp" port="20000">
                <serverProviders>
                    <formatter ref="binary" typeFilterLevel="Full" />
                </serverProviders>
                </channel>
            </channels>
             <client>
                <wellknown url="tcp://localhost:20001/TradingEngineAgent.rem"
```

```
                            type="Common.IController, Common" />
                    </client>
                </application>
            </system.runtime.remoting>
        </configuration>
```

Primary Controller Host

The Host class launches the primary controller shell and also invokes the application management service that is an agent-side service. The primary controller instructs this service to start the application, which is equivalent to launching a remote application.

Here's the code for the primary controller host:

```
using System;
using Common;
using System.Runtime.Remoting;

namespace AppController
{
  class Host
  {
    static void Main(string[] args)
    {
      //Start Primary Controller
      PrimaryController primaryController = new PrimaryController();
      RemotingConfiguration.Configure(@"AppController.exe.config");
      RemotingServices.Marshal(primaryController  ,
                 "PrimaryController.ref",typeof(PrimaryController));
      primaryController.Start();
      Console.WriteLine("Primary Controller Started");

      //Access trading agent, and invoke the application management service
      Console.WriteLine("Starting App Management Service..");
      AgentInfo agentInfo =
            primaryController["tcp://localhost:20001/TradingEngineAgent.rem"];
      DomainApp omeApp =  agentInfo.Applications["Order Matching"] as DomainApp;
      omeApp.AppManagement.Start();
      Console.ReadLine();
    }
  }
}
```

AgentController

This class represents an agent-side controller, so the code of this class is more or less similar to the server-side controller code. The important section in this class is the CreateApplication method; inside its method body, a new instance of DomainApp class is created, and also agent-side services are initialized. Remember, the CreateApplication method is invoked by the primary controller, which also happens to pass its remote reference of DomainApp, so you assign the proxy reference of server-side services to an instance of the agent-side DomainApp.

Here's the code for AppController:

```
using System;
using System.Collections;
using Common;
using AppAgent.Services;
```

```
namespace AppAgent
{
  public class AgentController : MarshalByRefObject,IController
  {
    Hashtable appCollections = new Hashtable();
    Hashtable dataBag;

    public AgentController ()
    {
    }

    public void InitializeDataBag(Hashtable data)
    {
      dataBag = data;
    }

    public DomainApp CreateApplication(AppInfo appInfo, DomainApp serverApp)
    {
      Console.WriteLine("Creating Application : " +appInfo.Name);
      DomainApp newApp = new DomainApp(appInfo);
      AppManagement appMgmt = new AppManagement(this,newApp);
      newApp.Logger = serverApp.Logger;
      appCollections[appInfo.Name] = newApp;
      return newApp;
    }

    public bool IsAgent
    {
      get{return true;}
    }
  }
}
```

AppManagement

AppManagement is an agent-side service that is responsible for launching and stopping the trading application. It creates a new application domain and a new thread and executes the trading application inside this newly created domain. Another interesting thing to note is that a reference to the agent-side instance of DomainApp is passed using the SetData method of the AppDomain class.

Here's the code for AppManagement:

```
using System;
using System.Threading;
using Common;

namespace AppAgent.Services
{
  public class AppManagement  : Service
  {
    AppDomain newDomain;
    Thread newThread;

    public AppManagement(IController controller, DomainApp app)
    :base(controller,app)
    {
      app.AppManagement = this;
```

```
        newThread = new Thread(new ThreadStart(LaunchApp));
    }

    public void LaunchApp()
    {
      newDomain = AppDomain.CreateDomain(domainApp.Info.Name);
      string appFullPath= domainApp.Info.AssemblyPath +"\\"
                          +domainApp.Info.AssemblyName;
      newDomain.SetData("SERVICE_DOMAINAPP",domainApp);
      newDomain.ExecuteAssembly(appFullPath);
    }

    public override void Start()
    {
      newThread.Start();
    }

    public override void Stop()
    {

    }

    public override void Resume()
    {

    }

    public override void Suspend()
    {

    }

  }
}
```

Agent Remoting Configuration

This is the agent remoting configuration:

```
<?xml version="1.0" encoding="utf-8" ?>
<configuration>
    <system.runtime.remoting>
        <application>
            <service>
                <wellknown mode="Singleton" objectUri="TradingEngineAgent.rem"
                           type="AppAgent.AgentController, AppAgent" />
            </service>
            <channels>
                <channel ref="tcp" port="20001">
                    <serverProviders>
                      <formatter ref="binary" typeFilterLevel="Full" />
                    </serverProviders>
                </channel>
            </channels>
        </application>
    </system.runtime.remoting>
</configuration>
```

Agent Host

This is the agent host:

```
using System;
using System.Runtime.Remoting;

namespace AppAgent
{
  class Host
  {
    static void Main(string[] args)
    {
      RemotingConfiguration.Configure(@"AppAgent.exe.config");
      Console.WriteLine("Service Controller Agent Started...");
      Console.ReadLine();
    }
  }
}
```

Order-Matching Application

If you peek at the primary controller code, you will see a reference to the order-matching application. On further digging inside the host code of the primary controller, you will also discover a startup call to the application management service, and you are already aware of the functionality provided by this service. The code inside the order-matching application retrieves a reference to an instance of DomainApp assigned by the application management service, and by using this instance, it invokes logging service. The actual logging is performed on the server and not on the client as depicted in the following program output:

```
using System;
using System.Threading;
using Common;

namespace OrderMatching
{
  class Class1
  {
    static void Main(string[] args)
    {
      DomainApp serviceApp =
              AppDomain.CurrentDomain.GetData("SERVICE_DOMAINAPP") as DomainApp;
      serviceApp.Logger.Log("Order Matching Started");
    }
  }
}
```

Figure 5-20 shows the console output of the application operation engine.

Figure 5-20. *Console output of the application operation engine*

Summary

In this chapter, we explained and implemented the following:

- We achieved fault isolation in managed applications using application domains. We demonstrated this concept by implementing a central service controller that is responsible for managing trading operation–related services such as the heartbeat service.

- We explored the remoting communication framework by implementing a distributed version of the central service controller example.

- We demystified the secrets behind the remoting proxy with the help of a service directory lookup example.

- We covered the mechanics of distributed garbage collection and demonstrated how the leasing and sponsorship feature is used in designing remote objects that are subject to garbage collection only after trading hours.

- We explained the aspect-oriented programming concept that allows the separation of crosscutting concerns from the functional modules.

- Finally, we designed and developed a small prototype of an application operation engine that enables the instrumentation and management of various subcomponents of a system.

CHAPTER 6

■■■

STP Security

Money holds strong reference with the rich and weak reference with the poor.

We introduced the concept of STP in Chapter 1 and described it as moving trades right from the order-entry stage to settlement without manual intervention. The explanation provided in Chapter 1 highlighted both the internal and external aspects of STP. In this chapter, we will cover the external STP aspect in more detail and also explain what type of security aspects are required for the process. Security in external STP becomes important because multiple entities are involved in moving every trade from origination to settlement. This chapter kicks off its discussion with a detailed business explanation and then slowly changes its rhythm to the technical side, which includes basic coverage of the cryptography- and security-related programming features supported by the .NET Framework.

Exploring the Business Context

Participants in any trade are many, and all are geographically spread out. They all need to settle trades in a time-bound manner. Hence, security in exchanging data becomes a key consideration. There is normally no time for trade rectification, and the cost of repair in the later stage of trade settlement is high. Chapter 1 covered the trading and settlement fundamentals. In this chapter, you will see the steps involved in STP in more detail. This will complete your understanding of settlement in the equities market. We will introduce two more entities here: custodian service providers and STP service providers. They both play important roles in the overall settlement and STP process.

Custodian Service Provider

Investors trust fund managers with their money. But that does not give fund managers ownership over an investor's assets. They are just money managers. From a governance perspective, it is required that a third-party entity holds securities in its name on behalf of the ultimate investors. This third-party entity is called the *custodian* of the securities. A custodian is responsible for delivering and receiving securities and cash on the instruction of the fund manager whenever a purchase or sale transaction takes place. A fund that invests securities in multiple markets and asset classes needs a custodian who can provide support in multiple locations and across asset classes. Custodians normally have presence across major locations, and wherever they don't, they enter into agreements with other custodians to provide such services. The second-level custodians that serve the bigger custodians are called *subcustodians*.

STP Service Provider

STP service providers have the responsibility of carrying and delivering STP-related instructions and messages. They provide connectivity to market entities such as brokers, custodians, and fund managers and bring them together in a common network. Once the entities enter the common network, they communicate with each other using standard messaging protocols such as Swift 15022. STP service providers invest in high-end fault-tolerant hardware and invest in creating a network that becomes the backbone in such message-based communication. For an STP service to succeed, it is important that it has a critical mass of institutions along with it. More institutions would mean higher volumes, which in turn mean higher margins (assuming a fixed cost regardless of the number of institutions signing in). In most countries, more than one STP service provider exists. This is to encourage competition so that users have a choice, which in turn yields better service for institutions. This raises another challenge of interoperability.

In markets where more than one STP service provider exists, institutions have a choice. They can sign up with one service provider after considering the cost structure, reliability, image, and reach of the service provider. In such cases, a possibility is that the fund manager, custodian, and broker involved in a particular transaction are on separate networks because they have subscribed to the services of different service providers. To settle transactions in such cases, messages need to be passed from one service provider (network) to another service provider (network). To achieve this, connectivity needs to exist between the three competing networks, and they also need to either be on the same protocol or understand the same protocols. This ability to seamlessly communicate with each other across service provider networks and settle transactions is called *interoperability*. Noncompliance to interoperability is an area of key concern for market participants, especially if they have a large customer base. This will alienate institutions that are not with the same service provider. Compliance to interoperability is normally monitored by the country's regulators or industry associations.

Driving Factors Behind STP

STP was initiated as part of the T+1 initiative by the equities market. Transactions are currently being settled on a T+3 basis. Industry participants are keen to push efficiencies across their own organization as well as in the overall markets. STP was the central theme around which the T+1 initiative rested. The T+1 initiative would have resulted in less risk, better capital deployment, and an overall strengthening of the financial markets. In fact, an association called Global Straight-Through Processing Association (GSTPA) was formed to drive the T+1 initiative. However, the initiative was abandoned in November 2002 because it was met with an unenthusiastic response from industry participants. Although the industry participants believe that STP is necessary, they were not convinced of T+1.

STP is driven by a couple of factors. We'll cover some of them in the following sections.

Standardization

Institutions work on a variety of applications, which are themselves on different hardware and software platforms. Different institutions work on different applications and used to communicate via phone calls, faxes, e-mails, and file transfers. Apart from reading these communications and acting on them, the recipient of these messages really did not have many other choices. There was no automation of processes. STP helps standardize the interinstitution communication in order to streamline operations.

Reduction in Costs

Security trading has become a commodity business. This means customers don't really perceive much difference between getting their trades executed through broker X versus broker Y unless the quantity of shares transacted (or their related value) is very large. This is much like buying an airline ticket today. For a 2-hour flight, passengers really don't care whether they are flying carrier A or carrier B as long as the services of both are reasonably comparable. This commoditization of services has happened even in the securities industry, and when service levels are comparable, customers really don't care whether they route transactions through broker X or broker Y. With the differentiation in service levels eroding, any differentiation with respect to cost leads to a comparative advantage for the broker. Brokers are hence taking proactive steps to reduce overall transaction costs and pass on the benefits in the form of a lower brokerage to customers. Moving toward STP has demonstrated significant cost savings.

Reduction in Settlement Time

To improve capital allocation and to contain settlement risk, reducing the settlement time from T+5 to T+2 and any initiative toward T+1 will compress the window available for managing settlement-related activities even further. This makes automation at all levels mandatory.

Reduction in Head Count

Traditional processes in settlements were such that institutions were forced to add staff with increasing volumes. A fixed number of staff could not take on additional volumes when market activity started to rise. With STP in place, an existing staff can manage even high volumes because the bulk of transactions pass through and settle through an automated process.

Addressing Exceptions

The settlement process is changing. It is now increasingly being seen as a cost center. The earlier approach was that every transaction was manually attended to for completing settlements, but now it is only the problematic transactions to which settlement managers pay attention. All transactions that don't have any issues are just allowed to go through.

Single-Point Transaction Fulfillment

While institutions are constantly upgrading their operations, they realized that handling multiple points of data entry, especially if they relate to the same transaction, is cumbersome and prone to errors. STP ensures that all trade data enters the STP network only once, and then the same transaction moves on. This results in a savings of effort and an error-free environment. Extensive manual work was also being done in post-trade activities such as calculating average rates, taxes, and other levies, and the level of accuracy that customers demanded was not possible in a manual environment.

A Perspective of STP

To appreciate the benefits of STP, you first need to understand the perspective under which STP happens. Historically, the process of settlements was fairly manual and involved a lot of phone conversations, faxing, and e-mailing. The settlement departments of brokers and custodians had to ensure that they met whatever their obligations were and met them on time. Despite this, trades used to fail in settlement because of manual involvement, and worse is that all failures used to come to light only after the process for settling all trades for that settlement were complete. The entire process of settlements was time-consuming and fraught with a lot of problems and risk involving time delays, failed settlements, and too much manual work.

To move toward STP, the two main challenges are getting all entities on a common platform so that they can communicate with each other and having a common protocol to understand seamlessly what others in the process are discussing. The STP service providers largely overcame this hurdle. It is also important that a critical mass of institutions be on the STP network. Currently, most institutions have adopted STP technology, and those who have not are running the risk of being alienated by other institutions because everyone is looking to do business with tech-savvy institutions that don't pose a risk when becoming a counterpart.

STP in an equities trade involves the following entities (see Figure 6-1):

- Investing institutions (fund managers)
- Custodians
- Brokers
- STP service providers

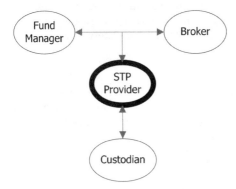

Figure 6-1. *Block diagram of participants in STP*

The STP service provider sells its STP services to fund managers, brokers, and custodians and expects them to join their service. Once they join, they are given a terminal through which they can connect to the common network and communicate through a common and standard protocol such as Swift 15022. Having a common protocol for communication is important. This ensures that from day one each participant can understand what the others are saying and ensures that no one organization has an edge over the other in this entire framework. The entire network is also independent of which systems or front/back office products the organizations are using. The network is platform neutral. Once these organizations are on a common network and have the ability of processing trade-related information electronically using the communication protocol, technically they are STP enabled.

Along with entities mentioned, the following also play a crucial role in enabling the STP process in the market:

- Stock exchanges
- Clearing corporations
- Depositories
- Banks

These other entities also play an important role in enabling the STP process and will continue to play a vital role, especially if the market again creates an initiative to move from T+3 to T+1. STP also will not be achieved until both institutional and retail trades are brought into the STP framework. In a T+3 to a T+1 environment, there is as much risk from retail trades as there is from institutional trades. Though the value of retail trades is a lot less than institutional trades, a lot of discipline is required on the retail side, especially when it comes to meeting commitments on time. Retail investors are normally required to deliver the shares in a sale transaction and provide money to brokers to meet their purchase commitments. This money ultimately has to move to the clearing corporation's account by T+3 (or T+1 as the case might be). Moving money normally happens through multiple accounts. A retail investor will first write a check in favor of his broker. The broker in turn will write a check in favor of the clearing corporation. Moving money may take time, especially when it is not the only thing investors are doing. Banks must be geared up in terms of systems to meet these challenges and move money fast.

Brokers and financial institutions have spent a lot of time, effort, and money on centralizing and consolidating their IT operations. To achieve true STP, this IT structure, especially the part related to decision making, will again have to be decentralized. This also means that just as fund managers, brokers, and custodians use a mix of their systems and the STP service providers' services, other entities such as a broker's franchises (if the broker operates on a franchise model), exchanges, and depositories must also devise their operations and processes in such a way that they are able to communicate and work effectively so that the market as a whole can come to the T+1 model. For example, for retail transactions, instead of expecting delivery of shares from the broker, if the depository also builds in the facility of accepting shares directly from the retail investor's accounts, then those investors who maintain their securities with a broker (other than the one who has executed the transaction) can deliver the securities directly by the pay-in date. This transaction could be tagged by the broker's code so that the clearing corporation also knows the name of the broker against whose obligations these securities could be deemed delivered. This will reduce the leg of investors first transferring shares in the broker's account and brokers in turn transferring them to the clearing corporation's account at the time of pay-in. Similarly, at the time of pay-out, the clearing corporation could directly transfer the shares.

In fact, true STP can be achieved only when all these entities come forward and participate in the STP process and only when interoperability issues have been addressed.

How Is STP Achieved?

We will attempt to explain STP with an example. Our emphasis in this example is on institutional transactions rather than retail. This is because STP is more relevant for institutional transactions because the number of entities and complexity involved in settling an institutional transaction is greater than when settling a retail transaction. Let's assume a buy transaction.

Fund managers run investment management services for individuals, governments, pension trusts, corporations, and virtually everyone who has money and wants to deploy in the market in search of returns. The complexity of the fund management process differs depending upon the customer for which the fund is being managed, the type and objectives of the fund, the number and category of securities the fund invests in, and the geographical diversification and investment of the fund.

Fund managers buy or sell depending upon their perception of the market and underlying securities. They buy when they are convinced the underlying securities will appreciate in value and sell when they believe the underlying securities will decline in value. They benchmark their returns with a broad-based index and also with other funds having a similar objective.

Fund managers route their orders through brokers. Fund managers try their best to keep the composition of the fund's portfolio aligned to the fund's objectives. This alignment, realignment, and fund manager's changing perception of a stock's value causes the purchase and sale of shares. The sales desk staff of brokering companies looking for business also engages fund managers and discusses the market trends and direction. They also discuss investment as well as divestment opportunities. Normally such discussions result in the fund managers giving orders to buy or sell one or more securities.

When an order is given to the trading desk, the fund manager may consolidate orders from multiple funds into one and forward it. This may happen frequently if the fund manager manages assets for multiple portfolios and funds. When the order reaches the trading desk, the dealer may aggregate those orders with orders from other clients/funds but put the same execution conditions into a single block and then send the block for execution.

A lot of clients and fund managers use their own order management systems (OMSs) to connect to the broker. They connect directly to the exchange where their orders are routed after passing risk management checks laid down by the brokers, or these orders get delivered to the broker who in turn enters the orders in the exchange trading system available. Establishing connectivity with brokers is a key challenge in itself. Some countries have regulations on the amount of business that can be passed to a single broker. Assuming regulators allow a maximum of 5 percent of transactions to be given to one broker, it logically follows that each fund must at least maintain relations with a minimum of 20 brokers. Establishing connectivity with each separately is impractical. Even if connectivity is assumed, establishing connectivity alone is not enough to deliver orders. Orders must also be delivered in a format that brokers can understand. This format also has to be fairly standardized so that *all* brokers understand it. The Financial Information Exchange (FIX) protocol has evolved as one of the most popular protocols for the electronic exchange of securities information, especially on the order delivery (front-office) side.

Returning to the example, execution on the exchange may or may not happen in the same block of quantity. In fact, the order will most likely result in multiple fills and will hence result in multiple trades. (Please refer to Chapter 2 to get more insight into this.)

The broker is required to regroup the executions and realign them according to the order. This will most times require averaging out the trades and arriving at a common average price. Once the average price is established, the broker will send out a "notice of execution" to the fund manager.

The notice of execution is sent through the STP service provider (see Figure 6-2). This notice of execution is usually generated automatically by the broker's system and passed to the STP service provider's system for further delivery.

Figure 6-2. *The fund manager submits the order, and the broker sends a notice of execution.*

It could be possible that by looking at good prospects or a buoyant market, the fund manager could have given a blanket buy order for multiple funds without disclosing the identity of individual funds to the broker. Once the broker communicates that all execution is done, the fund manager can then decide which part of execution will go into which fund. This information is returned to the broker through the STP service provider network. This process is called *allocation*. The broker uses the allocation details to calculate the fees and taxes applicable and prepares the contract in the name of the individual fund for which the transactions were originally meant. Once these details are ready, the broker forwards the contract to the fund manager through the STP service network (see Figure 6-3). In absence of such a mechanism, the broker would have to generate the contract notes, take hard-copy printouts, and fax them to fund managers and custodians. The fund managers and custodians would have to then pick up this fax and manually enter all the information in their system. Imagine the number of faxes that would have been required to send if the fund manger worked with 20 brokers and the broker catered to 20 fund managers. With digital signatures in place, the delivery of such digitally signed contracts is legally treated on par with the physical delivery that used to happen.

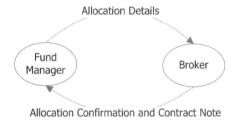

Allocation Details

Fund Manager

Broker

Allocation Confirmation and Contract Note

Figure 6-3. *The fund manager provides allocation, and the broker sends the contract note.*

Once the confirmation is received by the fund managers, the fund's respective custodians need to be informed about the executions so they can be ready for settling the transaction.

The custodian receives transaction details from the fund manager and execution details from the broker. The custodian matches the two and accepts the transaction from the broker if all the details match. Once a custodian accepts a transaction, settling this transaction becomes the responsibility of the custodian. Custodians are normally clearing members in the clearing corporations that clear the trades for exchanges on which brokers transact on behalf of fund managers. In case the contract parameters do not conform to what was expected to be executed by the fund manager, the custodian rejects the contract, and the profit or loss arising from transactions forming the contract becomes the liability of the broker. Normally the broker squares up such transactions on the same day by entering a reverse transaction in the stock exchange. In case the rejection has happened because of something minor like an erroneous calculation of commission or taxes, then the broker has the facility to correct the contents of the contract note and resubmit it to the custodian for acceptance.

One big benefit that brokers derive from being on the same network as the custodians is that they know their obligations in real time. This is because the moment custodians reject any contract, a message is sent to the broker as well. The broker can immediately take steps to square up the transactions or regenerate the contract note as the case may be. In addition to real-time clarity over the fate of contracts, everyone is aware and in complete control of what's happening and when. Such clarity and control is not present in a fax-based scenario. In the fax era, brokers knew that a fax had been received by the fund manager/custodian but didn't know whether they had acted on it also.

All communication between fund manager, custodian, and broker also happens through the STP service provider network (see Figure 6-4).

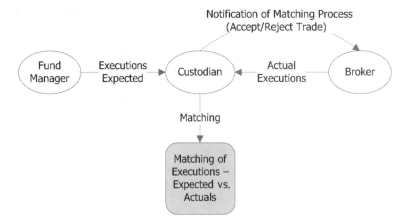

Figure 6-4. *The broker sends the contract details to the custodian; the custodian matches the details with transaction information submitted by the fund manager.*

Once the custodian accepts the transaction, they submit an instruction for receipt (remember, it was a buy transaction) of securities. Similarly, the counterparty of this transaction (who sold the shares) would have submitted an instruction for the delivery of securities. The submission of instruction is a confirmation that an institution is standing by the transaction and wants to receive/deliver securities in order to complete the settlement. Such instructions enter a database called a Standing Instructions Database (SID). Once both sides of instructions get matched, the depository will move securities from the seller's account to the buyer's account through the clearing corporation. Figure 6-5 shows the complete STP framework (post-trade).

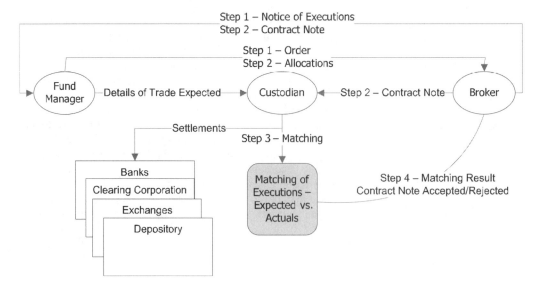

Figure 6-5. *Complete STP framework (post-trade)*

The settlement of funds happens through the usual banking channels.

Implementing Security in the STP Space

In this entire STP process, the exchange of information is key. Multiple actors are involved in the STP space, and an individual actor plays an important role in making a transaction successful (see Figure 6-6). When so many institutions are trying to get onto the same network and exchange messages with each other, the security and the reliability of the service provider's network become the main concerns.

Figure 6-6. *The STP space*

A quick flashback to bygone days will reveal that the primary communication mediums used to exchange information were telephone or fax. This type of communication involved quite a large amount of paperwork to be produced and exchanged on a regular basis. However, in today's modern age with the availability of advanced communication infrastructure, information exchange has become blazingly fast. Zero paperwork is involved; instead, the majority of information is made available in electronic form. This is certainly a boon, but unfortunately the electronic medium has the following problems:

Confidentiality: Confidentiality is related to the privacy of data; for example, when the broker sends a contract note to a fund manager, the information provided in the contract note (such as the number of trades executed and the price of individual trade) is very sensitive in nature. If this information is compromised during transit by a malicious user (a fund manager competitor), then it is sufficient to create havoc in the trading community. By gaining access to such information, the competitor can easily infer the trading strategy, which is the bread and butter of a fund manager.

Integrity: Data integrity is an important aspect of a transaction. Consider an order initiated by a fund manager to a broker to purchase 100 stocks of Microsoft Corporation. Before it is received by the broker, this order is altered by an unauthorized user, and the number of stocks is changed to 1,000. On receiving this order, the broker immediately transacts and sends a confirmation to purchase 1,000 stocks to the fund manager. No doubt it will come as a big blow to the fund manager, and the financial impact of such a transaction will be irrecoverable.

Authentication: In bygone days, trading usually happened over phones; fund managers used to directly place a call to a broker and submit the order. The advantage of such an approach is that both parties know each other's identity, but in a faceless world when a broker receives an order in an electronic form, it is important to know the sender information. It is equally important to the fund manager to know the source of data when the broker sends an order confirmation.

Nonrepudiation: Financial transactions are highly vulnerable to legal problems; the most notable is the sender denying performing an invalid operation. Consider the data integrity example where the quantity attribute of an order is changed from 100 to 1,000. It is expected that the fund manager will deny performing any such action, but without any strong evidence the broker has no way to prove this in a court of law.

The success of STP is solely dependent upon the mechanism implemented to protect the information: the security of the information. A weak security implementation will lose the credibility and acceptance of the STP. Therefore, to prevent loss of trust and to provide a strong sense of safety and privacy to an individual actor, a secure platform is required where information is safely exchanged. This is where the field of cryptography comes into action. *Cryptography* is a set of mathematical techniques implemented to protect information. It includes mechanisms that effectively solve the majority of problems encountered during the electronic exchange of information. By applying cryptography in the STP space, all kinds of data-sharing barriers are eliminated, and a secure environment is erected to conduct business.

Confidentiality

Cryptography addresses the confidentiality aspect of information by concealing it. The act of concealment includes disguising the existence of the actual information by converting it into a gibberish message that is hard to understand and doesn't convey any meaningful sense to the human eye. This process is called the *encryption* of a message; similarly, a reverse process is conducted where the encrypted message is transformed to its original message, and this process is known as the *decryption* of the message.

The secret of encryption/decryption lies in the algorithm that is devised based on the tenets of mathematics. This algorithm in cryptographic terminology is known as a *cipher*. A cipher contains a set of established rules that knows how to encrypt and decrypt a message. The rules depend upon a *cipher key* that is selected from a possible set of *key spaces* and that dictates the encryption/decryption process.

An important fact of cryptography is that *cipher*s should be publicly known, but *cipher keys*, which contain the actual information that needs to be protected, should be private. The safety of the data is ultimately dependent upon the safety of the key and not the cipher. If the safety of the data depended upon the cipher, then imagine the consequences if the cipher was broken. By carving out safety based on the cipher key, decrypting the message becomes complex and time-consuming because the attacker now has to play with all possible cipher keys in order to deduce the original message. This whole concept is explained clearly with the help of a simple substitution cipher (see Figure 6-7).

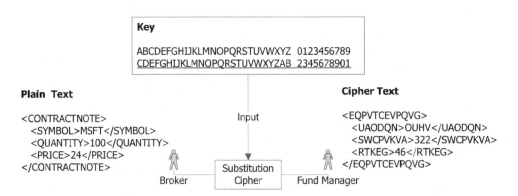

Figure 6-7. *Substitution cipher*

The strength of the substitution cipher resides in replacing every character with a mapped character. This mapping information represents the key that is fed to the substitution algorithm that swaps the original character with another one. By swapping characters, you produce a new encrypted message that is also popularly known as the *cipher text*. It is hard to weed out the original message from the cipher text, and the only way to recover it is to know the mapping rules (that is, the key). By feeding the correct key and cipher text back to the substitution cipher, you can generate the original message.

This example clearly demonstrates that the strength of encryption and decryption depends upon the key. Even though the inner workings of a cipher are straightforward, without a legitimate key the fund manager will fail to decode the encrypted message sent by the broker. Furthermore, the number of possible keys that could be envisaged is directly related to the possible number of ways that both alphabets and numbers can be arranged. Thus, an attacker has to build an exhaustive list of all possible combinations in order to recover the original message. This kind of attack is called a *brute-force attack*.

Besides the substitution cipher, a transposition cipher re-orders the arrangement of a message. For example, in Figure 6-8, when plain text is passed to the transposition cipher, it rearranges the message in a matrix fashion where an individual row represents *n* characters of the message. This *n* forms the key, and in this example we have arranged the message in a row of ten characters. If a message size is not a multiple of ten, then it is padded with a hyphen character. After splitting the message, another round of shuffling is conducted where the individual character is read from top to bottom in a columnar fashion to form the cipher text.

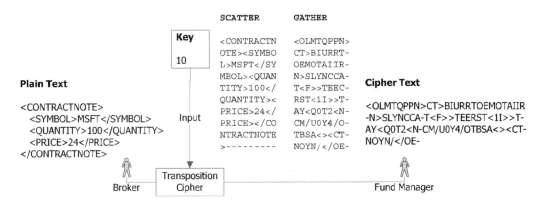

Figure 6-8. *Transposition cipher*

In both the transposition and substitution cipher examples, the whole encryption and decryption scheme is applied over the entire message, but in reality ciphers operate in two modes: block mode and stream mode (see Figure 6-9). *Block ciphers* divide a message in blocks of an appropriate size, and then an individual block is encrypted or decrypted. Similarly, *stream ciphers* are suitable to encrypt or decrypt a message of a smaller size where the encryption/decryption scheme is applied at an individual byte or bit level.

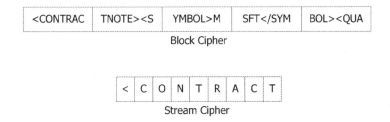

Figure 6-9. *Cipher mode*

Today's modern ciphers implement both a transposition technique and a substitution technique, which makes it harder for attackers to break the message. But it doesn't means it is an impossible task. With the help of an advanced processor, an attacker can easily crack messages that are founded upon a weak cipher or key. Therefore, the only approach to thwart an attacker attempt is to have a watertight cipher and a key of a large size. By increasing the length of the key, the number of possible combinations increases, which makes the attacker's job much tougher. It also means the security of data and a strong cipher are mainly dependent upon the key, and hence it is absolutely necessary to safeguard the key from prying eyes.

Symmetric Key

Symmetric keys are also called *shared keys* because they are known to both the sender and the receiver, and both the encryption and decryption tasks are achieved using this single key (see Figure 6-10). Security based on a symmetric key is considered to be a secret/private communication between the sender and the receiver. For example, if a broker is conducting business with multiple fund managers, then it involves generating multiple shared keys, and each key is unique and exclusive to a particular fund manager. By assigning a dedicated key to an individual fund manager, the broker is able to meet both the authentication and the confidentiality aspects of the data. Furthermore, the symmetric key–based ciphers are very fast and support the encryption/decryption of a large block of data without any hit on performance.

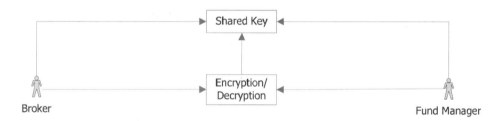

Figure 6-10. *Symmetric key*

The most popular symmetric algorithms are Data Encryption Standard (DES), Triple-DES, RC2, and Rijndael. These algorithms are extensively used in both the commercial and academic fields and are a success story in the field of security. However, the strength of these algorithms is determined by their key size, which is different for each individual algorithm. As a matter of fact, DES is almost on the verge of losing its market share because it implements a 56-bit key size, which is relatively small in comparison with Rijndael and RC2. Rijndael supports key sizes of 128, 196, and 256 bits; similarly, RC2 supports variable key sizes ranging from 1 byte to 128 bytes. Another important fact about symmetric algorithms is that different types of modes are available to encrypt or decrypt a message. This mode determines the granularity of the message that is considered for the encryption/decryption.

Electronic Code Book (ECB)

Electronic Code Book (ECB) is the simplest mode of all available modes (see Figure 6-11). Given plain text, it divides the message into a fixed block of *n* size. Then each individual block is encrypted or decrypted, and finally the output produced by an individual block is combined to form cipher text or plain text.

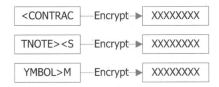

Figure 6-11. *ECB mode*

Cipher Block Chaining (CBC)

In Cipher Block Chaining (CBC) mode, the plain text is divided into a fixed block of *n* size, but each block of plain text before being encrypted is XORed with the previous encrypted block, and encryption is performed on the output produced from this bitwise XOR operation (see Figure 6-12). There is an exception that is applied only to the first block where the XORing operation is performed with an initialization vector (IV). IV is random information generated to act as input to the first block of plain text.

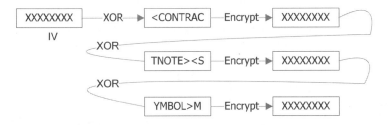

Figure 6-12. *CBC mode*

Cipher Feedback Mode (CFM)

Cipher Feedback Mode (CFM) is used to encrypt/decrypt data with a length smaller than block size (see Figure 6-13). The characteristics of CFM make it look like a stream cipher and are highly suited to encrypt a single byte or bit.

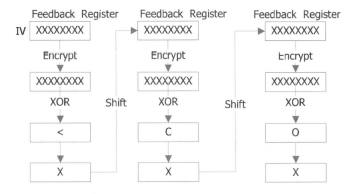

Figure 6-13. *CFM*

Figure 6-13 demonstrates the encryption of a single byte using CFM. The important element that pumps this mode is the feedback register that is initially filled with the IV. The length of this register is exactly equal to the underlying cipher block size; in this scenario, we have considered the length of the block cipher to be 64 bits. Encryption is first performed on the feedback register, and output produced from this operation is then XORed with the plain text. However, the number of bits considered for the XORing operation depends upon the length of the input bits; for instance, if the length of the plain text is 1 byte, then the leftmost 8 bits of output bit is XORed with 8 bit of input bits. The output after the XORing operation is fed back to the feedback register; it involves shifting the leftmost 8 bits. This entire operation is again repeated for the next stream of characters. A slight variant of CFM is Output Feedback Mode (OFB). In this mode, the feedback register is populated with bits that are produced after applying an encryption scheme, which is in contrast with CFM where the feedback register is populated with bits produced after the XOR operation.

As you can see, the behavior of different cipher modes is fine-tuned for a specific scenario. For example, if you come across an interactive-based application where every keystroke needs to be immediately transmitted to its recipient, then CFM and OFB are much more secure than CBC.

Symmetric Classes

The programmatic implementation of symmetric algorithms is defined inside the System.Security. Cryptography namespace. This namespace basically contains cryptographic classes related to symmetric algorithms, hashing, and asymmetric algorithms (discussed later in this chapter). Looking more closely at the cryptography implementation in .NET mainly at the class level, you will find two levels of inheritance followed. The first level is the abstract class that defines common operations. This class is then derived by an algorithm-specific class, which is abstract, and a final-level concrete class is defined that is used by the client to perform cryptographic operation.

Returning to the symmetric algorithms, the base class in which all common operations are defined is SymmetricAlgorithm. This class is further subclassed by an algorithm-specific class that is abstract and is further extended by the concrete class. The implementation of this final concrete class is either managed or unmanaged and is easy to determine by its suffix. Class names that contain the suffix CryptoServiceProvider are unmanaged implementations; similarly, class names that contain the suffix Managed are pure managed implementations. Figure 6-14 shows a class diagram of symmetric algorithms.

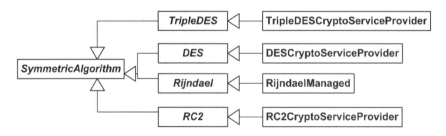

Figure 6-14. *Symmetric algorithm class hierarchy*

The individual symmetric algorithm is encapsulated in a separate class, and being inherited from a common base class, it is relatively simple to change the algorithm implementation with the flip of a switch. However, some exception cases exist where a particular feature is available in one algorithm and not in others. The key differentiator among these algorithms is the key size supported and how fast a message is encrypted or decrypted. Table 6-1 provides this information.

Table 6-1. *Key Sizes of Various Symmetric Ciphers*

Algorithm	Key Size
DES	56 bits
TripleDES	Three different keys of 56-bit key size to encrypt and decrypt a message
Rijndael	Variable key size (1 to 2,048 bits)
RC2	Supports 128-, 192-, and 256-bit key size only

The next step is to delve into the code-level implementation where a plain message is encrypted and decrypted using the Rijndael algorithm. Let's consider the interaction between the broker and fund manager where the contract note defined using XML is encrypted into an unreadable content and sent to the fund manager. The fund manager on receiving this encrypted information will be able to decipher the message only if he knows the symmetric key. The code shown in Listing 6-1 demonstrates both these scenarios. The code is broken down into two sections; the first section provides information about underlying cipher strength, and the last section covers the encryption and decryption task.

Listing 6-1. *Contract Note Information Encrypted by the Broker and Decrypted by the Fund Manager Using the Symmetric Key*

```
using System;
using System.Text;
using System.IO;
using System.Security.Cryptography;

namespace SymmetricAlgo
{
  class SymmetricExample
  {
    static void Main(string[] args)
    {

      //perform symmetric encryption using RijndaelManaged algorithm
      SymmetricAlgorithm algoProvider = RijndaelManaged.Create();
      Console.WriteLine("Crypto Provider Information");
      Console.WriteLine("--------------------");
      Console.WriteLine("Cipher Mode : " + algoProvider.Mode);
      Console.WriteLine("Padding Mode : " +algoProvider.Padding);
      Console.WriteLine("Block Size : " +algoProvider.BlockSize);
      Console.WriteLine("Key Size : " +algoProvider.KeySize);

      Console.WriteLine("Contract Note Encryption Stage - Broker end");
      Console.WriteLine("-------------------------------------------");

      //Generate Symmetric Key
      algoProvider.GenerateKey();

      //Generate IV
      algoProvider.GenerateIV();

      //create file that stores encrypted content of contract note
      FileStream fileStream = new
              FileStream(@"C:\ContractNote.enc",FileMode.Create);
```

```
//create symmetric encryptor object
ICryptoTransform cryptoTransform = algoProvider.CreateEncryptor();

//create cryptostream
CryptoStream cryptoStream = new
        CryptoStream(fileStream,cryptoTransform,CryptoStreamMode.Write);
string contractNote = "<CONTRACTNOTE>"
                    +"<SYMBOL>MSFT</SYMBOL>"
                    +"<QUANTITY>100</QUANTITY>"
                    +"<PRICE>24</PRICE>"
                    +"</CONTRACTNOTE>";
byte[] contentBuffer  = Encoding.ASCII.GetBytes(contractNote);

//write encrypted data
cryptoStream.Write(contentBuffer,0,contentBuffer.Length);
cryptoStream.Close();
fileStream.Close();

Console.WriteLine("Contract Note Decryption Stage - Fund Manager end");
Console.WriteLine("--------------------------------------------------");

//open encrypted content of contract note
fileStream = new FileStream(@"C:\ContractNote.enc",FileMode.Open);

//create symmetric decryptor object
cryptoTransform = algoProvider.CreateDecryptor();
cryptoStream = new
        CryptoStream(fileStream,cryptoTransform,CryptoStreamMode.Read);
byte[] readBuffer = new byte[fileStream.Length];

//decrypt data
cryptoStream.Read(readBuffer,0,readBuffer.Length);
string decryptedText =
        Encoding.ASCII.GetString(readBuffer,0,readBuffer.Length);
Console.WriteLine(decryptedText);

    }
  }
}
```

In Listing 6-1, a new instance of Rijndael is created that represents the Rijndael symmetric algorithm. This newly returned instance is then assigned to a variable of the SymmetricAlgorithm type. This cast operation is successfully executed without any errors because Rijndael is derived from SymmetricAlgorithm. A more elegant approach is to create a factory class with a factory method that returns the correct instance based on an argument passed to it. This way, the provider-level class details are completely hidden in the factory class, and any new symmetric algorithms can be easily introduced by modifying the factory class.

```
SymmetricAlgorithm algoProvider = RijndaelManaged.Create();
```

After constructing an instance of Rijndael, the next step is to list the features supported by the algorithm, which includes the cipher mode, key size, block size, and padding mode. The default cipher mode is CBC, and with the help of the Mode property, it can be changed; however, remember that it is also important to verify that the underlying algorithm supports the other mode. An exception will be thrown if a particular cipher mode is not supported by the provider.

```
Console.WriteLine("Crypto Provider Information");
Console.WriteLine("--------------------");
Console.WriteLine("Cipher Mode : " + algoProvider.Mode);
Console.WriteLine("Padding Mode : " +algoProvider.Padding);
```

Another important property that goes hand in hand with the cipher mode is Padding. Often, when a message is broken down into a block of particular size, the last block is left behind with empty bytes, and it needs to be padded. To address this problem, padding is performed, and three possible values exist:

None: No padding is performed.

PKCS7: This padding scheme fills up the empty bytes with a value equal to the number of padding bytes required.

Zeros: The value zero is padded.

The key and block size are determined with the help of the KeySize and BlockSize properties:

```
Console.WriteLine("Block Size : " +algoProvider.BlockSize);
Console.WriteLine("Key Size : " +algoProvider.KeySize);
```

You can change these values provided that they fall in a valid range, which is available in the form of the LegalKeySizes and LegalBlockSizes properties. Both these properties return only the values that are supported by the underlying algorithm provider. The default key size supported by Rijndael is 256 bits, and the block size is 128 bits.

Next, you initiate the encryption phase; the first step in this phase is to generate a key and IV that is used to encrypt the message:

```
Console.WriteLine("Contract Note Encryption Stage - Broker end");
Console.WriteLine("-------------------------------------------");
algoProvider.GenerateKey();
algoProvider.GenerateIV();
```

You can generate a key and IV in two ways. The first approach is let the user define the key and IV, and this is possible by assigning a value to the Key and IV properties of the SymmetricAlgorithm class. The major drawback of such an approach is it is very susceptible to brute-force attacks, and we as human beings are weak when it comes to coining a message that is truly unique and random in nature. The other approach is to rely on the underlying algorithm provider to produce a key automatically. This way, a strong key is generated that is hard to guess.

In Listing 6-1, with the help of the GenerateKey and GenerateIV methods, both the key and IV are autogenerated. This newly generated value is also assigned to the Key and IV properties. It is important to preserve both these values on some persistent storage medium because the fund manager on the other end will be able to decrypt the message only when the correct key and IV are fed to the algorithm.

Next, a new file is created that is forwarded to the fund manager, and the content of this file represents contract note information in encrypted form:

```
FileStream fileStream = new FileStream(@"C:\ContractNote.enc",FileMode.Create);
```

Once you have successfully created the file, the next task is to encrypt the contract note information. The encryption and decryption task is achieved using the CreateEncryptor and CreateDecryptor methods. Both these methods return an instance of a transform class that implements the ICryptoTransform interface. This newly returned instance contains logic to encrypt/decrypt the message.

```
ICryptoTransform cryptoTransform = algoProvider.CreateEncryptor();
```

Next, we create an instance of `CryptoStream` that is used in conjunction with any data stream to perform cryptographic transformation (encryption or decryption):

```
CryptoStream cryptoStream =
        new CryptoStream(fileStream,cryptoTransform,CryptoStreamMode.Write);
```

`CryptoStream` is in line with a file or socket stream that supports reading or writing data in a byte-oriented fashion. The same functionality is provided by `CryptoStream`; but instead of directly reading or writing a chunk of bytes, it is first submitted to the transformer that performs the cryptographic transformation (encryption/decryption), and then the output produced is chained with another stream-based object. In Listing 6-1, you chain the cryptographic stream with a file stream and configure it in a write mode, so any byte written through the cryptostream will get first encrypted, and this encrypted message is then directly written to the file.

The actual contract note message, before passing to `CryptoStream`, is converted into an array of bytes. Then the content is encrypted and finally redirected to a `FileStream`:

```
string contractNote = "<CONTRACTNOTE>"
                    +"<SYMBOL>MSFT</SYMBOL>"
                    +"<QUANTITY>100</QUANTITY>"
                    +"<PRICE>24</PRICE>"
                    +"</CONTRACTNOTE>";
byte[] contentBuffer  = Encoding.ASCII.GetBytes(contractNote);
cryptoStream.Write(contentBuffer,0,contentBuffer.Length);
cryptoStream.Close();
fileStream.Close();
```

Finally, we cover the last leg of this code, which in the real world mimics the fund manager who receives the encrypted content of the contract note and then uses the correct symmetric key to decrypt it and read the original message:

```
Console.WriteLine("Contract Note Decryption Stage - Fund Manager end");
Console.WriteLine("------------------------------------------------");
fileStream = new FileStream(@"C:\ContractNote.enc",FileMode.Open);
cryptoTransform = algoProvider.CreateDecryptor();
cryptoStream = new CryptoStream(fileStream,cryptoTransform,CryptoStreamMode.Read);
byte[] readBuffer = new byte[fileStream.Length];
cryptoStream.Read(readBuffer,0,readBuffer.Length);
string decryptedText = Encoding.ASCII.GetString(readBuffer,0,readBuffer.Length);
Console.WriteLine(decryptedText);
```

The decryption code (the fund manager end) is the same as the encryption code with the only difference being that the data is read from `CryptoStream`. Another important point to note is that we have reused the same instance of `SymmetricAlgorithm` in which both the key and IV are already populated, but in the real world the fund manager will initialize these values. Of course, the fund manager must know both the key and IV beforehand, and the broker must have communicated this information through some secure communication channel or storage medium.

Figure 6-15 shows the console output of Listing 6-1; it also displays the content of the contract note, which is in encrypted form.

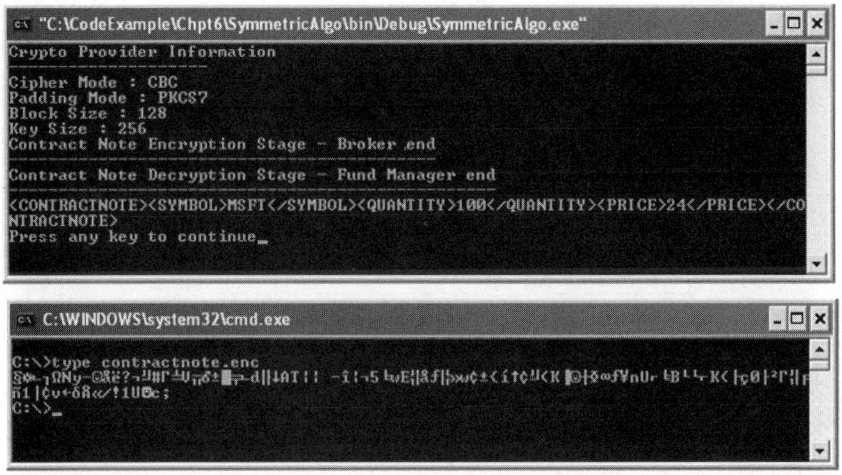
"C:\CodeExample\Chpt6\SymmetricAlgo\bin\Debug\SymmetricAlgo.exe"
Crypto Provider Information
Cipher Mode : CBC
Padding Mode : PKCS7
Block Size : 128
Key Size : 256
Contract Note Encryption Stage - Broker end
Contract Note Decryption Stage - Fund Manager end
<CONTRACTNOTE><SYMBOL>MSFT</SYMBOL><QUANTITY>100</QUANTITY><PRICE>24</PRICE></CONTRACTNOTE>
Press any key to continue_
C:\WINDOWS\system32\cmd.exe
C:\>type contractnote.enc
C:\>_

Figure 6-15. *Console output of the program using the symmetric key*

Asymmetric Key

An asymmetric key solves most of the problems in cryptography (see Figure 6-16). The most important one it addresses is the key exchange issue; the way this algorithm works is that a key pair containing a public key and private key is first generated. The public key, as the name indicates, is meant to be distributed to the masses, and the private key is confidential information and is kept secret. Both public and private keys generated are related to each other, and a message encrypted using a public key can be decrypted only by its corresponding private key. This logic also holds true for a reverse case where a message encrypted using a private key can be decrypted only with its corresponding public key.

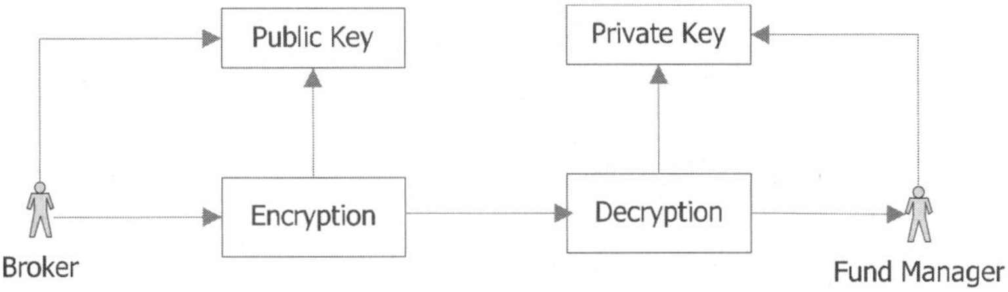
Public Key
Private Key
Encryption
Decryption
Broker
Fund Manager

Figure 6- 16. *Asymmetric key*

Using asymmetric algorithms, the fund manager generates a single key pair and distributes the public key to the broker. The fund manager can also publish the public key on a Web site, allowing it to be freely available for download. Now, when the broker sends a contract note to the fund manager, the plain-text message is encrypted with a public key, and the fund manager upon receiving it decrypts it with the private key. The decryption is performed successfully because only the fund manager is in possession of the private key.

Several asymmetric algorithms exist, but the most popular ones are RSA and DSA. (RSA stands for Rivest Shamir Adleman, and DSA stands for Digital Signature Standard.) Both algorithms are bundled inside the .NET Framework and have their own class hierarchy, as shown in Figure 6-17.

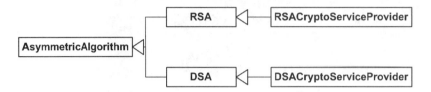

Figure 6- 17. *Asymmetric algorithm class hierarchy*

The depth of class hierarchy is similar to the symmetric algorithm's class hierarchy consisting of two levels of inheritance. AsymmetricAlgorithm is a base abstract class that is further extended by an algorithm-specific abstract class. The common functionality (such as encryption and decryption, key import, and export) is all bundled in one pack and exposed in the form of members by AsymmetricAlgorithm. You will look at this functionality with the help of the code shown in Listing 6-2, which uses an asymmetric key to exchange contract note information between the fund manager and the broker.

Listing 6-2. *Contract Note Information Encrypted by the Broker and Decrypted by the Fund Manager Using the Asymmetric Key*

```
using System;
using System.Text;
using System.IO;
using System.Security.Cryptography;


namespace AsymmetricAlgo
{
class Class1
{
  static void Main(string[] args)
  {
    //Generate public and private key
    GenerateKeyPair();

    //encrypt contract note using fund manager's public key
    ContractNoteBroker();

    //decrypt contract note encrypted by the broker
    //using the fund manager's private key
    ContractNoteFM();
  }

  public static void GenerateKeyPair()
  {
    //perform asymmetric encryption and decryption using the RSA algorithm
    RSACryptoServiceProvider cryptoProv = new RSACryptoServiceProvider();
    //extract public key
    string publicKey = cryptoProv.ToXmlString(false);
    //extract private key
```

```
    string privateKey = cryptoProv.ToXmlString(true);
    //persist private key
    StreamWriter writer = new StreamWriter(@"C:\PrivateKey.xml");
    writer.Write(privateKey);
    writer.Close();

    //persist public key
    writer = new StreamWriter(@"C:\PublicKey.xml");
    writer.Write(publicKey);
    writer.Close();
}

public static void ContractNoteBroker()
{
    Console.WriteLine("Contract Note Encryption Stage - Broker end");
    //parameters passed to cryptographic service provider
    CspParameters param = new CspParameters();
    param.Flags = CspProviderFlags.UseMachineKeyStore;

    //read public key, and initialize RSA with the fund manager's public key
    RSACryptoServiceProvider cryptoProv = new RSACryptoServiceProvider(param);
    StreamReader reader = new StreamReader(@"C:\PublicKey.xml");
    cryptoProv.FromXmlString(reader.ReadToEnd());

    string contractNote = "<CONTRACTNOTE>"
      +"<SYMBOL>MSFT</SYMBOL>"
      +"<QUANTITY>100</QUANTITY>"
      +"<PRICE>24</PRICE>"
      +"</CONTRACTNOTE>";

    byte[] contentBuffer  = Encoding.ASCII.GetBytes(contractNote);

    //encrypt contract note using public key, and write it to a file
    FileStream fileStream = new
               FileStream(@"C:\ContractNote.enc",FileMode.Create);
    byte[] encContent = cryptoProv.Encrypt(contentBuffer ,false);
    fileStream.Write(encContent,0,encContent.Length);
    fileStream.Close();

}

public static void ContractNoteFM()
{
    Console.WriteLine("Contract Note Decryption Stage - Fund Manager end");

    //parameters passed to cryptographic service provider
    CspParameters param = new CspParameters();
    param.Flags = CspProviderFlags.UseMachineKeyStore;
    RSACryptoServiceProvider cryptoProv = new RSACryptoServiceProvider(param);

    //initialize RSA with private key
    StreamReader reader = new StreamReader(@"C:\PrivateKey.xml");
    cryptoProv.FromXmlString(reader.ReadToEnd());
    reader.Close();
```

```
    //decrypt the encrypted contract note using private key
    FileStream fileStream = new FileStream(@"C:\ContractNote.enc",FileMode.Open);
    byte[] readBuffer = new byte[fileStream.Length];
    fileStream.Read(readBuffer,0,readBuffer.Length);
    byte[] decContent = cryptoProv.Decrypt(readBuffer,false);
    string contractNote = Encoding.ASCII.GetString(decContent);

    Console.WriteLine(contractNote);
  }
}
}
```

In Listing 6-2, we have redefined the interaction between the fund manager and the broker using an asymmetric key. The approach used here is that the individual fund manager generates both the public and private keys and communicates only the public key to the broker. The broker maintains a central database where public key information of an individual fund manager is stored. Now whenever the broker wants to send a contract note to the fund manager, the first step is to retrieve the correct public key belonging to that particular fund manager and then encrypt the message using this key. Since you know both the public key and the private key are interrelated and a message encrypted using the public key can be deciphered only by its private key, this means only the fund manager will be able to decrypt the message.

The code described in Listing 6-2 has been divided into three phases, starting with generation of key, and then the encryption phase, and finally the decryption phase. Here is the code that generates a key pair that in the real world is executed on the fund manager end:

```
public static void GenerateKeyPair()
{
RSACryptoServiceProvider cryptoProv = new RSACryptoServiceProvider();
string publicKey = cryptoProv.ToXmlString(false);
string privateKey = cryptoProv.ToXmlString(true);
```

By creating a new instance of RSACryptoServiceProvider, you started your journey into the asymmetric algorithm world. A parameterless constructor-based instantiation will automatically generate both the public and private keys. Both these keys' information is accessible with the help of the ToXmlString and ExportParameters methods. Even though both methods provide the same information, their purpose is different. ExportParameters is platform specific, and its usage is limited to the application level; when information needs to be exchanged across applications that are hosted on different platforms, then the only platform-neutral format that comes to the rescue is XML, and ToXmlString achieves it.

Both ExportParameters and ToXmlString expect a Boolean value that controls the amount of information to be returned. By passing the value true, both public and private keys are exported; the value false will return only the public key. In Listing 6-2, we have extracted this information and stored it in a separate variable.

The key information retrieved is finally persisted on disk. PrivateKey.xml contains the public key as well as the private key, and hence this file needs to be carefully guarded and protected against falling into the hands of a malicious person. Similarly, PublicKey.xml contains public key information and is meant to be distributed to brokers.

```
StreamWriter writer = new StreamWriter(@"C:\PrivateKey.xml");
writer.Write(privateKey);
writer.Close();
writer = new StreamWriter(@"C:\PublicKey.xml");
writer.Write(publicKey);
writer.Close();
```

You have completed the key generation phase; next is the encryption stage where the broker encrypts the message using the fund manager public key:

```
public static void ContractNoteBroker()
{
  Console.WriteLine("Contract Note Encryption Stage - Broker end");
  CspParameters param = new CspParameters();
  param.Flags = CspProviderFlags.UseMachineKeyStore;
  RSACryptoServiceProvider cryptoProv = new RSACryptoServiceProvider(param);
```

The big difference in the previous line of code is the way an instance of RSACryptoServiceProvider is created. You already know that during the construction phase, key pairs are automatically generated, but in the previous code we have overridden this behavior by passing an instance of CspParameters, which contains cryptographic-specific information.

After successfully creating an instance of RSACryptoServiceProvider, we then initialized with the public key that is uploaded from a file:

```
StreamReader reader = new StreamReader(@"C:\PublicKey.xml");
cryptoProv.FromXmlString(reader.ReadToEnd());
```

Next, the contract note information is converted into a byte array using Encoding:

```
string contractNote = "<CONTRACTNOTE>"
                    +"<SYMBOL>MSFT</SYMBOL>"
                    +"<QUANTITY>100</QUANTITY>"
                    +"<PRICE>24</PRICE>"
                    +"</CONTRACTNOTE>";

byte[] contentBuffer = Encoding.ASCII.GetBytes(contractNote);
```

Here comes the important part of code in which the information that is in byte array form is encrypted using Encrypt. The encryption is performed using the public key, and the final encrypted content is returned in the form of a byte array. Encrypt, along with the data that needs to be encrypted, also accepts additional padding information. The default padding available is PKCS padding and is used by passing the value false to this method. A value of true indicates a different padding scheme, which in this case is OAEP padding and is available only on computers running Microsoft Windows XP or later.

```
FileStream fileStream = new FileStream(@"C:\ContractNote.enc",FileMode.Create);
byte[] encContent = cryptoProv.Encrypt(contentBuffer ,false);
fileStream.Write(encContent,0,encContent.Length);
fileStream.Close();
```

Now you step into the last part of this example in which the fund manager decrypts the message using the private key. This code is now familiar to you; a new instance of RSACryptoServiceProvider is created, and both public and private keys are initialized:

```
public static void ContractNoteFM()
{
  Console.WriteLine("Contract Note Decryption Stage - Fund Manager end");
   CspParameters param = new CspParameters();
  param.Flags = CspProviderFlags.UseMachineKeyStore;
  RSACryptoServiceProvider cryptoProv = new RSACryptoServiceProvider(param);
   StreamReader reader = new StreamReader(@"C:\PrivateKey.xml");
  cryptoProv.FromXmlString(reader.ReadToEnd());
  reader.Close();
```

Let's assume the broker sends contract note information through some communication medium. After receiving it, the encrypted information is read and decrypted using the fund manager's private key. This is made possible by Decrypt, which accepts two arguments: data that needs to be decrypted and the padding mode.

```
FileStream fileStream = new FileStream(@"C:\ContractNote.enc",FileMode.Open);
byte[] readBuffer = new byte[fileStream.Length];
fileStream.Read(readBuffer,0,readBuffer.Length);
byte[] decContent = cryptoProv.Decrypt(readBuffer,false);
string contractNote - Encoding.ASCII.GetString(decContent);
Console.WriteLine(contractNote);
```

After the successful decryption, the original message is displayed on the console, as depicted in Figure 6-18.

Figure 6-18. *Console output of a program using the asymmetric key*

The example used asymmetric keys to encrypt and decrypt the message. But in reality asymmetric encryption when performed over large blocks of text is 1,000 times slower than symmetric encryption, and therefore it is highly unsuitable for encrypting/decrypting a message of a large size. So, the most well-known technique is to use the best of both asymmetric and symmetric algorithms. For example, you can slightly tweak the example to generate a symmetric key that is also known as the *session key* and use this key to encrypt the contract note information. The advantage gained is faster performance. After encrypting the message, the next step is to use the asymmetric key to encrypt the session key and send both the message and encrypted session key to the fund manager. To successfully decrypt the message, the fund manager must first decrypt the session key using the private key and then decrypt the encrypted message using the original session key.

Integrity

Data integrity refers to the consistency of data and that its content has not been compromised or unknowingly altered by an unauthorized user. For example, imagine the consequences if critical information such as quantity or price is tweaked, and the fund manager, based upon this manipulated information, undertakes some aggressive action that leaves a devastating effect on an entire business. The most effective way to deal with this problem is to calculate a cryptographic hash of the information that is also known as a *message digest*. The way this is calculated depends upon the underlying hashing algorithm, but in general a variable-length data is passed to a hash algorithm that then produces a relatively small fixed-size hash value (see Figure 6-19). The value produced is irreversible in nature and is considered a one-way function because it is impossible to reverse engineer the original message based on just the hash value. Furthermore, two identical inputs will always produce an identical hash value, but even a difference in bits is sufficient to create a distinct hash value.

Plain Text

```
<CONTRACTNOTE>
    <SYMBOL>MSFT</SYMBOL>
    <QUANTITY>100</QUANTITY>
    <PRICE>24</PRICE>
</CONTRACTNOTE>
```

Figure 6-19. *Data hashing*

So, the way the broker achieves data integrity is by calculating a cryptographic hash and sending it along with the original message. The fund manager on receiving it recalculates the hash value based on the original message received and compares it to the hash value calculated on the broker end. If there is a discrepancy found, then it confirms the message has been tampered with in transit. Of course, you can further strengthen this by using a keyed hash algorithm that uses a symmetric key to encrypt the hash value. The keyed hash algorithm provides both message authenticity and integrity.

The popular hash algorithms that are provided by the .NET Framework are Message Digest (MD5) and Secure Hash Algorithm (SHA). The MD5 algorithm produces a 128-bit hash value, whereas SHA supports 160-, 256-, 384-, and 512-bit hash values. SHA provides the hash size of a different length, and the greater the length of a hash size, the more difficult it is to break. Figure 6-20 shows the class layout of hash algorithm classes. HashAlgorithm is the abstract base class that is then derived by concrete classes.

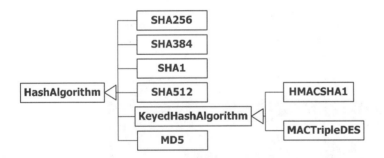

Figure 6-20. HashAlgorithm *class hierarchy*

Listing 6-3 shows the code that is used by the broker to generate a hash value, which is then verified by the fund manager to ensure that the message has not been tampered with.

Listing 6-3. *Hash Value Computed for Contract Note Data*

```
using System;
using System.Text;
using System.Security.Cryptography;
```

```
namespace HashAlgo
{
  class Class1
  {
    static void Main(string[] args)
    {
      //compute hash using SHA-1
      HashAlgorithm hashAlgo = new SHA1Managed();
      string contractNote = "<CONTRACTNOTE>"
                        +"<SYMBOL>MSFT</SYMBOL>"
                        +"<QUANTITY>100</QUANTITY>"
                        +"<PRICE>24</PRICE>"
                        +"</CONTRACTNOTE>";

      byte[] contentBuffer  = Encoding.ASCII.GetBytes(contractNote);
      //compute contract note hash value
      byte[] hashedData = hashAlgo.ComputeHash(contentBuffer);
      Console.WriteLine("Data Length : " +contentBuffer.Length);
      Console.WriteLine("Hashed Data Length : " +hashedData.Length);
    }
  }
}
```

As you can see, the code described in Listing 6-3 is pretty straightforward; the only missing part is that you are not encrypting the hash value, which is ideally done in a realistic scenario. For demonstration purposes, we have ignored those steps, so it is pretty simple to implement.

In Listing 6-3, a new instance of SHA1Managed is created, and then ComputeHash is invoked to calculate the hash value. ComputeHash is an overloaded method that accepts either a byte array or a Stream object and returns a fixed-size byte array. Since this code uses a 160-bit SHA algorithm, it is obvious that the length of the hash value generated is 20 bytes. All this information is displayed in the console output window, as shown in Figure 6-21.

Figure 6-21. *Console output of hash algorithm program*

Digital Signatures

You looked at how you can use hashing algorithms to achieve integrity; however, when combined with asymmetric algorithms, you can also use it to create digital signatures of information. *Digital signatures* are important aspects of a secure transaction and address authentication, integrity, and nonrepudiation issues (see Figure 6-22). Both authentication and nonrepudiation are achieved by asymmetric algorithms, and the integrity of data is achieved with the help of hashing algorithms. Digital signatures are widely accepted in the commercial world and are one of the formal requirements for conducting any type of legal transaction. Additionally, it is also considered to be important evidence and well respected in a court of law.

Plain Text

Figure 6-22. *Digital signature*

The first step in digitally signing information is to compute a message digest or hash value of the original message. The message digest is then encrypted with a private key to create a digital signature of the information. Remember, digital signatures can be created only by the individual who is also the sole owner of the private key. Unless the private key is leaked somehow, there is no other way to construct the digital signature. Both the original message and digital signature are then sent to recipients. Upon receiving this information, the receiver performs similar steps by first calculating the hash value of the original message. It is important that both the sender and receiver agree on common hashing algorithms that are used during the signing and verification stages. The digital signature is then decrypted by the corresponding public key; if decryption happens successfully, then it confirms that the message indeed originated from the authentic sender. Next, the decrypted hash value is then verified with the newly computed hash value; if both hash results differ, then it is concluded that the information has been tampered with.

The beauty of digital signing is that only the individual who is in possession of the private key will be able to create signed messages, so attackers can forge it only if they have access to a private key. An attacker cannot even alter the message because it would need a recomputation of the hash value. Similarly, a signature, once computed, can be verified by anyone who is in possession of only the public key, which is made publicly available. Another important fact about digital signatures is that only the hash value is encrypted, but the information is still retained in its original format. So, when information secrecy takes higher precedence, it is important to encrypt the message using symmetric algorithms.

Now let's look at the requirement where the broker, instead of encrypting the contract note information, agrees to digitally sign it before sending it to the fund manager. On receiving this information, the fund manager verifies it by decrypting the hash value with the broker's public key and comparing it with the newly computed hash value. The code implementation is pretty simple and uses both asymmetric and hash algorithm classes (see Listing 6-4).

Listing 6-4. *Signing and Verification of Contract Note Data*

```
using System;
using System.Text;
using System.Security.Cryptography;

namespace DigitalSignature
{
  class DigSign
  {
    static void Main(string[] args)
    {
      string contractNote = "<CONTRACTNOTE>"
                      +"<SYMBOL>MSFT</SYMBOL>"
                      +"<QUANTITY>100</QUANTITY>"
                      +"<PRICE>24</PRICE>"
                      +"</CONTRACTNOTE>";
      //perform digital signature using RSA
```

```
        RSACryptoServiceProvider rsCrypto = new RSACryptoServiceProvider();
        //export of private key
        RSAParameters privateRSA = rsCrypto.ExportParameters(true);
        //export of public key
        RSAParameters publicRSA = rsCrypto.ExportParameters(false);
        byte[] contentBuffer = Encoding.ASCII.GetBytes(contractNote);
        //compute digital signature of contract note using the broker's private key
        byte[] signedData = SignDataBroker(contentBuffer,privateRSA);
        //verify digital signature
        bool hashResult = VerifySignFM(contentBuffer,signedData,publicRSA) ;
        Console.WriteLine ( "Hash Result : " + hashResult);
    }


    public static byte[] SignDataBroker(byte[] data,RSAParameters privateRSA)
    {
        //create RSA provider, and initialize it with the broker's private key
        RSACryptoServiceProvider rsCrypto = new RSACryptoServiceProvider();
        rsCrypto.ImportParameters(privateRSA);
        //compute hash value of contract note
        HashAlgorithm hashAlgo = new SHA1Managed();
        byte[] hashedData = hashAlgo.ComputeHash(data);
        //sign hash value using private key
        string shaOID = CryptoConfig.MapNameToOID("SHA1");
        return rsCrypto.SignHash(hashedData,shaOID);
    }

    public static bool VerifySignFM(byte[] data,
                            byte[] signedData,RSAParameters publicRSA)
    {
        //create RSA provider, and initialize it with the broker's public key
        RSACryptoServiceProvider rsCrypto = new RSACryptoServiceProvider();
        rsCrypto.ImportParameters(publicRSA);
        //recompute hash value of contract note
        HashAlgorithm hashAlgo = new SHA1Managed();
        byte[] hashedData = hashAlgo.ComputeHash(data);
        string shaOID = CryptoConfig.MapNameToOID("SHA1");
        //verify the computed hash value with the digital signature
        return rsCrypto.VerifyHash(hashedData,shaOID,signedData);

    }

  }
}
```

In Listing 6-4, the code has two facets, with the first part covering the digital signing aspect of a transaction. The final phase is the verification process in which the signature is verified. Both these functionalities are encapsulated in the SignDataBroker and VerifySignFM methods.

Before invoking SignDataBroker and VerifySignFM, a new instance of RSACryptoServiceProvider is created that also creates the public and private keys. The key information is then stored in an instance of RSAParameters. In a real-world scenario, the broker will be in possession of both the public and private keys, but the fund manager will be aware of only the public key. Therefore, the key information is exported once with the private key and again without the private key.

In the next step, you invoke SignDataBroker, which mimics the broker end:

```
public static byte[] SignDataBroker(byte[] data,RSAParameters privateRSA)
{
  RSACryptoServiceProvider rsCrypto = new RSACryptoServiceProvider();
  rsCrypto.ImportParameters(privateRSA);
  HashAlgorithm hashAlgo = new SHA1Managed();
  byte[] hashedData = hashAlgo.ComputeHash(data);
  string shaOID = CryptoConfig.MapNameToOID("SHA1");
  return rsCrypto.SignHash(hashedData,shaOID);
}
```

The actual message is first flattened into bytes, and then its hash value is computed. The hash value is then passed to SignHash, which encrypts it with a private key, and the final result, which is the digital signature of the contract note itself, is returned in a byte array. SignHash accepts additional mandatory arguments that represent hashing algorithm information. This information cannot be passed directly; instead, its corresponding object identifier (OID) is supplied, which is located with the help of the MapNameToOID static method of the CryptoConfig class.

After signing the message, both the contract note information and the digital signature are delivered to recipients. In this case, the recipient is the fund manager and is mimicked by VerifySignFM:

```
public static bool VerifySignFM(byte[] data,byte[] signedData,
                                RSAParameters publicRSA)
{
  RSACryptoServiceProvider rsCrypto = new RSACryptoServiceProvider();
  rsCrypto.ImportParameters(publicRSA);
  HashAlgorithm hashAlgo = new SHA1Managed();
  byte[] hashedData = hashAlgo.ComputeHash(data);
  string shaOID = CryptoConfig.MapNameToOID("SHA1");
  return rsCrypto.VerifyHash(hashedData,shaOID,signedData);
}
```

The fund manager, upon receiving this message, immediately recomputes the hash value. The hash value is then verified with the digital signature by calling VerifyHash. During the verification process, the public key is used to decrypt the digital signature to obtain the original hash value. The original hash value is then compared with the newly computed hash value, and if both these hashes match, then it proves that the message indeed came from a legitimate source and that the integrity of information has not been compromised.

Digital Certificates

The first prerequisite before exchanging digital signature information is communicating the public key information. This exchange of a public key may happen through multiple sources, such as sending it through e-mail or downloading it from a public Web site. Multiple channels are available, but each of them gives rise to the problem of how a person is assured that the public key published belongs to the authentic party. A real-life example that addresses this concern is a passport issued to a citizen of a country. This passport forms the basis for individuals to prove their identities. Before issuing the passport to a person, a background check is conducted that includes the investigation of a criminal record. Such types of procedures are sufficient to create a level of trust. Because every country in the world honors passports, this provides a means to verify the identity of an individual.

In the digital world, a similar document is required that acts like a digital passport, and this is where digital certificates are used. Digital certificates prove the identity of an individual or organization, and they form a strong basis of authentication. The primary purpose of a digital certificate is to encapsulate the public key information that is then used to verify the digital signature. But how is it different from transmitting public key information through e-mails or a Web download? The first difference is that digital certificates are issued by a certificate authority (CA). A CA is an entity that establishes trust between two parties in a communication chain. The CA fills the needs for a trusted third party in an e-commerce world by verifying the identity of an individual or organization. Even though the digital certificate issued by a CA is sufficient to assure the authenticity, the important thing is that the CA must be reliable and well-known in the industry. CAs such as VeriSign and Thawte are quite popular in the e-commerce world and are the main issuers of digital certificates.

Digital certificates adhere to X.509 format and contain the following important information:

- Name
- Organization
- Serial number
- Validity date
- Public key
- CA name
- CA digital signature

There are no limits on the amount of information that can be embedded into a certificate, but the most important attribute is a CA digital signature that assures that the owner of the certificate is in fact who say they are and has been verified by the CA. This signature is the electronic counterpart to a signature signed by a legal authority on a legal paper. Remember, only the CA can generate the digital signature because only the CA knows the private key, and for an attacker to impersonate a CA, they need to have access to the private key. Furthermore, the CA public key is easily accessible, so anyone can verify the integrity of the certificate before initiating a transaction with the owner of the certificate.

Now it is time to use a digital certificate in the STP world; to keep the example simple and straightforward, we will rewrite the code described in Listing 6-4. The concept is the same; the only difference is that the broker's public key is published using a digital certificate. The information inside the digital certificate, mainly the public key, is then read by the fund manager to verify the digital signature of the contract note information received from the broker. Unfortunately, the .NET Framework provides very lean support for dealing with digital certificates. Even though information stored inside a certificate is readable with the help of the X509Certificate class defined in the System.Security.Cryptography.X509Certificates namespace, there is no direct way to derive an appropriate cryptographic class that can then verify the digital signature. Considering this drawback, we will introduce the Web Services Enhancement (WSE) framework that forms an add-on to the .NET Framework. WSE provides advanced features related to cryptography areas, and one of the important features directly supported is reading both the certificate and the key information.

The first step is to generate a digital certificate, and in the real world this involves a lot of steps; for testing purposes, there is a ready-to-use makecert utility, which is a certificate creation tool available as part of the .NET Framework tools. This utility allows you to create a self-signed certificate that is used by applications in development environments for testing purposes.

By executing the following command, a test certificate is created and persisted in C:\BrokerCertificate.cer:

```
makecert -sk STPKeyStore -a sha1 -r C:\BrokerCertificate.cer
                      -ss STPCertificateStore -n "CN=Broker A"
```

The makecert utility includes various options, and discussing each of them is outside the scope of this chapter. However, the essential information required for certification creation is as follows:

Key container name: The tool by default creates public and private keys and stores them in an STPKeyStore container. This information is provided with the help of the -sk switch.

Hashing algorithm: The underlying hashing algorithm of a digital signature is specified using the -a switch.

Certificate store: Certificates are usually managed through a central certificate store. Stores allow the easy management of certificates and provide functionality to store and retrieve certificates. This information is provided using the -ss switch.

Certificate subject: The information defined must conform to the X.500 standard.

Figure 6-23 is a graphical representation of a certificate launched by clicking BrokerCertificate.cer.

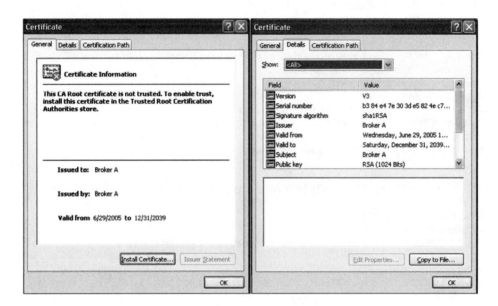

Figure 6-23. *Digital certificate*

The next step is to delve into the actual code that uses the digital certificate depicted in Figure 6-23 to verify the digital signature. Before compiling the code shown in Listing 6-5, ensure that the Microsoft. Web.Services2 assembly is referenced properly.

Listing 6-5. *Signing and Verification of Contract Note Data Using Digital Certificates*

```
using System;
using System.Text;
using System.Security.Cryptography;
using Microsoft.Web.Services2.Security.X509;

namespace DigitalCertificate
{
  class DigCert
  {
    static void Main(string[] args)
    {
      string contractNote = "<CONTRACTNOTE>"
                    +"<SYMBOL>MSFT</SYMBOL>"
                    +"<QUANTITY>100</QUANTITY>"
                    +"<PRICE>24</PRICE>"
                    +"</CONTRACTNOTE>";
```

```
      byte[] contentBuffer = Encoding.ASCII.GetBytes(contractNote);
      //compute digital signature using the broker's private key
      byte[] signedData = SignDataBroker(contentBuffer);
      //verify digital signature using the broker's public key
      bool hashResult = VerifySignFM(contentBuffer,signedData) ;
      Console.WriteLine("Verification Result : " +hashResult);
    }

    public static byte[] SignDataBroker(byte[] data)
    {
      //parameters passed to cryptographic service provider
      CspParameters param = new CspParameters();
      //assign the key store name generated by the makecert tool
      param.KeyContainerName = "STPKeyStore";
      //use the signature key pair
      param.KeyNumber = 2;
      //initialize RSA to use private key stored in STPKeyStore
      RSACryptoServiceProvider rsCrypto = new RSACryptoServiceProvider(param);
      //compute digital signature
      return rsCrypto.SignData(data, new SHA1Managed());
    }

    public static bool VerifySignFM(byte[] data,byte[] signedData)
    {
      //Open STP certificate store
      X509CertificateStore store =
              X509CertificateStore.CurrentUserStore("STPCertificateStore");
      store.OpenRead();
      //retrieve broker certificate
      X509Certificate brokerCertificate = store.Certificates[0];
      Console.WriteLine("Certificate Subject :" +
                      brokerCertificate.FriendlyDisplayName);
      Console.WriteLine("Valid From :" +
                      brokerCertificate.GetEffectiveDateString());
      Console.WriteLine("Valid To :" +
                      brokerCertificate.GetExpirationDateString());
      Console.WriteLine("Serial No:" + brokerCertificate.GetSerialNumberString());
      //initialize RSA to use public key stored in broker certificate
      RSAParameters publicParam =  brokerCertificate.Key.ExportParameters(false);
      RSACryptoServiceProvider rsCrypto = new RSACryptoServiceProvider();
      rsCrypto.ImportParameters(publicParam);
      //verify digital signature
      return rsCrypto.VerifyData(data,new SHA1Managed(),signedData);
    }
  }
}
```

The code described in Listing 6-5 is more or less similar to Listing 6-4. Both the signing and verification tasks are encapsulated inside SignDataBroker and VerifySignFM. Additionally, public and private keys are already generated using the makecert utility, and therefore you need to ensure that the appropriate keys are used during the signing and verification phases.

Let's take a look at the SignDataBroker method. Since asymmetric keys are already generated and stored in the STPKeyStore container, you directly assign it to the KeyContainerName property of CspParameters. Then you assign the value 2 to the KeyNumber property, which retrieves the signature key from the container.

This looks confusing, but the way the underlying cryptographic provider works is that two pairs of keys are generated. The first pair is known as the *exchange key*, and the second pair is known as the *signature key*. By default, the exchange key is used for encryption unless explicitly specified to use the signature key. The problem comes during the digital signature verification phase when the public key is directly read from the digital certificate. The public key embedded inside the digital certificate belongs to the signature key pair, and if the digital signature is constructed using the exchange key pair, then the verification of the signature will definitely fail.

Once you have populated CspParameters, you then create a new instance of RSACryptoServiceProvider. Then the signature of the data is produced using SignData. SignData is a dual-purpose method that computes the hash value of data and then signs it with the private key to produce a digital signature.

Now let's look at the verification process performed on the fund manager end. First, the digital certificate published by the broker is installed in a certificate store; in this case you have already installed it in STPCertificateStore, which is the custom certificate store. Then, the certificate store is accessed using the static CurrentUserStore method of X509CertificateStore, which returns an instance of X509CertificateStore that allows iterating through all stored certificates.

Then, the broker digital certificate is fetched from the store and is returned in the form of X509Certificate, which contains essential information about the certificate. The important one is the public key that is retrieved using the Key property of X509Certificate. This property returns a ready-to-use instance of RSA that is already populated with the public key published with the certificate. Remember, all this functionality is available out of the box because of the WSE framework.

It is time to recall the ExportParameters and ImportParameters functionality supported by RSA. With the help of these methods, you create a new instance of RSACryptoServiceProvider and initialize it with the public key read from the digital certificate. Then, the digital signature is verified by invoking VerifyData, which compares the signature by comparing it to the signature computed for the specified data. Figure 6-24 depicts the output of this example.

Figure 6-24. *Console output describing various field information embedded inside digital certificates*

Exploring the Business-Technology Mapping

It is clear from the earlier business sections that STP is not an individual effort; instead, to make this initiative successful, it requires a collective effort from various entities. It is also a major paradigm shift for the entire securities industry in which entities such as banks, clearing corporations, depositories, exchanges, brokers, and institutions converge toward one business goal. The goal is to reduce transaction turn-around time by eliminating tasks that demand manual paperwork or human intervention encountered during trade settlement and processing. STP, if properly planned and implemented, will revolutionize the securities industry, and the key driving force behind this is a robust and reliable infrastructure. This infrastructure is provided by the STP service provider that electronically connects different entities, and information is exchanged using a common, agreed-upon protocol.

The biggest challenge faced by a service provider is to safeguard the integrity of information exchanged between entities. Furthermore, an organization will participate under this STP umbrella only when various services offered by the service provider are secure and watertight. Therefore, most providers strongly advocate the use of smart cards and digital certificates that handle both the authentication and information-signing aspects of a transaction. A *smart card* is similar to a credit card and has its own microprocessor and storage disk. The disk capacity of a smart card is limited but sufficient enough to store private and confidential information. This storage characteristic of a smart card offers a convenient and secured solution of storing private key information that is read with the help of a smart card reader attached to a computer.

Although service providers are equipped with a strong infrastructure that tackles all the major concerns faced in conducting electronic transactions, this addresses external STP and not internal STP. To achieve internal STP, an organization needs to automate its internal business processes, and this requires a fair amount of integration-level plumbing among applications, including both home-grown and vendor-based applications. However, the truth of the matter is that regardless of which part of STP is automated, there is still a need for a data security framework that must meet the requirements of both internal and external STP.

The objective of this framework is to have a common security platform that is reused across a variety of applications inside an organization. Sometimes, the STP service provider bundles this framework as part of their service offering and allows an organization to integrate it with their internal applications. Additionally, this framework looks after only the data security aspect of an application; other features such as user authentication and role-based management that come under the purview of application security are not implemented. So let's start with the conceptual design, as depicted in Figure 6-25, before drilling into the code-level implementation details.

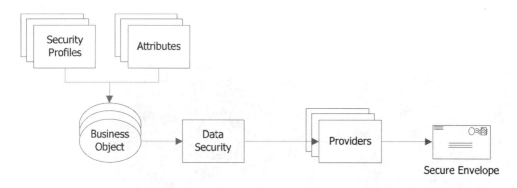

Figure 6-25. *Conceptual design*

Some of the salient features of this framework are as follows:

- This provides the ability to create a security profile that captures cryptographic-level details and allows associating this profile with the data that needs to be secured.

- The ability to hide the algorithm level details inside a security profile provides total flexibility when it comes to changing the implementation.

- Binding between security profiles and data is implemented using a declarative programming approach.

- This provides a unified API.

The term *data* in this context reflects the custom business object, and the field encapsulated inside it reflects the actual information. It is true that this information eventually needs to be converted into a suitable format that will be easily transmitted over the wire. But before data transmission takes place, the serialized data needs to be baked with security ingredients, and this is where you integrate the data security framework.

As depicted in Figure 6-25, the important part of information that acts as fuel to this framework is the security profile. There are multiple profiles created based on different types of requirements; for example, if a fund manager is doing business with broker A and they both agree to use the DES symmetric algorithm to encrypt/decrypt data, then this information forms a unique profile. If you extrapolate this scenario where the fund manager is conducting business with ten other brokers and each of them has distinct requirements, then this will result in the creation of ten additional types of security profile. Once the profile is set up, the next step is to bind them to the custom business object using a declarative programming technique. This binding is performed by annotating the class with security profile attributes.

After the profile binding, the next thing to do is identify the type of data security required. This means whether data needs to be encrypted (confidential), data needs to be digitally signed (nonrepudiation), or data needs to be verified for data integrity. To apply this option, special attributes are annotated with the class. These special attributes dictate the type of data security required and are directly related to information embedded inside the profiles. For example, if a class is decorated with a confidential attribute, then the symmetric algorithm details are determined from the security profile associated with it. This way, an individual will easily infer the security knowledge applied over this data by looking at the list of attributes annotated with the class. However, attributes are just information markers, and they still need to come with the proper implementation. This is where providers are defined. Providers contain the code that, based on profile information and attributes, performs the actual cryptographic task. The output produced by this task is a secure envelope that contains data that is secure and can be safely exchanged with other parties in the communication chain.

Class Details

Figure 6-26 shows the class hierarchy, and Figure 6-27 shows the security framework project structure.

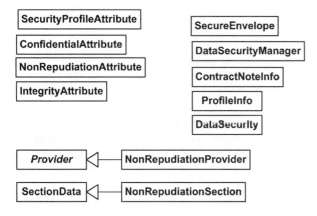

Figure 6-26. *Security framework class hierarchy*

We describe the design approach in terms of the classes introduced in Figure 6-26.

Figure 6-27. *Security framework project structure*

ConfidentialAttribute

Here's the code for ConfidentialAttribute:

```
using System;

namespace STP.Security
{
  //This attribute is annotated at the class level
  //to indicate that data needs to be encrypted
  [AttributeUsage(AttributeTargets.Class)]
  public class ConfidentialAttribute : Attribute
  {
    public ConfidentialAttribute()
    {
    }
  }
}
```

This attribute indicates that data needs to be encrypted using appropriate symmetric algorithms as described in the data security profile. It is annotated at the class level. Similarly, the integrity of data and nonrepudiation are achieved using IntegrityAttribute and NonRepudiationAttribute.

IntegrityAttribute

Here's the code for IntegrityAttribute:

```
using System;

namespace STP.Security
{
  //This attribute is annotated at the class level
```

```
//to indicate data needs to be protected by
//computing a strong hash value
[AttributeUsage(AttributeTargets.Class)]
public class IntegrityAttribute : Attribute
{
  public IntegrityAttribute()
  {
  }
}
}
```

NonRepudiationAttribute

Here's the code for NonRepudiationAttribute:

```
using System;

namespace STP.Security
{
  //This attribute is annotated at the class level
  //to indicate data needs to be protected by
  //applying a digital signature algorithm
  [AttributeUsage(AttributeTargets.Class)]
  public class NonRepudiationAttribute: Attribute
  {
    public NonRepudiationAttribute()
    {
    }
  }
}
```

SecurityProfileAttribute

Here's the code for SecurityProfileAttribute:

```
using System;

namespace STP.Security
{
  //The information about cryptography implementation
  //used to achieve data integrity, nonrepudiation, and confidential
  //is stored in a XML file or database and is identified
  //by profile name
  [AttributeUsage(AttributeTargets.Class)]
  public class SecurityProfileAttribute : Attribute
  {
    private string profileName;
    public SecurityProfileAttribute(string name)
    {
      profileName=name;
    }

    public string Profile
    {
      get{return profileName;}
    }
  }
}
```

This is the most important attribute that is annotated on the class to capture the data security profile information. It is a mandatory attribute because as you are aware the profile information not only contains implementation-level algorithm information but also the source information of various cryptographic keys.

ContractNoteInfo

Here's the code for ContractNoteInfo:

```
using System;

namespace STP.Security
{
  //A perfect example of applying cryptography infrastructure
  //to contract note data. The important information required
  //is profile name and type of protection we wanted to apply
  //to this data. In this case we have expressed data needs
  //to be digitally signed by annotating the NonRepudiation attribute.
  [SecurityProfile("BrokerA")]
  [NonRepudiation]
  [Serializable]
  public class ContractNoteInfo
  {
    public string Symbol;
    public int Quantity;
    public double Price;

    public ContractNoteInfo(string symbol,int quantity,double price)
    {
      Symbol = symbol;
      Quantity = quantity;
      Price = price;
    }
  }
}
```

This is an object-oriented representation of a contract note, and as you can see, it is annotated with NonRepudiation so the digital signature is computed based on the information encapsulated inside this class. Additionally, with the help of SecurityProfile, it also mentions the data security profile information to be used.

ProfileInfo

Here's the code for ProfileInfo:

```
using System;

namespace STP.Security
{
  public enum IntegrityAlgo
  {
    SHA1,
    MD5
  }

  public enum ConfidentialAlgo
  {
    DES,
```

```
    Rijndael
}

//This class represents object-oriented representation
//of security profile information stored in XML configuration
//or database
public class ProfileInfo
{
  IntegrityAlgo integrityAlgo;
  ConfidentialAlgo confidentialAlgo;
  string nonRepKeyPath;
  string profileName;

  public IntegrityAlgo Integrity
  {
    get{return integrityAlgo;}
  }

  public ConfidentialAlgo Confidential
  {
    get{return confidentialAlgo;}
  }

  public string ProfileName
  {
    get{return profileName;}
  }

  public string NonRepudiationKeyPath
  {
    get{return nonRepKeyPath;}
  }

  public ProfileInfo(ConfidentialAlgo confalgo,
                     IntegrityAlgo intalgo,string nonrepKey)
  {
    confidentialAlgo=confalgo;
    integrityAlgo=intalgo;
    nonRepKeyPath= nonrepKey;
  }

 }
}
```

This class provides information about various algorithms to be used that includes the hashing algorithm (integrity), the symmetric algorithm (confidential), and the digital signature algorithm (nonrepudiation). The information is populated from an XML-based configuration file or relational database system. However, in a real-life scenario there is more information to be captured, such as the cryptographic keys container name, certificate information, and so on; to keep the example simple, we have ignored all those aspects.

SecureEnvelope

Here's the code for SecureEnvelope:

```
using System;
using System.Collections;
```

```
namespace STP.Security
{
  [Serializable]
  //This class holds data produced by
  //applying cryptographic transformation on original data
  public class SecureEnvelope
  {
    string profileName;
    Hashtable sectionList = new Hashtable();

    public Hashtable Sections
    {
      get{return sectionList;}
    }

    public string Profile
    {
      get{return profileName;}
    }

    public SecureEnvelope(string profile)
    {
      profileName=profile;
    }
  }
}
```

SecureEnvelope is the object-oriented form of the envelope mentioned in Figure 6-25. The body of this envelope is built by combining sections, and each individual section represents information that is produced as a result of a provider-level transformation. For example, when ConfidentialAttribute and NonRepudiationAttribute are applied over ContractNoteInfo, then two types of information are generated. The first one is the encrypted content, and the second one is the digital signature. Both types of information are distinct and are constructed by different underlying providers; it is only during the consolidation phase that they are packaged inside a single envelope but internally separated in the form of a section.

SectionData

Here's the code for SectionData:

```
using System;

namespace STP.Security
{
  //Secure envelope is composed of multiple sections,
  //and each section is represented by this class.
  //For example, if a data supports both encryption and
  //a digital signature, then it will produce different output,
  //and both these outputs will be stored in a distinct
  //section of an envelope.
  [Serializable]
  public class SectionData
  {
    public byte[] secData;
```

```
    public byte[] Data
    {
      get{return secData;}
    }

    public SectionData(byte[] data)
    {
      secData=data;
    }
  }
}
```

SectionData represents a section of the secure envelope body.

NonRepudiationSection

Here's the code for NonRepudiationSection:

```
using System;

namespace STP.Security
{
  public class NonRepudiationSection : SectionData
  {
    byte[] signature;

    public NonRepudiationSection(byte[] data,byte[] hashedData)
    :base(data)
    {
      signature = hashedData;
    }

    public byte[] Signature
    {
      get{return signature;}
    }
  }
}
```

NonRepudiationSection is subclassed from SectionData to capture additional provider-specific information. This provider-specific information is none other than the digital signature.

Provider

Here's the code for Provider:

```
using System;

namespace STP.Security
{
  //This class represents an abstract implementation
  //of various cryptographic features the framework
  //is going to support.
  public abstract class Provider
  {
    ProfileInfo    profileInfo;
```

```
      public Provider(ProfileInfo profile)
      {
        profileInfo = profile;
      }
      //crytographic transformaton of outgoing data
      public abstract void Create(byte[] originalData,SecureEnvelope envelope);
      //crytographic transformaton of incoming data
      public abstract bool Verify(SecureEnvelope envelope);
  }
}
```

As you can see, Provider is declared as an abstract base class that is then inherited by concrete providers that provide a correct implementation for security attributes defined at the class level. In the same way, this abstract class is also given complete access to the underlying security profile information. The two most important methods are Create and Verify. Create is invoked to construct a new cryptographic message that is derived from the original message; similarly, Verify is invoked to verify or unpack the message.

It is apparent that the number of concrete providers will be equal to the number of security attributes supported. But for demonstration purposes, we have supplied concrete providers only for NonRepudiationAttribute, which is explained in a moment.

NonRepudiationProvider

Here's the code for NonRepudiationProvider:

```
using System;
using System.IO;
using System.Security.Cryptography;

namespace STP.Security
{
  //Digital signature implementation
  public class NonRepudiationProvider : Provider
  {
    RSACryptoServiceProvider rsaProvider = new RSACryptoServiceProvider();

    public NonRepudiationProvider(ProfileInfo profile)
    :base(profile)
    {
      //Read digital certificate information
      StreamReader reader = new StreamReader(profile.NonRepudiationKeyPath);
      string xmlContent = reader.ReadToEnd();
      rsaProvider.FromXmlString(xmlContent );
      reader.Close();
    }

    public override void Create(byte[] originalData,SecureEnvelope envelope)
    {
      //create signature
      byte[] signedData = rsaProvider.SignData(originalData,new SHA1Managed());
      //insert digital signature in secure envelope
      envelope.Sections.Add(typeof(NonRepudiationAttribute).ToString(),
              new  NonRepudiationSection(originalData,signedData));
    }
```

```
public override bool Verify(SecureEnvelope envelope)
{
  //extract digital signature from secure envelope
  NonRepudiationSection nonrepSection =
          envelope.Sections[typeof(NonRepudiationAttribute).ToString()] as
              NonRepudiationSection;
  //verify digital signature
  return rsaProvider.VerifyData(nonrepSection.Signature,
        new   SHA1Managed(),nonrepSection.Data);
}

  }
}
```

The name itself indicates the functionality of this class, and it addresses the nonrepudiation aspect by creating and verifying the digital signature. Both these requirements are encapsulated in the Create and Verify methods. The most important line of code is the way the digital signature is created and then encapsulated inside an instance of NonRepudiationSection and then finally appended to SecureEnvelope. Similarly, in Verify the digital signature is verified by fetching the correct section from SecureEnvelope. The result of this verification is then returned to the caller.

DataSecurityManager

Here's the code for DataSecurityManager:

```
using System;
using System.Collections;

namespace STP.Security
{
  //Class responsible for loading security profiles
  //from XML configuration file or database
  public class DataSecurityManager
  {
    Hashtable profileCollection = new Hashtable();

    public DataSecurityManager()
    {
      profileCollection["BrokerA"] = new ProfileInfo(ConfidentialAlgo.Rijndael,
                    IntegrityAlgo.SHA1,@"C:\PubPrivKey.txt");
    }

    public Hashtable Profiles
    {
      get{return profileCollection;}
    }

    public DataSecurity Secure(Type objType)
    {
      return new DataSecurity(this,objType);
    }
  }
}
```

This class is exposed to the external world, and it is a gateway through which the initialization of the security framework is performed. The first step is to initialize security profile information, and in this case we have hard-coded it; however, remember in the real world it is usually populated from an XML configuration file or database. Next, the most important method is Secure, which accepts the type as a method argument and returns a new instance of DataSecurity.

DataSecurity

Here's the code for DataSecurity:

```
using System;

namespace STP.Security
{
  //Orchestrates the cryptography process
  public class DataSecurity
  {
    Type objType;
    DataSecurityManager securityMgr;
    Provider nonrepProvider;
    bool isConfidential;
    bool isNonRepudiation;
    bool isIntegrity;
    ProfileInfo profInfo;

    public DataSecurity(DataSecurityManager mgr, Type type)
    {
      objType = type;
      securityMgr=mgr;
      ExtractAttributes();
    }

    private void ExtractAttributes()
    {
      //Retrieve the security profile attribute
      //to retrieve the name of the profile
      object[] attributes =
          objType.GetCustomAttributes(typeof(SecurityProfileAttribute),true);
      SecurityProfileAttribute profAttr = attributes[0] as
                          SecurityProfileAttribute;
      profInfo= securityMgr.Profiles[profAttr.Profile] as ProfileInfo;

      //Check for confidential attribute
      attributes =
            objType.GetCustomAttributes(typeof(ConfidentialAttribute),true);
      isConfidential = (attributes.Length == 0 ? false : true);

      //Check for nonrepudiation attribute
      attributes =
            objType.GetCustomAttributes(typeof(NonRepudiationAttribute),true);
      isNonRepudiation  = (attributes.Length == 0 ? false : true);

      //Check for integrity attribute
      attributes = objType.GetCustomAttributes(typeof(IntegrityAttribute),true);
      isIntegrity  = (attributes.Length == 0 ? false : true);
```

```
      //Instantiate the nonrepudiation provider
      //and pass on the profile information
      nonrepProvider = new NonRepudiationProvider(profInfo);
    }

    public SecureEnvelope Create(byte[] data)
    {
      //Create a new secure envelope
      SecureEnvelope envelope = new SecureEnvelope(profInfo.ProfileName);

      //Based on attribute declared, we instantiate
      //appropriate provider
      if ( isNonRepudiation == true )
        nonrepProvider.Create(data,envelope);
      return envelope;
    }

    public bool Verify(SecureEnvelope envelope)
    {
      //invoke the appropriate provider to verify data
      return nonrepProvider.Verify(envelope);
    }

  }
}
```

This class implements the core logic, which includes extracting security-related attributes from a type, instantiating the appropriate provider, and finally providing a way to construct or verify cryptographic messages.

Code Example

The following code demonstrates the usage of a security framework:

```
using System;
using System.Security.Cryptography;
using System.IO;
using System.Text;
using System.Runtime.Serialization.Formatters.Binary;

namespace STP.Security
{
  class CodeExample
  {
    static void Main(string[] args)
    {
      //An instance of ContractNoteInfo is created.
      ContractNoteInfo noteInfo = new ContractNoteInfo("MSFT",100,24);

      //ContractNoteInfo is decorated with the Serializable attribute,
      //so the entire object graph with help of BinaryFormatter is
      //flattened into raw bytes, and this task is achieved by
      //with the help of the SerializeContractNote method
      byte[] data = SerializeContractNote(noteInfo);
```

```
                    //Generate public and private key for demonstration purpose
                    GenerateKey();

                    //Security Framework is initialized, a new instance of DataSecurity
                    //is created, and this instance returned by DataSecurityManager
                    //is exclusively meant for instances of ContractNoteInfo. This
                    //behavior is similar to XmlSerializer where there exists strong
                    //coupling between an object instance and the type associated with it.
                    DataSecurityManager secMgr = new DataSecurityManager();
                    DataSecurity dataSec = secMgr.Secure(typeof(ContractNoteInfo));

                    //The serialized byte array of ContractNoteInfo is then passed to
                    //Create method of DataSecurity that is then handed internally to
                    //NonRepudiationProvider, which creates a digital signature and
                    //associates it with SecureEnvelope.  Also, the secure envelope itself
                    //is marked serializable so its entire object graph itself can now
                    //be serialized and transmitted over the wire.
                    SecureEnvelope secureEnvelope = dataSec.Create(data);
            }

            public static void GenerateKey()
            {
                RSACryptoServiceProvider rsaCrypto = new RSACryptoServiceProvider();
                string pubprivKey = rsaCrypto.ToXmlString(true);
                StreamWriter writer = new StreamWriter(@"C:\PubPrivKey.txt");
                writer.WriteLine(pubprivKey);
                writer.Close();
            }

            public static byte[] SerializeContractNote(ContractNoteInfo noteInfo)
            {
                MemoryStream memStream = new MemoryStream();
                BinaryFormatter binaryFormatter = new BinaryFormatter();
                binaryFormatter.Serialize(memStream,noteInfo);
                int dataLength = (int)memStream.Length;
                byte[] data = new byte[dataLength];
                memStream.Position = 0;
                memStream.Read(data,0,dataLength);
                memStream.Close();
                return data;
            }
        }
    }
```

Summary

The following are the salient features covered in this chapter:

- We explained the various business entities involved in STP and how essential it is to secure information exchanged between them in order to gain credibility and acceptance of STP.

- We highlighted the role played by the STP service provider in bringing all business entities to a common platform.

- We briefly discussed the fundamental concepts of cryptography and also covered cryptography terminology.

- We explained both symmetric and asymmetric algorithms and how they can be used to protect the confidential aspect of data.

- We demonstrated how integrity of data is achieved by calculating a cryptographic hash value that is irreversible in nature.

- We introduced the concept of digital signatures that address nonrepudiation issues encountered in a high-risk transaction.

- We explained that the support of digital certificates in the STP world will act as a digital passport to verify an individual business identity.

- We covered how the prototype of a security framework is implemented and is based on a declarative programming approach to secure information.

CHAPTER 7

■ ■ ■

STP Interoperability

Activities undertaken in life are like a one-way transaction that has only a commit phase.

In the previous chapter, we discussed the role of an STP service provider. Each entity (such as the broker, custodian, and fund manager) subscribes to the STP provider's services, which use a predefined format for communicating trade details. The entire trade takes place on the STP service provider's network. Several STP service providers exist in the settlement marketplace, and they compete with each other for business. The challenging issue for the financial industry is to enable seamless interoperability between the various STP providers. To achieve this, you need a technology platform that connects individual market participants and STP providers, understands their internal and external business processes, and, most important, integrates their technologies. In this chapter, we will cover how you can use Web services to enable STP, and we will briefly cover the various features of Web services and how each of these components fits together to achieve interoperability in the STP world.

What Is Interoperability?

With the advent of multiple service providers, it becomes imperative that they communicate with each other in an unbiased way so that trades originating in one network can be settled on a different network if the entities involved in settling the trades are on different networks. The communication between two or more service providers or components in an STP environment is called *interoperability*. Regulators and industry associations ensure that seamless interoperability is in place in the interest of brokers, custodians, and fund managers. In the absence of interoperability, only those networks that had subscriptions from the largest and most influential institutions would attract more customers and traffic. This would in turn create a vicious cycle, prevent competition from growing, and result in a monopolistic situation. You can appreciate the need for interoperability by drawing an analogy between STP service providers and mobile phone service providers in the telecom business. You probably know that a single service provider in the mobile phone industry would not be a desirable situation. Specifically, you wouldn't have much choice over the services you get, the quality of services, or even the rate at which you pay for services. It would be a take-it-or-leave-it kind of situation. People don't like to be forced to subscribe to one service or continue to be associated with one service provider. Therefore, having multiple service providers in the mobile phone industry is healthy for subscribers. Now assume there was a constraint that subscribers from one network could not call subscribers in other networks. This kind of restriction would be difficult to digest. In such situations, though, multiple service providers would exist, but you would rarely get any choice. Whenever you wanted a mobile telephone connection, you would have to see what service most of your contacts used, and you would have to simply subscribe to that network. In this case, it is immediately obvious that these networks should be in a position to talk to one another. Unless they talk to each other, you would not be able to talk to all your contacts. And these conversations must be supported regardless of which network the call originates from, which network the call utilizes as a mere carrier, and which network the call finally terminates on. In this entire communication process, you would also expect the call clarity to be intact, and as long as the conversation takes place effectively, you really wouldn't care which networks the call utilizes.

Similarly, in the STP marketplace, you expect the following:

Choice of service provider: As individuals we like to have control over who provides us with service. We like to choose who provides us with a telephone connection and who provides us with banking services. These choices are driven by parameters such as who is providing better services, who guarantees deliveries, and which service provider is cost competitive. Institutions choose their STP service providers in the same way. Some choose multiple service providers to have a failover plan—just in case the services of one STP service provider is disrupted, the institution can quickly switch to the other service provider without much loss in business. If interoperability were not implemented, brokers/custodians would have to sign up with each service provider and route the messages to the appropriate service provider where their final recipient resides.

Immediate delivery of trades: The timely delivery of trades is extremely crucial. Trades originating from one network have to be delivered to the ultimate recipient such as the custodian/fund manager immediately. The STP service provider has to ensure that congestions are forecasted and managed efficiently.

Seamless communication: STP service providers have to talk to each other and exchange data in a seamless way through predefined protocols. The user institution must not be saddled with the responsibility of coding data in different formats and building additional logic for separate networks. No additional service provider–specific hardware/software should be required.

Correct content delivery: Trades initiated from one network must be delivered to other networks with correct content. Financial information is critical, and a small error can lead to a lot of losses for the institutions involved.

In the examples discussed in the previous chapter about STP, we assumed only one service provider. In such cases, it is simple to exchange messages between brokers, custodians, and fund managers, because only one communication protocol is involved. The market entities' back offices are required to be configured to talk to only one STP service provider (see Figure 7-1).

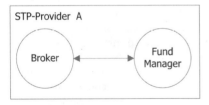

Figure 7-1. *Communication happens easily when all entities are on one network.*

We will now present another example that shows how STP interoperability works with several service providers in place. Assume there are three STP service providers: A, B, and C. And assume three market entities exist (see Table 7-1).

Table 7-1. *Market Entities and Their STP Providers*

Market Entity	Classification	Signed with Service Provider
X	Fund Manager	A
Y	Broker	B
Z	Custodian	C

Also assume fund manager X gives orders for execution on the exchange to broker Y. Broker Y will execute the order and will try to communicate the details to fund manager X. In this case, the fund manager is with service provider A, and broker Y is with service provider B. If both service providers don't talk to each other, the message initiated by broker Y will not get delivered to fund manager X.

Such an arrangement cannot work if there is no acceptable message format in which data will be exchanged. In such cases, regulators and industry associations normally come forward to formulate messaging protocols that are followed by each entity in the market, including the STP service providers. Once the messaging protocols get finalized, the market participants (brokers, fund managers, and custodians) modify their back offices and make them capable for communication with these protocols. Since all the entities understand these protocols, communication can take place easily amongst various STP service providers (see Figure 7-2).

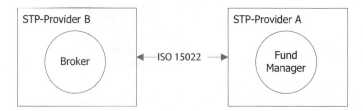

Figure 7-2. *Communication flows freely with a communication protocol in place.*

ISO 15022 is an acceptable communication protocol for achieving STP interoperability in several countries.

Why Is Interoperability Required?

As discussed in Chapter 1, STP is an approach to settlement that will reduce the time taken for settling transactions. Currently, settlements in U.S. equities markets happen on a T+3 basis. An ongoing effort is taking place through STP to bring it down to T+1. This means if you trade today, your transactions will get settled tomorrow. The task is enormous by any standard. STP will demand that a lot of the manual processes be automated. Since the same trade needs to flow between the fund manager, broker, and custodian and maybe even to the clearing corporation and depository, it is important that all such entities connect to a common network.

A common network in turn raises a lot of issues. Who will own this network, who will set it up, and who will manage it? Agencies such as exchanges or clearing corporations could be willing to set it up, but they might not provide enough features to suit individual institutions. Just as in other industries, having competition could be the answer. When multiple vendors exist, they will attempt to provide superior services to attract customers. The STP network also needs to communicate with the back offices of institutions; hence, it may also be desirable that one vendor provides a back office as well as STP services.

This is the case for having multiple vendors providing STP services. But we actually argue for having them on one network. Every vendor, however, has their own network. To achieve interoperability, a protocol needs to exist that enables each STP network to communicate with other STP networks.

Interoperability offers institutions the choice of having a preferred STP service provider. They can also sign up with multiple vendors to have redundancy.

Challenges in Achieving Interoperability

Although interoperability is highly desired, in many markets experience has shown that regulators and industry associations have to make a large amount of effort to implement interoperability. A variety of reasons exist for why interoperability does not take off on its own, especially in nonmature markets:

High cost of enhancements/interface development: This problem arises in the early stages when interoperability is implemented. Both STP service providers and their end customers have to make a large amount of investments to achieve a common messaging protocol and handshaking. This is more relevant for the first and early movers. A significant amount of investment is required for early movers to establish policies and processes and put an infrastructure in place. Late adopters simply learn from earlier adopters and hence have to invest less money. The entire industry thus adopts a wait-and-watch policy for many initiatives, causing the initiative itself to not take off.

Lack of messaging protocol: Each STP service provider may have its own technology framework, and there may not be any common protocol in which messaging takes place. Industry associations normally take the initiative in these cases, and they form committees to decide which messaging protocol is best for that market. STP service providers in those markets then adopt the decided messaging protocol as standard and implement interoperability using that standard.

Lack of common digital signature authentication process: When an STP service provider accepts transactions to be delivered to someone in its network, it needs to be sure the transaction content is digitally signed. Each STP service provider may sign up with a different certifying agency, giving rise to a need for a common body that verifies these signatures and certifies that the messages are genuine and can be accepted.

Other technology issues: Sometimes markets have agreed to a messaging protocol, but the back-office solutions of brokers/custodians and fund managers are not compliant to the agreed messaging formats. This gives rise to the need for the manual entry of data in such systems and causes a break in the chain for STP, leading to errors and delays.

Poor service-level agreements and legal infrastructure: Every STP service provider enters into a legal agreement with its customers for the delivery of messages. None of these service providers, however, guarantees the delivery of messages terminating on other networks. Since a failure of delivery means monetary loss that can at times be high, clients don't accept the risk and continue to sign up with multiple service providers rather than signing up with one and risking the delivery failure of a message and having no legal recourse.

High interconnectivity charges: Interconnectivity charges are charges that are levied to institutions for messages they send that terminate on a network different from the network of origination. Existing STP service providers levy high interconnect charges, especially to service providers that are new to this business. This deters institutions from joining the new service provider. However, strong regulatory guidelines exist for what interconnect charges can be levied and whether there can be differential pricing in interconnectivity.

Vested interests: Large players in the STP space don't want smaller vendors to come in and take away their business.

Central to all of these problems is integration and interoperability between STP providers. To resolve this, you need a computing platform that allows using industry standards but still takes advantage of investments made in the existing system. Additionally, it must allow architecting systems in a provider-neutral fashion where the external interface to the outside world is exposed using open standard and protocols regardless of the operating system or programming environment used to implement the core business logic. Such architectural style is important to survive in a highly dynamic environment and also to expand the reach of the business, particularly when the activities inside a business process demand a strong collaboration from its business partners. So, to meet this goal, STP service providers must embrace service-oriented architecture (SOA) principles.

Introducing Service-Oriented Architecture

SOA represents an architectural style of identifying and packaging applications in the form of a service. A *service* is an atomic processing unit that deals with a specific aspect of a business requirement. Collectively, a service forms a service suite (services) that facilitates building an end-to-end business solution. For example, Figure 7-3 identifies different pieces of an order management system and realizes them in the form of a service that is self-governed in nature. This idea of separating the business concerns is not a new concept and already exists in the component programming world, but what distinguishes the modern service-oriented approach (using Web services) is its ability to abstract away the knowledge about the implementation platform, data format, or transport protocol used by the service to communicate with its requestor. This is in contrast to the traditional distributed architecture world where it is absolutely necessary to understand the platform-specific details in order to leverage the functionality encapsulated inside a component. For example, if risk management functionality is exposed as DCOM components, then it would be difficult for the Java world to interoperate with it.

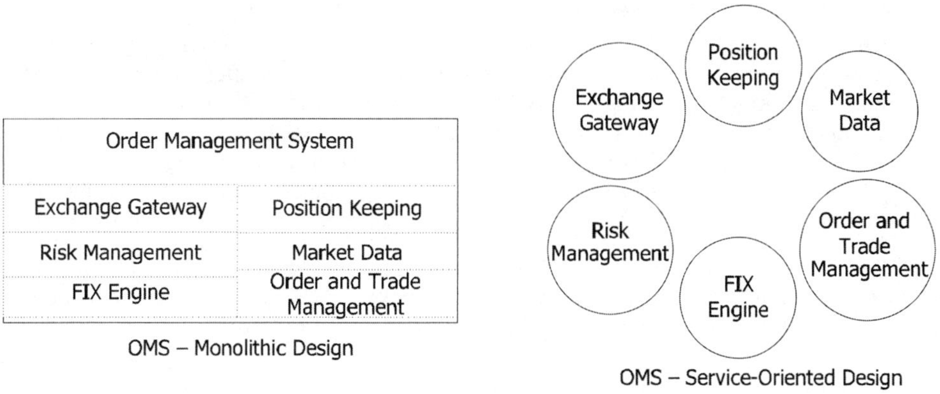

Figure 7-3. *OMS components represented using service-oriented design*

The modern SOA departs from the traditional architecture style and has characteristics that promote the strong reuse of the existing application by wrapping it in the form of services. It also allows interoperability between services that are spread across different computing platforms. The following are the important characteristics of SOA that make it so significant in today's computing world:

Loose coupling: Loose coupling is one of the important characteristics of SOA; it means both the service and its requestor are independent of each other's implementation. The details of the service are described through well-defined *service metadata* that outlines the business functionality, the structure of the message service's send or receive, and the transport protocol used to deliver messages. Furthermore, the content of the service description is laid out in a simple, machine-readable format. Significantly, this means the service metadata is the glue that establishes the link between the service provider and its requestor and allows them to discover and invoke functionality.

Autonomous: SOA requires that an individual service be an *autonomous* application. It must have complete control over its underlying processing logic. A service encapsulates logic that is either a business task or some kind of computational-related task, but its requestor is always shielded from its internal implementation. This proves to be highly flexible because it provides room to evolve and grow the business logic without impacting its consumers. This concept of autonomy is further applied to the message sent or received by the service. The service communicates using messages that are self-governed units and are platform agnostic. One valuable aspect of message-level autonomy is it allows you to transparently introduce value-added features such as message encryption, authentication, and so on.

Reusability: SOA promotes strong reusability both within the organization and outside the organization. It is natural in the service-oriented world because of the individual service that is designed to tackle a specific aspect of the business problem. Additionally, when an organization starts bundling its existing system in the form of the services, this automatically results in widespread reuse. So, by embracing SOA principles, an organization can easily integrate its modern systems with existing legacy systems regardless of the underlying platform or implementation language. This benefit of reuse will save organizations both time and money that otherwise would have been mobilized in migrating this legacy system to a new platform.

Abstraction: A service describes its functionality using service metadata. Even though a service internally must be using various business components that run on different platforms and demand a strict formalism, all this complexity is totally hidden to the consumer of the service. A service manages to abstract away the nitty-gritty details involved to achieve a specific business goal and act as a facade to the outside world. This degree of abstraction establishes a new service layer where the service acts as an entry point and coordinates among various internal business processing components.

The characteristics highlighted previously are equally applicable to other distributed application architectures; therefore, it is reasonable to wonder what makes SOA so different from the others. The difference is that SOA (using Web services) is the first architecture to promote interoperability from the inception stage. Moreover, SOA encourages organizations to leverage existing legacy systems, which drastically reduces cost and yields higher productivity. The tenets of SOA are an abstract architectural concept, and a technology implementation is needed that adheres to this principle and allows organizations to design and build service-oriented systems. Web services are one such implementation that lives up to the SOA expectation and provides a platform to build loosely coupled business solutions.

Web Services

Web services represent a new paradigm for building distributed applications that use industry-established open standards and protocols. They enable software components to be exposed as services over standard communication protocols and use a standard data representation format to exchange messages with consumers. They adopt XML as the key data exchange format and HTTP as the data delivery protocol. Because of this ubiquitous infrastructure, Web services have attracted the majority of organizations to follow the SOA path. With Web services, an organization can easily achieve its EAI and business-to-business integration goals that were in the past always seen as major hurdles. A much closer look at Web services will reveal that they provide the best of both the Web and component-oriented worlds. They facilitate the seamless integration between applications that are written in different languages and that run on different platforms. To fully understand Web services, it is essential to first know its pillars, as depicted in Figure 7-4.

Figure 7-4. *The pillars of Web services*

The important characteristics of Web services are as follows:

Web services use XML as the data representation format: The simplicity of XML technologies not only brought revolution in the Internet world but was also successful in establishing its place in the service-oriented world. Its innate ability to capture both data and metadata in an ordinary text format simplified the issues related to interoperability. It is through the use of XML that Web services interact and exchange messages with consumers. This unique strength of XML was soon realized by the industry, and it took the popularity of XML to a new height. Through the use of XML, vendors authored several standard specifications that form a part of today's basic architecture of a Web service.

The Web service messaging framework is founded upon SOAP: SOA preaches a message-oriented approach where the communication between a Web service and its consumer takes place by sending messages to each other. A request message initiated by a Web service requestor includes an action to be performed on the Web service along with the required data needed to support this action. Similarly, a response message triggered by a Web service includes the result of the action. To represent this interaction, a platform-agnostic messaging framework is required. As a result, Simple Object Access Protocol (SOAP) was designed; it uses XML to structure and format information. It is a highly extensible XML-based messaging framework designed to interoperate with any computing platform.

Web services use WSDL to define service metadata: Web Services Description Language (WSDL) is an XML document that defines the functionality offered by a Web service along with a list of messages it sends and receives. WSDL is the heart of a Web service because it is the only source of information provided to requestors in order to communicate with the service. Furthermore, the information provided contains sufficient knowledge that enables the requester to know the list of operations supported by the Web service, its physical location, the list of messages, and its underlying data types.

Web services use HTTP as their primary transport protocol: With the advent of the Internet, we were blessed with a new data delivery protocol that connected millions of systems across the globe. HTTP is an Internet protocol that is simple and has been widely used. Web services use HTTP to deliver SOAP messages. This combination of a ubiquitous Web protocol and language-agnostic messaging framework provides a strong platform to build an interoperable solution. Another important point is that the transport-level details are completely hidden from the Web service; therefore, organizations are not restricted to HTTP. Instead, they can use any communication protocol that suits their business requirement. But the only reason proponents of Web services advocate the use of HTTP is the inherent interoperability available off the shelf.

WSDL

WSDL is the foundation of a Web service. It describes crucial information about the Web service using XML vocabulary. The WSDL document contains the structure of messages, the data type of an individual message, the order in which the messages are arranged and exchanged with consumers, and the physical location of the Web service. Additionally, it contains details about the transport protocol used to deliver the message and the way messages are encoded over the wire. This aspect of WSDL makes it possible for any consumer to establish communication with a Web service without even knowing its internal implementation details. On the other hand, it achieves loose coupling and interoperability between Web services and their consumers. From a consumer point of view, the only critical information required is WSDL, which itself is described in a machine-readable format. Furthermore, a deep dive into WSDL will disclose the important fact that it contains information that is logically grouped into two parts: an abstract part and a concrete part.

The purpose of the abstract part is to define message-level characteristics that are independent of any platform or language. Similarly, the concrete part binds the implementation-level details to the abstract part; it describes the wire format of the message and the transport protocol used to deliver it. This ability to describe the data used by the Web service without any reference to technology and then dynamically bind it proves to be highly extensible. It provides multiple ways to interact with a service. For instance, the same service can be exposed over the multiple communication channels that are needed to achieve cross-platform interoperability.

Note This section does not cover WSDL in detail, but the explanation is good enough for you to understand the concept. Readers who want to further understand the nuts and bolts of individual elements can refer to the WSDL specification at `http://www.w3.org/TR/wsdl`.

WSDL borrows from XML Schema, which makes it possible to define/validate it using any good XML editor/parser. To give you a firsthand taste of WSDL, we have defined a WSDL document (see Listing 7-1) that represents a slimmed-down feature of the order management system and exposes the order submission functionality in the form of a Web service. This would enable a broker's trading partners to connect their internal systems directly to the broker's trading system.

Listing 7-1. *WSDL Document for Order Management Web Service*

```
<?xml version="1.0" encoding="utf-8"?>
<definitions xmlns:http="http://schemas.xmlsoap.org/wsdl/http/"
xmlns:soap="http://schemas.xmlsoap.org/wsdl/soap/"
xmlns:s="http://www.w3.org/2001/XMLSchema"
xmlns:s0="http://brokerxyz.com"
xmlns:soapenc="http://schemas.xmlsoap.org/soap/encoding/"
xmlns:tm="http://microsoft.com/wsdl/mime/textMatching/"
xmlns:mime="http://schemas.xmlsoap.org/wsdl/mime/"
targetNamespace="http://brokerxyz.com" xmlns="http://schemas.xmlsoap.org/wsdl/">
  <types>
    <s:schema elementFormDefault="qualified"
            targetNamespace="http://brokerxyz.com">
      <s:element name="SubmitOrder">
        <s:complexType>
          <s:sequence>
            <s:element minOccurs="0" maxOccurs="1" name="orderInfo"
                    type="s0:OrderInfo" />
          </s:sequence>
        </s:complexType>
      </s:element>
```

```xml
    <s:complexType name="OrderInfo">
      <s:sequence>
        <s:element minOccurs="0" maxOccurs="1" name="Instrument"
                   type="s:string" />
        <s:element minOccurs="1" maxOccurs="1" name="BuySell"
                   type="s0:BuySellEnum" />
        <s:element minOccurs="1" maxOccurs="1" name="Price" type="s:double" />
        <s:element minOccurs="1" maxOccurs="1" name="Quantity" type="s:int" />
      </s:sequence>
    </s:complexType>
    <s:simpleType name="BuySellEnum">
      <s:restriction base="s:string">
        <s:enumeration value="Buy" />
        <s:enumeration value="Sell" />
      </s:restriction>
    </s:simpleType>
    <s:element name="SubmitOrderResponse">
      <s:complexType>
        <s:sequence>
          <s:element minOccurs="0" maxOccurs="1" name="SubmitOrderResult"
                     type="s:string" />
        </s:sequence>
      </s:complexType>
    </s:element>
  </s:schema>
</types>
<message name="SubmitOrderSoapIn">
  <part name="parameters" element="s0:SubmitOrder" />
</message>
<message name="SubmitOrderSoapOut">
  <part name="parameters" element="s0:SubmitOrderResponse" />
</message>
<portType name="OrderManagementServiceSoap">
  <operation name="SubmitOrder">
    <input message="s0:SubmitOrderSoapIn" />
    <output message="s0:SubmitOrderSoapOut" />
  </operation>
</portType>
<binding name="OrderManagementServiceSoap" type="s0:OrderManagementServiceSoap">
  <soap:binding transport="http://schemas.xmlsoap.org/soap/http"
                style="document" />
  <operation name="SubmitOrder">
    <soap:operation soapAction="http://brokerxyz.com/SubmitOrder"
                    style="document" />
    <input>
      <soap:body use="literal" />
    </input>
    <output>
      <soap:body use="literal" />
    </output>
  </operation>
</binding>
<service name="OrderManagementService">
  <port name="OrderManagementServiceSoap"
        binding="s0:OrderManagementServiceSoap">
    <soap:address
         location="http://localhost/webservice3/OrderManagementService.asmx" />
```

```
      </port>
    </service>
</definitions>
```

In Listing 7-1, the abstract part of WSDL is represented by the `<types>`, `<message>`, and `<porttype>` elements, and the concrete portion is defined by the `<binding>`, `<port>`, and `<service>` elements. The WSDL document describes the complete information about the Web service; in this case, it provides a business feature where any consumer (a broker's trading partner) can directly submit an order and in response get a unique order number that is later used to find out the status of the order. To build this functionality, the first step is to define the structural characteristics of the message that forms the abstract part of the service and is encapsulated inside the `<types>` element.

The `<types>` element defines the data type of the message sent or received by the Web service. It relies on the grammar of the XML schema to define structural characteristics of the message, which can range from a simple type element to a complex type element. This is a remarkable quality of WSDL because instead of inventing its own type system, it directly adopted the industry-standard XML Schema as its official type system language. The following XML fragment defines the structural characteristics of the messages exchanged between a broker and his trading partners:

```
<types>
  <s:schema elementFormDefault="qualified"
            targetNamespace="http://brokerxyz.com">
    <s:element name="SubmitOrder">
      <s:complexType>
        <s:sequence>
          <s:element minOccurs="0" maxOccurs="1" name="orderInfo"
                     type="s0:OrderInfo" />
        </s:sequence>
      </s:complexType>
    </s:element>
    <s:complexType name="OrderInfo">
      <s:sequence>
        <s:element minOccurs="0" maxOccurs="1" name="Instrument"
                   type="s:string" />
        <s:element minOccurs="1" maxOccurs="1" name="BuySell"
                   type="s0:BuySellEnum" />
        <s:element minOccurs="1" maxOccurs="1" name="Price" type="s:double" />
        <s:element minOccurs="1" maxOccurs="1" name="Quantity" type="s:int" />
      </s:sequence>
    </s:complexType>
    <s:simpleType name="BuySellEnum">
      <s:restriction base="s:string">
        <s:enumeration value="Buy" />
        <s:enumeration value="Sell" />
      </s:restriction>
    </s:simpleType>
    <s:element name="SubmitOrderResponse">
      <s:complexType>
        <s:sequence>
          <s:element minOccurs="0" maxOccurs="1" name="SubmitOrderResult"
                     type="s:string" />
        </s:sequence>
      </s:complexType>
    </s:element>
  </s:schema>
</types>
```

With the support of the XSD type system, we constructed the content of the request-response message that will be accepted by the Web service. The request message maps to the structure of the order, and its definition is enclosed inside the <SubmitOrder> element. Similarly, the response message in this scenario represents a unique order number that is enclosed inside the <SubmitOrderResponse> element. The elements declared inside <types> are then referenced by the <message> element, which defines the actual composition of messages exchanged between a Web service and its consumer. Here is what the <message> element looks like for the order management Web service:

```
<message name="SubmitOrderSoapIn">
  <part name="parameters" element="sO:SubmitOrder" />
</message>
<message name="SubmitOrderSoapOut">
  <part name="parameters" element="sO:SubmitOrderResponse" />
</message>
```

Messages represent abstract definitions of data and are composed of multiple parts. Individual parts are described by one or more <part> child elements. Each <part> is tagged with a meaningful name along with its underlying data type that references a simple or complex type defined under the <types> element.

The next step is to group messages with the help of the <operation> element. This is analogous to a method declaration in the object-oriented world. Each operation contains input and output messages that are declared by the <input> and <output> constructs. The sequence in which the <input> and <output> elements are laid out determines the message exchange pattern. For example, the SubmitOrder operation described next represents a typical request-response message exchange pattern. An operation that contains only <input> messages represents a one-way message exchange pattern.

With the help of the <operation> element, messages are grouped; the <operation> elements are further grouped to form a <portType> element, which is the final leg of the abstract service definition. The <portType> element, as follows, basically lists all the operations supported by the Web service:

```
<portType name="OrderManagementServiceSoap">
  <operation name="SubmitOrder">
    <input message="sO:SubmitOrderSoapIn" />
    <output message="sO:SubmitOrderSoapOut" />
  </operation>
</portType>
```

So far we have covered the abstract part of WSDL that represents Web service metadata in a platform-agnostic fashion. But it is important to mention the implementation-level details about how messages are formatted over the wire and the underlying transport protocol used to deliver the message. This information is described inside a <binding> element. Here is what the <binding> element looks like that uses SOAP to format messages and HTTP to deliver these messages:

```
<binding name="OrderManagementServiceSoap" type="sO:OrderManagementServiceSoap">
  <soap:binding transport="http://schemas.xmlsoap.org/soap/http"
                style="document" />
  <operation name="SubmitOrder">
    <soap:operation soapAction="http://brokerxyz.com/SubmitOrder"
                    style="document" />
    <input>
      <soap:body use="literal" />
    </input>
    <output>
      <soap:body use="literal" />
    </output>
  </operation>
</binding>
```

The final leg of a WSDL document is the declaration of the `<service>` element, which contains `<port>` elements that supply the physical location of the Web service along with the appropriate binding information:

```
<service name="OrderManagementService">
  <port name="OrderManagementServiceSoap"
      binding="s0:OrderManagementServiceSoap">
    <soap:address
        location="http://localhost/webservice3/OrderManagementService.asmx" />
  </port>
</service>
```

This concludes the brief overview of various elements that collectively form a WSDL document. It is interesting to see how WSDL is used to capture the structural aspect of the Web service purely in terms of message interaction without disclosing any implementation-specific details; going further, you will learn how tools are used by Web service consumers to read the service description and generate the appropriate implementation code to interact with the Web service.

SOAP

SOAP is the messaging communication framework used by Web services to send or receive messages. The purpose of SOAP is to provide a standard wire format that allows binding on a variety of transport protocols and is not tied to any particular language or platform. To meet this requirement, SOAP uses XML technologies to construct messages. The key aspect of using SOAP is the simplicity it provides that facilitates loose coupling between the Web service and its requestor. It achieves message-level autonomy and provides a foundation to build higher-level application protocols. This results in the development of other advanced features that are evidenced in various distributed systems such as encryption, authentication, and routing.

A SOAP message represents an interaction between a Web service and its requestor; both the request and response messages use same SOAP structure. The structure of SOAP consists of a SOAP envelope that contains three important elements: header, body, and fault (see Figure 7-5). Each message contains a header element that is the primary driver behind SOAP extensibility. It records control information about data; for instance, if the actual data is encrypted, then information about the encryption algorithm such as its key size is recorded in the header. It is through the header element that Web services are able to separate the infrastructure aspect from the functional part and modularize each in the form of feature extensions that can then be composed by any Web service. The next element after the header element is the body element. It is an XML container that stores the actual message payload. It is a mandatory element, unlike the header element, that is optional. The last element is the fault element, which provides a generic structure used by the Web service to notify the error information to the sender.

Figure 7-5. *SOAP envelope*

Although SOAP is able to codify messages with the help of header, body, and fault elements, two important styles are prevalent in the SOAP messaging world. These styles dictate how to structure the content enclosed inside these elements. The first style represents the traditional RPC style where request-response messages are mapped in the form of a method name followed by method parameters. The second style represents modern document-style messages where the request-response messages contain the actual XML document and whose format is defined by the sender and receiver. The goal of the RPC style is to replace the proprietary protocol used by existing distributed applications and introduce a standard message format. But this initiative was not so widely welcomed and also was complex to understand. Therefore, Web services adopted a document-centric approach as its default style to exchange a message with its consumer.

Platform Infrastructure for Web Services

The concepts discussed so far regarding Web services such as SOAP and WSDL are specifications and not technology platforms. A *specification* is a document that is jointly prepared by vendors in order to achieve a common goal. The goal is to promote vendor-neutral communication and develop systems using open protocols and standards. The benefits are that no single vendor has complete control and that any significant changes in the specification require total consensus among vendors. However, you need an infrastructure that understands this specification and provides both the development and hosting platforms that would then allow you to build real-life business solutions that are based on the tenets of SOA. The infrastructure must also provide a development tool to build Web services using a suitable programming language. It must also have the ability to wrap the existing business components and expose them in the form of Web services.

The Microsoft .NET Framework has been designed to support this kind of infrastructure and offers strong development tools along with a reliable hosting platform. The framework provides support for building Web services in any .NET-aware programming language such as Visual Basic, C#, and so on. Furthermore, the CLR supplies so many goodies that it makes a developer's life simpler. The richness of the framework combined with the robustness provided by the CLR results in a perfect platform to build Web services.

Figure 7-6 illustrates a high-level architecture view of the Web service platform implemented in .NET. However, in reality there is no restriction on the selection of a platform; in other words, developers are free to choose any Web service platform.

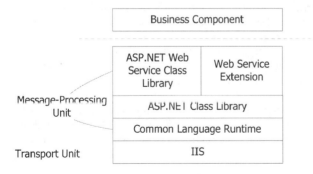

Figure 7-6. *High-level components of the Web service platform*

Regardless of which platform you select, you will always find the following basic software components:

Transport unit: This component is responsible for all kinds of communication aspects associated with Web services. It is bundled with various communication protocols that ensure the delivery of messages from one endpoint to another. In the .NET world, this role is played by the IIS server, and the communication between the Web service and its requestor is conducted using HTTP.

Message-processing unit: This component is known as the *message-handling engine* because at its core it is responsible for transforming and processing SOAP messages. It validates inbound and outbound SOAP messages and ensures they adhere to SOAP standards. It is equally responsible for dictating the wire-encoding format of the SOAP messages. In the .NET world, the Web service framework provides this feature. Obviously, the framework does more than message processing; one of the nice features it provides is an object-oriented abstraction over XML messages. Developers never deal with the tedious task of framing SOAP messages; instead, with the help of a declarative programming model, classes are decorated with the appropriate SOAP serialization attributes. The goal of this framework is to hide most of the complexities involved in creating a SOAP message. Additionally, the framework provides an extensibility hook that further offers opportunities to construct various value-added services.

Business processing unit: This component houses the actual business logic that is executed on receiving the request from the Web service consumer. There is no restriction on the use of the technology, and the business logic implemented may be truly proprietary in nature.

By introducing the previous three units, we have explained the basic architectural foundation of any Web service platform. Note that a vendor implementing such a platform may introduce additional layers, but the overall design characteristics will still revolve around the previously explained software pieces. In the next section, we will show how to leverage the Microsoft Web service platform, and you will see how easy it is to build your first Web service using Visual Studio .NET as the official Web service development tool.

STP and Web Services

Web services will be the greatest catalyst for enabling STP in the financial industry. Today, most financial firms depend upon both internal and external systems. Internal systems look after the internal needs of the organization, and external systems look after the business-to-business integration aspects. Additionally, the implementations of systems are spread across various platforms. So, in this scenario, the industry needs a platform that virtualizes all systems running inside and outside an organization as one single coherent system. Web services address this need by providing various industry standards that allow for the seamless integration between various systems. Using Web services, organizations can easily integrate their existing and new systems with minimal development effort; this will be the key incentive, and it will definitely entice a financial firm to participate in STP. Essentially, STP will be realized only on a platform that connects individual organizations in the financial industry, understands its internal and external business process, and integrates its technology.

Now it is time to wet your hands with your first Web service code using Visual Studio .NET. Let's say you were assigned the responsibility of automating STP; mainly your goal is to establish a framework to enable seamless, cross–STP provider integration. We already discussed the various problems faced by STP providers in the absence of a common, standard communication protocol. From here onward, we will show you step by step the implementation-level details, and at each step we will discuss the features available in Web services and give you background information about how Web services solve this problem.

The case study we will be explaining is based on Table 7-1 where the fund manager is registered with STP-Provider A and the broker with STP-Provider B. In this scenario, both the fund manager and the broker are registered with different STP providers. In order to enable seamless information flow between the broker and the fund manager, both STP-Provider A and STP-Provider B need to establish some form of communication medium. This will then allow the fund manager to submit an order for execution on the exchange to the broker and similarly will allow the broker to communicate the execution details to the fund manager. The only way this flow will be successful is when STP-Provider A (the fund manager's STP provider) routes the order to STP-Provider B (the broker's STP provider), and this requires agreement between both these providers. So, we will demonstrate how STP-Provider A and STP-Provider B use Web service technology to achieve this interoperability.

In Figure 7-7, you will notice post-execution interaction where the broker informs the fund manager about the trade details in the form of a contract note. Although the market entities are omitted in Figure 7-7, it is obvious that STP-Provider B, who is representing the broker, must somehow communicate the trade details to the fund manager via STP-Provider A. To support this interaction, STP-Provider A will expose a Web service that allows sending contract note information to all market entities falling under the STP-Provider A network in an interoperable fashion. This Web service will then be invoked by STP-Provider B to submit contract note information destined for the fund manager. STP-Provider A in Web service context is known as the *service provider*, and STP-Provider B is known as the *service consumer* or *service requestor*.

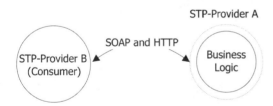

Figure 7-7. *STP-Provider B invoking the STP-Provider A Web service*

To create a Web service, the first prerequisite is to install and start IIS from the Service Control Panel. Keep in mind the steps we are discussing represent the activity performed by STP-Provider A in order to expose the Web service. The next step is to launch Visual Studio .NET, and select File ➤ New ➤ Project. This opens the New Project dialog box. Then, select ASP.NET Web Service in the Templates area, as shown in Figure 7-8. Next, enter a suitable name for this project, such as **STPProvider**. Click OK to create the project.

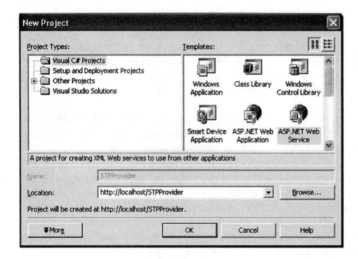

Figure 7-8. *Web service project created using Visual Studio .NET*

By default Visual Studio .NET creates various files that make up the Web service; the most important one to look at is the Web service file with the extension asmx (see Figure 7-9).

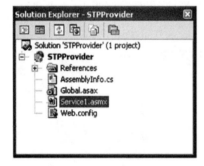

Figure 7-9. *STPProvider project structure*

By double-clicking Service1.asmx, you will be provided with a code editor view, as depicted in Figure 7-10.

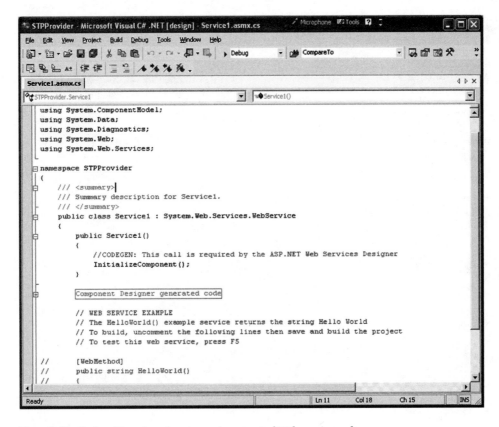

Figure 7-10. *Code editor view showing autogenerated Web service code*

You will now modify both the class name and filename so that they reflect the actual business functionality they intend to offer to the consumer (see Figure 7-11).

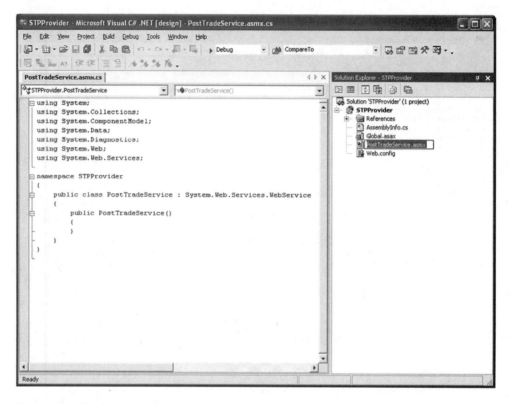

Figure 7-11. *Changing the Web service class name and filename*

Creating a Web service using Visual Studio .NET is easy; all you need to do is reference the System.Web assembly and import the System.Web.Services namespace. Then, create a new class and inherit it from System.Web.Services.WebService, which then automatically promotes it to a Web service. After completing this step, the next procedure is to describe the functionality provided by the service; you do this with the help of the WebMethod attribute decorated over the public method of the class. Listing 7-2 shows the revised code of PostTradeService that enables the contract note functionality.

Listing 7-2. *Web Service Exposed by STP-Provider A*

```
using System;
using System.Collections;
using System.ComponentModel;
using System.Data;
using System.Diagnostics;
using System.Web;
using System.Web.Services;

namespace STPProvider
{
  public class ContractNoteInfo
  {
    public string Symbol;
    public string Quantity;
```

```
  public string Price;
  public BuySellEnum BuySell;
}
public enum BuySellEnum
{
  Buy,
  Sell
}
public class PostTradeService : System.Web.Services.WebService
{
  public PostTradeService()
  {
  }

  [WebMethod]
  public int SubmitContractNote(ContractNoteInfo contractNote)
  {
    //Process the submitted information
    return 0;
  }
}
}
```

Notice that in Listing 7-2 a new operation, SubmitContractNote, is published by the Web service. This method accepts the contract note information as an input message and returns an acknowledgment number as an output message. ContractNoteInfo represents the contract note information. You already know Web services communicate through XML messages, but Visual Studio .NET provides an object-centric approach to building Web services. To take advantage of this strong-typing feature, Visual Studio .NET undertakes a lot of the complex steps and hides them from developers. In simpler terms, with just a few lines of the previous code, you defined the WSDL document and SOAP message structure. To construct this information, you need to compile the project by selecting Build ➤ Build Solution. The next step after compilation is to open Internet Explorer and retrieve the WSDL document simply by visiting http://localhost/STPProvider/PostTradeService.asmx?wsdl. This will fetch the complete information about the Web service, as shown in Listing 7-3.

Listing 7-3. *WSDL for Web Service Exposed by STP-Provider A*

```
<definitions xmlns:http="http://schemas.xmlsoap.org/wsdl/http/"
     xmlns:soap="http://schemas.xmlsoap.org/wsdl/soap/"
     xmlns:s="http://www.w3.org/2001/XMLSchema" xmlns:s0="http://tempuri.org/"
     xmlns:soapenc="http://schemas.xmlsoap.org/soap/encoding/"
     xmlns:tm="http://microsoft.com/wsdl/mime/textMatching/"
     xmlns:mime="http://schemas.xmlsoap.org/wsdl/mime/"
     targetNamespace="http://tempuri.org/"
     xmlns="http://schemas.xmlsoap.org/wsdl/">
  <types>
    <s:schema elementFormDefault="qualified"
            targetNamespace="http://tempuri.org/">
      <s:element name="SubmitContractNote">
        <s:complexType>
          <s:sequence>
            <s:element minOccurs="0" maxOccurs="1" name="contractNote"
                     type="s0:ContractNoteInfo" />
          </s:sequence>
        </s:complexType>
```

```
        </s:element>
        <s:complexType name="ContractNoteInfo">
          <s:sequence>
            <s:element minOccurs="0" maxOccurs="1" name="Symbol" type="s:string" />
            <s:element minOccurs="1" maxOccurs="1" name="Quantity" type="s:int" />
            <s:element minOccurs="1" maxOccurs="1" name="Price" type="s:double" />
            <s:element minOccurs="1" maxOccurs="1" name="BuySell"
                        type="s0:BuySellEnum" />
          </s:sequence>
        </s:complexType>

        <s:simpleType name="BuySellEnum">
          <s:restriction base="s:string">
            <s:enumeration value="Buy" />
            <s:enumeration value="Sell" />
          </s:restriction>
        </s:simpleType>
        <s:element name="SubmitContractNoteResponse">
          <s:complexType>
            <s:sequence>

              <s:element minOccurs="1" maxOccurs="1" name="SubmitContractNoteResult"
                          type="s:int" />
            </s:sequence>
          </s:complexType>
        </s:element>
      </s:schema>
  </types>
  <message name="SubmitContractNoteSoapIn">
    <part name="parameters" element="s0:SubmitContractNote" />
  </message>

  <message name="SubmitContractNoteSoapOut">
    <part name="parameters" element="s0:SubmitContractNoteResponse" />
  </message>
  <portType name="PostTradeServiceSoap">
    <operation name="SubmitContractNote">
      <input message="s0:SubmitContractNoteSoapIn" />
      <output message="s0:SubmitContractNoteSoapOut" />
    </operation>
  </portType>

  <binding name="PostTradeServiceSoap" type="s0:PostTradeServiceSoap">
    <soap:binding transport="http://schemas.xmlsoap.org/soap/http"
                   style="document" />
    <operation name="SubmitContractNote">
      <soap:operation soapAction="http://tempuri.org/SubmitContractNote"
                       style="document" />
      <input>
        <soap:body use="literal" />
      </input>
      <output>
        <soap:body use="literal" />

      </output>
    </operation>
  </binding>
```

```
    <service name="PostTradeService">
      <port name="PostTradeServiceSoap" binding="s0:PostTradeServiceSoap">
        <soap:address location="http://localhost/STPProvider/PostTradeService.asmx" />
      </port>
    </service>
</definitions>
```

In Listing 7-3, notice how `ContractNoteInfo` type is represented in XSD form; similarly, employing the `WebMethod` attribute over the `SubmitContractNote` method translates in the form of the `<operation>` element, and arguments of this method are enclosed inside the `<message>` element. Certainly, you can build the previous WSDL document by hand, but it would be lot of work and the chances of human mistake are very high.

With the WSDL document in place, it can now be shared with the other STP providers (STP-Provider B is one of them) who can then start building an appropriate interface to interact with the Web service.

This completes the discussion of the STP-Provider A end; the next step is to build a service consumer implementation that in this case is represented by STP-Provider B who will use the Web service interface of STP-Provider A to submit contract note information received from the broker to the fund manager.

In this example, we will assume both the Web service and its consumer are using the .NET platform, and therefore STP-Provider B can use the `wsdl` command-line tool to generate what we call a *service proxy* that emits a class based on a WSDL document. The proxy contains information about the method and the type that is represented in the form of `<operation>` and `<types>` inside WSDL. The intent of the proxy is to act as a mediator between the Web service and consumer and hide the low-level details involved in composing the request or response message using SOAP.

To build a service consumer (STP-Provider B), you will create a new console project using Visual Studio .NET, as illustrated in Figure 7-12.

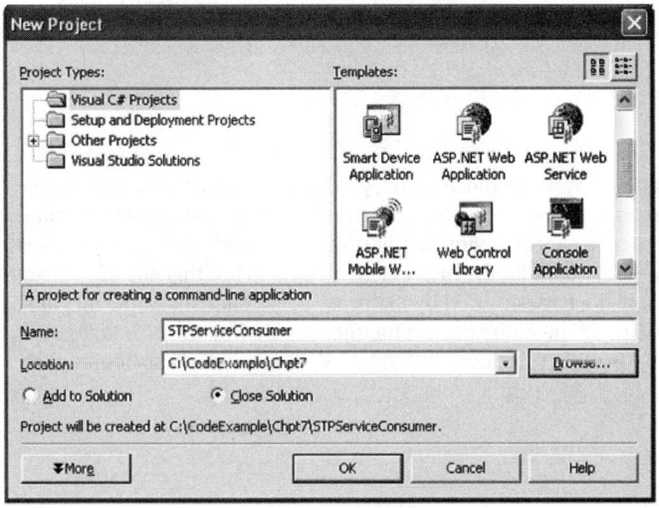

Figure 7-12. *Service consumer project created using Visual Studio .NET's New Project dialog box*

After the project is successfully created, the next step is to add a Web service reference; you can accomplish this task using the `wsdl` command-line tool. Alternatively, Visual Studio .NET provides an easy-to-use wizard that automatically generates the proxy class that no doubt under the hood uses the wsdl command-line tool. Additionally, the wizard also makes the necessary adjustments in the existing project to add the newly created proxy class. Now to bring up the wizard, right-click the project node, and select Add Web Reference. This opens the Search dialog box. In the Search dialog box's URL field, enter the physical location of the Web service, and click Go to continue. This will display the list of operations supported by Web service, as depicted in Figure 7-13.

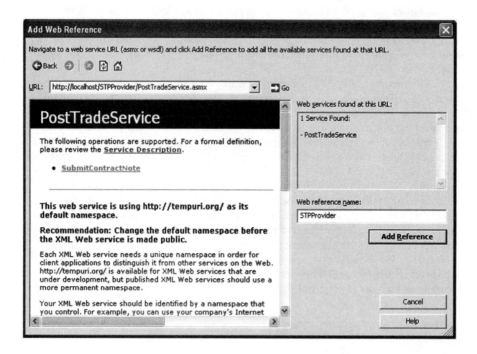

Figure 7-13. *Add Web Reference dialog box*

In Figure 7-13, after assigning a new Web reference name, you finally hook up this Web service reference to your project. You must have figured it by now how simple it is to add Web service references; it's similar to adding a reference to a local assembly. But under the hood a new proxy class is generated and included in the project. By default, the proxy class is hidden, but this doesn't restrict developers from looking at it. To view the code emitted by the proxy class, click the Show All Files icon in Solution Explorer. This will expand the entire project hierarchy including the Web References node, and you should see the proxy class beneath the individual Web references, as depicted in Figure 7-14.

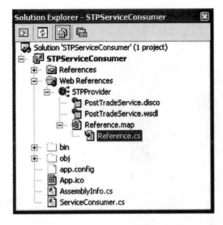

Figure 7-14. *Solution Explorer showing the autogenerated proxy class created when adding a new Web reference*

As you peek into the code of the proxy class, you will notice that it inherits from System.Web. Services.Protocols.SoapHttpClientProtocol, which provides an object model to interact with the Web service and also extend this model to programmatically manipulate SOAP request-response messages. After the proxy is generated, the next step is to write the code to invoke the contract note functionality exposed by the STP-Provider A Web service, as shown in Listing 7-4.

Listing 7-4. *STP-Provider B Invoking STP-Provider A Web Service*

```
using System;

namespace STPServiceConsumer
{
  class ServiceConsumer
  {
    [STAThread]
    static void Main(string[] args)
    {
      //instantiate Web service proxy
      STPProvider.PostTradeService postTradeSvc = new
                          STPProvider.PostTradeService();
      //prepare contract note information
      STPProvider.ContractNoteInfo contractNote = new
                          STPProvider.ContractNoteInfo();
      contractNote.Symbol = "MSFT";
      contractNote.Price = 25;
      contractNote.Quantity=100;
      contractNote.BuySell = STPProvider.BuySellEnum.Buy;
      //submit contract note information through Web service
      int ackId =postTradeSvc.SubmitContractNote(contractNote);
      //display the ack no. received from Web service
      Console.WriteLine("Acknowledgement Id: " + ackId);
    }
  }
}
```

To test your first Web service, compile the code described in Listing 7-4 and then run the program. You will see the output in Figure 7-15.

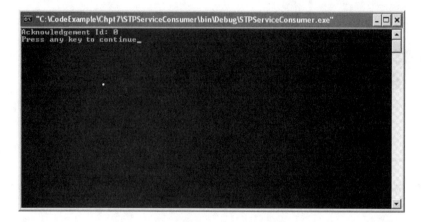

Figure 7-15. *Console application demonstrating successful invocation of STP-Provider A Web service*

The program executed without any errors; STP-Provider B was able to submit a contract note request to STP-Provider A and in response get an acknowledgment number. Clearly, with minimal effort, you were able to build and test the Web service. The primary reason for this is the strong support provided by the .NET Framework and Visual Studio .NET. Without their support, it would have been a difficult and time-consuming task.

STP Provider Consortium: Using UDDI

We demonstrated how STP-Provider A and STP-Provider B were able to shape and standardize both the message and transport protocol details. Because of this, any consumer who understands WSDL and SOAP can now directly communicate with STP-Provider A regardless of how proprietary the STP-Provider A implementation platform is. So, for communication to take place, the first thing the consumer must know is the exact location of the WSDL document. The example we illustrated involved only two STP providers, but in reality there would be multiple STP providers offering the same set of services in the STP space; it would be extremely difficult for the consumer to keep track of the individual STP provider service descriptions and their Web service locations. To circumvent this problem, you need a single well-known repository where information about the STP provider and the services offered are published. It will support basic and advance search capability that will be of tremendous value to consumers who can easily find a specific service that matches their business requirement. Furthermore, you can think of the registry as an *STP provider consortium* where the STP provider advertises itself along with its various service offerings.

To realize the STP provider consortium mission in the service-oriented world, what you need is a registry that is based on service-oriented concepts. Universal Description, Discovery, and Integration (UDDI) exactly fits this requirement (see Figure 7-16). It is a specification that describes a standard way to publish, discover, and integrate Web services. It plays an important role in providing a repository that not only contains technical information about Web services but also provides nontechnical details. The nontechnical details consist of business addresses along with contact information, geographic locations, and industry sectors. The role of the UDDI registry is just like a telephone directory where information about businesses is registered, categorized, and finally made available to the general public.

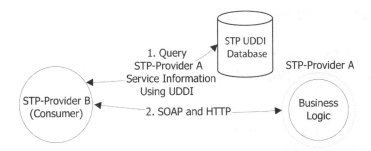

Figure 7-16. *Illustrates how the UDDI repository is used by STP-Provider B to find the STP-Provider A Web service*

At a high level, UDDI captures the following information during the Web service registration process:

Business entity: Represents Web service provider information that contains names, addresses, and contact details

Business service: Represents services provided by the business entity

Binding template: Provides implementation-level information about how to initiate a communication with the Web service

One of the main benefits of using UDDI is that it facilitates the consumer to bind to Web services at runtime simply by querying on any of the previous attributes, and on a successful match the consumer will receive the Web service network endpoint. This behavior is possible because a central repository exists, and one can use the UDDI API to find information by issuing an appropriate query. The UDDI API is exposed in the form of a Web service, so it is clear that XML is the language used to interact with the registry. Data structures are defined using XSD, and operations such as service discovery and publishing are defined in terms of the SOAP message. Many APIs are available in UDDI that are broadly classified under the discovery and publishing category. The discovery API is intended to retrieve service information based on specific search criteria, and the publishing API is intended to integrate service information with the registry. To invoke these APIs, you need to understand and frame correct SOAP messages, but considering the scope of this section, it is not possible to cover the individual message structure and operation of UDDI Web services. For readers who want to gain further insight, visit www.uddi.org.

In a typical STP world, you will require a repository based on UDDI standards. Currently, you have two options for building a UDDI repository. The first option is to host a private UDDI repository, and in the Microsoft world only Windows 2003 servers natively support it. The second option is to reserve a space in the public UDDI repository hosted by Microsoft (http://uddi.microsoft.com) and IBM (http://www.ibm.com/services/uddi). There are no entry barriers, and any organization can participate and register its Web services. Moreover, both IBM and Microsoft have provided a test repository database that allows organizations to experiment before touching the real repository; you can find these at http:/test.uddi.microsoft.com and https://uddi.ibm.com/testregistry/registry.html. Figure 7-17 shows the Microsoft test site.

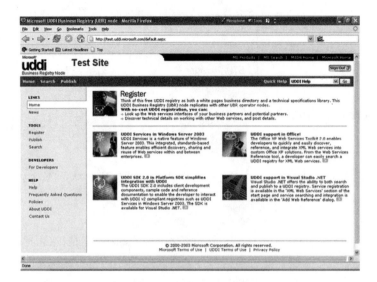

Figure 7-17. *UDDI test Web site*

With basic knowledge of UDDI, you are now ready to build the STP provider consortium, and to achieve this, you will use the Microsoft test registry database. So, the first step is to publish the Web service; to do this, you need to authenticate your identity using a Microsoft Passport account. To ease this authentication process, we have created the following Passport credential especially for this exercise:

- *Passport account*: stpinteroperability@hotmail.com
- *Password*: chapter7

To publish the Web service, click the Publish link; this will open the instruction page with a sign-in icon; by clicking this icon, you will be redirected to the Passport login page. Enter the previous credential to get successfully authenticated. After you have been authenticated, you will be presented with a page that enables you to register business- and service-related information, as shown in Figure 7-18.

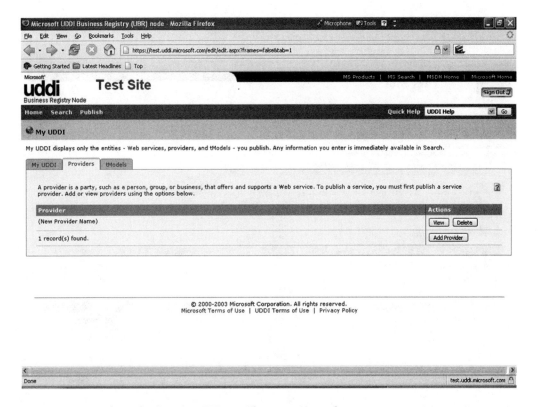

Figure 7-18. *Providers tab where new STP providers are registered*

The Providers tab is the starting point where individual STP providers are registered and are asked to enter business and service details. Since you are using the test registry, you are allowed to enter a maximum of only one provider, and it is created by default. Therefore, the only possible option is to update the default provider details. To edit provider information, simply click View. You will be presented with a new page, as shown in Figure 7-19.

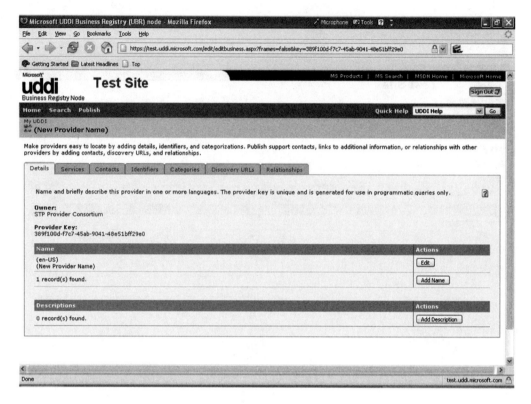

Figure 7-19. *Provider registration page with various other options represented in the form of tabs*

Figure 7-20 reflects updated information about the provider.

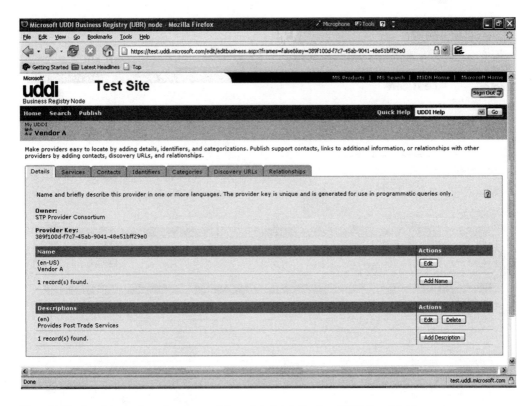

Figure 7-20. *Provider registration page with updated details about STP-Provider A*

The important section of the provider information is the Services tab that exposes the service-level details. It enables the STP providers to register Web service information along with the physical location of the WSDL document. Also, there are no restrictions on the number of Web services that are allowed to register. Figure 7-21 shows the details with a new service registered.

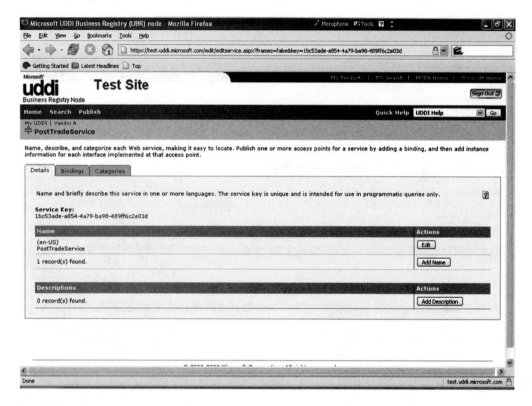

Figure 7-21. *A new service registered*

The Bindings tab records network endpoint details of the Web service and also a technical description of the service including the WSDL document. For demonstration purposes, we entered the URL of the PostTradeService Web service, as shown in Figure 7-22.

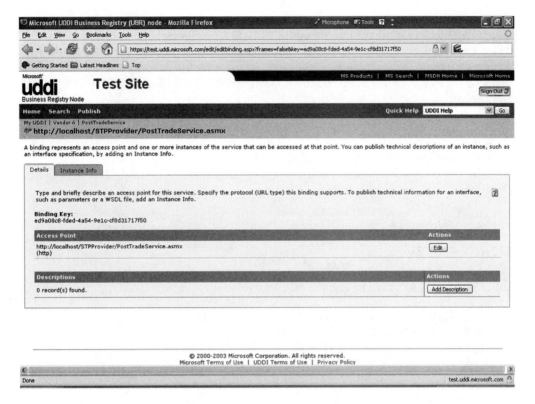

Figure 7-22. *Service registration page with updated information about PostTradeService*

After entering binding information, you complete the service registration process and also make this Web service endpoint information available to the outside world. Now, any consumer who wants to know the Web service endpoint must first construct a proper query request and submit it to the registry. Even though the UDDI Web site provided by Microsoft and IBM already offers a strong search capability that allows you to search for services based on business name, contact details, and so on, it requires manual user intervention. What you need is a programmatic way of integrating this search feature so that the application can dynamically select the implementation of a service at runtime. To build this feature, it is simply a matter of understanding the UDDI request and response XML structures and then using SOAP to submit them to the UDDI registry. There is nothing wrong with this approach except it demands a precise understanding of the UDDI specification. To simplify this task, Microsoft provides a managed .NET wrapper that ships with the UDDI SDK; you can download it from http://msdn.microsoft.com.

The UDDI .NET SDK enables .NET applications to interact with the UDDI registry at runtime; it also provides other goodies such as code samples and API documentation. The original motivation of the UDDI SDK was to provide an object-oriented abstraction over UDDI messages, similar to the one provided by Visual Studio .NET and the .NET Framework to create Web services. Using the UDDI SDK, developers can perform both discover and publish Web services.

Now we will demonstrate an example of how to use the UDDI .NET assembly that will further strengthen your understanding. In Listing 7-4, the location of the STP-Provider A Web service was hard-coded inside the proxy file. Nowhere did you make a provision to read the Web service location from an external source such as an application configuration file, which is the right way to do things. But with the STP provider consortium in place, STP-Provider B knows a central repository exists that provides all the necessary details required to handshake with the STP-Provider A Web service. Therefore, the STP-Provider B program will directly use the UDDI SDK to retrieve this information, mainly the network endpoint details of the Web service. Listing 7-5 illustrates how to handle this scenario.

Listing 7-5. *STP-Provider B Using the UDDI API to Programmatically Determine STP-Provider A Web Service Location*

```
using System;
using Microsoft.Uddi;
using Microsoft.Uddi.Api;
using Microsoft.Uddi.Business;
using Microsoft.Uddi.Service;
using Microsoft.Uddi.Binding;


namespace STPConsortium
{
  class ServiceConsumer
  {
    [STAThread]
    static void Main(string[] args)
    {
      //instantiate Web service proxy
      STPProvider.PostTradeService postTradeSvc = new
                           STPProvider.PostTradeService();
      //prepare contract note information
      STPProvider.ContractNoteInfo contractNote = new
                           STPProvider.ContractNoteInfo();
      contractNote.Symbol = "MSFT";
      contractNote.Price = 25;
      contractNote.Quantity=100;
      contractNote.BuySell = STPProvider.BuySellEnum.Buy;

      //Fetch service endpoint information using UDDI
      postTradeSvc.Url = GetServiceLocation();

      //submit contract note through Web service
      int contractNo =postTradeSvc.SubmitContractNote(contractNote);
      //display contract no received from Web service
      Console.WriteLine("Contract Note : " +contractNo);
    }

    public static string GetServiceLocation()
    {
      Console.WriteLine("Querying UDDI Registry...");
      //Assign the network endpoint of UDDI Web services
      Inquire.Url = "http://test.uddi.microsoft.com/inquire";

      //Find the provider
      FindBusiness findProvider = new FindBusiness();
      findProvider.Names.Add("STP-Provider A");
      BusinessList providerList = findProvider.Send();
      BusinessInfo  provider = providerList.BusinessInfos[0];
      ServiceInfo providerService = provider.ServiceInfos[0];
```

```
    //Find the service details
    GetServiceDetail findService = new GetServiceDetail();
    findService.ServiceKeys.Add(providerService.ServiceKey);
    ServiceDetail sd = findService.Send();
    BusinessService service = sd.BusinessServices[0];
    BindingTemplate template =  service.BindingTemplates[0];

    //Retrieve the service URL
    Console.WriteLine("Provider Endpoint : " +template.AccessPoint.Text);
    return template.AccessPoint.Text;
    }
  }
}
```

To compile the program described in Listing 7-5, the UDDI .NET assembly needs to be referenced from the GAC. Figure 7-23 displays the console output where the service endpoint information is dynamically determined at runtime by querying the UDDI registry.

Figure 7-23. *Console application showing how STP-Provider A Web service endpoint information is retrieved by querying the UDDI registry*

WS-*Specification* (WS-*)

You have learned how specifications such as WSDL, XML, XSD, SOAP, and UDDI offer a simple way to build distributed applications and bring a sense of order and smoothness to envisioning an STP platform where STP providers collaborate to offer various services in an interoperable fashion. Although these basic Web service standards prove useful in addressing a simple business requirement, they fail to handle a complex business scenario. For instance, the first concern raised by market participants who intend to transact in the Web service world is related to message security. Currently, you can think of leveraging transport protocol security such as SSL or IPSec. This kind of transport-level dependency will introduce a strong coupling between the Web service and its underlying transport, but the truth of the matter is that the Web service technology is not affinitized to any particular transport protocol. So, you require message-layer security that promises to bake security ingredients within the actual message instead of wrapping them up, which is what SSL or IPSec does.

Currently, the basic Web Service stack depicted in Figure 7-24 faces several technology limitations that restrict many financial organizations from embracing the Web service technology to its fullest extent. Clearly, message security is one of them, but you will also notice lack of support for problems that are linked to reliability and the transactional aspect of services. For the Web service technology to make it into today's STP mainstream, it is important that it addresses the QOS requirements needed to implement large-scale distributed systems. Furthermore, the goal must be to define quality service requirements in a technology-neutral manner and enable organizations to leverage them regardless of the underlying technology implementation. To address these requirements, a team consisting of Microsoft, IBM, BEA Systems, and VeriSign was formed. The ultimate mission of this team is to produce a set of specifications to incorporate various qualities of features required to enable the widespread acceptance and implementation of Web services. WS-* was the output of this collaboration effort.

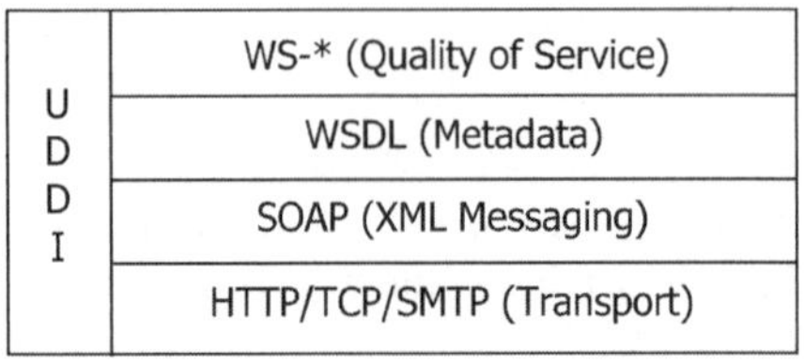

U D D I	WS-* (Quality of Service)
	WSDL (Metadata)
	SOAP (XML Messaging)
	HTTP/TCP/SMTP (Transport)

Figure 7-24. *Web service stack*

WS-* is a collection of specifications that sit on top of the standard Web service specification. WS-* is based on XML, SOAP, and WSDL and provides a first-class foundation to build such specifications in an interoperable and loosely coupled manner. WS-* is popularly known as second-generation Web services because it extends the capabilities of basic Web service functionality to a new level where it stands shoulder to shoulder with other popular distributed systems such as CORBA and COM in terms of its feature set. The features offered by WS-* are already available in legacy distributed technology, but replicating this feature in the Web service world is a revolutionary step. WS-* is composed of individual specifications, and each of these specifications is discrete and independent of one another. For example, the WS-Security specification provides the building block for building secure Web services. Similarly, the WS-Policy specification defines the rules and constraints of a Web service. Each specification outlines a modular solution to a particular requirement of the business.

Web Services Enhancement (WSE) 2.0

Web Services Enhancement (WSE) is an add-on framework to the existing ASP.NET Web service platform (see Figure 7-25). It is a development toolkit provided by Microsoft to integrate WS-* for building second-generation Web services. It is similar to the ASP.NET Web service infrastructure that addresses the basic requirement of Web services, but WSE is one step ahead and provides a programming model to use various quality of service (QOS) features offered by WS-*. It is designed to be used with Visual Studio .NET, which promises to bring higher productivity to a developer's desk. Without the WSE toolkit, it would be extremely time-consuming for developers to build WS-* features into an application; the developer would first have to understand the minute details of each individual specification and then accordingly build an implementation platform. WSE relieves developers from this effort by providing a developer-friendly API and abstracts away the internal message-level complexities related to each specification.

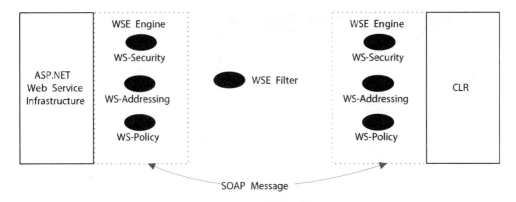

Figure 7-25. *WSE architecture*

From an architectural perspective, WSE is a message-processing engine that can be used both by the Web service and by its consumers. At the heart of the engine is the pipeline infrastructure that orchestrates the processing of SOAP messages. The pipeline is constructed by chaining together individual WSE filters. The idea behind filters is that they encapsulate the functionality of a particular specification of WS-*, which is then plugged into the pipeline. For example, WS-Security and WS-Addressing will be realized in two separate filters. The work done by the filter mainly depends on the direction of the message. For instance, if the nature of the message is inbound, then the responsibility of processing is assigned to an inbound filter; similarly, if it is an outbound message, then it is assigned to an outbound filter. The message processing and handling logic in both cases is completely different. Inbound filters are dedicated to parsing incoming SOAP messages and then applying specification-level processing. On other hand, outbound filters are dedicated to augmenting SOAP messages with specification-level details. This also proves that each filter has complete control over the message, and it can modify any part of a SOAP envelope. Often, a filter's favorite shelter place is the SOAP header where it records specification control information.

By modularizing specifications in the form of filters, WSE promotes higher extensibility because filters can be easily added or removed from the pipeline. It also means as WS-* evolves there will be new specifications rolled out, and to integrate them into the WSE platform, you need to develop an appropriate filter and then integrate it with the pipeline. The overall goal of WSE is to provide developers with a lot of power to deal with individual specifications by using a set of classes instead of directly interfacing with low-level message details that are cumbersome and prone to human error. However, WSE currently doesn't yet support the entire gamut of WS-*. One of the reasons is that most of the specifications are still evolving, and there is a high possibility that WSE may undergo several rounds of changes before it appears in the commercial world. Therefore, Microsoft bundled WSE with the most popular specifications such as WS-Security, WS-Policy, WS-Addressing, WS-Attachments, WS-Referral, WS-SecureConversation, and WS-Trust.

To start using WSE, you need to install the WSE 2.0 development kit, which is freely downloadable from the MSDN Web Services Developer Center. During the installation phase, you will be provided with various set-up types; you should choose the Visual Studio Developer option, which installs WSE runtime files and documentation and integrates with the Visual Studio .NET IDE (see Figure 7-26).

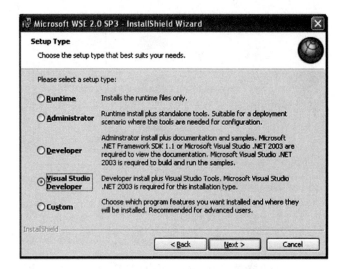

Figure 7-26. *WSE set-up options*

Assuming installation went through successfully, then you can begin to set up the WSE development environment. By choosing the Visual Studio Developer option during the installation stage, you install an additional GUI tool exclusively meant to specify WSE settings. This tool is available inside Visual Studio .NET and is activated by right-clicking the project in Solution Explorer and selecting WSE Settings 2.0, as illustrated in Figure 7-27.

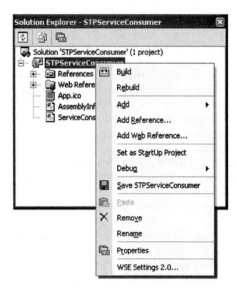

Figure 7-27. *Menu to invoke the WSE Configuration dialog box*

Figure 7-28 shows the WSE settings dialog box with the various configuration information organized in tabs. Each tab relates to information specific to a particular Web service specification supported by WSE. The most important one is the General tab, which is used to enable WSE support in the project. To trigger this support, check the Enable This Project for Web Services Enhancements box. After checking this box, the tool automatically reconfigures the project settings to reference the `Microsoft.Web.Services2` assembly from the GAC. Another immediate impact is a change in the application configuration file: a new section, `<microsoft.web.services2>`, is added especially to record WSE-related configuration settings.

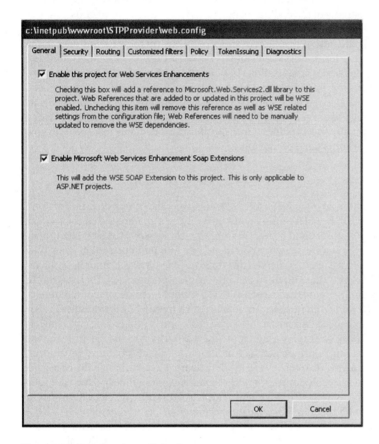

Figure 7-28. *WSE settings dialog box*

We demonstrated how to enable WSE support in Visual Studio .NET, but you still need to do a bit more tweaking. You need to marry the basic Web service infrastructure with the advanced infrastructure provided by WSE. So, obviously, you would expect both the Web service and its consumer to be affected by this change. Assuming the Web service is built on the ASP.NET infrastructure, which is very true in this case, then it is mandatory to check the Enable Microsoft Web Services Enhancement Soap Extensions box. This step integrates the WSE pipeline processing model with the ASP.NET infrastructure, which allows WSE filters to intercept the inbound/outbound message and perform the necessary actions on it. On the other hand, if WSE is enabled on the service consumer end that interacts with the Web service using a proxy class, then you need to update the base class of the proxy. As you are aware, the proxy class is generated whenever a new Web reference is added to the project, so the proxy base class change discussed is not required in the case of a new Web reference because Visual Studio .NET automatically creates WSE-aware proxy classes. It is required only when the existing proxy class needs to be changed. To implement this, you need to modify the base class, `System.Web.Services.Protocols.SoapHttpClientProtocol`, from which the proxy class inherits to `Microsoft.Web.Services2.WebServicesClientProtocol`. After applying this modification, the service consumer is fully compliant with WSE.

After making the changes recommended in this section, you are now ready to embrace the WSE class library in your code. In fact, you will notice how easy it is to configure the project to use the WSE framework both from the Web service and from its consumer. Going forward, you will also observe how WSE has simplified many of the coding-related tasks with the help of wizards. There is absolutely no doubt that WSE comes as a boon to organizations that intend to enter the Web service world. Without WSE support, organizations would have shown a lukewarm response because in the past couple of years there has been a huge surge in the number of Web service specifications proposed by vendors. This raised fear among many organizations because there has not been a single implementation platform that supports this specification; but then Microsoft stepped in and showed its commitment by periodically releasing new versions of WSE. In the upcoming section, we will dig in further to the programming level and cover some of the popular specifications supported by WSE. Although it is impossible to cover all aspects of individual specifications in detail, our goal is to give you a basic understanding of the important specifications.

WS-Security

The biggest concern raised by financial organizations is how to protect the sanctity of information exchanged with business partners. In broader terms, organizations want a guarantee that transactions conducted over a public network are safe and protected from eavesdroppers' eyes. Organizations encounter many aspects of security such as integrity, confidentiality, and nonrepudiation when they work across public networks. We have already covered this topic in Chapter 6; the domain problem we are addressing here is different. What you need is an interoperable approach for integrating security features. We already demonstrated the use of basic Web service technology to interconnect various STP providers in the STP world, but the environment in which these STP providers live is complex and hostile in nature. They need additional sophisticated QOS, and message security is one of these attributes. You could propose or employ a transport-level security such as SSL or IPSec to protect Web services, but this assumption breaks the fundamental rule of transport neutrality. Although SSL and IPSec might provide in-transit integrity, they do not have the capability to provide end-to-end message security. Additionally, for Web services to get maximum mileage, it is essential that they support security as part of their basic technology infrastructure. As a result, Microsoft and IBM collaborated and came up with the new WS-Security specification.

WS-Security provides a foundation to enable security in Web services. This specification aims to integrate important attributes of security such as encryption, authentication, and digital signing in an interoperable and technology-neutral manner. It provides a standard mechanism to package and transport security-related information using SOAP and XML. Its goal is not to replace the existing security infrastructure; instead, it provides a unified framework to leverage various security models such as Kerberos and Public Key Infrastructure (PKI). The specification clearly outlines the list of changes required for adding security to SOAP messages. Without going into too much detail, readers interested to know more about WS-Security can refer to `http://docs.oasis-open.org/wss/2004/01/oasis-200401-wss-soap-message-security-1.0.pdf`.

Returning to the WS-Security specification, you will notice three important XML elements that form part of a WS-Security–enabled SOAP header. The first is the security token that represents authentication information also known as a *claim*. The second is the signature element that contains the digital signature of the message enclosed inside the body element of the SOAP envelope. The final element is the encryption element that contains an encrypted version of the original message. Together these three elements form the foundation of the WS-Security message structure (see Figure 7-29).

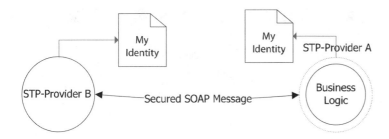

Figure 7-29. *Using WS-Security to secure SOAP message*

The next step is to focus on how to implement WS-Security features using WSE. To date, WSE is the first toolset to provide comprehensive support for implementing the WS-Security specification. To drive WS-Security in the STP world, you have to leverage its digital signature and encryption capability. Assuming STP providers have adopted a common medium of information exchange using the Web service platform, then the need for implementing digital certificates to meet authentication and message integrity purposes becomes apparent. Therefore, the next example beginning with a digital signature will show you how to implement this QOS in an interoperable manner using WSE 2.0.

The first prerequisite needed for the success of this scenario is a digital certificate. Digital certificates, as explained in Chapter 6, are the most reliable way to prove one's identity. Therefore, it makes sense to make it part of regulatory rule that individual market participants and STP providers in the STP world own a digital certificate that not only proves their identities but also is used to securely protect the integrity of a message. Getting a certificate is a formal process that requires the approval of a CA such as VeriSign. But for demonstration purposes, we will use the makecert tool to generate a self-signed certificate:

```
makecert -n "CN=STP-Provider A" -ss My -sr currentuser
        -sp "Microsoft Enhanced Cryptographic Provider v1.0" -sky exchange
        -sk "STP-Provider A Key Container"

makecert -n "CN=STP-Provider B" -ss My -sr currentuser
        -sp "Microsoft Enhanced Cryptographic Provider v1.0" -sky exchange
        -sk "STP-Provider B Key Container"
```

Execute the previous command under the Visual Studio .NET command prompt. This will generate two certificates and store them in a central location known as a *certificate store*. The certificate store is a physical repository that looks after the management of certificates. Each individual user or Windows service or machine can have its own certificate store. Additionally, each store is logically divided into a store category; there is always a Personal category, also known as a My category, used to store personal certificates. The two certificates recently generated are stored under the current user certificate store and available in the Personal category of that store. To view these certificates, launch the MMC, and add the Certificates snap-in that displays certificates according to their storage characteristics; in this case, it is the currently logged-in user. It also displays the category information about the store. Figure 7-30 depicts the certificates snap-in, which is a GUI tool to store, enumerate, delete, and verify certificates.

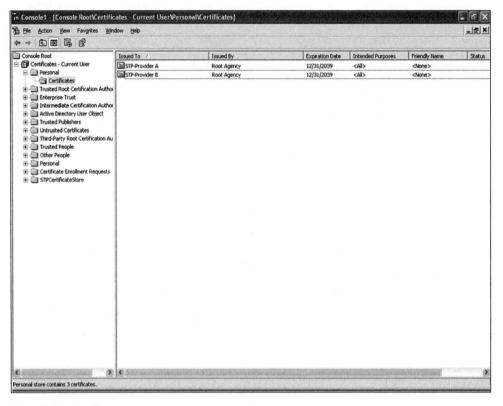

Figure 7-30. *Certificate store*

This completes the certificate installation process. Both STP-Provider A and STP-Provider B certificates are installed under the Personal category of the current user store. To reiterate, the STP-Provider A is the actual service provider, and STP-Provider B, which is a service provider, in this context plays the role of a service consumer that forwards the contract note information to STP-Provider A. The next step is to write the code implemented on the service consumer end: STP-Provider B. The overall goal of this code example is to secure the contract note information submitted by STP-Provider B to STP-Provider A using a digital signature. To start, you need to perform the following steps:

1. Create a new console application called **SecureSTPConsumer** using Visual Studio .NET.

2. Enable WSE 2.0 support for this project using the WSE GUI tool. This will automatically add a reference to the `Microsoft.Web.Services2` assembly.

3. Add a Web reference to the STP-Provider A Web service at `http://localhost/STPProvider/PostTradeService.asmx`. A WSE-aware proxy class will be automatically generated and added to the project. The final project structure must look like Figure 7-31.

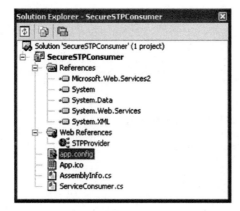

Figure 7-31. *Solution Explorer view of the consumer application*

4. Update the application configuration file; the `<x509>` element specifies how WSE verifies the certificate. Without this setting, WSE will raise an exception because a test root signs the test certificates. To instruct WSE to honor the certificates signed by the test root, the following changes are required:

```
<configuration>
  <configSections>
    <section name="microsoft.web.services2"
             type="Microsoft.Web.Services2.Configuration.WebServicesConfiguration,
                   Microsoft.Web.Services2, Version=2.0.0.0, Culture=neutral,
                   PublicKeyToken=31bf3856ad364e35" />
  </configSections>
  <microsoft.web.services2>
    <security>
    <x509 allowTestRoot="true"/>
    </security>
    <diagnostics />
  </microsoft.web.services2>
</configuration>
```

Now that you have completed the necessary configuration-related changes required on the consumer (STP-Provider B) end, the final step is to write code that digitally signs the contract note, as shown in Listing 7-6.

Listing 7-6. *STP-Provider B Digitally Signing Contract Note Information, Before Forwarding to STP-Provider A*

```
using System;
using System.Net;
using Microsoft.Web.Services2;
using Microsoft.Web.Services2.Security;
using Microsoft.Web.Services2.Security.Tokens;
using Microsoft.Web.Services2.Security.X509;
```

```
namespace SecureSTPConsumer
{
  class ServiceConsumer
  {
    [STAThread]
    static void Main(string[] args)
    {
      STPProvider.PostTradeServiceWse postTradeSvc= new
                           STPProvider.PostTradeServiceWse();
      STPProvider.ContractNoteInfo contractNote = new
                           STPProvider.ContractNoteInfo();

      //Digitally Sign the Contract Note
      SignContractNote(postTradeSvc);

      //Create new contract info, and submit it to the STP-Provider A Web service
      contractNote.Symbol = "MSFT";
      contractNote.Price = 25;
      contractNote.Quantity=100;
      contractNote.BuySell = STPProvider.BuySellEnum.Buy;
      int ackId =postTradeSvc.SubmitContractNote(contractNote);

      //Verify the response received from STP-Provider A
      VerifyAckResponse(postTradeSvc);
      Console.WriteLine("Acknowledgement ID : " +ackId);
    }

    public static bool VerifyAckResponse(STPProvider.PostTradeServiceWse
                                                       postTradeSvc)
    {
      SoapContext respCtx = postTradeSvc.ResponseSoapContext;

      //Iterate through all Security elements
      foreach(ISecurityElement secElement in respCtx.Security.Elements)
      {
        //Check whether message is digitally signed
        if ( secElement is MessageSignature)
        {
          MessageSignature signature = (MessageSignature)secElement;
          X509SecurityToken signingToken = signature.SigningToken
                                    as X509SecurityToken;
          //Authenticate the Sender using any one of the attributes of Certificate
          //More secure way is to verify using the STP-Provider A public key
          if ( signingToken != null &&
               signingToken.Certificate.FriendlyDisplayName == "STP-Provider A" )
          {
            return true;
          }
        }
      }
      return false;
    }
```

```
public static void SignContractNote(STPProvider.PostTradeServiceWse
                                    postTradeSvc)
{
  //Open the current user certificate store, and look for Personal category
  X509CertificateStore localStore =
        X509CertificateStore.CurrentUserStore(X509CertificateStore.MyStore);
  localStore.OpenRead();

  //Find STP-Provider B Certificate
  X509CertificateCollection certCollection =
            localStore.FindCertificateBySubjectString("STP-Provider B");
  X509Certificate provCert = certCollection[0];

  //Create a new security token that is of X509 type
  //Token represent claim (authentication information)
  X509SecurityToken token = new X509SecurityToken(provCert);
  postTradeSvc.RequestSoapContext.Security.Tokens.Add(token);

  //Instruct WSE inbound filter to sign the message before it is transmitted
  //over the wire
  //The signature is computed based on a security token
  postTradeSvc.RequestSoapContext.Security.Elements.Add(
                          new MessageSignature(token));
  }
 }
}
```

In Listing 7-6, you will notice how easy it is to integrate the digital signature functionality. The important thing in Listing 7-6 is the namespaces that are imported in this project.

WSE outlines a straightforward approach by naming individual namespaces based upon the specification supported by them. For instance, classes that correspond to WS-Security are grouped under Microsoft.Web.Services2.Security. Stepping into the heart of the WSE class framework, you will find SoapContext, which represents an object-oriented representation of the SOAP message. It allows you to inspect the header and body of incoming SOAP messages. For outgoing SOAP messages, it provides the capability to record specification-level information both at the header level and at the body level.

Now that you have STP-Provider B that uses WS-Security to digitally sign the contract note information, the next step is to reconfigure the STP-Provider A Web service to recognize this digital signature and accordingly authenticate the sender of the message in addition to verifying the integrity of the message. To incorporate these changes, you need to slightly modify the STP-Provider A ASP.NET Web service project as follows:

1. Open the existing ASP.NET Web service project STPProvider (the STP-Provider A Web service) using Visual Studio .NET.

2. Enable WSE 2.0 support for this project using the WSE GUI tool. Remember, this is an ASP.NET Web service project, so you need to also enable Microsoft WSE SOAP extensions.

3. Update the web.config file; the <x509> element is added that specifies how WSE verifies the certificate. Also, a few additional settings are specific to the authentication mechanism of the ASP.NET application. By default, the ASP.NET application is executed under the security context of the ASPNET user account, which has limited privileges. To get around this problem, you can tweak the configuration file to impersonate the currently logged-in user:

```
<?xml version="1.0" encoding="utf-8"?>
<configuration>
  <configSections>
```

```
            <section name="microsoft.web.services2"
                type="Microsoft.Web.Services2.Configuration.WebServicesConfiguration,
                    Microsoft.Web.Services2, Version=2.0.0.0, Culture=neutral,
                    PublicKeyToken=31bf3856ad364e35" />
        </configSections>
        <system.web>
          <identity userName=<Logged in user id> password=<Logged in user Password>
                impersonate="true" >
          </identity>
          <webServices>
            <soapExtensionTypes>
              <add type="Microsoft.Web.Services2.WebServicesExtension,
                      Microsoft.Web.Services2, Version=2.0.0.0, Culture=neutral,
                      PublicKeyToken=31bf3856ad364e35" priority="1" group="0" />
            </soapExtensionTypes>
          </webServices>
        </system.web>
        <microsoft.web.services2>
          <security>
            <x509 allowTestRoot="true"/>
          </security>
        </microsoft.web.services2>
      </configuration>
```

After the previous configuration changes have been updated successfully, then you are ready to update the Web service that will verify the digital signature received from STP-Provider B. The code will also include a modification to digitally sign the response message using the STP-Provider A certificate, which is then returned to STP-Provider B. Listing 7-7 shows how to achieve this functionality.

Listing 7-7. *STP-Provider A Digitally Verifying the Contract Note Information Submitted by STP-Provider B and Digitally Signing the Response Message Sent to STP-Provider B*

```
using System;
using System.IO;
using System.Threading;
using System.Collections;
using System.ComponentModel;
using System.Data;
using System.Diagnostics;
using System.Web;
using System.Web.Services;
using Microsoft.Web.Services2;
using Microsoft.Web.Services2.Security;
using Microsoft.Web.Services2.Security.Tokens;
using Microsoft.Web.Services2.Security.X509;

namespace STPProvider
{
  public class ContractNoteInfo
  {
    public string Symbol;
    public int Quantity;
    public double Price;
    public BuySellEnum BuySell;
  }
  public enum BuySellEnum
  {
```

```
    Buy,
    Sell
}
public class PostTradeService : System.Web.Services.WebService
{
    public PostTradeService()
    {
    }

    [WebMethod]
    public int SubmitContractNote(ContractNoteInfo contractNote)
    {
        //Verify the Sender Information ( STP-Provider B)
        VerifySignatureOrigin();

        //Send the digitally signed response to STP-Provider B using STP-Provider A
        //Certficate.
        SignAckResponse();
        return 1;
    }

    public void SignAckResponse()
    {
        //Open the current user certificate store, and look for Personal category
        X509CertificateStore localStore =
                X509CertificateStore.CurrentUserStore(X509CertificateStore.MyStore);
        localStore.OpenRead();

        //Find STP-Provider A Certificate
        X509CertificateCollection certCollection =
                localStore.FindCertificateBySubjectString("STP-Provider A");
        X509Certificate provCert = certCollection[0];

        //Create a new security token that is of X509 type
        //Token represent claim (authentication information)
        X509SecurityToken token = new X509SecurityToken(provCert);
        ResponseSoapContext.Current.Security.Tokens.Add(token);

        //Instruct WSE outbound filter to sign the message before it is transmitted
        //over the wire
        //The signature is computed based on a security token
        ResponseSoapContext.Current.Security.Elements.Add(new
                                MessageSignature(token));

    }

    public bool VerifySignatureOrigin()
    {
        SoapContext reqCtx = RequestSoapContext.Current;

        //Iterate through all Security elements
        foreach(ISecurityElement secElement in reqCtx.Security.Elements)
        {
            //Check if message is digitally signed
            if ( secElement is MessageSignature)
            {
```

```
                    MessageSignature signature = (MessageSignature)secElement;
                    X509SecurityToken signingToken = signature.SigningToken
                                        as X509SecurityToken;
                    //Authenticate the Sender using any one of the attributes of Certificate
                    //More secure way is to verify using STP-Provider B public key
                    if ( signingToken != null &&
                            signingToken.Certificate.FriendlyDisplayName == "STP-Provider B" )
                    {
                        return true;
                    }
                }
            }
            return false;
        }
    }
}
```

In Listing 7-7 not even a single line of code does the verification of the digital signature. This verification process is automatically built into the WSE framework. As you might you have guessed, the Web service doesn't have to write any code to verify the signature, but it is definitely interested in knowing the outcome of the verification process. First, if the signature is tampered with, it will ultimately fail the verification process, and then WSE raises a SOAP exception and communicates to the sender of the message. Otherwise, WSE populates the instance of SoapContext with the sender certificate information and invokes the Web service method.

Clearly, WSE abstracts away most of the coding complexities usually encountered during the message signing and verification process. In the absence of WSE, developers will be forced to accomplish this task manually, which is certainly prone to human errors. Building on WS-Security, WSE makes it easy to implement security. Digital signature capability is one aspect of WSE; it also supports encryption technology. Using encryption technology, SOAP messages are protected from prying eyes; this is a big leap from transport-level security to message-level security. Fortunately, WSE supports asymmetric encryption, and you will see how easy it is to include it in the existing code example.

For asymmetric encryption to work, STP-Provider B has to use the STP-Provider A public key to encrypt the message. This will ensure that only STP-Provider A, who is in possession of the private key, will be able to decrypt the message. On the Web service end, STP-Provider A, after the successful decryption of the message, encrypts the response message using the STP-Provider B public key. Again, only STP-Provider B, who owns the private key, will be able to interpret this message correctly. The following code describes how STP-Provider B encrypts the contract note information using the STP-Provider A public key:

```
using System;
using System.Net;
using Microsoft.Web.Services2;
using Microsoft.Web.Services2.Security;
using Microsoft.Web.Services2.Security.Tokens;
using Microsoft.Web.Services2.Security.X509;

namespace SecureSTPConsumer
{
    class ServiceConsumer
    {
        [STAThread]
        static void Main(string[] args)
        {
```

```
        STPProvider.PostTradeServiceWse postTradeSvc= new
                              STPProvider.PostTradeServiceWse();
        STPProvider.ContractNoteInfo contractNote = new
                              STPProvider.ContractNoteInfo();


        //Encrypt the Contract Note Information
        EncryptContractNote(postTradeSvc);

        //Create new contract info. and submit it to STP-Provider A Web service
        contractNote.Symbol = "MSFT";
        contractNote.Price = 25;
        contractNote.Quantity=100;
        contractNote.BuySell = STPProvider.BuySellEnum.Buy;

        int ackId =postTradeSvc.SubmitContractNote(contractNote);

        Console.WriteLine("Acknowledgement ID :" + ackId);
    }

    public static void EncryptContractNote(STPProvider.PostTradeServiceWse
                                    postTradeSvc)
    {
      //Open the current user certificate store, and look for Personal category
      X509CertificateStore localStore =
              X509CertificateStore.CurrentUserStore(X509CertificateStore.MyStore);
      localStore.OpenRead();

      //Find STP-Provider A Certificate
      X509CertificateCollection certCollection =
              localStore.FindCertificateBySubjectString("STP-Provider A");
      X509Certificate provCert = certCollection[0];

      //Create a new security token that is of X509 type
      //Token represent claim (authentication information)
      X509SecurityToken token = new X509SecurityToken(provCert);
      postTradeSvc.RequestSoapContext.Security.Tokens.Add(token);

      //Instruct WSE inbound filter to encrypt the message before it is
      //transmitted over the wire
      postTradeSvc.RequestSoapContext.Security.Elements.Add(new
                                    EncryptedData(token));
    }
  }
}
```

On the STP-Provider A end, when the Web service examines the SOAP header and determines that the actual message is encrypted, it retrieves the correct private key associated with the certificate used by STP-Provider B to encrypt the message and finally decrypts the message. If decryption happens successfully, then the Web service method is invoked. Otherwise, a SOAP fault is raised and communicated to the sender. Assuming decryption went through without any problems, then STP-Provider A constructs the acknowledgment confirmation message, encrypts it using the STP-Provider B public key, and forwards it to STP-Provider B. The following are the code modifications required on the STP-Provider A end:

```
using System;
using System.IO;
```

```
using System.Threading;
using System.Collections;
using System.ComponentModel;
using System.Data;
using System.Diagnostics;
using System.Web;
using System.Web.Services;
using Microsoft.Web.Services2;
using Microsoft.Web.Services2.Security;
using Microsoft.Web.Services2.Security.Tokens;
using Microsoft.Web.Services2.Security.X509;

namespace STPProvider
{
  public class ContractNoteInfo
  {
    public string Symbol;
    public int Quantity;
    public double Price;
    public BuySellEnum BuySell;
  }
  public enum BuySellEnum
  {
    Buy,
    Sell
  }
  public class PostTradeService : System.Web.Services.WebService
  {
    public PostTradeService()
    {
    }

    [WebMethod]
    public int SubmitContractNote(ContractNoteInfo contractNote)
    {

      //Encrypt the Response
      EncryptAckResponse();
      return 1;
    }

    public void EncryptAckResponse()
    {
      //Open the current user certificate store, and look for Personal category
      X509CertificateStore localStore =
          X509CertificateStore.CurrentUserStore(X509CertificateStore.MyStore);
      localStore.OpenRead();

      //Find STP-Provider B Certificate
      X509CertificateCollection certCollection =
            localStore.FindCertificateBySubjectString("STP-Provider B");
      X509Certificate provCert = certCollection[0];
```

```
    //Create a new security token that is of X509 type
    //Token represent claim (authentication information)
    X509SecurityToken token = new X509SecurityToken(provCert);
    ResponseSoapContext.Current.Security.Tokens.Add(token);

    //Instruct WSE inbound filter to encrypt the message before it is
    //transmitted over the wire
    ResponseSoapContext.Current.Security.Elements.Add(new EncryptedData(token));

   }
  }
}
```

The code for encrypting/decrypting a SOAP message is no different from the digital signing/verification code. Both share many similarities, mainly from a programmatic perspective; however, when it comes to actual execution, they emit completely different behavior. The important thing to take away from this brief tour of WS-Security is that it establishes a standard mechanism to protect a SOAP message, and it is a big step forward in promoting Web services in the STP world.

WS-Policy

The interaction between a service provider and a service requestor is deemed successful only when information provided by the requestor is complete and meets the provider expectation. The level of expectation depends directly upon the level of information shared by the service provider to its requestor. In a service-oriented environment, you already have WSDL that fleshes out the details of the functional description of the Web service published by the service provider to its requestor. However, WSDL falls short when it comes to outlining the nonfunctional characteristics of a Web service. For example, based on the STP-Provider A WSDL, you have no way to find out the quality of services, such as message signing or encryption. Additionally, STP-Provider A will enforce its own domain-level rules and constraints when accepting messages from other STP providers. This kind of information can be communicated only through documentation or some other communication channel. To close this gap, the specification WS-Policy was released (see Figure 7-32).

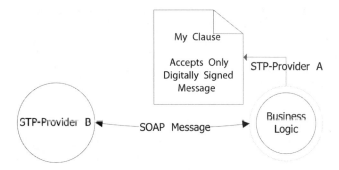

Figure 7-32. *Using WS-Policy to enforce constraints and rules*

WS-Policy allows you to associate rules and constraints to a Web service in an interoperable manner. It complements WSDL by separating out the nonfunctional aspects of a Web service. It is a general-purpose framework to formalize various kinds of policies within a Web service. Each of these specific policies encodes a discipline that needs to be enforced during the message-processing stage. For example, STP-Provider A may enforce digital signature technology, and any information that is not digitally signed will be blatantly rejected. This kind of assertion check is documented in the form of a policy. From a development perspective, WS-Policy is viewed as a declarative approach in listing the preferences and limitations of a Web service. This greatly increases development productivity because developers don't need to worry about writing any kind of validation code. Much of the grunt work is encapsulated inside a policy document, which is expressed using XML grammar.

WS-Policy represents a family of specifications that consists of WS-Policy, WS-PolicyAssertion, and WS-PolicyAttachment:

WS-Policy: This provides a generic XML-based framework to author the Web service policy.

WS-PolicyAsssertion: This represents rules or constraints imposed on the Web service in the form of individual policy assertions. These collections of policy assertions are implemented inside a policy expression document that itself is an XML document.

WS-PolicyAttachment: This refers to the association of a policy expression with a policy subject. *Policy subject* refers to any particular portion of a Web service; it can be the whole service, a particular operation, or a particular message.

The purpose of the WS-Policy specification is to provide a standard policy framework based on which specialized policies are defined. For example, the WS-SecurityPolicy specification extends WS-Policy to define WS-Security–specific policy assertions. WSE 2.0 enables support for WS-Policy by configuring and implementing various policy assertions in a configuration file. Furthermore, WSE has built-in support for the WS-Security policy and provides a wizard interface to activate individual policy assertions. WSE 2.0 also provides support for incorporating custom business validation rules in the form of policy assertions, and to implement it, developers have to undertake quite an amount of manual work. We clearly cannot explain the syntax-level functionality of WS-Policy within this short section, but you can refer to the WSE online documentation for more details. The primary focus of WS-Policy is to further enrich the metadata information of a Web service by documenting the required QOS properties and make it available to the service requestor.

WSE 2.0 already provides a set of predefined policy assertions falling under WS-SecurityPolicy and is integrated with VS .NET. To activate this policy, right-click the project node in VS .NET, and select WSE Settings, which opens a multitab configuration dialog box. The Policy tab allows you to configure security-related policy assertions such as that the body of SOAP messages must be digitally signed or encrypted (see Figure 7-33). It is also important to note that these policy assertions can be applied to both incoming and outgoing SOAP messages.

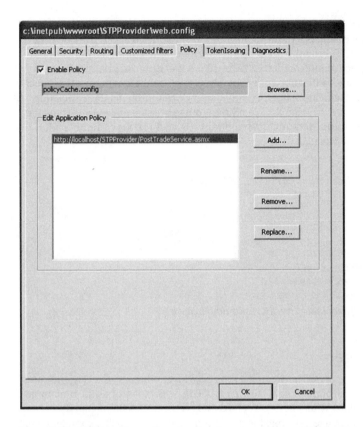

Figure 7-33. *WSE configuration showing how to configure Web service policies*

WS-Addressing

In a classic request-reply message exchange pattern implemented between STP-Provider A and STP-Provider B, there is strong dependency on HTTP as a default transport protocol. Because of HTTP's ubiquitous nature, it is highly favored over any other transport protocols. While this assumption works fine as long as the service requestor and provider are using the same transport protocols, in reality the message exchange may happen on protocols different from HTTP. For a message to be routed in a multitransport environment, you need a uniform addressing mechanism. Currently, the addressing information about the Web service is encoded inside the HTTP header, and the actual SOAP message forms part of the HTTP payload. This transport-level dependency needs to be removed in order to achieve transport standardization. Additionally, HTTP is a stateless protocol and is not suitable for interactions that are long running and stateful in nature.

The WS-Addressing specification promotes transport standardization by defining a common addressing mechanism and encapsulating it inside SOAP headers (see Figure 7-34). The attachment of addressing information further strengthens the mobility of a message and can be carried over multiple transport protocols. It is extremely useful in handling a multihop scenario where the message travels across multiple intermediaries before it reaches its final destination. The intent of this specification is to keep the original sender, destination, and reply address information intact. This specification serves as a building block to incorporate asynchronous behavior between Web services.

For example, it is possible for STP-Provider B to send a one-way request to STP-Provider A using HTTP. STP-Provider A, after processing the request, notifies STP-Provider B about the outcome using TCP. As you can see, both STP-Provider A and STP-Provider B were completely decoupled from each other, and the only piece of information STP-Provider A had is the original sender reply address, which itself is sufficient for notification purposes. There is no doubt that many other specifications such as WS-ReliableMessaging have been extended upon WS-Addressing. By associating additional sets of addressing headers, a message completely turns out to be self-sufficient and transport independent. Furthermore, it opens the door to implementing an asynchronous communication pattern between the requestor and provider.

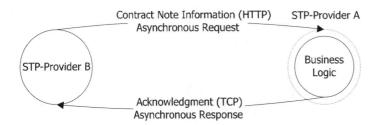

Figure 7-34. *Using WS-Addressing to achieve transport standardization*

WS-MetadataExchange

Metadata is the key to enabling interaction between a service provider and requestor. Currently, the service provider supplies three types of metadata. The first is WSDL, which describes the functional characteristics of a Web service along with wire-level details. Next is the XSD Schema that describes the structural aspect of the XML message. The final metadata information that further complements WSDL is WS-Policy, which describes the nonfunctional characteristics of a Web service. Together this metadata information plays an important role in enabling the loose-coupling behavior between the service requestor and provider. The service requestor based on this metadata information begins exchanging messages with the service provider. However, the key point here is before the real interaction kicks off, the service requestor must have complete access to metadata, and there is no standardized way to retrieve this information. Even though the provider may publish metadata information using some other communication medium, again it becomes native to that provider. What you really need is a standard way of accessing metadata-related information, and this is where WS-MetadataExchange comes to the rescue.

The WS-MetadataExchange specification allows the requestor to query metadata information directly from the service provider (see Figure 7-35). In other words, a bootstrap phase kicks off before the real interaction takes place between the provider and requestor. During this phase, the requestor can query the service metadata such as WSDL or WS-Policy directly from the service endpoint. This allows the requestor to get hold of a fresh copy of information and then incorporate any required modification. The dynamic retrieval of metadata also introduces run-time capabilities. For instance, by default during the handshaking phase, the service requestor can reconcile and verify the planned metadata with fresh metadata published by the service provider. Additionally, it also brings flexibility on the service provider end because it now allows for the easy modification of metadata. With WS-MetadataExchange it is possible for STP-Provider B to query the WS-Policy enforced by STP-Provider A for their interaction and apply that same set of policies on the message sent by STP-Provider B. Using this approach, exceptions can be easily caught on the requestor end instead of leaking on the provider end.

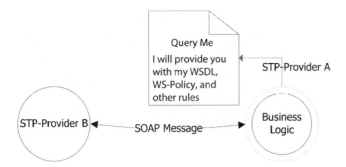

Figure 7-35. *Using WS-MetadataExchange to allow the consumer to query metadata information directly from the Web service*

WS-Referral

The major advantage of a SOAP message is it is complete and self-governed from all dimensions. By looking at the message, you can know its travel path and also the QOS applied on it. Furthermore, the loose-coupling nature between the sender and receiver of the SOAP message allows further message enrichment without any side effects on the sender or receiver. Keeping in mind this advantage, a new specification called WS-Referral is geared toward dictating the travel path of the message (see Figure 7-36). The WS-Referral specification transparently brings dynamic message-routing capabilities to the Web service world. This opens the door to implementing advanced features such as load balancing and content-based routing. Load balancing has been widely recognized and implemented in today's network topology; its important goal is to bring horizontal scalability by offloading the work-processing load on multiple machines. Similarly, content-based routing shares a similar spirit as load balancing, but its intention is different. The intent of content-based routing is to redirect messages received from the original sender to a different destination based on certain markups defined in message. This idea of content-based routing brings some elegant architectural style to the STP world.

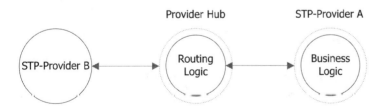

Figure 7-36. *Illustrates use of WS-Referral in implementing STP provider hub*

With WS-Referral in place, you can bring an additional important player known as an *STP provider hub* to the STP world. Imagine this hub as a virtual face representing all STP providers. STP providers will never directly communicate with each other; instead, all interaction will happen through this hub. STP providers will send the message to the STP provider hub that will then be routed automatically to the destined provider. This will definitely bring a major shift in the STP provider mind-set because it is obvious that the role of a hub will be played by a regulatory board that wants to oversee each transaction happening in the STP world and wants to maintain a healthy market practice. The STP provider hub will be equipped with the necessary intelligence of maintaining an audit of messages exchanged between different STP providers. Additionally, the hub can also act as a first line of defense for a provider that has built-in support to verify a digital message received from the sender. With a central hub in place, it brings an enormous amount of confidence to both the STP provider and the individual market participants. Both are assured that the regulations are fully followed and the regulatory board is in control of transactions occurring in the STP world.

Web Service Performance in the Financial Market

The performance of Web services is the most common concern in a capital market. However, there is no doubt Web services are the ideal technology platform for enabling business-to-business integration. But when discussed in terms of speed and performance, some issues hinder their adoption in real-time trading systems. In this chapter, we explained the benefit of Web services in the post-trade phase of the trading life cycle. However, in the pre-trade and trade phases, where the timely delivery of the data and the response is critical, it is essential to evaluate the suitability of Web services.

The primary issue with Web services is the large amount of XML data sent and received. XML has its own advantages, but it also contributes to an increase in network utilization and processing overhead, which is usually unacceptable in the pre-trade and trade phases of the trading life cycle. Real-time trading systems are engineered from a high-throughput and low-latency perspective, and the profit/loss of the trading desk to a large extent depends upon these systems.

Various strategies can address the performance problems of Web services, and they require a good amount of planning and evaluation:

Use of network accelerators: The processing demands of XML can be addressed by using specialized hardware accelerators that provide the end-to-end processing of XML and include XML schema validation, encryption, serialization, and so on.

XML compression: The higher network transmission cost associated with XML payload can be reduced to a large extent by applying a compression/decompression scheme.

Binary XML: Binary XML is a new approach to compact XML-based data and is already being used by the mobile industry. The WAP binary XML format is the standard officially recognized by the W3C to transfer content to mobile devices.

Use of faster transport protocol: Because of the request-response nature of HTTP, it is extremely difficult to introduce asynchronous communication. Therefore, it is always advisable to explore other transport protocols in search of better performance.

Avoid RPC style of invocation: Always design Web services with a message-based programming model in mind. This will result in fewer method calls and also reduce network round-trips.

Exploring the Business-Technology Mapping

Figure 7-37 represents the end-to-end interaction between market participants and the STP provider in the new Web-STP world. It demonstrates how the various components of Web services discussed so far fit together to streamline the overall process. The first and foremost requirement of Web-STP is the presence of an STP directory. The directory should be UDDI compliant and will publish information about the STP provider and market participants. With an STP directory in place, any market participant using UDDI can access information about the various STP providers and their offerings. Other prerequisites needed to complete this setup are an individual market participant and that the STP provider must have a valid digital certificate.

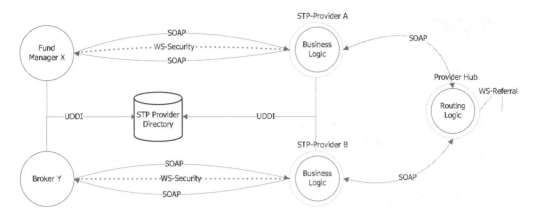

Figure 7-37. *Web-STP*

The communication with the STP provider is first initiated by market participants. The interaction involves a message sent by market participants to their registered STP providers through a Web service. This message is triggered by systems on the market participant end that may not necessarily be a Web service but that surely understands the protocols of Web services. The message is digitally signed using WS-Security and sent to the STP provider. On receiving this message, the STP provider verifies the signature and forwards it to the STP provider hub if the recipient of the message is registered with another STP provider. For instance, when the broker registered with STP-Provider B sends a message to the fund manager who is registered with STP-Provider A, then the message is routed to its final destination through the STP provider hub.

STP providers forward all messages meant for delivery with a different STP provider via the central hub, which in turn forwards the message to the terminating STP provider. The STP provider hub is a Web service that implements WS-Referral to incorporate smart routing logic. The role of hub can be played by any public or private agency, but generally it is preferable to assign this responsibility to a public agency. Additionally, the hub can act as a checkpoint where messages received from the STP provider are verified and are again digitally signed using the STP provider hub digital certificate. This step further strengthens the overall interaction because the recipient STP provider on receiving the message could verify whether the message is legitimate and approved by the STP provider hub.

By wiring the individual STP provider and market participant using Web service technology and other advanced WS-* specifications, we have illustrated the next-generation technology platform for automating end-to-end transaction processing in the financial trading world. Although the necessary infrastructure is in place, getting market participants and STP providers to come to this new Web-STP world will take some time. However, it is possible to start leveraging this infrastructure in a piece-by-piece manner. It is possible to start with WSDL, SOAP, and HTTPS and then slowly start augmenting this basic functionality with the advanced features provided by WS-*. It is clear that whatever strategy or vision the industry outlines, without reference to the Web service platform it would be incomplete.

Summary

In this chapter, we discussed following points:

- We talked about the need for interoperability between STP providers and how it will benefit business entities such as brokers, fund managers, and custodians in different ways.
- We discussed different types of challenges encountered in achieving interoperability.
- We covered the architecture of Web services and how the underlying principles ensure wide reach and enable interoperability between STP providers.
- We gave a brief overview of the building blocks of Web services such as SOAP and WSDL.
- We implemented a simple Web service that supports sending contract note information between STP providers in an interoperable fashion.
- We illustrated the advantage of a UDDI repository in establishing an STP provider consortium.
- We showed how WS-* extends the capabilities of basic Web service functionality by providing advanced features such as security, routing, and policy enforcement.
- We depicted a blueprint of Web-STP that demonstrates various components of Web services and how they connect an individual STP provider and market participants to represent the next-generation platform for automating STP.

CHAPTER 8
■ ■ ■

Equity Arbitrage

Dreams are the user interfaces of our goals.

In this chapter, we will explain the economics behind the arbitrage business. *Arbitrage* is a trading tactic exploited to make profits based on the price differences of stock quotes at two or more exchanges. The business-related sections of this chapter explain that price differences of stocks in multiple exchanges are not sufficient to determine profitability; instead, additional procedures are performed to arrive at a final decision. This chapter covers those additional steps. In the technical sections, we explain code-generation concepts and then provide comprehensive coverage of the CodeDOM framework. We also provide an outlook on .NET reflection features. This chapter is different from other chapters covered so far where we implemented a small prototype of the business framework; here we will skip the implementation part because it requires a considerable amount of effort that is simply outside the scope of this book. But our primary goal is to arm you with code-generation tactics that will help you automate most of the redundant tasks and also establish a strong foundation in building sophisticated arbitrage rule engines.

Introducing Arbitrage

Arbitrage is technically defined as profiting by buying something that is selling cheaper in one market and selling it simultaneously in another market where it is selling higher. A person who does arbitrage is called an *arbitrageur*.

Thus, every arbitrage has a buy leg and a sell leg, and in almost all cases they are executed simultaneously. The attempt is to lock and make profit on the price differential that the stock quotes at in two or more exchanges. Arbitrages can range from simple to complex. For the purposes of this chapter, we will discuss only the simple arbitrage strategy that involves equities traded on stock exchanges.

Assume an arbitrageur specializes in arbitrage in Advanced Micro Devices (AMD) shares. AMD shares would normally be quoting at the same price; assume it's trading at $40 in all exchanges where it trades. For some reason—say because of excessive demand in one of the exchanges—the price hits $40.25 while it continues to trade at $40 on all other exchanges. The arbitrageur tracking AMD will immediately buy AMD shares from exchanges where it is still quoting at $40 and sell an equal quantity of shares in the exchange where it is quoting at $40.25. By executing these two transactions simultaneously, the arbitrageur will make a neat profit of 25 cents per share.

However, even a price differential of $0.25 as cited in this example is rare, especially for highly liquid stocks. When price differentials arise in markets because of skewed demand or supply in one of the markets, arbitrageurs start selling where demand is more and start buying where demand is less, which in the process causes the prices to stabilize and makes them equal at both places.

Arbitrage is just another way of making money for market participants just as they make money using trades and investments. In fact, certain professionals specialize in making money only through arbitrage. Arbitrage opportunities in financial markets are rare; hence, specialized skills and specialized computer software are required to exploit them. Technically, regular retail investors can do arbitrage, but because of limited skill sets and limited capital, they are not exactly the right people to get into arbitrage. Arbitrageurs normally score over retail investors on arbitrage because of the following reasons:

They possess far more trading skill: They understand the markets well and understand the economics behind the price differentials. Sometimes price differentials are because of some genuine reason, and they will never converge. Lay traders would be lulled into believing that an arbitrage opportunity exists where actually there isn't any. Skilled arbitrageurs understand the precise risks associated and have access to vast pools of money and securities.

They have access to real-time information on multiple markets: The arbitrage business is all about cashing in on market opportunities fast. Difference in prices really don't exist for a long time, and they get bridged very fast—in fact, in a matter of subseconds. If real-time access to market data is not available, it is impossible to make decisions relating to arbitrage. Often, retail investors don't get ready access to real-time market data. Those retail investors who have regular jobs don't have the inclination to monitor the market on a subsecond basis. The arbitrage business has thus remained confined to arbitrage specialists.

They have complex trading software: Since price differentials are rare and the numbers of scrips listed on exchanges are high, arbitrageurs depend upon special arbitrage software that scours market data from each exchange of the arbitrageur's interests and keeps posting arbitrage opportunities. Either arbitrageurs act on these opportunities directly or they make the arbitrage systems interface with program trading systems that generate buy and sale orders automatically whenever arbitrage opportunities arise.

Costs Involved in Arbitrage Transactions

All transactions involve costs. If a transaction takes place through a broker, it involves brokerage. Otherwise, depending on the regulations, transactions include turnover taxes, transaction taxes, and clearing and settlement fees just as they are levied on any normal transaction. These are direct costs while doing any transaction. Then there are some indirect costs associated with such transactions. In the context of arbitrage, the biggest indirect cost involved is the interest cost involved in taking such arbitrage positions. One leg of arbitrage is a buy transaction. To execute such buy transactions, traders are required to pay margins and in some cases the full value of the transaction. If they pay the full value, a cost is associated with paying such money to the clearing corporation in the form of interest the money would have otherwise earned if it were simply kept in a bank fixed deposit. This interest is one component of the cost in arbitrage.

Similarly, the sale leg of the transaction has two scenarios. Either the arbitrageurs may have the securities with them for delivery or they may not. If they have the deliveries, they can deliver them at the time of pay-in. But if the arbitrage transaction is not completed and the arbitragers don't even have shares, they will have to borrow shares either privately or through established stock-lending facilities. Stock lending is a facility where shares can be borrowed just like money by paying interest. Institutions and individuals who have surplus shares try to generate interest income by lending their shares to the general public and trading fraternities that are in need of these shares to meet their delivery obligations. Arbitrageurs whose positions result in delivery to clearing corporations may utilize this facility by paying interest to the lender and using the securities for meeting delivery obligations. The interest they pay adds to their total arbitrage costs.

The cost involved in any arbitrage will thus be as follows:

Arbitrage costs = Direct transaction costs + Interest costs on buy leg + Interest costs on sale leg

It follows that arbitrages will be profitable only if the profit from the difference in the prices of the security at two places exceeds the cost of arbitrage. Otherwise, the arbitrage will be unviable. In this chapter, we will refer to these costs as *arbitrage cost* and *interest cost*.

In the earlier AMD example, $0.25 is the profit per share that the arbitrageur is making. However, this is the theoretical profit. In reality, several costs are associated with arbitrage. The arbitrageur will have to bear the transaction costs and will have to deliver shares in one exchange and receive shares from another exchange. There is a high chance that these will not be the same set of shares. Hence, to meet the payment commitment on one exchange and the delivery commitment on another, the arbitrageur will have to deploy cash on the exchange where the buy transaction was routed and give shares where they were sold (at the time of pay-in), and he will have to receive shares from the exchange where they were purchased and receive cash from where the shares were sold (at the time of pay-out). Hence, this implies that the arbitrageur will have to maintain an inventory of cash as well as AMD shares to complete this kind of transaction. Holding both cash and shares will involve interest cost. Cash is normally available to such operators usually in unlimited supply (limited by interest payment ability). Shares are in short supply because they are limited in numbers. Such arbitrage strategy will hence become dangerous if shares are in limited supply. Usually, a good stock-lending mechanism needs to be in place if these strategies have to be resolved.

Arbitrage and related operations have been criticized severely in the past, and many market crashes have been attributed to the orders that have been generated automatically by their systems. However, arbitrageurs benefit the market overall by bringing about liquidity where there is less liquidity and by helping to stabilize prices.

Other Forms of Arbitrage

In the previous examples, the arbitrage discussed is for the same security. However, arbitrage may happen on securities or assets that are either directly or inversely correlated with each other. Because of the scope of this book, we will limit this discussion only to equities shares. For example, assume there are two classes of shares issued by a company. Their prices must ideally move in tandem. Berkshire Hathaway, for example, has two classes of stocks: Class A and Class B (listed as BRKA and BRKB on the NYSE). A share of Class B common stock has 1/30th the right of a Class A stock. Holders of Class A shares have the option of converting the stock to Class B shares at their discretion. Holders of Class B shares cannot get their shares converted to Class A. The ratio of rights implies that Class B shares can never trade above a tiny fraction of 1/30th the price of a Class A share. Whenever the price differential exceeds 1/30th, arbitrageurs get active selling Class B stock and buying Class A stock, and this in turn pushes the prices of Class B stock back to 1/30th of the price of the Class A stock. Another interesting issue applies here. Since Class B shares don't hold the right to get their shares converted into Class A shares, this implies that holders of Class B shares are at a disadvantage compared to holders of Class A shares. This phenomenon may at times cause Class B shares to quote at a discount to the usual 1/30th of the price of Class A shares. However, if the discount becomes too large, once again the arbitrageurs will get active and bring the price differential close to 1/30th of the price of Class A shares.

Table 8-1 shows the prices of Class A stock and Class B stock of Berkshire Hathaway.

Table 8-1. *Prices of Class A and Class B Stocks of Berkshire Hathaway*

Name	Symbol	Closing Price
Berkshire Hathaway	BRKA	$84,375
Berkshire Hathaway	BRKB	$2,807

Here's the price ratio:

Price ratio = 843,75 / 2,807 = $30.05

Thus, you can see that the price of Class B stock is almost equal to 1/30th of the price of Class A stock.

This discussion showed a case of near-perfect price correlation between the two stocks. Arbitrage can also take place on stocks that are not perfectly correlated with each other. Correlation in prices means the prices of both move in tandem; a perfect *positive correlation* would mean that if one stock rises x percent, then the other stock will also rise by the same x percent. A negative correlation means the prices of both stocks are inversely related to each other. A perfect *negative correlation* would mean that if the price of one stock rises by x percent, then the price of other stock will fall by x percent. Stocks of different companies operating in the same economic environment could have prices heavily correlated to each other. An example is a company that mines and produces gold and a company that produces and sells gold jewelry. A large component of the value of stocks of these two companies (and hence the price) would be coming from the inventory of gold that both companies would be holding. The direction of the trend of the prices would be weighed heavily in favor of the direction of gold prices. In other words, the prices of both stocks would rise when gold prices rise, and the prices of both stocks would fall when prices of gold fall. A good demand of jewelry in the market would mean fortune for both companies. Arbitrageurs following both these stocks would be aware of the degree of correlation between the prices of stocks of both companies. When the prices of these two companies deviate from each other beyond the usual degree of correlation and arbitrageurs are convinced that this price variation cannot be attributed to other economic factors affecting the companies in isolation, they would get into it through arbitrage. This arbitrage will push the prices of both stocks toward the usual correlation between them.

Some arbitrage takes place because of takeovers and the fixing of swap ratios. Say, for example, company A is of interest to company B. Company A is quoting at $50. Company B thinks this price is not a reflection of its fair value, and it wants to acquire company A, maybe because of strategic reasons. Company B now makes an open offer to shareholders of company A to purchase shares of company A for $60 per share. In this case, the market prices will rise, but it may not touch $60 (because of the implicit fear that the takeover might fail). Assume it rises to $55. There is still a differential of $5. Any trader can now buy company A shares from the market at $55, wait for some time, and sell them to company B at $60 a share. However, traders encounter two risks here. One, which we have noted, is the risk that the takeover may not succeed. Such takeovers are subject to shareholder and regulator approval, and the risk that the takeover will not succeed is very high. Second, a longer-than-expected waiting period could take place. These bids go through a lot of pricing, repricing, and negotiations, which may take time.

Pure and Speculative Arbitrage

Arbitrage can be loosely divided into pure arbitrage and speculative arbitrage.

Pure arbitrage is where the arbitrageurs take a position, expecting prices to return to their fair values. The fair value is the inherent value of the stock around which the market price must be quoted. When a security trades at more than the fair value for some time, chances are high it will return to its fair value. Similarly, when it has been trading at less than the fair value for a long time, chances are its prices will rise. Arbitrageurs bet on this fact, and such arbitrage is pure arbitrage. An example of fair-value arbitrage is in the arbitrage of Class A and Class B securities of Berkshire Hathaway. Assume the price today of a Class A share is $84,375 and the price of a Class B share is $2,815. The ratio discussed earlier of 1:30 indicates that the price of a Class A share should not be lower than $2,815 \times 30 = $84,450. This means that either Class A shares are undervalued or Class B shares are overvalued. Traders investing in either of the stocks would be concerned to know whether a stock is genuinely underpriced, overpriced, or correctly priced. An arbitrageur, on the other hand, works only on the price differential. Hence, this issue will not bother the arbitrageurs much. They will simply buy a Class A stock at $84,375 and sell 30 shares of Class B stocks at $2,815 each. The two positions completely hedge each other so there is not much of a price risk in this arbitrage. They will wait for some time for the price ratio to hit 1:30 exactly. This phenomenon of prices returning to their expected ratios is called a *convergence of prices*. Once such a price is reached, the arbitrageur will quickly sell one Class A share and buy 30 Class B shares. This will close out their original arbitrage position (this action is called *winding up the arbitrage*) and generate profits for them. This type of arbitrage involving the simultaneous buy and sale of stocks that are highly correlated is covered (the effect of the price rise/decline in one is offsetting the other) and is therefore not very risky in the long term.

Speculative arbitrage is an arbitrage where the value of the hedge portfolio is not stationary. This essentially means there is no fair value where the value of the portfolio is expected to converge. The fair value estimate itself changes with time and in the environment under which the security trades. Speculative arbitrage is considered risky in the long run because there is no fair value around which the conversion will take place. Examples of speculative arbitrage include spreads, pair trading, and risk arbitrage. Discussing these types of arbitrage is beyond the scope of this book.

Risks Associated in Arbitrage

Making money through arbitrage looks simple. However, it is one of the most risk-prone ways of making profits. Arbitrageurs face several risks in implementing their arbitrage strategies. Some of these are basis risk, model risk, and arbitrage cost risk.

Basis is the net difference in prices of the two stocks when the arbitrage is done. If a stock is trading at $40 on one exchange and $40.10 on another exchange, the difference between the two ($0.10) is the basis. When an arbitrageur sells at $40.10 and buys simultaneously at $40, she assumes that the price difference will converge, and she will reverse the deals to pocket the difference. If the arbitrageur does not have much ability to carry forward the transaction, she will look forward to reversing the transaction as early as possible. It could, however, be that instead of prices converging, they diverge further and become $40 and $40.20. If the arbitrageur does not have the ability to carry forward the positions to the next day, she will have to close the transaction by selling at $40 and buying at $40.20. She will lose $0.10 in this entire arbitrage. The risk that the arbitrage position will move against the arbitrageur and prices will not converge as expected is called *basis risk*. In the Berkshire Hathaway example, the arbitrageur bought a Class A stock at $84,375 and sold 30 shares of Class B stocks at $2,815 each. He is expecting the prices to converge to a 1:30 ratio. There is a remote chance that this conversion might never take place. The prices could even diverge more. The conversion may finally happen sometime but may not be before the settlement comes. Both the transactions will then have to be settled individually by paying cash to take delivery on one exchange and deliver shares and receive cash on the other exchange. In such cases, the arbitrageur faces basis risk because the basis has gone against him.

Sometimes arbitrageurs have not understood the relative values and correlations of the instruments used for arbitrage. At times, the best of arbitrageurs make mistakes in arbitrage when they don't understand all the risks associated or when they think there is arbitrage opportunity where there is none. Such a risk is called *model risk*.

Arbitrage cost risk is risk that the cost of settling the arbitrage and the carrying costs associated with it exceed the profit expected from that arbitrage. Some unexpected costs could come up all of a sudden, or there could be a sudden increase in the margin that exposes the arbitrageur to more than the expected costs and makes the arbitrageur suffer losses, especially when the margin in arbitrage is low.

Building an Equity Arbitrage Engine: Arbitrage in Equity Shares

Let's build a case around five popular stocks traded in the United States. We will first try to fit in logic for the arbitrage engine and then try to extend it to regular program trading to show how orders are generated to bring profit to the arbitrageur. An *arbitrage system* scours the market data of multiple exchanges and markets and discovers arbitrage opportunities. A *program trading system* is a system that accepts criteria for generating and executing orders from its users and keeps track of the market. The moment the defined criteria are met, it automatically triggers orders in a relevant exchange without any human intervention. In a typical dealing room setup, the arbitrage engine would be set up to track data from multiple exchanges to look for arbitrage opportunities. Any opportunity would then be passed to the program trading engine for the generation of orders. Dealers themselves normally monitor these orders. However, in such cases, complexity of analysis and speed is of the essence. With thousands of analysts and traders tracking the prices of every stock every second, market opportunities due to price distortions are rare, and program trading engines coupled with arbitrage engines are programmed to exploit such opportunities. Some program trading engines are also programmed to look for arbitrage opportunities. In such cases the program trading engine itself doubles as the arbitrage engine.

Arbitrageurs usually have arbitrage interest in multiple exchanges. Assume you are building an arbitrage engine around such a case. The arbitrage engine will need to analyze data from these exchanges. It would be extremely difficult for one human being to track several shares across exchanges and keep a watch on prevailing prices on every exchange and differential in order to track arbitrage opportunities. Good arbitrage opportunities are rare and happen mostly on not-so-popular securities. Hence, arbitrageurs need a sophisticated program that will help them track arbitrage opportunities.

These computer programs simultaneously read broadcasts across different exchanges and go through an arbitrageur's requirements to seek out arbitrage opportunities. On any normal day, manually tracking five stocks may seem simple. But both these exchanges would have thousands of listed stocks, and there would be good arbitrage opportunities in only a few of them. To arrive at arbitrage opportunities across these five, the arbitrage engine would follow these steps:

1. Create a short list of securities of interest, and define the arbitrage costs and margin and the minimum expected returns from arbitrage.

2. Scan the prices prevailing of securities the arbitrageur is interested in by reading continuously available market data.

3. Arrive at price differentials between those stocks across various exchanges. These differentials will determine the returns to the arbitrageur.

4. Compute the percentage returns.

5. Calculate the annualized percentage returns; as discussed earlier, the absolute returns will not only determine whether the arbitrage opportunity is good or bad. They have to be annualized in terms of percentage for a comparison to be possible.

6. Compare the annualized percentage returns with the prevailing arbitrage cost and expected returns from the arbitrage; since a comparison has to be made, in most cases the arbitrage cost is also expressed as a percentage and is annualized for the comparison to be more meaningful.

7. Determine on which exchange to buy and on which exchange to sell. This depends upon the relative prices in each exchange. Arbitrageurs need to buy on the exchange where the stock is trading at a lower price and sell where it is trading at a higher price.

8. Present the opportunities to the arbitrageur in a meaningful form for them to take action.

When the arbitrage engine is interacting with a program trading engine, it will pass the details of these arbitrage opportunities to the program trading engine, and the program trading engine will generate orders to exploit these opportunities. We will run through the steps in the previous example to give you more clarity on this.

For this example, assume an arbitrage opportunity is feasible only if it generates a return of 2 percent per annum over and above the arbitrage cost of 6 percent. We will call this figure of 2 percent the *arbitrage margin*. The margin reflects a layer of safety over and above the arbitrage set-up costs. The costs will barely cover our arbitrageur on the essentials that they will have to directly or indirectly pay out for setting up the arbitrage. This arbitrage may have many other risks, as discussed earlier. They need to be adequately covered and compensated for these risks. They will therefore not be willing to look at an arbitrage opportunity where only the basic cost is met. Returns have to be a specific percentage over and above these costs. It is normal in such scenarios for the arbitrageur to say, "I am interested in having a look at the opportunity only if the returns are 2 percent over and above my costs." Even if something goes wrong in the arbitrage, the cushion of margin is still there to prevent the trader from going out of pocket.

The arbitrage cost of 6 percent assumed for this example is all inclusive of transaction costs, costs associated on the buy leg, and costs associated on the sale leg. The 2 percent (arbitrage margin) and 6 percent (arbitrage cost) return also means that the arbitrageur is interested in doing an arbitrage only if the return on it is 8 percent or higher.

These returns are normally quoted in two terms: for one particular arbitrage setup or on an annualized basis. The arbitrage-level return being quoted in percentage is understandable. Arbitrageurs would like to know how much return a particular arbitrage is giving them. Every arbitrage has a life span after which it is wound up consciously or the market conditions force arbitrageurs to close the arbitrage. Additionally, this life span is different for different arbitrage situations. Some may be closed intraday, some may continue for two to three days, and some may even span weeks. If an arbitrageur's talk of returns on an arbitrage take place where there is no standardization on the number of days it takes to generate the returns, comparison would be very difficult. Therefore, for a more standardized comparison, these arbitrage-specific return figures are converted into an annualized return figure for the purpose of comparison. When annualized figures are discussed, returns from every arbitrage can be compared to each other meaningfully.

Returning to the example, for the sake of brevity assume our arbitrageurs are interested in only two exchanges: the NYSE and Philadelphia Stock Exchange (PSE).

In any arbitrage, the choice of whether the arbitrage opportunity on a security will be acceptable to the arbitrageur changes from security to security. Securities that enjoy very high liquidity are more likely to be acceptable for arbitrage. Arbitrage on them normally comes at a low risk and a low cost. These securities are widely available, and in the eventuality of the delivery requirement, they can be sourced easily and delivered. The financials behind the companies are public domain information, and most events in such companies and their stocks are predicted in advance; therefore, surprises are rare. Although this level of transparency is welcome to the arbitrageur, this comfort usually comes at a price. The more the market knows about a stock and the company behind it, the better the price discovery process is in that particular stock across markets. Better price discovery and predictability of events attracts more trading interest from market participants. This keeps prices in sync across markets and makes arbitrage opportunities rare. To curtail the risk arbitrageurs face, they will normally create a short list of securities on which they will accept arbitrage opportunities and exploit them.

Assume that the arbitrageurs have a clear and unlimited supply of the shares listed in Table 8-2 lying in their demat account and ready for delivery, and these are the only stocks on which they want to accept arbitrage opportunities.

Table 8-2. *Short List of Securities of Interest for Arbitrage (Step 1)*

Stock	Symbol on NYSE	Assumed Arbitrage Cost	Arbitrage Margin*	Minimum Expected Return from Arbitrage**
The Coca-Cola Company	KO	6%	2%	8%
General Electric Company	GE	6%	2%	8%
Advanced Micro Devices	AMD	6%	2%	8%
The Walt Disney Company	DIS	6%	2%	8%
Wal-Mart Stores	WMT	6%	2%	8%

*Over and Above Costs
**Assumed Arbitrage Cost + Arbitrage Margin

This kind of short list that the arbitrageurs have created to classify securities of their interest is a good way to start because the arbitrage engine will now focus on market data available for only these securities and will ignore market data for thousands of other securities. This will improve the performance of the arbitrage engine tremendously.

We will now run through the steps listed earlier to show how the arbitrage engine works.

Step 1 has already been executed in Table 8-2; five securities are available, and a minimum expectation of 8 percent has been set from the arbitrage. It is important to set the minimum expectation from the arbitrage because otherwise the arbitrageur will be flooded by arbitrage opportunities. Notice that in arbitrage you are working on price differentials. Even though arbitrage opportunities are rare, price differentials are bound to exist. However, it is not all differentials that interest arbitrageurs. It is only those differentials that are big enough to be translated into effective profits that interest them.

Step 2 gets the latest prices on a real-time basis. Note that since the arbitrage opportunities will finally translate into orders to be executed on a stock exchange, it is important that the arbitrage engine works on absolute real-time prices. Stale prices will run a high risk of orders not getting through—or worse, only one of the two sides (buy/sale) getting transacted.

Assume Table 8-3 shows the prices prevailing for these five shares on the NYSE and PSE.

Table 8-3. *Current Market Prices in Exchanges of Interest (Step 2)*

Stock	NYSE	PSE
The Coca-Cola Company	$40	$40.05
General Electric Company	$39.60	$39.80
Advanced Micro Devices	$40	$41
The Walt Disney Company	$28.20	$28
Wal-Mart Stores	$46	$46

Step 3 involves computing price differentials. Here exchange pairs are created; one exchange is taken as a base, and price differentials are computed with respect to that exchange (see Table 8-4).

Table 8-4. *Price Differentials with Respect to NYSE (Step 3)*

Stock	Symbol	NYSE	PSE	Price Differential
The Coca-Cola Company	KO	$40	$40.05	$0.05
General Electric Company	GE	$39.60	$39.80	$0.20
Advanced Micro Devices	AMD	$40	$41	$1
The Walt Disney Company	DIS	$28.20	$28	($0.20)
Wal-Mart Stores	WMT	$46	$46	$0

In Table 8-4, the price differentials are computed with respect to the NYSE. Since prices on the PSE are higher for the Coca-Cola Company, General Electric Company, and Advanced Micro Devices, the price differentials are positive. However, in the case of the Walt Disney Company, the price differential is negative because the price for the Walt Disney Company is higher on the NYSE than on the PSE.

In step 4, the arbitrage engine would generate returns against these differentials. Percentage returns are computed by dividing the price differential with prices prevailing on the base exchange (the NYSE) and expressing them as percentages (see Table 8-5).

Table 8-5. *Calculating Percentage Returns (Step 4)*

Stock	NYSE	PSE	Price Differential	Percentage Returns = (Price Differential / NYSE Prices) $\times$ 100
The Coca-Cola Company	$40	$40.05	$0.05	0.125
General Electric Company	$39.60	$39.80	$0.20	0.51
Advanced Micro Devices	$40	$41	$1	2.50
The Walt Disney Company	$28.2	$28	($0.20)	-0.71
Wal-Mart Stores	$46	$46	$0	0

In step 5, returns will be computed on an annualized basis. Assume that the settlement for the transactions in Table 8-5 is on a T+3 basis. No arbitrageur would want the arbitrage position to close by going through settlements. They all aspire to close the arbitrage before settlements by reversing the buy and sale positions in order to avoid the hassles and cost associated with settlements. In a T+3 environment, from setting up the arbitrage through winding up would take a maximum of three days. For practical purposes, assume the channelization of funds and securities takes another four days for every arbitrage. This would mean a total of about seven days is involved to generate the returns in step 4. To annualize this, assuming 365 days a year, you need to multiply the returns by 365 / 7. This will give the annualized returns shown in Table 8-6.

Table 8-6. *Calculating Annualized Percentage Returns (Step 5)*

Stock	NYSE	PSE	Price Differential	Percentage Returns	Annualized Returns*
The Coca-Cola Company	$40	$40.05	$0.05	0.12%	6.51%
General Electric Company	$39.60	$39.80	$0.20	0.51%	26.33%
Advanced Micro Devices	$40	$41	$1	2.50%	130.36%
The Walt Disney Company	$28.20	$28	($0.20)	-0.71%	(36.98%)
Wal-Mart Stores	$46	$46	$0	0%	0%

*= Percentage Returns * 365 / Number of Days Arbitrage Position Is Kept Live

This tells you the relative returns on doing arbitrage on these securities; however, to find out whether these deals will be profitable, they have to be validated against the cost of doing the arbitrage. More important, the interest level of the arbitrageur will be determined by the returns they generate over and above the expected arbitrage returns.

The arbitrage engine in step 6 performs this comparison (see Table 8-7).

Table 8-7. *Selecting Profitable Arbitrage (Step 6)*

Stock	NYSE	PSE	Price Differential	Percentage Returns	Annualized Returns	Arbitrage Cost	Arbitrage Profitable?	Expectation from Arbitrage	Returns from Arbitrage Over and Above Expectations*
The Coca-Cola Company	$40	$40.05	$0.05	0.12%	6.52%	6%	Yes	8%	-1.48%
General Electric Company	$39.60	$39.80	$0.20	0.51%	26.33%	6%	Yes	8%	18.33%
Advanced Micro Devices	$40	$41	$1	2.50%	130.36%	6%	Yes	8%	122.36%
The Walt Disney Company	$28.20	$28	($0.20)	-0.71%	-36.98%	6%	Yes	8%	-44.98%
Wal-Mart Stores	$46	$46	$0	0%	0%	6%	No	8%	-8%

*Annualized Returns – Expectation from Arbitrage

As discussed earlier, arbitrage is profitable only if the returns from it exceed the costs. However, even that does not ensure that such positions will be taken. Positions are most likely to be taken only if annualized returns are over and above the expectation of arbitrage (the last column in Table 8-7 indicates positive returns). The figures show that three cases will generate negative returns. Let's examine them closely. Arbitrage on the Coca-Cola Company will be profitable but only marginally. When compared with expected returns from the arbitrage, it does not generate positive returns. This will thus be most likely dropped as a case for arbitrage or may be put in a watch list for the prices to be watched more carefully just in case the price differentials widen and better the arbitrage opportunity available in this scrip. The Walt Disney Company is also showing huge negative returns, but remember that this figure is negative because it is being measured with respect to the NYSE and the differential was negative because prices on the PSE were lower than prices on the NYSE. This has to be treated as a special case. This essentially means the arbitrage opportunity is very much there. Only the order type (buy/sale) has to be reversed while hitting the exchanges. Finally, Wal-Mart Stores is generating -8 percent over and above expectation, indicating that there is no arbitrage opportunity here. This is not surprising given that there was no price differential in its prices to start.

The two cases yielding positive results—General Electric Company and Advanced Micro Devices— are clear-cut cases for arbitrage and are likely to be taken up for execution.

Table 8-8 summarizes the cases.

Table 8-8. *Arbitrage Opportunity (Step 7)*

Stock	NYSE	PSE	Percentage Returns	Annualized Returns	Arbitrage Cost	Arbitrage Profitable?	Expectation from Arbitrage	Returns from Arbitrage Over and Above Expectations*	Case for Arbitrage
The Coca-Cola Company	$40	$40.05	0.12%	6.52%	6%	Yes	8%	-1.48%	No
General Electric Company	$39.60	$39.80	0.51%	26.33%	6%	Yes	8%	18.33%	Yes
Advanced Micro Devices	$40	$41	2.50%	130.36%	6%	Yes	8%	122.36%	Yes
The Walt Disney Company	$28.20	$28	-0.71%	-36.98%	6%	Yes	8%	-44.98%	Yes
Wal-Mart Stores	$46	$46	0%	0%	6%	No	8%	-8%	No

Annualized Returns – Expectation from Arbitrage

However, to make these cases actionable, specific buy and sell recommendations have to be generated as indicated in step 7.

For this, the arbitrage engine will have to refer to the prevailing prices and see in which exchange the prices are high and in which exchange they are low. Following the principles of arbitrage, it will recommend buying on the exchange where the prices are low and selling on the exchange where the prices are high.

Table 8-9 shows the recommendations.

Table 8-9. *Determine on Which Exchange to Buy and on Which Exchange to Sell (Step 8)*

Stock	NYSE	PSE	Price Differential	Case for Arbitrage	Recommendations
The Coca-Cola Company	$40	$40.05	$0.05	No	No action to be taken.
General Electric Company	$39.60	$39.80	$0.20	Yes	Buy on the NYSE, and sell on the PSE.
Advanced Micro Devices	$40	$41	$1	Yes	Buy on the NYSE, and sell on the PSE.
The Walt Disney Company	$28.20	$28	($0.20)	Yes	Buy on the PSE, and sell on the NYSE.
Wal-Mart Stores	$46	$46	$0	No	No action to be taken.

This is the usual information that any arbitrageur would want to see. Now let's move on to program trading and see how you can make the program trading engine use information generated by the arbitrage engine to generate orders automatically.

Assume the arbitrageur is willing to commit money in lots of $10,000 per deal. The arbitrage engine will have to refer to the market lot and prevailing prices to see how many shares can be bought in one order. Assume that all these shares can be bought and sold in lots of one share each. The program trading engine will arrive at the quantity of shares each order will contain. This will be equal to $10,000 per current prevailing price. Table 8-10 shows the numbers.

Table 8-10. *Orders Generated by Program Trading Engine*

Stock	NYSE	PSE	Price Differential	Number of Shares (Rounded Off)	Recommendations
The Coca-Cola Company	$40	$40.05	$0.05		No action to be taken.
General Electric Company	$39.60	$39.80	$0.20	252	Buy on the NYSE, and sell on the PSE.
Advanced Micro Devices	$40	$41	$1	250	Buy NYSE, and sell on the PSE.
The Walt Disney Company	$28.20	$28	($0.20)	354	Buy on the PSE, and sell on the NYSE
Wal-Mart Stores	$46	$46	$0		No action to be taken.

The final orders that will be generated are as follows:

- Buy 252 of the General Electric Company on the NYSE.

- Sell 252 of the General Electric Company on the PSE.

- Buy 250 of Advanced Micro Devices on the NYSE.

- Sell 250 of Advanced Micro Devices on the PSE.

- Buy 354 of the Walt Disney Company on the PSE.

- Sell 354 of the Walt Disney Company on the NYSE.

These orders, once executed, will result in successful arbitrage positions. The arbitrageur will later get the opportunity to unwind the arbitrage if the prices converge or proceed for settlements in cases where the prices don't converge until settlement. In both cases, the arbitrageur will make a profit because the cost incurred in settlements was already factored in while calculating the costs of settling the arbitrage.

Thus, you can see that arbitrage is an art of exploiting price differentials in multiple markets to one's advantage. Apart from making profits for the individual arbitrageur, it helps in the price discovery process and brings prices in multiple markets closer to each other. This is an important economic function that arbitrageurs fulfill.

This completes the business journey of arbitrage. The design of an arbitrage engine is mainly centered on the functionality you want to provide to traders. The most sophisticated arbitrage engine uses a rule engine to capture arbitrage rules defined by the traders. The rules are defined through a trader-friendly language that is then processed by the rule engine, which translates the rules into an appropriate language-level implementation. Automated code-generation tactics prove extremely useful in this kind of scenario; in the rest of the chapter, we will discuss the code-generation topic in detail.

Introducing Code Generation

Building good software involves a tremendous amount of planning, rock-solid architectural design, efficient code, and a rigorous quality testing environment. Undoubtedly, each stage is time-consuming, but the most important one—especially in large-scale projects—is the build phase in which code is continuously churned out. The build phase accounts for the majority of the project time and budget because the real work is performed in this stage; this includes writing real code, test cases, database stored procedures, build scripts, and so on. However, this may not be true in other fields of engineering; for instance, an automobile engineering's development cycle is more or less aligned with the software development life cycle, but the build time is shorter compared to the planning and design time. The primary reason for such differences is because for a particular type of automobile there is already a well-defined template that captures the detail specification of every component of the automobile, which is then fed to sophisticated machines that understand and generate components in accordance with the template. This kind of end-to-end automation is difficult to implement in the software development world, particularly during the build phase, because the nature of the business requirements is different for different customers. However, with the recent advancement in software engineering, most of the repetitive tasks encountered during the software construction stage are now automated, and this has deeply aided in speeding up the development life cycle. Code generation is an advanced area that has evolved over a period of time, and in today's world it represents a novel way of building any type of application.

Code generation is the technique of producing language-specific code during either design time or runtime based on some input information. This input information could be high-level code or an abstract model defined using domain-oriented languages. Regardless of the type of input provided, the output produced is always program source code. This power to automatically generate source code has greatly benefited developers and absolved them from writing repetitive and monotonous code.

For example, consider back-office applications that are Online Transaction Processing (OLTP) systems and contain hundreds of database tables. In such applications, a strong audit is required that tracks changes applied to the underlying tables. To implement such requirements, developers will first immerse themselves in creating triggers, and the number of triggers created in this case will be exactly equal to the number of tables. Furthermore, the trigger logic formulated will be simple; it will contain a single-line SQL statement that copies rows from the original table to the audit table. This same logic will get repeated and replicated across all tables. Now, such repetitive and menial tasks when assigned to developers become a chore and can also be a source of frustration. To rescue developers from such mundane tasks and to mobilize their efforts in building more productive parts of the system, the development team must embrace automatic code-generation techniques. At a surface level, such automation may not sound like an easy-to-achieve task, but we will show that all that is required is a list of the table names and their underlying fields. This information is already available and forms part of the database metadata that is separately stored in tables also known as *system tables*. By writing the appropriate query, this information can then be retrieved and, with the help of additional processing logic trigger code, can be automatically emitted. Such automation tasks require a one-time investment in terms of development effort, but after that it forms part of the reusable components and can be applied to other systems. There is no doubt that such automation when implemented in the large scale will always lead to shipping great applications on schedule and on budget.

Code generation is not a new concept and has been prevalent from the genesis of computing days. It is rooted in high-level programming languages where code written in a user-friendly language is compiled into low-level assembly instructions. This compilation process is a classic example of automatic code generation that has consistently evolved from one generation to another, abstracting away the complexities and layering another abstraction level that brings a higher degree of automation and consistency to day-to-day application development.

The following are the three components required as the fuel to ignite the code-generation process (see Figure 8-1):

Metadata: Metadata is a repository of information that describes application data. For example, information about database tables and their field-level information forms part of metadata. This information is stored in system tables and can be easily retrieved by framing and executing an appropriate query.

Code generators: Code generators are key components that know the structure of the metadata, understand the template, and weave this information together to produce program source code.

Code templates: Code templates represent the layout of the code and are composed of both static and dynamic information. For example, in Figure 8-1, the trigger syntax forms part of the static information, but the table name and list of fields form part of the dynamic information that is populated by code generators during the code-generation phase.

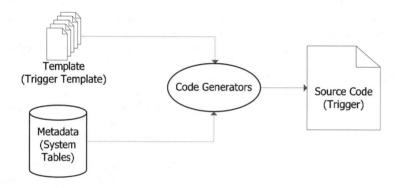

Figure 8-1. *Code generator components*

Types of Code Generators

Automated code generation forms one of the powerful weapons in a developer's arsenal. Its immediate impact is a change in developer thinking when solving a complex problem, particularly during cases where problems are repetitive in nature. Such a drastic shift in developer attitude has institutionalized the concept of code generation in every phase of the software development life cycle, spanning from the design to the deployment of systems. This has resulted in various forms of code generation that are distinguished based on their applicability and which specific aspect of software development they are trying to automate. The following are the most commonly used generators in day-to-day application development:

Code wizards: Code generation using wizards is popular and also an important selling point of any good IDE tools. Wizard-based techniques are commonly used to generate boilerplate code, but they are also used to generate end-to-end full-blown code.

User interface: A user interface is certainly one of the most important parts of an application; it is an external visual representation of the system to the outside world. The UI code generator provides the developer with a novel way of designing UI-based applications. It allows developers to visually design the UI applications instead of understanding and writing the low-level code details.

Specialized class: This type of generator is used to generate a highly specialized class that forms the building blocks of the system. The specialized class generated is never compiled independently; rather, it forms an important part of a larger set of classes and is included before building the final executables.

Code inflator: A code inflator produces inline code based on a placeholder defined inside the code. This kind of feature is mainly seen during the code-editing phase where the developer is busy writing code and desperately looking for a shortcut to achieve a specific programming goal such as writing safe multithreaded code, automatic resource cleanup, and so on.

Model-driven generator: Modeling plays an important role in the development of good software. It captures and communicates the requirements and interaction between systems. With the help of a model, individual components in the systems are visualized and represented in a domain-specific language. Unified Modeling Language (UML) is a perfect example that is widely adopted and is a graphical language for designing any kind of system. This visual model is fed to the model-driven generator, which takes the responsibility of interpreting and producing language-specific code.

Code documentation: Code documentation is not the most pleasant task encountered in a day-to-day routine, but there is no way to escape it. It is a mandatory task because it captures the design essence behind the code that is later used for reference. Therefore, both comments and the actual code reside side by side, and with the help of the specialized code documentation generator, the comments are extracted and polished into finished documentation represented in .html, .doc, or .pdf format.

Just-in-time code cutting: Just-in-time code cutting is a modern way of generating code and compiling it on the fly, and all this activity is executed during runtime, which is in contrast with other types of code generators discussed so far that are meant to work during design time.

Code generation brings efficiency, agility, higher productivity, and consistency to software development. Obviously, all this contributes to a lower maintenance cost. It is an extremely valuable asset, and when properly leveraged, it provides a totally a new gear that boosts the application development. That is why most of the components inside the .NET Framework and VS .NET leverage code-generation techniques. We will discuss important areas where it is used in the subsequent section.

Code Generation and Reflection

In the .NET world, the *assembly* is a unit of deployment, and besides encapsulating IL code, it stores complete metadata information about types and its members. This metadata information is emitted by CLR-aware compilers during the compilation phase and seen as a major improvement over traditional compilers that used to capture limited information about the underlying types and their dependencies. Such self-describing characteristics of an assembly provide complete information about the program without needing the program source code, and retrieving this information at runtime is made possible with reflection.

Reflection allows self-introspection of an assembly. Using reflection, you can examine classes encapsulated inside assemblies and further drill down to the programming elements of a class, including the properties, members, fields, and so on. Reflection works only with compiled code and is not concerned with the programming language used to write the code. This ability has opened up a plethora of opportunities and is utilized effectively by various tools such as visual designers, assembly inspectors, class browsers, IntelliSense tools, and so on. Another interesting fact about reflection is that it is not limited to examining type information and its underlying programming element; it is also capable of modifying the object state during runtime such as invoking a method, accessing a property value, or directly modifying a field value. This type of dynamic behavior, when introduced, properly saves tons of lines of code and motivates developers to design highly dynamic and extensible applications.

Reflection also enables building an assembly on the fly and allows loading it in memory; all this is possible at runtime. This is a new development path available to developers that leads toward code-generation techniques. Both code-generation and reflection share a bloodline relationship, and nowadays it is certainly impossible to talk about code generation in isolation without discussing reflection. Code generation is all about generating code, whereas reflection is about providing enough information to produce this code, load it in memory, and then provide instant access to the functionality exposed by this code.

Certainly such a combination is considered an advanced programming technique mainly practiced to implement programs whose behavior is dynamic in nature and hard to predict or capture its intent during design time. For example, highly complex trading algorithms are difficult to specify and impossible both for traders and developers to document and implement inside code. The various parameters used for algorithms tend to change frequently based on market conditions. Often the most elegant solution to this problem is to capture the business input during runtime and then dynamically emit code that is specific to a particular algorithm specification. This is definitely a win-win deal to both traders and developers because developers now can mobilize their efforts in producing a program that can not only understand business inputs fed by traders but also can reorganize and retune the behavior of the program at runtime to suit this specific need.

User Interface

A user interface is one of the most visible parts of an application and directly gives a feel of how the system works to users. A badly designed user interface can be a fertile source of frustration, and users may even dislike the application despite its other components such as the database logic and middle tier performing way beyond user expectations. It also means no matter how much effort is invested in developing and fine-tuning the hidden part of the system, it is always the usability aspect that determines the fate of the application. Therefore, it is important to provide a consistent and easy-to-access user interface that is fairly intuitive and increases user efficiency in performing any complex task.

To keep up with this goal, developers always strive to provide a consistent look and feel across the application. The whole point of a user interface is to capture the data from the users. To do this, developers need to present the correct visual cues. From a UI development perspective, this task involves identifying UI elements (UI *widgets*) and then rendering them on a UI canvas (UI *form*). The final task is to apply finishing touches, which again require good aesthetic taste. All these tasks demand a rigorous amount of coding, and handcrafting it manually can be a primary reason for developers to avoid this task. But the Windows Form Designer built into the VS .NET IDE makes it a breeze to do.

The Windows Form Designer internally uses code-generation techniques, but it provides a drawing surface at design time and allows developers to place UI widgets directly onto it. Developers can then control the aesthetic aspect of widgets by tweaking their properties through the Properties window. Figure 8-2 depicts a Form Designer view with the left panel displaying the widget Toolbox window, the center view displaying the drawing surface with various types of widgets rendered on it, and the right panel representing the widget Properties window.

As you can see, developers do not have to write a single line of code in order to lay out and configure widgets. Developers just have to drag and drop widgets onto the form and then use the Properties window to tweak them. However, in reality, the Form Designer is churning out lots of code in the background that is completely transparent to developers. In a broader sense, the Form Designer is an additional resource provided for free that is 100 percent dedicated to UI development–related tasks.

Fortunately, autogenerated code is not kept secret in some sort of opaque files; rather, it forms part of the source code and is neatly grouped under the `Windows Form Designer generated` code region. By expanding this code region, developers get an opportunity to take a closer look at the code generated by the Windows Form Designer. Figure 8-3 represents the editor view of the autogenerated source code.

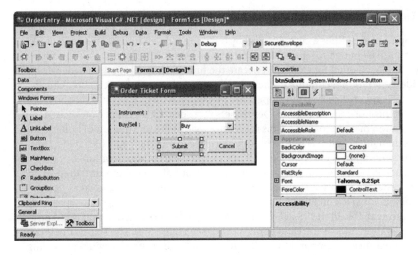

Figure 8-2. *Windows Form Designer*

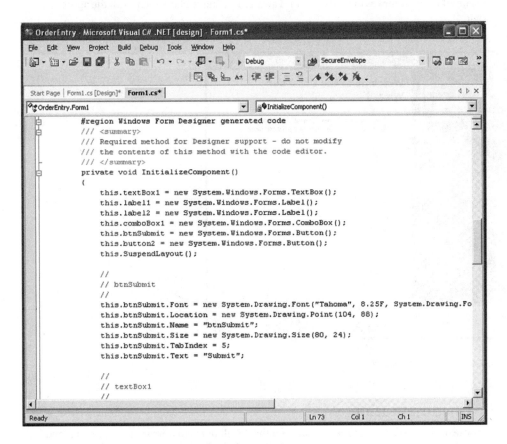

Figure 8-3. *Windows Form Designer editor view*

Code Wizards

Wizard-based development simplifies a complex task by breaking it down into a series of subtasks that are simple and intuitive enough for the user to understand. At each step, enough information is gathered that is then finally chained together to generate the final output. Similarly, a code wizard is a special form of code-generation technique implemented to ease the coding task by breaking it into a sequence of steps, and at each step developers are presented with a dialog box that collects information required to produce the final code. Developers first seek the assistance of wizards in establishing the foundation of complex code. This assistance leads to the formation of boilerplate code, and developers then are absolutely free to modify the code to suit their specific needs. However, this form of code generation is different from UI designer–based code generation, because once the boilerplate code is generated, the wizard is completely out of the picture, and there is no relationship between code and wizards. Therefore, code wizards are sometimes known as *jump-starters* because of their ability kick off any complex task.

Various wizards are available in the VS .NET IDE, but the most important one that is directly related to the code-generation topic is the Data Form Wizard (see Figure 8-4). The Data Form Wizard automates the task of creating a data-bound form. It runs through the entire procedure of loading data from a database, displaying it on a grid, and updating the data back to the database. The wizard creates several files such as a typed dataset, a Windows form, and so on. It also constructs the appropriate UI widgets, makes them data bound aware, and finally backs them with the appropriate code logic.

Figure 8-4. *Data Form Wizard*

Code Documentation

The purpose of getting code documentation from the developer is to mirror their ideas hatched during the development stage on paper. It is only through documentation that developers demonstrate the nuts and bolts of the system to the outside world. This initial effort proves to be extremely handy and pays off during the maintenance stage when developers struggle to recollect a particular code trace or try to diagnose a peculiar system problem. Additionally, it helps newcomers quickly get on board. Also, it helps other stakeholders of the system, such as quality assurance people and technical writers, to get a better grip on the system. But it has always been hard to produce a single and consistent copy of documentation that could then be shared with all interested parties. Much of this can be attributed to the lack of strong tools that are not only difficult to use but also hard to integrate with the existing development environment.

Even though developers happen to document their code using the language-specific code inline documentation feature, this will not make other people in the team happy. To satisfy their appetites, developers now need to undertake the same documentation task and present it in a nicer format such as .html, .doc, .pdf, and so on. However, this solves the problem temporarily but leads to another big problem—document synchronization. Developers now need to ensure that any change in a comment at one place also is updated in another location. Keeping both copies synchronized is sufficient to drive anyone crazy, and this is where documentation generators solve many of the problems faced during code documentation.

Documentation generators never produce code; instead, they parse the source code and extract the comments embedded inside it to produce a finished, readable document. For example, the C# language allows in-place code commenting using XML comments. Predefined tags supported by XML comments are classified based on their usage and applicability. Tags are mainly applied over code constructs such as types and type members. Table 8-11 describes a few important tags.

Table 8-11. *XML Tags for Documentation Comments*

Tag	Description
`<summary>`	This tag describes a type or type member.
`<param>`	This tag describes a method parameter.
`<return>`	This tag describes the return value of a method or property.
`<exception>`	This tag is applied to a method, and it lists the exceptions a method can throw.

The following is an example of using these tags:

```
/// <summary>
/// Submits a limit price order to exchange
/// </summary>
/// <param name="instrument">Name of the underlying</param>
/// <param name="quantity">Total Quantity of the order</param>
/// <param name="price">Price at which this order is traded in the market</param>
public void SubmitOrder(string instrument,long quantity,double price)
{
}
```

As you can see, comments are nested inside XML tags, but an individual comment line begins with three slashes. The documentation generator recognizes this as an XML comment identifier and directly extracts the line into a separate file. This feature is already built into the C# compiler (csc.exe), and with the help of the /doc switch, comments are extracted in an XML file. In this way, comments are exported in a well-formed XML format, and now developers can easily produce any presentation format using XSLT. Using an XSLT template is the most common technique to read XML and produce HTML pages. Open source tools such as NDoc (http://ndoc.sourceforge.net/) understand these XML documentation tags and generate MSDN-style help documentation.

The advantage of a code documentation generator is that it allows both the code and the actual documentation to reside in one central place and thus avoids the scattering of developer knowledge. Furthermore, it provides the developer with a complete liberty to design a custom generator to suit a particular need; for instance, quality assurance will demand documentation in test-plan format.

Similarly, a technical manual writer will demand it in an API documentation format. Both of these expectations can easily be met by creating two different types of XSLT while the actual documentation still resides inside the code.

Code Inflator

A code inflator is an inline expansion of code performed during the code compilation or editing phase. The generator that does this code expansion basically reads a source file and looks for special markup inside the code, and upon locating this markup, replaces it with the actual intended code. This markup is called *code tags*. For developers, code tags are a way to boost productivity by having their common programming task linked with keywords. This means a task that requires 20 lines of code can be represented by defining a code tag and then inserting it inside the code. The beauty of a code tag is that it brings all the platinum quality that good code must possess such as code clarity, readability, and simplicity. A good example is the use of the lock keyword used in the C# programming language to ensure mutually exclusive access to a shared resource in a multithreaded environment. The lock statement takes the following form:

```
object lockObj = new object();
lock(lockObj)
{
    //Thread-Safe Code
}
```

This is inflated by the compiler during the compilation phase into the following:

```
object lockObj = new object();
Monitor.Enter(lockObj);
try
{
        //Thread-Safe Code
}
finally
{
    Monitor.Exit(lockObj);
}
```

As you can see from the previous code, the lock keyword is a much cleaner and convenient approach for writing thread-safe code compared to its expanded version. Another example of a code inflator is the inherent refactoring support provided by VS .NET 2005 during the code-editing phase. Refactoring is a technique adopted to modify the existing code structure, thus improving code readability and maintainability. VS .NET 2005 supports many refactoring features, but the most useful one is field-level refactoring. As part of good OO practices, we always adhere to its encapsulation tenet where publicly accessible fields are not exposed directly to the external world; instead, they are made available through a getter property and a setter property. Developers face this kind of requirement in their day-to-day development routines, and they have to manually implement it. But VS .NET 2005 automates this process with just a few mouse clicks, and the code for the get/set method is automatically generated during design time.

Model-Driven Generator

Model-driven generators build code based on an abstract model. The abstract model represents system requirements at a much higher abstraction layer. UML is a good example of a model-driven generator in which the system is modeled using a graphical language. It enables the developer to visualize and construct models in a manner that is easy to express and understand. The model represents the functional requirements of the system at a high level that is independent of the language implementation. This kind of language-neutral model is precise enough to generate code. Furthermore, code can be generated for any kind of programming language because UML decouples the implementation aspect from the model. Several UML-related commercial tools are available that allow custom plug-ins of various types of code generators. Microsoft offers the Visio technology that facilitates end-to-end software modeling. Additionally, it is tightly integrated with VS .NET and provides tight support for both forward and reverse engineering. *Forward engineering* refers to generating code based on an abstract model; *reverse engineering* implies the construction of a model based on source code.

Specialized Class

In this type of generator, code is generated based on metadata information that is defined in an XML file. The metadata contains information that is mainly related to the type of application code the generator is supposed to produce. For instance, if you need to autogenerate database triggers, then all that is required is the name of the tables and type of trigger (insert, update, and delete) to create. All this information then forms part of the metadata and is included in the XML file. Another good example of this kind of generator is the ADO.NET strongly type DataSet. The ADO.NET DataSet is a general-purpose in-memory container with a relational programming model flavor. The internal structure of a DataSet is organized in the form of rows and columns. It is mainly used to cache rows populated from a database.

A typed DataSet is a sophisticated version of a dataset that provides strongly typed methods, events, and properties. It means tables and columns are accessed by name instead of following ordinal-based methods, thereby improving code readability. It is completely possible to construct the entire relational database model inside a dataset, which includes tasks such as defining the primary key, relations between tables using foreign keys, unique constraints, and so on. So, the foundation for creating a typed dataset is the metadata information defined inside an XSD file. The structure of this information is in accordance to the XSD standard, and it is then fed to an XSD tool (xsd.exe) that generates a strongly typed dataset. The code inside this tool has sufficient knowledge to understand and interpret the metadata and accordingly produce output.

Just-in-Time Code Cutting

Just-in-time code cutting (JIT-CC) is an ability to dynamically generate and compile code on the fly at runtime. This behavior is different from other types of code generators discussed so far that generate code during design time and that are compiled later with another production set of classes. Obviously, generating code on the fly at runtime requires support from the underlying execution run-time system, and the CLR is well equipped to blend with such techniques. A perfect example of it is the way XmlSerializer is designed.

As discussed in Chapter 3, XmlSerializer enables you to serialize and deserialize objects into and from XML documents, but a deep dive into its internal implementation will reveal some cool programming techniques. It allows you to work with strongly typed classes where an individual field or property is mapped with elements or attributes of the XML document, and this mapping information is controlled through a special set of XmlSerializer attributes. At the core implementation level, every time a new instance of XmlSerializer is constructed, a new assembly and a new class are dynamically created. This newly created class strictly contains type-specialized code to transfer data between objects and XML and is determined at runtime. That is the reason why you notice a slowness in execution whenever a new instance of XmlSerializer is created. The instantiation process includes the dynamic generation and compilation of code, which chews a fair amount of CPU cycles; therefore, it is always a good programming practice to cache the instance of XmlSeralizer instead of re-creating it again and again.

With this example, we have completed the discussion of the various forms of code generators. Now we will cover the real implementation technique that includes a code generator framework available in the .NET Framework. The rest of the chapter will cover this topic in detail and lay a strong foundation for building code generator–based solutions.

Introducing the CodeDOM

Code generators that possess the ability to generate code in a language-independent manner will always earn the highest respect from the developers, and this is true with the Code Document Object Model (CodeDOM) that is bundled with the .NET Framework. Using the CodeDOM, source code is written in a language-neutral manner. This is possible because of its internal object model where there is a one-to-one relationship between a language construct and its corresponding object-oriented representation. This type of abstraction allows representing source code in an object-oriented fashion, which results in a CodeDOM graph. The CodeDOM graph is analogous to a tree where multiple nodes are linked with each other and also hierarchically arranged. Similarly, the CodeDOM graph is a collection of objects arranged in a tree structure, and an individual object describes a language structure in abstract terms. This abstract graph is then traversed and processed to generate source code that is specific to a particular language implementation such as C#, VB .NET, JScript.NET, and so on.

Certainly, the CodeDOM is a promising framework available to a developer, and Microsoft has shown its commitment to it by developing several of its tools based on it. However, developers will face certain pitfalls when it comes to implementing a language construct that is specific to a particular language. For instance, a *conditional statement* is a generic programming construct and is supported by almost all modern programming languages. Hence, it makes sense to define an abstract representation of this statement, but now let's consider a *fixed statement* provided by C# used to prevent the relocation of a variable by the garbage collector. This statement is not available in any other language and hence would be difficult to generalize and consider it under a general-purpose code object model. However, this shouldn't be the bottleneck; if you look at the brighter side, the CodeDOM provides a rich object model that is truly appealing and compels developers to integrate it in their day-to-day tasks. Let's walk through Figure 8-5 to see how.

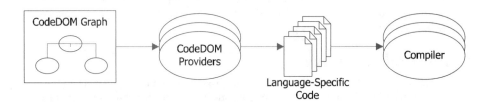

Figure 8-5. *Conceptual flow of how abstract code is processed using the CodeDOM framework*

Figure 8-5 represents a conceptual flow of generating and compiling source code using the CodeDOM framework. At a high level, there are three stages, and each stage plays an important role in the overall code-generation process. The first stage is to create the CodeDOM graph that is populated with objects defined in the System.CodeDOM namespace. This namespace contains classes used to model the structure and elements of the source code. After successfully populating the object graph, it is then fed to CodeDOM providers. CodeDOM providers are code generators that understand the CodeDOM object graph and generate source code in a particular programming language. In this way, the code-generation logic is encapsulated in its own component, and such flexibility allows representing code in any new language without undertaking any code rewriting. Additionally, it is possible to directly compile the object graph into an executable form. Both the code generation and compilation tasks are defined inside the System.CodeDom.Compiler namespace, and shortly we will discuss this topic in detail.

To illustrate the implementation aspect of the CodeDOM, we will present the C# code in Listing 8-1, which represents a custom class of a stock price. It contains attributes such as the name of the stock, ask price, bid price, and so on. To keep the code simple, we have omitted most of the essential attributes that usually form part of the stock information.

Listing 8-1. *Sorting of Stock Data*

```
using System;
using System.Collections;

//Stock Domain Model
public class StockData
{
  public string Symbol;
  public double AskPrice;
  public double BidPrice;
}

//Custom Comparer to sort stock data
public class StockSorter : IComparer
{
  string fldName;
  public StockSorter(string fld)
  {
    //since we want to provide sorting on individual field
    //of stock class, the name of the field on
    //which the sort is performed is accepted as the constructor
    //argument
    fldName=fld;
  }

  public int Compare(object x, object y)
  {
    StockData leftObj= x as StockData;
    StockData rightObj=y as StockData;
    //If sorting is to be done on symbol field
    if ( fldName == "Symbol" )
    {
      return leftObj.Symbol.CompareTo(rightObj.Symbol);
    }
    //If sorting is to be done on ask price field
    if ( fldName == "AskPrice" )
    {
      return leftObj.AskPrice.CompareTo(rightObj.AskPrice);
    }
    return 1;
  }
}

class SortNormal
{
  [STAThread]
  static void Main(string[] args)
  {
    //create stock list
    ArrayList stockList = new ArrayList();

    //create msft stock
    StockData stkData1 = new StockData();
    stkData1.Symbol = "MSFT";
```

```
//create ibm stock
StockData stkData2= new StockData();
stkData2.Symbol = "IBM";

//add both msft and ibm stock
stockList.Add(stkData1);
stockList.Add(stkData2);

while(true)
{
  //prompt name of the field to sort
  Console.WriteLine("Enter name of the field to sort on : ");
  string fldName = Console.ReadLine();

  //instantiate the custom comparer, passing the field name
  StockSorter stockSorter = new StockSorter(fldName);

  //sort the list
  stockList.Sort(stockSorter);

  //display the sorted stock item
  Console.WriteLine(fldName +" ----------------------" );
  foreach(StockData stkData in stockList)
  {
    Console.WriteLine("Symbol {0} AskPrice {1} BidPrice {2}
    ",stkData.Symbol,stkData.AskPrice,stkData.BidPrice);
  }
  Console.WriteLine("------------------------------");
}
}
}
```

In Listing 8-1, particularly in the application entry point method, we have declared the StockData class that represents stock information, and an individual instance of it is stored in an array. The important section to explore is the loop code that prompts for a field name, based on which the elements stored in the array are sorted using quick-sort functionality, which was already discussed in depth in Chapter 2. The trick in this code example is to provide sorting on any valid field; to accomplish this, we identified and defined all possible field lists in the Compare method of StockSorter. However, the disadvantage of this approach is that the field list is defined during design time, and if a new field is introduced in the class, then it will trigger a fair amount of modification in the implementation of the comparer class and also a recompilation of the program. To escape this problem, we will demonstrate the practical use of both the CodeDOM and reflection. Before we proceed, we need to slightly modify the code structure to suit this new example, as shown in Figure 8-6.

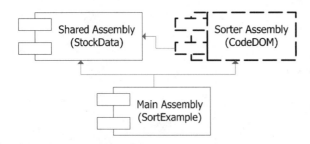

Figure 8-6. *New assembly structure*

From Figure 8-6 it should be clear the kind of code refactoring we are envisaging. The comparison logic that was enclosed inside the main assembly (that is, StockSorter) will now be dynamically generated using the CodeDOM. Similarly, the stock information is separated in a new shared assembly and will be referenced by both the main and dynamically generated assemblies. The first installment of this exercise is to define StockData in a shared assembly:

```
using System;

namespace SharedAssembly
{
  public class StockData
  {
    public string Symbol;
    public double AskPrice;
    public double BidPrice;
  }
}
```

The next installment is the revised code of the main assembly that triggers the code-generation process:

```
using System;
using System.Collections;
using SharedAssembly;

class SortCodeDOM
{
  static void Main(string[] args)
  {
    //create empty arraylist
    ArrayList stockList = new ArrayList();
    //create msft stock
    StockData stkData1 = new StockData();
    stkData1.Symbol = "MSFT";
    stkData1.AskPrice = 10;
    stkData1.BidPrice = 12;

    //create ibm stock
    StockData stkData2= new StockData();
    stkData2.Symbol = "IBM";
    stkData2.AskPrice = 12;
    stkData2.BidPrice = 9;

    //create GE stock
    StockData stkData3 = new StockData();
    stkData3.Symbol = "GE";
    stkData3.AskPrice = 13;
    stkData3.BidPrice = 10;

    //add stock
    stockList.Add(stkData1);
    stockList.Add(stkData2);
    stockList.Add(stkData3);

    while(true)
    {
      //prompt name of the field to sort
      Console.WriteLine("Enter name of the field to sort on : ");
```

```
      string fldName = Console.ReadLine();
      //generate custom comparer code using CodeDOM
      SortByCodeDOM sort = new SortByCodeDOM(fldName);
      //sort the list
      stockList.Sort(sort.GetComparer());
      //display the sorted stock item
      Console.WriteLine(fldName +" ----------------------" );
      foreach(StockData stkData in stockList)
      {
        Console.WriteLine("Symbol {0} AskPrice {1} BidPrice {2}
              ",stkData.Symbol,stkData.AskPrice,stkData.BidPrice);
      }
      Console.WriteLine("------------------------------");
    }
  }
}
```

There is nothing extraordinary in the previous code except that a new class, SortByCodeDOM, is instantiated, and its GetComparer method is invoked, which returns an instance of IComparer, as shown in Listing 8-2.

Listing 8-2. *Sorting of Stock Data (Using the CodeDOM)*

```
using System;
using System.Collections;

public class SortByCodeDOM
{
  string fldName;
  public SortByCodeDOM(string fld)
  {
    fldName=fld;
  }

  public IComparer GetComparer()
  {
    //Dynamic Generation of Code using CodeDOM
    return null;
  }
}
```

The real food will be cooked inside GetComparer, whose method body is currently empty. But you are now going to populate this method with suitable logic to generate the correct sorting implementation that is based on a particular field of StockData. Listing 8-3 shows the code that will get dynamically generated. This code will not get compiled; it is still in unfinished form, and we have purposely described it to further strengthen your understanding.

Listing 8-3. *Customizing the Sort Order of the Stock Data*

```
using System;
using System.Collections;
using SharedAssembly;

namespace SorterAssembly
{
  public class SortCode : IComparer
  {
```

```
    public int Compare(object x, object y)
    {
      StockData leftObj;
      StockData rightObj;
      leftObj= x as StockData;
      rightObj=y as StockData;
      return leftObj.<Field Name>.CompareTo(rightObj.<Field Name>);
    }
  }
}
```

If you were told to translate the code described in Listing 8-3 in a pseudo-code format, then it is simply a matter of breaking up the code into fine-grained steps, as follows:

1. Reference SharedAssembly, which will allow you to access StockData.

2. Declare the new namespace SorterAssembly.

3. Import the System, System.Collections, and SharedAssembly namespaces.

4. Create a new class under the SorterAssembly namespace. Name this class SortCode. This class will also implement the IComparer interface.

5. Create the new method Compare. The method return type is int, and it accepts two method arguments of type Object.

6. Populate the method body. The first two lines of the body are to cast both input arguments to StockData. The last line of the code is to invoke the CompareTo method on one of the input parameters.

Now let's look at how to leverage the CodeDOM classes with a step-by-step translation of the previous pseudo-code into an abstract hierarchy of code elements.

The first and foremost requirement of the CodeDOM is to construct an instance of CodeCompileUnit, which provides a container for the CodeDOM object graph and is a representation of an assembly. The two most important attributes provided by this class are ReferencedAssemblies and AssemblyCustomAttributes. ReferencedAssemblies is a string collection that contains the filenames of the referenced assemblies. Similarly, the AssemblyCustomAttributes property represents custom attributes of the assembly and is defined with the help of CodeAttributeDeclarationCollection. For example:

```
CodeCompileUnit compileUnit = new CodeCompileUnit();
```

The next step after declaring the container is to define a new namespace, so accordingly you use CodeNameSpace to represent a namespace:

```
//Step2 - create a new namespace
CodeNamespace newNameSpace = new CodeNamespace("SorterAssembly");
```

Next, you declare the list of namespaces referenced by the program, which is equivalent to the using namespace directive in C#. The Imports property of CodeNameSpace represents namespaces referenced by assembly. This property returns CodeNamespaceImportCollection, which represents a collection of CodeNamespaceImport objects. After populating this namespace collection, the newly created instance of CodeNameSpace is then added to CodeCompileUnit, like so:

```
//Step3 - Import namespaces
newNameSpace.Imports.Add(new CodeNamespaceImport("System"));
newNameSpace.Imports.Add(new CodeNamespaceImport("System.Collections"));
newNameSpace.Imports.Add(new CodeNamespaceImport("SharedAssembly"));
compileUnit.Namespaces.Add(newNameSpace);
```

The next step is to define the SortCode class using CodeTypeDeclaration, which is also used to represent the structure, interface, or enumeration. The IsClass, IsStruct, IsEnum, and IsInterface methods of CodeTypeDeclaration indicate the underlying type. Additionally, you also derive the SortCode class from IComparer by populating the BaseTypes property of CodeTypeDeclaration, and finally you group it under the newly created namespace:

```
//Step4 - Defines new Type
CodeTypeDeclaration newType = new CodeTypeDeclaration("SortCode");
newType.BaseTypes.Add(typeof(IComparer));
newNameSpace.Types.Add(newType);
```

Next, you declare the Compare method using CodeMemberMethod. This class represents a declaration for a method, and both the name of the method and its accessibility are assigned, respectively, by setting the Name and Attributes properties. This newly created member is then added to the SortCode class by populating the Members property of CodeTypeDeclaration:

```
//Step5 - Declare Method
CodeMemberMethod compareMethod = new CodeMemberMethod();
compareMethod.ReturnType = new CodeTypeReference(typeof(int));
compareMethod.Name = "Compare";
compareMethod.Attributes = MemberAttributes.Public | MemberAttributes.Final;
newType.Members.Add(compareMethod);
```

CodeMemberMethod is also extended by other classes:

- CodeConstructor: Represents a constructor member declaration

- CodeEntryPointMethod: Defines an executable entry point

- CodeTypeConstructor: Represents a static constructor member declaration

If you look at the code described in Listing 8-3, the Compare method accepts two input arguments, and accordingly you define both these arguments with CodeParameterDeclarationExpression. This class represents code that declares arguments for a method, property, or constructor. As you can guess, the individual instance of CodeParameterDeclarationExpression is then added to the Parameters collection of the CodeMemberMethod (the Compare method), which also completes the method declaration step:

```
CodeParameterDeclarationExpression param1 = new
               CodeParameterDeclarationExpression(typeof(object),"x");
CodeParameterDeclarationExpression param2 = new
               CodeParameterDeclarationExpression(typeof(object),"y");
compareMethod.Parameters.Add(param1);
compareMethod.Parameters.Add(param2);
```

CodeParameterDeclarationExpression is derived from CodeExpression, which forms a base class for declaring any type of code expression. The following are the derived classes that represent the various types of code expression:

- CodeArgumentReferenceExpression: Represents a reference to the value of an argument passed to a method

- CodeArrayCreateExpression: Represents an array creation expression

- CodeArrayIndexerExpression: Represents a reference to an index of an array

- CodeBaseReferenceExpression: Represents a reference to the base class

- CodeBinaryOperatorExpression: Represents a binary operation between two expressions

- CodeCastExpression: Represents a cast expression

- CodeDelegateCreateExpression: Represents an expression to create a delegate

- `CodeDelegateInvokeExpression`: Represents an expression that raises an event

- `CodeEventReferenceExpression`: Represents a reference to an event

- `CodeFieldReferenceExpression`: Represents a reference to a field

- `CodeMethodInvokeExpression`: Represents an expression that invokes a method

- `CodeObjectCreateExpression`: Represents an expression that creates a new instance of a type

- `CodeParameterDeclarationExpression`: Represents a parameter declaration for a method, property, or constructor

- `CodePropertyReferenceExpression`: Represents a reference to the value of a property

- `CodePropertySetValueReferenceExpression`: Represents the value argument of a property set method call within a property set method

- `CodeThisReferenceExpression`: Represents a reference to the current local class instance

- `CodeTypeOfExpression`: Represents a typeof expression

- `CodeTypeReferenceExpression`: Represents a reference to a data type

- `CodeVariableReferenceExpression`: Represents a reference to a local variable

- `CodeSnippetExpression`: Represents a literal expression

After adding the parameter declaration for the `Compare` method, the next step is to populate the body of the method; you do this using the `Statements` property of `CodeMemberMethod`. This property returns `CodeStatementsCollections`, which represents a collection of `CodeStatement` objects. `CodeStatement` represents individual code constructs that appear within method bodies, properties, and so on. For instance, local variable declaration is one type of code statement, so to accommodate different types of code statements, `CodeStatement` is further extended. In the following code, you declare two local variables of type `StockData` using `CodeVariableDeclarationStatement`, which basically represents the first and second lines of code in the `Compare` method described in Listing 8-3:

```
//Step6 - Populate Method Body
//Declare the Variable
CodeVariableDeclarationStatement leftObj = new
            CodeVariableDeclarationStatement("StockData","leftObj");
CodeVariableDeclarationStatement rightObj = new
            CodeVariableDeclarationStatement("StockData","rightObj");
compareMethod.Statements.Add(leftObj);
compareMethod.Statements.Add(rightObj);
```

The following are the classes that directly derive from `CodeStatement`:

- `CodeAssignStatement`: Represents an assignment statement.

- `CodeAttachEventStatement`: Represents the attachment of an event handler.

- `CodeCommentStatement`: Represents a single-line comment statement.

- `CodeConditionStatement`: Represents a conditional branch statement.

- `CodeExpressionStatement`: Represents a statement that consists of a single expression.

- `CodeGotoStatement`: Represents a goto statement.

- `CodeIterationStatement`: Represents a loop statement.

- `CodeMethodReturnStatement`: Represents a return value statement.

- `CodeRemoveEventStatement`: Represents the removal of an event handler.

- `CodeSnippetStatement`: `CodeSnippetStatement` can represent a statement using a literal code fragment that will be included directly in the source without modification.

- `CodeThrowExceptionStatement`: Represents a statement that throws an exception.

- `CodeTryCatchFinallyStatement`: Represents a `try-catch-finally` statement.

- `CodeVariableDeclarationStatement`: Represents a variable declaration.

Next, a cast operation is performed on both input arguments, and the result of it is assigned to a local variable. Another important thing is even though method bodies are populated using `CodeStatement`, usually `CodeStatement` is composed from `CodeExpression`. This step represents the third and fourth lines of code in the `Compare` method described in Listing 8-3:

```
//Cast x argument
CodeCastExpression leftcastExp = new
CodeCastExpression("StockData",new CodeVariableReferenceExpression("x"));
CodeAssignStatement leftcastStmt = new
  CodeAssignStatement(new CodeVariableReferenceExpression("leftObj"),leftcastExp);
compareMethod.Statements.Add(leftcastStmt );
//Cast y argument
CodeCastExpression rightcastExp = new
  CodeCastExpression("StockData",new CodeVariableReferenceExpression("y"));
CodeAssignStatement rightcastStmt = new
  CodeAssignStatement(new
    CodeVariableReferenceExpression("rightObj"),rightcastExp);
compareMethod.Statements.Add(rightcastStmt);
```

Finally, a closer look at the following code will reveal that the code generated is specialized to access a particular field; to be precise, the field name mentioned refers to the argument supplied to the `SortByCodeDOM` constructor:

```
//Compare both field value and return the result
CodePropertyReferenceExpression leftExp= new
  CodePropertyReferenceExpression(new
    CodeVariableReferenceExpression("leftObj"),fldName);
CodePropertyReferenceExpression rightExp = new
  CodePropertyReferenceExpression(new
    CodeVariableReferenceExpression("rightObj"),fldName);
CodeMethodInvokeExpression methodExp = new
  CodeMethodInvokeExpression(leftExp,"CompareTo",rightExp);
CodeMethodReturnStatement retStmt = new
  CodeMethodReturnStatement(methodExp);
compareMethod.Statements.Add(retStmt);
```

This brings an end to the population of the CodeDOM object graph. At this stage, the CodeDOM object graph is populated in a language-neutral manner, and this tree is now ready for parsing in order to produce language-specific code. The parsing functionality happens via CodeDOM providers. CodeDOM providers are responsible for translating the CodeDOM tree into a language-specific implementation. Since the multiple languages would result into multiple implementations of code providers, each provider needs to inherit from `CodeDOMProvider`. `CodeDOMProvider` is the abstract base class and provides interfaces for code generation and code compilation. The code-generation feature is retrieved with a call to `CreateGenerator`, which returns an object that implements the `ICodeGenerator` interface. Similarly, the code compilation feature is retrieved with a call to `CreateCompiler`, which returns an object that implements `ICodeCompiler`. `Microsoft.CSharp.CSharpCodeProvider` and `Microsoft.VisualBasic.VBCodeProvider` are the default CodeDOM providers available in the .NET Framework.

So, the next step is to construct a language-specific code provider, which in this case is the C# code provider itself, and transform the abstract code graph into C# source code. The following code demonstrates this:

```
Console.WriteLine("Translating CodeDOM object graph into text...");
//create C# code provider
CodeDomProvider csharpProv = new CSharpCodeProvider();
ICodeGenerator csharpCodeGen = csharpProv.CreateGenerator();
StringBuilder builder = new StringBuilder();
StringWriter writer = new StringWriter(builder);
//code-generation option
CodeGeneratorOptions opt = new CodeGeneratorOptions();
//convert CodeDOM graph into source code
csharpCodeGen.GenerateCodeFromCompileUnit(compileUnit,writer,opt);
```

After getting an instance of ICodeGenerator, you then convert the object graph to text using GenerateCodeFromCompileUnit. This method takes three arguments; the first argument is an instance of CodeCompileUnit, the second argument refers to StringWriter into which the output is redirected, and the third argument is an instance of CodeGeneratorOptions that allows modifying the output format of the generated code.

The final phase is to translate the CodeDOM object graph into a compiled form, and you do this with the help of CompileAssemblyFromDom defined in ICodeCompiler. CompileAssemblyFromDom is supplied with an instance of CompilerParameters that provides various tweaking features required during the compilation process. One of the features it provides is compiling the CodeDOM object graph either into a class library or into an executable form. It also provides options to persist the assembly either in memory or to disk. In the following code, the CodeDOM object graph is compiled in memory, and the result of the compilation is collected with the help of CompilerResults:

```
Console.WriteLine("Translating CodeDOM object graph into assembly...");
//create c-sharp compiler
ICodeCompiler csharpCompiler = csharpProv.CreateCompiler();
CompilerParameters param = new CompilerParameters(new
                    string[]{"System.dll","SharedAssembly.dll"});
param.GenerateExecutable=false;
param.GenerateInMemory=true;
//compile the source code
CompilerResults results =
          csharpCompiler.CompileAssemblyFromDom(param,compileUnit);
foreach(CompilerError error in results.Errors)
{
  Console.WriteLine(error.ErrorText);
}
//check for any errors
if ( results.Errors.Count > 0 ) return null;
```

The advantage of in-memory generation of an assembly is that a reference to the generated assembly can be obtained from the CompiledAssembly property of CompilerResults. Similarly, if the assembly is written to disk, then the path to the newly generated assembly is obtained from the PathToAssembly property of CompilerResults. In both cases, the assembly is loaded into the current application domain, and with the help of reflection you instantiate the new class that implements the IComparer interface and contains comparison logic specific to a particular field of StockData:

```
IComparer comparer=
  results.CompiledAssembly.CreateInstance("SorterAssembly.SortCode") as IComparer;
return comparer;
```

This completes the GetComparer implementation of SortByCodeDOM. Now let's compile and run the SortCodeDOM assembly. Figure 8-7 shows the console output of SortCodeDOM.

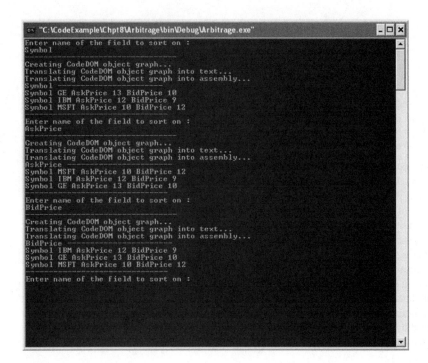

Figure 8-7. *Console output of sort-by-CodeDOM program*

Introducing Reflection

As you are aware, reflection is about examining and querying type information at runtime. It provides rich metadata that is available only during runtime, and based on this information, developers can implement more advanced programming techniques. Developers often resort to writing tons of code when implementing a complex feature, but in this section we will discuss the reflection class library and also highlight the fact that you can develop some cool features using reflection.

The Reflection API is defined inside the System.Reflection namespace. It contains classes and interfaces that provide an object-oriented representation of loaded assemblies, modules, types, and methods. If you look at Figure 8-8, the individual types are organized in a hierarchy fashion, and they depict a traversing path in which metadata is accessed. At the top of the hierarchy is AppDomain, which provides information about the loaded assemblies in the form of Assembly. Assembly is composed of multiple modules. A module is represented by Module, and it contains types and interfaces. The most important element of reflection is a class and is represented by Type. With access to Type, the entire information about a class including the list of fields, methods, properties, interfaces, nested types, custom attributes, and so on, can be retrieved.

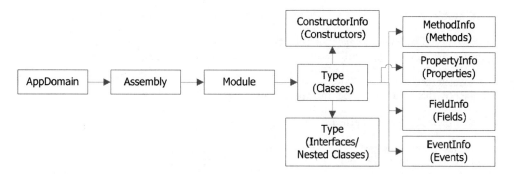

Figure 8-8. *Traversing path using reflection*

The following is a class search example that uses reflection to locate a class based on user input. On a successful search, the program lists the class methods, fields, and properties.

```
using System;
using System.Reflection;

class Reflector
{
  static void Main(string[] args)
  {
    Console.WriteLine("Enter name of the type to search for : " );
    //Prompt for type name
    string typeName = Console.ReadLine();
    //Initiate the search
    SearchType(typeName);
  }

  public static void SearchType(string typeName)
  {
    //iterate thru assembly
    foreach(Assembly curAssem in AppDomain.CurrentDomain.GetAssemblies())
    {
      //iterate through module
      foreach(Module curModule in curAssem.GetModules())
      {
        //iterate through type
        foreach(Type curType in curModule.GetTypes())
        {
          if ( curType.Name == typeName )
          {
            Console.WriteLine("Found inside Assembly : " +curAssem.FullName);
            //on successful search, display the type information
            RetrieveTypeInfo(curType);
            break;
          }
        }
      }
    }
  }
}
```

```
public static void RetrieveTypeInfo(Type type)
{
  //display all methods defined in this type
  Console.WriteLine("Type Full Name : " +type.FullName);
  Console.WriteLine("List of Methods");
  Console.WriteLine("----------------");
  foreach(MethodInfo curMethod in type.GetMethods())
  {
    Console.WriteLine(curMethod.Name);
  }
  //display properties defined in this type
  Console.WriteLine("List of Properties");
  Console.WriteLine("------------------");
  foreach(PropertyInfo propInfo in type.GetProperties())
  {
    Console.WriteLine(propInfo.Name);
  }
  //display fields defined in this type
  Console.WriteLine("List of Fields");
  Console.WriteLine("--------------");
  foreach(FieldInfo fldInfo in type.GetFields())
  {
    Console.WriteLine(fldInfo.Name);
  }
}
}
```

Figure 8-9 shows the console output of the class search program.

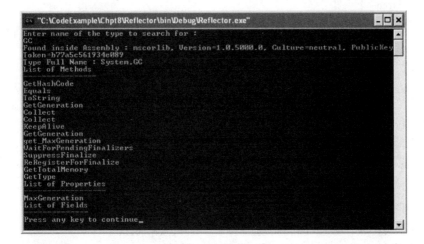

Figure 8-9. *Console output of class search program*

Another mechanism provided by reflection is late binding. *Late binding* is a technique in which an instance of a class or a method invocation takes place at runtime instead of compile time. The only downside to using late binding is that you lose the type safety–related checks done by compilers. However, the upside is that this ability of reflection allows you to build a highly extensible and pluggable application. For instance, you can locate a specific method in a type, determine the number of arguments required and their underlying types, and finally invoke this method. You can achieve this entire task dynamically.

To give you an idea of what we are talking about, let's rewrite the stock sort example using reflection, as shown in Listing 8-4.

Listing 8-4. *Sorting of Stock Data (Using Reflection)*

```
using System;
using System.Reflection;
using SharedAssembly;
using System.Collections;

class ReflectionComparer   : IComparer
{
  string fldName;
  public ReflectionComparer(string fld)
  {
    fldName = fld;
  }

  public int Compare(object x, object y)
  {
    StockData leftObj = x as StockData;
    StockData rightObj = y as StockData;

    //Retrieve field meta data
    FieldInfo leftField= leftObj.GetType().GetField(fldName);
    FieldInfo rightField= rightObj.GetType().GetField(fldName);

    //Retrieve field value
    object leftValue = leftField.GetValue(leftObj);
    object rightValue = rightField.GetValue(rightObj);

   //Retrieve method metadata
    MethodInfo leftMethod = leftField.FieldType.GetMethod("CompareTo",new
                          Type[]{leftValue.GetType()});
    //invoke the method
    object retValue = leftMethod.Invoke(leftValue,new object[]{rightValue});
    return (int)retValue;
  }
}

public class SortByReflection
{
  string fldName;

  public SortByReflection(string fld)
  {
    fldName=fld;
  }

  public IComparer GetComparer()
  {
    return new ReflectionComparer(fldName);
  }
}
```

The corresponding impact in the main assembly now sorts the list using reflection:

```
using System;
using System.Collections;
using SharedAssembly;

class SortReflection
{
  static void Main(string[] args)
  {
    ArrayList stockList = new ArrayList();
    StockData stkData1 = new StockData();
    stkData1.Symbol = "MSFT";
    stkData1.AskPrice = 10;
    stkData1.BidPrice = 12;

    StockData stkData2= new StockData();
    stkData2.Symbol = "IBM";
    stkData2.AskPrice = 12;
    stkData2.BidPrice = 9;

    StockData stkData3 = new StockData();
    stkData3.Symbol = "GE";
    stkData3.AskPrice = 13;
    stkData3.BidPrice = 10;

    stockList.Add(stkData1);
    stockList.Add(stkData2);
    stockList.Add(stkData3);

    while(true)
    {
      Console.WriteLine("Enter name of the field to sort on : ");
      string fldName = Console.ReadLine();
      SortByReflection sort = new SortByReflection(fldName);
      stockList.Sort(sort.GetComparer());
      Console.WriteLine(fldName +" ----------------------" );
      foreach(StockData stkData in stockList)
      {
        Console.WriteLine("Symbol {0} AskPrice {1} BidPrice {2}
                  ",stkData.Symbol,stkData.AskPrice,stkData.BidPrice);
      }
      Console.WriteLine("------------------------------");
    }
  }
}
```

You have seen in Listing 8-4 how reflection is used to dynamically determine the field, query the field, and then invoke the CompareTo method. Certainly, you can achieve this kind of flexibility only using reflection, but it comes with a cost. The cost is impact both in performance and maintenance. First, it is hard to debug code that uses reflection, and any errors produced as a result of dynamic invocation are often not so friendly to diagnose. Second, this impacts performance; it is obvious that early-binding method calls will always be faster than late-binding ones. But sometimes it is impossible to escape using reflection. Reflection is a privilege offered by the .NET Framework, and a balanced use of it will lead to the design of highly extensible applications.

Code Generation Using Reflection.Emit

Another approach to dynamically generating code is using `Reflection.Emit`, which is an extremely powerful code-generation weapon that directly emits raw MSIL code. This is in contrast to the CodeDOM, which has the ability to generate code in multiple languages such as C#, VB .NET, and so on, which is then translated by compilers into low-level MSIL code. Using `Reflection.Emit`, you avoid the intermediate compilation step because the code emitted is already in its lowest common denominator form. This certainly boosts the code-generation time. But, the biggest problem is that developers need to be proficient with MSIL instructions, and this restricts its usage to the hands of a few developers. It also begs the question as to why anyone would want to dirty their hands with `Reflection.Emit`. The primary reason is it provides tighter control to structure the IL code, which is nearly impossible to achieve from high-level languages. This is similar to system programmers shying away from the C language and using low-level assembly code to achieve machine-specific optimizations.

You will now see how classes defined in the `System.Reflection.Emit` namespace are used to emit MSIL. We are assuming you are familiar with MSIL syntax. Based on this assumption, we will now show how to rewrite the sort implementation. Before we delve into the code-level details, though, the following are the important classes:

- `AssemblyBuilder`: Defines an assembly.

- `ModuleBuilder`: Defines a module.

- `TypeBuilder`: Defines a class.

- `ConstructorBuilder`: Defines a constructor for a class.

- `FieldBuilder`: Defines a field for a class.

- `EventBuilder`: Defines events for a class.

- `MethodBuilder`: Defines methods for a class.

- `PropertyBuilder`: Defines properties for a class.

- `ILGenerator`: Defines MSIL instructions. This class is referenced by both `ConstructorBuilder` and `MethodBuilder` to implement the body of the method.

- `OpCodes`: Provides field representations of the MSIL instructions used by the `ILGenerator` class members.

We will now show how to rewrite the sort example using `Reflection.Emit`. Listing 8-5 provides you with the first taste of how to emit raw IL code at runtime.

Listing 8-5. *Sorting of Stock Data (Using* `Reflection.Emit`*)*

```
using System;
using System.Collections;
using System.Reflection;
using System.Reflection.Emit;
using SharedAssembly;

public class SortByReflectionEmit
{
  string fldName;
  public SortByReflectionEmit(string fld)
  {
    fldName = fld;
  }
```

```csharp
public IComparer GetComparer()
{
  AssemblyName asmName = new AssemblyName();
  asmName.Name = "SorterAssembly";

  //Define a new in-memory assembly
  AssemblyBuilder asmBuilder = AppDomain.CurrentDomain.DefineDynamicAssembly
                           (asmName,AssemblyBuilderAccess.Run);

  //Define a new module
  ModuleBuilder modBuilder = asmBuilder.DefineDynamicModule("SorterModule");

  //Create a new Type, and implement IComparer interface
  TypeBuilder typeBuilder = modBuilder.DefineType
                           ("SortCode",TypeAttributes.Public);
  typeBuilder.AddInterfaceImplementation(typeof(IComparer));

  //Create Compare Method with 2 input arguments and also declare return type
  //as int
  MethodBuilder methodBuilder = typeBuilder.DefineMethod
      ("Compare",MethodAttributes.Public | MethodAttributes.Virtual,typeof(int),
      new Type[] {typeof(object),typeof(object)});

  //Implements IComparer Compare Method
  MethodInfo compareMethod = typeof(IComparer).GetMethod("Compare");
  typeBuilder.DefineMethodOverride(methodBuilder,compareMethod);

  //Generate IL code for the above declared method
  ILGenerator ilGenerator = methodBuilder.GetILGenerator();


  //Declare two local variables i.e. leftObj and rightObj
  ilGenerator.DeclareLocal(typeof(StockData));
  ilGenerator.DeclareLocal(typeof(StockData));
  //Declare local variable to hold result returned by CompareTo method
  ilGenerator.DeclareLocal(typeof(int));

  //Cast x object to StockData type, and store it inside local variable
  ilGenerator.Emit(OpCodes.Ldarg_1);
  ilGenerator.Emit(OpCodes.Isinst,typeof(StockData));
  ilGenerator.Emit(OpCodes.Stloc_0);

  //Cast y object to StockData type, and store it inside local variable
  ilGenerator.Emit(OpCodes.Ldarg_2);
  ilGenerator.Emit(OpCodes.Isinst,typeof(StockData));
  ilGenerator.Emit(OpCodes.Stloc_1);

  //Access field of x object using reflection
  FieldInfo xField = typeof(StockData).GetField(fldName);

   //Access the field of x object
  ilGenerator.Emit(OpCodes.Ldloc_0);

  if ( xField.FieldType.IsValueType == true )
    ilGenerator.Emit(OpCodes.Ldflda,xField);
  else
    ilGenerator.Emit(OpCodes.Ldfld,xField);
```

```
    //Access field of y object using reflection
    FieldInfo yField = typeof(StockData).GetField(fldName);

    //Access the field of y object
    ilGenerator.Emit(OpCodes.Ldloc_1);
    ilGenerator.Emit(OpCodes.Ldfld,yField);

    //Boxing Operation in case field value returns a value type
    if ( yField.FieldType.IsValueType == true )
    {
      ilGenerator.Emit(OpCodes.Box,yField.FieldType);
    }

    //Invoke Compare Method, and return the comparison result
    MethodInfo invokeCompare = yField.FieldType.GetMethod("CompareTo",
            new Type[]{typeof(object)});
    ilGenerator.Emit(OpCodes.Call,invokeCompare);
    ilGenerator.Emit(OpCodes.Stloc_2);

    Label codeBranch = ilGenerator.DefineLabel();
    ilGenerator.Emit(OpCodes.Br_S,codeBranch);
    ilGenerator.MarkLabel(codeBranch);
    ilGenerator.Emit(OpCodes.Ldloc_2);
    ilGenerator.Emit(OpCodes.Ret);

    //Create the Type
    typeBuilder.CreateType();

    //Instantiate the dynamic type
    IComparer comparer=  asmBuilder.CreateInstance("SortCode",true)
                      as IComparer;
    return comparer;
  }
}
```

The corresponding impact in the main assembly now sorts the list using Reflection.Emit:

```
using System;
using System.Collections;
using SharedAssembly;


class SortReflectionEmit
{
  static void Main(string[] args)
  {
    ArrayList stockList = new ArrayList();
    StockData stkData1 = new StockData();
    stkData1.Symbol = "MSFT";

    stkData1.AskPrice = 10;
    stkData1.BidPrice = 12;

    StockData stkData2= new StockData();
    stkData2.Symbol = "IBM";
    stkData2.AskPrice = 12;
    stkData2.BidPrice = 9;
```

```
        StockData stkData3 = new StockData();
        stkData3.Symbol = "GE";
        stkData3.AskPrice = 13;
        stkData3.BidPrice = 10;

        stockList.Add(stkData1);
        stockList.Add(stkData2);
        stockList.Add(stkData3);

        while(true)
        {
          Console.WriteLine("Enter name of the field to sort on : ");
          string fldName = Console.ReadLine();
          SortByReflectionEmit sort = new SortByReflectionEmit(fldName);
          stockList.Sort(sort.GetComparer());

          Console.WriteLine(fldName +" ----------------------" );
          foreach(StockData stkData in stockList)
          {
            Console.WriteLine("Symbol {0} AskPrice {1} BidPrice {2}
                   ",stkData.Symbol,stkData.AskPrice,stkData.BidPrice);
          }
          Console.WriteLine("------------------------------");
        }
      }
    }
}
```

Examining the Business-Technology Mapping

The most important element in designing an arbitrage engine is the type of strategy with which the market participant wants to experiment. The strategy can range from a simple one that has less risk to a complex one. In either case, the goal is to make money and get the maximum mileage from this short window of opportunity provided to the participant. Another interesting fact is only a few vendors offer off-the-shelf products that address the arbitrage requirements of an organization. Such limited support from commercial vendors is because each individual organization has its own requirements that are difficult to generalize. Therefore, organizations most of the times tend to settle on building such engines in-house (see Figure 8-10).

Figure 8-10. *Simple arbitrage engine*

As you know, arbitrage trading is another tactic to make money, but it can be exploited only by automation. This may start with a simple arbitrage engine that tracks opportunities based on stock price differences. The first prerequisite in this case is to subscribe to market data from various exchanges; also, it is important that data is made available in a timely manner. The whole concept of arbitrage is based on that there are imbalances in stock prices that will last for short period of times. Therefore, even a fraction of a delay in receiving market data is sufficient to lose such opportunities.

Another way of building an arbitrage engine is by using various arbitrage models (see Figure 8-11). An arbitrage model contains core logic that seeks out arbitrage opportunities. This logic is usually complex in nature and is defined using mathematical models and analyzing historical data. The engine provides a plug-and-play approach where traders have complete freedom to come out with their own model and then associate it with the engine. Such flexibility often results in the creation of various models specialized for a particular stock or event. These models are often coded in a programming language that traders are comfortable with; most of the time it is C++, but this trend is changing. Nowadays they are written in C#. Microsoft Excel is the favorite candidate and is an ideal choice for building calculation-intensive applications.

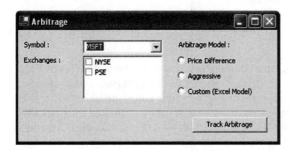

Figure 8-11. *Arbitrage engine architected based on different type of arbitrage models*

Considering the popularity of the Office suite, Microsoft released Office Primary Interop Assemblies (PIA), which allows the seamless integration of .NET applications with Microsoft Office. With the help of Office PIA, it is possible to define arbitrage models using Excel macro programming features and then integrate them with engines that are .NET applications. Such mix-and-match capability proves to be extremely beneficial both to traders and to developers. Developers do not need to worry about business logic and can concentrate on the infrastructure aspect of the engine such as the faster processing of market data, multithreading, and so on. Similarly, traders are not dependent upon developers and are in complete charge of the underlying business logic. No doubt such separation of responsibility provides much tighter control to traders, but a word of caution is that the performance of the application needs to be closely examined. As you know, an arbitrage opportunity exists for a very short interval, so the system must not only capture this opportunity but must also undertake several computation steps to determine whether this opportunity is favorable and healthy for the business. This decision-making process needs to be highly optimized; therefore, the code written by traders needs to be thoroughly reviewed before it is integrated with the system.

Another sophisticated version of an arbitrage engine is to provide a rule-driven interface to traders (see Figure 8-12). This allows traders to capture all types of arbitrage strategies in the form of rules. The rules defined are then interpreted by the rule engine, which serves as the execution engine for the arbitrage strategy. They allow flexibility by externalizing the business logic from the system logic and representing the logic with rules that are then easy to modify. Rules are defined from business vocabulary definitions.

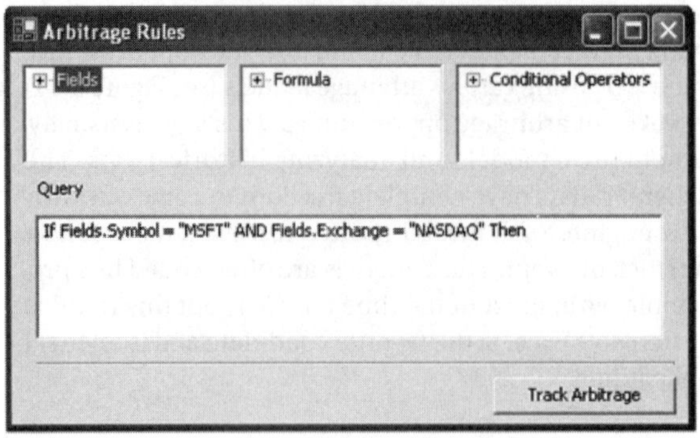

Figure 8-12. *Rule-based arbitrage engine*

The rule engine consists of design and run-time components. Design-time components provide the appropriate interface that allows the rules to be defined. These rules are then parsed and validated to detect both syntax and semantic errors. On the other hand, run-time components look after the execution aspect of rules, which is achieved by identifying the stock information that the rules are processed against to produce the desired output. The motivation behind the rule engine is it avoids the need of translating the business requirements in a procedural instructions language, which is usually done by developers. With the help of the engine, the task is directly assigned to traders, and they can directly define the rules in their own business language. Furthermore, to simplify such tasks, traders are presented with an easy-to-use GUI-based rule management tool.

From an implementation perspective, the rule engine can leverage an automated code-generation approach where the rules after interpretation are directly translated into a binary executable form. This obviously results in the faster execution of rules and provides the best of both worlds. Developers will concentrate on fine-tuning the code-generation aspect, and traders will mobilize their efforts in defining business logic without knowing its language implementation details.

Automated code generation is a perfect implementation technique in designing and implementing any type of business rule engine. Another area in the financial world where code-generation techniques come in handy is when building a finite state machine compiler. A *finite state machine* is composed of state, transition, and actions. A *state* represents information, a *transition* refers to a change in state, and an *action* defines the activity that is executed because of a change in state. Such information when graphically depicted results in a state diagram, and systems are then modeled on this concept. State machine compilers provide GUI-based state modeling tools that allow you to chart the system states, and then the compiler generates boilerplate code.

Code-generation techniques bring higher productivity to developers, but there is initial investment in terms of time and resources that need to be deployed. In most projects, it is hard to justify their usage. Certainly this is true in small-scale projects where using code generation doesn't seem to be a viable solution because of the nature of the tasks. For instance, there is no need to consider a code-generation technique when building a simple arbitrage engine. But when it comes to building a highly complex arbitrage engine, then the whole concept of code generation falls squarely in line with a rule engine. Also, when the nature of the task is repetitive and exists in large numbers, then code generation becomes an extremely useful tool.

Summary

In this chapter, we described the following topics:

- We explained the economics behind the equities arbitrage business and how an arbitrageur attempts to lock and make profit by exploiting price differentials in multiple markets.

- We discussed the various forms of the arbitrage business and showed the basic mathematics calculation applied to find out a profitable arbitrage.

- Next, we started the journey into various code-generation techniques and how they are leveraged to automate day-to-day tasks.

- We explained the strengths offered by the CodeDOM framework in writing language-independent code.

- We illustrated the advantage provided by `Reflection.Emit` over the .NET CodeDOM.

- We provided a brief overview of using reflection, which enables you to self-introspect .NET assembly.

CHAPTER 9

■ ■ ■

.NET 2.0

Writing is a hard thing, but it is only through writing we come to know how far we can stretch our imagination.

This chapter is unlike the other chapters where the main theme was mixing business case studies with technical implementations. The main focus of this chapter is to highlight the new wealth of technical features introduced in .NET 2.0. Although you can find enhancements in every nook and cranny of the framework, in this chapter we will address only the major enhancements.

Language Improvements

In .NET 2.0, you will discover language-level improvements such as generics, anonymous methods, and partial classes that provide ways to increase development productivity. These enhancements can be generally classified into two levels: compiler-driven features and run-time features. Compiler-driven features are those that are solely implemented by compilers. A classic example of a compiler-driven feature is the `lock` keyword used in C# to achieve thread synchronization; the real magic is performed by the compiler, which interprets the keyword and accordingly emits `Monitor.Enter` and `Monitor.Exit` statements. Similarly, in .NET 2.0, anonymous methods, partial classes, and iterators are compiler-driven features aimed at providing greater functionality with less code. On the other hand, generics are run-time features that have a deep impact on both the IL instruction set and the CLR system. They are aimed at improving application performance, which is absolutely true in the case of generics.

Generics

With generics in place, the CLR provides the powerful concept of *parametric polymorphism*, which has been popular in the object-oriented community. Parametric polymorphism provides a mechanism to parameterize the data types declared inside classes, interfaces, and structures. For example, using parametric polymorphism, an array can be declared to hold any type of object without knowing its actual type; it can store an array of integers, an array of strings, and so on. This provides an opportunity to write code in a generic and reusable manner without binding it to any specific data type. As you might have guessed, the name *generic* was coined because of its capability to write code without committing to an actual data type and, more important, not compromising the type-safety feature provided by the CLR. To further illustrate generics, Listing 9-1 demonstrates some serious problems that have plagued software developers without the support of generics.

Listing 9-1. *Order Container*

```
using System;
using System.Collections;

class NonGenericOrderContainer
{
  //reference type order
  public class OrderObj
  {
    public string Instrument;
    public double Quantity;
  }
  //value type order
  public struct OrderStruct
  {
    public string Instrument;
    public double Quantity;
  }
  static void Main(string[] args)
  {
    //create order container to store reference type orders
    OrderContainer orderObjContainer = new OrderContainer(10);
    //Adding orders of reference type
    orderObjContainer.AddOrder(new OrderObj());
    //Cast Operation
    OrderObj orderObj = orderObjContainer.GetOrder(0) as OrderObj;

    //create order container to store value type orders
    OrderContainer orderStructContainer = new OrderContainer(10);
    //Adding orders of value type
    //Boxing Cost
    orderStructContainer.AddOrder(new OrderStruct());
    //Unboxing Cost
    OrderStruct orderStruct = orderStructContainer.GetOrder(0)
                                           as  OrderStruct;
  }
}

public class OrderContainer
{
  object[] dataContainers;
  int ctr = 0;

  //allocate array elements with specified capacity
  public OrderContainer(int orderCapacity)
  {
    dataContainers = new object[orderCapacity];
  }

  //Add a new Order
  public void AddOrder(object order)
  {
    dataContainers[ctr] = order;
    ctr++;
  }
```

```
//Retrieve a specific order
public object GetOrder(int index)
{
  return dataContainers[index];
}
}
```

As you recall from Chapter 2, we discussed how you can use various types of collections to implement an order container. The container adds an extra layer of abstraction over the internal data structure used to store orders, thereby providing freedom to tweak the storage implementation when needed. To examine how this is done, take another look at Listing 9-1, which shows the partial implementation of an order container. This container is capable of storing any order type. The code is pretty straightforward and begins with a declaration of a System.Object array. The reason we chose System.Object was because it is the base class from which both reference and value type classes are derived.

From a functionality perspective, the code achieves its goal of providing a common order container for storing all types of orders; however, when looked at from a performance viewpoint, you will find some serious problems. The first problem is the performance penalty incurred as a result of the boxing and unboxing operations. For example, OrderStruct is a value type, and when an instance of it is passed to the Add method of OrderContainer, it first needs to be boxed in order to be stored in an array of the System.Object type. Similarly, to retrieve an instance of OrderStruct from the order container, it needs to be unboxed. Both boxing and unboxing are expensive operations that involve memory allocation resulting in frequent garbage collections. Certainly, to avoid the performance tax associated with value types, you can use reference types. But with reference types, you lose compile-time type-safety features; therefore, type mismatch errors that are detected early during the compilation phase can be traced only at runtime. Second, a performance penalty is incurred as a result of the cast operation that occurs when System.Object is assigned to an actual reference type. Unfortunately, you do not have an easy way to create a type-specific data structure that provides compile-time type safety without jeopardizing performance.

However, with the advent of generics in .NET 2.0, developers do not need to worry about type safety and performance issues and can achieve the long-dreamed-of task of creating type-specific data structures. Generics are first-class citizens of the CLR, and they allow developers to parameterize classes based on the type of data they store. The parameterization is dictated by the consumer code, and to show how to incorporate this new language feature, we will build a generic version of the order container example, as shown in Listing 9-2.

Listing 9-2. *Order Container (Using Generics)*

```
public class OrderContainer<T>
{
  T[] dataContainers;
  int ctr = 0;

  //allocate array elements with specified capacity
  public OrderContainer(int orderCapacity)
  {
    dataContainers = new T[orderCapacity];
  }

  //Add a new Order
  public void AddOrder(T order)
  {
    dataContainers[ctr] = order;
    ctr++;
  }
```

```
    //Retrieve a specific order
    public T GetOrder(int index)
    {
      return dataContainers[index];
    }
}
```

At first glance, the code for OrderContainer looks similar to its predecessor, but the important element that is missing is that the details of the data type used to hold orders; instead, the data type is represented by T. The character T in generics is known as a *type parameter* and is enclosed in angle brackets. The type parameter acts as a placeholder for the data type that is filled later by the consumer code. The presence of angle brackets immediately after the class name makes it easy to recognize a generic type versus its nongeneric counterpart. Additionally, angle brackets enclose multiple type parameters whose details are unspecified and are referenced all over the code. For instance, you will notice that in the generic version of OrderContainer, the role played by System.Object is taken over by type parameter T. Another important note about naming conventions of type parameters is that they can be any valid C# identifier.

OrderContainer<T> is known as a generic type because it contains code about the functionality it is going to provide, but what is not known is the kind of data on which it intends to execute its logic. This missing information is filled by the consumer of the generics and is demonstrated in the next code example:

```
class GenericOrderContainer
{

  //reference type order
  public class OrderObj
  {
    public string Instrument;
    public double Quantity;
  }
  //value type order
  public struct OrderStruct
  {
    public string Instrument;
    public double Quantity;
  }

  static void Main(string[] args)
  {
    //Generic type instantiation using reference type
    OrderContainer<OrderObj> orderObjContainer = new
                        OrderContainer<OrderObj>(10);
    //Add and retrieve reference type order
    orderObjContainer.AddOrder(new OrderObj());
    OrderObj orderObj = orderObjContainer.GetOrder(0);

    //Generic type instantiation using value type
    OrderContainer<OrderStruct> orderStructContainer =
                    new OrderContainer<OrderStruct>(10);
    //Add and retrieve value type order
    orderStructContainer.AddOrder(new OrderStruct());
    OrderStruct orderStruct = orderStructContainer.GetOrder(0);
  }
 }
}
```

To create an instance of a generic type, the consumer must supply the list of concrete data types that need to be substituted for the type parameters defined. For example, by instantiating OrderContainer<OrderObj>, which is also called the *closed constructed* type, every occurrence of type parameter T is replaced with OrderObj, which is a concrete type. This action immediately gives new life to the order container, because it knows the concrete data type it intends to store and operate. Similarly, the instantiation of OrderContainer<OrderStruct> allows the storage of only value types.

You can easily see the power behind generics from the generic version of the order container code where both reference and value types are instantiated without incurring any kind of performance penalty. Both the compiler and runtime provide a necessary type-safety guarantee to an instance of a generic type. In this way, any attempt to add orders to OrderContainer<OrderStruct> other than OrderStruct will not be allowed. Additionally, generics bring higher productivity to both the producer and consumer of the generic type because, along with code clarity, generics provide the opportunity to design types in a completely generic fashion by offloading most of the internal data type details to the consumer.

Inheritance on Generic Types

Generics in .NET are not restricted to just pure types; they can be applied to interfaces and abstract types and also participate in forming a generic-based inheritance chain. By default, the base class of a generic type is System.Object, but the truth of the matter is a generic type can also be derived from a base generic type or closed constructed type. In either of these cases, the type parameters declared in the derived class can be propagated to its base class. For example, if you look at the following code, we declared Order<T>, which forms the base type for DayOrder<T> and LimitOrder<T>. The only difference is that LimitOrder<T> is extended from a concrete type, unlike DayOrder<T>, which propagates the subclass type parameter to its generic base class.

```
public class Order<T>
{
    public T OrderID;
}
public class DayOrder<T> : Order<T>
{}
public class LimitOrder<T> : Order<string>
{}
```

When a subclass is a generic type and is derived from a generic interface or generic abstract classes, then an abstract or virtual method declared in a base type can be overridden in the derived class. In these cases, the signature of the overridden method must match its base type or interface. For example, let's assume you have been given a new requirement to implement comparison functionality between two orders; the most ideal way is to subclass the order generic type from the IComparable interface:

```
public interface IComparable<T>
{
    int CompareTo(T other);
}
```

Currently, there are two version of the IComparable interface. The original version is a nongeneric type, but the new version is meant to handle the generic requirement:

```
public class OrderObj : IComparable<OrderObj>
{
    public string Instrument;
    public double Quantity;
```

```
   int IComparable<OrderObj>.CompareTo(OrderObj x)
   {
     return x.Quantity.CompareTo(this.Quantity);
   }
}
public struct OrderStruct : IComparable<OrderStruct>
{
  public string Instrument;
  public double Quantity;

  int IComparable<OrderStruct>.CompareTo(OrderStruct x)
  {
    return x.Quantity.CompareTo(this.Quantity);
  }
}
```

Constraints on Generic Types

Generic *constraints* permit you to associate rules with the generic type parameter. The rules help you further narrow down the list of possible types an individual generic type parameter can use. By default, a generic type parameter with no constraints is known as an *unbounded type*, and it restricts generic code to use only methods and properties defined in System.Object. As a result, any attempt to invoke methods or properties not supported by System.Object will result in compile-time errors. This behavior is completely acceptable because if you look at it from a compiler point of view, it has no additional information to ensure compile-time type safety:

```
//Compile-time error
public class OrderContainer<T>
{
  public void AddOrder(T order)
  {
    //Quantity cannot be negative
    if (order.Quantity < 0)
            throw new ApplicationException("Quantity cannot be negative");
  }
}
```

Constraints are additional inputs to compilers, and based on this information, they expand the reach of generic code to invoke methods or properties of different types. Without constraints, the only possible way to incorporate this feature is to perform a run-time cast, but that leads to performance overhead. Additionally, if a cast operation is unsuccessful, then it throws a run-time exception. To address these problems, constraints were incorporated into generics; to use them, you need to first understand various types of constraints.

Class/Interface Constraint

The code syntax of constraints are specified using the where keyword, which is followed by a generic type parameter and colon. Given this declaration, a constraint can be classified as a class type or interface type. Class type constraints define a list of types that a type parameter can support. Similarly, interface type constraints define a list of interfaces that a type parameter can implement. For example, in following code by constraining OrderContainer<T>, you are allowed to access members of OrderObj inside generic code:

```
//Compiles successfully
public class OrderContainer<T> where T:OrderObj
```

```
{
  public void AddOrder(T order)
  {
    //Quantity cannot be negative
    if (order.Quantity < 0)
     throw new ApplicationException("Quantity cannot be negative"); successfully
  }
}
```

Similarly, by applying interface type constraints, you can enforce a rule that any item added in OrderContainer<T> must implement the IComparable<T> interface:

```
public class OrderContainer<T> where T : IComparable<T>
{
  //....
}
```

Furthermore, it is also possible to associate multiple constraints on a generic type parameter; for example, OrderContainer<T> is tagged with both class and interface type constraints:

```
public class OrderContainer<T> where T : OrderObj,IComparable<T>
{
  //....
}
```

Reference/Value Type Constraint

Using this type of constraint, it is possible to specify that a generic type parameter must be of a reference type (such as class, delegate, or interface) or value type (such as int, double, or enum):

```
//Allow only reference type
public class OrderContainer<T> where T : class
{
  //....
}
```

```
//Allow only value type
public class OrderContainer<T> where T : struct
{
  //....
}
```

Parameterless Constructor Constraint

This constraint enforces a rule that a generic type parameter must have a public parameterless constructor. As a result, code inside a generic class can instantiate a new generic object of a generic parameter type:

```
public class OrderContainer<T> where T: OrderObj,new()
{
  public T CreateNewOrder()
  {
    //This line compiles because OrderObj has a default public constructor
    T newOrder = new T();

    //Assign Default Value
    newOrder.Quantity = 10;
    return newOrder;
  }
}
```

Inheritance Constraint

This is not a new constraint but must be considered as a mandatory step that needs to be followed in establishing a constraint-enabled, generics-based inheritance chain. When a generic type is derived from a base generic type, then generic constraints declared at a base type must be repeated at a subclass level. Failing to honor this rule will result in compile-time errors:

```
public class Order<T> where T:IComparable<T>
{
  //unique order identifier
  public T OrderID;
}

//Constraints needs to be repeated
public class DayOrder<T> : Order<T> where T:IComparable<T>
{
}

//Constraints are not repeated because it is derived from the closed constructed
//type
//but the compiler will ensure that the concrete type specified in the closed
//constructed type
//implements the IComparable interface
public class LimitOrder<T> : Order<string>
{
}

//This will result into compilation error, because we are trying to
//use the byte array as the underlying data type to identify unique order,
//and the byte array doesn't implement the IComparable interface
public class IOCOrder<T> : Order<byte[]>
{
}
```

Generic Methods and Delegates

A generic method is a method that parameterizes both input and output arguments. It is syntactically similar to a generic class with the only difference being that access to the type parameter defined at the generic method level is limited to its execution scope. Using a generic method, it is possible to sprinkle generic ingredients inside a nongeneric class. Additionally, it enjoys the same benefit of a generic class.

To demonstrate how powerful a generic method is, we will incorporate sort functionality inside the generic version of the order container. Instead of hard-coding this functionality, it is delegated to consumer code that then dictates the sorting behavior using the generic method, as shown in Listing 9-3.

Listing 9-3. *Generic Method*

```
using System;
using System.Collections.Generic;
using System.Text;

public class Order
{
  public string OrderID;
  public string Instrument;
}
```

```
public class SortByOrderID<T> : IComparer<T> where T: Order
{
   int IComparer<T>.Compare(T x,T y)
                 { return x.OrderID.CompareTo(y.OrderID);}
}

public class SortByInstrument<T> : IComparer<T> where T : Order
{
   int IComparer<T>.Compare(T x, T y)
       { return x.Instrument.CompareTo(y.Instrument);}
}

public class OrderContainer<T>
{
   //Customize the Sorting behavior using the generic method
   public void SortOrder<U>(U orderComparer) where U:IComparer<Order>
   {
      //....
   }
}
```

In Listing 9-3, we presented multiple ways to sort a list of orders, either by instrument name or by order ID. SortByOrderID<T> and SortByInstrument<T> provide this functionality. To integrate this sort feature with OrderContainer<T>, we defined a generic method, SortOrder<U>, that is declared with type parameters and constrained to be compatible with the IComparer<Order> type. This generic method is then used to sort orders, as described in the following code example:

```
class GenericSortMethod
{
   static void Main(string[] args)
   {
      OrderContainer<Order> container = new OrderContainer<Order>();

      //Sort By Instrument
      SortByInstrument<Order> sortInst = new SortByInstrument<Order>();
      container.SortOrder<SortByInstrument<Order>>(sortInst);

      //Sort By Order ID
      SortByOrderID<Order> sortID = new SortByOrderID<Order>();
      container.SortOrder<SortByOrderID<Order>>(sortID);
   }
}
```

The discussion on generics would be incomplete without talking about generic delegates. You know delegates are managed function pointers and are used extensively in implementing event notification features. A generic delegate shares the same spirit of a conventional delegate but proves extremely useful in building generic event handling. For example, using a generic delegate, you can build a generic event notification feature in the order container code that is capable of providing a strongly typed item to its subscriber:

```
using System;
using System.Collections.Generic;
using System.Text;

public class Order
{}
```

```
public class DayOrder
{}

public class OrderContainer<T>
{
  //Generic Delegate Declaration
  public delegate void InsertOrderDelegate<U>(U orderComparer);
  public event InsertOrderDelegate<T> OrderInsert;

  public void Add(T order)
  {
    //Notify Consumer of this event
    if (OrderInsert != null)
    {
      OrderInsert(order);
    }
  }
}

class GenericDelegate
{
  static void Main(string[] args)
  {
    OrderContainer<Order> orderCont= new OrderContainer<Order>();
    orderCont.OrderInsert += new
    OrderContainer<Order>.InsertOrderDelegate<Order>
                          (orderCont_OrderInsert);

    OrderContainer<DayOrder> dayorderCont = new
                            OrderContainer<DayOrder>();

    dayorderCont.OrderInsert += new
                    OrderContainer<DayOrder>.InsertOrderDelegate<DayOrder>
                    (dayorderCont_OrderInsert);
  }

  //Event notification for day orders
  static void dayorderCont_OrderInsert(DayOrder orderComparer)
  {
  }

  //Event notification for regular orders
  static void orderCont_OrderInsert(Order orderComparer)
  {
  }
}
```

Generic Collections

Collections in .NET are the most commonly used types to store in-memory items. As highlighted in Chapter 2, you know that there are various flavors of collections, and their characteristics are determined based on how individual items are stored and searched. Considering that data structures are the most basic necessity, Microsoft released a new generic version of collection classes. This generic version resides side by side with its nongeneric counterpart but is grouped in a different namespace. The generic collection classes are defined in the System.Collections.Generic namespace. This includes most of the familiar data structures such as implementing queues, stacks, dictionaries, and lists. The primary benefit of using generic collections is it brings strong typing, which was badly required in the pregeneric days:

```
using System;
using System.Collections.Generic;
using System.Text;

public class Order
{}

class GenericCollections
{
  static void Main(string[] args)
  {
    //Generic Queue
    Queue<Order> orderQueue = new Queue<Order>();

    //Generic Stack
    Stack<Order> orderStack = new Stack<Order>();

    //Generic List
    List<Order> orderList = new List<Order>();

    //Generic Hashtable
    Dictionary<string, Order> orderHashTable = new
                        Dictionary<string, Order>();

    //Generic SortedList
    SortedDictionary<string, Order> orderSortDict = new
                        SortedDictionary<string, Order>();

    //Generic LinkedList
    LinkedList<Order> linkList = new LinkedList<Order>();
  }
}
```

Anonymous Methods

Anonymous methods aim to reduce the amount of code developers have to write to implement event handlers or callbacks that are invoked through a delegate. This is a kind of code-inflator trick employed by compilers to bring higher productivity to a developer's desk. Anonymous methods allow for the inline recruitment of code associated with a delegate, which is in direct contrast to the conventional approach where a new instance of a delegate and a separate method handler are required. For example, the following code is a conventional approach for offloading processing tasks using a CLR thread-pool implementation:

```
using System;
using System.Text;
using System.Threading;

public class Order
{
  public string OrderId;
}
```

```
class NonAnonymousMethods
{
  static void Main(string[] args)
  {
    //Create a new Order
    Order newOrder = new Order();
    newOrder.OrderId = "1";

    ThreadPool.QueueUserWorkItem(new
                       WaitCallback(ProcessOrders),newOrder);
    Console.ReadLine();
  }

  public static void ProcessOrders(object state)
  {
    Order curOrder = state as Order;
    Console.WriteLine("Processing Order : " + curOrder.OrderId);
  }
}
```

Using anonymous methods, Listing 9-4 appears in its condensed form, which is succinct when compared to its conventional approach.

Listing 9-4. *Anonymous Methods*

```
using System;
using System.Text;
using System.Threading;

public class Order
{
  public string OrderId;
}

class AnonymousMethods
{
  static void Main(string[] args)
  {
    //Create a new Order
    Order newOrder = new Order();
    newOrder.OrderId = "1";

    //Process this newly created order using ThreadPool
    ThreadPool.QueueUserWorkItem
         (delegate(object state)
            {
              Order curOrder = state as Order;
              Console.WriteLine("Processing Order : " +curOrder.OrderId);
            },newOrder
         );

    Console.ReadLine();
  }
}
```

The code declaration of an anonymous method begins with the delegate keyword and an optional parameter list. As you will notice, the actual method body is enclosed inside { and } delimiters, which are also known as an *anonymous method block*. Code inside this block can declare variables similar to local variables defined in the conventional method; the only twist is that the lifetime of such variables is limited to the execution of the anonymous method. Additionally, the code block can also reference outer variables that are defined at the class level.

In Listing 9-4, we demonstrated how to create an anonymous method, and it can be used wherever a delegate is expected. Even though it enjoys most of the benefits of the conventional method, certain things are not permitted inside anonymous method blocks. One of a developer's favorite features is .NET attributes, and sadly it is not possible to annotate attributes over an anonymous method. Furthermore, an anonymous method cannot reference ref or out parameters except those specified in an anonymous method signature. It is also not possible for an anonymous method block to contain an unsafe/goto/break/continue statement. Despite such restrictions, you will find the anonymous method to be useful in your day-to-day development.

Iterators

Iterators in C# provide a uniform way to iterate over various types of data structures using the foreach keyword. They achieve this kind of standardization using the IEnumerable and IEnumerator interfaces. These interfaces need to be implemented by a class in order to support the foreach iteration. Although the implementation looks straightforward, to support a simple iteration, quite a large amount of code needs to be written. Moreover, the development effort keeps on mounting with the addition of iteration flavors such as top-to-bottom traversal and bottom-to-top traversal. To simplify this task, C# 2.0 introduced iterators in which most of the work is lifted by compilers. Using this new construct, there is no need to provide implementation for the entire IEnumerable interface; instead, what is required is an iterator statement block, as shown in Listing 9-5.

Listing 9-5. *Iterators*

```
using System;
using System.Collections.Generic;
using System.Text;

public class Order {}

public class OrderContainer<T>
{
  List<T> orderList = new List<T>();

  //Default foreach Implementation
  public IEnumerator<T> GetEnumerator()
  {
    for (int ctr = 0; ctr < orderList.Count; ctr++)
    {
      yield return orderList[ctr];
    }
  }

  //Best Five Orders
  public IEnumerable<T> BestFive()
  {
    for (int ctr= 0; ctr < orderList.Count; ctr++)
    {
      if (ctr > 4)
        //Stop Iteration Phase
        yield break;
```

```
      yield return orderList[ctr];
    }
  }

  //Iteration of only limit orders
  public IEnumerable<T> LimitOrders()
  {
    for (int ctr = 0; ctr < orderList.Count; ctr++)
    {
      //Check for limit order, and return
      yield return orderList[ctr];
    }
  }
}

class Iterators
{
  static void Main(string[] args)
  {
    OrderContainer<Order> orderContainer = new OrderContainer<Order>();

    //Iterate all orders
    foreach (Order curOrder in orderContainer)
    {}

    //Iterate Best Five
    foreach (Order curOrder in orderContainer.BestFive())
    {}

    //Iterate limit order
    foreach (Order curOrder in orderContainer.LimitOrders())
    {}
  }
}
```

In Listing 9-5, the iterator statement block is identified by the presence of yield statements enclosed inside a method, and its return type is either IEnumerator<T> or IEnumerable<T>. It is composed of two types of statement: yield return and yield break. The yield return indicates the beginning of the iteration phase and dictates the iteration behavior by producing the next value in the iteration. Similarly, yield break indicates the completion of the iteration phase. Based on this keyword, the C# compiler under the hood generates classes (also known as *compiler-generated classes* and hidden from developers) that maintain navigation information about the individual iterator. As a result, you can have multiple iterators defined inside a class, and each of these individual iterators can slice and dice data from a different perspective.

Partial Types

Partial types enable the spanning of source code into multiple files. To be precise, they allow the definition of a class, a structure, or an interface to split across multiple files that are later combined as one large chunk of source code by the compilers. At a surface level, you may fail to recognize the advantage of a code split, but if you flash back to Chapter 8 where we mentioned the different types of code generators and their implementation tactics, then partial types prove to be a perfect fit. For example, we discussed how the VS .NET Windows Form Designer automates the task of UI development by autogenerating most of the code. The code generated by the designer resides side by side with the user code and is differentiated by logically grouping it inside the Windows Form Designer generated code region. However, using partial types, both the designer code and the user code are now separated into two files. The advantage of such separation brings a tremendous amount of flexibility to augment both the designer and user code.

A partial type is identified by the presence of the partial keyword, which appears immediately before the class, struct, or interface keywords. For example, the following code illustrates a strategy class that is separated into two parts. The first part represents code generated by a trading strategy tool, and the second part represents code defined by traders:

```
//In the real world this class is generated by tool
public partial class TradingStrategy
{
  public void InitializeStrategy()
  {}
}

//In the real world this class is defined by traders
public partial class TradingStrategy
{
  public void CalculateRisk()
  {}
}

class PartialTypes
{
  static void Main(string[] args)
  {
    TradingStrategy tradStrat = new TradingStrategy();
  }
}
```

The benefit of using a partial type is twofold. First, it proves to be extremely useful in the automatic code generation world where the majority of the code is generated by tools, and it provides an intelligent approach of keeping system-generated code separate from user code and finally merging them during the compilation stage. Second, it helps to further strengthen day-to-day version-control activities. A large class can be easily shared with a group of developers by branching it into multiple files; this allows them to work on it independently.

Nullable Types

In the computer programming world, the value null has always played a special role in defining a state that is either unacceptable or unknown. For example, instances of reference types in .NET are by default initialized to the null value to indicate that the instance is in an undefined state and that attempting to perform any kind of operation on it will result in an exception. Similarly, you will also find support for *nullability* in the relational database world, which denotes a column value and is used to convey data that is either unknown or undefined. Over the years, null values have stretched their wings in many other computing disciplines, but when it comes to the .NET value type, it seriously lacks support for it. It is not possible to assign null values to value types; this leads to a serious problem, particularly when data fetched from a database is mapped to the appropriate .NET value type. This limitation of the value type was carefully given thought, and as a result *nullable* types were introduced.

Nullable types provide the ability to store null values to value types. Additionally, this feature is standardized and integrated as part of the language framework. A nullable type is a generic structure and is represented by Nullable<T>. The internal implementation of Nullable<T> is composed of a value type that is passed as a generic type argument and, more important, a flag variable that is a null indicator. While it is true that to define a nullable value type you need to instantiate a new instance of Nullable<I>, different code syntax is available to achieve the same task. The new syntax allows constructing nullable types simply by appending a question mark after the name of a value type. For example, int? is the nullable representation of the int data type. In the following code, we demonstrate how to use the nullable type by assigning the null value to the Quantity and Price fields of the Order class:

```
using System;

public class Order
{
  public string Instrument;

  //Nullable Value type, null is assigned as default value
  public int? Quantity = null;
  public double? Price = null;
}
class NullableTypes
{
  static void Main(string[] args)
  {
    Order newOrder = new Order();

    //This will return true because quantity value is null
    Console.WriteLine("Is Quantity Null : " + ( newOrder.Quantity == null ) );

    //Null coalescing operator
    //If quantity value is null, then by default assign value 10
    newOrder.Quantity = newOrder.Quantity ?? 10;
    Console.WriteLine("Quantity : " +newOrder.Quantity);

    //Addition operator
    newOrder.Quantity = newOrder.Quantity + 5;
    Console.WriteLine("Quantity : " + newOrder.Quantity);

  }
}
```

Counting Semaphore

The *counting semaphore* is a new addition to the existing list of managed synchronization objects and is represented by System.Threading.Semaphore. It defines a threshold value on the number of times a shared resource can be accessed. This resource-counting mechanism proves extremely useful in multithreaded applications where a limit can be set on the number of threads allowed to access a particular resource. Threads use the semaphore to create a pool of tokens that is issued each time a thread enters the semaphore and is recycled back to the pool when the thread leaves the semaphore. In the case of the unavailability of tokens, the thread requesting it is blocked until other threads release the token back to the pool. Even though semaphores are similar to mutexes and monitors, when it comes to ensuring the synchronization of shared resources, semaphores are one step ahead; they enable the metering of shared resources. Additionally, mutexes and monitors are meant to grant exclusive access on shared resources to only one thread at a time, which is in contrast to semaphores, which grant access to multiple threads on shared resources. Listing 9-6 shows an example:

Listing 9-6. *Semaphore*

```
using System;
using System.Collections.Generic;
using System.Text;
using System.Threading;

class Order
{}

class SemaphoreLock
{
  static Semaphore orderSemaphore;
  static void Main(string[] args)
  {
    ManualResetEvent waitEvent = new ManualResetEvent(false);
    int initialTokens = 3;
    int maxTokens = 3;

    //Assume some sort of order container that stores the order
    List<Order> orderContainer = new List<Order>();

    //Create a new semaphore, which at any time allows
    //only three concurrent threads to access the order container
    //and process an individual order
    //The first parameter represents initial tokens available in the pool
    //and the last parameter represents the maximum available tokens
    orderSemaphore = new Semaphore(initialTokens, maxTokens);
    for (int ctr = 0; ctr <= 10; ctr++)
    {
      ThreadPool.QueueUserWorkItem(new WaitCallback(ProcessOrders),ctr);
    }

    //Prevent program from exiting
    waitEvent.WaitOne();
  }

  public static void ProcessOrders(object state)
  {
    //Acquire the Semaphore lock
    //If lock is successfully acquired then semaphore count is decremented
    orderSemaphore.WaitOne();

    //insert order into order book
    Console.WriteLine("Order Processed . " +state);
    Console.WriteLine("Press any key to Continue");
    Console.ReadLine();

    //Release the lock, which will increment the semaphore count
    orderSemaphore.Release();
  }
}
```

In Listing 9-6, notice how you can limit the number of threads that can access the order book concurrently. You created a semaphore that can handle up to three concurrent requests, with an initial count of three so it is immediately available on the pool. To process individual orders, you use worker threads from the thread pool. A thread enters the semaphore by calling the WaitOne method and, after inserting the order into the order book, releases the semaphore by calling the Release method.

Memory Gate

The *memory gate* functions as a checkpoint in managed code and is used to ensure the availability of sufficient memory before initiating any kind of memory-intensive operation. Although the CLR is responsible for managing memory, sometimes it fails to satisfy memory requests issued by an application. On such occasions, the failure result is notified to the application in the form of OutOfMemoryException. This exception signifies that a disaster has already taken place, and most of the times the application lands in an inconsistent state that is hard to recover from. Using the memory gate, it is possible to minimize such incidents by doing upfront estimation of the memory required, and if the specified amount of memory is not available, then it is notified in the form of InsufficientMemoryException. Here's an example:

```
using System;
using System.Runtime;

namespace MemoryGate
{
  class Program
  {
    static void Main(string[] args)
    {
      //Check whether application can allocate 20MB of
      //memory to perform file copy operation
      using (new MemoryFailPoint(20))
      {
        //Perform File Copy Operation
      }
    }
  }
}
```

Garbage Collector

The .NET Framework provides an end-to-end platform to build both client-side and server-side applications. Client-side applications are generally GUI driven and intended to run on the desktop. Server-side applications are computational intensive and usually require high-end servers. The performance need of the client and server applications are different, so the CLR ships with two flavors of the garbage collector: Workstation GC and Server GC. Workstation GC is the default collector used by managed code. It is highly optimized for GUI-based applications to provide greater user responsiveness. On the other hand, Server GC is optimized for multiprocessor machines and highly suitable for server-side applications that need high throughput.

Both these GCs undertake a different strategy when it comes to the garbage collection process. Workstation GC creates a single managed heap and a dedicated thread to perform garbage collection regardless of the number of processors available in the machine. This is in contrast to Server GC where the number of managed heaps and threads created is equal to the number of processors installed in the machine. This setup definitely boosts the performance because garbage collection takes place in parallel on all available CPUs. Server GC is highly recommended for mission-critical applications, and with the advent of .NET 2.0, it can be easily enabled by adding a new <gcServer> element in an application configuration file:

```
<configuration>
  <runtime>
    <!-- Server GC Enabled -->
    <gcServer enabled="true"/>
```

```
    </runtime>
</configuration>
```

A new helper class, GCSettings, introduced in the .NET 2.0 specifies the garbage collection settings. With the help of this class, you can find out the type of garbage collection used by the currently running process:

```
using System;
using System.Runtime;

namespace GCConfig
{
  class Program
  {
    static void Main(string[] args)
    {
      if (GCSettings.IsServerGC == true)
        Console.WriteLine("Server GC enabled");
      else
        Console.WriteLine("Workstation GC enabled");
    }
  }
}
```

SGen

To boost the start-up performance of XMLSerializer, .NET 2.0 toolkits are packaged with a new tool known as SGen. You learned in Chapter 3 about the capability of XMLSerializer to serialize and deserialize objects into and from XML documents. In addition, you also understand its implementation technique that under the hood applies the code-generation technique to emit serialization and deserialization code. The code generated is then compiled into an assembly and loaded into the currently running process. That is the reason you always notice a delay when a new instance of XMLSerializer is created. The magnitude of this delay depends upon the depth of the object graph.

To cut down on this start-up delay, SGen creates XML serialization and deserialization code in advance. It generates an XML serialization assembly that is then referenced by applications. The immediate advantage of statically linking serialization logic at compile time is that there is no code-generation activity involved at runtime; this drastically reduces the application start-up cost. But it doesn't mean this approach is free of any side effects. You lose the flexibility offered by dynamic code generation, particularly any kind of modification; for example, adding or removing the property/field at the class level now requires a recompilation to keep the serialization assembly synchronized with the XML serializable type. However, this additional step is amortized over the cost of generating serialization code for a large number classes at runtime that is bit expensive.

SGen is a command-line tool that accepts the name of the assembly for which the serialization and deserialization code is generated. By default, it generates the serialization code for all the classes defined in the assembly, but using the /type switch, it is possible to generate serialization code for only a particular class.

Assume the following code is compiled in the form of an executable assembly and is named PreGenXMLSerializer.exe:

```
using System;
using System.Collections.Generic;
using System.Text;
```

```
namespace PreGenXMLSerializer
{
  public class Order
  {
    public string OrderID;
    public int Quantity;
    public double Price;
  }

  class Program
  {
    static void Main(string[] args)
    {
    }
  }
}
```

To generate an XML serialization assembly, the following is the command to be executed in the VS .NET 2005 command prompt window:

```
sgen /assembly:pregenxmlserializer.exe /type:Order
```

The output of the tool is a set of classes persisted in the PreGenXMLSerializer.XmlSerializers. dll assembly that can be referenced from code that needs to serialize or deserialize the Order type. The following code bypasses the conventional XML serialization path and uses the pregenerated assembly to serialize and deserialize an instance of the Order type:

```
using System;
using System.Collections.Generic;
using System.Text;
using System.Xml;
using System.IO;

//Include namespace from the PreGenXMLSerializer.XMLSerializers assembly
using Microsoft.Xml.Serialization.GeneratedAssembly;

namespace PreGenXMLSerializer
{
  public class Order
  {
    public string OrderID;
    public int Quantity;
    public double Price;
  }

  class Program
  {
    static void Main(string[] args)
    {
      Order dayOrder = new Order();
      dayOrder.OrderID = "1";
      dayOrder.Quantity = 50;
      dayOrder.Price = 25;

      //Serialize Order using pregenerated serializers
      OrderSerializer orderSzer = new OrderSerializer();
      XmlTextWriter txtWriter = new XmlTextWriter(
                          new StreamWriter(@"C:\Order.xml"));
```

```
        orderSzer.Serialize(txtWriter, dayOrder);
        txtWriter.Close();

        //Deserialize Order using pregenerated deserializers
        XmlTextReader txtReader = new XmlTextReader(
                                new StreamReader(@"C:\Order.xml"));
        Order newOrder = orderSzer.Deserialize(txtReader) as Order;
        Console.WriteLine(newOrder.OrderID);
    }
  }
}
```

Data Compression

In building networked applications, an important goal followed by developers is to ensure the efficient utilization of network bandwidth. The success of a networked application depends upon various factors; one of them is to apply a data compression technique to save network bandwidth, resulting in the much faster transmission of data. Additionally, you can also apply a compression technique to condense log files generated by the application. Nowadays, it is mandatory for an organization to maintain an archive of application log files that is subject to a periodic internal audit check. In such scenarios it is sensible to preserve the files in their compressed formats instead of their original formats, which translates into a huge savings of disk space.

.NET 2.0 introduces a new System.IO.Compression namespace that provides exactly what you need to do so. It provides basic compression and decompression services out of the box. The two most important classes defined in this namespace are DeflateStream and GZipStream. DeflateStream represents the industry-standard Deflate algorithm. GZipStream is a wrapper around the DeflateStream class and defines additional meta-information around compressed data.

Here's the code that demonstrates the compression and decompression of in-memory data:

```
using System;
using System.Collections.Generic;
using System.Text;
using System.IO;
using System.IO.Compression;

namespace IOCompression
{
  class Program
  {
    static void Main(string[] args)
    {
      MemoryStream memStream = new MemoryStream();
      string orderXml =
          "<Order><OrderID>1</OrderID><Quantity>50</Quantity>"
        +"<Price>25</Price></Order>";
      byte[] data = Encoding.UTF8.GetBytes(orderXml);

      //Data Compression
      DeflateStream compressedStream =
          new DeflateStream(memStream , CompressionMode.Compress,true);
      compressedStream.Write(data, 0, data.Length);
      compressedStream.Close();

      //Reset seek pointer that is mandatory in order to decompress data
      memStream.Position = 0;
```

```
        //Data Decompression
        DeflateStream decompressedStream =
            new DeflateStream(memStream, CompressionMode.Decompress);
        byte[] decompBuffer = new byte[memStream.Length];
        decompressedStream.Read(decompBuffer, 0, decompBuffer.Length);
        string orgData = Encoding.UTF8.GetString(decompBuffer);
        Console.WriteLine("Decompressed Data : " + orgData);


    }
  }
}
```

Network Information

.NET 1.1 had no easy way to gather information about the network traffic status at runtime. Developers often would resort to P/Invoke or use the Windows Management Instrumentation (WMI) API to incorporate this feature, resulting in an increase in the developer's learning curve. But with .NET 2.0, this has changed. A new namespace, System.Net.NetworkInformation, is dedicated solely to providing network-related information. It contains classes that enable querying information on almost all layers of the TCP/IP core stack. In addition to gathering information about network traffic status, it also provides the ability to query information about the underlying network adapter and allows you to conduct standard tests for network connectivity. This offers a great advantage in the .NET world, and taking into account the breadth and depth of individual classes defined in this namespace, it is possible to develop a managed version of a commonly used network utility such as ping.exe, ipconfig.exe, or netstat.exe. Furthermore, developers can tune their applications to sense network behavior and accordingly react to it. For example, in distributed applications, there is often a need to detect a disconnected network cable and accordingly preserve any further changes performed by a user into the local database. Such kind of intelligence makes an application more reliable and increases user confidence.

We will now explore some of the important classes available in the System.Net.NetworkInformation namespace. We begin with some first trivial code that more or less covers the features of the netstat.exe utility. You can use this utility to find out the following information:

- Active TCP connections, which includes the IP address and port number of the local and foreign host

- A list of TCP and UDP connections configured in listening mode

- Statistical information about TCP, UDP, and IP

Here's an example:

```
using System;
using System.Net;
using System.Net.NetworkInformation;

namespace NetStat
{
  class Program
  {
    static void Main(string[] args)
    {
      IPGlobalProperties properties = IPGlobalProperties.GetIPGlobalProperties();
      Console.WriteLine("Domain Name : " + properties.DomainName);
      Console.WriteLine("Host Name : " + properties.HostName);
```

```
      //Get Active TCP Connections
      TcpConnectionInformation[] connections =
                    properties.GetActiveTcpConnections();

      //Get Active TCP Listener
      IPEndPoint[] endPointsTCP= properties.GetActiveTcpListeners();

      //Get Active UDP Listener
      IPEndPoint[] endPointsUDP = properties.GetActiveUdpListeners();

      //Get IP statistics information
      IPGlobalStatistics ipstat = properties.GetIPv4GlobalStatistics();

      //Get TCP statistical information
      TcpStatistics tcpstat = properties.GetTcpIPv4Statistics();

      //Get UDP statistical information
      UdpStatistics udpStat = properties.GetUdpIPv4Statistics();
    }
  }
}
```

The next step in the network data collection phase is to interact with the underlying network adapter and retrieve interface-level information such as the physical address, the operational status of the individual interface, the data transfer speed supported by the interface, and the logical IP address:

```
using System;
using System.Collections.Generic;
using System.Text;
using System.Net.NetworkInformation;

namespace NetAdapterStat
{
  class Program
  {
    static void Main(string[] args)
    {
      NetworkInterface[] nics = NetworkInterface.GetAllNetworkInterfaces();

      foreach (NetworkInterface adapter in nics)
      {
        Console.WriteLine("Adapter Name : " +adapter.Name);
        Console.WriteLine("Physical Address : "
                      + adapter.GetPhysicalAddress().ToString());
        Console.WriteLine("Data Transfer Speed :"
                      + adapter.Speed +" bits per second ") ;
        Console.WriteLine("Operational Status :"
                      + adapter.OperationalStatus);
        Console.WriteLine("");
      }
    }
  }
}
```

Up until now we have demonstrated features that focused on gathering statistical data information about a network and its underlying transport. But the next topic we will discuss will prove extremely useful in detecting network-related changes. In other words, a managed application can incorporate a network detector that will sense the underlying network and raise notification when the IP address or network adapter changes:

```
using System;
using System.Collections.Generic;
using System.Text;
using System.Net.NetworkInformation;

namespace NetDetector
{
  class Program
  {
    static void Main(string[] args)
    {
      //This event is raised when IP address of network is changed
      NetworkChange.NetworkAddressChanged += NetworkChange_NetworkAddressChanged;

      //This event is raised when network availability is changed
      //For example, the application will be able to get notification about the
      //network
      //cable disconnect by subscribing to this event
      NetworkChange.NetworkAvailabilityChanged +=
                                NetworkChange_NetworkAvailabilityChanged;
      Console.ReadLine();
    }

    static void NetworkChange_NetworkAvailabilityChanged(object sender,
                                    NetworkAvailabilityEventArgs e)
    {
      Console.WriteLine("Network Disconnected");
    }

    static void NetworkChange_NetworkAddressChanged(object sender, EventArgs e)
    {
      Console.WriteLine("IP Address Changed");
    }
  }
}
```

Another important class that brings tremendous value to the developer's desk is Ping. This class is a programmatic representation of the ping.exe command-line tool. ping.exe is one of the most well-known network troubleshooting tools and is primarily used to conduct machine reachability tests. Additionally, it also enables you to perform various kinds of network diagnostic checks, such as tracking the number of intermediate hops between the source and destination hosts and measuring the total round-trip time. The benefit offered by ping.exe is tremendous, and there is definitely a need for it in the managed programming world. The Ping class brings the same benefit and features; applications can directly integrate it in their code to perform various kinds of network diagnostic checks.

Using Ping, applications can implement a heartbeat between machines. It is also possible for applications to determine the network round-trip time or the underlying network speed and accordingly tune their communication strategies. For example, a distributed application, before establishing communication with the server, can initiate a ping request to collect the round-trip time and underlying network capacity. If the results of the round-trip time or network bandwidth are poor, then the application can apply a data compression scheme to reduce the size of the data. For example:

```
using System;
using System.Collections.Generic;
using System.Text;
using System.Net.NetworkInformation;

namespace NetPing
{
  class Program
  {
    static void Main(string[] args)
    {

      Ping pingSender = new Ping();

      //Ping Apress Web site with timeout of 1 seconds (1,000 milliseconds)
      //The result of ping is stored in instance of PingReply
      PingReply reply =  pingSender.Send("www.apress.com",1000);

      //Analyze the result
      if (reply.Status == IPStatus.Success)
      {
        Console.WriteLine("Roundtrip Time : " + reply.RoundtripTime);
      }

    }
  }
}
```

The outcome of the ping request is checked with the help of the Status property defined in Ping. Also keep in mind that because of security risks, most organizations configure their firewalls or proxy servers to reject ICMP requests. In such situations, the ping request will definitely fail, so it is always advisable to check the network environment before utilizing this class.

Remoting

The remoting framework in .NET 2.0 bundles a new communication channel, IpcChannel, which is specifically targeted for remoting between application domains on the same computer. This new channel is defined under the System.Runtime.Remoting.Channels.Ipc namespace. The primary motive behind the design of this channel is to increase interprocess communication performance on the same machine. Before IpcChannel, the highly recommended way is to follow the TCP channel route. The problem with the TCP channel is regardless of where the data is destined, it will always be processed by an individual layer of the TCP/IP core stack. So even though both the sending and receiving applications are hosted on the same machines, the individual messages exchanged by them will always incur additional TCP/IP overhead. The IPC channel addresses this problem by providing a communication pipe that is free from any kind of network overhead, and it internally uses the IPC system of the Windows operating system to enable the faster exchange of messages.

It is now possible for back-office applications to use the IPC channel to implement a market information cache server. Usually, back-office GUI applications involve quite a large amount of data-entry activity; to speed up the task, users are provided with a selection list such as combo boxes, grids, or list boxes populated with information retrieved from the database or middle-tier components. The information populated is huge in number, and usually they are cached during the application start-up phase. But as soon as the user exits from the GUI application, the cached information is lost, and it needs to be repopulated again, which increases the application loading time. By implementing the information cache server that is running as a separate process, the overall performance of the

GUI application increases tremendously because the information is locally cached by the server and the GUI application retrieves it using the IPC channel.

We will now demonstrate the full-fledged remoting code that is based on the market information example and that uses the IPC channel.

Shared Assembly

The following is the shared assembly referenced by the market information cache server and back-office applications:

```
using System;
using System.Data;
using System.Collections.Generic;
using System.Text;

namespace Common
{
  public interface ICacheInfo
  {
    DataSet RetrieveCache();
  }
}
```

Implementation of Market Info Cache Server

The following is the code implementation of the market information cache server:

```
using System;
using System.Data;
using System.Collections.Generic;
using System.Text;
using Common;

namespace MktInfoCacheServer
{
  public class MktInfoCacheImpl : MarshalByRefObject, ICacheInfo
  {

    public DataSet RetrieveCache()
    {
      Console.WriteLine("Request Received...");
      return null;
    }
  }
}
```

Remoting Configuration of Market Info Cache Server

The following is the remoting configuration of the market information cache server:

```
<?xml version="1.0" encoding="utf-8" ?>
<configuration>
  <system.runtime.remoting>
    <application>
      <service>
        <wellknown mode="SingleCall"
```

```
                    type="MktInfoCacheServer.MktInfoCacheImpl, MktInfoCacheServer"
                    objectUri="MktInfoCacheImpl.rem" />
      </service>
      <channels>
        <channel ref="ipc" portName="InfoCacheServer" />
      </channels>
    </application>
  </system.runtime.remoting>
</configuration>
```

Market Info Cache Server Host

The following code is the host market information cache server:

```csharp
using System;
using System.Collections.Generic;
using System.Text;
using System.Runtime.Remoting;
using System.Runtime.Remoting.Channels;
using System.Runtime.Remoting.Channels.Ipc;

namespace MktInfoCacheServer
{
  class Program
  {
    static void Main(string[] args)
    {
      RemotingConfiguration.Configure(@"MktInfoCacheServer.exe.config");
      Console.WriteLine("Market Information Cache Server started.. ");
      Console.WriteLine("Press enter to exit.");
      Console.ReadLine();
    }
  }
}
```

Market Info Cache Client (Back-Office Applications)

The following code connects to the market information cache server and retrieves the cached information:

```csharp
using System;
using System.Data;
using System.Collections.Generic;
using System.Text;
using Common;

namespace InfoCacheClient
{
  class Program
  {
    static void Main(string[] args)
    {
      //Retrieve Cached object from the market information cache server
      //which is locally hosted
      ICacheInfo remoteCache = (ICacheInfo)Activator.GetObject(typeof(ICacheInfo),
                               "ipc://InfoCacheServer/MktInfoCacheImpl.rem");
```

```
         DataSet cacheObj = remoteCache.RetrieveCache();
         Console.WriteLine("Information Successfully Retrieved...");
         Console.ReadLine();
      }
   }
}
```

Remoting and Generics

The remoting framework respects and recognizes generics and provides the necessary infrastructure to allow developers to define generic-aware remote classes. The only prerequisite of generic-aware remote classes is that the generic type parameters declared inside either must be a serializable type or must be derived from MarshalByRefObject. To learn how generics can be applied in remoting applications, consider a remote order container that allows you to store and retrieve the order of any data type. This example is similar to one discussed in the "Generics" section of this chapter, but in this case the order container is instantiated and updated on a remote machine.

Shared Assembly

The following is the shared assembly:

```
using System;
using System.Collections.Generic;
using System.Text;

namespace GenericsShared
{
  [Serializable]
  public class Order
  {}

  [Serializable]
  public struct LimitOrder
  {}

  public interface IRemoteContainer<T>
  {
    void Add(T item);
    T this[string id] { get;}
  }
}
```

Generic-Aware Remote Order Container

The following is the generic-aware remote order container:

```
using System;
using System.Collections.Generic;
using System.Text;
using GenericsShared;

namespace RemoteServer
{
  public class RemoteOrderContainer<T> : MarshalByRefObject,IRemoteContainer<T>
  {
    //Add a new item
```

```
    public void Add(T newOrder)
    {
      Console.WriteLine("Order of Type " +newOrder.ToString() +" Added" );
    }

    //Retrieve a specific item
    public T this[string orderId]
    {
      get { return default(T); }
    }
  }
}
```

Remoting Configuration of Remote Order Container

The following is the remote configuration of the remote order container:

```
<?xml version="1.0" encoding="utf-8" ?>
<configuration>
  <system.runtime.remoting>
    <application>
      <service>
        <wellknown mode="SingleCall"  type="RemoteServer.RemoteOrderContainer`1
                    [[GenericsShared.Order,GenericsShared]], RemoteServer"
                    objectUri="OrderContainer.rem" />
        <wellknown mode="SingleCall" type="RemoteServer.RemoteOrderContainer`1
                    [[GenericsShared.LimitOrder,GenericsShared]], RemoteServer"
                    objectUri="LimitOrderContainer.rem" />
      </service>
      <channels>
        <channel ref="tcp" port="17000">
          <serverProviders>
            <formatter ref="binary" typeFilterLevel="Low" />
          </serverProviders>
        </channel>
      </channels>
    </application>
  </system.runtime.remoting>
</configuration>
```

Client Instantiating Remote Generic Type

The following is the client that is instantiating the remote generic type:

```
using System;
using System.Collections.Generic;
using System.Text;
using GenericsShared;

namespace RemoteClient
{
  class Program
  {
    static void Main(string[] args)
    {
      //Instantiating remote container that allows only regular order
      IRemoteContainer<Order> ordCont =
```

```
        Activator.GetObject(typeof(IRemoteContainer<Order>),
            "tcp://localhost:17000/OrderContainer.rem") as IRemoteContainer<Order>;
    Order newOrder = new Order();
    ordCont.Add(newOrder);

    //Instantiating remote container that allows only limit order
    IRemoteContainer<LimitOrder> limitOrdCont =
            Activator.GetObject(typeof(IRemoteContainer<LimitOrder>),
            "tcp://localhost:17000/LimitOrderContainer.rem") as
            IRemoteContainer<LimitOrder>;
    LimitOrder newLimit= new LimitOrder();
    limitOrdCont.Add(newLimit);

    Console.ReadLine();
    }
  }
}
```

Summary

In this chapter, we provided an overview of some important features introduced by .NET 2.0. But you will find a treasure of other exciting new features added in ADO.NET, Windows Forms, and ASP.NET that we didn't discussed. .NET 2.0 makes the development task much simpler and promises some major improvements in the overall performance of managed applications. There is no doubt that .NET 2.0 is going to be the future, and Microsoft has given you an easy migration path by providing backward compatibility with applications designed on the .NET 1.*x* Framework.

APPENDIX A

■ ■ ■

.NET Tools

The following are .NET tools you may find useful.

Reflect Assemblies Using .NET Reflector http://www.aisto.com/roeder/dotnet/
 .NET Reflector is an extremely valuable tool that allows you to examine various classes and methods defined in .NET assemblies. The real strength of this tool resides in the automatic decompilation of IL code into C# or VB .NET code.

Export Reverse-Engineered Source Code to a File Using Reflector.FileDisassembler
http://www.denisbauer.com/NETTools/FileDisassembler.aspx
 Reflector.FileDisassembler is an add-on extension to .NET Reflector and is used to export the content of a .NET assembly (binary form) into C# or VB .NET files.

Perform Code Obfuscation Using Dotfuscator http://www.gotdotnet.com/team/dotfuscator/
 Code obfuscation is a technique applied to MSIL binaries to make the reverse-engineering task extremely difficult. .NET assemblies are rich in metadata and contain information that can be easily deciphered using various kinds of reflection tools, such as ILDASM. .NET Reflector is one of them. Using these kinds of tools, anyone can reverse engineer the original source code, and to foil this attempt, a code obfuscation technique is used.

Unit Test Source Code Using NUnit http://sourceforge.net/projects/nunit and http://sourceforge.net/projects/nunitaddin
 NUnit is an open source unit-testing framework that brings Test Driven Development (TDD) practices to .NET.

Perform .NET Programming Compliance Checks Using FxCop http://www.gotdotnet.com/team/fxcop/
 FxCop is a peer review tool for code that analyzes assemblies and checks them for compliance using a number of rules. By default, it comes with predefined rules that check code for conformance to the .NET Framework design guidelines.

Automate the Build Process Using NAnt http://sourceforge.net/projects/nant
 NAnt is an open source framework tasked with the responsibility of automating the build process of .NET projects using NAnt scripts defined in XML.

Produce Documentation of Source Code Automatically Using NDoc http://ndoc.sourceforge.net/
NDoc is an open source framework that generates code documentation from .NET assemblies in MSDN-style Help format (.chm) or VS .NET Help format (HTML Help 2).

Build and Test Regular Expressions Using Regulator http://regex.osherove.com/
The Regulator tool makes creating and testing extremely complex regular expressions a breeze.

Build Networked Applications with Indy.Sockets http://www.indyproject.org/Sockets/index.en.iwp
Indy.Sockets is an open source .NET library that provides an exhaustive collection of various communication protocols such as TCP, UDP, NNTP, HTTP, POP3, and SMTP.

Use the Centralized Connection Strings Database http://www.connectionstrings.com/
This site provides an excellent resource of database connection strings for all the available database drivers.

Develop MMC Snap-ins Using MMC.NET Library http://sourceforge.net/projects/mmclibrary/
The MMC.NET Library provides a managed library that enables MMC snap-in–style development.

Understand P/Invoke Signatures Through P/Invoke .NET Wiki http://pinvoke.net
This site provides a repository that contains predefined P/Invoke signatures that can be used in managed code in a copy-and-paste manner.

Explore Advanced Data Structures Using Power Collections for .NET http://www.wintellect.com/powercollections/
Power Collections provides high-quality advanced data structures that use .NET 2.0 generic features and is entirely developed in C#.

Measure the Quality of .NET Assemblies Using NDepend http://smacchia.chez-alice.fr/NDepend.html
The NDepend tool analyzes .NET assemblies and generates design-quality metric reports.

Build Grid Computing in .NET Using Alchemi http://www.alchemi.net/
Alchemi is an open source .NET-based grid computing framework that offers an infrastructure to collaborate multiple computers on networks in order to execute large-scale computational tasks.

Provide Code Coverage Using CoverageEye.NET http://www.gotdotnet.com/Community/UserSamples/Details.aspx?SampleGuid=881a36c6-6f45-4485-a94e-060130687151
CoverageEye.NET analyzes an assembly and generates reports about IL instructions that have been executed. This tool will help discover the code coverage percentage of any .NET assembly.

Solve Complex Scientific Problems Using Math.NET http://www.cdrnet.net/projects/nmath/default.asp
Math.NET is an open source library used to perform some highly advanced numerical computations.

Harness the Power of log4Net http://logging.apache.org/log4net/
log4Net is a highly advanced logging and tracing framework that enables you to log/trace statements to a variety of output targets.

Profile Applications Using CLR Profiler `http://www.microsoft.com/downloads/`
`details.aspx?FamilyId=86CE6052-D7F4-4AEB-9B7A-94635BEEBDDA&displaylang=en`
CLR Profiler is one of the most well-known profiling tools for managed code available from Microsoft. It includes a number of useful views of the allocation profile, including a histogram of allocated types, allocation and call graphs, a timeline showing garbage collectors of various generations and the final state of the managed heap after those collections, and a call tree showing per-method allocations and assembly loads.

Analyze Network Using Ethereal `http://www.ethereal.com/`
Ethereal is an open source network troubleshooting and protocol analyzer tool. It provides a detailed analysis of low-level network protocols and several other features that are not available in any other product.

Perform TCP Tunneling Using TCPTrace `http://www.pocketsoap.com/tcptrace/`
The TCPTrace tool is useful to debug socket/.NET remoting applications.

Source Code Metrics Using SourceMonitor `http://www.campwoodsw.com/index.html`
This tool measures source code metrics in terms of the number of classes, methods, and total lines of code.

Explore the Enterprise Library for .NET Framework 1.1 `http://msdn.microsoft.com/practices/`
`default.aspx?pull=/library/en-us/dnpag2/html/entlib.asp`
The Enterprise Library contains application blocks such as a caching block, a configuration block, a data access block, an exception management block, a cryptography block, and a security block that are designed to solve basic development problems.

Use Windows System Utilities `http://www.sysinternals.com`
This site provides advanced low-level Windows utilities that are extremely helpful in diagnosing performance-sensitive applications.

Build a Business Rule Engine `http://sourceforge.net/projects/nxbre/`
This is an open source framework for the .NET platform to build an XML-driven rule engine.

Use Advance .NET Assembly Instrumentation with the Runtime Assembly Instrumentation Library (RAIL)
`http://rail.dei.uc.pt/`
This framework provides a low-level hook that allows .NET assemblies to be manipulated and instrumented before they are loaded and executed.

Use Spring.NET `http://www.springframework.net`
Spring.NET provides a framework to incorporate a dependency injection pattern in managed applications.

Perform Advanced Debugging with Windows Debugger (WinDbg) `http://www.microsoft.com/whdc/`
`devtools/debugging/installx86.mspx`
WinDbg is the official Windows debugging tool that supports both user-mode and kernel-mode debugging. It is a must-have tool for developers architecting server-side applications in order to analyze low-level performance and hard-to-produce problems.

Debug CLR Internals Using Son of Strike (SOS) http://www.microsoft.com/whdc/devtools/debugging/
default.mspx

Bundled with the Windows Debugger Package, SOS is a WinDbg extension that provides low-level
information about the CLR internal data structures and is extremely handy to detect problems related
to memory and thread deadlock issues. This tool is a must-have for managed developers designing
mission-critical applications.

Use .NET on Linux: Mono http://www.mono-project.com

Mono is an open source initiative that provides a complete end-to-end framework to run .NET
applications on the Linux and Solaris platforms.

APPENDIX B

■ ■ ■

References

The following are some useful references:

- MSDN (http://msdn.microsoft.com)

- *MSDN Magazine* (http://msdn.microsoft.com/msdnmag)

- MSDN Web Services and Other Distributed Technologies Developer Center (http://msdn.microsoft.com/webservices)

- Microsoft Patterns & Practices (http://msdn.microsoft.com/practices)

- O'Reilly Network (http://www.oreillynet.com)

- *Applied Microsoft .NET Framework Programming* by Jeffrey Richter (0735614229; Microsoft Press, 2002)

- *Microsoft Windows Internals, Fourth Edition* by Mark E. Russinovich and David A. Solomon (0735619174; Microsoft Press, 2004)

- *Professional XML* by Mark Birbeck, Michael Kay, Steven Livingstone, Stephen F. Mohr, Jonathan Pinnock, Brian Loesgen, Steven Livingston, Didier Martin, Nikola Ozu, Mark Seabourne, and David Baliles (1861003110; Wrox, 2000)

- *.NET and XML* by Niel M. Bornstein (0596003978; O'Reilly, 2003)

- *Pro .NET 1.1 Network Programming* by Christian Nagel, Ajit Mungale, Vinod Kumar, Nauman Laghari, Andrew Krowczyk, Tim Parker, Srinivasa Sivakumar, and Alexandru Serban (1590593456; Apress, 2004)

- *TCP/IP* by Sidnie Feit (0070220697; McGraw-Hill, 1998)

- *Pattern-Oriented Software Architecture* by Douglas Schmidt, Michael Stal, Hans Rohnert, and Frank Buschmann (0471606952; John Wiley & Sons, 2000)

- *C++ Network Programming, Volume 1* by Douglas C. Schmidt and Stephen D. Huston (0201604647; Addison-Wesley, 2010)

- *TCP/IP Sockets in C#* by David Makofske, Michael J. Donahoo, and Kenneth L. Calvert (0124660517; Morgan Kaufmann, 2004)

- *Advanced .NET Remoting* by Ingo Rammer (1590590252; Apress, 2002)

- *AspectJ in Action* by Ramnivas Laddad (1930110936; Manning, 2003)

- *.NET Security and Cryptography* by Peter Thorsteinson and G. Gnana Arun Ganesh (013100851X; Prentice Hall, 2003)

- *.NET Security* by Jason Bock, Tom Fischer, Nathan Smith, and Pete Stromquist (1590590538; Apress, 2002)

- *Expert Service-Oriented Architecture in C#* by Jeffrey Hasan (1590593901; Apress, 2004)

- *Service-Oriented Architecture* by Thomas Erl (0131858580; Prentice Hall, 2005)

- *Code Generation in Action* by Jack Herrington (1930110979; Manning, 2003)

- *Code Generation in Microsoft .NET* by Kathleen Dollard (1590591372; Apress, 2004)

- *Essential .NET, Volume 1* by Don Box (0201734117; Addison Wesley, 2002)

- *Distributed Systems* by George Coulouris, Jean Dollimore, and Tim Kindberg (0321263545; Addison Wesley, 2005)

- *Security Engineering* by Ross J. Anderson (0471389226; Wiley, 2001)

- *Web Service Platform Architecture* by Sanjiva Weerawarana, Francisco Curbera, Frank Leymann, Tony Storey, and Donald F. Ferguson (0131488740; Prentice Hall, 2005)

Index

Numbers

255.255.255.255 broadcast address, significance of, 210
32-bit IP address, explanation of, 180

Symbols

80-20 rule
    applying to clean reference data, 114
    applying to market capitalization, 13
    abstract model, basing code on, 422

A

abstract part of WSDL
    explanation of, 354
    representing, 356
    abstraction, availability in SOA, 352
    Accept, calling for market data producer with TCP, 193
    account activity statement, explanation of, 22
accounts, availability from depositories, 16
activation mode, defining in RPC, 258
Activator class, creating instance of remote object with, 260
active (pre-insert) order, explanation of, 88
Add method
    overriding for collections and multithreading, 78
    using with Hashtable class, 57
addresses in IP header, explanations of, 182
addressing specification. See WS-Addressing specification
ADO.NET DataSet, significance of, 423
Advanced Micro Devices
    buying for arbitrage, 414
    price differential for, 411
advice in AOP, explanation of, 279
affirmation and confirmation of trades, processes of, 23–24
agent host code sample for trading application, 297
agent remoting configuration code sample for trading application, 296
agent-side services, relationship to application operation engine, 284

AgentController class, using with application operation engine, 294
AgentInfo class, implementing for application operation engine, 292–293
Alchemi framework, description of, 478
algorithm efficiency, measuring via Big-O novation, 48
algorithms
    applying to collections of data elements, 48
    determining efficiency of, 48
    of thread pools, 59
    relationship to data storage, 85
    relationship to data structures, 48
allocation details, explanation of, 23
allocation process, relationship to STP, 304
AMD (Advanced Micro Devices) arbitrage example, 403
AMD example, 405
AMEX (American Stock Exchange), significance of, 8
analysis, role of market data in, 173
annualized percentage returns, calculating for arbitrage, 412
anonymous methods, reducing amounts of code with, 457, 459
AOP (aspect-oriented programming), overview of, 275–276, 282
AopAlliance assembly, referencing, 279
APIs, invoking in UDDI, 371
AppDomain class, using with heartbeat service, 247
AppDomain type, properties and events of, 253
AppDomainSetup class
    storing binding information in, 252
    using with shadow copying, 253
AppInfo class, using in application operation engine, 287
AppInfo interface, using in application operation engine, 288
application configuration details, defining, 250
application design, factors involved in, 36

application layer of TCP/IP, explanation of, 179
application management operational component, description of, 237
application operation engine. *See also* trading applications
  assembly structure for, 285
  class details for, 284, 290
  class diagram for, 285
  framework of, 283
  implementing AgentInfo class for, 292–293
  implementing LogManagement service for, 293
  implementing PrimaryController for, 290, 292
  project structure of, 285
  using AgentController class with, 294
application operator GUI, role in application operation engine, 284
application processes, communication between, 258
application-monitoring engine, significance of, 39
ApplicationName property, using with shadow copying, 253
applications
  efficiency of, 35
  measuring responsiveness of, 35
  programmatic perspective of, 36
AppManagement agent-side service, stopping and starting trading application with, 295
AppSettings property, exposing with ConfigurationSettings class, 251
arbitrage. *See also* equity arbitrage engine
  definition of, 403
  explanation of, 5
  forms of, 405–406
  overview of, 403–404
  profitability of, 405, 412
  pure arbitrage, 406
  risks associated in, 407
  speculative arbitrage, 407
arbitrage cost risk in arbitraged, explanation of, 407
arbitrage margin, explanation of, 409
arbitrage model, building arbitrage engine with, 443
arbitrage opportunities, examples of, 413
arbitrage system versus program trading system, 408
arbitrage transactions, costs involved in, 404–405
arbitrageurs, reasons for success of, 404
architects, types of, 34
array of bytes, converting contract note message into, 316

array lists
  overcoming fixed-size problems with, 50
  role in .NET collections, 49, 51
array size, problem associated with, 49
Array.BinarySearch static method, calling, 52
ArrayList
  driving sort and search behaviors in, 87
  properties of, 78–79
arrays
  locating items in, 52
  redimensioning, 49–50
  role in .NET collections, 48–49
  type coupleness behavior associated with, 50
  using parametric polymorphism with, 447
  using quick sort algorithm with, 51
  using with market data producer, 187
ascending order, sorting orders in, 53–54
.asmx extension, using with Web services, 362
aspect in AOP, explanation of, 279
Aspect# assemblies
  downloading, 278
  referencing, 279
AspectEngine, injecting rules dynamically with, 282
AspectLanguageEngineBuilder, injecting rules dynamically with, 282
AspectSharp assembly, referencing, 279
assemblies. *See also* shared assembly for remoting and generics code sample
  definition of, 417
  in-memory generation of, 433
assembly structure for sample RPC, 254
AssemblyCustomAttributes attribute, using with CodeDOM, 429
asymmetric encryption
  ridexamples of, 318
  implementing for STP and Web services, 392–393
  versus symmetric encryption, 322
asymmetric keys, using in STP-space security, 317, 322
AsymmetricAlgorithm base abstract class, explanation of, 318
AsyncCallback delegate, using in asynchronous callback notification, 63
asynchronous delegate infrastructure, relationship to multithreading, 60, 63
asynchronous market data producers and consumers, overview of, 196, 200
AsyncWaitHandle property of IAsyncResult, using with delegates, 62
atomic operation, relationship to multithreading, 73

attributes
  descriptions of, 134
  support for, 132
authentication information, representing in
      WS-Security, 384
authentication of data, explanation of, 307
Authorization advice, injecting in AOP, 281
Authorization aspect, defining in AOP,
      280–281
AuthorizationAdvice class, constructing in
      AOP, 279
automatic code generation, using partial
      types for, 461
automatic deserialization, remoting support
      for, 275
AutoResetEvent class, role in interthread
      notification, 70

B

back office
  relationship to STP, 28
  role of market data in, 175
  routing trades to, 109
back-office applications, using IPC channel
      with, 471
back-office systems
  characteristics of, 30
  design of, 30
Band class, using in data conversion
      framework, 153–154
BandParser class, using in data conversion
      framework, 158–159
bands in data conversion framework,
      explanation of, 146
banks
  versus depositories, 15
  two roles of, 15
base types, forming for generic types, 451
basis risk in arbitrage, explanation of, 407
BCastPipe class, using with broadcast
      engine, 229–230
BCL (base class library), significance of, 38
bearish trader, definition of, 4
BeginAccept, calling for market data
      producer with TCP, 197
BeginInvoke method, using with delegates,
      60–61
BeginInvoke thread-safe member, exposing
      in Windows control collection, 82
BeginSend method, sending data
      asynchronously with, 197–198
beneficiary accounts, availability from
      depositories, 16
Berkshire Hathaway arbitrage example,
      405
Berkshire Hathaway example, 407
bid price, relationship to two-way quote, 4

Big-O notation, representing algorithm
      efficiency in, 48
binary formatter
  description of, 258
  serializing object graphs with, 202
binary search algorithm
  availability of, 87
  locating array items with, 52, 54
binary serializer, explanation of, 132
BinaryClientFormatter class, using in hosting
      service controller, 260
BinaryFormatter, using as data-encoding
      standard, 284
BinaryReader and BinaryWriter specialized
      Stream classes, overview of, 120–121
BinaryServerFormatterSinkProvider class,
      description of, 258
Bind method
  using with market data consumer, 189
  using with market data producer and TCP,
      193
binding information, storing in
      AppDomainSetup class, 252
<binding> element, using with WSDL
      documents, 357
bits, role in networking, 179
BizDomain class of order-matching engine,
      overview of, 100–101
block cipher, definition of, 309
BlockSize property, using with symmetric
      classes, 315
bonds, definition of, 1
bookkeeping, performing with order
      processor, 86
Boolean value, returning for
      IsTransparentProxy static method,
      261
BooleanCursor class, using in data
      conversion framework, 156–157
boxing and unboxing operations,
      considering for containers, 449
boxing process, relationship to array lists, 50
broadcast
  relationship to networking, 209–210
  unsolicited broadcast, 210, 213
broadcast engine
  primary role of, 220
  significance of, 39
broadcast engine class details
  BCastPipe, 229–230
  DataSerializerModule, 230–231
  Dispatcher, 226
  Host, 233
  IBCastMessage, 222–224
  IMessageStore, 224
  IModule, 228
  InMemoryStore, 224–225

MktDataMessage, 231, 233
PipeContext, 228–229
RoundRobinDispatcher, 226–227
StoreCollection, 225–226
TransportModule, 231
broadcast engines, building, 221–222
broadcast event, launching with dispatcher, 222
broadcast message, receiving, 212
broadcast pipe component of broadcast engine, description of, 222
broadcasts
relationship to market data, 172
solicited broadcasts, 213, 216
BrokerCertificate.cer, launching digital certificate with, 329
brokers. *See also* stock-exchange members
definition of, 7
floor brokers, 8, 10
interactions with fund managers, 320
interactions with custodians, 305
role in order matching, 42–43
specialists, 10–11
brute-force attack, explanation of, 309
buckets, assigning for orders, 43
BufferedStream subclass of Stream class, description of, 118
buffers, using with Socket, 219
bulk order upload forms, implementing parallelism in, 81
BulkOrderUpload, executing, 82
bullish trader, definition of, 4
business components
abstract view of, 235
examples of, 236
versus operational components, 236–237
relationship to trading operational requirement, 235
business concerns, separating with SOA, 351
business domain, explanation of, 85
business infoset
overview of, 106–107
reference data elements in, 107
business logic layer, uniformity of data at, 144
business requirements, significance of, 238
business rule engine, resource for building of, 479
business-processing unit, role in Web-service platforms, 360
business-technology mapping
BizDomain snippet for, 100
class details for, 284, 290
class details of, 88
Container snippet for, 92–93
ContainerCollection snippet for, 93–94

EquityMatchingLogic snippet for, 101–102
EquityOrder snippet for, 91
examining, 143, 148
for STP security, 331, 333
for Web services, 400
LeafContainer snippet for, 94, 96
of equity arbitrage, 442, 444
OMEHost snippet for, 102–103
Order snippet for, 89, 91
OrderBook snippet for, 96, 98
OrderEventArgs snippet for, 98
OrderProcessor snippet for, 99–100
overview of, 84, 88, 220, 222, 283–284
PriceTimePriority snippet for, 91–92
Buy and Sell, specifying nodes for, 87
buy or sell attribute of orders, explanation of, 89
buy orders
processing, 21
sorting in order matching, 42
bytes, extracting for market data consumer, 190
bytes array, converting contract note information into, 321

■**C**
C/C++
bright and dark side of, 31
using with front-office systems, 30
CachePath property, using with shadow copying, 253
callback method, execution of, 84
callback notification approach, using with asynchronous operations, 62
CAOs (client-activated objects)
versus local objects, 243
role in .NET Remoting, 242
capital markets
definition of, 1
I's (Intelligence) of performance in, 35, 38
proprietary class libraries provided for, 70
CAs (certificate authorities), issuing digital certificates with, 327–328
CBC (Cipher Block Chaining) mode, using with symmetric keys, 311
CellsAttribute abstract class, using in data conversion framework, 152–153
central order book, example of, 86
centralized application controllers, building, 284
certificate store
installing certificate published by broker in, 331
relationship to WS-Security, 385
certificates. *See* digital certificates
CFM (Cipher Feedback Mode), using with symmetric keys, 311–312

channel configuration, setting up in hosting service controller, 260

channel information, separating remote object registration from, 271

channel layer, relationship to proxy in .NET Remoting, 242

<channel> element of remoting configuration, explanation of, 271

channels in RPC, listening supported by, 259

cipher modes
  behaviors of, 312
  and Padding, 315

cipher text, producing, 308

ciphers, types of, 308–309

Class A stock and Class B stock of Berkshire Hathaway, prices of, 405

Class A-C network addresses, explanations of, 181

class details for application operation engine
  AppInfo, 287–288
  DomainApp, 288–289
  IConfiguration, 289
  IController, 286–287
  ILogger, 289
  overview of, 285
  Service, 289–290

class details for STP security
  ConfidentialAttribute class, 334
  ContractNoteInfo class, 336
  DataSecurity class, 342–343
  DataSecurityManager class, 341–342
  IntegrityAttribute class, 334
  NonRepudiationAttribute class, 335
  NonRepudiationProvider class, 340–341
  NonRepudiationSection class, 339
  ProfileInfo class, 336–337
  Provider class, 339–340
  SecrityProfileAttribute class, 336
  SectionData class, 338–339
  SecureEnvelope class, 337–338

class diagrams, of application operation engine, 285

class generic type constraint, overview of, 452

class names, changing for Web services, 363

class search example using reflection, 435–436

classes, relationship to objects, 238

cleansing stage of information based on external data sources, overview of, 143

clearing accounts, opening, 15

clearing and settlement, processes of, 24, 28

clearing banks, explanation of, 15, 26

clearing corporations, overview of, 14–15

CLI (Common Language Infrastructure), significance of, 32

client configuration details, separating from server in remoting, 273

<client> element of remoting configuration, explanation of, 271

CLR (common language runtime)
  explanation of, 32
  role in remoting framework, 241

CLR Profiler tool, features of, 479

CLR thread-pool implementation, offloading processing tasks with, 457–458

CLR types and an XML documents, using XmlSerializer class with, 133

clubbing orders, explanation of, 7

Coca-Cola Company
  arbitrage on, 412
  price differential for, 411

COD (context-oriented data), relationship to XML, 116

code, basing on abstract model, 422

code access security, significance of, code documentation generators, features of, 417, 420–422

code editor view, using with STP and Web services, 362

code expressions, declaring in CodeDOM, 430–431

code generation
  overview of, 415–416
  with Reflection.Emit, 439, 442

code generation and reflection, overview of, 417–418

code generators, types of, 416–417

code inflator generators, features of, 417, 422

code splits, advantages of, 460

code synchronization, relationship to manual thread management, 63, 65

code tags, boosting productivity with, 422

code templates, role in code generation, 416

code wizard generators, features of, 416, 420

code-generation process, triggering in CodeDOM, 427–428

code-reentrancy problem, occurrence with callback methods, 84

CodeCompileUnit instance, constructing with CodeDOM of, 429

CodeDOM
  declaring code expressions in, 430–431
  overview of, 424, 433

CodeDOM classes, leveraging, 429

CodeDOM object graph
  converting to text, 433
  translating into compiled form, 433

CodeDOM providers, purpose of, 432

CodeMemberMethod, declaring Compare method with, 430

CodeNameSpace, defining with CodeDOM, 429

CodeStatement, classes derived from, 431–432

CodeStatementsCollections, returning in CodeDOM, 431

CodeTypeDeclaration, defining SortCode class with, 430

collections. *See* generic collections; .NET collections

Column class, using in data conversion framework, 155

ColumnParser class, using in data conversion framework, 160–161

columns in data conversion framework, explanation of, 147

COM (Component Object Model) technology, introduction of, 31

communication handshaking, occurrence of, 260

communication services, providing with middleware, 240

Compare method
adding parameter declaration for, 430
declaring with CodeMemberMethod, 430

CompileAssemblyFromDom, compiling CodeDOM object graph with, 433

compiler-driven feature example of, 447

CompilerResults, using with CodeDOM object graph, 433

complex type, example of, 141

complex type elements, nesting under xs:schema element, 138

compressing in-memory data, 467–468

computed data element of business infoset, overview of, 108

ComputeHash, invoking, 324

concrete part of WSDL, representing, 356

concurrency. *See* multithreading

ConfidentialAttribute class, using in STP security, 334

confidentiality
of data, 307
in STP space, 308, 322

configuration file
composition of, 250
location of, 250

configuration framework, overview of, 250–251

configuration operational component, description of, 237

configuration path, assigning to ConfigurationFile property of AppDomainSetup class, 252

ConfigurationFile property of AppDomainSetup class, assigning configuration path to, 252

ConfigurationSettings class, exposing AppSettings property with, 251

Configure method of RemotingConfiguration class, booting remoting infrastructure with, 271

confirmation and affirmation of trades, processes of, 23–24

constraints, using with generic code, 452

constraints and rules, associating with Web services, 396

constructor method
updating LogicalProcess class with, 251
using with infrastructure services, 265

consumers, binding to Web services at runtime, 371

Container class of order-matching engine, overview of, 92

ContainerCollection class of order-matching engine, overview of, 93

containers, tweaking storage implementation for, 449

context switching, relationship to thread scheduling, 74

contexts, relationship to objects, 239

contract note, explanation of, 22

contract note data
hash value computed for, 323–324
signing and verification of, 325–326
signing and verification with digital certificates, 329–330

contract note functionality, enabling with PostTradeService, 364

contract note information
converting into bytes array, 321
encrypting, 315
encrypting with STP-Provider A public key, 392–393
exchanging with asymmetric algorithm, 318
securing, 386, 389

contract note message, converting into array of bytes, 316

contract notes
digital signing of, 387, 389
encrypting and decrypting, 313–314
sending, 305

ContractNoteInfo class, using in STP security, 336

ContractNoteInfo type, representing in XSD form, 367

conversion rule, producing XML output with, 167–168

conversion stage of information based on external data sources, overview of, 143

Convert method, using in data conversion example, 166

converter, role in data conversion framework, 147

core lookup service class, using with service directory, 263–264

corporate stocks versus indexes, 12

correlation in prices, relationship to arbitrage, 406

cost savings, realizing with STP, 301

costs of arbitrage transactions, 404–405

Count property, using with stacks, 56

counting semaphores, using with shared resources, 462–463

CoverageEye.NET tool, features of, 478

Create method
using with NonRepudiationProvider class, 341
using with Provider class, 340

CreateApplication method, using with AgentController class, 294

CreateDecryptor method, decrypting contract notes with, 315

CreateEncryptor method, encrypting contract notes with, 315

CreateInstanceAndUnwrap method, using with heartbeat service, 247

credit checks, performance by clearing corporations, 14

critical section, relationship to code synchronization, 64

cryptography, definition of, 308

CryptoServiceProvider suffix, significance of, 312

CryptoStream, creating instance of, 316

CryptoStream subclass of Stream class, description of, 118

CspParameters, contents of, 321

CSV conversion rule, using with data conversion framework, 148, 151

CSV versus XML, 116

current time, checking for sponsors, 270

custodian, role in trading, 23–24

custodian service provider, relationship to STP, 299

custodians
characteristics of, 305
interactions with brokers, 305
submissions of instruction initiated by, 306

custom sink layer, relationship to proxy in .NET Remoting, 242

■D

data
authentication of, 307
confidentiality of, 307
defining security type for, 333
integrity of, 307, 322, 324
nonrepudiation of, 307
plotting in matrix, 145

reading and writing, 117, 119

receiving on separate thread, 200

data arrangement uniformity, relationship to XML, 116

data cleansing, explanation of, 112

data compression, overview of, 467–468

data containers, design of, 84–85

data conversion
definition of, 105
definitions of, 111
example of, 166–167

data conversion example, XML output for, 167

data conversion framework
architecting, 143
Band class in, 153–154
BandParser class in, 158–159
bands in, 145–146
BooleanCursor class in, 156–157
CellsAttribute abstract class in, 152–153
Column class in, 155
ColumnParser class in, 160–161
columns in, 147
CSV conversion rule in, 148, 152
DataConverter class in, 162, 166
goals of, 144
IWriter class in, 161
Matrix class in, 155–156
Parser class in, 157–158
relationship to reference data, 111, 114
Row class in, 154
RowParser class in, 159
rows in, 146
rule schema in, 149
XmlDataWriter class in, 161–162

data elements, costs associated with location of, 51

data elements of business infoset
computed data, 108
derived data, 107
reference data, 107–108, 115
relationship to order attributes, 106–107
static data, 108
variable data, 107

data in silos, issues related to, 112

data length in IP, significance of, 182

data management, overview of, 105–106

data management operational component, description of, 237

data security, importance of, 39

data security versus code access security, 32

data store, explanation of, 117

data structures
relationship to algorithms, 48
relationship to order matching, 85

data type, defining for Web-service messages, 356

data uniformity at business logic layer, significance of, 144
data-quake, definition of, 37
data-quakes, relationship to broadcast engines, 220
database connection string resource, 478
DataConverter class, using in data conversion framework, 162, 166
datagrams, role in networking, 179
DataSecurity class, using in STP security, 342–343
DataSecurityManager class, using in STP security, 341–342
DataSerializerModule class, using with broadcast engine, 230–231
DataSet, internal structure of, 423
DataSet writer, role in data conversion framework, 148
dates, pay-in and pay-out dates, 26
dce element, representing with Matrix class, 155
DCOM, relationship to .NET Remoting, 240
deadlock prevention, relationship to multithreading, 65, 68
dealers versus investors and traders, 3
debit instructions, providing for depositories, 17
debugging, managing in remoting, 275
decompressing in-memory data, 467–468
Decrypt, using with asymmetric keys, 322
decryption of contract notes, 315
decryption process, explanation of, 308
DeflateStream class in System.IO.Compression namespace, definition of, 467
delegate execution, arranging on UI threads, 82
delegate keyword, using with anonymous methods, 458
delegates, relationship to multithreading, 60
delegates, overview of, 456
delimited file format, example and description of, 144
demutualization of exchanges, explanation of, 8
depositories
    overview of, 15, 17
    risks eliminated by, 17
Dequeue methods, using with queues, 55
derived data element of business infoset, overview of, 107
DES (Data Encryption Standard) symmetric algorithm
    key size of, 313
    significance of, 310
descending order, sorting orders in, 53–54

deserialization
    definition of, 131
    example of, 135–136
    in message framing, 207
    process of, 202
    remoting support for, 275
destination address in IP header, significance of, 182
destination unreachable ICMP message, description of, 183
development team, relationship to operations team, 283
diagrams. See figures
digital certificates
    generating, 328
    inclusion in WS-Security, 385
    role in STP-space security, 327, 331
    verifying with WSE, 387
digital signatures
    inclusion in WS-Security, 384
    role in STP-space security, 324, 327
    verifying, 326
    verifying hash values with, 327
Dispatcher class, using with broadcast engine, 226
dispatcher component of broadcast engine, description of, 222
distributed garbage collection, overview of, 267, 270
distributed systems, relationship to networking, 177
dividend, definition of, 2
DJIA (Dow Jones Industrial Average) index, description of, 12
DLL locking problem, occurrence of, 252
DNS (Domain Name System), relationship to TCP/IP, 183
document root elements, nesting under xs:chema element, 139
documentation generators, features of, 421
domain intelligence, overview of, 37
domain knowledge, relationship to XML, 116
DomainApp class
    description of, 284
    using in application operation engine, 288
DomainApp interface, using in application operation engine, 289
Dotfuscator tool, features of, 477
DTC (depository trust corporation), significance of, 15

■E
EAI (enterprise application integration), relationship to XML, 115
EASDAQ (European Association of Securities Dealers Automated Quotation), significance of, 8

ECB (Electronic Code Book) mode, using with symmetric keys, 310

echo reply and request ICMP messages, descriptions of, 183

Encoding
converting contract note information with, 321
in System.Text namespace for market data producer, 188

Encrypt, using with information in byte array, 321

encryption
implementing asymmetric encryption for STP and Web services, 392–393
of contract notes, 315
of keys, 321

encryption element, inclusion in WS-Security, 384

encryption phase, initiating for symmetric classes, 315

encryption process, explanation of, 308

EndInvoke method, using with delegates, 60, 62

EndPoint
defining for market data producer with TCP, 193
resolving in market data producer, 188

EndSend, invoking to complete asynchronous send operation, 198

Enqueue method, using with queues, 55

enrichment stage of information based on external data sources, overview of, 144

Enterprise Library, description of, 479

entities for STP in equities trade, 302

enumeration of orders, problem associated with, 79

envelope, object-oriented form of, 338

equilibrium position and price, explanations of, 11

equities market, .NET in, 30, 34

equities market entities
banks, 15
clearing corporations, 14–15
depositories, 15, 17
indexes, 12–13
stock exchanges, 6, 8

equities trade, STP in, 302

equity and equity shares, overview of, 2

equity arbitrage, business-technology mapping of, 442, 444

equity arbitrage engine, building, 407–408, 414. See also arbitrage

EquityMatchingLogic class of order-matching engine, overview of, 101–102

EquityOrder class of order-matching engine, overview of, 91

error handling, managing in remoting, 274–275

Ethereal tool, features of, 479

event, definition of, 83

<exception> XML tag for documentation comments, description of, 421

exceptions, support in remoting, 274–275

Exchange element, XML Schema of, 140

Exchange information, generating, 130

exchange interactions, synchronizing with Mutex, 71–72

exchange keys, using with digital certificate, 331

exchanges. See stock exchanges

ExchangesModel complex type, example of, 140

ExportParameters method
using with keys, 320
external STP
using with digital certificates, 331

■F

factory classes, using with symmetric classes, 314

fast-forward parsers, overview of, 122–123

fault isolation, achieving with CLR and Win32 process, 241

field layout, rearranging with runtime, 204

field marshaling behavior, changing, 204

FIFO (first-in, first-out) data structures, queues as, 54

FIFO manner, processing orders in, 55

Figures
Add Web Reference dialog box, 368
affirmation and confirmation process, 23
allocation and contract note, 305
AOP architecture, 279
application design versus time, 35
application operation engine, 283
arbitrage engine, 442
arbitrage engine based on arbitrage models, 443
array lists used in linear arrangement of heterogeneous order, 49
arrays used in linear arrangement of homogeneous order, 48
asymmetric algorithm class hierarchy, 318
asymmetric key, 317
BCastServer console output, 234
bridging networks with routers, 180
broadcast engine class diagram, 223
broadcast engine implementation overview, 222
broadcast engine project structure, 223
brokers help investors, 9

bulk order upload form, 82
business component, 236
buy orders of retail clients, 21
byte ordering, 201
CBC (Cipher Block Chaining) mode, 311
central order book, 87
centralization of operational services, 238
certificate store, 386
CFM (Cipher Feedback Mode), 311
changing Web service class name and
    filename, 364
cipher mode, 309
class search program using reflection, 436
cleansing reference data, 113
clearing process, 25
code editor view showing autogenerated
    Web service code, 363
code generator components, 416
CodeDOM, 434
CodeDOM processes abstract code, 424
COM days, 31
communication with entities on one
    network, 348
communication protocol, 349
console application demonstrates
    invocation of STP-Provider A Web
    service, 370
console output describing field
    information embedded in digital
    certificates, 331
console output of AOP-enabled heartbeat
    service, 282
console output of hash algorithm
    program, 324
console output of program using
    asymmetric key, 322
console output of program using
    symmetric key, 317
console output of service controller and
    heartbeat service, 260–261
console output of service directory, 267
conversion framework, 147
data conversion framework class diagram,
    151
data conversion framework project
    structure, 151
Data Form Wizard, 420
data hashing, 323
digital certificate, 329
digital signature, 325
front, middle, and back offices, 29
HashAlgorithm class hierarchy, 323
information originating from multiple
    sources in different formats, 106
instrument mapping in front office, 110
integrating operational and functional
    requirements, 278

intelligence levels, 36
life cycle of a trade, 18
market data, 173
market data producers and consumers,
    221
MCastClient console output, 216
MCastServer console output, 216
MDC (Async-TCP) console output, 200
MDC (UDP) console output, 190
MDP (Async-TCP) console output, 200
MDP (market data producer) and MDC
    (market data consumer), 186
MDP (TCP) console output, 195
MDP (UDP) console output, 190
.NET days, 31
.NET Framework and solutions for
    financial world, 38
network byte order console output, 202
object facets, 239
order management system components in
    service-oriented design, 351
order processed in FIFO manner, 54
order processed in LIFO manner, 56
order submission and notice of execution,
    304
order-matching engine, 86
order-matching engine class diagram, 88
order-matching engine VS.NET project
    structure, 89
parsing console output for message
    framing, 209
PING output, 183
pre-.NET days, 31
Provider registration page, 374
Providers tab for registering STP providers,
    373
record represented as matrix, 145
reference data is central to all functions,
    108
reflection used in path traversal, 435
remote proxies receiving remote calls, 261
remoting framework, 240
remoting object facets, 243
requirement distillation, 238
rule-based arbitrage engine, 444
securities clearing account, 27
security framework and class hierarchy,
    333
security framework project structure, 334
sell orders are validated, 21
service consumer project created with
    Visual Studio .NET, 367
service controller and heartbeat service,
    244
service directory, 263
Service registration page with information
    about PostTradeService, 377

settlement comprises pay-in and pay-out, 28
SOAP envelope, 358
solicited broadcast, 213
Solution Explorer shows autogenerated
    proxy class, 369
Solution Explorer view of consumer
    application, 387
specialists provide quotes on request, 10
STP (straight through processing), 29
STP framework (post-trade), 306
STP participants, 302
STP Provider project structure, 362
STP security conceptual design, 332
STP space, 307
STP-Provider A Web service endpoint
    information is retrieved, 379
STP-Provider B invokes STP-Provider
    A Web service, 361
substitution cipher, 308
symmetric algorithm class hierarchy, 312
symmetric key, 310
TCP/IP layers, 179
thread scheduling, 74
trade confirmation, 111
trade with and without novation, 47
trades happen due to differences in
    opinion, 4
transparent and real proxies, 261
transposition cipher, 309
two-way quote comprising bid price and
    offer price, 4
UDDI repository finds STP-Provider A Web
    service, 371
UDDI test Web site offered by Microsoft,
    372
UI thread, 81
unicast communication model, 210
unsolicited broadcast, 211
UnsolicitedBCastClient console output,
    213
UnsolicitedBCastServer console output,
    213
Web service registration, 376
Web service stack, 380
Web services, 353
Web-service platform high-level
    components, 359
Web-service project created with Visual
    Studio .NET, 362
Web-STP, 401
while loop code, 126
Windows Form Designer, 419
WS-Addressing achieves transport
    standardization, 398
WS-MetadataExchange, 399
WS-Policy enforces constraints and rules,
    395

WS-Referral implements STP provider
    hub, 399
WS-Security secures SOAP message, 385
WSE architecture, 381
WSE configuration configures Web service
    policies, 397
WSE Configuration dialog box, 382
WSE set-up options, 382
WSE settings dialog box, 383
file formats, examples of, 144
filenames, changing for Web services, 364
FileStream subclass of Stream class,
    description of, 117
fills, relationship to orders, 7
financial marketplace, primary objectives in,
    41
financial markets, anonymity in, 42
finite state machine, components of, 444
firm quote, definition of, 10
FIX (Financial Information Exchange)
        protocol
    popularity of, 304
    significance of, 19
flags, relationship to fragmentation and IP,
    182
floor brokers, overview of, 8, 10
foreach keyword, using with iterators, 459
formatter configuration, setting up in
        hosting service controller, 260
formatter layer, relationship to proxy in .NET
        Remoting, 241
formatters. *See* remoting formatters
forward engineering, explanation of, 423
forward lookup, relationship to DNS, 184
forward-only parsers, types of, 122–123
fragment offset, relationship to IP, 182
fragmentation
    disabling in IP, 217
    relationship to IP (Internet protocol),
        182
frames, role in networking, 179
front office
    instrument mapping in, 109
    origination of orders in, 109
    relationship to STP, 28
front running, explanation of, 10
front-office systems
    characteristics of, 30
    using C/C++ with, 30
full-covered concept, relationship to risk
        management, 20
full-duplex TCP connection, explanation of,
    194
full-type fidelity mode of serialization
        engine, explanation of, 132
functional requirements, integrating
        operational requirements with, 277

fund managers
    activities of, 303
    interactions with brokers, 320
funds settlement, overview of, 26–27
FxCop tool, features of, 477

■**G**

garbage collection, automation in .NET, 32
GCs (garbage collectors), types of, 464
<gcServer> element, adding to configuration
    file, 464
GCSettings helper class, example of, 465
General Electric Company
    buying for arbitrage, 414
    price differential for, 411
GenerateCodeFromCompileUnit, converting
    object graph to text with, 433
generic classes versus generic methods, 454
generic collections, overview of, 456–457
    See also .NET collections
generic delegates, overview of, 456
generic methods, overview of, 454, 456
generic type constraints
    class constraint, 452–453
    inheritance constraint, 454
    interface constraint, 453
    overview of, 452
    parameterless constructor constraint,
        453–454
    reference constraint, 453
    value type constraint, 453
generic type parameters
    associating multiple constraints on,
        453
    associating rules with, 452
generic types
    base class of, 451
    creating instances of, 451
    inheritance on, 451
generic-aware remote classes, prerequisite
    for, 474
generic-aware remote order container code
    sample, 474
generics
    role in .NET 2.0, 447, 451
    using with order container, 449–450
GetLifetimeService method, returning lease
    objects with, 270
GetObject of Activator class, using with
    instances of remote objects, 260
GetString method of Encoding.ASCII class,
    extracting bytes with, 190
GTC (good till cancelled) order, explanation
    of, 43
GTD (good till date) order, explanation of, 44
GZipStream class in System.IO.Compression
    namespace, definition of, 467

■**H**

handshaking
    occurrence of, 261
    relationship to transport layer, 191
hardware components, role in networking,
    178
hash algorithms
    examples of, 323
    passing data to, 322
hash tables, using, 57
hash values
    generating, 323–324
    verifying with digital signature, 327
Hashtable
    creating proxy references in, 265
    declaring for service directory, 264
head count, reducing with STP, 301
header checksum field, relationship to IP, 182
heartbeat, implementing between machines
    with Ping, 470
heartbeat interval information, capturing in
    key-value pair, 251
heartbeat messages
    exchange of, 83
    sending with server timer, 83
    targeting to monitor NASDAQ exchange
        gateway, 277
    targeting to monitor NYSE exchange
        gateway code sample, 276
heartbeat operational component,
    description of, 237
heartbeat service
    accessing core knowledge about, 260
    connecting service controller to,
        259–260
    creating proxy instance for, 260
    defining LogicalProcess class for, 246
    enabling in AOP, 282
    explanation of, 244–245
    in AOP, 281
    interaction with service controller, 265
    modifying to demonstrate configuration
        framework, 250
    returning proxy reference to, 266
    RPC version of, 255–256
    URL location of, 260
HeartBeatService class, code for, 245–246
HeartBeatServiceInfo class, emitting
    metadata information with, 256
HeartBeatServiceInfo type
    description of, 260
    registering in RPC, 258–259
hitting the bid, explanation of, 5
Host class
    in hosting service controller, 260
    using with broadcast engine, 233
    using with infrastructure services, 257

using with primary controller, 294

using with service directory, 263–264

host ID, relationship to IP addresses, 181

host name, resolving to IP address, 184

hosts in networks

identifying, 185

multihomed hosts, explanation of, 189

house accounts, explanation of, 9

HTTP, use by Web services, 353

HTTP channel, description of, 258

HttpServerChannel class, description of, 258

human intelligence, overview of, 37

HybridDictionary specialized collection, overview of, 58

I's (Intelligence) of performance in capital markets

domain intelligence, 37

human intelligence, 37

machine intelligence, 36

overview of, 35

IAsyncResult, using with delegates, 61

IBCastMessage class, using with broadcast engine, 223–224

IBM UDDI repository website, 371

ICMP (Internet Control Message Protocol), relationship to IP layer, 182

ICodeCompiler, implementing in CodeDOM, 432

ICodeGenerator interface, implementing in CodeDOM, 432

IComparable interface, using generic types with, 451

IComparer instance, returning with CodeDOM, 428

IComparer interface, sorting with, 53

IConfiguration interface, using in application operation engine, 289

IController interface

implementing with PrimaryController, 290, 292

using in application operation engine, 286–287

ICryptoTransform interface, implementing, 315

identification field, relationship to fragmentation and IP, 182

identifier attribute

explanation of, 146

using in CSV conversion rule, 148

IGMP (Internet Group Management Protocol), relationship to routers, 214

IIS, DLL locking problem associated with, 252

ILease interface, controlling Lease class with, 268

ILogger interface, using in application operation engine, 289

ILookUp interface

implementing for service directory, 264

using with service directory, 263

IMessageStore class, using with broadcast engine, 224

IMethodInterceptor interface, implementing with AuthorizationAdvice class in AOP, 280

IModule class, using with broadcast engine, 228

impact cost, relationship to stock exchanges, 6

ImportParameters functionality, using with digital certificates, 331

in- versus out-memory matching, 85

in-memory data, compressing and decompressing, 467–468

in-memory generation of assemblies, advantage of, 433

in-memory matching

explanation of, 85

options available for, 85

rationale for, 85

inactive (removed) order, explanation of, 88

indexes

computing, 12

overview of, 12–13

Indy.Sockets .NET library, features of, 478

information, relationship to transactions, 3

infrastructural services, providing with middleware, 240

infrastructure components versus business components, 237

infrastructure service controller, hosting, 266

infrastructure services

configuring, 250, 252

hosting, 257

operations supported by, 248

server-side implementation for, 255–256

shadow copying of, 252–253

storing proxy references of, 264

inheritance, performing on generic types, 451

inheritance generic constraint, overview of, 454

inheritance levels in cryptography, explanations of, 312

InitializeLifetimeService class, invoking for lease objects, 268

InitializeLifetimeService member, using with RPC version of heartbeat service, 256

InMemoryStore class, using with broadcast engine, 224

<input> construct, using with WSDL documents, 357

insider, definition of, 11

institutional investor, explanation of, 19

institutional transactions, using STP in, 303

institutions versus retail customers, 20

instrument attribute of orders, explanation of, 89

instrument master, using in trading chain, 109

instrumentation operational component, description of, 237

instruments, mapping trees to, 87

instruments. *See* stocks

InsufficientMemoryException, generating, 464

integrity of data
  explanation of, 307
  overview of, 322, 324

IntegrityAttribute class, using in STP security, 334

interdepository transfers, management by depositories, 16

interface generic type constraints, overview of, 452–453

Interlocked class, relationship to atomic operation, 73

internal STP, explanation of, 29

Internet layer of TCP/IP, explanation of, 179

interop attributes, using with message framing, 204

interoperability. *See also* STP interoperability
  overview of, 347, 349
  of service providers, explanation of, 300

interprocess communication performance, creating on same machine, 471

interthread notification, relationship to multithreading, 68, 70

investors versus traders and dealers, 3

Invoke method, calling for bulk order form, 82–83

Invoke thread-safe member, exposing in Windows control collection, 82

IOC (immediate or cancel) order, explanation of, 44

IP (Internet protocol)
  addressing in, 182
  data length field in, 182
  fragmentation and reassembling process related to, 182
  maintaining message integrity in, 182, 185
  overview of, 179, 181
  tweaking, 217

IP addresses
  resolving host name to, 184
  significance of, 180
  subnet IDs in, 181

IP fragmentation, disabling, 217

IP MulticastLoopback, tweaking, 218

IP TTL and multicast TTL, tweaking, 217–218

IpcChannel, relationship to remoting, 471

IPEndPoint instance, using with market data consumer, 189

IPHostEntry class, relationship to DNS, 185

IPO (initial public offering), explanation of, 2

IService
  declaring for RPC, 254
  declaring in .NET Remoting, 245

IServiceInfo interface, using with RPC, 254

ISIN codes
  exchange code mapped to, 111
  significance of, 109

ISIN element, XML Schema of, 139–140

ISIN master
  example of, 148, 152
  reading XML version of, 124–125
  using XML with, 115–116
  XML Schema of, 137–138

ISIN master XML document
  assumptions made in, 136
  validating with XmlValidatingReader class, 141–142
  writing, 128, 130

ISINInfo type, annotating Serializable attribute on, 133

ISINMaster root element, contents of, 141

ISO file format, example and description of, 145

ISponsor interface, implementing, 270

issuers, participation in market data industry, 172

IsTransparentProxy helper static method, using with transparent proxies, 261

IT structure, decentralizing for STP, 303

iterators, using with data structures, 459–460

IVs (initialization vectors)
  generating, 315
  relationship to CBC, 311

IWriter class, using in data conversion framework, 161

■J

JIT-CC (just-in-time code cutting), features of, 417, 423

JUSTRIGHT

■K

key information, storing in instance of RSAParameters, 326

key pairs, generating and executing, 320

Key property of X509Certificate, retrieving public key with, 331

key sizes
  determining, 315
  of symmetric ciphers, 313

support by symmetric algorithms, 310
supported by Rijndael, 315
key-value pair, capturing heartbeat interval
information in, 251
keys
encrypting, 321
generating, 315, 320–321
role in encryption and decryption, 309

■L

language-specific code provider,
constructing with CodeDOM,
432–433
late binding, providing with reflection, 436
latency, definition of, 35
layers of TCP/IP, relationship to networking, 179
lazy-loading technique, implementation in
remoting framework, 275
lead manager, definition of, 2
LeafContainer class of order-matching
engine, overview of, 94, 96
lease behavior, overriding default for, 268
Lease class, controlling with ILease interface,
268
lease manager, registering lease objects with,
269
Lease objects
associating new instance of, 268
getting reference to, 270
invoking InitializeLifetimeService class
for, 268
returning with GetLifetimeService
method, 270
leases
preventing renewal of, 270
renewing for remote objects, 269
leasing architecture of remote object
destruction, illustration of, 267
legacy systems, populating data from, 112
LegalBlockSizes property, using with
symmetric classes, 315
LegalKeySizes property, using with
symmetric classes, 315
lifetime management, performing in
remoting, 273
<lifetime> element of remoting
configuration, explanation of, 271
LIFO (last-in, first-out) data structures, stacks
as, 55–56
limit price order, explanation of, 44
liquidity
definition of, 4
measurement of, 41
relationship to transactions, 3
liquidity providers, specialists as, 10
list data structure, relationship to collections
and multithreading, 78

ListDictionary specialized collection,
overview of, 58
Listen method, using with market data
producer and TCP, 193
listing securities, effect of, 2
Listings
anonymous methods, 458–459
AOP-based heartbeat service, 281
asynchronous market data consumer
using TCP, 198–199
asynchronous market data producer with
TCP, 196–197
attributes, 132
client receiving broadcast message, 212
configuration file, 251
contract note information encrypted and
decrypted, 313–314
contract note information digitally
verified, 390, 392
contract note information encrypted and
decrypted, 318, 320
digitally signing contract note
information, 387, 389
Exchange element, 140
generic method, 454
generics used with order container, 449–450
hash value computed for contract note
data, 323–324
heartbeat message targeted to monitor
NYSE exchange gateway, 276–277
heartbeat message targeted to monitor
NASDAQ exchange gateway, 277
heartbeat service (RPC version), 255–256
heartbeat service configuration settings, 251
heartbeat service meta-information, 256
Heratbeat service (LPC version), 245
host translator, 184
hosting infrastructure service controller, 266
hosting infrastructure services, 257
hosting of service directory, 265
hosting service controller, 259–260
infrastructure service lookup, 263–264
ISIN master, 115
ISIN master CSV conversion rule file, 149
iterators, 459–460
market data (stock price) class, 203–204
market data consumer, 188–189
market data producer using TCP, 192–193
market data producer using UDP, 186–187
message framing, 204, 206
message header, 203
meta-information about infrastructure
service, 255
operations supported by infrastructure
services, 248
order container example related to
generics, 448–449

overriding remote object lease time, 268

reading XML version of ISIN master, 124

semaphore, 463–464

service controller remoting configuration, 272

signing and verification of contract note data, 325–326

signing and verification of contract note data using digital certificates, 325–330

solicited broadcast of market data, 214

sorting stock data, 425–426

stock data sort order customization, 428

stock data sorted using reflection, 437–438

stock data sorted with Reflection.Emit, 439, 442

STP-Provider B invokes STP-Provider A Web service, 369

UDDI API programmatically determines STP-Provider A Web service location, 378–379

unsolicited broadcast of market data, 211–212

Web service exposed by STP-Provider A, 364

writing ISIN master XML document, 128, 130

WSDL document for order management Web service, 354, 356

WSDL for Web service exposed by STP-Provider A, 365, 367

XML Schema of Exchange element, 140

XML Schema of ISIN element, 139–140

XML Schema of ISIN master, 137–138

XML Schema of root element, 141

lists, locking to ensure thread-safety of, 79

little-endian machine, explanation of, 201

local broadcasts
    overview of, 210, 213
    versus solicited broadcasts, 213

local objects
    versus CAO objects, 243
    definition of, 239

Location field, including in infrastructure service, 255

location transparency, relationship to proxy serialization, 263

lock keyword, as compiler-drive feature, 447

lock statement
    form of, 422
    using in code synchronization, 65

locks
    acquiring in multithreading, 66
    acquiring with Mutex, 70
    heavyweight and lightweight locks, 70

log4Net framework, description of, 478

logging operational component, description of, 237

logging service, invoking with order-matching application, 297

LogicalProcess class
    defining for heartbeat service, 246–247
    introducing shadow copying in, 252–253
    updating with overloaded constructor method, 251
    using service controller with, 249

LogManagement service, implementing for application operation engine, 293

LookUp method
    invoking in infrastructure service controller, 266
    using with proxy cache container, 265

loop attribute, using in CSV conversion rule, 148

loop attribute of bands, explanation of, 146

loopback address, example of, 181

loose coupling, availability in SOA, 351

LPC (local process communication)
    overview of, 244, 249
    relationship to .NET Remoting, 241

LPC Assembly Structure, overview of, 244–245

LPC projects, descriptions of, 244

LSB (least significant byte), relationship to Intel-based machines, 201

■M

machine intelligence, overview of, 36

machine.config file, location of, 250

makecert utility
    generating self-signed certificate with, 385
    using with digital certificates, 328

managed objects
    computing unmanaged size of, 207
    field layout of, 204

Managed suffix, using with class names, 312

manual thread management, relationship to code synchronization, 63–65. *See also* multithreading; threads

ManualResetEvent class
    role in interthread notification, 70
    using with OrderProcessor, 98

margin trading, explanation of, 9

margining, implementing risk management by means of, 22

market capitalization, relationship to indexes, 13

market data
availability of, 177
example of, 173
overview of, 171–172
role in financial trading value chain, 173, 175
sending to multicast groups, 215
serializing into raw bytes, 194
timeliness of, 175, 177
market data consumers
asynchronous type of, 200
building for unsolicited broadcast, 212
for market data on multicast addresses, 215–216
overview of, 188, 190
using multicast groups with, 214–215
using TCP with, 194–195
market data engine, explanation of, 221
market data farm, explanation of, 220
market data industry, participants in, 172–173
market data producers
asynchronous type of, 195, 200
using TCP with, 192–193
market data service code sample, 72
market data service providers
differentiators in, 175
participation in market data industry, 172
market data vendors, significance of, 221
market entities and STP providers, examples of, 348
market info cache client code sample, 473–474
market info cache server host code sample, 473
market information cache server
code implementation of, 472
implementing with IPC channel, 471
remoting configuration of, 472
market makers, overview of, 10–11
market price order, explanation of, 44
market transfers, management by depositories, 16
market width and depth, relationship to liquidity, 4
MarshalByRefObject, inheritance by HeartBeatService class, 246
marshaling byte array from unmanaged section of memory, 208
master detail file format, example and description of, 145
matching process. *See* order-matching engines
Math.NET open source library, description of, 478
matrix, plotting data in, 145
Matrix class, using in data conversion framework, 155–156
MBR (marshal-by-reference) objects. *See* remote objects
MBV (marshal-by-value) objects. *See* mobile objects
MD5 algorithm, hash values produced by, 323
MDP (market data producer) and MDC (market data consumer) example, 186, 190
members. *See* brokers; stock-exchange members
memory gate, overview of, 464
MemoryStream subclass of Stream class, description of, 117
merchant banker, definition of, 2
message digest
computing for digital signature, 325
relationship to data integrity, 322
message framing, relationship to networking, 202, 209
message integrity, maintaining in IP, 182, 185
<message> element looks like for the order management Web service, 357
message-processing unit, role in Web-service platforms, 360
message-routing capabilities, availability in Web services, 399–400
messages
grouping with <operation> element, 357
in SOAP, 358–359
managing for STP and Web services, 401
representing in WSDL documents, 357
triggering in networks, 179
messaging backbones, examples of, 235
meta-information
about infrastructure service, 255
defining for RPC version of heartbeat service, 256
metadata, role in code generation, 416
metadata specification, overview of, 398
Microsoft Corporation, arbitrage on, 413
Microsoft test registry database, using with Web services, 372, 378
Microsoft UDDI repository website, 371
middle office
reference data held by, 109
relationship to STP, 29
middle-office systems, implementation of, 30
middleware
role in .NET Remoting, 240
services offered by, 240
MktDataMessage class, using with broadcast engine, 231, 233
MMC.NET Library website, 478

mobile objects
    definition of, 239
    using in .NET Remoting, 248
mode attribute value in custom Errors
        element, managing remoting error
        handling with, 274
model risk in arbitrage, explanation of, 407
model-driven code generators, features of,
        417, 422
Monitor class
    ensuring thread-safe access to shared
        resources with, 64
    implementing order book with, 64–65
    versus Mutex synchronization
        mechanism, 70
    solving deadlock problems with, 67
monitors and mutexes versus semaphores,
        462
Mono implementation of CLR standard, web
        resource for, 32
Mono initiative, description of, 480
MSB (most significant byte), relationship to
        Intel-based machines, 201
MSFT order book processing, thread priority
        of, 43, 75–76
MSIL, emitting with classes in
        System.Reflection.Emit namespace,
        439
MSS (maximum segment size), relationship
        to TCP, 191
MTU (maximum transmission unit),
        relationship to IP, 182
multibyte value, converting from host byte
        order to network byte order, 201–202
multicast address, example of, 216
multicast groups
    defining, 215
    formation of, 214
    receiving data published on, 216
    sending market data to, 215
    using with market data consumers,
        214–215
multicast server and client, running, 216
multicast TTL scope, description of, 217
multicasts, overview of, 213, 216
multihomed host, explanation of, 189
multithreaded behavior, providing with
        Socket, 196
multithreaded problems, guarding timer
        code from, 84
multithreading. See also manual thread
        management; threads
    and asynchronous delegate infrastructure,
        60, 63
    and atomic operation, 73
    and collections, 77–78, 80–81
    and deadlock prevention, 65, 68

    and interthread notification, 68
    and manual thread management, 63, 84
    and Mutex synchronization mechanism,
        70, 72
    and server timer, 83–84
    and thread pools, 59–60
    and thread scheduling, 74, 77–78
    and UI widgets, 81, 83
    overview of, 59
Mutex synchronization mechanism,
        overview of, 70, 72
mutexes and monitors versus semaphores,
        462
mutual fund managers, building of positions
        in indexes by, 12

■N
Nagle algorithm, relationship to TCP, 220
namespaces
    representing in CodeDOM, 429
    System.Collection namespace, 85
    System.Threading namespace, 83
NAnt tool, features of, 477
NASDAQ (National Association of Securities
        Dealers Automated Quotation),
        significance of, 8
NASDAQ exchange gateway, heartbeat
        message targeted to monitoring of,
        277
NASDAQHeartBeatService class
    authorization logic in, 280
    requirements for, 277
navigation methods, using with XML,
        127–128
NDepend tool, features of, 478
NDoc tool, features of, 478
negative correlation in price, relationship to
        arbitrage, 406
.NET
    features of, 32, 34
    in equities market, 30, 34
.NET 2.0
    and generics, 447, 451
.NET collections. See also generic collections
    and arrays, 48–49
    and hash tables, 57
    and multithreading, 78, 81
    and queues, 54
    and stacks, 55–56
    overview of, 48
.NET Compact Framework, explanation of,
        33
.NET executable, role in remoting
        framework, 241
.NET Framework BCL (base class library),
        significance of, 38
.NET objects. See objects

.NET Reflector tool, features of, 477
.NET Remoting infrastructure, overview of, 240–242. *See also* remoting framework
.NET specialized collections
    HybridDictionary, 58
    ListDictionary, 58
netstat.exe utility, features of, 468
network adapters, interacting with, 469
network address classes, list of, 181
network address type, defining for market data producer, 188
network byte order, overview of, 201–202
network endpoint details, recording for Web services, 185, 376
network hosts, identifying, 185
network information, gathering, 468, 471
network interface layer of TCP/IP, explanation of, 179
network-related changes, detecting, 470
network-related problems, diagnosing with PING, 183
networking
    and broadcast, 209–210
    and Internet protocol, 179–180, 185
    and message framing, 202, 209
    and transport layer, 185, 191, 195
    overview of, 177, 179
networks, components of, 178
NetworkStream subclass of Stream class, description of, 118
nodes
    relationship to networks, 178
    specifying for Buy and Sell, 87
NodeType property, using with XML, 126
nonrepudiation of data, explanation of, 307
NonRepudiationAttribute class, using in STP security, 335
NonRepudiationProvider class, using in STP security, 340–341
nonsignal state, relationship to interthread notification, 70
notice of execution, issuing, 304
novation, relationship to order matching, 47
NSCC (National Securities Clearing Corporation), relationship to NYUSE, 15
null values, returning for remoting classes, 269
nullable types, overview of, 461–462
NUnit tool, features of, 477
NYSE (New York Stock Exchange), significance of, 8
NYSE arbitrage example, 409, 414
NYSE Composite Index, description of, 12
NYSE exchange gateway, heartbeat message targeted to monitoring of, 276

NYSEHeartBeatService class, requirements for, 277

■ **O**

OAEP padding, using with asymmetric keys, 321
object endpoint information, assigning in RPC, 259
object lifetime with leasing, 267
objects. *See also* remoting objects
    characteristics of, 241
    multiple facets of, 238–239
    relationship to classes, 238
    types of, 239
ObjRef class, relationship to proxy serialization, 262
OBook.orderSync, requesting locks on, 67
off-market transfers, management by depositories, 16
offer price, relationship to two-way quotes, 4
Office PIA (Primary Interop Assemblies), defining arbitrage models with, 443
OMEHost class of order-matching engine, overview of, 102–103
online trading, enablement by banks, 15
<operation> element, grouping messages with, 357
operational components versus business components, 237
operational requirements, integrating with functional requirements, 277
operations team, importance of, 283
oral auction
    explanation of, 42
    order precedence rules for, 44
order, definition of, 42
order attributes, examples of, 107
order books
    conceptualizing, 86
    example of, 43
    implementing with Monitor, 64–65
    for matching, 46
    versus position books, 66
    pre-match version of, 45
    segregating into tree structure, 87
Order class of order-matching engine, overview of, 89–90
order containers
    instantiating and updating on remote machine, 474
    providing, 449
    using generics with, 449–450
order dispatcher, monitoring operations performed by, 86
order ID
    explanation of, 89
    generating and assigning, 73

order initiation and delivery, process of,
    19–20
order management Web service
    mimicking functionality of, 71
    WSDL document for, 354, 356
order matching
    and containment of credit risk, 47
    and conversion into trades, processes of,
        22
    and novation, 47
    example of, 46
    exchanges and brokers in, 42–43
    in-memory matching, 85
    logic of, 42–43
    need for efficiency in, 41–42
    order precedence rules related to,
        44, 47
    out-memory matching, 85
    price priority rule in, 44
    types of orders in, 43–44
order precedence ranking, example of, 45
order price, sorting, 53–55
order processors
    foundation of, 86
    performing bookkeeping with, 86
    realizing queue of, 86
order routing and risk management,
        processes of, 20, 22
order type attribute of orders, explanation of,
        89
Order type instance, serializing and
        deserializing, 466–467
    data structures related to, 85
    order-matching applications reference to
        instance of DomainApp in, 297
order-matching engine classes
    BizDomain class, 100–101
    Container class, 92–93
    ContainerCollection class, 93–94
    EquityMatchingLogic class,
        101–102
    EquityOrder class, 91
    LeafContainer class, 94, 96
    OMEHost class, 102–103
    Order class, 89–90
    OrderBook class, 96, 98
    PriceTimePriority class, 91–92
order-matching engines
    designing for efficiency, 84
    high-level implementation of, 86
    Order class, 88
    overview of, 38
    VS .NET project structure of, 89
OrderBook class of order-matching engine,
        overview of, 96, 98
OrderContainer<OrderObj>, instantiating,
        451

OrderContainer<T> generic type,
        significance of, 450
OrderEventArgs class of order-matching
        engine, overview of, 98
OrderObj members, accessing inside generic
        code, 452
OrderProcessor class of order-matching
        engine, overview of, 98, 100
orders
    adding, retrieving, and removing,
        50–51
    attributes of, 89
    designing data containers for, 84
    enumeration of, 79
    generating with program trading engine,
        414
    matching component of, 88
    originating in front office, 109
    placing, 7
    processing concurrently with thread
        pools, 59
    processing in FIFO manner, 55
    ranking in order matching, 46
    ranking with PriceTimePriority class,
        91–92
    sorting with generic method, 454
    states of, 88
    storing, 87
    storing in hash tables, 57
orderSync, acquiring lock on, 66
out- versus in-memory matching, 85
out-memory matching, explanation of, 85
OutOfMemoryException, generating, 464
<output> construct, using with WSDL
        documents, 357

■P

P/Invoke service, using with message
        framing, 204
P/Invoke signatures website, 478
packets, determining ages of, 217
Padding, relationship to cipher mode, 315
padding information, including in
        MessageHeader, 203
paired method, relationship to
        XmlTextWriter object, 130
<param> XML tag for documentation
        comments, description of, 421
parameterless constructor generic
        constraint, overview of, 454
parametric polymorphism, relationship to
        generics in .NET 2.0, 447
Parser class, using in data conversion
        framework, 157–158
parsers. See XML parsers
parsing approach, implementing for
        message framing, 204

partial types, spanning source code into multiple files with, 460

partial-type fidelity mode of serialization engine, explanation of, 132

passive (insert) order, explanation of, 88

Passport credential, using to publish Web services, 372

pay-in and pay-out, in settlement, 28

pay-in and pay-out dates, explanations of, 26

PBook.posSync, requesting lock on, 67

percentage returns, calculating for arbitrage, 411

performance of applications, importance of, 35, 38

PING (Packet Internet Groper) Utility, features of, 183

ping request, checking outcome of, 471

ping.exe command-line tool, features of, 470

pipe, relationship to proxy in .NET Remoting, 242

PipeContext class, using with broadcast engine, 228–229

PKCS padding, using with asymmetric keys, 321

pledges, management by depositories, 16

point-cut in AOP, explanation of, 279

point-cut methods, identifying in AOP, 281

policies, overview of, 395–396

polling value, changing for lease manager, 269

Pop methods, using with stacks, 56

port 12000, honoring service controller request on, 265

<port> elements, using with WSDL documents, 358

<portType> element, using with WSDL documents, 357

position books versus order books, 66

positional file format, example and description of, 145

positive correlation in price, relationship to arbitrage, 406

posSync, acquiring lock on, 67

post-trade activity, explanation of, 19

PostTradeService, enabling contract note functionality with, 364

Power Collections tool, features of, 478

power of attorney, requirement by brokers, 17

pre-opening session, explanation of, 8

pre-trade, explanation of, 19

PreGenXMLSerializer.exe code sample, 465–466

price and time, basing order-matching logic on, 42

price attribute of orders, explanation of, 89

price conditions order, explanation of, 44

price differentials
computing in arbitrage, 410
exploiting with arbitrage, 414

price priority order precedence rule, explanation of, 44

prices, touchline prices, 7, 43

PriceTimePriority class of order-matching engine, overview of, 91–93

primary controller
code sample, 294
explanation of, 284
remoting configuration for, 293–294
role in application operation engine, 283

PrimaryController, implementing for application operation engine, 290, 292

principal transactions, explanation of, 9

private keys
decrypting messages with, 321–322
versus public keys, 317

PrivateKey.xml, contents of, 320

ProcessInfo property of LogicalProcess class, using ServiceHost with, 249–250

processing tasks, offloading with CLR thread-pool implementation, 457–458

processor balance, establishing between multiple threads, 76

ProcessOrder static method, using with thread pools, 60

producer components of broadcast engines, descriptions of, 221–222

profile binding, performing in STP security, 333

ProfileInfo class, using in STP security, 336–337

profitable arbitrage, selecting, 412

program execution, consistency of, 63

program trading, explanation of, 19

program trading engine versus arbitrage engine, 414

program trading system versus arbitrage system, 408

protocol tweaking
IP DontFragment, 217
IP MulticastLoopback, 218
IP TTL and multicast TTL, 217–218
overview of, 216
Socket buffers, 219
Socket ReuseAddress, 218
Socket timeout, 219
TCP NoDelay, 220

protocols
FIX (Financial Information Exchange), 304
importance of, 302
relationship to networks, 178

Provider class, using in STP security, 339–340

proxies. *See also* real proxies; transparent proxies
  creating for remotable services, 260
  overview of, 261, 266
  real proxies, 261–262
  role in caller interaction with remote objects, 241–242
  successful instantiation of, 260
  transparent proxies, 261–262
proxy cache container, populating and making available to service controller, 265
proxy classes
  using with WSE, 383
  viewing code emitted by, 368
proxy instance, creating for heartbeat service, 260
proxy objects, types of, 261
proxy references
  returning to heartbeat service, 247, 266
  returning to service controller, 263
  storing for infrastructure services, 264
proxy serialization
  secret behind, 262
  significance of, 262
PSE (Philadelphia Stock Exchange) arbitrage example, 409, 414
public key information, communicating, 327
public keys
  initializing, 321
  versus private keys, 317
  retrieving with Key property of X509Certificate, 331
public offering, definition of, 2
PublicKey.xml, contents of, 320
Pull forward-only parsers, description of, 123
pure arbitrage, explanation of, 406
Push forward-only parsers, description of, 122
Push method, using with stacks, 56

Q

quantity attribute of orders, explanation of, 89
quantity precedence, role in order matching, 45
QueryServiceInfo method, using in .NET Remoting, 249
queues, storing and retrieving data with, 54–55
QueueUserWorkItem static method, calling for tasks in thread pools, 60
quick sort algorithm
  availability of, 87
  using with arrays, 51
quotes
  receiving firm and soft quotes from specialists, 10–11
  receiving from specialists, 10

quotes for stock, two-way quotes, 4
quotes for stocks, referring to, 4

R

race condition, explanation of, 64
RAIL (Runtime Assembly Instrumentation Library) framework, description of, 479
RC2 symmetric algorithm, key sizes supported by, 310, 313
Read method, using with XML, 125
reading comma-delimited version of ISIN master, 119
real proxies, explanation of, 261–262. *See also* proxies; transparent proxies
ReceiveFrom, invoking for market data consumer, 189
recipients, participation in market data industry, 173
refactoring, improving code readability and maintainability with, 422
reference data
  and framework for data conversion, 111, 115
  cleaning, 112
  overview of, 107–108, 115
  role in order flow chain, 110
reference generic constraints, overview of, 453
reference types, using with containers, 449
ReferencedAssemblies attribute, using with CodeDOM, 429
reflection
  overview of, 434, 438
  relationship to code generation, 417–418
Reflection API, definition of, 434
Reflection.Emit, code generation with, 439, 442
Reflector.FileDisassembler tool, features of, 477
Register method, using with sponsors, 270
RegisterChannel of ChannelServices class, using in remoting infrastructure, 258
RegisterWellKnownServiceType static member, using in RPC, 258
registry for STP provider consortium, using UDDI as, 370
Regulator tool, features of, 478
remotable services, creating proxies for, 260
remotable type and channel, relationship between, 259
remote generic type, client instantiation of, 475–476
remote object registration, separating from channel information, 271
remote objects
  controlling destruction of, 267
  creating instance of, 260

default lease times assigned to, 268
definition of, 239
extending life of, 268
providing infinite lifetimes to, 269
registering, 258
renewing leases for, 269
remote order container, remoting
    configuration of, 475
remoting
    and debugging, 275
    and error handling, 274–275
    and lifetime management, 273
    and security, 275
    and versioning, 274
    configuring, 271, 275
    separating client and server configuration
        details in, 273
remoting applications, applying generics in,
    474
remoting architecture, extensibility of, 242
remoting channels, examples of, 258
remoting classes, packaging of, 257
remoting code
    for configuration of market info cache
        server, 472–473
    for implementation of market info cache
        server, 472
    for market info cache client, 473
    for market info cache server host, 473
    shared assembly component of, 472
remoting components, identifying, 284
remoting configuration
    code sample with service controller, 272
    example of, 271
    for primary controller, 293
remoting formatters, types of, 258
remoting framework, overview of, 471. *See
    also* .NET Remoting infrastructure
remoting infrastructure, booting with
    Configure method of
    RemotingConfiguration class, 271
remoting objects, types of, 242–243. *See also*
    objects
Remove method
    overriding for collections and
        multithreading, 79
    using with Hashtable class, 57
Renewal method, using with ISponsor
    interface, 270
repository for STP provider consortium,
    using UDDI as, 370
requirement distillation, explanation of, 238
requirements. *See* business requirements
Resolve operation, using with DNS, 184
resources, relationship to networking, 178
responsiveness of applications,
    measurement of, 35

retail customers
    explanation of, 19
    versus institutions, 20
retail transaction, process of, 20, 22
<return> XML tag for documentation
    comments, description of, 421
returns on arbitrage, factors involved in,
    409
reusability, availability in SOA, 352
reverse engineering, explanation of, 423
reverse lookup, relationship to DNS, 184
Rijndael symmetric algorithm
    key sizes supported by, 310, 313, 315
    listed features supported by, 314
    using, 313–314
risk management
    and order routing, processes of,
        20, 22
    role of market data in, 174–175
risks, for physical securities, 17
root element of XML Schema, example of,
    141
round-turn transaction, relationship to
    spread, 5
RoundRobinDispatcher class, using with
    broadcast engine, 226–227
routers
    relationship to multicast messages,
        214
    role in networks, 180
Row class, using in data conversion
    framework, 154
RowParser class, using in data conversion
    framework, 159
rows in data conversion framework,
    explanation of, 146
RPC (remote process communication)
    overview of, 254, 260
    relationship to .NET Remoting, 241
RPC style, using with SOAP messages,
    359
RPC.ServiceDirectory console project,
    creating for service directory, 263
RPC.Services.exe.config configuration file,
    creating, 272
RSACryptoServiceProvider
    creating instance of, 321
    creating new instance for digital
        certificates, 331
    creating new instance of, 320–321, 326
RSAParameters, storing key information in,
    326
RTT (round-trip time (RTT), inclusion in
    PING output, 183
rule file, role in data conversion framework,
    147
rule schema, example of, 149, 151

rules
    associating with generic type parameters, 452
    capturing arbitrage strategies in form of, 443–444
rules and constraints, associating with Web services, 396

■S

SAOs (server-activated objects), role in .NET Remoting, 242
scalability, definition of, 35
scheduler, maintaining thread priority level with, 75
Schemas property, using with XmlValidatingReader class, 142
screen-based trading, explanation of, 7
search cost, reducing, 6
search costs, avoiding, 42
SectionData class, using in STP security, 338–339
SecureEnvelope class, using in STP security, 337–338
SecureSTPConsumer console application, creating, 386
securities. *See also* stocks
    considering in arbitrage, 410
    examples of, 6
securities clearing account, logical breakdown of, 27
securities obligation, overview of, 27–28
security. *See also* WS-Security specification
    considering in remoting, 275
    STP security, 39
    types of, 32
security code mapping, examples of, 110
security framework code sample, 343–344
security in STP space. *See* STP-space security
security profile, role in STP security, 333
security type, defining for data, 333
SecurityProfileAttribute class, using in STP security, 336
SEDOL (Stock Exchange Daily Official List) codes, using, 109
SEDOL code mapping, example of, 110
segments, role in networking, 179
self-describing document, XML as, 116
Sell, specifying node for, 87
sell orders
    processing, 21
    sorting in order matching, 42
semaphores, counting semaphores, 462–463
SendData, completing asynchronous send with, 198
Serializable attribute
    annotating in .NET Remoting, 248
    example of, 133

serialization
    definition of, 131
    example of, 135–136
serialization code for message framing, 206
serialization engines
    modes of, 132
    types of, 132
serialization logic, static linking of, 465
serialization process, explanation of, 202
server configuration details, separating from client in remoting, 273
Server GC, description of, 464
server timers
    enabling, 84
    relationship to multithreading, 83–84
    sending heartbeat messages with, 83
server-side implementation, defining for infrastructure services, 255–256
server-side services, relationship to application operation engine, 284
Service base class, using in application operation engine, 289–290
service consumers, building with Visual Studio .NET, 367
service controller and heartbeat service, console output for, 260
service controller remoting configuration code sample, 272
service controller request, honoring on port 12000, 265
service controllers
    building, 244, 249
    connecting to heartbeat service in RPC, 259–260
    making proxy cache container available to, 265
    returning proxy reference to, 263
    versus sponsorship, 270
    updating to interact with heartbeat service, 265
    using LogicalProcess class with, 249
service directory
    console output of, 267
    hosting, 265
    hosting as executable, 263
    implementing functionality for, 263
    interaction with heartbeat service, 265
    relationship to proxy serialization, 263
service providers
    custodian service provider, 299
    STP service provider, 300
service proxies, using with STP and Web services, 367
<service> element
    explanation of, 271
    using with WSDL documents, 358
ServiceHost, using with heartbeat service, 247

ServiceInfo class
  using in .NET Remoting, 248
  using in RPC, 254–255
ServiceLookUp class, creating instance of, 265
session key, explanation of, 322
SetSocketOption, using in unsolicited broadcast, 212
settled transaction, explanation of, 28
settlement
  between clearing members and clearing corporations, 15
  process of, 15
  role of market data in, 175
settlement and clearing, processes of, 24, 28
settlement cycle, acceleration by depositories, 17
settlement time
  reducing with STP, 301
  reduction by STP, 30
SGen tool, boosting start up performance of XMLSerializer with, 465, 467
SHA algorithm, hash values produced by, 323
SHA1Managed, creating new instance of, 324
shadow copy mechanism, relationship to infrastructure services, 252
share quantity, hiding, 44
shared assembly for remoting and generics code sample, 474. *See also* assemblies
shared keys. *See* symmetric keys
shared resources, using counting semaphores with, 462–463
shareholders, definition of, 2
Shutdown, implementing with TCP half-close feature, 194
signal state, relationship to interthread notification, 70
signature keys, using with digital certificates, 331
SignData method, producing signature of data with, 331
SignDataBroker method
  invoking, 326
  using with digital certificates, 330
  verifying digital signatures with, 326
SignHash, passing hash value to, 327
simple type elements, nesting under xs:schema element, 139
SingleCall objects, relationship to .NET Remoting, 242
Singleton objects, role in .NET Remoting, 243–244
Singleton remotable classes, modeling primary controller and agent as, 284
Singleton type, using in RPC, 258
size precedence, role in order matching, 45

SL (stop loss) order, explanation of, 44
smart card, explanation of, 332
SOA (service-oriented architecture)
  and SOAP, 358–359
  and Web services, 352–353
  and WSDL, 354, 358
  relationship to STP interoperability, 351–352
SOAP (Simple Object Access Protocol)
  relationship to SOA, 358–359
  relationship to Web services, 353
SOAP formatter, description of, 258
SOAP messages
  processing by WSE, 381
  securing with WS-Security, 385
SOAP serializer, explanation of, 132
SoapServerFormatterSinkProvider class, description of, 258
Socket buffers, tweaking, 219
socket exception handler, including in market data consumer, 189
Socket instance, creating for market data producer, 187
Socket ReuseAddress, tweaking, 218
Socket timeout, tweaking, 219
Socket.Send, using with TCP, 202
Sockets
  advisory about closing of, 188
  creating for market data producer with TCP, 193–194
  providing multithreaded behavior with, 196
  role in networking, 186
  support for blocking and nonblocking operations, 195
  using asynchronous methods of, 197
soft quotes, receiving from specialists, 10
software components, role in networking, 178
solicited broadcasts, overview of, 213, 216
Sony Corporation, arbitrage on, 412
sort functionality, incorporating inside generic order container, 454
SortCode class, defining in CodeDOM, 430
sorting
  applying on user-defined attributes of data elements, 52
  data elements, 87
SOS (Son of Strike) WinDbg extension, features of, 480
source address in IP header, significance of, 182
SourceMonitor tool, features of, 479
space, role in measuring algorithm efficiency, 48
specialists, overview of, 10–11
specialized class code generators, features of, 417, 423

specialized Stream classes. *See also* streams
  BinaryReader and BinaryWriter, 120–121
  TextReader and TextWriter, 120
  XmlReader and XmlWriter, 122
specification, definition of, 359
speculative arbitrage, explanation of, 407
sponsors
  building relative to current system time,
      270
  relationship to remote objects and leases,
      269
  using Register and Unregister methods
      with, 270
spread
  relationship to bid and offer prices, 5
  relationship to stock exchanges, 6
Spring.NET framework, description of, 479
stacks, using, 55–56
Standard & Poor's 500 index, description of,
      12
standing instructions, providing for
      depositories, 17
Start method
  declaring virtual for
      NASDAQHeartBeatService, 280
  invoking for heartbeat service, 260
  using with HeartBeatService class, 246
state-change event, explanation of, 83
stateful objects, description of, 243
stateless objects, description of, 242
static data element of business infoset,
      overview of, 108
stock data
  sorting, 424, 426
  sorting with Reflection.Emit, 439, 442
stock exchanges
  buying and selling on related to arbitrage,
      413
  examples of, 8
  forms of trading supported by, 42
  overview of, 6, 8
  participation in market data industry, 172
  role in order matching, 42–43
  transitions in, 6
stock ownership, benefits of, 2
stock price custom class example of
      CodeDOM, 424, 426
stock sort example using reflection,
      37–438
stock-exchange members. *See also* brokers
  becoming, 11–12
  floor brokers, 8, 10
  relationship to classes, 238
  specialists, 10–11
  trades between, 25
StockData, defining in shared assembly,
      427

stocks. *See also* securities
  versus bonds, 1
  risks associated with, 17
Stop method, declaring virtual for
      NASDAQHeartBeatService, 280
storage mechanism, considering for data
      containers, 85
store component of broadcast engine,
      description of, 222
StoreCollection class, using with broadcast
      engine, 225–226
STP (straight through processing)
  achieving, 303, 306
  achieving internal STP, 332
  and custodian service providers, 299
  and single-point transaction fulfillment,
      301
  and Web services, 360, 370
  cost savings associated with, 300
  development of, 300
  goal of, 331
  implementing WS-Security in, 385
  overview of, 28, 30
  perspective of, 301, 303
  reducing head count with, 301
  reduction in settlement time associated
      with, 301
  standardizing interinstitution
      communication with, 300
  success of, 307
STP framework, illustration of, 306
STP interoperability. *See also* interoperability
  challenges in achievement of, 350
  overview of, 347
  requirement of, 349
  with several service providers, 348–349
STP marketplace, expectations related to, 348
STP process, enabling, 302–303
STP provider consortium
  building, 372, 378
  relationship to UDDI, 370, 379
STP provider hub, making available with WS-
      Referral specification, 399
STP providers
  activities of, 302
  initiating communication with, 401
  overview of, 300
  registering, 373
STP security
  conceptual design of, 332
  importance of, 39
STP service provider network,
      communication in, 305
STP settlements, significance of, 15
STP space
  confidentiality in, 308, 322
  illustration of, 307

STP-Provider A ASP.NET Web service project, modifying to recognize digital signature, 389–390
STP-space security
  asymmetric keys in, 317, 322
  confidentiality in, 308, 310
  digital certificates in, 327, 331
  digital signatures in, 324, 327
  integrity in, 322, 324
  overview of, 307–308
  symmetric classes in, 312, 316
  symmetric keys in, 310, 312
STPCertificateStore, installing certificate published by broker in, 331
stream cipher, definition of, 309
Stream class, properties and methods provided by, 118
streams, relationship to data stores, 117. *See also* specialized Stream classes
subclasses as generic types, derivation of, 451
submission of instruction, initiation by custodian, 306
SubmitContractNote operation, publishing by Web service, 365
subnet ID in IP address, significance of, 181
substitution ciphers, strength of, 308
<summary> XML tag for documentation comments, description of, 421
symmetric algorithms
  examples of, 310
  programmatic implementation of, 312
symmetric ciphers, key sizes of, 312
symmetric classes, relationship to STP-space security, 312, 316
symmetric encryption versus asymmetric encryption, 322
symmetric keys
  in STP-space security, overview of, 310
  using CBC (Cipher Block Chaining) mode with, 311
  using CFM (Cipher Feedback Mode) mode with, 311–312
  using ECB (Electronic Code Book) mode with, 310
SymmetricAlgorithm class, subclassing and extending, 312
SyncArrayList, deriving from ArrayList, 78
Synchronized static method defined in the ArrayList class, using with thread-safe lists, 78
SyncRoot property of ArrayList, relationship to collections and multithreading, 79
System.Collections namespace data structures
  array lists, 49, 51
  arrays, 48–49

hash tables, 56–57
  and relationship to in-memory matching, 85
queues, 54–55
quick sort and binary search, 51, 54
stacks, 55–56
System.Collections.ArrayList, storing orders in, 87
System.Collections.Generic namespace, contents of, 456
System.IO.Compression namespace, compressing data with, 467–468
System.Net.NetworkInformation namespace, classes available in, 468
  providing network-related information with, 468
System.Object array, declaring for container, 449
System.Runtime.Remoting assembly, remoting classes in, 257
System.Runtime.Remoting.ObjRef class, relationship to proxy serialization, 262
System.Security.Cryptography namespace, programmatic implementation of symmetric algorithms in, 312
System.Threading namespace, Timer class in, 83
System.Threading.ThreadPool class
  functionality of, 74
  representing thread pools in, 59

■T

T type parameter, replacing with OrderObj, 451
T+1 and T+2 settlements, prerequisite for, 17
T+1 initiative, significance of, 300
T+1 settlements
  move toward, 29
  significance of, 15
T+2 and T+3 environments, explanations of, 25
T+3 versus T+1, 349
T+3 to T+1 environment, relationship to STP, 302
taking the offer, explanation of, 5
TCP (Transmission Control Protocol)
  using Socket.Send with, 202
  using with asynchronous market data consumer, 198–199
  using with asynchronous market data producers, 196–197
  using with market data consumer, 194–195
  using with market data producer, 192, 194

TCP buffer, role as sender window size and
    receive window size, 192
TCP channel
    description of, 258
    remoting-related problem with, 471
TCP half-close, implementing with
    Shutdown, 194
TCP NoDelay, tweaking, 220
TCP/IP, relationship to DNS, 183–184
TCPChannel, using as primary
    communication channel, 284
TcpClientChannel class, using in hosting
    service controller, 260
TcpServerChannel class, description of, 258
TCPTrace tool, features of, 479
techno-domain architects, overview of, 34
TextReader and TextWriter specialized
    Stream classes, overview of, 120
thread affinity, support for, 76
Thread class, instantiating instance of, 70
thread pools, overview of, 59
thread priority levels, examples of, 75
thread safety, ensuring, 79, 81
thread scheduling, overview of, 74, 78
thread-safe list, example of, 78
threads. *See also* manual thread
        management; multithreading
    execution of, 74
    limiting access by, 463
    use of counting semaphores by, 462
throughput, definition of, 35
ticker plant, market data farm as, 220
time, role in measuring algorithm efficiency,
    48
time and price, basing order-matching logic
    on, 42
time stamp attribute of orders, explanation
    of, 89
time to live field, relationship to IP, 182
timer architecture, importance of, 83
Timer class defined in the System.Threading
    namespace, using, 83–84
timer code, guarding from multithreaded
    problems, 84
timer event, explanation of, 83
TimeSpan.Zero value, returning for leases,
    270
top-five functionality orders, enumerating, 79
touchline price, explanation of, 7, 43
ToXmlString method, using with keys, 320
trade book, example of, 46
trade confirmation, process of, 111
trade guarantee funds, relationship to
    clearing corporations, 14
trade life-cycle steps
    affirmation and confirmation, 23
    clearing and settlement, 24, 28

order initiation and delivery, 19–20
order matching and conversion into trade,
    22
order matching and conversion into trade
    step of, 22
overview of, 18–19
risk management and order routing, 20
trade reconciliation process, initiation of, 24
traders versus investors and dealers, 3
trades
    back-office functions of, 18
    between members, 25
    front-office functions of, 18
    notifying with callback mechanism, 62–63
    pre- and post-trades, 19
trading, justifications for, 3, 5
trading applications. *See also* application
        operation engine
    launching, 284
    modularizing, 236
    stopping and starting, 295–296
trading chain, using instrument master in,
    109
trading operation-related services, example
    of, 244
trading operational requirement, overview
    of, 235, 238
trading session, definition of, 8
trading terminals, using, 19
trading value chain, division of, 109
transactions
    addressing exceptions related to, 301
    factors related to, 3
    management by depositories, 16
    settlement of, 28
    settling with depositories, 15
    splitting via novation, 47
    using STP in institutional transactions,
        303
Transmission Control Protocol/Internet
        Protocol (TCP/IP), relationship to
        networks, 178
transmission media, role in networking,
    178
transparent proxies. *See also* proxies; real
        proxies
    explanation of, 261–262
    serializable nature of, 262
transport layer of TCP/IP, overview of, 179,
    185–186, 190–191, 195
transport unit, role in Web-service platforms,
    360
TransportModule class, using with broadcast
    engine, 231
transposition cipher, explanation of, 309
tree structure, segregating order books into,
    87

tree-based parsers
  overview of, 122
  support for, 123
trees, implementing, 87
TripleDES, key size of, 313
TryEnter, using with Monitor class and
    deadlocks, 67
two-way quotes
  explanation of, 4
  receiving from specialists, 10
Type class, relationship to reflection, 434
type parameter in generics, explanation of,
    450
type safety
  providing to instances of generic types,
    451
  resolving with generics, 449
typed DataSet, explanation of, 423
TypeLoadException, throwing in remoting
    framework, 274
types
  nullable types, 461–462
  using partial types, 461
<types> element, using with WSDL
    documents, 356

U
UDDI (Universal Description, Discovery, and
    Integration), using with STP provider
    consortium, 370, 379
UDDI .NET assembly, using, 377, 379
UDDI .NET SDK, description of, 377
UDDI repository, building, 371
UDP (User Datagram Protocol)
  drawbacks of, 190–191
  relationship to transport layer, 186
  versus TCP, 191
  using with market data consumer, 188,
    190
  using with market data producer, 187
  using with market data producer, 186
UI actions, examples of, 81
UI messages, generating, 81
UI threads
  explanation of, 81
  receipt of messages by, 82
UI widgets
  creating in Windows Form Designer,
    418
  relationship to multithreading, 81, 83
UML model-driven generator, description of,
    422
unbound type, relationship to generic type
    parameters, 452
unboxing process, relationship to array lists, 50
unicast communication model, example of,
    209

UnRegister method, using with sponsors, 270
unsolicited broadcasts
  overview of, 210, 213
  versus solicited broadcasts, 213
upload activity, making interactive, 81
Upload button, clicking for bulk order
    upload form, 82
URI (uniform resource identifier), defining in
    RPC, 258
URL location of heartbeat service, storage of,
    260
Use the Centralized Connection Strings
    Database website, 478
user authentication and profile operational
    component, description of, 237
user event, explanation of, 83
user interface code generators, features of,
    416, 418
user requirements, relationship to
    application design, 36

V
value type generic constraints, overview of,
    453
value types
  allowing storage of, 451
  using with containers, 449
variable data element of business infoset,
    overview of, 107
variables, relationship to classes, 238
Verify method
  using with NonRepudiationProvider class,
    341
  using with provider class, 340
VerifyData, invoking for digital certificates,
    331
VerifySignFM
  mimicking fund manager with, 327
  using with digital certificates, 330
  verifying digital signatures with, 326
versioning, relationship to remoting, 274
virtual methods, using with Service base
    class, 289
Visual Studio .NET
  creating service consumer with, 367
  creating Web services with, 364
  creating Web-service project with, 361
  enabling WSE support in, 381

W
WaitCallBack delegates, using with thread
    pools, 60
Wal-Mart Stores, arbitrage on, 413
Walt Disney Company
  arbitrage on, 413
  buying for arbitrage, 414
  price differential for, 411

weaving rules, composing in AOP-based
    heartbeat service, 280–281
Web References node, expanding, 368
Web service references, adding with wsdl
    command-line tool, 367
Web service registration process, UDDI
    information captured during, 371
Web services
    addressing performance associated with,
        400
    and STP, 360, 370
    associating rules and constraints to, 396
    business-technology mapping for, 400
    changing class names and filenames for,
        363
    creating with Visual Studio .NET, 364
    expanding project hierarchy for, 368
    fetching complete information about, 365
    performance in financial market, 400
    platform infrastructure for, 359–360
    prerequisites for creation of, 361
    publishing, 372
    recording network endpoint details of, 376
    relationship to SOA, 352–353
    testing, 370
    updating to verify digital signatures, 390,
        392
Web-STP, requirements of, 400
websites
    Alchemi framework, 478
    Aspect#, 278
    CLR Profiler tool, 479
    CoverageEye.NET tool, 478
    database connection strings, 478
    Dotfuscator tool, 477
    Enterprise Library, 479
    Ethereal tool, 479
    FxCop tool, 477
    Indy.Sockets .NET library, 478
    log4Net framework, 478
    Math.NET open source library, 478
    MMC.NET Library, 478
    Mono CLR standard, 32
    Mono initiative, 480
    NAnt tool, 477
    NDepend tool, 478
    NDoc tool, 478
    .NET Reflector, 477
    NUnit tool, 477
    P/Invoke signatures, 478
    Power Collections tool, 478
    RAIL (Runtime Assembly Instrumentation
        Library), 479
    Reflector.FileDisassembler, 477
    Regulator tool, 478
    SOS (Son of Strike)WinDbg extension, 480
    SourceMonitor tool, 479
    Spring.NET framework, 479
    TCPTrace tool, 479
    UDDI repositories, 371
    Use the Centralized Connection Strings
        Database, 478
    WinDbg tool, 479
    Windows System Utilities, 479
    WS-Security, 384
    WSDL specification, 354
well-formed document, example of, 116
"what" portion of the clearing problem,
    answering, 25–26
"when" portion of the clearing problem,
    answering, 25
where keyword, specifying code syntax of
    generic constraints with, 452
"where" portion of the clearing problem,
    answering, 25
while loop
    using with Start method of
        HeartBeatService class, 246
    using with XML, 125
whitespace, managing in XML documents,
    126
"whom" portion of the clearing problem,
    answering, 25
Win32 process, role in remoting framework,
    241
WinDbg tool, features of, 479
window size, relationship to TCP, 192
Windows Form Designer, code-generation
    techniques in, 418
Windows scheduler, maintaining thread
    priority level with, 75
Windows service manager versus service
    controller, 244
Windows System Utilities website, 479
WinForm applications, bulkorder upload
    form, 82
wizards, availability in VS .NET IDE, 420
worker threads
    modifying UI widget properties from, 82
    sending messages from, 82
Workstation GC, description of, 464
WrapClass factory method, using new
    instance of
    NASDAQHeartbeatService with, 282
writers in data conversion framework,
    examples of, 148
WS-* specifications, overview of, 379–380
WS-Addressing specification, overview of,
    397–398
WS-MetadataExchange specification,
    overview of, 398
WS-Policy specification, overview of, 395–396

WS-Referral specification, overview of, 399–400

WS-Security specification, overview of, 384, 392–393, 395. *See also* security

WS-SecurityPolicy, activating, 396

WSDL (Web Services Description Language)
explanation of, 353
relationship to SOA, 354, 358

wsdl command-line tool, adding Web service references with, 367

WSDL document, retrieving for use with Web services, 365

WSE (Web Services Enhancement) framework
implementing WS-Security features with, 385
overview of, 380, 384
using with digital certificates, 328
verifying digital certificates, 387

■ **X**

<x509> element, explanation of, 387

X509CertificateStore, returning instance of, 331

XML (eXtensible Markup Language)
and COD (context-oriented data), 116–117
versus CSV, 116
and data arrangement uniformity, 116
and domain knowledge, 116
extensibility of, 117
overview of, 115–116
reading, 123, 128
use in Web services, 353
writing, 128, 131

XML data cleansing stages
cleansing, 113
enrichment, 114
import and conversion, 113

XML data writer, role in data conversion framework, 148

XML documents
requirements for, 141
validating, 141

XML documents and CLR types, using XmlSerializer class with, 133

XML fragment of messages between broker and trading partners, 357

XML output
for data conversion example, 167
for refined conversion rule, 167–168

XML parsers
fast-forward parsers, 122–123
features of, 123
forward-only parsers, 122–123
overview of, 122

tree-based parsers, 122

using with bands, rows, and columns, 148

XML Schema
information captured by, 137
relationship to WSDL, 354

XML serialization, overview of, 131, 136

XML serializer, explanation of, 132

XML tags for documentation comments, examples of, 421

XmlAnyAttribute attribute, description of, 134

XmlAnyElement attribute, description of, 134

XmlArray attribute, description of, 134

XmlArrayItem attribute, description of, 134

XmlAttribute attribute, description of, 134

XmlDataWriter class, using in data conversion framework, 161–162

XmlElement attribute, description of, 134

XmlEnum attribute, description of, 134

XmlIgnore attribute, description of, 134

XmlNodeReader inherited class, using with XmlReader, 123

XmlReader and XmlWriter specialized Stream classes, overview of, 121

XmlReader class
explanation of, 123
inherited classes of, 123

XmlRoot attribute, description of, 134

XmlSerializer class
boosting start up performance of, 465, 467
relationship to JIT-CC, 423
using attributes with, 133–134

XmlTextReader class
properties and methods of, 126–127
role in data conversion framework, 147

XmlTextReader inherited class
using with XmlReader, 123
writing XML-aware code with, 123, 125

XmlTextWriter class
description of, 128
members and properties of, 130–131

XmlTextWriter object, instantiating, 130

XmlValidatingReader class
role in data conversion framework, 147
validating ISIN master of XML document with, 141–142

XmlValidatingReader inherited class, using with XmlReader, 123

XOR operations, using with CFM (Cipher Feedback Mode), 312

XSD (XML schema definition)
overview of, 136, 143
using with conversion rule file, 149, 151

XSD document, role in data conversion framework, 147

XSD form, representing ContractNoteInfo
type in, 367
XSD type system, using with WSDL
documents, 357
xs:schema element, elements nested under,
138–139

 Y

yield return and yield break statements, with
iterators, 460

You Need the Companion eBook

Your purchase of this book entitles you to its companion eBook for only $10.

We believe this Apress title will prove so indispensable that you'll want to carry it with you everywhere, which is why we are offering the companion eBook for $10 to customers who purchase this book now. Convenient and fully searchable, the eBook version of any content-rich, page-heavy Apress book makes a valuable addition to your programming library. You can easily find, copy, and apply code—and then perform examples by quickly toggling between instructions and the application. Even simultaneously tackling a donut, diet soda, and complex code becomes simplified with hands-free eBooks!

Once you purchase this book, getting the $10 companion eBook is simple:

❶ Visit **www.apress.com/promo/tendollars/**.

❷ Complete a basic registration form to receive a randomly generated question about this title.

❸ Answer the question correctly in 60 seconds and you will receive a promotional code to redeem for the $10 eBook.

2560 Ninth Street • Suite 219 • Berkeley, CA 94710

Offer valid through 10/06.